VALENCIA AND MURCIA
Pages 232–253

ARAGÓN
Pages 216–231

CATALONIA
Pages 196–215

Donostia
(San Sebastián)

Iruña
(Pamplona)

0 kilometres   100

0 miles   100

Zaragoza

Lleida

Barcelona

EASTERN SPAIN

BARCELONA
Pages 132–185

Cuenca

THE BALEARIC ISLANDS

Palma de
Mallorca

Valencia

Albacete

Alacant
(Alicante)

Murcia

THE BALEARIC ISLANDS
Pages 482–503

Almeria

ANDALUSIA
Pages 434–477

THE CANARY ISLANDS

THE CANARY ISLANDS
Pages 504–527

Santa Cruz
de Tenerife

Las Palmas
de Gran Canaria

EYEWITNESS *TRAVEL GUIDES*

SPAIN

EYEWITNESS *TRAVEL GUIDES*

SPAIN

DORLING KINDERSLEY

LONDON • NEW YORK • SYDNEY • MOSCOW

A DORLING KINDERSLEY BOOK

Project Editor Nick Inman
Art Editors Jaki Grosvenor, Janis Utton
Editors Catherine Day, Lesley McCave, Seán O'Connell
Designers Susan Blackburn, Dawn Davies-Cook,
Joy Fitzsimmons, Helen Westwood
Map Co-ordinators Michael Ellis, David Pugh

Managing Editors Vivien Crump, Helen Partington
Managing Art Editor Steve Knowlden
Deputy Editorial Director Douglas Amrine
Deputy Art Director Gillian Allan

Production Kate Hayward, David Proffit
Picture Researchers Monica Allende, Helen Stallion
DTP Designer Ingrid Vienings

Main Contributors
John Ardagh, David Baird, Vicky Hayward, Adam Hopkins,
Lindsay Hunt, Nick Inman, Paul Richardson, Martin Symington,
Nigel Tisdall, Roger Williams

Maps
Jennifer Skelley, Phil Rose, Jane Hanson (Lovell Johns Ltd)
Gary Bowes, Richard Toomey (ERA-Maptec Ltd)

Photographers
Max Alexander, Joe Cornish, Neil Lukas, Neil Mersh,
John Miller, Kim Sayer, Linda Whitwam, Peter Wilson

Illustrators
Stephen Conlin, Richard Draper, Isidoro González-Adalid Cabezas
(Acanto Arquitectura y Urbanismo S.L.), Claire Littlejohn, Maltings
Partnership, Chris Orr & Assocs, John Woodcock

Text film output by Graphical Innovations (London)
Reproduced by Colourscan (Singapore)
Printed and bound by Graphicom (Italy)

First published in Great Britain in 1996
by Dorling Kindersley Limited
9 Henrietta Street, London WC2E 8PS
Reprinted with revisions 1997

Copyright 1996, 1997 © Dorling Kindersley Limited, London
Visit us on the World Wide Web at http://www.dk.com

ALL RIGHTS RESERVED. NO PART OF THIS PUBLICATION MAY BE
REPRODUCED, STORED IN A RETRIEVAL SYSTEM, OR TRANSMITTED IN ANY
FORM OR BY ANY MEANS, ELECTRONIC, MECHANICAL, PHOTOCOPYING,
RECORDING OR OTHERWISE, WITHOUT THE PRIOR WRITTEN PERMISSION
OF THE COPYRIGHT OWNER.

A CIP CATALOGUE RECORD IS AVAILABLE FROM THE BRITISH LIBRARY.

ISBN 0 7513 9406 8

Every effort has been made to ensure that the information in this
book is as up-to-date as possible at the time of going to press.
However, details such as telephone numbers, opening hours,
prices, gallery hanging arrangements and travel information are
liable to change. The publishers cannot accept responsibility for
any consequences arising from the use of this book.

We would be delighted to receive any corrections and
suggestions for incorporation in the next edition. Please write to:
Deputy Editorial Director, Eyewitness Travel Guides,
Dorling Kindersley, 9 Henrietta Street, London WC2E 8PS.

Previous pages: Pilgrimage of the Virgin of the Bridges, Belalcázar, near Córdoba in Andalusia

CONTENTS

King Alfonso X the Learned

INTRODUCING
SPAIN

NORTHERN SPAIN

BARCELONA

Statue of Alfonso XII, Madrid

Grapes growing in La Mancha, the world's largest expanse of vineyards

Iglesia de Santa María del Naranco in Asturias

HOW TO USE THIS GUIDE

THIS GUIDE helps you to get the most from your visit to Spain. It provides detailed practical information and expert recommendations. *Introducing Spain* maps the country and sets it in its historical and cultural context. The five regional sections, plus *Barcelona* and *Madrid*, describe important sights, using maps, photographs and illustrations. Features cover topics from food and wine to fiestas and beaches. Restaurant and hotel recommendations can be found in *Travellers' Needs*. The *Survival Guide* has tips on everything from transport to using the telephone system.

BARCELONA, MADRID AND SEVILLE

These cities are divided into areas, each with its own chapter. A last chapter, *Further Afield*, covers peripheral sights. Madrid Province, surrounding the capital, has its own chapter. All sights are numbered and plotted on the chapter's area map. Information on each sight is easy to locate as it follows the numerical order on the map.

Sights at a Glance lists the chapter's sights by category: Churches and Cathedrals, Museums and Galleries, Streets and Squares, Historic Buildings, Parks and Gardens.

All pages relating to Madrid have green thumb tabs. Barcelona's are pink and Seville's are red.

A locator map shows where you are in relation to other areas of the city centre.

1 Area Map
For easy reference, sights are numbered and located on a map. City centre sights are also marked on Street Finders: Barcelona *(pages 175–81);* Madrid *(pages 297–303);* Seville *(pages 429–33).*

2 Street-by-Street Map
This gives a bird's-eye view of the key areas in each chapter.

Stars indicate the sights that no visitor should miss.

A suggested route for a walk is shown in red.

3 Detailed information
The sights in the three main cities are described individually. Addresses, telephone numbers, opening hours, admission charges, tours, photography and wheelchair access are also provided, as well as public transport links.

1 Introduction
The landscape, history and character of each region is outlined here, showing how the area has developed over the centuries and what it has to offer to the visitor today.

SPAIN AREA BY AREA
Apart from Barcelona, Madrid and Seville, the country has been divided into 12 regions, each of which has a separate chapter. The most interesting cities, towns and villages, and other places to visit are numbered on a *Pictorial Map*.

2 Pictorial Map
This shows the road network and gives an illustrated overview of the whole region. All interesting places to visit are numbered and there are also useful tips on getting to, and around, the region by car and public transport.

Fiesta boxes highlight the best traditional fiestas in the region.

Each area of Spain can be quickly identified by its colour coding, shown on the inside front cover.

3 Detailed information
All the important towns and other places to visit are described individually. They are listed in order, following the numbering on the Pictorial Map. *Within each town or city, there is detailed information on important buildings and other sights.*

For all top sights, a Visitors' Checklist provides the practical information you will need to plan your visit.

4 Spain's top sights
These are given two or more full pages. Historic buildings are dissected to reveal their interiors. The most interesting towns or city centres are shown in a bird's-eye view, with sights picked out and described.

INTRODUCING
SPAIN

Putting Spain on the Map

S PAIN, IN SOUTHWESTERN Europe, covers the greater part of the Iberian Peninsula. The third largest country in Europe, it includes two island groups: the Canaries in the Atlantic and the Balearics in the Mediterranean, and two small territories in North Africa. Its southernmost point faces Morocco across a strait, making Spain a bridge between continents.

Satellite image showing the Iberian Peninsula

KEY

✈	International airport
⚓	Ferry service
▬	Motorway
▬	Major road
—	Main railway line
▬	AVE high-speed railway line

◁ *Rooftops, Fortna Lux, Mallorca* (1969) by Frederick Gore

THE CANARY ISLANDS

Cádiz

Arrecife

Santa Cruz
de la Palma

Puerto de
la Cruz

Santa Cruz
de Tenerife

Puerto del
Rosario

San
Sebastián
de la Gomera

Las Palmas de
Gran Canaria

Valverde

Maspalomas

Spain's Most Southerly Islands
This chain of seven islands in the Atlantic is 1,150 km (700 miles) southwest of Cádiz and 150 km (70 miles) off Morocco.

Biarritz

Bilbo
(Bilbao)

Donostia
(San Sebastián)

F R A N C E

Iruña
(Pamplona)

Perpignan

ANDORRA

Girona

Huesca

Ebro

Soria

Zaragoza

Lleida

Barcelona

Tarragona

Cuenca

Maó

M e d i t e r r a n e a n   S e a

Palma de
Mallorca

Valencia

Júcar

Albacete

Eivissa (Ibiza)

0 kilometres   100

0 miles   50

Alacant
(Alicante)

Múrcia

Segura

Spain's Frontiers
Spain has land borders with France, Portugal, Andorra and Gibraltar (a British territory on the south coast). The Strait of Gibraltar is only 13 km (8 miles) wide between Tarifa, the peninsula's southernmost point, and northern Morocco.

Almería

Oran

Melilla

EUROPE AND NORTH AFRICA

NORWAY

FINLAND

SWEDEN

DENMARK

ESTONIA

RUSSIAN
FED.

LATVIA

LITHUANIA

RUSSIAN
FED.

BELORUSSIA

REPUBLIC
OF
IRELAND

UNITED
KINGDOM

NETHERLANDS

POLAND

GERMANY

BELGIUM

LUXEMBOURG

CZECH
REPUBLIC

UKRAINE

FRANCE

SWITZERLAND

AUSTRIA

SLOVAKIA

HUNGARY

ROMANIA

ITALY

SLOVENIA

CROATIA

BOSNIA AND
HERZEGOVINA

YUGOSLAVIA

BULGARIA

ALBANIA

GREECE

PORTUGAL

Madrid

SPAIN

MOROCCO

TUNISIA

ALGERIA

LIBYA

Regional Spain

Spain has a population of 39 million and receives more than 57 million visitors a year. It covers an area of 504,780 sq km (194,900 sq miles). Madrid is the largest city, followed by Barcelona and Valencia. The country is dominated by a central plateau drained by the Duero, Tagus (Tajo) and Guadiana rivers. This book divides Spain into 15 areas, but officially it has 17 independent regions called *comunidades autónomas*.

GETTING AROUND

Spain's regional capitals and islands are linked by regular flights and there is a shuttle service between Madrid and Barcelona. The TALGO and AVE high-speed trains provide fast rail services between many provincial cities and are backed up by regional and local rail networks. Some motorways have expensive tolls, but are fast. Other roads range from rapid, modern highways to scenic, but often rough, byways. The Balearic and Canary islands are served by regular ferries from the mainland.

KEY

━━ Motorway

━━ Major road

══ Minor road

| 0 kilometres | 100 |
| 0 miles | 100 |

Eyewitness Spain Regions

Each of the chapters in this guide has a colour code. The chapters are grouped into five sections: Northern, Eastern, Central and Southern Spain and Spain's Islands; and two cities: Madrid and Barcelona.

KEY TO COLOUR CODING

Northern Spain

- Galicia
- Asturias and Cantabria
- The Basque Country, Navarra and La Rioja

Eastern Spain

- Barcelona
- Catalonia
- Aragón
- Valencia and Murcia

Central Spain

- Madrid
- Castilla y León
- Castilla-La Mancha
- Extremadura

Southern Spain

- Seville
- Andalusia

Spain's Islands

- The Balearic Islands
- The Canary Islands

stia
(Sebastián)

Iruña
(Pamplona)

N135
N240
N330
N121
N240
Tudela
N330
N232
N330
Zaragoza
N232
Ebro
N234
N330
N330
Teruel
N330
N234
N420
N211
N230
N232

Huesca
N123
N240
N260
N330
Lleida
N240
Reus
N420
Tortosa
N232
C1412
N330
N234
N332
N237
CS801
CS230

La Seu
d'Urgell
N260
N260
N260
N260
Vic
NT-S
Manresa
N152
A18
A2
N11
Barcelona
A7
Tarragona

Figueres
Girona
A7
N11

Castelló de la Plana

Sagunt
Valencia

C238
Turia
N111
N430

N330
N340
mansa
N430
N344

Alcoi
Benidorm
A7
Alacant
(Alicante)

Elx
N301
Murcia
Cartagena

THE BALEARIC ISLANDS

Ciutadella
C721
Menorca
Maó

Mallorca
Palma de
Mallorca
PM1
PM27
Manacor

Cabrera

Ibiza
C733
Eivissa (Ibiza)

Formentera

THE CANARY ISLANDS

Lanzarote
Arrecife

La Palma
Santa Cruz
de la Palma

Fuerteventura
GC10
Puerto del
Rosario

Puerto de
la Cruz
Santa Cruz
de Tenerife

La Gomera
Tenerife

San Sebastián
de la Gomera

Las Palmas
de Gran Canaria
GC10

El Hierro
Valverde
Gran Canaria
Maspalomas

Spain's Atlantic Territories

The Canary Islands, in the Atlantic Ocean off the coast of Africa, are an integral part of Spain. They are one hour behind the rest of the country.

A PORTRAIT OF SPAIN

THE FAMILIAR IMAGES OF SPAIN – *flamenco dancing, bullfighting, tapas bars and solemn Easter processions – do no more than hint at the diversity of the country. Spain has four official languages, two major cities of almost equal importance and a greater range of landscapes than any other European country. These remarkable contrasts make Spain an endlessly fascinating country to visit.*

Separated from the rest of Europe by the Pyrenees, Spain reaches south to the coast of North Africa. It has both Atlantic and Mediterranean coastlines, and includes two archipelagos – the Balearics and the Canary Islands.

The climate and landscape vary from snow-capped peaks in the Pyrenees, through the green meadows of Galicia and the orange groves of Valencia, to the desert of Almería. Madrid is the highest capital in Europe, and Spain its most mountainous country after Switzerland and Austria. The innumerable sierras have always hindered communications. Until railways were built it was easier to move goods from Barcelona to South America than to Madrid.

In early times, Spain was a coveted prize for foreign conquerors including the Phoenicians and the Romans. During the Middle Ages, much of it was ruled by the Moors, who arrived from North Africa in the 8th century. It was reconquered by Christian forces, and unified at the end of the 15th century. A succession of rulers tried to impose a common culture, but Spain remains as culturally diverse as ever. Several regions have maintained a strong sense of their own independent identities. Many Basques and Catalans, in particular, do not consider themselves

Statue of Don Quixote and Sancho Panza, Madrid

Landscape with a solitary cork tree near Albacete in Castilla-La Mancha

◁ The outlandishly dressed *Peliqueiros* who take to the streets during Carnival in Laza, Galicia

Peñafiel castle in the Duero valley (Castilla y León), built between the 10th and 13th centuries

to be Spanish. Madrid may be the nominal capital but it is closely rivalled in commerce, the arts and sport by Barcelona, the main city of Catalonia.

THE SPANISH WAY OF LIFE

The inhabitants of this very varied country have few things in common except for a natural sociability and a zest for living. Spaniards commonly put as much energy into enjoying life as they do into their work. The stereotypical *"mañana"* (leave everything until tomorrow) is a myth, but time is flexible in Spain and many people bend their work to fit the demands

"Vinegar Face" in Pamplona's Los Sanfermines fiesta

of their social life, rather than let themselves be ruled by the clock. The day is long in Spain and Spanish has a word, *madrugada*, for the time between midnight and dawn, when city streets are often still lively.

Spaniards are highly gregarious. In many places people still go out in the evening for the *paseo*, when the streets are crowded with strollers. Eating is invariably communal and big groups often meet up for tapas or dinner. Not surprisingly, Spain has more bars and restaurants per head than any other country.

Underpinning Spanish society is the extended family. Traditionally, the state in Spain has been very inefficient at providing public services – although this has improved in the last 20 years. The Spanish have therefore always relied on their families and personal connections, rather than institutions, to find work or seek assistance in a crisis. This attitude has sometimes led to a disregard for general interests – such as the environment – when they have conflicted with private ones.

Most Spaniards place their family at the centre of their lives. Three generations may live together under one roof, or at least see each other often. Even

Tables outside a café in Madrid's Plaza Mayor

lifelong city-dwellers refer fondly to their *pueblo* – the town or village where their family comes from and where they return whenever they can. Children are adored in Spain and, consequently, great importance is attached to education. The family in Spain, however, is under strain as couples increasingly opt for a higher income and better lifestyle rather than a large family. One of the most striking transformations in modern Spain has been in the birth rate, from one of the highest in Europe, at 2.72 children for every woman in 1975, to one of the lowest in the world, only 1.2 in 1995.

The windmills and castle above Consuegra, La Mancha

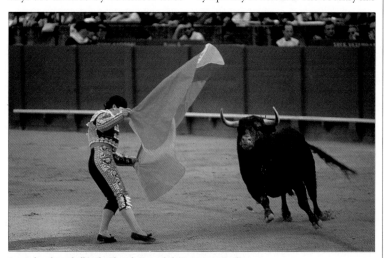

Virgin of Guadalupe in Extremadura

Catholicism is still a pervasive influence over Spanish society, although church attendance among those under 35 has declined in recent years to below 25 per cent. The images of saints watch over some shops, bars and lorry drivers' cabs. Church feast days are marked by countless traditional fiestas which are enthusiastically maintained in modern Spain.

SPORT AND THE ARTS

Spanish cultural life has been reinvigorated in recent years. Spanish-made films – notably those of cult director Pedro Almodóvar – have been able to compete effectively with Hollywood productions for audiences. Despite the low overall level of reading (fewer than one in ten buy a daily newspaper), contemporary literature has steadily gained a wider readership. The performing arts have been restricted by a lack of facilities, but recent major investments have provided new venues, regional arts centres and new symphony orchestras. The country has

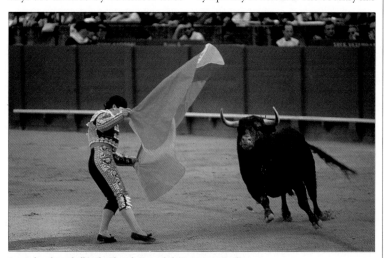

A matador plays a bull in the Plaza de Toros de la Maestranza, Seville

Poster for a Pedro Almodóvar film

produced many remarkable opera singers including Montserrat Caballé, Alfredo Kraus, Plácido Domingo and José Carreras. Spain has also excelled in design, particularly evident in the interior furnishings shops of Barcelona.

Spaniards are the most avid TV-watchers in Europe after the British. In many parts of the country there are six channels: two state-owned channels, three private networks and a regional station. Sports are one of the mainstays of TV programming. Recently, Spanish sportsmen and women have been very successful – for example, tennis players Conchita Martínez and Arantxa Sánchez, cyclist Miguel Induráin, and golfer Severiano Ballesteros. Such role models have encouraged participation in sport and new facilities have been provided to meet this demand. Most popular are basketball and, above all, soccer.

Bullfighting has enjoyed renewed popularity since the late 1980s. For aficionados, a *corrida* is a unique occasion that provides a link to Spain's roots, and the noise, colour and argumentative attitude of the crowd are as much of an attraction as the bullfight itself.

SPAIN TODAY

In the last 40 years Spain has undergone more social change than anywhere else in western Europe. Until the 1950s, Spain was predominantly a poor, rural country, in which only 37 per cent of the population lived in towns of over 10,000 people. By the 1990s, the figure was 65 per cent. As people flooded into towns and cities many rural areas became depopulated. The 1960s saw the beginning of

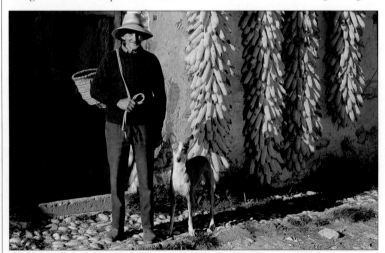

A farmer with his crop of maize hanging to dry on the outside of his house in the hills of Alicante

Beach near Tossa de Mar on the Costa Brava

terrorist group ETA is a constant thorn in the side of Spanish democracy.

During the 1980s Spain enjoyed an economic boom as service industries and manufacturing expanded. Even so, GDP remains below the European Union average and growth has been very unevenly spread around the country. Agriculture is an important industry but while it is highly developed in some regions, it is inefficient in others. Tourism provides approximately ten per cent of the country's earnings. Most tourists still come for beaches. But increasingly, foreign visitors are drawn by Spain's rich cultural heritage and spectacular countryside. Anyone who knows this country, however, will tell you that it is the Spanish people's capacity to enjoy life to the full that is Spain's biggest attraction.

spectacular economic growth, partly the result of a burgeoning tourist industry. In that decade alone the number of car owners went from 1 in 100 to 1 in 10.

After the death of the dictator General Franco in 1975 Spain became a constitutional monarchy under King Juan Carlos I. The post-Franco era, up until the mid-1990s, has been dominated by the

King Juan Carlos I and Queen Sofía

Socialist Prime Minister Felipe González. As well as presiding over major improvements in roads, education and health services, the Socialists increased Spain's international standing. Spain joined the European Community in 1986, triggering a spectacular increase in the country's prosperity. The country's fortunes seemed to peak in the extraordinary year of 1992, when Barcelona staged the Olympic Games and Seville hosted a world fair, Expo '92.

With the establishment of democracy, the 17 autonomous regions of Spain have acquired considerable powers. Several have their own languages which are officially given equal importance to Spanish (strictly called Castilian). A significant number of Basques favour independence for the Basque Country. The Basque

Demonstration for Catalan independence

Architecture in Spain

S PAIN HAS ALWAYS IMPORTED its styles of architecture: Moorish from North Africa, Romanesque and Gothic from France and Renaissance from Italy. Each style, however, was interpreted in a distinctively Spanish way, with sudden and strong contrasts between light and shady areas; façades alternating between austerity and extravagant decoration; and thick walls pierced by few windows to lessen the impact of heat and sunlight. Styles vary from region to region, reflecting the division of Spain before unification. The key design of a central patio surrounded by arcades has been a strong feature of civil buildings since Moorish times.

The 15th-century Casa de Conchas in Salamanca *(see p343)*

ROMANESQUE AND EARLIER (8TH–13TH CENTURIES)

Romanesque churches were mainly built in Catalonia and along the pilgrim route to Santiago *(see p79)*. Their distinctive features include round arches, massive walls and few windows. Earlier churches were built in Pre-Romanesque *(see 102)* or Mozarabic *(see p335)* style.

Round arch   **Multiple apses**

The Romanesque Sant Climent, Taüll *(p201)*

MOORISH (8TH–15TH CENTURIES)

The Moors *(see pp48–9)* reserved the most lavish decoration for the interior of buildings, where ornate designs based on geometry, calligraphy and plant motifs were created in *azulejos* (tiles) or stucco. They made extensive use of the horseshoe arch, a feature inherited from the Visigoths *(see pp46–7)*. The greatest surviving works of Moorish architecture *(see pp404–5)* are in Southern Spain.

The Salón de Embajadores *in the Alhambra* (see p466) *has exquisite Moorish decoration.*

GOTHIC (12TH–16TH CENTURIES)

Gothic was imported from France in the late 12th century. The round arch was replaced by the pointed arch which, because of its greater strength, allowed for higher vaults and taller windows. External buttresses were added to prevent the walls of the nave from leaning outwards. Carved decoration

Gothic arched window

was at its most opulent in the Flamboyant Gothic style of the 15th century. After the fall of Granada, Isabelline, a late Gothic style, developed. Meanwhile, Moorish craftsmen working in reconquered areas created the highly decorative hybrid Christian-Islamic style Mudéjar *(see p51)*.

Rose window   **Tracery**
Pointed arch   **Flying buttress**

The nave *of León Cathedral (see pp336–7), built in the 13th century, is supported by rib vaulting and is illuminated by the finest display of stained glass in Spain.*

Sculptural decoration *above the doorways of León cathedral's south front depicted biblical stories for the benefit of the largely illiterate populace.*

RENAISSANCE (16TH CENTURY)

Around 1500 a new style was introduced to Spain by Italian craftsmen and Spanish artists who had studied in Italy. The Renaissance was a revival of the style of Ancient Rome. It is distinguished by its sense of symmetry and the use of the round arch, and Doric, Ionic and Corinthian columns. Early Spanish Renaissance architecture is known as Plateresque because its fine detail resembles ornate silverwork (*platero* means silversmith).

The Palacio de las Cadenas *in Úbeda* (see p473) *has a severely Classical façade.*

Medallions   Classical columns   Sculpted parapet   Round arch

The Hostal de San Marcos in León *(see p335)*, one of Spain's finest Plateresque buildings

BAROQUE (17TH–18TH CENTURIES)

Baroque was driven by a desire for drama and movement. Decoration became extravagant, with exuberant sculpture and twisting columns. Although the excessive Baroque style of Churrigueresque is named after the Churriguera family of architects, it was their successors who were its main exponents.

The ornamentation on the Baroque façade of Valladolid University (see p348) *is concentrated above the doorway.*

Finials   Statues on parapet

The façade of the Museo Municipal in Madrid *(pp294–5)*

MODERN (LATE 19TH CENTURY ONWARDS)

Modernisme *(see pp136–7)*, a Catalan interpretation of Art Nouveau, is seen at its best in Barcelona. Its architects experimented with a highly original language of ornament. In recent decades, Spain has seen an explosion of bold, functionalist architecture in which the form of a building reflects its use and decoration is sparingly used.

Torre de Picasso in Madrid

Curving parapet   Spiral chimney   Decorative ironwork

Casa Milà, *in Barcelona (see p161), was built in 1910 by Modernisme's most famous and best-loved architect, Antoni Gaudí, who drew much of his inspiration from nature.*

Vernacular Architecture

Window in Navarra

As well as its cathedrals and palaces, Spain has a great variety of charming vernacular buildings. These have been constructed by local craftsmen to meet the practical needs of rural communities and to take account of local climate conditions, with little reference to formal architectural styles. Due to the high expense involved in transporting raw materials, builders used whatever stone or timber lay closest to hand. The three houses illustrated below incorporate the most common characteristics of village architecture seen in different parts of Spain.

A cave church in Artenara *(see p521)*, on Gran Canaria

STONE HOUSE

The climate is wet in the north and houses like this one in Carmona *(see p107)*, in Cantabria, are built with overhanging eaves to shed the rain. Wooden balconies catch the sun.

Supporting pillar

Large doors accommodate carts and animals.

The walls are built of irregularly shaped stones.

Detail of stonework

Family and farm often share rural houses. The ground floor is used to stable animals, or store tools and firewood.

TIMBER-FRAMED HOUSE

Spain, in general, has few large trees and wood is in short supply. Castilla y León is one of the few regions where timber-framed houses, such as this one in Covarrubias *(see p352)*, can be found. These houses are quick and cheap to build. The timber frame is filled in with a coarse plaster mixed from lime and sand, or adobe (bricks dried in the sun).

Portico

Gently sloping roof

The verandah runs the length of the building.

Balcony

The ends of the beams supporting the floorboards are visible.

Stone plinths below upright timbers provide protection from damp.

Half-timbered wall

In town squares, upright struts of timber supporting horizontal beams were used to form porticoes. A shady space was created for people to meet, talk and trade.

WHITEWASHED HOUSE

Houses in the south of Spain – often built of baked clay – are regularly whitewashed to deflect the sun's intense rays. Andalusia's famous white towns *(see p444)* exemplify this attractive form of architecture.

Irregularly shaped houses are joined together.

Few, small windows

Shallow-pitched roof

Clay-tiled roof

Windows are small and few in number, and deeply recessed, in order to keep the interior cool.

Whitewashed walls

THE PLAZA MAYOR

Almost every town in Spain centres on a main square, the *plaza mayor*, like this one in Pedraza de la Sierra *(see p347)*, near Segovia. More than a market square, it acts as a focus for local life. It is usually overlooked by the church, the town hall, shops and bars and the mansions of aristocratic families.

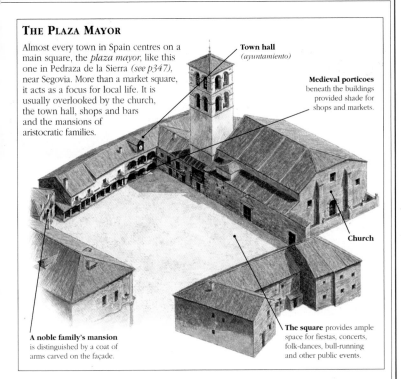

Town hall
(ayuntamiento)

Medieval porticoes beneath the buildings provided shade for shops and markets.

Church

A noble family's mansion is distinguished by a coat of arms carved on the façade.

The square provides ample space for fiestas, concerts, folk-dances, bull-running and other public events.

RURAL ARCHITECTURE

A variety of distinctive buildings dots the countryside.

Where the rock is soft and the climate hot, subterranean dwellings have been excavated. Insulated from extremes of temperature, they provide a comfortable place to live.

Hórreos, granaries raised on stone stilts to prevent rats climbing up into the grain, are a common sight in Galicia (where they are stone-built) and Asturias (where they are made of wood). In fields you will often see shelters for livestock or for storing crops, such as the *teitos* of Asturias.

Windmills provided power in parts of Spain where there was little running water but plentiful wind, like La Mancha and the Balearic Islands.

Almost everywhere in the Spanish countryside you will come across *ermitas*, isolated chapels or shrines dedicated to a local saint. An *ermita* may be opened only on the patron saint's feast day.

Cave houses in Guadix near Granada *(see p469)*

Teito **in Valle de Teverga in Asturias** *(see p101)*

Hórreo, **a granary, on the Rías Baixas** *(see p91)* **in Galicia**

Windmill above Consuegra *(see p376)* **in La Mancha**

Farming in Spain

S PAIN'S VARIED geography and climate have created a mosaic of farming patterns ranging from lush dairylands to stony hillsides where goats graze. Land can be broadly divided into *secano*, or dry cultivation (used for olives, wheat and vines), and much smaller areas of *regadío*, irrigated land (planted with citrus trees, rice and vegetables).

Donkey in Extremadura

Farming in many parts is a family affair relying on traditional, labour-intensive methods but it is becoming increasingly mechanized.

Plains of cereals *make up much of the farmland of the central* meseta *of Spain. Wheat is grown in better-watered, more fertile western areas; barley is grown in the drier south.*

Cork oaks thrive in Extremadura and western Andalusia.

MADRID

SEVILLA

0 kilometres 200
0 miles 100

Sheep *grazed on the rough pastures of Central Spain are milked to make cheese, especially* manchego, *which is produced in La Mancha (see p321).*

THE AGRICULTURAL YEAR

	Jul–Aug Wheat harvested in Central Spain	**Sep** Rice harvest in Eastern Spain. Grape harvest at its height	**Oct** Maize harvested in Northern Spain **Oct–Nov** Table olives picked	**Dec–Mar** Olives for making oil picked
Spring	**Summer**		**Autumn**	**Winter**
Mar–Apr Orange trees in blossom on Mediterranean coast			**Nov–Dec** Oranges picked	**Feb** Almond trees in blossom
Jun–Aug Haymaking in Northern Spain		**Sep** Start of wild mushroom season	**Dec** Pigs are slaughtered when cold weather arrives	

The high rainfall and mild summers of Northern Spain make it suitable for dairy farming. Farms are often small, especially in Galicia, one of the country's most under-developed regions. Crops such as maize and wheat are grown in small quantities.

Cork oaks stripped of their bark every ten years

Wine is produced in many parts of Spain *(see pp576–7)*. The country's best sparkling wine grapes are grown in Catalonia.

BARCELONA ●

Rice is grown mainly in the Ebro delta in Catalonia, around L'Albufera near Valencia and also at Calasparra in Murcia.

Oranges, lemons and clementines are grown on the irrigated coastal plains beside the Mediterranean. The region of Valencia is the prime producer of oranges.

CROPS FROM TREES

The almond, orange and olive create the three most characteristic landscapes of rural Spain but several other trees provide important crops. Wine corks are made from the bark of the cork oak. Tropical species, such as avocado and cherimoya, a delicious creamy fruit little known outside Spain, have been introduced to the so-called Costa Tropical of Andalusia *(see p459)*; and bananas are a major crop of the Canary Islands. Elsewhere, peaches and loquats are also grown commercially. Figs and carobs – whose fruit is used for fodder and as a substitute for chocolate – grow semi-wild.

Almonds grow on dry hill-sides in many parts of Spain. The spring blossom can be spectacular. The nut, enclosed by a fleshy green skin, is used in a variety of sweetmeats including the Christmas treat turrón (see p191).

Olive trees grow slowly and often live to a great age. The fruit is harvested in winter and either pickled in brine for eating as a tapa or pressed to extract the oil which is widely used in Spanish cuisine.

Sweet oranges are grown in dense, well-irrigated groves near the frost free coasts. The sweet smell of orange blossom in spring-time is unmistakeable. Trees of the bitter orange are often planted for shade and decoration in parks and gardens.

Olive trees are planted in long, straight lines across large swaths of Andalusia, especially in the province of Jaén. Spain is the world's leading producer of olive oil.

Spain's National Parks

EW OTHER COUNTRIES in western Europe have such unspoiled scenery as Spain, or can boast tracts of wilderness where brown bears live and wolves hunt. More than 200 nature reserves protect a broad range of ecosystems. The most important areas are the 11 national parks, the first of which was established in 1918. Natural parks *(parques naturales),* regulated by regional governments, are also vital to the task of conservation.

Giant orchid

Clear mountain river, Ordesa

MOUNTAINS

Some of Spain's finest scenery is to be found in the three national parks in the north. Rivers have carved stupendous gorges between the high peaks of the Picos de Europa. Ordesa and Aigüestortes between them share some of the most dramatic landscapes of the Pyrenees.

Rough terrain in the Picos de Europa

Eagle owls are Europe's largest owl, easily identified by their large ear tufts. At night they hunt small mammals and birds.

Chamois are well adapted to climbing across slopes covered in scree. They live in small groups, always alert to predators, and feed on grass and flowers.

WETLANDS

Wetlands, including coastal strips and freshwater marshes, are ever-changing environments. Seasonal floods rejuvenate the water providing nutrients for animal and plant growth. These areas are rich feeding grounds for birds. Spain's best-known wetland is Doñana. Tablas de Daimiel, in La Mancha, is much smaller.

Lynx, endangered by hunting and habitat loss, can occasionally be spotted in Doñana (see pp440–41).

Black-winged stilts, with their long, straight legs, are adept at stalking tiny freshwater crustaceans.

Laguna del Acebuche, Parque Nacional de Doñana

ISLANDS

Cabrera, off Mallorca, is home to rare plants, reptiles and seabirds, such as Eleonara's falcon. The surrounding waters are important for their marine life.

Lizards are often found in rocky terrain and on cliff faces.

Cabrera archipelago, Balearic Islands

NATIONAL PARKS

① Mountains

④ Wetlands

⑥ Islands

⑦ Woods and Forests

⑨ Volcanic Landscapes

MOUNTAINS

① Picos de Europa *pp104–105*

② Ordesa y Monte Perdido *pp222–3*

③ Aigüestortes y Estany de Sant Maurici *p201*

WETLANDS

④ Tablas de Daimiel *p381*

⑤ Doñana *pp440–41*

ISLANDS

⑥ Archipiélago de Cabrera *p493*

WOODS AND FORESTS

⑦ Cabañeros *p369*

⑧ Garajonay *p509*

VOLCANIC LANDSCAPES

⑨ Caldera de Taburiente *p508*

⑩ Teide *pp514–15*

⑪ Timanfaya *pp524–5*

VISITORS' CHECKLIST

All but one of the national parks are managed by ICONA (Instituto para la Conservación de la Naturaleza). **[** *(91) 347 59 71. Parque Nacional d'Aigüestortes y Estany de Sant Maurici is administered by Catalonia's Department of Agriculture.* **[** *(973) 62 40 36. Most, but not all, of Spain's national parks have visitors' centres.*

WOODS AND FORESTS

Deciduous broad-leaved forests grow in the northwest of Spain, and stands of Aleppo and Scots pine cover many mountainous areas. On the central plateau there are stretches of open woodland of evergreen holm oak and cork oak in the Parque Nacional de Cabañeros. Dense, lush *laurasilva* woodland grows in the Parque Nacional de Garajonay, on La Gomera, one of the smaller Canary Islands.

Black vultures *are the largest birds of prey in Europe, with an enormous wingspan of over 2.5 m (8 ft).*

Hedgehogs, *common in woodlands, root among fallen leaves and grass to find worms and slugs.*

Parque Nacional de Garajonay

VOLCANIC LANDSCAPES

Three very different parks protect parts of the Canary Islands' amazing volcanic scenery. Caldera de Taburiente on La Palma is a volcanic crater surrounded by woods. Mount Teide in Tenerife has unique alpine flora, and Lanzarote's Timanfaya is composed of barren but atmospheric lava fields.

Rabbits *are highly opportunistic, quickly colonizing areas in which they can burrow. In the absence of predators, populations may increase, damaging fragile ecosystems.*

Colonizing plant species, Mount Teide (Tenerife)

Canaries *belong to the finch family of songbirds. The popular canary has been bred from the wild serin, native to the Canaries.*

Spanish Art

THREE SPANISH PAINTERS stand out as milestones in the history of Western art. Diego de Velázquez was a 17th-century court portrait painter and his *Las Meninas* is a seminal work. Francisco de Goya depicted Spanish life during one of its most violent periods. The prolific 20th-century master, Pablo Picasso, is recognized as the founder of modern art. To these names must be added that of El Greco – who was born in Crete but who lived in Spain, where he painted religious scenes in an individualistic style. The work of these and Spain's many other great artists can be seen in world-renowned galleries, especially the Prado *(see pp282–5)*.

The king and queen, reflected in a mirror behind the painter, may be posing for their portrait.

Self-portrait of Velázquez

In his series, **Las Meninas** *(1957), Picasso interprets the frozen gesture of the five-year-old Infanta Margarita. Altogether, Picasso produced 44 paintings based on Velázquez's canvas. They can be seen in Barcelona's Museu de Picasso* (see p149).

RELIGIOUS ART IN SPAIN

The influence of the Catholic Church on Spanish art through the ages is reflected in the predominance of religious imagery. Many churches and museums have Romanesque altarpieces or earlier icons. El Greco *(see p373)* painted from a highly personal religious vision. Baroque religious art of the 17th century, when the Inquisition *(see p264)* was at its height, often graphically depicts physical suffering and spiritual torment.

The Burial of the Count of Orgaz by El Greco (see p372)

LAS MENINAS *(1656)*
In Velázquez's painting of the Infanta Margarita and her courtiers, in the Prado *(see pp282–5)*, the eye is drawn into the distance where the artist's patron, Felipe IV, is reflected in a mirror.

TIMELINE OF GREAT SPANISH ARTISTS

The Saviour by José de Ribera

1285–1348 Ferrer Bassá	**1390–1410** Pere Nicolau			**1598–1664** Francisco de Zurbarán
	1363–95 Jaume Serra	**1428–1460** Luis Daimau		**1591–1652** José de Ribera
1300		**1400**		**1500**
	1388–1424 Luis Borrassa		**1474–95** Bartolomé Bermejo	**1565–1628** Francisco Ribalta
			1450–1504 Pedro Berruguete	**1599–1660** Diego de Velázquez
Virgin and Child by Ferrer Bassá	**1427–52** Bernat Martorell		**1541–1614** El Greco	

José Nieto, the queen's chamberlain, stands in the doorway in the background of the painting.

Court jester

MODERN ART

The early 20th-century artists Joan Miró *(see p168)*, Salvador Dalí *(see p205)* and Pablo Picasso *(see p148)* all belonged to the Paris School. More recent artists of note include Antonio Saura and Antoni Tàpies *(see p160)*. Among many great Spanish art collections, the Centro de Reina Sofía in Madrid *(see pp288–9)* specializes in modern art. Contemporary artists are accorded great prestige in Spain. Their work is to be seen in town halls, banks and public squares, and many towns have a museum dedicated to a local painter.

Salvador Dalí's painting of the *Colossus of Rhodes* (1954)

***Collage* (1934) by Joan Miró**

The Family of King Charles IV *was painted in 1800 by Francisco de Goya (see p229), nearly 150 years after* Las Meninas. *Its debt to Velázquez's painting is evident in its frontal composition, compact grouping of figures and in the inclusion of a self-portrait.*

The Holy Children with the Shell *by Murillo*

1746–1828 Francisco de Goya

1893–1983 Joan Miró

1881–1973 Pablo Picasso

1863–1923 Joaquín Sorolla

1904–89 Salvador Dalí

1923– Antoni Tàpies

1700

1800

1900

1642–93 Claudio Coello

1618–82 Bartolomé Esteban Murillo

Jug and Glass *(1916) by Juan Gris*

1887–1927 Juan Gris

1930– Antonio Saura

Literary Spain

DON QUIXOTE, considered the first modern novel, is the best-known work of Spanish literature. However, Spain has produced many major works over the last 2,000 years. The Roman writers Seneca, Lucan and Martial were born in Spain. Later, the Moors developed a flourishing, but now little-known, literary culture. Although Spanish (Castilian) is the national tongue, many enduring works have been written in the Galician and Catalan regional languages. Basque literature, hitherto an oral culture, is a more recent development. Many foreign writers, such as Alexandre Dumas, Ernest Hemingway and Karel Capek, have written accounts of their travels in Spain.

The 14th-century *El Libro de Buen Amor*

MIDDLE AGES

AS THE ROMAN EMPIRE fell, Latin evolved into several Romance languages. The earliest non-Latin literature in Spain derives from an oral tradition that arose before the 10th century. It is in the form of *jarchas*, snatches of love poetry written in Mozarab, the Romance language that was spoken by Christians living under the Moors.

In the 12th century, the first poems appeared in Castilian. During the next 300 years, two separate schools of poetry developed. The best-known example of troubadour verse is the anonymous epic, *El Cantar del Mío Cid*, which tells of the heroic exploits of El Cid *(see p352)* during the Reconquest. Works of clerical poetry – for example, Gonzalo de Berceo's *Milagros de Nuestra Señora*, relating the life of the Virgin – convey a moral message.

Spanish literature evolved in the 13th century after Alfonso X the Learned *(see p51)* replaced Latin with Castilian

Alfonso X the Learned (1221–84)

Romance (later called Spanish) as the official language. Under his supervision a team of Jews, Christians and Arabs wrote scholarly treatises. The king himself was a poet, writing in Galician Romance.

The first great prose works in Spanish appeared in the 14th and 15th centuries. *El Libro de Buen Amor,* by an ecclesiastic, Juan Ruiz, is a tale of the love affairs of a priest, interleaved with other stories. Fernando de Rojas uses skilful characterization in *La Celestina* to tell a tragic love story about two nobles and a scheming go-between. This was an age in which tales of chivalry were also popular.

GOLDEN AGE

The prolific Golden Age dramatist, Félix Lope de Vega

THE 16TH CENTURY hailed the start of Spain's Golden Age of literature. But it was also a period of domestic strife. This found expression in the picaresque novel, a Spanish genre originating with the anonymous *El Lazarillo de Tormes*, a bitter reflection on the misfortunes of a blind man's guide.

Spiritual writers flourished under the austere climate of the Counter-Reformation. St John of the Cross's *Cántico Espiritual* was influenced by oriental erotic poetry and the Bible's *Song of Songs*.

The 17th century saw the emergence of more great talents. The life and work of Miguel de Cervantes *(see p315)* straddles the two centuries of the Golden Age. He published his masterpiece, *Don Quixote*, in 1605. Other important writers of the time include Francisco de Quevedo and Luis de Góngora.

Corrales (public theatres) appeared in the 17th century, opening the way for Lope de Vega *(see p280)*, Calderón de la Barca and other dramatists.

Don Quixote's adventures portrayed by José Moreno Carbonero

18TH AND 19TH CENTURIES

INFLUENCED BY the French Enlightenment, literature in the 18th century was seen as a way to educate the people. Such was the aim, for instance, of Leandro Fernández de Moratín's comedy *El Sí de las Niñas*. This period saw the development of journalism as well as the emergence of the essay as a literary form. Romanticism had a short and late life in Spain. *Don Juan Tenorio*, a tale of the legendary irrepressible Latin lover by José Zorrilla, is the best-known Romantic play.

José Zorrilla (1817–93)

The satirical essayist Larra stands out from his contemporaries at the beginning of the 19th century. Towards the end of the century, the novel became a vehicle for realistic portrayals of Spanish society. Benito Pérez Galdós, regarded by many to be Spain's greatest novelist after Cervantes, studied the human condition in his *Episodios Nacionales*. The heroine in Clarín's *La Regenta* is undone by the reactionary prejudices of provincial town society.

20TH CENTURY

WRITERS AT THE turn of the century, including Pío Baroja *(see p60)*, Miguel de Unamuno and Antonio Machado, described a Spain falling behind the rest of Europe. Exploring the grotesque, the only way he could describe society, led Ramón María del Valle-Inclán to lay the foundations for modern Spanish theatre. In poetry, the Nobel Prize winner, Juan Ramón Jiménez, strived for pureness of form.

The so-called "Generation of 27" combined European experimental art with Spain's traditional literary subjects and forms. The best known of them is the poet and playwright Federico García Lorca who was executed by a Fascist firing squad in 1936 *(see p63)*. He drew on the legends and stereotypes of his native Andalusia to make universal statements in his poems and plays, such as *Yerma*.

In the aftermath of the Civil War, many intellectuals who had backed the Republic were forced into exile. The Franco regime tried to create its own propagandist culture. Yet the finest literature of the period was written in spite of the prevailing political climate. Camilo José Cela's *La Colmena*, a description of everyday life in the hungry, postwar city of Madrid, set a mood of social realism that inspired other writers.

Poster for a Lorca play

The novel has had a rebirth in Spain since the 1960s, with the emergence of writers like Juan Goytisolo, Joan Benet, Julio Llamazares, Antonio Muñoz Molina, José Manuel Caballero Bonald and Juan Marsé.

The 20th century has also witnessed a surge of great Spanish literature from Latin America. Prominent authors include Jorge Luis Borges and Gabriel García Márquez.

Camilo José Cela, Nobel Prize-winning novelist, by Alvaro Delgado

The Art of Bullfighting

Poster for a bullfight

BULLFIGHTING is a sacrificial ritual in which men (and also a few women) pit themselves against an animal bred for the ring. In this "authentic religious drama", as poet García Lorca described it, the spectator experiences vicariously the fear and exaltation felt by the matador. Although some Spaniards oppose it on grounds of its cruelty, nowadays it is as popular as ever. Many Spaniards see talk of banning bullfighting as striking at the essence of their being, for they regard the *toreo*, the art of bullfighting, as a noble part of their heritage. Bullfights today, however, are often debased by practices which weaken the bull, especially shaving its horns to make them blunt.

***Plaza de Toros de la Maestranza**, Seville. This ring is regarded, with Las Ventas in Madrid, as one of the top venues for bullfighting in Spain.*

The matador wears a *traje de luces* (suit of lights), a colourful silk outfit embroidered with gold sequins.

The passes are made with a *muleta*, a scarlet cape stiffened along one side.

***Well treated at the ranch**, the toro bravo (fighting bull) is specially bred for qualities of aggressiveness and courage. As aficionados of bullfighting point out in its defence, the young bull enjoys a full life while it is being prepared for its 15 minutes in the ring. Bulls must be at least four years old before they fight.*

THE BULLFIGHT

The *corrida* (bullfight) has three stages, called *tercios*. In the first one, the *tercio de varas*, the matador and *picadores* (horsemen with lances) are aided by *peones* (assistants). In the *tercio de banderillas*, *banderilleros* stick pairs of darts in the bull's back. In the *tercio de muleta* the matador makes a series of passes at the bull with a *muleta* (cape). He then executes the kill, the *estocada*, with a sword.

***The matador** plays the bull with a capa (red cape) in the tercio de varas. Peones will then draw the bull towards the picadores.*

Horses are now padded.

***Picadores** goad the bull with steel-pointed lances, testing its bravery. The lances weaken the animal's shoulder muscles.*

THE BULLRING

The *corrida* audience is seated in the *tendidos* (stalls) or in the *palcos* (balcony), where the *presidencia* (president's box) is situated. Opposite are the *puerta de cuadrillas*, through which the matador and team arrive, and the *arrastre de toros* (exit for bulls). Before entering the ring, the matadors wait in a corridor (*callejón*) behind *barreras* and *burladeros* (barriers). Horses are kept in the *patio de caballos* and the bulls in the *corrales*.

Plan of a typical bullring

KEY

- Tendidos
- Palcos
- Presidencia
- Puerta de cuadrillas
- Arrastre de toros
- Callejón
- Barreras
- Burladeros
- Patio de caballos
- Corrales

Banderillas, barbed darts, are thrust into the bull's already weakened back muscles.

Manolete is regarded by most followers of bullfighting as one of the greatest matadors ever. He was eventually gored to death by the bull Islero at Linares, Jaén, in 1947.

Manolete (portrait)

The bull may go free if it shows courage – spectators wave white handkerchiefs, asking the *corrida* president to let it leave the ring alive.

Joselito is one of Spain's leading matadors today. He is famous for his purist approach and for his flair and technical skill with both the capa and the muleta.

The bull weighs about 500 kg (1,100 lb).

***Banderilleros** enter to provoke the wounded bull in the* tercio de banderillas, *sticking pairs of* banderillas *in its back.*

***The matador** makes passes with the cape in the* tercio de muleta, *then lowers it and thrusts in the sword for the kill.*

***The estocada recibiendo** is a difficult kill, rarely seen. The matador awaits the bull's charge rather than moving to meet it.*

The Fiestas of Spain

ON ANY DAY of the year there is a fiesta happening somewhere in Spain – usually more than one. There isn't a village, town or city in the country which doesn't honour its patron saint, the Virgin or the changing seasons with processions, bull-running, fireworks, re-enacted battles, some ancestral rite or a *romería* – a mass pilgrimage to a rural shrine. Whatever the pretext, a fiesta is a chance for everyone to take a break from normal life (most shops and offices close) and let off steam, with celebrations sometimes going on around the clock.

The Passion, Semana Santa

Many *romerías* wind through the countryside during the year

SPRING FIESTAS

THE END OF WINTER and the start of spring are marked by Valencia's great fire festival, Las Fallas *(see p245)*, in which huge papier-mâché sculptures are set alight in a symbolic act of burning the old in order to make way for the new.

Alcoi's noisy mock battles between costumed armies of Moors and Christians in April *(see p245)* are the most spectacular of the countless fiestas which commemorate the battles of the Reconquest.

Seville's great April Fair *(see p413)*, is the biggest celebration held in Andalusia.

During Los Mayos, on 30 April and the following days, crosses are decorated with flowers in parts of Spain.

EASTER

EASTER IS SPAIN'S main fiesta. Almost every community observes it in some form with pomp and solemnity.

It is heralded by the processions of Palm Sunday. The most impressive of these is in Elx, where intricate sculptures are woven from blanched leaves cropped from the most extensive forest of palm trees in Europe *(see p251)*.

The best Semana Santa (Easter Week) processions are those held in Seville *(see p413)*, Málaga, Murcia and Valladolid. Brotherhoods of robed men carry *pasos*, huge sculptures depicting the Virgin, Christ or scenes of the Passion, through the streets. They are accompanied by people dressed as biblical characters or penitents, in tall conical hats. In some towns passion plays are acted out. In others, people carry heavy crosses. Sometimes the centuries-old ritual of self-flagellation can be witnessed.

SUMMER FIESTAS

THE FIRST MAJOR fiesta of the summer is Pentecost (also known as Whitsun), in May or June, and its most famous celebration is at El Rocío *(see p439)*, where many thousands of people gather in a frenzy of religious devotion.

At Corpus Christi (in May or June) the consecrated host is carried in procession through many cities in an ornate silver monstrance. The route of the procession is often covered with a carpet of flowers. The main Corpus Christi celebrations take place in Valencia, Toledo and Granada.

On Midsummer's Eve, bonfires are lit all over Spain, especially in the areas along the Mediterranean coast, to

The Brotherhood of Candlemas, Semana Santa (Easter Week) in Seville

herald the celebration of St John the Baptist on 24 June.

St Peter, the patron saint of fishermen, is honoured in many ports with flotillas of decorated boats on 29 June.

During Los Sanfermines *(see p128)* in Pamplona in July, young people run through the streets in front of six bulls.

The important Catholic holiday of Assumption Day, 15 August, is marked by a huge number and variety of fiestas.

AUTUMN FIESTAS

THERE ARE FEW FIESTAS in autumn, but in most wine regions the grape harvest is fêted. The annual pig slaughter has become a jubilant public event in some villages, especially in Extremadura. In Galicia it is traditional to roast chestnuts on street bonfires.

On All Saints' Day, 1 November, people remember the dead by visiting cemeteries to lay flowers, especially chrysanthemums, on graves.

CHRISTMAS AND NEW YEAR

NOCHEBUENA (Christmas Eve) is the main Christmas celebration, when families gather for an evening meal before attending Midnight Mass, known as *misa del gallo* (Mass of the rooster). During the Christmas period, *belenes* (crib scenes) of painted figurines abound. You may also see a "living crib", peopled by costumed actors.

The losers end up in the harbour in Dénia's July fiesta *(see p245)*

Spain's "April Fools' Day" is 28 December, the Day of the Holy Innocents, when people play practical jokes on each other. Clown-like characters may act out the role of mayor and make fun of passers-by.

To celebrate New Year's Eve *(Noche Vieja)*, crowds gather beneath the clock in Madrid's central square, the Puerta del Sol *(see p262)*.

Spanish children do not receive their Christmas presents until Epiphany, on 6 January, when the Three Kings parade through large cities throwing sweets into the crowds.

WINTER FIESTAS

ANIMALS HOLD centre stage in a variety of fiestas on 17 January, the Day of St Anthony, patron saint of animals, when pets and livestock are blessed by priests.

St Agatha, the patron saint of married women, is honoured on 5 February when women, for once, are the protagonists of many fiestas. In Zamarramala (Segovia), for example, women take over the mayor's privileges and powers for this particular day *(see p350)*.

St Anthony's Day in Villanueva de Alcolea (Castellón province)

CARNIVAL

CARNIVAL, in February or early March (depending on the date of Easter), brings a chance for a street party as winter comes to an end and before Lent begins. The biggest celebrations are held in Santa Cruz de Tenerife *(see p512)* – comparable with those of Rio de Janeiro – and in Cádiz *(see p439)*. Carnival was prohibited by the Franco regime because of its licentiousness and frivolity. It ends on or after Ash Wednesday with the Burial of the Sardine, a "funeral" in which a mock sardine, representing winter, is ritually burned or buried.

A spectacularly costumed choir singing during Carnival in Cádiz

SPAIN THROUGH THE YEAR

ESTIVALS, cultural events and sports competitions crowd the calendar in Spain. Even small villages have at least one traditional fiesta, lasting a week or more, when parades, bull-fights and fireworks displays replace work (*see pp34–5*). Many rural and coastal towns celebrate the harvest or fishing catch with a gastronomic fair at which you can sample local produce.

Matador with a cape playing a bull

Music, dance, drama and film festivals are held in Spain's major cities throughout the year. Meanwhile, the country's favourite outdoor sports – football, basketball, cycling, sailing, golf and tennis – culminate in several national and international championships.

It is a good idea to confirm specific dates of events with the local tourist board as some vary from year to year.

SPRING

LIFE IN SPAIN moves outdoors with the arrival of spring, and terrace-cafés begin to fill with people. The countryside is at its best as wild flowers bloom before the onset of the summer heat, and irrigation channels flow to bring water to the newly sown crops. The important Easter holiday is a time of solemn processions.

MARCH

International Vintage Car Rally *(first Sun)*, from Barcelona to Sitges.
Las Fallas *(week ending 19 Mar)*, Valencia *(see p245)*. A spectacular fiesta which also marks the start of the bull-fighting *(see pp32–3)* season.

APRIL

Vuelta Ciclista a España *(Apr or Sep)*. Bicycle race around Spain.
Religious Music Week *(mid-Apr)*, Cuenca.

Feria del Caballo (Festival of the Horses) in Jerez de la Frontera

Trofeo Conde de Godó *(mid-Apr)*, Barcelona. Spain's premier international tennis championship.
Moors and Christians *(third week)*, Alcoi *(see p249)*. Celebration of the Christian victory over the Moors in 1276.
April Fair *(two weeks after Easter)*, Seville. Exuberant Andalusian fiesta *(see p413)*.
Feria Nacional del Queso *(late Apr/early May)*, Trujillo (Cáceres). Festival celebrating Spanish cheese *(see p389)*.

MAY

Feria del Caballo *(first week)*, Jerez de la Frontera. Horse fair showing Andalusia at its most traditional, with fine horses, and beautiful women in flamenco dresses.
Spanish Motorcycle Grand Prix *(May)*, Jerez de la Frontera race track.
Fiesta de San Isidro *(8–15 May)*, Madrid *(see p280)*. Bullfights at Las Ventas bull-ring are the highlights of the taurine year.
National Flamenco Competition *(mid-May, every third year: 1998, 2001)*, Córdoba.
Peugeot Open de España *(mid-May)*, Club de Campo, Madrid. Golf tournament.
Spanish Formula One Grand Prix *(May/Jun)*, Montmeló circuit, Barcelona. International motor race.
A Rapa das Bestas *(May and Jun)*, Pontevedra (Galicia). Wild horses are rounded up so that their manes and tails can be cut *(see p94)*.

Onlookers lining the street during the Vuelta Ciclista a España

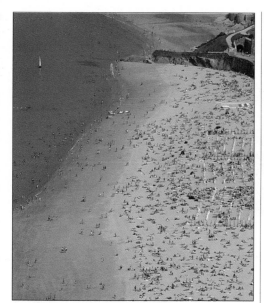

San Sebastián, one of the most popular resorts on the north coast

SUMMER

AUGUST is Spain's big holiday season. The cities empty as Spaniards flock to the coast or to their second homes in the hills. Their numbers are swelled by millions of foreign tourists, and beaches and camp sites are often full to bursting. As the heat starts in the centre and south, entertainment often takes place only in the evening, when the temperature has dropped. In late summer the harvest begins and there are gastronomic fiestas everywhere to celebrate food and drink, from the fishing catches of the north coast to the sausages of the Balearic Islands.

JUNE

International Festival of Music and Dance (*mid-Jun–early Jul*), Granada. Many events are staged in the Alhambra or the Generalife.
Grec Arts Festival (*Jun–Jul*), Barcelona. Theatre, music and dance by Catalan, Spanish and international performers.
Copa del Rey (*Apr–Jun*) Football cup final.

JULY

Classical Theatre Festival (*Jul–Aug*), Mérida. Staged in the Roman theatre and amphitheatre (*see p392*).
Guitar Festival (*first two weeks*), Córdoba. Performances range from classical to flamenco (*see pp406–7*).
National Classical Theatre Festival of Almagro (*4–28 Jul*). Spanish and international classical repertoire performed in one of the oldest theatres in Europe (*see p381*).

The pouring and tasting of cider in Asturias's Cider Festival

Cider Festival (*second Sat, even years only*), Nava (Asturias). Includes traditional cider-pouring competitions.
International Festival of Santander (*Jul–Aug*). Celebration of music, dance and theatre.
Pyrenean Folklore Festival (*late Jul/early Aug, odd years only*), Jaca (Aragón). Display of folk costumes, music and dance.
International Jazz Festivals in San Sebastián (*third week*) and Vitoria (*mid-Jul*).

AUGUST

Certamen Internacional de Habaneras y Polifonía (*late Jul–early Aug*), Torrevieja (Alicante). Musical competition of 19th-century seafarers' songs.
HM the King's International Cup (*first week*), Palma de Mallorca. Sailing competition in which Juan Carlos I participates.
Descent of the Río Sella (*first Sat*). Canoe race in Asturias from Arriondas to Ribadesella (*see p103*).
Assumption Day (*15 Aug*) The Assumption is celebrated in cities, towns and villages throughout the country.

Participants in the Descent of the Río Sella canoe race

Semanas Grandes (*early–mid-Aug*), Bilbao and San Sebastián. "Great Weeks" of sporting and cultural events.
Misteri d'Elx (*14–15 Aug*), Elx (*see p251*). Unique liturgical drama performed in a church and featuring spectacular special effects.

Vines and the village of Larouco in the Valdeorras wine region of Galicia *(see p74)* in autumn

AUTUMN

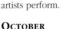

Wild mushrooms

AUTUMN USUALLY brings rain after the heat of summer, and with the high tourist season over, a large number of resorts practically close down. Harvest festivities continue, however, and the most important celebrations are in honour of the grape. The first pressings are blessed and, in some places, wine is served for free.

In woodland areas, freshly picked wild mushrooms start to appear in various dishes on local restaurant menus. The hunting season begins in the middle of October and runs until February. Autumn is also the start of the new drama and classical music seasons in the major cities of Spain.

SEPTEMBER

International Folklore Gala *(late Aug/early Sep)*, Ronda (Málaga). Music and dancing.
Grape Harvest *(first week)*, Jerez de la Frontera. Celebration of the new crop in the country's sherry capital.
Madrid Autumn Festival *(mid-Sep–mid-Nov)*. Classical and modern drama, dance and music by national and visiting foreign companies.
San Sebastián Film Festival *(last two weeks)*. International gathering of film-makers which includes screenings of new releases *(see p119)*.
Bienal de Arte Flamenco *(last two weeks, even years only)*, Seville. Top flamenco artists perform.

OCTOBER

Día de la Hispanidad *(12 Oct)*. Spain's national holiday marks Columbus's discovery of America in 1492. The biggest celebration in the country is the exuberant fiesta of Día del Pilar in Zaragoza *(see p229)*, which marks the end of the bullfighting year.

Driving down the fairway in the Volvo Masters Golf Championship

IBERFLORA *(mid-Oct)*, Valencia. Flower show.
Saffron Festival *(late Oct)*, Consuegra (Toledo).
Volvo Masters Golf Championship *(late Oct)*, Valderrama (Cádiz).

NOVEMBER

All Saints' Day *(1 Nov)*. The traditional start of the *matanza* (pig slaughter) in rural areas of Spain.
Os Magostos *(11 Nov)*. Various towns in Galicia hold chestnut-harvest fairs.
Latin American Film Festival *(last two weeks)*, Huelva *(see p438)*.

Lana Turner on centre-stage at the San Sebastián Film Festival

PUBLIC HOLIDAYS

Besides marking the national holidays below, each region *(comunidad autónoma)* celebrates its own holiday and every town and village has at least one other fiesta each year. If a holiday falls on a Tuesday or a Thursday shops, offices and monuments may also be closed on the intervening Monday or Friday, making a long weekend called a *puente* ("bridge").

Año Nuevo *(New Year's Day)* (1 Jan)
Día de los Reyes *(Epiphany)* (6 Jan)
Jueves Santo *(Maundy Thursday)* (Mar/Apr)
Viernes Santo *(Good Friday)* (Mar/Apr)
Día de Pascua *(Easter Sunday)* (Mar/Apr)
Día del Trabajo *(Labour Day)* (1 May)
Asunción *(Assumption Day)* (15 Aug)
Día de la Hispanidad *(National Day)* (12 Oct)
Todos los Santos *(All Saints' Day)* (1 Nov)
Día de la Constitución *(Constitution Day)* (6 Dec)
Inmaculada Concepción *(Immaculate Conception)* (8 Dec)

Assumption Day in La Alberca (Salamanca)

Navidad *(Christmas Day)* (25 Dec)

WINTER

WINTER VARIES greatly from region to region. In the mountains, snowfalls bring skiers to the slopes; while in lower areas, olive and orange picking are in full swing. The higher parts of Central Spain can become very cold. Andalusia, the east coast and the Balearic Islands have cool nights but often sunny days. The winter warmth of the Canary Islands brings the high tourist season. Christmas is a special time of celebration – an occasion for families to re-unite, share food and attend religious celebrations.

Skiers in the Sierra de Guadarrama, north of Madrid *(see p311)*

"El Gordo", the largest Spanish lottery prize, being drawn

DECEMBER

El Gordo *(22 Dec)*. Spain's largest lottery prize, "the Fat One", is drawn *(see p622)*.
Noche Buena *(24 Dec)* is a family Christmas Eve, followed by Midnight Mass for the devout *(see p35)*.
Santos Inocentes *(28 Dec)*, Spain's version of April Fools' Day, when people play tricks.
Noche Vieja *(31 Dec)*. New Year's Eve is most celebrated in Madrid's Puerta del Sol.

JANUARY

Canary Islands International Music Festival *(Jan–Feb)*. Classical concerts are held on all of the major islands.
Opera Season *(Jan–Apr)*, Teatro Coliseo, Bilbao.

Vigo Video Festival *(last week)*. Screenings and other events exploring all aspects of video film-making.

FEBRUARY

Festival of Ancient Music *(Feb–Mar)*, Seville. Early music is played on period instruments.
ARCO *(mid-Feb)*, Madrid. International contemporary art fair attracting galleries from across the world.
IMAGENMODA and **IBERMODA** *(mid-Feb)*, Madrid. Women's and men's fashion shows.
Carnival *(Feb/Mar)*. Final fiesta before Lent, with colourful costumes. Those in Santa Cruz de Tenerife and Cádiz are among the best.

The Climate of Spain

SPAIN'S LARGE LANDMASS, with its extensive high plateaus and mountain ranges, and the influences of the Mediterranean and Atlantic produce a wide range of climatic variation, especially in winter. The north is wettest year round, the eastern and southern coasts and the islands have mild winters, while winter temperatures in the interior are often below freezing. Summers everywhere are hot, except in upland areas.

BASQUE COUNTRY, NAVARRA & RIOJA

°C 36 / 25 / 25.5 / 9.5 / 15 / 0.5 / 2 / -7

month	Apr	Jul	Oct	Jan
☀	6.0 hrs	9.5 hrs	5 hrs	2.5 hrs
☂	83 mm	46 mm	107 mm	120 mm

ARAGÓN

°C 37 / 26 / 26.5 / 13.5 / 17.5 / 3.5 / 4.5 / -3.5

month	Apr	Jul	Oct	Jan
☀	8 hrs	11.5 hrs	6.5 hrs	5 hrs
☂	34 mm	15 mm	34 mm	17 mm

CATALONIA

°C 37.5 / 27.5 / 27.5 / 13 / 17.5 / 3 / 2.5 / -5

month	Apr	Jul	Oct	Jan
☀	8.5 hrs	11.5 hrs	6.5 hrs	4 hrs
☂	46 mm	24 mm	30 mm	22 mm

THE BALEARIC ISLANDS

°C 33 / 23.5 / 26.5 / 16.5 / 18 / 6.0 / 8.5 / 2

month	Apr	Jul	Oct	Jan
☀	7.5 hrs	11.5 hrs	6 hrs	5.0 hrs
☂	32 mm	3 mm	77 mm	39 mm

CASTILLA-LA MANCHA

°C 35.5 / 23.5 / 25.5 / 8.0 / 16 / -1.5 / -1 / -9.5

month	Apr	Jul	Oct	Jan
☀	7.5 hrs	12 hrs	6 hrs	4.5 hrs
☂	48 mm	19 mm	52 mm	43 mm

VALENCIA AND MURCIA

°C 36 / 27 / 29.5 / 16.5 / 22.5 / 6.5 / 9 / 1

month	Apr	Jul	Oct	Jan
☀	8.5 hrs	11.5 hrs	7 hrs	6 hrs
☂	40 mm	4 mm	52 mm	30 mm

THE CANARY ISLANDS

°C 32 / 26 / 30 / 17 / 25 / 11.5 / 15.5 / 10.5

month	Apr	Jul	Oct	Jan
☀	7.5 hrs	9.5 hrs	7 hrs	6.5 hrs
☂	13 mm	0 mm	28 mm	36 mm

Map labels:
onostia (Sebastián)
Iruña (mplona)
Zaragoza
Lleida
Barcelona
Palma de Mallorca
Valencia
Alacant (Alicante)
Murcia
Santa Cruz de Tenerife
Las Palmas de Gran Canaria

THE HISTORY OF SPAIN

THE IBERIAN PENINSULA, first inhabited around 800,000 BC, has long been subject to foreign influences. From the 11th century BC it was colonized by sophisticated eastern Mediterranean civilizations, starting with the Phoenicians, then the Greeks and Carthaginians.

The Romans arrived in 218 BC to fight the Carthaginians, thus sparking off the Second Punic War. They harvested the peninsula's agricultural and mineral wealth and established cities with aqueducts, temples and theatres.

Gold Aztec statue from America

With the fall of the Roman Empire in the early 5th century AD, Visigothic invaders from the north assumed power. Their poor political organization, however, made them easy prey to the Moors from North Africa. In the 8th century, the peninsula came almost entirely under Moorish rule. Europe's only major Muslim territory, the civilization of Al Andalus excelled in mathematics, geography, astronomy and poetry. In the 9th and 10th centuries Córdoba was Europe's leading city.

From the 11th century, northern Christian kingdoms initiated a military reconquest of Al Andalus. The marriage, in 1469, of Fernando of Aragón and Isabel of Castile, the so-called Catholic Monarchs, led to Spanish unity. They took Granada, the last Moorish kingdom, in 1492. Columbus discovered the Americas in the same year, opening the way for the Spanish conquistadors, who plundered the civilizations of the New World.

The succeeding Habsburg dynasty spent the riches from the New World in endless foreign wars. Spain's decline was exacerbated by high inflation and religious oppression. Although the Enlightenment in the late 18th century created a climate of learning, Spain's misfortunes continued into the next century with an invasion by Napoleon's troops and the loss of her American colonies. A new radicalism began to emerge, creating a strong Anarchist movement. The political instability of the late 19th and early 20th centuries led to dictatorship in the 1920s and a republic in the 1930s, which was destroyed by the Spanish Civil War. Victorious General Franco ruled by repression until his death in 1975. Since then Spain has been a democratic state.

Bullfighting in Madrid's Plaza Mayor in the 17th century

◁ Moors paying homage to Fernando and Isabel, the 15th-century Catholic Monarchs

Prehistoric Spain

Helmet of Celt-Iberian warrior

T HE IBERIAN PENINSULA was first inhabited by hunter-gatherers around 800,000 BC. They were eclipsed by a Neolithic farming population from 5000 BC. First in a wave of settlers from over the Mediterranean, the Phoenicians landed in 1100 BC, to be followed by the Greeks and Carthaginians. Invading Celts mixed with native Iberian tribes (forming the Celtiberians). They proved a formidable force against the Romans, the next conquerors of Spain.

SPAIN IN 5000 BC

☐ *Neolithic farming settlements*

Iron Dagger *(6th century BC)*
Weapons, like this dagger from Burgos, represent the later Iron Age, in contrast to earlier metal objects which were for domestic use.

Stone Age Man
This skull belongs to a Palaeolithic man, who hunted deer and bison with tools made of wood and stone.

Incised geometric pattern

The 28 bracelets have perforations and moulded decorations.

Small silver bottle

La Dama de Elche
Dating from the 4th century BC, this stone statue is a fine example of Iberian art. Her austere beauty reveals traces of Greek influence.

THE VILLENA TREASURE

Discovered in 1963 during works in Villena, near Alicante, this Bronze Age find consists of 66 dazzling objects mostly of gold, including bowls, bottles and jewellery *(see p250)*. The treasure dates from around 1000 BC.

TIMELINE

800,000 BC *Homo erectus* arrives in Iberian Peninsula	**35,000 BC** Cro-Magnon man evolves in Spain	**2500 BC** Los Millares *(p477)* is inhabited by early metalworkers with belief in the afterlife	**1800–1100 BC** Civilization of El Argar, an advanced agrarian society, flourishes in southeast Spain
300,000 BC Tribes of *Homo erectus* live in hunting camps in Soria and Madrid			

800,000 BC		2500	2000
500,000 BC Stones used as tools by hominids (probably *Homo erectus*)	**100,000–40,000 BC** Neanderthal man in Gibraltar	**5000 BC** Farming begins in Iberian Peninsula	
Bison cave drawing, Altamira		**18,000–14,000 BC** Drawings by cave dwellers at Altamira (Cantabria), near Ribadesella (Asturias) and at Nerja (Andalusia)	

Greek Ceramic Vase
The Greek colonizers brought new technology, including the potter's wheel, as well as refined artistic ideals. Ceramics, such as this 6th-century BC vase depicting the Labours of Hercules, provided sophisticated models.

WHERE TO SEE PREHISTORIC SPAIN

The most famous cave paintings in Spain are at Altamira *(see p108)*. There are dolmens in many parts of the country; among the largest are those at Antequera *(see p451)*. The Guanches – the indigenous inhabitants of the Canary Islands – left behind more recent remains *(see p523)*.

La Naveta d'es Tudons is one of the many prehistoric stone monuments scattered across the island of Menorca (see p503).

An excavated Celtic village, with its round huts, can be seen near A Guarda in Pontevedra (see p92).

The largest of the treasure's five bottles, made of silver, stands 22.5 cm (9 in) high.

Bowls of beaten gold may have originated in southwest Spain.

Brooches with separate clasps

The smaller pieces are of unknown use.

Astarte *(8th century BC)*
Worship of Phoenician deities was incorporated into local religions. One of the most popular was the fertility goddess Astarte, shown on this bronze from the kingdom of Tartessus.

Phoenician gold ornament

1100 BC Phoenicians believed to have founded modern-day Cádiz

600 BC Greek colonists settle on northeast coast of Spain

228 BC Carthaginians occupy south-east Spain

1500 — 1000 — 500

1200 BC The "talaiotic" people of Menorca erect three unique types of stone building: *taulas*, *talaiots* and *navetas*

Taula *in Menorca*

775 BC Phoenicians establish colonies along the coast near Málaga

300 BC *La Dama de Elche* is carved *(p286)*

700 BC Semi-mythical kingdom of Tartessus thought to be at its height

Carthaginian glass necklace

Romans and Visigoths

THE ROMANS CAME TO SPAIN to fight the Cartha-ginians and take possession of the Iberian Peninsula's huge mineral wealth. Later, Hispania's wheat and olive oil became mainstays of the empire. It took 200 years to subdue the penin-sula, which was divided in three provinces: Tarraconensis, Lusitania and Baetica. In time, cities with Roman infrastructure developed.

Roman vase

The fall of the empire in the 5th century left Spain in the hands of the Visigoths, invaders from the north. Politically disorganized, they fell victim to the Moors in 711.

SPAIN (HISPANIA) IN 5 BC

☐ *Tarraconensis*

☐ *Lusitania*

☐ *Baetica*

Trajan *(AD 53–117)*
Trajan was the first Hispanic Roman emperor (AD 98–117). He improved public administration and expanded the empire.

Portico over-looking the gardens

Good acoustics at every level

A Classical façade served as a backdrop for tragedies. Additional scenery was used for comedies.

Seneca *(4 BC– AD 65)*
Born in Córdoba, the Stoic philosopher Seneca lived in Rome as Nero's adviser.

The orchestra, a semicircular open space for the choir

Visigothic Relief
This crude Visigothic stone carving, based on a Roman relief, is in the 7th-century church of Quintanilla de las Viñas, near Burgos (p352).

The auditorium seated over 5,000. The audience was placed according to social status.

TIMELINE

218 BC Scipio the Elder lands with a Roman army at Emporion *(p206)*. The Second Punic War begins	**c.200 BC** Romans reach Gadir (modern Cádiz) after driving Carthaginians out of Hispania	**26 BC** Emerita Augusta (Mérida) is founded and soon becomes capital of Lusitania
	155 BC Lusitanian Wars begin. Romans invade Portugal	**19 BC** Augustus takes Cantabria and Asturias, ending 200 years of war

200 BC	**100**	**AD 1**	**AD 100**

| **219 BC** Hannibal takes Saguntum *(p239)* for Carthaginians *Hannibal* | **133 BC** Celt-Iberian Wars culminate in destruction of Numantia, Soria *(p359)* | **61 BC** Julius Caesar, governor of Hispania Ulterior, begins final conquest of northern Portugal and Galicia **82–72 BC** Roman Civil War. Pompey founds Pompaelo (Pamplona) in 75 BC | **AD 74** Emperor Vespasian grants Latin status to all towns in Hispania, completing process of Romanization |

Gladiator Mosaic
Mosaics were used as decoration both indoors and out. Themes range from mythical episodes to portrayals of daily life. This 4th-century AD mosaic shows gladiators in action and has helpful labels to name the fighters and show who is dead or alive.

WHERE TO SEE ROMAN SPAIN

Like Mérida, Tarragona *(see p214)* has extensive Roman ruins and Itálica *(see p452)* is an excavated town. A magnificent Roman wall rings Lugo in Galicia *(see p95)*. Built in Trajan's rule, the bridge over the Tagus at Alcántara *(see p392)* has a temple on it.

Emporion, *a Roman town, was built next to a former Greek colony in the 3rd century BC. The ruins include grand villas and a forum (see p206).*

Segovia's Roman aqueduct *(see p347), a huge monument with 163 arches, dates from the end of the 1st century AD.*

The gardens were used as a foyer during intervals by the Hispanic nobility, dressed in elegant togas.

Stage building in granite and marble

Scaena, the platform on which the actors performed

ROMAN THEATRE, MÉRIDA
Theatre was an extremely popular form of entertainment in Hispania. This reconstruction shows the theatre at Mérida *(see p392)*, built in 16–15 BC.

Visigothic Cross
Although Visigothic kings seldom ruled long enough to make an impact on society, the early Christian Church grew powerful. Fortunes were spent on churches and religious art.

Mosaic from Mérida

258 Franks cross Pyrenees into Tarraconensis and sack Tarragona

312 Christianity officially recognized as religion under rule of Constantine, the first Christian emperor

The Codex Vigilianus, a Christian manuscript

409 Vandals and their allies cross Pyrenees into Tarraconensis

415 Visigoths establish their court at Barcelona

446 Romans attempt to win back rest of Hispania

476 Overthrow of the last Roman emperor leads to end of Western Roman Empire

589 Visigothic King Reccared converts from Arianism to Catholicism at Third Council of Toledo

200	300	400	500

Al Andalus: Muslim Spain

THE ARRIVAL OF ARAB and Berber invaders from North Africa, and their defeat of the Visigoths, gave rise to the most brilliant civilization of early medieval Europe. These Muslim settlers, often known as the Moors, called Spain "Al Andalus". A rich and powerful caliphate was established in Córdoba and mathematics, science, architecture and the decorative arts flourished. The caliphate eventually broke up into small kingdoms or *taifas*. Meanwhile small Christian enclaves expanded in the north.

SPAIN IN 750

☐ *Extent of Moorish domination*

Alhambra Vase
(see p467)

The palace, dating from the 11th century, was surrounded by patios, pools and gardens.

Water Wheel
Moorish irrigation techniques, such as the water wheel, revolutionized agriculture. New crops, including oranges and rice, were introduced.

Astrolabe
Perfected by the Moors around AD 800, the astrolabe was used by navigators and astronomers.

Remains of a Roman amphitheatre

Silver Casket of Hisham II
In the Caliphate of Córdoba, luxury objects of brilliant craftsmanship were worked in ivory, silver and bronze.

Fortified entrance gate

Curtain wall with watch towers

TIMELINE

711 Moors, led by Tariq, invade Spain and defeat Visigoths at battle of Guadalete

732 Moors' advance into France is halted by Charles Martel at Poitiers

778 Charlemagne's rearguard defeated by Basques at Roncesvalles *(p130)*

785 Building of great mosque at Córdoba begins

Charlemagne (742–814)

	750		800		850

722 Led by Pelayo, Christians defeat Moors at Covadonga *(p105)*

Pelayo (718–37)

756 Abd al Rahman I proclaims independent emirate in Córdoba

744 Christians under Alfonso I of Asturias take León

822 Abd al Rahman II begins 30-year rule marked by patronage of the arts and culture

c.800 Tomb of St James (Santiago) is supposedly discovered at Santiago de Compostela

Puerta de Sabbath in Córdoba's Mezquita
Wealth and artistic brilliance were lavished on mosques, especially in Córdoba (see pp456–7). Calligraphy was a major element in decoration.

WHERE TO SEE MOORISH SPAIN

The finest Moorish buildings are found in Andalusia, especially in the cities of Córdoba *(see pp454–7)* and Granada *(see pp462–8)*. Almería *(see p477)* has a large, ruined *alcazaba* (castle). In Jaén *(see p469)* there are Moorish baths. Further north, in Zaragoza, is the castle-palace of La Aljafería *(see p227)*.

Medina Azahara *(see p453), sacked in the 11th century but partly restored, was the final residence of Córdoba's caliphs.*

Torre del Homenaje, the keep, was built by Abd al Rahman I (756–88).

Baths

Patio with Moorish decoration

ALCAZABA AT MÁLAGA

An *alcazaba* was a castle built into the ramparts of a Moorish city, often protected by massive concentric walls. In Málaga *(see p450)* – the principal port of the Moorish kingdom of Granada – the vast Alcazaba was built in the 8–11th centuries on the site of a Roman fortress, and incorporated massive curtain walls and fortified gates.

Moorish Sword
A fine example of late Moorish craftsman-ship, this sword has a golden pommel. The blade is inscribed with Arabic writing.

Warrior Helmet
Practical as well as ornate, this Islamic nobleman's helmet, made of iron, gold and silver, incorporates inscriptions, a coat of arms and chain mail.

905 Emergent Navarra becomes Christian kingdom under Sancho I

976 Al Mansur, military dictator, usurps caliphal powers and sacks Barcelona. Córdoba Mezquita finished

1010 Medina Azahara sacked by Berbers

900

950

1000

913 Christian capital is established at León

936 Building of Medina Azahara palace starts near Córdoba

Bronze stag from Medina Azahara

1013 Caliphate of Córdoba breaks up. Emergence of *taifas*: small, independent Moorish kingdoms

The Reconquest

THE INFANT CHRISTIAN KINGDOMS in the north – León, Castile, Navarra, Aragón and Catalonia – advanced south gradually in the 11th century, fighting in the name of Christianity to regain land from the Moors. After the fall of Toledo in 1085, the struggle became increasingly a holy war. Militant North African Muslims – Almoravids and Almohads – rallied to the Moorish cause and ultimately took over Al Andalus in the 12th century. As the Christians pushed further south, soon only Granada remained under Moorish control.

Cross of the Knights of St James

SPAIN IN 1173

☐ *Christian kingdoms*

☐ *Al Andalus*

Golden Goblet
The exquisite goblet (1063) of Doña Urraca, daughter of Alfonso VI, shows the quality of medieval Christian craftsmanship.

Fernando I
Fernando formed the first Christian power bloc in 1037 by uniting León with Castile, which was emerging as a major military force.

Armies of Castile, Aragón and Navarra

The Almohads
fight until the bitter end, although many comrades lay slain.

LAS NAVAS DE TOLOSA

The Christian victory over the Almohads in the Battle of Las Navas de Tolosa (1212) led to Moorish Spain's decline. The army of Muhammad II al Nasir was no match for the forces of Sancho VII of Navarra, Pedro II of Aragón and Alfonso VIII of Castile. A stained-glass window in Roncesvalles (see p130) depicts the battle.

Alhambra, Palace of the Nasrids
Moorish art and architecture of singular beauty continued to be produced in the Nasrid kingdom of Granada. Its apogee is the exquisite Alhambra (see pp466–7).

TIMELINE

Uniforms of military orders

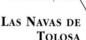

1037 León and Castile united for first time under Fernando I

1065 Death of Fernando I precipitates fratricidal civil war between his sons

1086 Almoravids respond to pleas for help from Moorish emirs by taking over *taifas* (splinter states)

1158 Establishment of the Order of Calatrava, the first military order of knights in Spain

|1050|1100|1150|120|

El Cid

1085 Toledo falls to Christians under Alfonso VI of Castile

1094 The legendary El Cid *(see p352)* captures Valencia

1137 Ramón Berenguer IV of Catalonia marries Petronila of Aragón uniting the two kingdoms under their son, Alfonso II

1147 Almohads arrive in Al Andalus and make Seville their capital

1143 Portugal becomes separate kingdom

1212 Combined Christian forces defeat Almohads at battle of Las Navas de Tolosa

Cantigas of Alfonso X *(1252–84)*
This detail of a manuscript by Alfonxo X portrays the confrontation between Moorish and Christian cavalry. Alfonso the Learned encouraged his scholars to master Arab culture and translate ancient Greek manuscripts brought by the Moors.

WHERE TO SEE MUDÉJAR SPAIN

The Mudéjares – Muslims who remained in territories under Christian occupation – created a distinctive architectural style distinguished by its ornamental work in brick, plaster and ceramics. Aragón, particularly Zaragoza *(see pp226–7)* and Teruel *(see pp230–31)*, boasts some of the finest Mudéjar buildings. Seville's Reales Alcázares is an exquisitely harmonious collection of patios and halls built under Pedro I *(see pp422–3)*.

The Mudéjar tower of Teruel cathedral combines both brick and colourful ceramics to highly decorative effect.

Sancho VII of Navarra leads the Christian forces.

St James (Santiago)
Known as the Moor-slayer, St James is said to have miraculously intervened at the Battle of Clavijo in 844. This powerful figurehead is the patron saint of Spain.

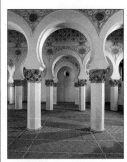

Santa María la Blanca (see p373), *a former synagogue and church, shows the fusion of cultures in medieval Toledo.*

---

15 Foundation of amanca University

1230 Fernando III reunites Castile and León

Crest of Castile and León

1385 Portuguese defeat Castilians at Aljubarrota, crushing King Juan's aspirations to throne of Portugal

1388–9 Treaties end Spanish phase of Hundred Years War

1250	1300	1350	1400

1250 Toledo at its height as a centre of translation and learning, influenced by Alfonso X, the Learned

1386 Invasion of Galicia by the English, ended by Bayonne Treaty

1232 Granada becomes capital of future Nasrid kingdom. Building of the Alhambra begins

Alfonso X

1401 Work starts in Seville on what was then the world's largest Gothic cathedral

The Catholic Monarchs

Fernando of Aragón

THE FOUNDATION of the Spanish nation-state was laid by Isabel I of Castile and Fernando II of Aragón *(see p66)*. Uniting their lands in military, diplomatic and religious matters, the "Catholic Monarchs", as they are known, won back Granada, the last Moorish kingdom, from Boabdil. The Inquisition gave Spain a reputation for intolerance, yet in art and architecture brilliant progress was made and the voyages of Columbus opened up the New World.

SPAIN'S EXPLORATION OF THE NEW WORLD

— *Route of Columbus's first voyage*

Tomb of El Doncel *(15th century)*
This effigy of a page who died in the fight for Granada combines ideals of military glory and learning (see p364).

Boabdil, the grief-stricken king, moves forward to hand over the keys to Granada.

The Inquisition
Active from 1478, the Inquisition (see p264) persecuted those suspected of heresy with increasing vigour. This member of the Brotherhood of Death took victims to the stake.

Alhambra

Baptizing Jews
After the Christian reconquest of Granada, Jews were forced to convert or leave Spain. The conversos (converted Jews) were often treated badly.

THE FALL OF GRANADA *(1492)*
This romantic interpretation by Francisco Pradilla (1846–1921) reflects the chivalry of Boabdil, ruler of Granada, as he surrenders the keys of the last Moorish kingdom to the Catholic Monarchs, Fernando and Isabel, following ten long years of war.

TIMELINE

1454 Enrique IV, Isabel's half-brother, accedes to throne of Castile

1465 Civil war erupts in Castile

1478 Papal bull authorizes Castilian Inquisition with Tomás de Torquemada as Inquisitor General

Torquemada

1450	1460	1470	1480

1451 Birth of Isabel of Castile

Fernando and Isabel on 15th-century gold coin

1469 Marriage of Fernando and Isabel in Valladolid unites Castile and Aragón

1474 Death of Enrique IV leads to civil war; Isabel triumphs over Juana la Beltraneja, Enrique's supposed daughter, to become queen

1479 Fernando becomes Fernando II of Aragón

Columbus Arriving in the Americas
The Catholic Monarchs financed Columbus's daring first voyage partly because they hoped for riches in return, but also because they expected him to convert infidels.

Boabdil
As the forlorn king left Granada, his mother reputedly said, "Don't cry as a child over what you could not defend as a man".

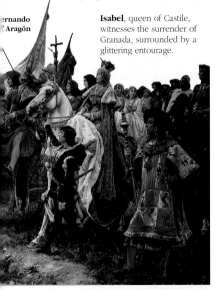

ernando ** Aragón**

Isabel, queen of Castile, witnesses the surrender of Granada, surrounded by a glittering entourage.

WHERE TO SEE GOTHIC ARCHITECTURE IN SPAIN

Spain has many great Gothic cathedrals, especially in Seville *(pp418–19)*, Burgos *(pp354–5)*, Barcelona *(pp144–5)*, Toledo *(pp374–5)* and Palma de Mallorca *(pp496–7)*. Secular buildings from this era include commodity exchanges like La Lonja in Valencia *(p241)* and castles *(pp326–7)*.

León cathedral (pp336–7) *has a west front covered in statuary. Here Christ is seen presiding over the Last Judgment.*

Crown of Isabel
Worn at the surrender, Isabel's crown is now in her final resting place, the Capilla Real in Granada (see p462).

1494 Treaty of Tordesillas divides the New World territories between Portugal and Spain		**1509** Cardinal Cisneros' troops attack Oran in Algeria and temporarily occupy it
	1496 Foundation of Santo Domingo, on Hispaniola, first Spanish city in the Americas	*Cardinal Cisneros*
1490	**1500**	**1510**
1492 Fall of Granada after ten-year war. Columbus reaches America. Expulsion of Jews from Spain	**1502** Unconverted Moors expelled from Spain	**1516** Death of Fernando
	Columbus's ship, the Santa María	**1512** Annexation of Navarra, leading to full unification of Spain
	1504 Following death of Isabel, her daughter Juana la Loca becomes queen of Castile with Fernando as regent	

The Age of Discovery

FOLLOWING COLUMBUS'S ARRIVAL in the Bahamas in 1492, the conquistadors went into Central and South America, conquering Mexico (1519), Peru (1532) and Chile (1541). In doing so, they destroyed Indian civilizations. In the 16th century, vast quantities of gold and silver flowed across the Atlantic to Spain. Carlos I and his son Felipe II spent some of it on battles to halt the spread of Protestantism in Europe, and in the Holy War against the Turks.

Aztec god (c.1540)

SPANISH EMPIRE IN 1580

☐ *Dominions of Felipe II*

Mapping the World
This 16th-century German map reflects a new world, largely unknown to Europe before the era of conquistadors.

Galleons were armed with cannons as a defence against pirates and rival conquerors.

Aztec Mask
In their great greed and ignorance, the Spanish destroyed the empires and civilizations of the Aztecs in Mexico and the Incas in Peru.

The lookout
was essential for spotting enemies and making landfall.

Forecastle

Seville
Granted the trading monopoly with the Americas, Seville, on the banks of the Guadalquivir, was Europe's richest port in the early 16th century.

TIMELINE

1519 Magellan, Portuguese explorer, leaves Seville under Spanish patronage to circumnavigate the globe

1520-21 Revolt by Castilian towns when Carlos I appoints foreigner, Adrian of Utrecht, as regent

1532 Pizarro takes Peru with 180 men and destroys Inca empire

1554 International Catholic alliance created by marriage of future king Felipe II with Mary Tudor of England

Pizarro

1520	1530	1540	1550

1519 Conquest of Mexico by Cortés. Carlos I crowned Holy Roman Emperor Charles V

Conquistador Hernán Cortés

1540 Father Bartolomé de las Casas writes book denouncing the oppression of Indians

Bartolomé de las Casas

Defeat of the Spanish Armada
Spain's self-esteem suffered a hard blow when its "invincible" 133-ship fleet was destroyed in an attempt to invade Protestant England in 1588.

NEW WORLD CROPS

Not only did Spain profit from the gold and silver brought across the ocean from the Americas, but also from an amazing range of new crops. Some, including potatoes and maize, were introduced for cultivation in Spain while others, such as tobacco and cacao, were mainly grown in native soil. Cocoa, from cacao beans, gained favour as a drink.

Cacao plant

Peruvian with exotic New World fruit

Armour of Felipe II
Felipe II (1556–98) was a cunning administrator, who claimed to rule the world with paper rather than military might.

Flag of Spain (until 1785)

Storage space for New World treasures

SPANISH GALLEON

Although sturdily built to carry New World treasure back to Spain, these ships were hard to manoeuvre except with the wind behind. They were often no match for smaller, swifter pirate vessels.

Carlos I (1516–56)
During his tumultuous 40-year reign, Carlos I (Holy Roman Emperor Charles V) often led his troops on the battlefield.

1557 First of a series of
artial bankruptcies of Spain

1561 Building of
El Escorial, near
Madrid, begins

El Escorial
(see pp312–3)

1588 Spanish
Armada fails in
attack on Britain

1560	1570	1580	1590

1561 Madrid
becomes capital
of Spain

1571 Spanish victory
over Turks in naval
battle of Lepanto

1580 Portugal unites
with Spain for the
next 60 years

1568 Moriscos (converted Moors)
the Alpujarras (Granada) rebel
inst high taxes and persecution

1569 Bible published
for first time in Castilian

The Golden Age

SPAIN'S GOLDEN AGE was a time of great artistic and literary achievement led by the painters – El Greco and Velázquez *(see pp28–9)* – and writers *(see pp30–31)*, especially Cervantes and the prolific dramatists, Lope de Vega and Calderón de la Barca. This brilliance occurred, however, against a background of economic deterioration and ruinous wars with the Low Countries and France. Spain was gradually losing its influence in Europe and the reigning house of Habsburg entered irreversible decline.

THE SPANISH EMPIRE IN EUROPE IN 1647

☐ *Spanish territories*

Don Quixote and Sancho Panza
Cervantes' satire on chivalrous romance, Don Quixote, *contrasts the fantasy of the main character with his servant's realism.*

A clock is a reminder of the inevitable passage of time.

The knight is dressed in mid-17th-century fashion.

Money represents worldly wealth.

Duke of Lerma
This bronze statue depicts the Duke of Lerma (c.1550–1625), a favourite of King Felipe III.

THE KNIGHT'S DREAM *(1650)*
This painting, attributed to Antonio de Pereda, is on a familiar Golden Age theme: human vanity. A young gentleman sits asleep beside a table piled with objects symbolizing power, wealth and mortality. The pleasures of life, we are told, are no more real than a dream.

TIMELINE

Felipe III	**1609** Felipe III orders the expulsion of the Moriscos	**1621** Low Countries war resumes after 12-year truce	**1643** Fall of Count-Duke Olivares. Spain heavily defeated by France at battle of Rocroi
1600 Capital temporarily moves to Valladolid	**1619** Construction of Plaza Mayor, Madrid	**1625** Capture of Breda, Netherlands, after one-year siege	
1600	**1610**	**1620**	**1630**	**164**
1605 Publication of first of two parts of Cervantes' *Don Quixote*	**1609** Lope de Vega publishes poem on the art of comic drama	**1622** Velázquez moves from Seville to Madrid to become court painter the following year	**1640** Secession of Portugal, amalgamated with Spain since 1580
		Lope de Vega (1562–1635)	

Fiesta in the Plaza Mayor in Madrid
This famous square (see p263) *became the scene for pageants, royal celebrations, bullfights and executions, all overlooked from the balconies.*

An angel warns that death is near.

The banner says, "It (death) pierces perpetually, flies quickly and kills".

A mask symbolizes the Arts.

Weapons represent power.

The skull on the book shows death triumphant over learning.

SEVILLE SCHOOL OF ART

Seville's wealth, together with the patronage of the Church, made it a centre of the arts, second only to the royal court. Velázquez, who was born in Seville, trained under the painter Pacheco. Sculptor Juan Martínez Montañés and painters Zurbarán and Murillo created great works which are displayed in the Museo de Bellas Artes (see p412).

San Diego de Alcalá Giving Food to the Poor **(c.1646) by Murillo**

Expulsion of the Moriscos
Although they had converted to Christianity, the last Moors were still expelled in 1609.

Surrender of Breda
Spain took the Dutch city of Breda on 5 June 1625 after a year-long siege. The event was later painted by Velázquez.

1652 Spanish troops regain Catalonia, following 12-year war with France

Calderón de la Barca

1669 Calderón de la Barca's last work, *La Estátua de Prometeo*, is published

1683–4 Louis XIV attacks Catalonia and Spanish Netherlands

1650	1660	1670	1680	1690	1700

1648 Holland achieves independence from Spain by Treaty of Westphalia, ending Thirty Years War

1659 Peace of the Pyrenees signed with France. Louis XIV marries Felipe IV's daughter María Teresa, leading to Bourbon succession in Spain

Coin from the reign of Felipe IV

1700 Death of Carlos II brings Habsburg line to an end. Felipe V, the first Bourbon king, ascends the throne

Bourbons to First Republic

THE WAR OF THE SPANISH SUCCESSION ended in triumph for the Bourbons, who made Spain a centralized nation. Their power was at its height during the reign of the enlightened despot, Carlos III. But the 19th century was a troubled time. An invasion by revolutionary France led to the War of Independence (Peninsular War). Later came the Carlist Wars – caused by another dispute over the succession – liberal revolts and the short-lived First Republic.

Isabel II

SPAIN IN 1714

☐ *Domain after Treaty of Utrecht*

The Enlightenment
The Enlightenment brought new learning and novel projects. On 5 July 1784 this Montgolfier balloon rose above Madrid.

A Franciscan friar is among the innocent victims.

Queen María Luisa
The dominating María Luisa of Parma, portrayed by Goya, forced her husband Carlos IV to appoint her lover, Manuel Godoy, prime minister in 1792.

Spanish rebel faces death in a gesture of crucifixion.

Battle of Trafalgar
The defeat of the Franco-Spanish fleet by the British admiral, Lord Nelson, off Cape Trafalgar in 1805 was the end of Spanish sea power.

Hundreds of lives were taken in the executions, which lasted several days.

TIMELINE

1702–14 War of the Spanish Succession. Spain loses Netherlands and Gibraltar by Treaty of Utrecht

1724 Luis I (son of Felipe V) gains throne when his father abdicates, but dies within a year; Felipe V reinstated

1767 Carlos III expels Jesuits from Spain and Spanish colonies

| 1700 | 1720 | 1740 | 1760 | 17 |

1714 Siege and reduction of Barcelona by Felipe V

Felipe V, the first Bourbon king (1700–24)

Count of Floridablanca (1728–1808)

1762–3 English government declares war on Spanish over colonies in America

1782 Count of Floridablanca helps to recover Menorca from England

Carlos III Leaving Naples
When Fernando VI died without an heir in 1759, his half-brother Carlos VII of Naples was put on the Spanish throne as Carlos III. His enlightened reign saw the foundation of academies of science and art and the beginning of free trade.

French soldiers, operating on orders from Marshal Murat, execute Spanish patriots.

General Prim *(1814–70)*
General Prim was one of 19th-century Spain's most influential figures. He forced the abdication of Isabel II, and pursued liberal policies until assassinated in Madrid.

French infantry helmet

THE 3RD OF MAY BY GOYA *(1814)*
On 2 May 1808, in reaction to Napoleon's occupation of Spain, the people of Madrid rose in vain against the occupying French forces. The next day the French army took its revenge by executing hundreds of people, both rebels and bystanders. These events sparked off the War of Independence.

Baroque Magnificence
The sacristy of the Monasterio de la Cartuja in Granada is typical of Spanish Baroque, more sumptuous than anywhere else in Europe.

1805 Battle of Trafalgar. Nelson defeats French and Spanish at sea

1809 Wellington's troops join with Spanish to triumph over French at Talavera

Duke of Wellington

1841–3 María Cristina, followed by General Espartero, acts as regent for Isabel II

1868 Revolution under General Prim forces Isabel II into exile. Amadeo I is king for three years from 1870

1800	1820	1840	1860

1808–14 Joseph Bonaparte on throne. War of Independence

1812 Promulgation of liberal constitution in Cádiz leads to military uprising

1824 Peru is the last South American country to gain independence

1833–9 First Carlist War

1836 Mendizábal seizes monastic property for the Spanish state

1847–9 Second Carlist War

Carlist soldiers

Republicans and Anarchists

SPAIN'S FIRST REPUBLIC lasted only a year (1873) and consumed four presidents. The late 19th century was a time of national decline, with Anarchism developing in reaction to rampant political corruption. The loss of Cuba, in 1898, was a low point for Spain, although there was a flurry of literary and artistic activity in the following years. The country's increasing instability was briefly checked by the dictatorship of Primo de Rivera. Spanish politics, however, were becoming polarized. Alfonso XIII was forced to abdicate and the ill-fated Second Republic was declared in 1931.

Primo de Rivera

THE LEGACY OF SPANISH COLONIZATION IN 1900

☐ *Spanish-speaking territories*

Anarchist Propaganda
Anarchism was idealistic, though often violent. This poster states, "Anarchist books are weapons against Fascism".

Workers unite, calling for radical social reform.

Pío Baroja
Baroja (1872–1956) was one of the most gifted novelists of his day. He was too original to be grouped with the writers of the Generation of 1898, who tried to create a national renaissance after the loss of Spain's colonies.

POWER TO THE PEOPLE
Political protest was rife under the Second Republic, as shown by this Communist demonstration in the Basque Country in 1932. Industrial workers banded together, forming trade unions to demand better pay and working conditions, and staging strikes. The Spanish Communist Party developed later than the Anarchists, but eventually gained more support.

TIMELINE

1873 Declaration of First Republic, lasting only one year

First Republic's last president, Emilio Castelar (1832–99)

1888 Universal Exhibition in Barcelona creates new buildings and parks, such as the Parc de la Ciutadella

1897 Prime Minister Cánovas del Castillo assassinated by an Italian Anarchist

| 1870 | 1880 | 1890 | 1900 |

1875 Second Bourbon restoration puts Alfonso XII on throne

Alfonso XII and Queen María

1893 Anarchists bomb opera-goers in the Barcelona Liceu

1898 Cuba and Philippines gain independence from Spain following the Spanish-American War

1870–75 Third Carlist War

Tragic Week
Led by Anarchists and Republicans, workers in Barcelona took to the streets in 1909 to resist a military call-up. The reprisals were brutal.

Universal Exhibitions
In 1929, Seville and Barcelona were transformed by exhibitions promoting art and industry. The fairs brought international recognition.

EXPOSICION
INTERNACIONAL
BARCELONA 1929

The banner appeals for working-class solidarity.

Picasso
Born in Málaga in 1881, the artist Pablo Picasso spent his formative years as a painter in the city of Barcelona (see p148) before moving to Paris in the 1930s.

Cuban War of Independence
Cuba began its fight for freedom in 1895, led by local patriots such as Antonio Maceo. In the disastrous campaign, Spain lost 50,000 soldiers and most of its navy.

The Garrotte
Convicted Anarchists were executed by the garrotte – an iron collar that brutally strangled the victim while crushing the neck.

1912 Prime Minister José Canalejas murdered by Anarchists in Madrid

Second Republic election poster

1921 Crushing defeat of Spanish army at Anual, Morocco

1931 Proclamation of Second Republic with a two-year coalition between Socialists and Republicans

1933 General election returns right-wing government

1910

1920

1930

1909 Semana Trágica (Tragic Week) in Barcelona. Workers' revolt against conscription for Moroccan Wars quashed by Government troops

1923 Primo de Rivera stages victorious coup to become military dictator under Alfonso XIII

1930 Primo de Rivera resigns after losing military support

1931 Republicans win local elections, causing Alfonso XIII to abdicate

1934 Revolution of Asturian miners suppressed by army under General Franco

Civil War and the Franco Era

NATIONALIST GENERALS rose against the government in 1936, starting the Spanish Civil War. The Nationalists, under General Franco, were halted by the Republicans outside Madrid, but with support from Hitler and Mussolini they inched their way to victory in the north and east. Madrid finally fell in early 1939. After the war, thousands of Republicans were executed in reprisals. Spain was internationally isolated until the 1950s, when the United States brought her into the western military alliance.

Franco

SPAIN ON 31 JULY 1936

☐ *Republican-held areas*

☐ *Nationalist-held areas*

Franco's Ideal World
Under Franco, Church and State were united. This poster shows the strong influence of religion on education.

Nationalist Poster
A Nationalist poster adorned with Fascist arrows reads "Fight for the Fatherland, Bread and Justice".

Anguished mother with dead child

Composition reflecting total chaos

GUERNICA *(1937)*
On behalf of advancing Nationalists, the Nazi Condor Legion bombed the Basque town of Guernica *(see p114)* on 26 April 1937 – a busy market day. This was Europe's first air raid on civilians, and it inspired Picasso's shocking *Guernica (see p289)*. Painted for a Republican Government exhibition in Paris, it is full of symbols of disaster.

TIMELINE

1936 Republican Popular Front wins the general election on 16 January. On 17 July, Nationalist generals rise against Republicans

1938 On 8 January, Republicans lose battle for Teruel in bitter cold

1939 In March, Madrid, Valencia and Alicante fall in quick succession to Franco's troops

1945 By end of World War II, Spain is diplomatically and politically isolated

1947 Spain declared monarchy with Franco as regent

1935	1940	1945	1950

1936 Nationalists declare Franco head of state on 29 September

1937 On 26 April, Nazi planes bomb Basque town of Guernica (Gernika-Lumo)

1939 Franco declares end of war on 1 April and demands unconditional surrender from Republicans

1938 On 23 December, Nationalists bomb Barcelona

1953 Deal with US permits American bases on Spanish soil in exchange for aid

Soldiers surrendering to Nationalist troops

GARCÍA LORCA

Federico García Lorca (1898–1936) was Spain's most brilliant dramatist and lyric poet of the 1920s and '30s. His homosexuality and association with the left, however, made him a target for Nationalist assassins. He was shot by an ad hoc firing squad near his home town of Granada.

Scene from his play *Blood Wedding*

Anarchist Poster
Anarchists fought for the Republic, forming agricultural collectives behind the lines. Their influence waned when they were discredited by the Communist Party.

A wounded horse representing the Spanish people

Witnesses to the massacre stare in wonder and disbelief.

Crucifixion gesture

The flower is a symbol of hope in the midst of despair.

The Hungry Years
Ration cards illustrate the postwar period when Spain nearly starved. Shunned by other nations, she received aid from the US in 1953 in return for accepting military bases.

Spanish Refugees
As the Nationalists came closer to victory, thousands of artists, writers, intellectuals and other Republican supporters fled Spain into indefinite exile.

1962 Tourism on the Mediterranean coast is boosted by official go-ahead

Sunbathers

1969 Franco declares Prince Juan Carlos his successor

1973 ETA assassinates Admiral Carrero Blanco, Franco's hard-line prime minister

1955	1960	1965	1970	1975

1959 Founding of ETA, Basque separatist group

1955 Spain joins United Nations

Franco's funeral, 23 November 1975

1970 "Burgos trials" of the regime's opponents outrage world opinion

1975 Death of Franco results in third Bourbon restoration as Juan Carlos is proclaimed king

Modern Spain

FRANCO'S DEATH left Spain's political future hanging in the balance. But few people wanted to preserve the old regime and the transition from dictatorship to democracy proved surprisingly swift and painless. The previously-outlawed Socialist Workers' Party, under Felipe González, won the general election in 1982 and set about modernizing Spain. Considerable power has since been devolved to the regions. A major threat facing central government has been the persistent violence of ETA, the Basque separatist organization. Spain's international relations have been strengthened by her membership of NATO and the European Union.

Contemporary Spanish fashion

SPAIN TODAY

☐ *Spain*

▨ *Other European Union states*

Castilla and León's modern pavilion was one of EXPO's 150 pavilions built to innovative designs.

Hi-tech floodlight

Coup d'Etat, 23 February 1981
Civil Guard colonel, Antonio Tejero, held parliament at gunpoint for several hours. Democracy survived because King Juan Carlos refused to support the rebels.

Anti-NATO Protest Rally
When Spain joined NATO in 1982, some saw it as a reversal of Socialist ideals. To others it represented an improvement in Spain's international standing.

EXPO '92
Over 100 countries were represented at the Universal Exposition which focused world attention on Seville in 1992. The many pavilions displayed scientific, technological and cultural exhibits.

TIMELINE

1977 First free elections return centrist government under Adolfo Suárez. Political parties, including Communists, are legalized

1982 Landslide electoral victory brings Socialist Workers' Party (PSOE), under Felipe González, to power

Felipe González

1980

1985

1981 Military officers stage attempted coup d'etat to overthrow democracy

1983 Semi-autonomous regional governments are established to appease Basque Country and Catalonia

1986 Spain joins EC (now EU)

1982 World Cup held in Spain. Spain joins NATO

Spanish royal family

Tourism
From 1959–73 the number of annual visitors to Spain grew from 3 million to 34 million, transforming the once-quiet coasts and islands.

Felipe González Elected
In 1982 the Spanish Socialist Workers' Party (PSOE) leader was elected prime minister. González transformed Spain during his 13 years in power.

Leaning blue tower rises above Andalusia's pavilion.

Ana Belén
Spanish women have enjoyed ever greater freedom and opportunity since the advent of democracy. In a 1980s opinion poll, they voted the singer and actress, Ana Belén, the woman they most admired.

El País
Founded in Madrid in 1976, the liberal daily El País is the best-selling newspaper in Spain. During the transition to democracy it had a great influence on public opinion.

A monorail carried visitors around the site.

Barcelona Olympic Games
The opening ceremony of the Barcelona Olympics included stunning displays of music, dance and colourful costumes.

	1992 Spain celebrates quincentenary of Columbus's voyage to America	**1995** ETA attempts to assassinate opposition leader José María Aznar
1991 Madrid hosts Bush-Gorbachev summit	**1993** González wins third term in office	**1996** In the general election on 3 March, González loses to a coalition led by Aznar
1990		**1995**
1989 Spain holds presidency of European Community	**1994/5** Corruption scandals rock the long-serving government	
	1992 Barcelona Olympics and Seville Expo '92 place Spain firmly within community of modern European nations	

Cobi, Barcelona Olympic Mascot

Rulers of Spain

SPAIN BECAME A NATION-STATE under Isabel and Fernando, whose marriage eventually united Castile and Aragón. With their daughter Juana's marriage, the kingdom was delivered into Habsburg hands. Carlos I and Felipe II were both capable rulers, but in 1700 Carlos II died without leaving an heir. After the War of the Spanish Succession, Spain came under the French Bourbons, who have ruled ever since – apart from an interregnum, two republics and Franco's dictatorship. The current Bourbon king, Juan Carlos I, a constitutional monarch, is respected for his support of democracy.

1665–1700
Carlos II

1479–1516
Fernando, King
of Aragón

1516–56 Carlos I of
Spain (Holy Roman
Emperor Charles V)

1598–1621 Felipe III

1474–1504 Isabel,
Queen of Castile

1400	1450	1500	1550	1600	1650
INDEPENDENT KINGDOMS		**HABSBURG DYNASTY**			
1400	1450	1500	1550	1600	1650

1469 Marriage of
Isabel and Fernando
leads to unification
of Spain

1504–16 Juana la
Loca (with Fernando
as regent)

1621–65 Felipe IV

Fernando and Isabel, the Catholic Monarchs

UNIFICATION OF SPAIN

In the late 15th century the two largest kingdoms in developing Christian Spain – Castile, with its military might, and Aragón (including Barcelona and a Mediterranean empire) – were united. The marriage of Isabel of Castile and Fernando of Aragón in 1469 joined these powerful kingdoms. Together the so-called Catholic Monarchs defeated the Nasrid Kingdom of Granada, the last stronghold of the Moors (see pp52–3). With the addition of Navarra in 1512, Spain was finally unified.

1556–98
Felipe II

1843–68 Isabel II reigns following
the regency of her mother María
Cristina (1833–41) and Espartero
(1841–3)

1814–33 First
Bourbon restoration,
following French
rule: Fernando VII

1871–3 Break in
Bourbon rule:
Amadeo I of Savoy

1939–75
General Franco
Head of State

1724 Luis I
reigns after
Felipe V's
abdication,
but dies
within a
year

1931–9
Second Republic

1759–88 Carlos III

1875–85
Second Bourbon
restoration:
Alfonso XII

'00	1750	1800	1850	1900	1950
OURBON DYNASTY		BOURBON	BOURBON		
'00	1750	1800	1850	1900	1950

1808–13 Break in
Bourbon rule:
Napoleon's brother,
Joseph Bonaparte,
rules as José I

1746–59
Fernando VI

1724–46 Felipe V
reinstated as king
upon the death of
his son, Luis I

1788–1808
Carlos IV

1902–31 Alfonso XIII

1886–1902 María-Cristina of
Habsburg-Lorraine as regent
for Alfonso XIII

1873–4
First Republic

'00–24
lipe V

1868–70 The
Septembrina Revolution

1975 Third Bourbon
restoration: Juan Carlos I

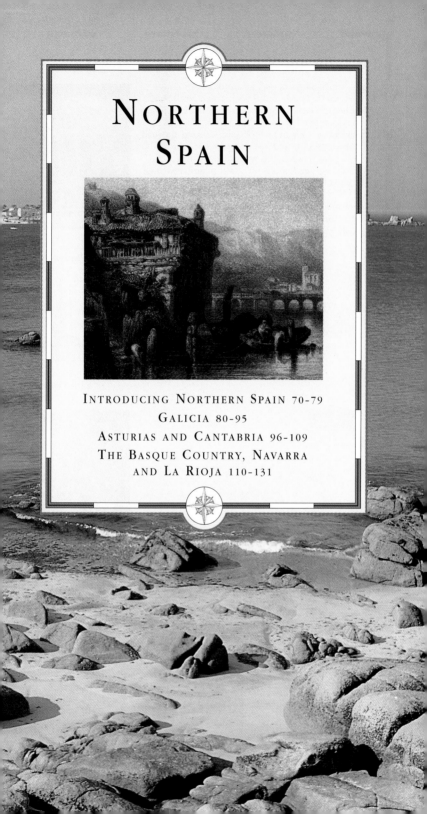

NORTHERN
SPAIN

Introducing Northern Spain

INCREASING NUMBERS of visitors are discovering the quiet, sandy beaches and deep green landscapes of Northern Spain. The Atlantic coast, from the Pyrenees to the Portuguese border, is often scenic but at its most attractive in the cliffs and rias of Galicia. Inland, the mild, wet climate has created lush meadows and broad-leaved forests, making this area ideal for a peaceful, rural holiday. The famous medieval pilgrimage route to the city of Santiago de Compostela crosses Northern Spain, its way marked by magnificent examples of Romanesque architecture. Plentiful seafood and dairy produce, and the outstanding red wines of La Rioja, add to the pleasure of a tour through this part of Spain.

Oviedo (see p102) *has a number of Pre-Romanesque churches, most notably the graceful Santa María del Naranco, and a fine Gothic cathedral.*

GALICIA
(see pp80–95)

Lugo

A Coruña

Asturias

ASTURIAS AND CANTABRIA
(see pp96–109)

Pontevedra

Ourense

The Rías Baixas (see p91) *is one of Spain's prettiest coastlines. Scattered around its pretty towns and villages are many quaint* hórreos, *grain stores, raised on stone stilts.*

Santiago de Compostela (see pp86–9) *attracts thousands of pilgrims and tourists each year. Its majestic cathedral was one of the most important shrines in medieval Christendom.*

The Picos de Europa *mountain range* (see pp104–105) *dominates the landscape of Asturias and Cantabria. Rivers have carved deep gorges through the mountains and there are many footpaths through a variety of spectacular scenery.*

0 kilometres   50

0 miles   25

◁ **The coast of Galicia, south of Cabo Fisterra**

Santillana del Mar (see p108), *with its well-preserved medieval streets, is one of the most picturesque towns in Spain. The Convento de Regina Coeli houses a small museum containing a collection of painted wooden figures and other works of religious art.*

San Sebastián (see p118), *the most elegant holiday resort in the Basque Country, is sited around a beautiful horseshoe bay of golden sandy beaches. The city hosts international arts events, including Spain's premier film festival.*

Cantabria

Vizcaya

Guipúzcoa

Álava

Navarra

THE BASQUE COUNTRY, NAVARRA AND LA RIOJA
(see pp110–31)

La Rioja

Pamplona (see pp128–9), *the capital of Navarra since the 9th century, is best known for its annual fiesta, Los Sanfermines. The climax of each day of riotous celebration is the* Encierro, *in which bulls stampede through the streets of the city.*

The Monasterio de Leyre (see p131), *founded in the early 11th century, was built in a lonely but attractive landscape. The monastery was once the burial place of the kings of Navarra and its crypt is among the finest examples of early Romanesque art in Spain.*

Regional Food: Northern Spain

Txangurro relleno *is a Basque dish made with spider crab. The meat is cleaned, stuffed into the shell and cooked au gratin.*

THE CUISINE of Northern Spain is distinguished by abundant fish and seafood from the Atlantic. The region is also Spain's dairy and the source of some of the country's finest cheeses. Year-round rainfall yields a variety of fresh vegetables, particularly potatoes, cabbages and sweetcorn. Vast mountain ranges mean plentiful game, hams and cured sausages, which are combined with beans to form hearty stews. The Basques, with their famous gastronomical societies and New Basque Cuisine, are said to produce the most sophisticated and varied food in Spain: intriguing sauces boost even salted cod to gourmet heights. Asturias is recognized for its plentiful fish, vegetables and the production of dry cider from apples; while inland Navarra is famed for its locally grown white asparagus, which it cans for the whole of Spain, as well as supplying the country with the essential, spicy, pointed pepper *pimiento piquillo*.

White asparagus

***Beans** are an essential element of northern cooking, and there are many specially cultivated varieties. The best, and the most expensive, are La Granja beans from Asturias. Costing double the price of lamb, they are probably the best beans in the world. Tolosa, in the Basque Country, is famous for its red and black beans.*

Revuelto, *creamy scrambled egg, is served all along the north coast. It is tastiest accompanied by prawns and turnip tops.*

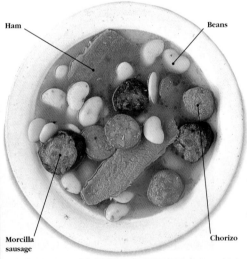

Ham

Beans

Morcilla sausage

Chorizo

Fabada, *the regional dish of Asturias, is a savoury stew combining pork and beans. Fat buttery fava beans are simmered with* tocino *(salt pork),* morcilla *(black sausage), smoky chorizo sausage and ham. Beef is also included sometimes. The beans take on the rich flavour of the meat, especially the* tocino.

Empanada, *the Galician flat pie, is stuffed with salted cod or tuna. Shellfish and pork are alternative fillings.*

Angulas *(elvers), a winter luxury in the Basque dining clubs, are cooked lightly with oil, garlic and chilli.*

Pimientos rellenos, *from Navarra, are the local spicy pointed red pepper stuffed with fish, seafood or meat.*

Truchas a la Navarra *are cleaned and deboned mountain trout which are stuffed with serrano ham and fried or grilled.*

Vieras de Santiago *are scallops (the symbol of St James) in the shell, covered in a tomato and brandy sauce and grilled.*

Casadielles   Carajitos

Sobaos

Lacón con grelos *is the Galician national dish of cured pork shoulder with turnip tops and sausage.*

Chilindrón de cordero, *a rich dish of spicy lamb stewed with local dried or fresh peppers, is a speciality of Navarra.*

Cakes and biscuits *include sobaos (a Cantabrian break- fast sponge), hazelnut carajitos and walnut-stuffed casadielles.*

CHEESES

From the Cantabrian mountains come the famous pungent blue Cabrales and Picón. Galicia is noted for soft cheeses, especially *tetilla*. Pear-shaped San Simón, smoked Basque Idiazábal and Roncal are also recommended.

Idiazábal

Cabrales

Tetilla

Mussels

Canned tuna

Scallops

FISH AND SEAFOOD

Some of the most delicious seafood in Europe comes from the Atlantic coast of Spain. Specialities include mussels, scallops, lobsters, octopus, and un- usual tall, black barnacles known as *percebes*. The north coast also supplies spider crabs, fat anchovies, and top quality tuna, much of which is canned. The Basques fish for cod off the coasts of Iceland and Norway. Most of the catch is salted, dried and sold throughout Spain as the ever popular *bacalao*.

Bacalao   Anchovies   Spider crab

Wines of Northern Spain

SPAIN'S MOST PRESTIGIOUS wine region, Rioja is best known for its red wines, matured to a distinctive vanilla mellowness. Some of the most prestigious bodegas were founded by émigrés from Bordeaux, and Rioja reds are similar to claret. Rioja also produces good white and rosé wines. Navarra reds and some whites have improved dramatically, thanks to a government research programme. The Basque region produces a tiny amount of the prickly, tart *txacoli* (*chacolí*). Larger quantities of a similar wine are made further west in Galicia, whose best wines are full-bodied whites.

Repairing barrels in Haro, Rioja

Ribeiro, *the popular everyday wine of Galicia, is slightly fizzy. It is often served in white porcelain cups* (tazas).

KEY

- Rías Baixas
- Ribeiro
- Valdeorras
- Txacoli de Guetaria
- Rioja
- Navarra

Lagar de Cervera is from Rías Baixas, where Spain's most fashionable whites are made from the Albariño grape.

WINE REGIONS

The wine regions of Northern Spain are widely dispersed. Cradled between the Pyrenees and the Atlantic are the important regions of Rioja and Navarra. Rioja is divided into the sub-regions of Rioja Alavesa, Rioja Alta and Rioja Baja, divided by the Río Ebro. The river also cuts through the wine region of Navarra. To the north are the only vineyards of the Basque country: the miniscule Txacoli de Guetaria region. In the far west lie the four wine regions of rugged, wet Galicia: Rías Baixas, Ribeiro, Valdeorras, and the newly created Ribera Sacra.

Wine village of El Villar de Álava in Rioja Alta

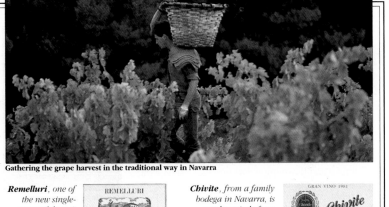

Gathering the grape harvest in the traditional way in Navarra

Remelluri, one of the new single-estate "Château" Riojas, from the vineyards of Rioja Alavesa, is soft and not too oaky.

Chivite, from a family bodega in Navarra, is made entirely from Tempranillo and aged in the barrel, resulting in a style similar to Rioja.

SANTANDER

BILBO (BILBAO)   Getaria   Zumaia   DONOSTIA (SAN SEBASTIÁN)

GASTEIZ (VITORIA)   IRUÑA (PAMPLONA)

Lizarra (Estella)   Tafalla

Haro   Logroño   Olite

Nájera   Calahorra

Arnedo   Alfaro

Corella   Tudela

Viña Ardanza is blended, as are most red Riojas. The best, like this reserva, are aged for two or more years in American oak casks.

KEY FACTS ABOUT WINES OF NORTHERN SPAIN

Location and Climate
Rioja and Navarra are influenced by both Mediterranean and Atlantic weather systems. The hillier, northwestern parts receive some Atlantic rain while the hot Ebro plain has a Mediterranean climate. The Basque region and Galicia are both cool, Atlantic regions with high rainfall. Soils everywhere are stony and poor, except in the Ebro plain.

Grape Varieties
The great red grape of Rioja and Navarra is Tempranillo. In Rioja it is blended with smaller quantities of Garnacha, Graciano and Mazuelo, while in Navarra Cabernet Sauvignon is permitted and blends excitingly with Tempranillo. Garnacha, also important in Navarra, is used

for the excellent *rosados* (rosés). Whites of Navarra and Rioja are made mainly from the Viura grape. Galicia has many local varieties, of which the most important are Albariño, Loureira and Treixadura, which is now taking over from the inferior Palomino.

Good Producers

Rías Baixas: Fillaboa, Lagar de Fornelos, Morgadío, Santiago Ruiz. *Ribeiro:* Cooperativa Vinícola del Ribeiro. *Rioja:* Bodegas Riojanas (Canchales, Monte Real), CVNE (Imperial, Viña Real Oro), Faustino Martínez, Federico Paternina, Marqués de Cáceres, Marqués de Murrieta, Martínez Bujanda, Remelluri, La Rioja Alta (Viña Ardanza). *Navarra:* Bodega de Sarría, Guelbenzu, Julián Chivite (Gran Feudo), Magaña, Ochoa, Príncipe de Viana.

Forests of the North

Purple emperor butterfly

M UCH OF SPAIN was once blanketed by a mantle of trees. Today, just ten per cent of the original cover remains, mostly in the mountainous north, where rainfall is high and slopes too steep for cultivation. Large areas of mixed deciduous forest – mainly beech, Pyrenean oak and chestnut, with some ash and lime – dominate the landscape, particularly in Cantabria and the Basque Country. The undergrowth of shrubs and flowering plants provides habitats for many insects, mammals and birds. The forests are also the refuge of Spain's last brown bears *(see p100).*

Forest in Northern Spain in autumn

REGENERATION OF THE FOREST

Dead materials – leaves, twigs and the excrement and bodies of animals – are broken down by various organisms on the forest floor, especially fungi, bacteria and ants. This process releases nutrients which are absorbed by trees and other plants, enabling them to grow.

Fly agaric mushrooms

Lichens grow slowly and are sensitive to pollution. Their presence in a forest often indicates that it is in good health.

The stag beetle takes its name from the huge antler-like mandibles of the male. Despite their ferocious appearance, these beetles are harmless to humans.

Millipede and fungus on a woodland floor

BEECH FOREST

Beech, the dominant species in the Cantabrian mountains and Pyrenees, grows on well-drained soils. Some trees retain their distinctive copper-red leaves through the winter. Beech mast (nuts) are collected to feed to pigs.

Beech leaf and mast

The thick crown shuts out light, inhibiting undergrowth.

Long, thin orange buds

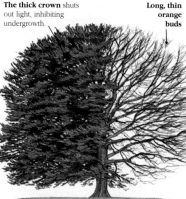

Male golden orioles, among the most colourful European birds, are hard to spot because they spend much of their time in the thick cover provided by old woodlands. Females and juveniles are a duller yellow-green with a brownish tail.

Beech martens are nocturnal. By day, they sleep in a hollow tree or another animal's abandoned nest. At night they feed on fruit, birds and small mammals.

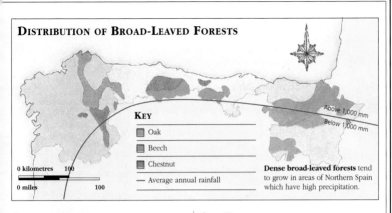

DISTRIBUTION OF BROAD-LEAVED FORESTS

KEY

- Oak
- Beech
- Chestnut
- Average annual rainfall

Above 1,000 mm

Below 1,000 mm

0 kilometres   100

0 miles   100

Dense broad-leaved forests tend to grow in areas of Northern Spain which have high precipitation.

CHESTNUT FOREST

Chestnut trees grow on well-drained acidic soils. They have slender yellow flowers and in summer produce their fruit, which is eaten by wild boar, dormice, squirrels and mice. The wood is hard and durable but splits easily.

Leaf and chestnut

OAK FOREST

Three main species of oak tree – pedunculate, Pyrenean and the evergreen holm oak – dominate the ancient woodlands of the north. Over 300 species of animal, such as wild boar, squirrels and nuthatches, feed off oaks.

Oak leaf and acorn

Large leaves have sharp, serrated edges.

Few massive, spreading branches

Grey twigs ending in numerous buds

Deep spiral ridges on trunk

The pipistrelle bat is a nocturnal species common in woodlands. It catches and eats small insects in flight. Larger insects are taken to a perch. The bat hibernates in winter in a hollow tree or cave.

The jay, a member of the crow family, is a common but somewhat shy woodland bird with a distinctively raucous cry. It can be identified in flight by its white rump, black tail and above all by its bright blue wing patch.

Blue tits feed mainly in the tree canopy of broad-leaved woods and rarely come down to the ground. The male and female have similar, distinctive plumage. They may raise the back feathers of the crown if alarmed.

Red squirrels bury large numbers of acorns during autumn to last through winter, since these diurnal creatures do not hibernate. Many of the acorns are left to sprout into seedlings.

The Road to Santiago

According to legend, the body of Christ's apostle James was brought to Galicia. In 813 the relics were supposedly discovered at Santiago de Compostela, where a cathedral was built in his honour (see pp88–9). In the Middle Ages half a million pilgrims a year flocked there from all over Europe, crossing the Pyrenees at Roncesvalles (see p130) or via the Somport Pass (see p220). They often donned the traditional garb of cape, long staff and curling felt hat adorned with scallop shells, the symbol of the saint. The various routes, marked by the cathedrals, churches and hospitals built along them, are still used by travellers today.

St James on horseback

19th-century painting of the Pórtico da Gloria of Santiago cathedral

Astorga (see p334), *once a Roman city, was an important halt on the pilgrim route in the Middle Ages. The museum within its cathedral has a collection of gold and silver plate including a 13th-century gold filigree cross.*

A certificate *is given to pilgrims covering at least 100 km (62 miles) of the route on foot, bicycle or horseback.*

O Cebreiro (see p95) has a 9th-century church and some of the ancient *pallozas* the pilgrims often used for shelter.

León *was one of the main pilgrim stops. Its cathedral* (see pp336–7) *contains one of Spain's finest collections of stained glass.*

Ribadeo

A Coruña

Oviedo

SANTIAGO DE COMPOSTELA

Maritime Route

Vilar de Donas

Ligonde

Portuguese Route

PORTO LISBOA

Vigo

O Cebreiro

Villafranca del Bierzo

Ponferrada's huge Templar castle stands close to the town centre (see p334).

Ponferrada

Silver Route

Astorga

Hospital de Órbigo

LEÓN

Sahagún

Scallop shells, staffs and gourds to carry water are symbols of the pilgrimage.

0 kilometres   50

0 miles   50

SALAMANCA

ROMANESQUE CHURCH ARCHITECTURE

The Romanesque style of architecture *(see p20)* was brought to Spain from France during the 10th and 11th centuries. As the pilgrimage to Santiago became more popular, many glorious religious buildings were constructed along its main routes. Massive walls, few windows, round heavy arches and barrel vaulting are typical features of Romanesque architecture.

Carved capital

Octagonal lantern **Twin round towers** **Barrel vault**

Thick walls **Round arch**

Façade Cross-section

Parallel apses **Aisle** **Nave**

San Martín de Frómista (see p350), *built in the 11th century, is the only complete example of the "pilgrimage" style of Romanesque. The nave and aisles are almost the same height and there are three parallel apses.*

Floorplan

Pamplona's *(see p128) Gothic cathedral was one of the pilgrims' first stops after crossing the Pyrenees at Roncesvalles.*

Santo Domingo de la Calzada's *(see p124)* pilgrim hospital is now a parador.

Puente la Reina (see p127) *takes its name from the 11th-century humpbacked bridge (puente), built for pilgrims and still used by pedestrians.*

Frómista preserves one of the finest Romanesque churches on the French route.

Santander

Donostia (San Sebastián) → PARIS

thern Route   Bilbo (Bilbao)

LE PUY VEZELAY

Orreaga (Roncesvalles) • Valcarlos

↑ ARLES

Iruña (Pamplona)

Lizarra (Estella) • Puente la Reina • Sangüesa • Jaca

Santo Domingo de la Calzada   French Route   San Juan de la Peña

San Juan de Ortega

mista   Nájera   Logroño

BURGOS

ROUTES TO SANTIAGO

Several traditional pilgrimage roads converge on Santiago de Compostela. The main road from the Pyrenees is known as the French Route, with the Aragonese Route as a variation.

Burgos has a magnificent Gothic cathedral *(see pp354–5).*

GALICIA

··

LUGO · A CORUÑA · PONTEVEDRA · OURENSE

REMOTE IN THE NORTHWEST CORNER *of the peninsula, Galicia is the country's greenest region. In its hilly interior, smallholdings are farmed by traditional methods. Galicia is Spain's main seafaring region – three of its four provinces have an Atlantic coastline, and its cuisine is based on superb seafood. The Galicians, whose origins are Celtic, are fiercely proud of their culture and language.*

Much of Galicia still has a medieval quality. Some inland farms are divided into plots too tiny or steep for tractors to work, so oxen and horses are used for ploughing. Grain is stored in quaint, pillared granaries called *hórreos*. The misty, emerald countryside abounds with old granite villages and is dotted with *pazos* – traditional stone manor houses.

The discovery of the supposed tomb of St James the Apostle, in the 9th century, confirmed medieval Santiago de Compostela as Europe's most important religious shrine after St Peter's in Rome. Pilgrims and tourists still follow this ancient route of pilgrimage across Northern Spain. The Galician coast is incised by many fjord-like rias; the loveliest of these are the Rías Baixas in the west. Elsewhere it juts defiantly into the Atlantic in rocky headlands, such as Cabo Fisterra, Spain's most westerly point. Many people still make a living from the sea. Vigo in Pontevedra is the most important fishing port in Spain.

Galicia's official language, used on most signs, is *gallego*. It has similarities to the language of Portugal, which borders Galicia to the south. The Celtic character of this haunting land is still evident in the Galicians' favourite traditional instrument, the bagpipes.

Staple crops – maize, cabbages and potatoes – growing on the harsh land around Cabo Fisterra

◁ **The west façade of Santiago de Compostela's cathedral, overlooking the Praza do Obradoiro**

Exploring Galicia

SANTIAGO DE COMPOSTELA is Galicia's major tourist attraction. This beautiful city is the centrepiece of a region with many fine old towns, especially Betanzos, Mondoñedo, Lugo and Pontevedra. The resorts along the coastline of the wild Rías Altas, with their backdrop of forest-covered hills, offer good bathing. The Rías Baixas, the southern part of Galicia's west coast, has sheltered coves and sandy beaches, and excellent seafood in abundance. Travelling through the interior, where life seems to have changed little in centuries, is an ideal way to spend a peaceful, rural holiday.

Students in traditional dress playing music in Pontevedra

SIGHTS AT A GLANCE

The isolated monastery at Ribas de Sil

SEE ALSO

GETTING AROUND

The region's main airports are at A Coruña, Santiago de Compostela and Vigo. A motorway (A9) connects Vigo and A Coruña. The roads are generally good, but traffic along the coast can be heavy. Rail lines link Galicia's major cities; and towns along the north coast are served by the attractive FEVE (see p631) line running from the Basque Country. There are coach services between the major cities and also between Santiago de Compostela and France.

Calvary in Pontevedra's
Praza de la Herrería

KEY

▬▬▬	Motorway
▬▬▬	Major road
▬▬▬	Minor road
▬▬▬	Scenic route
⌒	River
☼	Viewpoint

0 kilometres 25

0 miles 15

Carved coat of arms on a house-front in Mondoñedo

Rías Altas ❶

Lugo & A Coruña. 🚉 Ribadeo. 🚌 Viveiro. ℹ Foz, (982) 14 00 27.

DEEP RIAS are interspersed with coves and headlands along the beautiful north coast from Ribadeo to A Coruña. Inland are hills covered with forests of pine and eucalyptus. Many of the small resorts and fishing villages are charming.

The lovely, winding **Ría de Ribadeo** forms the border with Asturias. To the west of it is the small fishing port of **Foz**, which has two good beaches. Nearby, the 10th-century Iglesia de San Martín de Mondoñedo, standing alone on a hill, contains carvings of biblical scenes on its transept capitals – note the story of Lazarus. **Viveiro**, a summer holiday resort, is a handsome old town surrounded by Renaissance walls and gateways, typically Galician glassed-in balconies or *galerías*, and a Romanesque church. Near the pretty fishing village of O Barqueiro is the headland of Estaca de Bares, with its lighthouse and wind turbines.

Westward along the coast, the lovely **Ría de Ortigueira** leads to the fishing port of the same name, characterized by neat white houses. Around this area there are also many wild and unspoiled beaches.

High cliffs rise out of the sea near the village of **San Andrés de Teixido**, whose church is the focal point for pilgrims every 8 September. According to local legend, all those who fail to visit the church in their own lifetime will come back to it as an animal in the afterlife. The village of **Cedeira**, which sits in seclusion on a quiet bay, is a prosperous summer resort with neat lawns, modern houses with *galerías*, and a long, curving beach.

Mondoñedo ❷

Lugo. 🏘 5,100. 🚉 🚌 ℹ Rua Alfonso VII, 31 (982) 52 11 02. 🗓 Thu & Sun. 🎉 San Lucas (18 Oct).

THIS DELIGHTFUL TOWN, an old provincial capital, is set in a fertile inland valley. There are stately houses with carved coats of arms and *galerías* in the main square. This is dominated by the **cathedral**, a building of golden stone in an unusual mix of styles. It has 18th-century Baroque towers, a Romanesque portal with a 16th-century stained-glass rose window and 17th-century cloisters. A poly-chromatic statue in the south ambulatory, Nuestra Señora la Inglesa, was rescued from St Paul's cathedral in London during the Reformation. The **Museo Diocesano** contains statues, altarpieces and works by Zurbarán and El Greco.

🏛 **Museo Diocesano**
Plaza de la Catedral. 📞 (982) 52 19 48. 🕐 Jun–Sep: daily. 🎫

Ornate tomb in the Iglesia de San Francisco in Betanzos

Betanzos ❸

A Coruña. 🏘 14,000. 🚉 🚌 ℹ Plaza Constitución 1, (981) 77 29 08. 🗓 Tue, Thu & Sat. 🎉 San Roque (14–25 Aug).

THE HANDSOME TOWN of Betanzos lies in a fertile valley slightly inland. Its broad main square has a replica of the Fountain of Diana at Versailles. In its steep narrow streets are some fine old houses and Gothic churches. The **Iglesia de Santiago**, built in the 15th century by the tailors' guild, has a statue of St James on horseback above the door. The **Iglesia de San Francisco**, dated 1387, has statues of wild boars and a heraldic emblem of Count Fernán Pérez de Andrade, whose 15th-century tomb is inside the church. For centuries his family were the overlords of the region.

ENVIRONS: 15 km (9 miles) north is the large, though pretty, fishing village of **Pontedeume**, with its narrow, hilly streets. Its medieval bridge still carries the main road to the large industrial town of **Ferrol**, to the north. This port became an important naval base and dock-yard town in the 18th century, and its Neo-Classical buildings survive from that time. General Franco *(see pp62–3)* was born in Ferrol in 1892, and an imposing equestrian statue of him stands in the Praza de España.

Pavement cafés in Betanzos' Plaza de García Hermanos

Stone cross standing above the perilous waters of the Costa da Morte

A Coruña ❹

A Coruña. 🏙 *200,000.* ✈ 🚉 🚌
🛈 *Dársena de la Marina, (981) 22
18 22.* 🎭 *Fiestas de María Pita (Aug),
Semana Grande (first fortnight of Aug).*

THIS PROUD CITY and busy
port has played a sizeable
role in Spanish maritime
history. Felipe II's doomed
Armada sailed from here to
England in 1588 *(see p55).*
Today, the sprawling industrial
suburbs contrast with the
elegant town centre, which is
laid out on an isthmus leading
to a headland. The **Torre de
Hércules**, Europe's oldest
working lighthouse, is a
famous local landmark. Built
by the Romans and rebuilt in
the 18th century, it still flashes
across the deep. Climb its 242
steps for a wide ocean view.

On the large, arcaded Praza
María Pita, the city's main
square, is the handsome town
hall. The sea promenade of
La Marina is lined with tiers
of glass-enclosed balconies or
galerías. Built as protection
against the strong winds, they
explain why A Coruña is often
referred to as the City of Glass.
The peaceful, tiny Praza de
Santa Bárbara is enchanting.

A Coruña has several fine
Romanesque churches such as
the **Iglesia de Santiago**, with
a carving of its saint on horseback situated beneath the

tympanum, and the **Iglesia de
Santa María**. This church, featuring a tympanum carved with
the Adoration of the Magi, is
one of the best-preserved 12th-
century buildings in Galicia.

The quiet Jardín de San
Carlos contains the tomb of the
English general Sir John Moore,
killed by the French in battle.
This old part of town is still
somewhat military, and army
jeeps are a common sight in
its narrow streets.

**The lofty Torre de Hércules
lighthouse at A Coruña**

Costa da Morte ❺

A Coruña. 🚌 *A Coruña, Malpica,
Santiago de Compostela.* 🛈 *A Coruña,
(981) 22 18 22.*

FROM MALPICA to Fisterra the
coast is wild and remote. It
is called the "Coast of Death"
because of the many ships
lost in storms or smashed on
the rocks by gales over the
centuries. But the headlands
are majestic and the sunsets
beautiful. Inland, the countryside is breezy and open. There
are no coastal towns, only simple villages, where fishermen
gather gastronomic *percebes*
(barnacles), destined for the
region's restaurants.

One of the most northerly
points of the Costa da Morte,
Malpica, has a seabird sanctuary. Laxe has good beaches
and safe bathing. **Camariñas**,
one of the most appealing
places on this coast, is a fishing
village where women make
bobbin-lace in the streets.
Beside the lighthouse on
nearby Cabo Vilán, a group
of futuristic wind turbines, tall
and slender, swirl in graceful
unison – a haunting sight.

To the south is Corcubión,
exuding a faded elegance,
and lastly, **Cabo Fisterra**
"where the land ends". This
cape, with its lighthouse, is a
good place to watch the sun
go down over the Atlantic.

Street-by-Street: Santiago de Compostela ❻

Vegetable stall in
Santiago market

IN THE MIDDLE AGES Santiago de Compostela was Christendom's third most important place of pilgrimage *(see pp78–9)*, after Jerusalem and Rome. Around the Praza do Obradoiro is an ensemble of historic buildings that has few equals in Europe. The local granite gives a harmonious unity to the mixture of architectural styles. With its narrow streets and old squares, the city centre is compact enough to explore on foot. Two other monuments worth seeing are the Convento de Santo Domingo de Bonaval, to the east of the centre, housing a Galician folk museum, and the Colegiata del Sar, a 12th-century Romanesque church, located to the south of the city.

★ Convento de San Martiño Pinario
The Baroque church of this monastery has a huge double altar and an ornate Plateresque façade with carved figures of saints and bishops.

Pazo de Xelmírez

RÚA DA TROI

RÚA DA TROI

RUELA DO VAL DE DEUS

RÚA DE SAN FRANCISCO

PRAZA D INMACULA

PRAZA D

★ Hostal de los Reyes Católicos
Built by the Catholic Monarchs as an inn and hospital for sick pilgrims, and now a parador (see p537), this magnificent building has an elaborate Plateresque doorway.

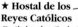

PRAZA OBRADO

Praza do Obradoiro
This majestic square is one of the world's finest and the focal point for pilgrims arriving in the city. The cathedral's Baroque façade dominates the square.

The Pazo de Raxo
with its Classical façade, was built i 1772 and houses the town hall.

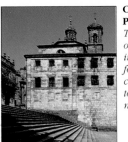

Convento de San Paio de Antealtares
This is one of the oldest monasteries in Santiago. It was founded in the 9th century to house the tomb of St James, now in the cathedral.

VISITORS' CHECKLIST

A Coruña. 👥 100,000. ✈ 10 km (6 miles) north. 🚌 Calle Hórreo, (981) 52 02 02. 🚌 Avenida Rodriguez de Viguri, (981) 58 77 00. 🛈 Calle Rúa do Villar 43, (981) 58 40 81. 🗓 Thu. 🎉 Semana Santa (Easter Week), Ascensión (May), Santiago (25 Jul).

Praza da Quintana, under the cathedral clock tower, is one of the city's most elegant squares.

Praza das Praterias
The Goldsmiths' Doorway of the cathedral opens on to this charming square with a 17th-century fountain in the centre.

KEY

– – – Suggested route

– – – Pilgrims' route

Rúa Nova is a handsome arcaded old street leading from the cathedral to the newer part of the city.

RÚA DE ACEVECHERIA

SACRA

RÚA DE GELMIREZ

RÚA NOVA

RÚA DO VILAR

RÚA DA RAINA

RÚA DO FRANCO

To tourist information

| 0 metres | 100 |
| 0 yards | 100 |

Colegio de San Jerónimo

STAR SIGHTS

★ Convento de San Martiño Pinario

★ Hotel de los Reyes Católicos

★ Cathedral

★ Cathedral
This grand towering spectacle has welcomed pilgrims to Santiago for centuries. Though the exterior has been remodelled over the years, the core of the building has remained virtually unchanged since the 11th century.

Santiago Cathedral

W ITH ITS TWIN BAROQUE TOWERS soaring high over the Praza do Obradoiro square, this monument to St James is a majestic sight, as befits one of the great shrines of Christendom *(see pp78–9)*. The present building dates from the 11th–12th centuries and stands on the site of the original 9th-century basilica built by Alfonso II. Through the famous carved Pórtico da Gloria, one of the great wonders of Christian art, is the same lofty interior that welcomed pilgrims in medieval times.

The gigantic *botafumeiro*

"Passport" – proof of a pilgrim's journey

The twin towers are the cathedral's highest structures at 74 m (243 ft).

Statue of St James

★ **West Façade**
The richly sculpted Baroque Obradoiro façade was added in the 18th century.

★ **Pórtico da Gloria**
The sculpted Doorway of Glory, with its statues of apostles and prophets, is 12th century.

The Santos dos Croques (Saint of Bumps) has greeted pilgrims since the 12th century. Touching this statue with the forehead is said to impart luck and wisdom.

Tapestry Museum
Some of the tapestries on show in the museum above the chapterhouse and the library date from the early 16th century. Others are based on cartoons by Goya.

STAR FEATURES

★ West Façade

★ Pórtico da Gloria

★ Porta das Praterias

The *botafumeiro*, a giant censer, is swung high above the altar by eight men during important services.

Mondragon Chapel (1521) contains fine wrought-iron grilles and vaulting.

Clock Tower

VISITORS' CHECKLIST

Praza do Obradoiro. **(** (981) 58 35 48. **□** 7am–9pm daily. **†** regular services during the day. **&** west entrance only. **Museum** **□** Jun–Sep: 10:30am–1:30pm & 4–6:30pm daily; Oct–May: 11am–1pm & 4–6pm daily.

High Altar
Visitors can pass behind the ornate high altar to kiss the silver mantle of the 13th-century statue of St James.

Cloisters

★ **Porta das Praterias**
The 11th-century Gold-smiths' Doorway is rich in bas-relief sculptures of biblical scenes.

Crypt
The relics of St James and two disciples are said to lie in a tomb in the crypt, under the altar, in the original 9th-century foundations.

Chapterhouse

Padrón ❼

A Coruña. 🏠 10,700. 🚌 🚏 ℹ️
*Calle General Franco 27, (981) 81 04
51.* 🏛 *Sun.* 🎭 *Santiago (24–5 Jul).*

THIS QUIET TOWN on the Río
Ulla, known for its piquant
green peppers, was a major
seaport until it silted up. Legend has it the boat carrying
the body of St James to Galicia
(see p78) arrived here. The
supposed mooring stone, or
padrón, lies below the altar
of the church by the bridge.

The leafy avenue beside the
church features in the poems of
one of Galicia's greatest writers,
Rosalia de Castro (1837–85).
Her creeper-covered home on
the edge of town, where she
spent her final years, has been
converted into a museum.

ENVIRONS: The estuary town
of Noia (Noya) lies on the
coast 20 km (12 miles) west.
Its Gothic church has a finely
carved portal. East of Padrón is
Pazo de Oca, a manor house,
with a crenellated tower, idyllic
gardens and a lake.

🏛 **Museo Rosalia de Castro**
La Matanza. 📞 *(981) 81 12 04.*
🔵 *Tue–Sun.* ♿

The picturesque gardens and lake of Pazo de Oca

A Toxa ❽

Near O Grove. 🚌 ℹ️ *Ayuntamiento,
O Grove, (986) 73 09 75.*

A TINY pine-covered island
joined to the mainland by
a bridge, A Toxa (La Toja) is
one of the most stylish resorts
in Galicia. The *belle époque*
palace-hotel *(see p537)* and
luxury villas add to the island's
elegant atmosphere. A Toxa's
best-known landmark is the
small church covered with
scallop shells. Across the bridge
is O Grove (El Grove), a
thriving family resort and fishing port on a peninsula, with
holiday hotels and flats alongside glorious beaches.

Scallop-covered roof of the church on A Toxa island

Pontevedra ❾

Pontevedra. 🏠 65,000. 🚌 🚏
ℹ️ *Calle General Mola 3, (986) 85
37 16.* 🏛 *Sat.* 🎭 *Fiestas de la
Peregrina (second week in Aug).*

PONTEVEDRA lies inland, at the
head of a long ria that is
backed by green hills. The delightful old town is typically
Galician and has a network of
cobbled alleys and tiny graceful squares with granite calvaries, arcades, flower-filled balconies and excellent tapas bars.
On the south side of the old
town is the Gothic **Convento
de Santo Domingo**. It is now
a museum containing Roman
steles and Galician coats of
arms and tombs. To the west,
the 16th-century **Iglesia de
Santa María la Mayor** contains a magnificent Plateresque
(see p21) façade that includes
richly carved figures of oars-
men and fishermen at the top.

On the **Praza de la Leña**, a
small, shaded square, two 18th-
century mansions form the
Museo de Pontevedra, one of
the best museums in Galicia.
The gold bracelets, torques and
other Celtic Bronze Age treasures found locally are superb.
Among the paintings on display are 15th-century Spanish
primitives, and canvases by
Zurbarán and Goya. On the
top floor is the museum's star
display: a collection of drawings and paintings by Alfonso
Castelao, a 20th-century Galician artist, writer and nationalist,
who forcefully depicted the
misery endured by his people
during the Spanish Civil War.

🏛 **Museo de Pontevedra**
Calle Pasanteria 10. 📞 *(986) 85
14 55.* 🔵 *Tue–Sun.*

Rías Baixas

THIS SOUTHERN PART of Galicia's west coast consists of four large rias or inlets between pine-covered hills. The beaches are good, the scenery is lovely, the bathing safe and the climate much milder than on the wilder coast to the north. Though areas such as Vilagarcía de Arousa and Panxón have become popular holiday resorts, much of the Rías Baixas (Rías Bajas) coastline is unspoiled, such as the quiet stretch from Muros to Noia. This part of the coastline provides some of Spain's most fertile fishing grounds. Mussel-breeding platforms are positioned in neat rows along the rias, looking like half-submerged submarines; and in November, the women harvest clams.

Muros, a pretty little fortified port, has well-preserved examples of typical Galician architecture.

Mirador da Curota

Between Muros and Noia *the coast is less built-up than further south. This beautiful open coast, bare and rocky, is backed by hills.*

Vilagarcía de Arousa is a popular resort with a pleasant waterfront promenade and good sailing and water sports facilities.

Cambados, known for its white wine, has a paved square, the Plaza de Fefiñanes, lined by fine old houses.

Pontevedra is the lively provincial capital and has a picturesque setting by a deep ria.

Hío, a small fishing village with a good beach, is noted for having one of the finest carved calvaries in Galicia.

Mirador da Madroa

Combarro *is a picturesque fishing village known for its hórreos (see p23) on the seafront.*

The Illas Cíes have white sand, clear water and a bird sanctuary.

Panxón, *across the broad bay from Baiona (see p92), is a popular holiday resort with excellent sandy beaches.*

Muros • • Noia
Porto do Son
Illa de Arousa • Vilagarcía de Arousa
• Ribeira   Vilanova de Arousa
           • Cambados
Illa de Sálvora   Illa da Toxa
              Combarro
Illa de Ons • Pontevedra
Sanxenxo • Marín
        Mirador de Cotorredondo
Hío •
• Illas Cíes   Cangas
           Vigo
Panxón
Baiona

0 kilometres   10
0 miles   5

Cannons on the battlements of Monterreal fortress, Baiona

Vigo ⑩

Pontevedra. 🏠 *300,000.* ✈ 🚐
🚌 ℹ *Estación Marítima, (986) 43
05 77.* 🚤 *Sun.* 🎭 *Cristo de los
Afligidos (Jul).*

GALICIA'S LARGEST TOWN is
also the biggest fishing
port in Spain. It is situated in
an attractive setting near the
mouth of a deep ria spanned
by a high suspension bridge,
and is surrounded by wooded
hills. Vigo isn't noted for its
old buildings but does have
striking modern
sculptures such as
local artist Juan José
Oliveira's horses
statue in the Praza
de España. The
oldest part of the
town, Barrio del Berbes,
is near the port and
used to be the
sailors' quarter.
Its cobbled alleys
are teeming with
bars, and here
you can find
some of the
finest

Bronze sculpture by Oliveira in
Vigo's Praza de España

tapas bars, which serve mainly
seafood. The Mercado de la
Piedra, near the port, sells
reasonably priced fish and
shellfish – particularly oysters.

Baiona ⑪

Pontevedra. 🏠 *10,000.* 🚌 ℹ *Calle
Lorenzo de la Carrera 17, (986) 35 52
50.* 🚤 *Mon.* 🎭 *Santa Marina (18 Jul).*

THE PINTA, one of the cara-
vels from the fleet of
Christopher Columbus, arrived
at this small port on 10 March
1493, bringing the first news
of the discovery of the New
World. Today Baiona (Bayona),
which is sited on a broad bay,
is a popular summer resort,
its harbour a mix of pleasure
and fishing boats. The 12th-
century **collegiate church** is
Romanesque and Gothic. Symbols, such as knives, chisels
and axes, carved on the arches,
indicate the local guilds that
helped build the church.
    A royal fortress once stood
on Monterreal promontory, to
the north of town. Its huge
defensive walls remain, but the
interior has been converted
into a smart parador *(see
p536)*. The cannons used as
protection against pirates can
still be seen. A walk around
the battlements offers superb
views of the coast.
    On the coast about 3 km
(2 miles) further south is a
huge granite statue of the
Virgen de la Roca. During
important religious festivals,
visitors climb up inside and
on to the ship she holds.

A Guarda ⑫

Pontevedra. 🏠 *10,000.* 🚌
ℹ *Plaza de España 1, (986) 61 00
00.* 🚤 *Sat.* 🎭 *Monte de Santa Tecla
(second week of Aug).*

THE LITTLE FISHING PORT of A
Guarda (La Guardia) has a
reputation for good seafood
and is particularly well known
for the quality of its lobsters.
    On the slopes of Monte de
Santa Tecla are the remains of
a Celtic settlement of some
100 round stone dwellings
which are dated around
600–200 BC. The **Museo de
Monte de Santa Tecla** is
situated on a nearby hilltop.

ENVIRONS: About 10 km
(6 miles) north, the tiny
Baroque **Monasterio de Santa
María** stands by the beach at
Oia. Semi-wild horses roam
the surrounding hills and, in
May and June, are rounded
up for branding in a series of
day-long fiestas *(see p94).*

🏛 **Museo de Monte de
Santa Tecla**
A Guarda. 🎫 *(986) 61 00 00.*
🔓 *daily.*

Circular foundations of Celtic
dwellings at A Guarda

Tui ⑬

Pontevedra. 🏠 *16,400.* 🚌 🚐 ℹ
Avda Portugal, (986) 60 17 89. 🚤 *Thu.*
🎭 *San Telmo (week after Easter),
Descent of the Río Miño (Aug).*

SPAIN'S main frontier town
with Portugal, Tui (Tuy)
stands on a hillside above the
Río Miño. Its graceful old
streets curve up to an old quarter and the 13th-century hilltop
cathedral. The two countries
were often at war during the
Middle Ages, and as a result
the church is built in the style

FISHING IN SPAIN

The Spanish eat more seafood per head of population than any other European nation except Portugal. Half of this is caught by Galician fishing fleets. Some 90,000 fishermen and 20,000 boats land over a million tonnes of fish and shellfish a year, much of this caught offshore where sardines, tuna, lobster and clams are plentiful. In recent years, the stocks in the seas around Spain have become depleted by overfishing, forcing deep-sea trawlers to travel as far as Canada and Iceland.

Unloading the catch in Spain's largest fishing port, Vigo

ornate altarpiece and Gothic choir stalls. In the garden is the 10th-century Mozarabic **Iglesia de San Miguel**.

ENVIRONS: At **Santa Comba de Bande**, 26 km (16 miles) to the south, is an even older little church. The features of this Visigothic (*see pp46–7*) church, which is thought to be 7th century, include a lantern turret and a horseshoe arch that has carved marble pillars.

Verín ⑮

Ourense. 11,500. 🏠 🛈 *Plaza do Concello 1, (988) 41 00 00.* 🗓 *3rd, 11th & 23rd of month.* 🎉 *Santa María la Mayor (15 Aug).*

THOUGH IT STANDS amid vineyards, Verín produces more than wine. Its thermal springs have given it a thriving bottled water industry. The town has a number of 17th-century houses with arcades and glass balconies, or *galerías*. The **Castillo de Monterrei**, built during the wars with Portugal, is 4 km (2.5 miles) to the west. Inside its three rings of walls are a square 15th-century keep, an arcaded courtyard, and a 13th-century church with a delicately carved portal. The castle once housed a monastery and hospital.

of a fortress, with towers and battlements. It has a cloister and choir stalls and a richly decorated west porch.

Nearby is the **Iglesia de San Telmo**, dedicated to the patron saint of fishermen, whose Baroque ornamentation shows a Portuguese influence. Below the cathedral is an iron bridge, the **Puente Internacional**, built by Gustave Eiffel in 1884 to stretch across the river to Valença do Minho in Portugal.

The Gothic **Iglesia de Santo Domingo**, situated beside the Parque de la Alameda, contains ivy-covered cloisters and tombs with delicately carved effigies. The church overlooks the river, which is filled with boats in August for the Descent of the Río Miño, a canoe race and fiesta.

Celanova ⑭

Ourense. 6,200. 🏠 🛈 *Plaza Mayor 1, (988) 43 14 81.* 🗓 *Thu.* 🎉 *San Roque (15 Aug).*

ON THE MAIN SQUARE of this little town is the massive **Monasterio de San Salvador**, which was formerly one of the most important monasteries in Spain. Founded during the 10th century and later rebuilt, it is mainly Baroque, though one of its two lovely cloisters is Renaissance. The enormous church of this Benedictine monastery has an

Ceramic tiled floor of the Iglesia de San Miguel

The Castillo de Monterrei, standing high above the town of Verín

GALICIA'S FIESTAS

Os Peliqueiros
(Carnival, Feb/Mar), Laza
(Ourense). Dressed up in
grinning masks and out-
landish costumes, with
cowbells tied to their belts
and brandishing sticks, *Os
Peliqueiros* take to the
streets on Carnival Sunday.
They are licensed to lash
out at onlookers, who are
forbidden to retaliate. On
Carnival Monday morning
a battle takes place, with
flour, water and live ants
used as ammunition. Laza's
carnival comes to on end
on the Tuesday with a
reading of the satirical
"Donkey's Will" and the
burning of an effigy.

The outrageous costumes of
Os Peliqueiros **in Laza**

A Rapa das Bestas
(May and Jun), Oia
(Pontevedra). Semi-wild
horses are rounded up by
local farmers for their
manes and tails to be cut.
What was once a chore is
now a popular fiesta.
Flower pavements
(Corpus Christi, May/Jun),
Ponteareas (Pontevedra).
The streets of the town
along which the Corpus
Christi procession passes
are carpeted with intricate
designs made from brightly
coloured flower petals.
St James's Day *(25 Jul)*,
Santiago de Compostela.
On the night before, there
is a firework display in
the Praza do Obradoiro.
The celebrations are es-
pecially wild when 25
July falls on a Sunday.

Ourense ⑯

Ourense. 🏘 *100,000*. 🚇 🚍
ℹ *Curros Enríquez 1, (988) 37 20 20.*
📅 *7th & 17th of each month.* 🎭
Os Maios (3 May), San Martín (11 Nov).

THE OLD QUARTER of Ourense
was built around the city's
well-known thermal springs,
Fonte as Burgas. Even today,
these spout water at a temperature of 65°C (150°F) from
three fountains.

This old part of the town is
the most interesting, particularly the small area around the
arcaded Plaza Mayor. Here the
cathedral, founded in 572 and
rebuilt in the 12th–13th centuries, has a vast gilded reredos
by Cornelis de Holanda. On
the triple-arched doorway are
carved multicoloured figures
reminiscent of the Pórtico da
Gloria at Santiago *(see p88)*.
Nearby is the elegant 14th-
century cloister, the **Claustro
de San Francisco**.

One of the city's landmarks
is the 13th-century **Puente
Romano**, a seven-arched
bridge which crosses the Río
Miño, north of the town. It is
built on Roman foundations
and still used by traffic.

ENVIRONS: Allariz, 25 km (16
miles) south, and Ribadavia,
to the west, have old Jewish
quarters with narrow streets
and Romanesque churches.
Ribadavia is also noted for its
Ribeiro wines – a dry white
and a port-like red *(see p74)*
– and has a wine museum.

**Ornate Gothic reredos in the
cathedral at Ourense**

Monasterio de Ribas de Sil ⑰

Ribas de Sil. 🚍 *San Esteban de Sil.*
🚍 *from Ourense.* 📞 *(988) 20 10 54.*
🕐 *Tue–Sun.* ♿

NEAR ITS CONFLUENCE with the
Miño, the Río Sil carves
a deep curving gorge in which
dams form two reservoirs of
dark green water. A hairpin
road winds to the top of the
gorge, where the Romanesque-
Gothic Monasterio de Ribas de
Sil is situated high on a crag
above the chasm. Partly dilapi-
dated, partly over-restored – it
has an enormous glass wall
in one of the three cloisters –
it nevertheless has a certain
ghostly grandeur.

The Río Sil winding its way through the gorge

The grandiose Monasterio de Oseira surrounded by the forests of the Valle de Arenteiro

Monasterio de Oseira ⑱

Oseira. 🚌 🚍 *from Ourense.* ☎ *(988) 28 20 04.* ☐ *daily.* 📷

Tʜɪs ᴍᴏɴᴀsᴛᴇʀʏ stands on its own in a wooded valley near the village of Oseira, named after the bears *(osos)* that once lived in this region. It is a big grey building with a Baroque façade dating from 1708. On the doorway is a statue of the Virgin as nurse, with St Bernard kneeling at her feet. The interior of the 12th–13th-century church is typically Cistercian in its simplicity. The cloisters, main stairway, and vaulted chapterhouse are impressive.

Fresco of a *dona* in the monastery at Vilar de Donas

Vilar de Donas ⑲

Lugo. 🏠 80. 🛈 *Ctra de Santiago 28, (982) 38 00 01.* 🎉 *San Antonio (13 Jun), San Salvador (6 Aug).*

Tʜɪs ʜᴀᴍʟᴇᴛ on the Road to Santiago *(see pp78–9)* has a small church, situated just off the main road, with a Romanesque doorway. Inside are tombs of some of the Knights of the Order of Santiago, and 15th-century frescoes of the

nuns *(donas)* who lived here until the 15th century and who gave the village its name. Some frescoes are on biblical themes.

The Cistercian **Monasterio Sobrado de los Monjes**, to the northwest, has a medieval kitchen and chapterhouse, and a church with attractive domes.

Lugo ⑳

Lugo. 🏠 80,000. 🚌 🚍 🛈 *Praza de España 27–9, (982) 23 13 61.* 🚍 *Tue & Fri.* 🎉 *San Froilán (4–12 Oct).*

Cᴀᴘɪᴛᴀʟ of Galicia's largest province, Lugo has also an important centre under the Romans. Attracted to the town by its thermal springs, they constructed what is now the finest surviving **Roman wall** in Spain. The wall, which encircles the city, is about 6 m (20 ft) thick and 10 m (33 ft) high with ten gateways. Six of these have stairways to the top of the wall, from where there is a good view of the city.

Inside the wall, the old town is lively though dignified, with pretty squares. In the **Praza de Santo Domingo** is a black statue of a Roman eagle, built to commemorate Augustus' capture of Lugo from the Celts in the 1st century BC. The Romanesque **cathedral** is large and rambling, and modelled on that of Santiago. It features an elegant Baroque cloister, and a chapel containing the alabaster statue of Nuestra Señora de los Ojos Grandes (Virgin of the Big Eyes). The **Museo Provincial** exhibits Celtic gold

torques, local Roman finds, a life-size model of a farm kitchen, modern Galician paintings and a curious statue of a kneeling peasant woman holding a miniature priest.

Eɴᴠɪʀᴏɴs: The stone hamlet of **Santa Eulalia**, situated in lovely open country to the west, conceals a curious building excavated in 1924: a tiny temple, with lively, bright frescoes of birds and leaves. Though its exact purpose is unknown, it is thought to be an early Christian church and has been dated at around the 3rd century AD.

🏛 **Museo Provincial**
Plaza de la Soledad. ☎ *(982) 24 21 12.* ☐ *daily.* ♿

O Cebreiro ㉑

Lugo. 🏠 16. 🚍 🛈 *(982) 36 70 25.* 🎉 *Santo Milagro (8 Sep).*

Uᴘ ɪɴ ᴛʜᴇ ʜɪʟʟs in the east of Galicia, close to the border with León, is one of the most unusual villages on the Road to Santiago. Its 9th-century church was supposedly the scene of a miracle in 1300 when the wine was turned into blood and the bread into flesh. Near the church there are several *pallozas*, round thatched stone huts of a Celtic design. Some of these ancient dwellings, which often had annexes for livestock and grain, have been restored. One of them is now a folk museum.

Painted gourd in O Cebreiro's museum

🏛 **Museo Etnográfico**
O Cebreiro. ☐ *Wed–Sun.*

ASTURIAS AND CANTABRIA

ASTURIAS · CANTABRIA

THE SPECTACULAR PICOS DE EUROPA *massif sits astride the border between Asturias and Cantabria. In this rural region cottage crafts are kept alive in villages in remote mountain valleys and forested foothills. There are many ancient towns and churches, and pretty fishing ports on the coasts. Cave paintings, such as those at Altamira, were made by people living here over 10,000 years ago.*

Asturias is proud that it resisted invasion by the Moors. The Reconquest of Spain is held to have begun in 718 when a Moorish force was defeated by Christians at Covadonga in the Picos de Europa.

The Christian kingdom of Asturias was founded in the 8th century, and in the brilliant, brief artistic period that followed many churches were built around the capital, Oviedo. Some of these pre-Romanesque churches still stand. Today, Asturias is a province and a principality under the patronage of the heir to the Spanish throne. In the charming, unspoiled Asturian countryside cider is produced and a quaint dialect, *bable,* is spoken.

Cantabria centres on Santander, its capital, a port and an elegant resort. It is a mountainous province with a legacy of Romanesque churches in isolated spots. It also has well-preserved towns and villages such as Santillana del Mar, Carmona and Bárcena Mayor.

Mountains cover more than half of both provinces, so mountain sports are a major attraction. Expanses of deciduous forests remain in many parts, some sheltering Spain's last wild bears. Along the coasts are pretty fishing ports and resorts, such as Castro Urdiales, Ribadesella and Comillas, and sandy coves for bathing. Both the coastal plains and uplands are ideal for quiet rural holidays.

Peaceful meadow around Lago de la Ercina in the Picos de Europa massif

◁ One of the pretty cobbled streets of Santillana del Mar, Cantabria

Exploring Asturias and Cantabria

THE MOST OBVIOUS ATTRACTION in this area is the group of mountains that straddles the two provinces – the Picos de Europa. These jagged peaks offer excellent rock climbing and rough hiking, and in certain parts can be explored by car or bicycle. These and several other nature reserves in the area are home to rare species of flora and fauna, including the capercaillie and brown bear. The coast offers many sandy coves for bathing. Santander and Oviedo are lively university cities with a rich cultural life. There are innumerable unspoiled villages to explore, especially the ancient town of Santillana del Mar. Some of the earliest examples of art exist in Cantabria, most notably at Altamira, where the cave drawings and engravings are among the oldest to be found in Europe.

Typical flower-covered balcony in the village of Bárcena Mayor

A view along the crowded beach of Playa del Camello, Santander

SIGHTS AT A GLANCE

Cantabrian dairy farmers loading hay on to their cart

RIBADESELLA
● LLANES
NGAS DE ONÍS
N634
⑬
COMILLAS
⑯
⑰ SANTILLANA
DEL MAR
CUEVAS DE ALTAMIRA
⑲ SANTANDER
● SANTOÑA
⑳ LAREDO
A8
RQUE NACIONAL
DE LOS PICOS
DE EUROPA
⑱ PUENTE VIESGO
N29
CASTRO
URDIALES
㉑
A8
⑪
⑫
POTES
⑭
VALLE DE
CABUÉRNIGA
● VILLACARRIEDO
N623
*Donostia
(San Sebastián)
Bilbo (Bilbao)*
N621
ALTO CAMPOO ⑮
N611
REINOSA
●
Embalse del Ebro
Burgos
Palencia

0 kilometres   25
0 miles   15

GETTING AROUND

The main road through the region is the N634, which is still narrow and hilly in places, and often suffers from heavy lorry traffic. Most other major roads follow the directions of the valleys and run north to south. Minor roads are generally good but can be slow and winding. The private FEVE railway, which follows the coast from Bilbao to Ferrol in Galicia, is both useful and extremely scenic. A twice-weekly Brittany Ferries service links Santander with Plymouth. Asturias has a small international airport near Avilés. Parts of Cantabria are closer to Bilbao airport.

**Carved figure in the
Convento de Regina
Coeli, Santillana del Mar**

SEE ALSO

• *Where to Stay* pp538–40

• *Restaurants and Bars* pp580–81

KEY

	Motorway
	Major road
	Minor road
	Scenic route
	River
☆	Viewpoint

Craftsman making knife blades in a forge at Taramundi

Taramundi ●

Asturias. 🏠 *1,000.* ℹ *Plaza del Poyo,
(98) 564 67 02.* 🎉 *San José (19 Mar),
Día del Turista (last Sun of Jul).*

Situated in the remote Los
Oscos region, this small
village houses a rural tourism
centre which organizes tours
of the forests in four-wheel
drive vehicles. Taramundi has
a long tradition of wrought-
iron craftsmanship. Iron ore
was first mined in the area by
the Romans. There are approximately two dozen forges in
and around the village, where
craftsmen can still be seen
making their traditional knives
and penknives with attractively
decorated wooden handles.

Environs: About 20 km
(12 miles) to the east, at **San
Martín de Oscos**, there is an
18th-century palace. At
Grandas de Salime, 10 km
(6 miles) further southeast,
the Museo Etnográfico has
displays showing local crafts,
traditional life and farming.

🏛 **Museo Etnográfico**
Calle el Ferreiro 17. 📞 *(98) 562
72 43.* ⭕ *Tue–Sun.* 🎫 &

Castro de Coaña ●

Southwest of Navia. 🚌 *from Navia.* 📞
(98) 597 84 01. ⭕ *Tue–Sun.* 🎫 &

One of the most important
Celtic settlements in Spain,
Castro de Coaña was established in the Iron Age and later
occupied by the Romans. Located on a hillside in the Navia
valley are the well-preserved
remains of its fortifications

and the stone foundations of
a number of circular dwellings,
some of which stand head
high. Inside the walls can be
found several hollowed-out
stones which may once have
been used as funerary urns or
for crushing corn.

The museum on the site displays many of the finds that
have been unearthed at Castro
de Coaña. Among the interesting remains on display are pottery, tools and Roman coins.

**Circular stone foundations of
dwellings at Castro de Coaña**

Costa Verde ●

Asturias. 🚉 *Avilés.* 🚉 *Oviedo, Gijón.*
ℹ *Plaza del Ayuntamiento, Castropol,
(98) 563 50 01.*

The aptly named "green coast"
is a succession of attractive
sandy coves and dramatic cliffs,
punctuated by deep estuaries
and numerous fishing villages.
Inland, there are lush meadows, and pine and eucalyptus
forests, backed by mountains.
This stretch of coastline has
been less spoiled than most in
Spain; the resorts tend to be
modest in size, like the hotels.

Two pretty fishing ports,
Castropol and **Figueras**, stand
by the eastern shore of the Ría
de Ribadeo, forming the border
with Galicia. To the east are
other picturesque villages such
as Tapia de Casariego and
Ortiguera, in a small rocky
cove. Following the coast,
Luarca lies below a church
and a quiet cemetery on a
headland, and has a neat little
harbour packed with red, blue
and white boats. The village
of **Cudillero** is even more
delightful – outdoor cafés and
excellent seafood restaurants
crowd the tiny plaza beside the
port, all of which are squeezed
into a narrow cove. Behind,
white cottages are scattered
over the steep hillsides.

Further along the coast is
the rocky headland of Cabo
de Peñas where, in the fishing
village of **Candas**, bullfights
are sometimes held on the
sand at low tide. East of Gijón,
Lastres is impressively located below a cliff, and **Isla**
has a broad open beach.
Beyond Ribadesella is the

The Brown Bear

The population of Spain's brown
bears *(Ursus arctos)* has dwind-
led from about 1,000 at the
beginning of the 20th century
to less than 100. Hunting by
man and the destruction of the
bear's natural forest habitat have
caused the decline. But now,
protected by nature reserves
such as Somiedo, where most of
the bears in Asturias are found,
together with new conservation
laws, it is hoped this magnificent
omnivore will thrive again.

**One of the few remaining
bears in the forests of Asturias**

Church and cemetery overlooking the sea from the headland at Luarca

lively town of **Llanes**. Among the attractions of this old fortified seaport, with its dramatic mountain backdrop, are ruined ramparts and good beaches.

Teverga **4**

Asturias. 🚌 *La Plaza.* ℹ *Plaza del Ayuntamiento La Plaza, (98) 576 42 02.*

THIS AREA, southwest of Oviedo, is rich in scenery, wildlife and ancient churches. Near the southern end of the narrow Teverga gorge is **La Plaza**. Its 12th-century church, the Iglesia de San Pedro, is a beautiful example of Romanesque architecture.

Just to the west of La Plaza is **Villanueva**, with its Romanesque Iglesia de Santa María. To the east, the Quirós valley, with hamlets dotted around its hillsides, is picturesque.

The pretty 12th-century Iglesia de San Pedro at La Plaza

ENVIRONS: The large **Parque Natural de Somiedo** straddles the mountains bordering León. Its high meadows and forests of chestnut, beech and oak are a sanctuary for wolves, brown bears and capercaillies, as well as a number of rare species of wild flowers.

The park has 18 glacial lakes, and is peppered with herdsmen's traditional thatched huts, known as *teitos (see p23).*

Avilés **5**

Asturias. 🏛 *88,000.* ✈ 🚌 🚉 ℹ *Plaza de España 1, (98) 512 21 00.* 🛒 *Mon.* 🎉 *San Agustín (28 Aug).*

AVILÉS BECAME the capital of Asturias' steel industry during the 19th century, and is still ringed by big factories. Even though it is sometimes criticized for having little to offer

the visitor, the town hides a medieval heart of some character, especially around the Plaza de España. The **Iglesia de San Francisco** is decorated with ancient frescoes and has a Renaissance cloister. The **Iglesia de San Nicolás** contains a fine 14th-century chapel and holds the tomb of the first Governor of the US state of Florida. All around are arcaded streets with lively bars. The international airport outside Avilés serves all Asturias.

Gijón **6**

Asturias. 🏛 *260,000.* 🚌 🚉 ℹ *Calle Marqués de San Esteban 1, (98) 534 60 46.* 🛒 *Sun.* 🎉 *San Antonio (13 Jun), La Virgen de Begoña (15 Aug).*

THE PROVINCE's largest city, this industrial port has been much rebuilt since the Civil War when it was bombarded by the Nationalist navy. The city's most famous son is Gaspar Melchor de Jovellanos, an eminent 18th-century author, reformer and diplomat.

Gijón's old town is on a small isthmus and headland. It centres on the arcaded Plaza Mayor and the 18th-century **Palacio de Revillagigedo**, a Neo-Renaissance folly with towers and battlements. The long sandy beach, near the city centre, is popular in summer.

🏛 **Palacio de Revillagigedo** Plaza del Marqués. 📞 *(98) 534 69 21.* ⭕ *Tue–Sun.* ⬤ *public hols.*

Oviedo **❼**

Alfonso II El Casto, 6. 🏛 *180,000*. 🚉
🚌 ℹ *Plaza de Alfonso II el Casto 6,
(98) 521 33 85.* 🏪 *Thu & Sun.*
🎉 *San Mateo (21 Sep).*

OVIEDO, A UNIVERSITY city and
the cultural and commer-
cial capital of Asturias, stands
on a raised site on a fertile
plain. The nearby coal mines
have made it an important
industrial centre since the 19th
century. It retains some of the
atmosphere of that time, as
described by Leopoldo Alas
("Clarín") in his great novel
La Regenta (see p31).

In and around Oviedo are
many Pre-Romanesque buildings. This style flourished in
the 8th–10th centuries and was
confined to a small area of the
kingdom of Asturias, one of
the few enclaves of Spain not
invaded by the Moors.

The nucleus of the medieval
city is the stately Plaza Alfonso
II, bordered by a number of
handsome old palaces. On this
square is situated the Flamboyant Gothic *(see p20)* **cathedral**
with its high tower and asym-
metrical west façade. Inside are
tombs of Asturian kings and a
majestic 16th-century gilded
reredos. The cathedral's
supreme treasure is the Cámara
Santa, a restored 9th-century
chapel containing statues of
Christ and the apostles. The

**Cross of Angels in the treasury of
Oviedo cathedral**

chapel also houses many
works of 9th-century Asturian
art including two crosses and
a reliquary – all made of gold,
silver and precious stones.

Also situated in the Plaza
Alfonso II is the **Iglesia de
San Tirso**. This church was
originally constructed in the
9th century, but subsequent
restorations have left the east
window as the only surviving
Pre-Romanesque feature.

Sited immediately behind
the cathedral is the **Museo
Arqueológico**, which is
housed in an old monastery
with fine cloisters. It contains
local prehistoric, Roman and
Romanesque treasures.

The **Museo de Bellas Artes**,
in the handsome 18th-century
Velarde Palace, has a good
range of Asturian and Spanish
paintings, such as Carreño's
portrait of Carlos II *(see p66).*

Two of the most magnificent
Pre-Romanesque churches are
on Mount Naranco, to the north.

SANTA MARÍA DEL NARANCO

This church, on Mount Naranco, was originally built as a
summer palace for Ramiro I in the 9th century. It is one of
the finest examples of Pre-Romanesque or Asturian
architecture, a style characterized by the
slender proportions of its buildings and
their original and graceful
ornamentation.

The Hall has an
unusually high
ceiling.

**Arcaded
galleries** at
both ends of the
building were designed
to let in an enormous
amount of light and were
an architectural innovation.

Columns carved with
soqueado or rope effect,
were typical of the Pre-
Romanesque style.

Vaultings of this
size were a technical
achievement and not
adopted throughout Europe
until the 11th century.

Church overlooking the sea at Ribadesella

Santa María del Naranco has a large barrel-vaulted hall on the main floor and arcaded galleries at either end. Some of the intricate reliefs on the door jambs of the nearby **San Miguel de Lillo** show acrobats and animal tamers in a circus.

The early 9th-century church of **San Julián de los Prados** stands on the road leading northeast out of Oviedo. It is the largest of all the Pre-Romanesque churches and is particularly noted for the frescoes which once covered the whole of its interior.

🏛 Museo Arqueológico
Calle San Vicente 3. 📞 (98) 521 54 05. ◯ Tue–Sun.
🏛 Museo de Bellas Artes
Calle La Rua 8. 📞 (98) 521 30 61. ◯ Tue–Sun.

Valdediós ❽

Asturias. 👥 150. 🛈 Villaviciosa, (98) 589 01 66.

SET ALONE in a field near this hamlet, the tiny 9th-century **Iglesia de San Salvador** is a jewel of Pre-Romanesque art. Its ceiling has vivid Asturian frescoes, and by the portal are stone recesses where pilgrims slept. The church in the monastery next door is 13th-century Cistercian, with cloisters dating from the 15th century.

ENVIRONS: To the north, the graceful little resort town of **Villaviciosa** lies amid apple orchards and glorious hilly scenery, and has glass-fronted mansions in its narrow streets. In nearby **Amandi**, the hilltop Iglesia de San Juan has a 13th-century portal and delicate carvings and friezes.

Iglesia de San Salvador de Valdediós in its idyllic setting

Ribadesella ❾

Asturias. 👥 6,400. 🚌 🚉 🛈 Plaza Reina María Cristina 1, (98) 586 02 55. 🛒 Wed. 🎉 Descent of the Río Sella (first Sat of Aug).

THIS ENCHANTING little seaside town bestrides a broad estuary. On one side is the lively old seaport full of tapas bars below a clifftop church. Across the estuary is a holiday resort. A multicoloured flotilla of kayaks arrives here from Arriondas (upstream) in an international regatta that is held every year on the first Saturday in August.

On the edge of town is the **Cueva de Tito Bustillo**. This cave is rich in stalactites but is best known for its many prehistoric drawings, which were discovered in 1968, some dating from around 18,000 BC. These include red and black pictures of stags and horses. To protect the paintings, only 400 visitors are allowed in per day, so in the high season it is advisable to arrive early. A museum on the site includes an artist's impressions of prehistoric living conditions.

⛰ Cueva de Tito Bustillo
Ribadesella. 📞 (98) 586 11 75. ◯ Tue–Sun. ● Oct–Apr. 🎥

Cangas de Onís ❿

Asturias. 👥 3,300. 🚉 🛈 Avenida de Covadonga 21, (98) 584 80 43. 🛒 Sun. 🎉 Fiesta del Pastor (25 Jul).

CANGAS DE ONÍS, one of the gateways to the Picos de Europa (see pp104–105), is where Pelayo, the 8th-century Visigothic nobleman and early hero of the Reconquest, set up his court. The town has a graceful Roman bridge and the 15th-century chapel of Santa Cruz with an engraved Bronze Age dolmen.

ENVIRONS: About 5 km (3 miles) east of Cangas de Onís is the **Cueva del Buxu**, which has rock-drawings and engravings which are over 10,000 years old. Arenas de Cabrales, some 25 km (16 miles) east of Cangas de Onís, is the home of Cabrales, a smooth but pungent cheese (see p73).

Parque Nacional de los Picos de Europa ⓫

THESE BEAUTIFUL mountains were reputedly christened the "Peaks of Europe" by returning sailors for whom this was often the first sight of their homeland. The range, now Europe's biggest national park, straddles three regions – Asturias, Cantabria and Castilla y León – and has diverse terrain. In some parts, deep winding gorges cut through craggy rocks while elsewhere verdant valleys support orchards and dairy farming. The celebrated creamy blue cheese, Cabrales *(see p73),* is made here. The Picos offer rock climbing and upland hiking as well as a profusion of flora and fauna. Tourism is well organized, with good roads and many hotels and refuges.

Lefebvre's Ringlet

Covadonga
The Neo-Romanesque basilica, built between 1886 and 1901, stands on the site of Pelayo's historic victory.

Lago de la Ercina
Together with the nearby Lago Enol, this lake lies on a wild limestone plateau above Covadonga and below the peak of Peña Santa.

Desfiladero de los Beyos
This deep, narrow gorge with its high limestone cliffs winds spectacularly for 10 km (6 miles) through the mountains. Tracing the route of the Río Sella below, it carries the main road from Cangas de Onís to Riaño.

KEY

═══	Major road
══	Minor road
-- -	Footpath
▬▬	National park boundary
🅸	Tourist information
✹	Viewpoint

Desfiladero del Río Cares
The River Cares forms a deep gorge in the heart of the Picos. A dramatic footpath follows the gorge, passing through tunnels and across high bridges up to 1,000 m (3,280 ft) above the river.

Map labels: RIBADESELLA, Cangas de Onís, AS114, Covadonga, DESFILADERO DE LOS BEYOS, Sella, LAGO ENOL, LAGO DE LA ERCINA, N625, Posada de Valdeón, Cares, Oseja de Sajambre, Puerto de Panderruedas, LE244, Puerto de Pontón, RIAÑO, GR

Dramatic view of the mountains of the Picos de Europa

Panes
SAN VICENTE DE LA BARQUERA
AS114
Arenas de Cabrales
AS264
Poncebos
Bulnes
DESFILADERO DE LA HERMIDA
Santa María de Lebeña
Deva
Parador de Fuente Dé
Monasterio de Santo Toribio de Liébana
Potes
N621
de Randetrave
LE243
RIAÑO
Puerto de San Glorio

0 kilometres 5
0 miles 5

VISITORS' CHECKLIST

ℹ️ *Cangas de Onis, (985) 84 86 14.* 🚌 *from Oviedo to Cangas de Onis.* **Fuente Dé cable car** ◯ *Jul–Sep: 9am–8pm daily, Oct–Jun: 10am–6pm daily.* ⚫ *Dec.*

PELAYO THE WARRIOR

A statue of this Visigothic nobleman who became king of Asturias guards the basilica at Covadonga. It was close to this site, in 722, that Pelayo and a band of men – though vastly outnumbered – are said to have defeated a Moorish army. The victory inspired Christians in the north of Spain to reconquer the peninsula *(see pp48–51)*. The tomb of the warrior is in a cave which has become a shrine, also containing a painted image of the Virgin.

Pelayo's statue

Naranjo de Bulnes, with its tooth-like crest, is in the heart of the massif. At 2,519 m (8,264 ft) it is one of the highest summits in the Picos de Europa.

Fuente Dé Cable Car

The 900-m (2950-ft) ascent from Fuente Dé takes visitors up to a wild rocky plateau pitted with craters. From here there is a spectacular panorama of the Picos' peaks and valleys.

Statue of the Virgin, San Vicente de la Barquera

ASTURIAS AND CANTABRIA'S FIESTAS

La Folía *(Apr)*, San Vicente de la Barquera (Cantabria). The statue of the Virgen de la Barquera is said to have arrived at San Vicente in a boat with no sails, oars or crew. Once a year, it is put in a fishing boat decorated with flags and flowers, which sails at the head of a procession to bless the sea. Groups of young girls, called *picayos,* stand on the shore singing traditional songs of the region in honour of the Virgin. La Folía usually falls at the end of April, but its date is dependent on the local tides.
Fiesta del Pastor *(25 Jul),* near Cangas de Onís (Asturias). Regional songs and dances are performed at the annual Shepherds' Festival beside the shores of Lake Enol in the Picos de Europa National Park.
Battle of the Flowers *(last Fri of Aug),* Laredo (Cantabria). Floats adorned with flowers are paraded through this small resort. A flower-throwing free-for-all follows the procession.
Nuestra Señora de Covadonga *(8 Sep),* Picos de Europa (Asturias). Huge crowds converge on the shrine of Covadonga *(see p104)* to pay homage to the patron saint of Asturias.

Potes ⓬

Cantabria. 🏘 *1,500.* 🛈 *Calle de la Independencia, (942) 73 00 06.* 🚌 *Mon.* 🎉 *Santisima Cruz (15 Sep).*

A SMALL ANCIENT TOWN, with old balconied houses lining the river, Potes is the main centre of the eastern Picos de Europa. It is situated in the broad Valle de Liébana, whose fertile soil yields prime crops of walnuts, cherries and grapes. A potent spirit called *orujo* is made in the town. The **Torre del Infantado**, in the main square, is a defensive tower built in the 15th century.

ENVIRONS: Between Potes and the coast runs a gorge, the **Desfiladero de la Hermida**. Halfway up it is **Santa María de Lebeña**, a 10th-century Mozarabic *(see p335)* church with horseshoe arches.
West of Potes is the monastery church of **Santo Toribio de Liébana**, one of the most revered spots in the Picos de Europa. Founded during the 7th century, it became known throughout Spain a century later when it received reputedly the largest fragment of the True Cross, kept in a silver reliquary. An 8th-century monk, St Beatus of Liébana, wrote the *Commentary on the Apocalypse,* later much copied and illuminated. The restored Romanesque buildings of the monastery, which was rebuilt in the 13th century, are now occupied by Franciscan monks.

Comillas ⓭

Cantabria. 🏘 *2,500.* 🛈 *Calle la Aldea 6, (942) 72 07 68.* 🚌 *Fri.* 🎉 *El Cristo (16 Jul).*

THIS PRETTY RESORT is known for its unusual buildings by Catalan Modernista architects *(see pp136–7).* Antonio López y López, a shipping tycoon who became the first Marquis of Comillas, commissioned Joan Martorell to design the **Palacio Sobrellano** (1881), an enormous Neo-Gothic edifice.

Stone bridge and houses in the ancient town of Potes

Surviving Classical columns among the ruins of the Roman town of Juliobriga, near Reinosa

Comilla's best-known monument, is Antoni Gaudí's *(see p160)* **El Capricho**, now a restaurant *(see p580)*. It was designed for a rich businessman from 1883–9 by Gaudí and is a Mudéjar-inspired fantasy with a minaret-like tower covered in green and yellow tiles. Another of the town's Modernista buildings is the **Universidad Pontificia**, which overlooks the sea from a hilltop. It was designed by Joan Martorell to plans by Domènech i Montaner *(see p136).*

Wall tile on the façade of El Capricho

ENVIRONS: The fishing port of **San Vicente de la Barquera** has arcaded streets, ramparts and the Gothic Romanesque church of Nuestra Señora de los Ángeles.

Valle de Cabuérniga ⑭

Cantabria. 🚂 *Bárcena Mayor.* 🅷 *Ayuntamiento, Ruente, (942) 70 91 04.*

Two exceptionally picturesque towns, notable for their superb examples of rural architecture, draw visitors to the Cabuérniga Valley. A good road takes you to the once-remote **Bárcena Mayor**. Its cobbled streets are furnished with old lamps and filled with boutiques, and restaurants serving a range of regional dishes. The pretty houses have flower-covered balconies, and cattle byres on the ground floor.

Carmona is an old, unspoiled village approximately 20 km (12 miles) to the northwest of Bárcena Mayor. Its solid stone houses, with pantiled roofs and wooden balconies, are typically Cantabrian *(see p22)*. Woodcarving, the traditional craft of the region, is still practised in this village, where men work outside their houses on a variety of artifacts including bowls, fiddles, *albarcas* (clogs) and chairs. The 13th-century Palacio de los Mier, a manor house in the centre of the village, has been restored and is now a hotel.

The extensive, wild beech woods near **Saja** have been designated a nature reserve.

Traditional balconied houses in Bárcena Mayor

Alto Campoo ⑮

Cantabria. 🏔 *1,900.* 🚗 🅿 🅷 *Estación de Montaña, (942) 779223.* 🚌 *Mon.* ⛄ *Nuestra Señora de las Nieves (5 Aug), San Roque (16 Aug).*

SITED HIGH in the Cantabrian mountains, this winter resort lies below the Pico de Tres Mares (2,175 m/7,000 ft), the "Peak of the Three Seas", so called because the rivers rising near it flow into the Mediterranean, the Atlantic and the Bay of Biscay. The Río Ebro, one of Spain's longest rivers, rises in this area and its source, at Fontibre, is a beauty spot. A road and a chair lift reach the summit of Tres Mares for a breathtaking panorama of the Picos de Europa and other mountain chains. The resort is small, with ten pistes totalling 17 km (10 miles) in length, and has few facilities for après-ski.

ENVIRONS: Reinosa, some 26 km (16 miles) to the east of Alto Campoo, is a handsome market town with old stone houses. Further southeast is Retortillo, a hamlet where the remains of **Juliobriga**, a town built by the Romans as a bastion against the wild tribes of Cantabria, can be seen.

The main road south out of Reinosa leads to **Cervatos**, where the former collegiate church has erotic carvings on its façade. This novel device was meant to deter the villagers from pleasures of the flesh.

At **Arroyuelo** and **Cadalso**, to the southeast, are two churches built into rock faces in the 9th and 10th centuries.

One of the many paintings of bison at Altamira

Cuevas de Altamira ⑯

Cantabria. 【 (942) 81 80 05 🚌
Santillana del Mar. **Caves** ◯ write in
advance for permission. **Museum** ◯
Tue–Sun. ⬤ 24, 25, 31 Dec & 1 Jan.

THESE CAVES contain some of
the world's finest examples
of prehistoric art. The earliest
of these engravings and
drawings, which were
discovered in 1869, date
back to around 18,000
BC *(see p44)*. The caves'
famous bison, dated
around 13,000 BC,
are painted in bold
colours using the
rock contours to
emphasize shape
and movement.   **Carved figure of Christ in**
Admission to the **the Convento de Regina Coeli**
caves is restricted
to prevent deterioration of the
paintings. You should apply
for permission months in advance. Displays in a museum
on the site explain the significance of the paintings.

Santillana del Mar ⑰

Cantabria. 🏘 4,000. 🚌 🛈 Plaza
Mayor, (942) 81 80 75. 🎎 Santa
Juliana (28 Jun), San Roque (16 Aug).

SET JUST INLAND, belying its
name, this town is one the
prettiest in Spain. Its ensemble
of 15th- to 17th-century golden
stone houses survives largely
intact despite the many tourists and souvenir shops.

The town grew up around
a monastery, which was an
important pilgrimage centre,
the Romanesque **La Colegiata**.
The church houses the tomb
of the local early-medieval
martyr St Juliana, and contains
a 17th-century painted reredos
and a carved south door. In its
lovely cloisters, vivid biblical scenes have been
sculpted on the capitals.

On the town's two main
cobbled streets there are
houses built by local
noblemen. These
have either fine
wooden galleries
or iron balconies,
and coats of arms
inlaid into their
stone façades. In
the past, farmers
used the open ground floors as
byres for stabling their cattle.

In the enchanting **Plaza
Mayor**, in the centre of town,
is a mansion-turned-parador

(see p540). The **Museo
Diocesano** is housed in the
restored Convento de Regina
Coeli, east of the town centre,
and has a collection of painted
carvings of religious figures.

🏛 **Museo Diocesano**
Calle Le Dorat 2. 【 (942) 81 80 04.
◯ Thu–Tue. 🎦

Puente Viesgo ⑱

Cantabria. 🏘 2,500. 🚌 🛈 Calle
Manuel Pérez Maso, (942) 59 81 05.
🎎 San Miguel (28–9 Sep).

THE SPA of Puente Viesgo is
best known for the caves
– especially **Cueva de El
Castillo** – dotted around the
limestone hills above the town,
which were decorated by prehistoric man. It is thought the
late Palaeolithic cave dwellers
the deep interior as a kind of
sanctuary. In these caves they
left drawings of horses, bison
and other animals, and some
50 hand prints – almost always
the left hand. The ochre and
other colours used to create
the images were extracted
from minerals in the cave.

ENVIRONS: The lush Pas valley,
to the southeast, is home to
transhumant dairy farmers, the
Pasiegos. In the main town of
Vega de Pas, you can buy two
Pasiego specialities – sobaos,
or sponge cakes *(see p73)*,
and quesadas, a sweet which
is made from milk, butter and
eggs. In **Villacarriedo** there
is a handsome 18th-century
mansion, with two Baroque
façades of carved stone hiding
a medieval tower.

⋔ **Cueva de El Castillo**
Puente Viesgo. 【 (942) 59 84 25.
◯ Mon.

Main façade of La Colegiata in Santillana del Mar

The Palacio de la Magdalena in El Sardinero

Santander **⑲**

Cantabria. 🏠 *200,000.* ✈ 🚌 🚂 ⛴ 🛈 *Estación Marítima, (942) 31 07 08.* 📅 *Mon & Thu.* 🎭 *Santiago (25 Jul), La Virgen la Bien Aparecida (15 Sep).*

CANTABRIA'S CAPITAL, a busy port, enjoys a splendid site near the mouth of a deep bay. The town centre is modern – after being ravaged by fire in 1941 it was completely reconstructed. The **cathedral** was rebuilt in Gothic style after the 1941 fire, but retains its 12th-century crypt. Worth visiting is the **Museo de Bellas Artes**, which houses works by Goya, Zurbarán and Mengs, as well as regional artists. The town's **Museo de Prehistoria y Arqueología** displays finds from caves in Cantabria, such as Neolithic axe heads, and Roman coins, pottery and figurines. The **Museo Marítimo** has rare whale skeletons and 350 species of local fish.

The town extends along the coast around the Península de la Magdalena, a headland on which there is a park, a zoo and the **Palacio de la Magdalena** – a summer palace built for Alfonso XIII in 1912, reflecting the resort's popularity at the time with the Royal Family.

The seaside suburb of **El Sardinero**, north of the headland, is a smart resort with a long graceful beach, backed by gardens, elegant cafés and a majestic white casino. A cultured, self-confident place, in July and August El Sardinero plays host to a major theatre and music festival.

🏛 **Museo de Bellas Artes**
Calle Rubio 5. 📞 *(942) 23 94 85.* ⏰ *Mon–Sat.*
🏛 **Museo de Prehistoria y Arqueología**
Calle Casimiro Saenz 4. 📞 *(942) 20 71 05.* ⏰ *Tue–Sun.*
🏛 **Museo Marítimo**
Promontorio de San Martín. 📞 *(942) 27 49 62.* ⏰ *Tue–Sun.*

Laredo **⑳**

Cantabria. 🏠 *14,000.* 🚌 🛈 *Calle Lopez Seña, (942) 61 10 96.* 🎭 *Batalla de Flores (last Fri of Aug), San Martín (11 Nov).*

THE EXCELLENT long, sandy beach of this small town has made it one of Cantabria's most popular bathing resorts. The old part of the town is attractive: narrow streets with balconied houses lead up to the 13th-century **Iglesia de la Asunción**, with its Flemish altar and enormous bronze lecterns. One of the highlights of the year in Laredo is the colourful fiesta of the Battle of the Flowers *(see p106)*.

Castro Urdiales **㉑**

Cantabria. 🏠 *15,500.* 🚌 🛈 *Plaza del Ayuntamiento, (942) 85 90 00.* 📅 *Thu.* 🎭 *Coso Blanco (27 Jun), Santa Ana (26 Jul).*

CASTRO URDIALES, a busy fishing town and popular holiday resort, is built around a picturesque natural harbour full of boats. Above the port, on a high promontory, stands the pinkish Gothic **Iglesia de Santa María**, as big as a cathedral. Beside it there is a half-ruined castle built by the Knights Templar, which has been converted into a lighthouse. Handsome glass-fronted houses, or *galerías*, line the elegant promenade. The small town beach often becomes crowded but there are bigger ones to the west, such as the Playa de Ostende.

ENVIRONS: Near the village of **Ramales de la Victoria**, 20 km (12 miles) south, are prehistoric caves containing etchings and engravings, reached by a very steep mountain road.

Small boats moored in the harbour at Castro Urdiales

THE BASQUE COUNTRY, NAVARRA AND LA RIOJA

VIZCAYA · GUIPÚZCOA · ÁLAVA · LA RIOJA · NAVARRA

GREEN HILLS MEET ATLANTIC BEACHES *in the Basque Country, land of an ancient people of mysterious origin. Navarra, also partly Basque, was a powerful medieval kingdom. The beautiful western Pyrenees form part of its charming countryside. The vineyards of La Rioja, to the south, produce many of Spain's finest wines.*

The Basques are a race apart – they will not let you forget that theirs is a culture different from any in Spain. Although the Basque regional government enjoys considerable autonomy, there is a strong separatist movement seeking to sever links with the government in Madrid.

The Basque Country (Euskadi is the Basque name) is an important industrial region. The Basques are great deep-sea fishermen and fish has a major role in their imaginative cuisine, regarded by many as the best in Spain.

Unrelated to any other tongue, the Basque language, *Euskera,* is widely used on signs and several towns have two names; the fashionable resort of San Sebastián, for example, is known to locals as Donostia. *Euskera* is also spoken in parts of Navarra, which is counted as part of the wider (unofficial) Basque Country. Many of its finest sights – the towns of Olite and Estella, and the monastery of Leyre – date from the Middle Ages when Navarra was a kingdom straddling the Pyrenees. Pamplona, its capital, is best known for its daredevil bull-running fiesta, which is held in July.

As well as its vineyards and bodegas, La Rioja is a region of market gardens. Among its many historic sights are the cathedral of Santo Domingo de la Calzada and the monasteries of San Millán de la Cogolla and Yuso.

Basque farmhouse near Gernika-Lumo in the Basque Country

◁ **A street in the village of Roncal, in the foothills of the Navarrese Pyrenees**

Exploring the Basque Country, Navarra and La Rioja

THESE GREEN, HILLY REGIONS have diverse attractions. The Pyrenees in Navarra offer skiing in winter and climbing, caving and canoeing the rest of the year. The cliffs of the Basque Country are broken by rocky coves, rias, and wide bays with beaches of fine yellow sand, interspersed with fishing villages. Inland, minor roads wind through wooded hills, valleys and gorges past lonely castles and isolated homesteads. In La Rioja, to the south, they cross vineyards, passing villages and towns clustered round venerable churches and monasteries.

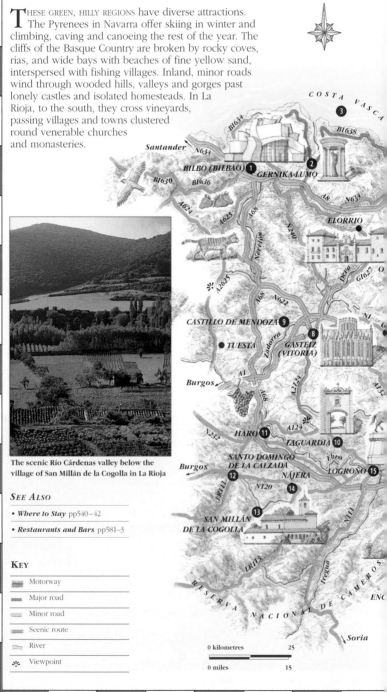

The scenic Río Cárdenas valley below the village of San Millán de la Cogolla in La Rioja

SEE ALSO

- *Where to Stay* pp540–42
- *Restaurants and Bars* pp581–3

KEY

	Motorway
	Major road
	Minor road
	Scenic route
	River
✹	Viewpoint

0 kilometres   25

0 miles   15

SIGHTS AT A GLANCE

Bilbo (Bilbao) **1**
Castillo de Javier **29**
Costa Vasca **3**
Donostia (San Sebastián) **4**
Elizondo **25**
Enciso **16**
Gasteiz (Vitoria) **8**
Gernika-Lumo **2**
Haro **11**

Hondarribia (Fuenterrabia) **5**
Iruña (Pamplona) **23**
Laguardia **10**
Lizarra (Estella) **22**
Logroño **15**
Monasterio de Leyre **28**
Monasterio de La Oliva **18**
Nájera **14**
Olite **20**
Oñati **7**

Orreaga (Roncesvalles) **26**
Puente la Reina **21**
Regata de Bidasoa **24**
Sangüesa **30**
San Millán de la Cogolla **13**
Santo Domingo de la Calzada **12**
Santuario de Loiola **6**
Tudela **17**
Ujué **19**
Valle de Roncal **27**

GETTING AROUND

Motorways give access to much of the area. The main road in the north, the A8, runs between Irún and Bilbao. The A68 runs southwards from Bilbao via Haro and follows the Ebro Valley, the area's east–west communications corridor, past Tudela. Motorway spurs extend to Vitoria and Pamplona. The rail network connects the cities and the larger towns, and most towns are served by coach. Bilbao has an international airport.

The fashionable Playa de Ondarreta, one of San Sebastián's three beaches

19th century, when iron ore began to be extracted from deposits northwest of the city. Soon, steelworks and chemical factories became a major part of the local landscape.

The city is not beautiful, but it is prosperous and its once heavy pollution is now much reduced. An urban development scheme includes a new metro system and a European branch of the Guggenheim Museum, a gallery of modern art. The airport and the harbour are soon to be extended.

The *casco viejo* (old town) by the river, built in the 14th century, is the most attractive district. Here, amid alleys lively with tapas bars, is the arcaded Plaza Nueva and the **Catedral Basílica de Santiago**. The **Museo Arqueológico, Etnográfico e Histórico Vasco** displays Basque art, folk artifacts, and photographs and *tableaux vivants* of Basque life. In the cloister is the Idol of Mikeldi, an animal-like carving from the 3rd–2nd century BC.

In the newer town is the large **Museo de Bellas Artes** (Museum of Fine Art), one of Spain's best art museums. It displays art ranging from 12th-century Catalan masterpieces to works by modern artists of international fame, including Vasarely, Kokoschka, Bacon, Delaunay and Léger. Spanish art is represented, among others, by Murillo, Zurbarán, El Greco, three Goyas and Ribera's fine *St Sebastian*. There are also several rooms of paintings by Basque artists.

Buildings overlooking the Río Nervión in Bilbao

Bilbao ❶

Vizcaya. 🏛 375,000. ✈ 🚆 🚍 🚢
🛈 *Plaza de Arriaga 1, (94) 416 02 88.*
📅 *Santiago (25 Jul), San Ignacio (31 Jul), La Asunción (15 Aug), Semana Grande (mid-Aug).*

BILBAO (BILBO) is the centre of Basque industry, Spain's leading commercial port and the largest Basque city. It is surrounded by high, bare hills. Its suburbs spread 16 km (10 miles) along the Río Nervión (Nerbioi) to its estuary. The river between Las Arenas and the fishing port of Portugalete is crossed via the **Puente Colgante**. This iron transporter bridge, built in 1893, has a suspended cabin for cars and passengers. On the east bank of the estuary is Santurtzi (Santurce), from where ferries sail to the UK *(see p628)*.

Bilbao has flourished as an industrial city since the mid-

West of the city, a road and a funicular railway ascend to the village of La Reineta, from where there is a wide urban panorama across the old dockyards. On the estuary's east bank is Algorta, a beach resort with handsome holiday villas.

🏛 **Museo Arqueológico, Etnográfico e Histórico Vasco**
Calle Cruz 4. 📞 *(94) 415 54 23.*
🕐 *Tue–Sun.* ● *public hols.* ♿
🏛 **Museo de Bellas Artes**
Plaza del Museo 2. 📞 *(94) 441 01 54.* 🕐 *Tue–Sun.* ● *public hols.*

The historic Oak of Gernika, the symbol of Basque nationalism

Gernika-Lumo ❷

Vizcaya. 🏛 15,400. 🚆 🚍
🛈 *Arte Calle 8, (94) 625 58 92.*
🔒 *Mon.* 📅 *Aniversario del Bombardeo de Guernica (26 Apr).*

THIS LITTLE TOWN is of great symbolic significance to the Basques. For centuries, Basque leaders met in democratic assembly under an oak on a hillside here. On 26 April 1937 Gernika-Lumo (Guernica) was the target of the world's first saturation bombing raid, carried out by Nazi aircraft at the request of General Franco. Picasso's powerful painting *(see pp62–3)* of this outrage can be seen in Madrid *(see p289)*.

The town has since been rebuilt and is rather dull. But in a garden, inside a pavilion and closely guarded, is the 300-year-old petrified trunk of the oak tree, the *Gernikako Arbola*, or Oak of Gernika, symbol of the ancient roots of the Basque people. A younger oak, its successor, is planted beside it. The Basque people make visits to this ancient tree as if on a pilgrimage.

Zuloaga's *Condesa Mathieu de Noailles* (1913), Bilbao Museum of Fine Art

Basque fishermen depicted in the stained-glass ceiling of the Casa de Juntas in Gernika-Lumo

The **Casa de Juntas**, nearby, is a former chapel where the parliament of the province of Vizcaya has convened since 1979, when the Basque provinces regained their autonomy. In one room a stained-glass ceiling depicts the Oak of Gernika with Basque citizens debating their rights.

The Europa Park, next door, has peace sculptures by Henry Moore and Eduardo Chillida.

ENVIRONS: Five km (3 miles) northeast of Gernika, near Kortézubi (Cortézubi), are the **Cuevas de Santimamiñe**. On the walls of a small chamber are drawings in charcoal of bison and other animals made by Cro-Magnon cave dwellers around 11,000 BC. They were discovered in 1917. A guide shows visitors these ancient drawings and then leads them down the Long Gallery, an underground passage full of oddly shaped stalagmites and stalactites, some of them shot through with brilliant colours. Santimamiñe is one of several huge cave complexes in this mountain area, but most are closed to the public.

⌂ Casa de Juntas
C/ Allende Salazar. **[** (94) 625 11 38. **◯** daily. **●** 15 Aug & 25 Dec. **&**
⋒ Cuevas de Santimamiñe
Barrio Basondo, Kortézubi. **[** (94) 625 29 75. **◯** Mon–Fri. **●** public hols.

Costa Vasca ❸

Vizcaya & Guipúzcoa. **☐** Bilbao. **☐** Bilbao. **ℹ** Getxo, (94) 491 08 00.

THE BASQUE COUNTRY's 176 km (110 miles) of coastline is heavily indented: rugged cliffs alternate with inlets and coves, the whole backed by wooded hills. Some of the fishing villages are over-developed, but the scenery inland is attractive.

There are good beaches north of Algorta (near Bilbao). Plentzia is a pleasant estuary town with a marina. Eastwards on the coast is Bakio, a large fishing village also known for its beaches. Beyond it the BI3101, a dramatic corniche road, winds high above the sea past the tiny island hermitage,

Anglers on the quayside at Lekeitio, a port on the Costa Vasca

San Juan de Gaztelugatxe, and Matxitxaco, a headland lighthouse. It passes Bermeo, a port with a fishery museum, the **Museo del Pescador**, and Mundaka, a small surfing resort. On the serene Ría de Guernica there are two sandy beaches, Laida and Laga.

Lekeitio, a fishing port to the east, has a pretty shoreline. Old Basque houses line the seafront below the 15th-century church of Santa María. One long beach, good for swimming, sweeps round the village of **Saturrarán** and the old port of **Ondarroa**. The Lekeitio–Ondarroa road is pleasantly planted with pines.

Zumaia is a beach resort with an old quarter. In the **Museo de Ignacio Zuloaga**, the former home of the well-known Basque painter who lived from 1870–1945, colourful studies of Basque rural and maritime life are on display. **Getaria**, along the coast, is a trawler port with lively cafés, and the 14th-century Iglesia de San Salvador. **Zarautz**, once a fashionable resort, has sizeable beaches and elegant mansions.

🏛 Museo del Pescador
Plaza Torrontero 1. **[** (94) 688 11 71. **◯** Tue–Sun. **●** public hols. **&**
🏛 Museo de Ignacio Zuloaga
Casa Santiago Zumaya, Carretera de San Sebastián. **[** (94) 386 10 15. **◯** Jan–Sep: Wed–Sun.

San Sebastián's Playa de Ondarreta, with its view across the bay

San Sebastián ❹

Guipúzcoa. 🏠 180,000. 🚆 🚌 ℹ️
Paseo de los Fueros 1, (94) 342 62 82.
🚢 Sun. 🎭 San Sebastián (20 Jan),
Semana Grande (around 15 Aug for
one week), Regatta (early Sep).

Gloriously situated on a neat, shell-shaped bay, San Sebastián (Donostia) is the most elegant and fashionable Spanish seaside resort. At either end of the bay is a tower-topped hill – Monte Urgull in the east and Monte Igueldo in the west. Between the two, in the mouth of the bay, lies a small island, the Isla de Santa Clara.

San Sebastián became a smart resort in the late 19th century and has been popular with the Spanish aristocracy ever since, although it no longer has quite the allure it held in decades past. It still has many smart shops and one of Spain's grandest luxury hotels, the María Cristina *(see p542)*, but San Sebastián is now primarily a family resort.

The city is renowned for its great summer arts festivals. A jazz festival is held in July, a classical music festival in late August, and the San Sebastián International Film Festival in September. The Semana Grande in August focuses on traditional Basque folk culture.

Cuisine also plays a huge part in local life: many Basque men in San Sebastián belong to gastronomic clubs where they gather to cook, eat, drink and talk. Even these days, women are seldom invited to such gatherings.

The Old Town
San Sebastián's fascinating old town, called the Parte Vieja, is wedged between the bay and the Río Urumea. Although few of its buildings predate 1813, when it was rebuilt after a devastating fire, it still has plenty of character. The alleys of the old town, packed with restaurants and tapas bars, are intensely animated at night. In the large local fish market, stalls piled high with delicacies, such as *kokotxa* (cheek of hake), testify to the key role of fish in the life of the town.

The heart of the old town is the **Plaza de la Constitución**, a handsome, arcaded square with blue and orange shutters. The numbers on the balconies date from when the square was used as a bullring – organizers sold a ticket for each numbered place. The church of **Santa María del Coro**, nearby, has a rich Baroque portal.

Monte Urgull rises behind the old town. It is well worth climbing up to the top for a panorama of the coast and the city encircled by knobbly hills. On the summit are a statue of Christ and the ruined **Castillo de Santa Cruz de la Mota**, with old cannons.

Beaches
San Sebastián's two principal beaches follow the bay round to **Monte Igueldo**. The **Playa de Ondarreta** is the more fashionable of the two while the **Playa de la Concha** is the larger. They are separated by a rocky outcrop. Between them is the **Palacio Miramar**, built in 1889 by the Basque architect, José Goicoa, to designs by Selden Wornum, a British architect. The palace, built for Queen María Cristina as a summer residence, helped to establish San Sebastián as an aristocratic resort. The gardens are open to the public and events are occasionally held in the palace.

At the water's edge near the Playa de Ondarreta is a striking modern iron sculpture, *The Comb of the Winds* by Eduardo Chillida. A road and a funicular railway lead to the top of Monte Igueldo, where there is an amusement park.

To the east of the Playa de la Concha is another beach, the **Playa de la Zurriola**, which is overlooked by the resort's third hill, **Monte Ulía**.

The Comb of the Winds by Eduardo Chillida

◁ The russet and green hills of Guipúzcoa province in the Basque Country, south of the Río Oyarzun

Josep Maria Sert's murals of Basque life in the Museo de San Telmo

🏛 Museo de San Telmo

Plaza Zuloaga. 📞 *(94) 342 49 70.*
🕐 *Tue–Sun.* 🚻

This is a large museum in a 16th-century monastery below Monte Urgull. In the cloister is a collection of Basque tombstones: rounded, inscribed funerary columns dating from the 15th to the 17th centuries.

The museum also contains displays of headdresses worn by women of the region, furniture, tools and other artifacts, and paintings by several local Basque artists. Among them are vivid 19th-century works by Antonio Ortiz Echagüe and modern paintings by Ignacio Zuloaga. There are also portraits by Vicente López and masterpieces by El Greco and other classic Spanish artists. In the chapel are 16 murals in sepia and gold by the Catalan artist, Josep Maria Sert, depicting Basque legends, culture and the region's seafaring life.

🏨 Palacio del Mar

Paseo Muelle 34. 📞 *(94) 342 19 05.*
🕐 *Tue–Sun.* ⬤ *1 Jan & 25 Dec.* 📷

A local architect, Juan Carlos Guerra, incorporated traditional Basque architectural styles in the design of this building. It opened in 1828 as the headquarters of the Guipúzcoa Oceanographic Society. The Aquarium features a unique collection of marine life from the local coastal waters. The museum contains exhibits of Basque maritime life, ranging from shipbuilding to profiles of Basque sailors.

ENVIRONS: Approximately 5 km (3 miles) east of San Sebastián is **Pasaia Donibane** (Pasajes de San Juan), a picturesque fishing village consisting of a jumble of houses with pretty painted balconies and a cobbled main street which has some good fish restaurants.

The waterfront of the tiny fishing village of Pasaia Donibane

Old balconied houses in the upper town, Hondarribia

Hondarribia ❺

Guipúzcoa. 🚹 *14,000.* 🏠 *Calle Javier Ugarte 6, (94) 364 54 58.* 🎉 *La Kutxa Entrega (25 Jul), Alarde (6–8 Sep).*

Hᴏɴᴅᴀʀʀɪʙɪᴀ (Fuenterrabía), the historic town at the mouth of the Río Bidasoa, was attacked by the French over many centuries. The upper town is protected by 15th-century walls and entered via their original gateway, the handsome **Puerta de Santa María**. They enclose alleys of old houses with carved eaves, balconies and coats of arms.

The streets cluster round the church of **Santa María de la Asunción**, with its massive buttresses, tall Baroque tower, and, inside, a gold reredos. At the town's highest point is the **castle**, which was founded in the 10th century and is now a parador *(see p541)*.

Hondarribia is a fishing port and there are seafront cafés in La Marina, the lively fishermen's quarter. It is also a seaside resort, with beaches stretching to the north.

ENVIRONS: A hill road climbs westwards to the shrine of the Virgin of Guadalupe. Further along this road are panoramic views of the coast and the mountains. From the **Ermita de San Marcial**, which stands on a hill 9 km (6 miles) to the south, there are views of the Bidasoa plain straddling the border – the French towns are neatly white, the Spanish ones are greyer.

Sᴀɴ Sᴇʙᴀsᴛɪᴀ́ɴ Fɪʟᴍ Fᴇsᴛɪᴠᴀʟ

This festival, founded in 1953, is one of the five leading European annual film festivals. It is held in late September, drawing more than 100,000 spectators. The special Donostia Prize is awarded as a tribute to the career of a star or director: it went to Lana Turner in 1994, and Susan Sarandon in 1995. Other visitors have included Quentin Tarantino, Greta Scacchi and William Hurt. Prizes also go to individual new films. An early winner was Hitchcock's *Vertigo*. The festival is strongly international, representing film from many countries.

Lauren Bacall receiving an award

The Renaissance façade of the former Basque university in Oñati

Santuario de Loiola ❻

Loiola (Guipúzcoa). ☎ (94) 381 65 08. 🚌 ⭘ daily.

SAINT IGNATIUS OF LOIOLA (San Ignacio de Loyola), founder of the Jesuits, was born in the 1490s in the Santa Casa (holy house), a stone manor near Azpeitia. In the 17th century it was enclosed by the Basílica de San Ignacio, and the rooms in which the aristocratic Loiola family lived were converted into chapels. The Chapel of the Conversion is the room in which Ignatius, as a young soldier, recovered from a war injury, and had a profound religious experience.

A diorama depicts episodes in the saint's life: dedicating his life to Christ at the Monastery of Montserrat *(see pp208–209)*; writing his *Spiritual Exercises* in a cave at Manresa; his imprisonment by the Inquisition; and his pilgrimage to the Holy Land. The basilica, built from 1681–1738, has a Churrigueresque dome and a circular nave, in which almost every surface is richly carved.

Oñati ❼

Guipúzcoa. 🏘 10,000. 🚌 🎫 Plaza de los Fueros 4, (94) 378 34 53. 🚍 Sat. 🎉 Corpus Christi (May/Jun), San Miguel (29 Sep).

THE HISTORIC TOWN of Oñati (Oñate) in the Udana Valley has a distinguished past. In the First Carlist War, 1833–9 *(see p59)*, it was a seat of the court of Don Carlos, brother of King Fernando VII and pretender to the throne. Its former **university**, built in about 1540, was for centuries the only one in the Basque Country. It has a Renaissance façade, decorated with statues of saints, and an elegant patio.

In the Plaza de los Fueros is the **Iglesia de San Miguel**, a Gothic church with a stone cloister in Plateresque *(see p21)* style. It contains the tomb of Bishop Zuázola of Ávila, the founder of the university. Opposite is the Baroque **town hall** *(ayuntamiento)*.

ENVIRONS: A mountain road ascends to the **Santuario de Arantzazu**, overshadowed by the peak of Aitzgorri. In 1469 a shepherd reported seeing a vision of the Virgin here. Over the door of the church, built in the 1950s, are sculptures of the apostles by Jorge Oteiza.

🏛 **Universidad de Sancti Spiritus**
Avenida de la Universidad Vasca. ☎ (94) 378 30 64. ⭘ Mon–Fri for guided tours (phone in advance). 🎧

The imposing Santuario de Loiola, with its Churrigueresque cupola

THE FOUNDING OF THE JESUIT ORDER

The Society of Jesus was founded in Rome in 1539 by Saint Ignatius and a group of priests who were dedicated to helping the poor. Pope Paul III soon approved the order's establishment, with Ignatius as Superior General. The order, which grew wealthy, vowed military obedience to the Pope and became his most powerful weapon against the Reformation. Today, there are approximately 24,000 Jesuits working, mainly in education, in 110 countries.

Saint Ignatius of Loiola

Basque Culture

THE BASQUES may be Europe's oldest race. Anthropologists think they could be descended from Cro-Magnon people, who lived in the Pyrenees 40,000 years ago. The dolmens and carved stones of their ancestors are evidence of the Basques' pagan roots.

Long isolated in their mountain valleys, the Basques preserved their unique language, myths and art for millennia, almost untouched by other influences.

Basque policeman

Many families still live in the isolated, chalet-style stone *caseríos*, or farmhouses, built by their forebears. Their music and high-bounding dances are unlike those of any other culture, and their cuisine is varied and imaginative.

The *fueros* or ancient Basque laws and rights were suppressed under General Franco, but since the arrival of democracy in 1975 the Basques have had their own parliament and police force, having won great autonomy over their own affairs.

THE BASQUE REGION

Areas of Basque culture

The national identity *is symbolized by the region's flag:* La Ikurriña. *The white cross symbolizes Christianity. The green St Andrew's Cross commemorates a battle won on his feast day.*

Bertsolaris *are bards. They improvise witty, sometimes humorous songs, whose verses relate current events or legends. Bertsolaris sing, unaccompanied, to gatherings in public places, such as bars and squares, often in competition. This oral tradition has preserved Basque folklore, legends and history. No texts were written in* Euskera (Basque) *until the 16th century.*

The Basque economy has always relied on fishing and associated industries, such as shipbuilding and agriculture. In recent history, heavy industries have made this region prosperous.

Traditional sports *are highly respected in Basque culture. In pelota (frontón), teams hit a ball at a wall then catch it with a wicker scoop or their hands. Sports involving strength, such as log-splitting and weightlifting, are the most popular.*

VITORIA CITY CENTRE

Catedral de Santa María ③
Iglesia de San Miguel ⑥
Museo de Arqueología ②
Museo de Naipes ⑤
Palacio de Escoriaza-Esquibel ④
Plaza de la Virgen Blanca ⑦
El Portalón ①

0 metres   250
0 yards   250

KEY

🚌 Coach station
🅿 Parking
✝ Church

Vitoria ❽

Álava. 🏛 *210,000.* ✈ 🚍 🚆
ℹ *Avenida de Gasteiz, (94) 516 15
98.* 🚍 *Thu.* 🎉 *Romería de San
Prudencio (28 Apr), Fiestas de la Virgen
Blanca (4–9 Aug), Romería de Olárizu
(second Mon of Sep).*

VITORIA (GASTEIZ), the seat
of the Basque government,
was founded on a hill – the
province's highest point and
the site of an ancient Basque
town, Gasteiz. Vitoria's oldest
part, El Campo Suso, was rebuilt after a victory over the
Moors. The city later grew rich
on the iron and wool trades.

The old town focuses on the
Plaza de la Virgen Blanca,
with its monument to a battle

fought nearby in 1813, when
the British Duke of Wellington
defeated the French. Around
the plaza are old houses with
miradores (glazed balconies).

On the hillside above the
plaza is the Gothic **Iglesia de
San Miguel**. An outside niche
contains a statue of the Virgen
Blanca (White Virgin), Vitoria's
patron saint. A big festival *(see
p128)* begins on her feast day,
4 August. On the wall of San
Miguel facing the **Plaza del
Machete** there is a recess that
once held a machete on which
the city's rulers swore to up-
hold the laws or be slain.

The old town has several
Renaissance palaces, including
the 16th-century **Palacio de
Escoriaza-Esquibel**, which

has a Plateresque *(see p21)*
patio. Around it is a charming
area of old alleys linked by
steep steps. Young people
throng the bars at night.

The city has two cathedrals.
The oldest, on the old town's
limit, is the Gothic **Catedral
de Santa María**, with a sculpted west porch. Close by, in
Calle Correría, a street of old
houses, is the enchanting **El
Portalón**, a merchant's house
and hostel from the 15th century. The building, which is full
of Basque country furniture
and art, is now a restaurant.

Among the city's later architectural gems are an arcaded
street, **Los Arquillos**, and the
adjoining **Plaza de España**,
also arcaded. They were built
in the late 18th century to link
the old town with the new
quarter then being built. South
of the old town is the Neo-
Gothic **Catedral de la Virgen
Inmaculada**, begun in 1907
and in use, though unfinished.

🏛 Museo de Arqueología
Calle Correría 116. 📞 *(94) 518
19 22.* 🕐 *Tue–Sun.*
The exhibits in this museum, in
a 16th-century half-timbered
house, include dolmens erected more than 4,000 years ago,
Roman sculptures found in
Álava, and medieval artifacts.

The quiet Plaza de España in the centre of Vitoria

The Gothic west door of Vitoria's Catedral de Santa María

🏛 Museo de Naipes

Palacio de Vendaña, C/ Cuchillería 54. ☎ (94) 518 19 20. ☐ Tue–Sun. ♿
The grandson of Heraclio Fournier, who founded a playing cards factory in Vitoria in 1868, displays his collection of more than 6,000 items in this museum. The oldest exhibits are late 14th-century Italian cards. Among the many sets of tarot cards are some designed by Salvador Dalí in the 1980s.

🏛 Museo de Armería

Paseo Fray Francisco 3. ☎ (94) 518 19 25. ☐ Tue–Sun.
The weapons exhibited in this museum range in age from prehistoric axes to 20th-century pistols. There are also displays of medieval armour and an exhibit tracing the events of the 1813 Battle of Vitoria.

🏛 Museo de Bellas Artes

Paseo Fray Francisco 8. ☎ (94) 518 19 18. ☐ Tue–Sun.
Exhibits in this art gallery, in a Neo-Renaissance mansion, range in date from ancient to modern times. They include 14th-century wood sculptures, 16th-century Flemish triptychs, paintings by Spanish masters – such as Ribera – and modern Basque and Spanish works by Zuloaga, Picasso and others.

Castillo de Mendoza ❾

Mendoza (Álava). ☎ (94) 518 16 17. ☐ Tue–Sun.

IN THE CENTRE of Mendoza village, 8 km (5 miles) west of Vitoria, stands this small, square, much restored fortress dating from the 13th century. There are marvellous views from the tops of the four towers. Once a ducal residence, the thick-walled castle now houses the **Museo Heráldica**. In it are displayed the coats of arms of noble Basque families and items relating to them.

ENVIRONS: On the A2622 Pobes–Tuesta road are the **Salinas de Añana**, a group of tiered saltpans that are fed by mineral springs. The nearby village of **Tuesta** boasts a Romanesque church with a decorated portal. Inside are capitals carved with historical scenes, and a medieval wood sculpture of St Sebastian.

Laguardia ❿

Álava. 👥 1,500. 🚌 Paseo Sancho Abarca, (94) 110 08 45. 🛒 Tue. 🎉 San Juan and San Pedro (24 Jun).

THIS LITTLE WINE TOWN is the capital of La Rioja Alavesa, a part of southern Álava province where Rioja wines (see pp74–5) have been produced for centuries. It is a fertile, vine-clad plain, sheltered by high hills to the north. There are fine panoramic views from the road that climbs up to the Herrera pass. Laguardia is a medieval hill town, its encircling ramparts, towers and fortified gateways visible from afar. Along its steep, narrow cobbled streets there are many **bodegas** (wine cellars), offering wine tastings and tours throughout the year. It is usually necessary to make a booking in advance.
The Gothic **Iglesia de Santa María de los Reyes** has an austere façade and unusual portal. A delicate statue of the Virgin and Child is displayed inside the church.

Virgin and child statue in Laguardia

Vineyards near Laguardia, capital of La Rioja Alavesa, a wine-producing region since the Middle Ages

Haro ⑪

La Rioja. 👥 9,000. 🚉 🚌 ℹ️ *Plaza de la Paz 1, (941) 31 01 05.* 🛒 *Tue & Sat.* 🎉 *Wine Battle (29 Jun), Virgen de la Vega (8 Sep).*

A GRACEFUL TOWN on the Río Ebro, Haro has a lively old quarter with wine taverns and mansions. It is crowned by the hilltop **Iglesia de Santo Tomás**, a Gothic church with a Plateresque *(see p21)* portal.

Haro is the centre for the vineyards and bodegas of the Rioja Alta wine region, which is higher and cooler than the Rioja Baja *(see pp74–5)*. The clay soil and the climate – Haro is sheltered by a sierra to the north – create the conditions in which the famous regional wines are produced. Many bodegas run tours of their cellars, including tastings. To join one, you usually need to book ahead at the bodega or the tourist office. There is sometimes a small charge.

The cafés in the main square offer local wines at low prices and a convivial atmosphere, especially in the evenings.

A wine-throwing orgy is the climax of the town's fiesta *(see p128)* held every June.

Tomb of St Dominic in the cathedral of Santo Domingo de la Calzada

Rows of Rioja vines on the rolling hills near Haro

Santo Domingo de la Calzada ⑫

La Rioja. 👥 5,800. 🚌 ℹ️ *Plaza de España 4, (941) 34 00 07.* 🛒 *Sat.* 🎉 *Día del Patrón (12 May), San Jerónimo Hermosilla (19 Sep).*

T HIS TOWN on the Road to Santiago de Compostela *(see pp78–9)* is named after the 11th-century saint who built bridges and roads *(calzadas)* to help pilgrims. To tend sick travellers, St Dominic also built a hospital, which now serves as a parador *(see p542)*.

Miracles performed by the saint are recorded in carvings on his tomb in the town's part-Romanesque, part-Gothic **cathedral**, and in paintings on the wall of the choir. The most obvious and bizarre record is a sumptuously decorated cage set in a wall in which, for centuries, a live cock and hen have been kept. The cathedral has a carved walnut reredos at the high altar, the last work, in 1541, of the artist Damià Forment. The restored 14th-century ramparts of the town are also well worth seeing.

THE COCK AND HEN OF ST DOMINIC

A live cock and hen are kept in the cathedral of Santo Domingo de la Calzada as a tribute to the saint's miraculous life-giving powers. Centuries ago, it is said, a German pilgrim refused the advances of a local girl, who denounced him as a thief. He was hanged as a consequence, but later his parents found him alive on the gallows. They rushed to a judge, who said, dismissively, "Nonsense, he's no more alive than this roast chicken on my plate". Whereupon, the chicken stood up on the plate and crowed.

The cock and hen in their decorated cage

San Millán de la Cogolla ⓭

La Rioja. ᗏ 300. 🅸 Calle Mayor 50, (941) 37 30 35. 🎪 Traslación de las Reliquias (26 Sep), San Millán (12 Nov).

This village grew up around two monasteries. On a hillside above the village is the **Monasterio de San Millán de Suso**. It was built in the 10th century on the site of a community founded by St Emilian, a shepherd hermit, in 537. The church, hollowed out of pink sandstone, has Romanesque and Mozarabic features. It contains the carved alabaster tomb of St Emilian and also the tomb of the 13th-century writer, Gonzalo de Berceo (see p30), who was a monk here.

The **Monasterio de San Millán de Yuso** is below it, in the Cárdenas Valley. It was built between the 16th and 18th centuries on the site of an earlier monastery. The part-Renaissance church has Baroque golden doors and a rococo sacristy, where 17th-century paintings are hung.

In the treasury there is a collection of ivory plaques. They were once part of two 11th-century jewelled reliquaries, which were plundered by French troops in 1813.

Medieval manuscripts are also displayed in the treasury. Among them is a facsimile of one of the earliest known texts in Castilian Romance (see p30). It is a commentary by a 10th-century Suso monk on a work by St Augustine, the *Glosas Emilianenses*.

The Monasterio de San Millán de Yuso in the Cárdenas valley

Cloister of the Monasterio de Santa María la Real, Nájera

Nájera ⓮

La Rioja. ᗏ 7,200. 🚋 🅸 Plaza de España 1, (941) 36 36 66. 🚌 Thu. 🎪 Fiestas de Nájera (24 Jun), Santa Maria la Real (16, 17 Sep).

The old town of Nájera, west of Logroño, was the capital of La Rioja and Navarra until 1076, when La Rioja was incorporated into Castile. The royal families of Navarra, León and Castile are buried in the **Monasterio de Santa María la Real**. It was founded in the 11th century beside a sandstone cliff where a statue of the Virgin was found in a cave. A 13th-century Madonna can be seen in the cave, beneath the carved choir stalls of the 15th-century church.

The 12th-century carved tomb of Blanca of Navarra, the wife of Sancho III, is the finest of many royal sarcophagi.

♦ Monasterio de Santa María la Real
Nájera. 🅲 (941) 36 36 50. ◻ Tue–Sun. ◼ public hols. 🎫 &

Logroño ⓯

La Rioja. ᗏ 130,000. 🚋 🚌 🅸 Paseo del Espolon 10, (941) 29 12 60. 🎪 San Bernabé (11 Jun), Grape Harvest (21 Sep).

The capital of La Rioja is a tidy, modern city of wide boulevards and smart shops. It is the commercial centre of a fertile plain where quality vegetables are produced, in addition to Rioja wines.

In Logroño's pleasant old quarter of narrow streets abutting the Río Ebro is the Gothic **cathedral**, with twin towers. Above the south portal of the nearby **Iglesia de Santiago el Real** is a Baroque equestrian statue of St James in his role as Moorslayer (see p51).

Environs: About 50 km (30 miles) south of Logroño, the N111 winds through the dramatic **Iregua Valley**, through tunnels and gorges and under twisted crags, before climbing into the Sierra de Cameros.

The ornate Baroque west door of Logroño cathedral

Enciso ⓰

La Rioja. ᗏ 220. 🚌 from Logroño. 🅸 Plaza Mayor, (941) 39 60 05. 🎪 San Roque (16 Aug).

Near this remote hill village west of Calahorra is Spain's "Jurassic Park". Signposts point to the *huellas de dinosaurios* (dinosaur footprints). Embedded in rocks overhanging a stream are the prints of many giant, three-toed feet, up to 30 cm (1 ft) long. They were made around 150 million years ago, when dinosaurs moved between the marshes of the Ebro valley, at that time a sea, and these hills. Prints can also be seen at other locations in the area.

Environs: **Arnedillo**, 10 km (6 miles) to the north, is a spa with thermal baths once used by Fernando VI. In **Autol**, to the east, there are two unusual limestone peaks.

The intricately carved portal of Tudela cathedral

Tudela ⑰

Navarra. 🚹 25,600. 🚉 🚌
🅘 Plaza Vieja 1, (948) 82 15 39.
🛳 Sat. 🎉 Santa Ana (26 Jul).

NAVARRA'S SECOND CITY is the great commercial centre of the vast agricultural lands of the Ebro valley in Navarra, the Ribera. Although much of Tudela consists of modern developments, its origins are ancient. Spanning the Ebro is a 13th-century bridge with 17 irregular arches. The old town has well-preserved Mudéjar and Jewish districts.

The delightful **Plaza de los Fueros** is old Tudela's main square. It is surrounded by houses with wrought-iron balconies. On their façades are paintings of bullfights, a reminder that the plaza was formerly used as a bullring.

The **cathedral**, begun in 1194, exemplifies the religious toleration under which Tudela was governed after the Reconquest. It is Early Gothic, with a carved portal depicting the Last Judgement. The Romanesque cloister encloses the ruins of a 9th-century mosque, and a Mudéjar chapel, which may have been a synagogue.

ENVIRONS: To the north is the **Bárdenas Reales**, an arid area of limestone cliffs and crags. About 20 km (12 miles) west of Tudela is the spa town of **Fitero**, with the 12th-century Monasterio de Santa María.

Monasterio de La Oliva ⑱

Carcastillo (Navarra). 📞 (948) 72 51 11. 🚌 from Pamplona. ◯ daily.

FRENCH CISTERCIAN MONKS built this small monastery on a remote plain in the 12th century. The church is simple, in typical Cistercian style, but adorned with rose windows.

One of the cloisters in the Monasterio de La Oliva

The serene cloister, dating from the 15th-century, adjoins a 13th-century chapterhouse. The church also has a tower, erected in the 17th century.

Today, the monks survive by selling their honey, cheese and wine, and by accepting paying guests (see p532).

Ujué ⑲

Navarra. 🚹 280. 🅘 Plaza Municipal, (948) 73 90 23. 🎉 Virgen de Ujué (8 Sep).

ONE OF SPAIN'S least spoiled hill villages, Ujué commands a high spur at the end of a winding road. It has quaint façades, cobbled alleys and steep steps. The **Iglesia de Santa María** is in Gothic style with a Romanesque chancel and an exterior lookout gallery. Beside the church is a ruined fortress. From its terrace there are views of the Pyrenees.

On 25 April every year, pilgrims in black capes come here to visit the Virgin of Ujué, whose Romanesque image is displayed in the church.

Olite ⑳

Navarra. 🚹 3,000. 🚉 🅘 Galerias de la Plaza Carlos III el Noble, (948) 71 24 34. 🛳 Wed. 🎉 Exaltación de la Santa Cruz (14–20 Sep).

THE HISTORIC TOWN of Olite was founded by the Romans and later chosen as a royal residence by the kings of Navarra. Part of the town's old walls can be seen. They

THE KINGDOM OF NAVARRA

Navarra emerged as an independent Christian kingdom in the 10th century, after Sancho I Garcés became king of Pamplona. Sancho III the Great expanded the kingdom, and at his death, in 1035, Navarra stretched all the way from Ribagorza in Aragón to Valladolid. Sancho VI the Wise, who reigned 1150–94, recognized the independent rights (fueros) of many towns. In 1234, Navarra passed by marriage to a line of French rulers. One, Carlos III the Noble, built Olite castle. His grandson, Carlos de Viana, wrote the Chronicle of the Kings of Navarra in 1455. In 1512 Navarra was annexed by Fernando II of Castile, as part of united Spain, but it kept its own laws and currency until the 1800s.

Prince Carlos de Viana, Carlos III's grandson

enclose a delightful jumble of steep, narrow streets and little squares, churches and the **Monasterio de las Clarisas**, begun in the 13th century. The houses along the Rúa Cerco de Fuera and the Rúa Mayor were built between the 16th and 18th centuries.

The castle, the **Palacio Real de Olite**, was built about 1406 by Carlos III, and has earned Olite its nickname "the Gothic town". It was heavily fortified, but was brilliantly decorated inside by Mudéjar artists with *azulejos* (ceramic tiles) and marquetry ceilings. The walkways were planted with vines and orange trees, and there was an aviary and a lions' den.

In the 19th century the castle was sacked by Carlists *(see pp58–9)* and the French. Since the 1920s, however, it has been restored to a semblance of its former glory. Part of it houses a parador *(see p541)*.

Today, the castle is a complex of courtyards, passages, steep stairs, large halls, royal chambers, battlements, towers and turrets. From the "windy tower" monarchs were able to watch tournaments.

Adjoining the castle is a 13th-century former royal chapel, the **Iglesia de Santa María la Real**, with a richly carved Gothic portal. Inside there is a 16th-century reredos.

Olite is in the Navarra wine region *(see pp74–5)* and the town has several bodegas.

⚜ Palacio Real de Olite
Plaza de Carlos III. ((948) 74 00 35.
◯ daily. ◪

The five-arched, medieval pilgrims' bridge at Puente la Reina

Puente la Reina ㉑

Navarra. ⌂ 2,200. ⓘ Plaza de Mena 1, (948) 34 00 07. 🅐 Sat. 🎉 Santiago (25 Jul).

FEW TOWNS along the Road to Santiago de Compostela *(see pp78–9)* evoke the past as vividly as Puente la Reina. The town takes its name from the graceful, humpbacked pedestrian bridge over the Río Arga. The bridge was built for pilgrims during the 11th century by royal command.

On Puente la Reina's narrow main street is the **Iglesia de Santiago**, which has a gilded statue by the west door showing the saint as a pilgrim. On the edge of town is the **Iglesia del Crucifijo**, another pilgrim church which was built in the 12th century by the Knights Templar. Contained within the church is a

Distinctive crucifix in Puente la Reina

Y-shaped wooden crucifix of a sorrowful Christ with arms upraised, which is said to have been a gift from a German pilgrim in the 14th century.

ENVIRONS: Isolated in the fields about 5 km (3 miles) to the east is the 12th-century **Iglesia de Santa María de Eunate**. This octagonal Romanesque church may once have been a cemetery church for pilgrims, as human bones have been unearthed here. Pilgrims would shelter beneath the church's external arcade. West of Puenta la Reina is the showpiece hill village of **Cirauqui**. It is also charming, if rather over-restored. Chic little balconied houses line tortuously twisting alleys linked by steps. The Iglesia de San Román, built in the 13th century on top of the hill, has a sculpted west door.

The battlements and towers of the Palacio Real de Olite

BASQUE COUNTRY, NAVARRA AND LA RIOJA'S FIESTAS

Los Sanfermines *(6–14 Jul)*, Pamplona (Navarra). In the famous *encierro* (bull running) six bulls are released early each morning to run from their corral through the narrow, cobbled streets of the old town. On the last night of this week-long, non-stop party, crowds with candles sing Basque songs in the main square. The event gained worldwide fame after Ernest Hemingway described it in his novel *The Sun Also Rises.*

Bulls scattering the runners in Pamplona

Wine Battle *(29 Jun)*, Haro (La Rioja). People dressed in white clothes squirt each other with wine from leather drinking bottles in the capital of the Rioja Alta wine region. **Danza de los Zancos** *(22 Jul and last Sat of Sep)*, Anguiano (La Rioja). Dancers on stilts, wearing ornate waistcoats and yellow skirts, hurtle down the stepped alley from the church to the main square. **La Virgen Blanca** *(4 Aug)*, Vitoria (Álava). A dummy holding an umbrella (the *celedón*) is lowered from San Miguel church to a house below – from which a man in similar dress emerges. The mayor fires a rocket and the crowds in the square light cigars.

Pilgrims drinking from the wine tap near the monastery at Irache

Estella ②

Navarra. 🏠 13,000. 🚊 🚌 **i** *Calle de San Nicolás 3, (948) 55 40 11.* 🛒 *Thu.* 🎉 *San Andrés (early Aug).*

IN THE MIDDLE AGES Estella (Lizarra) was the centre of the royal court of Navarra and a major stopping point on the pilgrims' Road to Santiago de Compostela *(see pp78–9)*. The town was a stronghold of the Carlists *(see p59)* in the 19th century. A memorial rally is held here on the first Sunday of May every year.

The most important monuments in Estella are sited on the edge of town, across the bridge over the Río Ega. Steps climb steeply from the arcaded Plaza de San Martín to the remarkable 12th-century **Iglesia de San Pedro de la Rúa**, built on top of a cliff. It features a Mudéjar-influenced, sculpted doorway. The carved capitals are all that now remain of the Romanesque cloister, which was destroyed when a castle overlooking the church was blown up in 1592. The **Palacio de los Reyes de Navarra**, on the other side of the Plaza de San Martín, is a rare example of civil Romanesque architecture. It also houses a gallery of Navarrese art.

In the town centre, on the arcaded Plaza de los Fueros, the **Iglesia de San Juan Bautista** has a Romanesque porch. The north portal of the **Iglesia de San Miguel** has Romanesque carvings of St Michael slaying a dragon.

ENVIRONS: The **Monasterio de Nuestra Señora de Irache**, 3 km (2 miles) southwest of Estella, was built by Cistercian monks, who sheltered pilgrims on their way to Santiago. The church is mainly Transitional Gothic in style, but it has Romanesque apses and a cloister in Plateresque style. It is capped by a remarkable dome.

A bodega next to the monastery provides pilgrims with wine from a tap in a wall.

A small road branches off the NA120 north of Estella and winds through a wooded gorge to reach the **Monasterio de Iranzu**, built in the 12th century. The graceful austerity of its church and cloisters are typically Cistercian features.

The Lizarraga Pass, further up the NA120, offers views of attractive beech woods.

Pamplona ②

Navarra. 🏠 183,000. ✈ 🚊 🚌 **i** *Calle Duque de Ahumada 3, (948) 22 07 41.* 🎉 *Sanfermines (6–14 Jul), San Saturnino (29 Nov).*

THE OLD FORTRESS city of Pamplona (Iruña) is said to have been founded by the Roman general, Pompey. In the 9th century it became the capital of Navarra. This otherwise quiet city explodes into life in July during the fiesta of Los Sanfermines, with its daredevil bull running.

From the old **city walls** *(murallas)* you can get a good overview of Pamplona. The nearby **cathedral**, which is

Sumptuous interior of the Palacio de Navarra, Pamplona

Stone tracery in the elegant cloister of Pamplona cathedral

built in ochre-coloured stone, looks down on a loop in the Río Arga. It was built on the foundations of its 12th-century predecessor, and is mainly Gothic in style, with twin towers and an 18th-century façade. Inside there are lovely choir stalls and the alabaster tomb of Carlos III and Queen Leonor.

The southern entrance to the cloister is the beautifully carved, medieval Puerta de la Preciosa. The cathedral priests would gather here to sing an antiphon (hymn) to La Preciosa (Precious Virgin) before the night service.

The Museo Diocesano in the cathedral's 14th-century kitchen and refectory (closed for restoration) displays Gothic altarpieces, polychrome wood statues from all over Navarra, and a French 13th-century reliquary of the Holy Sepulchre.

West of the cathedral is the old town, the former Jewish quarter, cut through with many alleys. The Baroque **Palacio de Navarra** is near the Plaza del Castillo. Its opulent throne room of the kings of Navarra contains a portrait of King Fernando VII by Goya. Outside, a statue of 1903 shows a symbolic queen upholding the *fueros* (historic laws) of Navarra *(see*

p126). North of the palace are the medieval **Iglesia de San Saturnino**, built on the site where St Saturnino is said to have baptized some 40,000 pagan townspeople, and the Baroque **town hall** *(ayuntamiento)*.

Beneath the old town wall, in a 16th-century hospital with a Plateresque doorway, is the **Museo de Navarra**. This is a museum of regional archaeology, history and art. Exhibits include Roman mosaics and an 11th-century, Islam-inspired ivory casket. There are murals painted during the 14th–16th centuries, a portrait by Goya, and a collection of paintings by Basque artists.

To the southeast is the city's massive 16th-century **citadel**, erected in Felipe II's reign. It is designed with five bastions in a star shape. Beyond it are the spacious boulevards of the new town, and also the university's green campus.

Sculpture in Pamplona depicting the *encierro*

🏛 **Museo de Navarra**
Calle Santo Domingo. 📞 *(948)* 42 64 92. ⏰ *Tue–Sun.* 🚫♿
🏛 **Palacio de Navarra**
Avenida Carlos III 2. 📞 *(948) 42 70 00.* ⏰ *by appointment.* ♿

PAMPLONA CITY CENTRE

Cathedral ③
City walls ②
Iglesia de San Saturnino ⑤
Museo de Navarra ①
Palacio de Navarra ⑥
Town Hall ④

Aeropuerto Estación de RENFE GASTEIZ (VITORIA) DONOSTIA (SAN SEBASTIAN)

| 0 metres | 250 |
| 0 yards | 250 |

KEY

〰 Bull-running route

🚌 Coach station

🅿 Parking

ℹ Tourist information

✝ Church

⛪ Convent or monastery

Basque houses in the picturesque town of Etxalar, Regata de Bidasoa

Regata de Bidasoa ㉔

Navarra. 🚌 *Pamplona, San Sebastián.* **ℹ** *Oieregi, (948) 59 22 36.*

FIVE ATTRACTIVE Basque towns lie in or near this valley, the most northerly being **Bera** (Vera). The houses in **Lesaka** have wooden balconies under deep eaves. The road south passes hills dotted with white farmsteads to reach **Igantzi**, (Yanci), with its red-and-white half-timbered houses. **Arantza**, further south, is the most remote town. Since the 12th century, pigeons have been caught in huge nets strung across a pass above **Etxalar** (Echalar). From the summit of La Rhune, on the French border above the valley, there is a great view of the Pyrenees.

Elizondo ㉕

Navarra. 🚹 *3,000.* 🚌 **ℹ** *Plaza de los Fueros, (948) 58 00 06.* 🔄 *Thu. Santiago (25 Jul), Feria (late Oct).*

THIS IS THE BIGGEST of a string of typical Basque villages in the very beautiful valley of Baztán. By the river are noble houses bearing coats of arms.

Arizkun, further up the valley, has old fortified houses and a 17th-century convent. The **Cueva de Brujas**, near Zugarramurdi, was once a meeting place for witches.

Canopy over the Virgin and Child in the Colegiata Real

Roncesvalles ㉖

Navarra. 🚶 *20.* **ℹ** *Roncesvalles, (948) 76 01 93.* 🎉 *Día de la Virgen de Roncesvalles (8 Sep).*

RONCESVALLES (ORREAGA), on the Spanish side of a pass through the Pyrenees, is a major halt on the Road to Santiago *(see pp78–9)*. Before it became associated with the pilgrim's way, Roncesvalles was the site of a major battle in 778, in which the Basques of Navarra slaughtered the rearguard of Charlemagne's army as it marched homeward. This event is described in the 12th-century French epic poem, *The Song of Roland*.

The 13th-century **Colegiata Real**, which has served travellers down the centuries, has a silver-plated Virgin and Child below a high canopy. In the graceful chapterhouse, off the cloister, is the white tomb of Sancho VII the Strong (1154–1234), looked down upon by a stained-glass window of his great victory, the Battle of Las Navas de Tolosa *(see pp50–51)*. Exhibits in the church museum include "Charlemagne's chessboard", an enamelled reliquary which is so-called because of its chequered design.

Valle de Roncal ㉗

Navarra. 🚌 *from Pamplona.* **ℹ** *Roncal, (948) 47 51 36.*

RUNNING perpendicular to the Pyrenees, this valley is still largely reliant on sheep, and the village of **Roncal** is known for its cheeses. Because of the relative isolation of the valley, the inhabitants have preserved their own identity and local costumes are worn

The forested countryside around Roncesvalles

during fiestas. The ski resort of **Isaba**, further up the valley, has a museum of local life and history. A spectacular road winds from Isaba to the tree-lined village of Ochagavia in the parallel **Valle de Salazar**. To the north, the pines and beeches of the **Bosque de Irati**, one of Europe's largest woodlands, spread over the Pyrenees into France, below the snowy summit of Monte Ori at 2,017 m (6,617 ft).

Colourful balconies of houses in the village of Roncal

Monasterio de Leyre 🟤28

Yesa (Navarra). 📞 (948) 88 40 11. 🚃 Yesa. ⬜ daily. 📷 ♿

THE MONASTERY of San Salvador de Leyre is situated high above a reservoir, alone amid grand scenery, backed by limestone cliffs. The abbey has been here since the 11th

century when it was a great spiritual centre. Sancho III and his successors made it the royal pantheon of Navarra.

The monastery began to decline in the 12th century. It was abandoned from the 19th century until 1954, when it was restored by Benedictines. They turned part of it into a modestly priced hotel (see p542). To see the monastery you must join one of the tours run by the monks every morning and afternoon.

The big church, unadorned in the Cistercian manner, has three lofty apses. On its west portal are weatherworn carvings of strange beasts, as well as biblical figures. The 11th-century crypt has unusually short columns with chunky capitals. The monks' Gregorian chant (see p358) during services is wonderful to hear.

Castillo de Javier 🟤29

Javier (Navarra). 📞 (948) 88 40 24. 🚃 from Pamplona. ⬜ daily. ♿

ST FRANCIS XAVIER, the patron saint of Navarra, a missionary and a co-founder of the Jesuit order (see p120), was born in this romantic-looking 13th-century castle in 1506. It has since been completely re-stored and is now used by the Jesuits as a college. Visitors can see the saint's bedroom and a museum in the keep devoted to his life. In the oratory is a 13th-century polychrome Christ and a macabre 15th-century mural of grinning skeletons entitled *The Dance of Death*.

Crucifix in the oratory of the Castillo de Javier

Sangüesa 🟤30

Navarra. 🚶 4,500. 🚉 ℹ️ Calle Alfonso el Batallador 20, (948) 87 03 29. 🚩 Fri. 🎉 San Sebastián (11 Sep).

SINCE MEDIEVAL TIMES this small town beside a bridge over the Río Aragón has been a stop on the Aragonese pilgrimage route to Santiago (see pp78–9).

The richly sculpted south portal of the **Iglesia de Santa María la Real** is a 13th-century treasure of Romanesque art (see p20). It is crammed with figures and details. Above the door, God is shown rejecting sinners and welcoming the chosen. This scene is surrounded by angels, musicians, warriors, artisans, geometric motifs and mythical animals.

The Romanesque **Iglesia de Santiago** and the 14th-century Gothic **Iglesia de San Francisco** are also worth seeing. On the main street is the **town hall** (ayuntamiento), formerly the palace of the Prince of Viana and a residence of the kings of Navarra. The interior is not open to visitors, but the Gothic and Baroque façades can be seen.

ENVIRONS: To the north of Sangüesa there are two deep, narrow gorges. The most impressive of them is the **Hoz de Arbayún**, whose limestone cliffs are inhabited by colonies of vultures. It is best seen from the NA178 north of Domeño. The **Hoz de Lumbier** can be seen from a point on the N240.

The roughly carved columns in the crypt of the Monasterio de Leyre

BARCELONA

Introducing Barcelona

BARCELONA, one of the Mediterranean's busiest ports, is more than the capital of Catalonia. In culture, commerce and sport it not only rivals Madrid, but also considers itself on a par with the greatest European cities. The success of the 1992 Olympic Games, staged in the Parc de Montjuïc, confirmed this to the world. Although there are plenty of historical monuments in the Old Town (Ciutat Vella), Barcelona is best known for the scores of buildings in the Eixample left by the artistic explosion of Modernisme *(see pp136–7)* in the decades around 1900. Always open to outside influences because of its location on the coast, not too far from the French border, Barcelona continues to sizzle with creativity: its bars and the public parks speak more of bold contemporary design than of tradition.

Casa Milà (see p161) *is the most avant-garde of all the works of Antoni Gaudí* (see p160). *Barcelona has more Art Nouveau buildings than any other city in the world.*

Palau Nacional (see p168), *on the hill of Montjuïc, dominates the monumental halls and fountain-filled avenue built for the 1929 International Exhibition. It now houses the Museu Nacional d'Art de Catalunya, an exceptional collection of medieval art, rich in Romanesque frescoes.*

MONTJUIC
(see pp164–9)

Montjuïc Castle (see p169) *is a massive fortification dating from the 17th century. Sited on the crest of the hill of Montjuïc, it offers panoramic views of the city and port, and forms a sharp contrast to the ultra-modern sports halls built nearby for the 1992 Olympic Games.*

Christopher Columbus *surveys the waterfront from the top of a 60-m (200-ft) column (see p152) in the heart of the Port Vell (Old Port). From the top, visitors can look out over the new promenades and quays that have revitalized the area.*

| 0 kilometres | 1 |
| 0 miles | 0.5 |

◁ **The Ramblas and the Old Town stretching out behind Barcelona's monument to Columbus**

The Sagrada Família (see pp162–3), Gaudí's unfinished masterpiece, begun in 1882, rises above the streets of the Eixample. Its polychrome ceramic mosaics and sculptural forms inspired by nature are typical of his work.

EIXAMPLE
(see pp154–63)

Barcelona cathedral (see pp144–5) is a magnificent 14th-century building in the heart of the Barri Gòtic (Gothic Quarter). It has 28 side chapels which encircle the nave and contain some splendid Baroque altarpieces. The keeping of white geese in the cloisters is a centuries-old tradition.

OLD TOWN
(see pp138–53)

Parc de la Ciutadella (see p150), between the Old Town and the Vila Olímpica, has something for everyone. The gardens full of statuary offer relaxation, the boating lake and the zoo are fun, while the three museums within its gates cover art, geology and zoology.

Las Ramblas (see pp146–7) is the most famous street in Spain, alive at all hours of the day and night. A stroll down its length to the seafront, taking in its palatial buildings, shops, cafés and street vendors, makes a perfect introduction to Barcelona life.

Gaudí and Modernisme

Chimney, Casa Vicens

Towards the end of the 19th century a new style of art and architecture, Modernisme, a variant of Art Nouveau, was born in Barcelona. It became a means of self-expression for Catalan nationalism and counted Josep Puig i Cadafalch, Lluís Domènech i Montaner and, above all, Antoni Gaudí i Cornet *(see p160)* among its major exponents. Barcelona's Eixample district *(see pp154–63)* is full of the highly original buildings that they created for their wealthy clients.

All aspects of decoration in a Modernista building, even interior design, were planned by the architect. This door and its tiled surround are in Gaudí's 1906 Casa Batlló (see p160).

A dramatic cupola covers the central salon, which rises through three floors. It is pierced by small round holes, inspired by Islamic architecture, giving the illusion of stars.

Upper galleries are richly decorated with carved wood and cofferwork.

The spiral carriage ramp is an early sign of Gaudí's predilection for curved lines. He would later exploit this to the full in the wavy façade of his masterpiece, the Casa Milà (see p161).

THE EVOLUTION OF MODERNISME

1859 Civil Engineer Ildefons Cerdà i Sunyer submits proposals for expansion of Barcelona

1900 Josep Puig i Cadafalch builds Casa Amatller *(see p160)*

1878 Gaudí graduates as an architect

1903 Lluís Domènech i Montaner builds Hospital de la Santa Creu i de Sant Pau *(see p161)*

Hospital detail

1850 | 1865 | 1880 | 1895 | 1910 | 1925

1883 Gaudí takes over design of Neo-Gothic Sagrada Família *(see pp162–3)*

Detail of Sagrada Família

1888 Barcelona Universal Exhibition gives impetus to Modernisme

1910 Casa Milà completed

1926 Gaudí dies

1905 Domènech i Montaner builds Casa Lleó Morera *(see p160)*. Puig i Cadafalch builds Casa Terrades *(see p161)*

Bizarrely decorated chimneys became one of the trademarks of Gaudí's later work. They reach a fantastic extreme on the gleaming, hump-backed roof of the Casa Batlló.

Elaborate wrought iron lamps light the grand hall.

Ceramic tiles decorate the chimneys.

GAUDÍ'S MATERIALS

Gaudí designed, or collaborated on designs, for almost every known media. He combined bare, undecorated materials – wood, rough-hewn stone, rubble and brickwork – with meticulous craftwork in wrought iron and stained glass. Mosaics of ceramic tiles were used to cover his fluid, uneven forms.

Stained-glass window in the Sagrada Família

Mosaic of ceramic tiles, Parc Güell *(see p174)*

Detail of iron gate, Casa Vicens *(see p160)*

Ceramic tiles on El Capricho *(see p107)*

Parabolic arches, used extensively by Gaudí, beginning in the Palau Güell, show his interest in Gothic architecture (see p20). *These arches form a corridor in his 1890 Colegio Teresiano, a convent school in the west of Barcelona.*

Escutcheon alludes to the Catalan coat of arms.

PALAU GÜELL *(1889)*

Gaudí's first major building in the centre of the city *(see p147)* established his international reputation for outstandingly original architecture. Built for his life-long patron, the industrialist Eusebi Güell, the mansion stands on a small plot of land in a narrow street, making the façade difficult to view. Inside, Gaudí creates a sense of space by using carved screens, galleries and recesses. His unique furniture is also on display.

Organic forms inspired the wrought iron around the gates to the palace. Gaudí's later work teems with wildlife, such as this dragon, covered with brightly coloured tiles, which guards the steps in the Parc Güell.

OLD TOWN

THE OLD TOWN, traversed by Barcelona's most famous avenue, the Ramblas, is one of the most extensive and harmonious medieval city centres in Europe. The Barri Gòtic (Gothic Quarter) contains the cathedral and ancient royal palace. Adjoining it is La Ribera, full of 14th-century mansions, one of which is occupied by the Museu Picasso. This area is bounded by the beautiful Parc de la Ciutadella, which contains the Museu d'Art Modern and the zoo. The revitalized seafront has several kilometres of reclaimed beaches, stretching from the modern Olympic Village to the Old Port, where there are historic shipyards, a fashionable marina and a promenade.

SIGHTS AT A GLANCE

Museums and Galleries
Museu d'Art Modern **20**
Museu Frederic Marès **2**
Museu de Geologia **18**
Museu d'Història de la Ciutat **4**
Museu Marítim and Drassanes **27**
Museu Picasso **13**
Museu de Zoologia **17**

Streets and Districts
Barceloneta **23**
Carrer Montcada **12**
Las Ramblas **9**
El Raval and Barri Xinès **8**

Harbour Sights
Golondrinas **26**
Port Vell **24**

Churches
Basílica de Santa Maria del Mar **11**
Cathedral (pp144–5) **7**

Historic Buildings
Casa de l'Ardiaca **1**
Casa de la Ciutat **5**
La Llotja **10**
Palau de la Generalitat **6**
Palau de la Música Catalana **14**
Palau Reial Major **3**

Modern Architecture
Vila Olímpica **22**

Monuments
Arc del Triomf **15**
Homenatge a Picasso **19**
Monument a Colom **25**

Parks and Gardens
Parc de la Ciutadella **16**
Parc Zoològic **21**

GETTING THERE
The area is well served by metro lines 1, 3 and 4; Jaume I station is in the heart of the Barri Gòtic. Many buses pass the Plaça de Catalunya, the centre of the modern city.

KEY

▨	Street-by-Street map *pp140–41*
Ⓜ	Metro station
🚆	Railway station
🚌	Main bus stop
ℹ	Tourist information
🅿	Parking

0 metres 500
0 yards 500

◁ **Stunning floral mosaic pillars in the Palau de la Música Catalana**

Street-by-Street: Barri Gòtic

Wax candle,
**Cereria
Subirà**

THE BARRI GOTIC (Gothic Quarter) is the true heart of Barcelona. The oldest part of the city, it was the site chosen by the Romans in the reign of Augustus (27 BC–AD 14) on which to found a new *colonia* (town), and has been the location of the city's administrative buildings ever since. The Roman forum was on the Plaça de Sant Jaume, where now stand the medieval Palau de la Generalitat, Catalonia's parlia- ment, and the Casa de la Ciutat, Barcelona's town hall. Close by are the Gothic cathedral and royal palace, where Columbus was received by Fernando and Isabel on his return from his voyage to the New World in 1492 *(see p53)*.

Casa de l'Ardiaca
Built on the Roman city wall, the Gothic-Renaissance archdeacon's residence now houses Barcelona's historical archives **❶**

To Plaça de Catalunya

★ Cathedral
The façade and spire are 19th- century additions to the original Gothic building. Among the artistic treasures inside are medieval Catalan paintings **❼**

**Palau de la
Generalitat**
Catalonia's parlia- ment retains superb Gothic features, which include the chapel and a stone staircase rising to an open-air, arcaded gallery **❻**

PLAÇA DE
SANT JAUME

CARRER DE FERRAN

To Las Ramblas

Casa de la Ciutat
Barcelona's town hall was built in the 14th and 15th centuries. The façade is a Neo-Classical addition. In the entrance hall stands Three Gypsy Boys *by Joan Rebull (1899– 1981), a 1976 copy of a sculpture he originally created in 1946* **❺**

KEY

– – – – Suggested route

Museu Frederic Marès
This medieval doorway is from an extensive display of Spanish sculpture – the mainstay of this museum's extraordinarily eclectic and high-quality collections ❷

LOCATOR MAP
See Street Finder map 5

Roman city wall

Saló del Tinell

★ **Palau Reial Major**
The 14th-century Capella Reial de Santa Àgata, with a 1466 altarpiece, is one of the best surviving sections of the palace ❸

TAPINERIA

CARRER DELS COMTES DE BARCELONA

Capella Reial de Santa Àgata

Plaça del Rei

Palau del Lloctinent

Cereria Subirà candle shop

VIA LAIETANA

CARRER DE JAUME I

Ⓜ Jaume I Metro

Museu d'Historia de la Ciutat
Housed in a 14th-century mansion, which was moved from the Carrer dels Mercaders in 1931, the museum focuses on Barcelona's development in the 13th and 14th centuries, when commerce expanded dramatically ❹

CARRER DAGUERIA

SOTS–TINENT NAVARRA

The Centre Excursionista de Catalunya, housed in a medieval mansion, displays Roman columns from the Temple of Augustus, whose site is marked by a millstone in the street outside.

STAR SIGHTS
★ **Cathedral**
★ **Palau Reial Major**

0 metres   100
0 yards   100

Decorated marble letterbox, Casa de l'Ardiaca

Casa de l'Ardiaca ❶

Carrer de Santa Llúcia 1. **Map** 5 B2.
[(93) 318 11 95. ⊛ Jaume I.
☐ Sep–Jul: 9am–8:45pm Mon–Fri,
9am–2pm Sat; Aug: 9am–2pm
Mon–Fri. ● public hols.

STANDING BESIDE what was originally the Bishop's Gate in the Roman wall is the Archdeacon's House. It was built in the 12th century, but its present appearance dates from around 1500 when it was remodelled and a colonnade added. In 1870 this was extended to form the Flamboyant Gothic *(see p20)* patio around a fountain. The Modernista architect Domènech i Montaner (1850–1923) added the fanciful marble letterbox, carved with three swallows and a tortoise, beside the Renaissance portal. The Municipal Institute of Barcelona History is upstairs.

Museu Frederic Marès ❷

Plaça de Sant Iu 5. **Map** 5 B2.
[(93) 310 58 00. ⊛ Jaume I.
☐ 10am–5pm Tue–Sat, 10am–2pm
Sun & public hols. ● 1 Jan, Good
Fri, 1 May, 25 Dec. ⧉

THE SCULPTOR Frederic Marès i Deulovol (1893–1991) was also a traveller and collector, and this extraordinary museum is a monument to his eclectic taste. The building is part of the Royal Palace complex and was occupied by 13th-century bishops, 14th-century counts of Barcelona, 15th-century judges, and 18th-century

nuns, who lived here until they were expelled in 1936. Marès, who had a small apartment in the building, opened his museum in 1948. It is one of the most fascinating in the city and has an outstanding collection of Romanesque and Gothic religious art. In the crypt there is an extensive assemblage of stone sculpture and two complete Romanesque portals. Exhibits on the three floors above range through clocks, crucifixes, costumes, antique cameras, pipes, tobacco jars and pin-up postcards to an amusement room full of children's toys.

Virgin, Museu Frederic Marès

Palau Reial Major ❸

Plaça del Rei. **Map** 5 B2. [(93) 315 11 11. ⊛ Jaume I. ☐ 10am–2pm, 4–8pm Tue–Sat, 10am–2pm Sun. ● 1 Jan, Good Fri, 25 & 26 Dec. ⧉

THE ROYAL PALACE was the residence of the count-kings of Barcelona from its foundation in the 13th century. The complex includes the 14th-century Gothic Saló del Tinell, a massive room with semicircular arches spanning 17 m (56 ft). This is where Isabel and Fernando *(see p66)* received Columbus after his triumphal return from America. It is also where the Inquisition *(see p264)* sat, believing the walls would move if lies were told.

On the right, built into the Roman city wall, is the royal chapel, the Capella de Santa Àgata, with a painted wood

Gothic nave of the Capella de Santa Àgata, Palau Reial

BARCELONA'S EARLY JEWISH COMMUNITY

Hebrew tablet

From the 11th to the 13th centuries Jews dominated Barcelona's commerce and culture, providing doctors and founding the first seat of learning. But in 1243, 354 years after they were first documented in the city, violent anti-Semitism led to the Jews being consigned to a ghetto, El Call. Ostensibly to provide protection, the ghetto had only one entrance, which led into the Plaça de Sant Jaume. Jews were heavily taxed by the monarch, who viewed them as "royal serfs"; but in return they also received privileges, as they handled most of Catalonia's lucrative trade with North Africa. However, official and popular persecution finally led to the disappearance of the ghetto in 1401, 91 years before Judaism was fully outlawed in Spain *(see p53)*.

Originally there were three synagogues, the main one being in Carrer Sant Domènec del Call, but only the foundations are left. A 14th-century Hebrew tablet is embedded in the wall at No. 1 Carrer de Martlet, which reads: "Holy Foundation of Rabbi Samuel Hassardi, for whom life never ends".

ceiling and an altarpiece (1466) by Jaume Huguet. Its bell tower is formed by part of a watchtower on the Roman wall. Stairs through a small door on the right of the altar lead to the 16th-century tower of Martí the Humane (who reigned from 1396–1410), the last ruler of the 500-year dynasty of the count-kings of Barcelona. From the top of the tower there are fine views over the royal complex.

Museu d'Història de la Ciutat ❹

Plaça del Rei. **Map** 5 B2. (93) 315 11 11. Jaume I. 10am–2pm, 4–8pm Tue–Sat, 10am–2pm Sun. 1 Jan, Good Fri, 25 & 26 Dec.

THE CITY MUSEUM occupies the Casa Clariana-Padellàs, a Gothic building which was brought here stone by stone in 1931 from its original site in Carrer dels Mercaders. During excavation of its new site, the remains of Roman water and drainage systems, baths, mosaic floors and a road were found. These can be seen in the basement, which extends beneath the Plaça de l'Angel. A short stretch of the Roman city wall is accessible from the upper floors, which are devoted to Barcelona's post-Roman development.

Casa de la Ciutat ❺

Plaça de Sant Jaume. **Map** 5 A2. (93) 402 73 62. Jaume I. write in advance for permission.

THE MAGNIFICENT city hall (*ajuntament*), dating from the 14th century, faces the Palau de la Generalitat across the Plaça de Sant Jaume. Flanking the entrance of the Casa de la Ciutat are statues of Jaime (Jaume) I, who granted the city rights to elect councillors in 1249, and Joan Fiveller, who in the 1500s successfully levied taxes on members of the court.

Inside is the huge council chamber, the 14th-century Saló de Cent, built for the city's 100 councillors. The Saló de les Cròniques, on the first floor, was commissioned for the 1929 International Exhibition and decorated by Josep-Marià Sert with murals of momentous events in Catalan history.

Palau de la Generalitat ❻

Plaça de Sant Jaume. **Map** 5 A2. (93) 402 46 00. Jaume I. 23 Apr for groups only (write in advance for permission).

SINCE 1403, the Generalitat has been the seat of the Catalonian Government. Above the entrance, in its Renaissance

The Italianate façade of the Palau de la Generalitat

façade, is a statue of Sant Jordi (St George) – the patron saint of Catalonia – and the Dragon. The late Catalan-Gothic courtyard is by Marc Safont (1416).

Among the fine interiors are the Gothic chapel of Sant Jordi, also by Safont, and Pere Blai's Italianate Saló de Sant Jordi. The building is open to the public only on the saint's feast day. At the back, one floor above street level, lies the *Pati dels Tarongers*, the Orange Tree Patio, by Pau Mateu, which has a bell tower built by Pere Ferrer in 1568.

The Catalan president has offices here as well as in the Casa dels Canonges. The two buildings are connected by a bridge across Carrer del Bisbe, built in 1928 and modelled on the Bridge of Sighs in Venice.

The magnificent council chamber, the Saló de Cent, in Casa de la Ciutat

Barcelona Cathedral ❼

THIS COMPACT GOTHIC CATHEDRAL, with a Romanesque chapel (Capella de Santa Llúcia) and beautiful cloister, was begun in 1298 under Jaime (Jaume) II, on the foundations of a Roman temple and Moorish mosque. It was not finished until the late 19th century, when the main façade was completed. A white marble choir screen, sculpted in the 16th century, depicts the martyrdom of St Eulalia, the city's patron. Next to the font, a plaque records the baptism of six Caribbean Indians, whom Columbus brought back from the Americas in 1493.

Statue of St Eulalia

The twin octagonal bell towers date from 1386–93. The bells were installed in this tower in 1545.

The main façade was not completed until 1889, and the central spire until 1913. It was based on the original 1408 plans of the French architect Charles Galtés.

Nave Interior
The Catalan-style Gothic interior has a single wide nave with 28 side chapels. These are set between the columns supporting the vaulted ceiling, which rises to 26 m (85 ft).

★ Choir Stalls
The top tier of the beautifully carved 15th-century stalls contains painted coats of arms (1518) of several European kings.

Capella del Santíssim Sagrament
This small chapel houses the 16th-century Christ of Lepanto crucifix.

Capella de Sant Benet
This chapel, dedicated to the founder of the Benedictine Order and patron saint of Europe, houses a magnificent altarpiece showing The Transfiguration *by Bernat Martorell (1452).*

VISITORS' CHECKLIST

Plaça de la Seu. **Map** 5 A2.
(93) 315 15 54. Urquinaona, Liceu. 17, 19, 45. 8am–1:30pm, 4–7:30pm daily.
9am, noon, 7pm daily.
Sacristy Museum 10am–1pm daily. **Choir** 9am–1:30pm, 4–7 pm Mon–Fri, 9am–1pm Sat.

★ **Crypt**
In the crypt, beneath the main altar, is the alabaster sarcophagus (1339) of St Eulalia, martyred for her beliefs by the Romans during the 4th century AD.

★ **Cloisters**
The fountain, set in a corner of the Gothic cloisters and decorated with a statue of St George, provided fresh water.

Porta de Sta Eulàlia, entrance to Cloisters

The Sacristy Museum has a small treasury. Pieces include an 11th-century font, tapestries and liturgical artifacts.

Capella de Santa Llúcia

STAR FEATURES

★ Choir Stalls

★ Crypt

★ Cloisters

TIMELINE

400	700	1000	1300	1600	1900
	559 Basilica dedicated to St Eulalia and Holy Cross	**1339** St Eulalia's relics transferred to alabaster sarcophagus		**1913** Central spire completed	
	877 St Eulalia's remains brought here from Santa Maria del Mar	**1046–58** Romanesque cathedral built under Ramon Berenguer I		**1889** Main façade completed, based on plans dating from 1408 by architect Charles Galtés	
4th century Original Roman (paleo-Christian) basilica built	**985** Building destroyed by the Moors	**1257–68** Romanesque Capella de Santa Llúcia built	**1493** Indians brought back from the Americas are baptized		
		1298 Gothic cathedral begun under Jaime II		*Plaque of the Indians' baptism*	

The former dissecting room of the Antic Hospital de la Santa Creu

El Raval and the Barri Xinès ❽

Map 2 E3. Ⓜ *Catalunya, Liceu.*
Museu d'Art Contemporani Pl dels Angels 1. █ *(93) 412 08 10.* ◯ *noon–8pm Tue–Fri, 10am–8pm Sat, 10am–3pm Sun & public hols.* ▨ &

T HE DISTRICTS of El Raval and the Barri Xinès occupy the streets south of the Ramblas. Having grown up outside the city walls, they may lack the Barri Gòtic's architecture, but they are full of atmosphere and have some grand buildings.

The huge 14th-century Casa de la Caritat (Charity House) is now a cultural centre. Next to it stands the stunning, white Museu d'Art Contemporani, which opened in 1995. Close by, off the Carrer de l'Hospital, which has some of Barcelona's most intriguing shops, is the 15th-century Hospital de la Santa Creu, now housing the city's main library.

The Barri Xinès (Chinese Quarter), towards the port, is Barcelona's red light district. There is, in fact, nothing at all Chinese about it save its name, which was given to it in the 1920s by a local journalist after he had seen a film about San Francisco's Chinatown.

On Carrer Nou de la Rambla are Gaudí's Palau Güell *(see p137)*; the Hotel Espanya *(see p543)*, with its superb Modernista interior by Domènech i Montaner; and the city's most complete Romanesque church, Sant Pau del Camp, where Franciscans still sing Mass.

Las Ramblas ❾

T HE HISTORIC AVENUE OF Las Ramblas (Les Rambles in Catalan) is busy around the clock, especially in the evenings and at weekends. Newsstands, caged bird and flower stalls, tarot readers, musicians and mime artists throng the wide, tree-shaded central walkway. Among its famous buildings are the Liceu Opera House, the huge Boqueria food market and some grand mansions.

Exploring Las Ramblas
The name of this long avenue, also more simply known as La Rambla, comes from the Arabic *ramla*, meaning the dried-up bed of a seasonal river. Barcelona's 13th-century city wall followed the left bank of one such river that flowed from the Collserola hills down to the sea.

Convents, monasteries and the university were built on the opposite bank in the 16th century. As time passed, the riverbed was filled in and those buildings demolished, but they are remembered in the names of the five Ramblas that make up the great avenue between the Plaça de Catalunya and Port Vell (Old Port). Today, it is lined with hotels, mansions, shops and cafés.

Palau Güell C/ Nou de la Rambla 3.
Map 2 F3. █ *(93) 317 39 74.* Ⓜ *Liceu.* ◯ *10am–2pm, 4–8pm Mon–Sat.* ● *public hols.* ▨ **Museu de Cera** Pg de la Banca 7. **Map** 2 F4.
█ *(93) 317 26 49.* Ⓜ *Drassanes.*
◯ *10am–1:30pm, 4–7:30pm Mon–Fri, 10am–1:30pm, 4:30–8pm Sat, Sun & public hols* ▨ &

The monument to Columbus at the bottom of the tree-lined Ramblas

Font de Canaletes ①
Saying that someone "drinks the waters of Canaletes" – from this 19th-century fountain – indicates he or she is from Barcelona.

Reial Acadèmia de Ciències i Arts ②
Converted to a theatre in 1910, this building has Barcelona's first official public clock.

Palau de la Virreina ④
The first occupant of this great palace, in 1777, was the *virreina* (viceroy's wife) of Spain in Peru.

Mercat de Sant Josep ⑤
Popularly known as "La Boqueria", this is Barcelona's most colourful food market.

Gran Teatre del Liceu ⑦
The opera house has had to be restored twice after fires – in 1861 and 1994.

Palau Güell ⑨
This Neo-Gothic palace is considered to be one of Gaudí's most important works *(see p137)*.

KEY

🚉	FF CC railway station
Ⓜ	Metro station
P	Parking
✝	Church

0 metres   100
0 yards   100

Palau Moja ③
The Baroque first-floor salon of this Classical building of 1790 is used for exhibitions.

Plaça de la Boqueria ⑥
This square features a mosaic pavement by Miró and an Art Deco dragon designed for a former umbrella shop.

Plaça Reial ⑧
Barcelona's most lively square was built in the 1850s. The Neo-Classical lampposts were designed by Gaudí.

Museu de Cera ⑩
This waxwork museum, in an atmospheric 19th-century building, contains about 300 exhibits.

Monument a Colom
Plaça del Portal de la Pau

Statue of Poseidon in the courtyard of La Llotja

La Llotja ⑩

Carrer de Consolat del Mar 2. **Map** 5 B3. (93) 401 35 55. Jaume I. 10am–12:30pm Mon–Fri.

ORIGINALLY BUILT in the 14th century as the customs house for Barcelona's busy port, the Stock Exchange's Classical appearance dates from a complete remodelling in the 18th century. The main trading room, however, which can be glimpsed through the large ground-floor windows, is an impressive three-aisled Gothic room which has been beautifully preserved.

The Catalan Academy of Fine Arts occupied the upper floors between 1849 and 1970. It was attended by the young Picasso *(see p28)*, whose father taught there, and also by Joan Miró (1893–1983) *(see p168)*.

Basílica de Santa Maria del Mar ⑪

Passeig del Born 1. **Map** 5 B3. (93) 310 23 90. Jaume I. 9am–noon, 4:30–8:15pm daily.

THIS BEAUTIFUL building, the city's favourite church with superb acoustics for concerts, is the only example of a church entirely in the Catalan Gothic style. It took just 55 years to build, with money donated by merchants and shipbuilders. The speed – unrivalled in the Middle Ages – gave it a unity of style both inside and out. The west front has a 15th-century rose window of the Coronation of the Virgin. More stained glass, dating from the 15th to the 18th centuries, lights the wide nave and high aisles.

The choir and furnishings were burned in the Civil War *(see p63)*, adding to the sense of space and simplicity.

Carrer Montcada ⑫

Map 5 B3. Jaume I. **Museu Tèxtil i de la Indumentària** (93) 310 45 16. 10am–5pm Tue–Sat, 10am–2pm Sun & public hols. 1 & 5 Jan, 25 Dec.

THE MOST AUTHENTIC medieval street in Barcelona is a narrow lane, overshadowed by gargoyles and protruding roofs which almost touch overhead. The Gothic palaces that line it, entered through great wooden doors and built around magnificent courtyards, date back to the expansion of Catalonia in the 13th century. A mural of the conquest of Mallorca, a rare secular Romanesque painting once in the 13th–15th century Palau Berenguer d'Aguilar, is now in the Museu Nacional d'Art de Catalunya *(see p168)*.

Carrer Montcada's buildings were all modified over the years, particularly in the 17th

A wedding service in the Gothic interior of Santa Maria del Mar

Pablo Picasso, *Self-Portrait* in charcoal (1899–1900)

PABLO PICASSO IN BARCELONA

Picasso (1881–1973) was born in Málaga and was almost 14 when he came to Barcelona, where his father had found a job in the city's art academy. Picasso enrolled, and was a precocious talent among his contemporaries. He was a regular visitor to Els Quatre Gats, an artists' café still in existence in Carrer Montsió, where he held his first exhibition. He also exhibited in Sala Parks, a gallery still functioning in Carrer Petritxol. The family lived in Carrer Mercé and Picasso had a studio in Carrer Nou de la Rambla. It was among the prostitutes of Carrer d'Avinyò that he found inspiration for the work that many art historians see as the wellspring of modern art, *Les Demoiselles d'Avignon* (1906–7). Picasso left Barcelona for Paris in his early twenties and initially returned several times. After the Civil War his opposition to Franco kept him in France, but he designed a frieze for Barcelona's College of Architects in 1962 and was persuaded to allow the city to open a museum of his work, which it did the following year.

century when the Renaissance style prevailed. The only one to retain its original façade is the Casa Cervelló-Guidice at No. 25. The **Museu Tèxtil i de la Indumentària** in the Palau dels Marquesos de Lió at No. 12 (also called the Palau Mora) displays textiles and clothing from the 4th century onwards. The street also has the city's best-known champagne bar, *El Xampanyet (see p185)*.

Museu Picasso 🕕

Carrer Montcada 15–19. **Map** 5 B1.
📞 *(93) 319 63 10.* 🚇 *Jaume I.*
🕐 *10am–8pm Tue–Sat & public hols, 10am–3pm Sun.* 🎫

ONE OF BARCELONA'S most popular attractions, the Picasso Museum, is housed in three palaces on the Carrer Montcada: the Baroque Meca, and the medieval Berenguer d'Aguilar and Baró de Castellet.

The museum opened in 1963 using works donated by Jaime Sabartes, a great friend of Picasso. Following Sabartes' death in 1968, Picasso himself donated paintings, including early examples which had been kept by his sister. These were complemented by graphic works, left in his will, and 141 ceramic pieces given by his widow, Jacqueline.

The works are divided into three sections: paintings and drawings, engravings, and ceramics. But the strength of the 3,000-piece collection is Picasso's early drawings and paintings. These demonstrate that even at the ages of 15 and 16 he was painting major

Painting in Picasso's series *Las Meninas* (1957), Museu Picasso

works, such as *The First Communion* (1896). There are only a few pictures from his Blue and Rose periods. The most famous work is his series *Las Meninas*, based on Velázquez's masterpiece *(see p28)*, which is displayed in its entirety.

Palau de la Música Catalana 🕖

Carrer de Sant Francesc de Paula 2.
Map 5 B1. 📞 *(93) 268 10 00.*
🚇 *Catalunya, Urquinaona.* 🕐 *for concerts, or by appointment at 3–4:30pm Tue & Thu, 10am–noon Sat.* 🚫 *Aug.* 🎫

THIS is a real palace of music, a Modernista celebration of tile-work, sculpture and glorious stained glass. It is the only concert hall in Europe lit by natural light. Designed by Lluís Domènech i Montaner, it was completed in 1908 on the site of a monastery dissolved in the 19th century. Although a few extensions have been

Glorious stained-glass dome, Palau de la Música Catalana

added, the building still retains its original appearance. The elaborate red brick façade is hard to appreciate fully in the confines of the narrow street. It is lined with mosaic-covered pillars topped by busts of Palestrina, Bach and Beethoven. The large stone sculpture of St George and other figures at the corner of the building is an allegory of Catalan folksong by Miquel Blay.

But it is the interior of the building which is truly inspiring. The auditorium on the first floor is lit by a huge inverted dome of stained glass depicting angelic choristers.

Two sculptures, designed by Domènech but finished by Pau Gargallo, decorate the proscenium arch: *Wagner* represents international music, and *Clavé*, Catalan music. Josep Anselm Clavé's (1824–74) work in promoting Catalan song led to the creation of the Orfeó Català choral society in 1891, a focus of Catalan nationalism and the inspiration behind the Palau.

The pink brick façade of the late 19th-century Arc del Triomf

Arc del Triomf ⓯

Passeig Lluís Companys. **Map** 5 C1.
Ⓜ *Arc de Triomf.*

T HE MAIN GATEWAY to the 1888 Universal Exhibition, which filled the Parc de la Ciutadella, was designed by Josep Vilaseca i Casanovas. It is built of brick in the Mudéjar style *(see p51)*, with sculptured allegories of crafts, industry and business. The frieze by Josep Reynés on the main façade represents the city of Barcelona welcoming foreign visitors. The one at the rear by Josep Llimona is of a prize-giving ceremony.

Parc de la Ciutadella ⓰

Avda del Marqués de l'Argentera. **Map** 6 D2. Ⓜ *Barceloneta, Ciutadella-Vila Olímpica.* ◯ *9am–9pm daily.* ♿

T HIS POPULAR park has a large boating lake, orange groves and scores of naturalized parrots living in the palm trees. The 30-ha (75-acre) park was pre-viously the site of a massive star-shaped citadel. Designed by Prosper Verboom, this was built for Felipe V between 1715 and 1720 following a 13-month siege of the city, brought about by Barcelona's opposition to the Bourbon succession *(see p58)*. The fortress was intended to house soldiers to help keep law and order, but was never used for this purpose. It was converted into a prison, which became particularly notorious during the Napoleonic occupation *(see p59)*, and during the 19th-century liberal repressions, when it was hated as a symbol of centralized power.

In 1878, under the enlightened dictator General Prim, whose statue stands in the middle of the park, the citadel was pulled down and the park was given to the city, to become, in 1888, the venue of the Universal Exhibition.

Three buildings, however, survived: the arsenal, which was redesigned in 1932 for use by the Catalan parliament and is today shared by the Museu d'Art Modern; the Governor's Palace, which is now a school; and the chapel, still sometimes used by the military.

The gardens in the Plaça de Armes were laid out by the French landscape gardener Jean Forestier. They centre on a cascade based around a triumphal arch and partly inspired by the Trevi Fountain in Rome. It was designed by architect Josep Fontseré, with the help of Antoni Gaudí, who was then still a young student.

One of the galleries inside the spacious Museu de Zoologia

Museu de Zoologia ⓱

Passeig de Picasso. **Map** 5 C2. ☎ *(93) 319 69 12.* Ⓜ *Arc de Triomf.* ◯ *10am–2pm Tue–Sun & public hols.* ▨

A T THE ENTRANCE to the Parc de la Ciutadella is the fortress-like Castell dels Tres Dragons (Castle of the Three Dragons), named after a play by Frederic Soler that was popular at the time it was built.

This brick edifice, crenellated and decorated with a frieze of ceramic shields, was built as a café-restaurant for the 1888 Universal Exhibition. The architect, Lluís Domènech i Montaner, modelled it on Valencia's Lonja *(see p241)*. He later used it as a workshop for Modernista design, and it became a focus of the movement. It has housed the city's Zoological Museum since 1937.

Ornamental cascade in the Parc de la Ciutadella designed by Josep Fontseré and Antoni Gaudí

Museu de Geologia ⑱

Parc de la Ciutadella. **Map** 5 C3.
📞 *(93) 319 68 95.* Ⓜ *Arc de Triomf, Jaume I.* 🕐 *9am–2pm Tue–Sun & public hols.* ⬤ *1 May, 25 Dec.* 📷

BARCELONA'S OLDEST MUSEUM opened in 1882, the same year the Parc de la Ciutadella became a public space for the city. It has a large collection of fossils and minerals, including specimens from Catalonia and around the country.

Beside it is the Hivernacle, an iron-framed glasshouse by Josep Amargós which is often used for concerts. Nearby is the Umbracle, a brick and wood conservatory built by the park's architect, Josep Fontseré, to shelter tropical plants.

Glass cube of the *Homenatge a Picasso*, Parc de la Ciutadella

Homenatge a Picasso ⑲

Passeig de Picasso. **Map** 5 C3.
Ⓜ *Barceloneta.*

AT THE EDGE OF THE Parc de la Ciutadella, opposite the Avinguda del Marqués de l'Argentera, is Catalan sculptor Antoni Tàpies' intriguing 1983 work, *Homenatge to Picasso*.

Built to pay homage to Picasso's Cubist works, it is an intellectual sculpture that does not immediately suggest its title. A large, plain glass cube sits in a square pond, with water streaming down the sides. The cube contains an old sofa, chairs and a sideboard skewered by metal poles and draped with a blanket. The elements have not treated it kindly, and an air-conditioning system has had to be installed to prevent the glass from cracking.

Dusk on the River Loing **by Alfred Sisley (1839–99)**

Museu d'Art Modern ⑳

Parc de la Ciutadella. **Map** 6 D3.
📞 *(93) 319 50 23.* Ⓜ *Arc de Triomf.* 🕐 *10am–7pm Tue–Sat & public hols, 10am–2pm Sun.* 📷

THE NAME OF THIS MUSEUM is slightly misleading, as it really houses a collection of 19th- and 20th-century Catalan art, in which the main players – Miró, Picasso, Dalí and Tàpies – are under-represented as they have museums of their own. This should not, however, put potential visitors off, as much of the work is excellent and of great help in understanding Catalan life and culture.

In particular there are works by Catalonia's two main early 20th-century painters, Santiago Rusiñol (1861–1931) and Ramón Casas (1866–1932), considered to be the region's first Impressionist. Casas' line drawings record the faces of the great men of his day. Chief among them is a picture of Pablo Picasso, newly arrived in Montmartre in Paris. There is also a painting of Casas himself on a tandem with Pere Romeu; the two men were founders of Barcelona's Els Quatre Gats café *(see p148)*, where the painting was originally hung.

Picasso's contemporaries, the painters Joaquim Mir (1873–1940) and Isidre Nonell (1873–1911), are represented here, and there are some sculptures by Miquel Blay (1866–1936). There is also a landscape by Alfred Sisley (1839–99), *Dusk on the River Loing.*

The museum has a few excellent examples of Modernista furniture from homes around the Eixample, including an entire private altar.

Parc Zoològic ㉑

Parc de la Ciutadella. **Map** 6 D3.
📞 *(93) 221 25 06.* Ⓜ *Ciutadella-Vila Olimpica.* 🕐 *Mar: 10am–6pm, Apr & Sep: 10am–7pm, May–Aug: 9:30am–7:30pm, Oct–Feb: 10am–5pm.* 📷

BARCELONA'S ZOO was laid out in the 1940s to a relatively enlightened design in which the animals are separated by moats instead of iron bars. The zoo is strong on primates and for years its mascot has been Floquet de Neu (Snowflake), a rare white gorilla. Dolphin and whale shows are held in one of the aquariums. By the entrance is Roig i Soler's romantic 1885 fountain sculpture, *The Lady with the Umbrella*, so well-loved that it has become a symbol of Barcelona.

Floquet de Neu, Barcelona zoo's rare white gorilla

Tree lined beach, Vila Olímpica

Vila Olímpica ㉒

Map 6 F4. ⊗ *Ciutadella-Vila Olímpica.*

THE MOST DRAMATIC rebuilding for the 1992 Olympics took place along the old industrial waterfront of Poble Nou, an area now known as the Vila Olímpica. A promenade and ring road were built to replace old shacks and shunting yards. Running parallel are 4 km (2 miles) of rehabilitated sandy beaches, which are packed with locals during the summer.

The factory district behind was replaced by a new 65-ha (160-acre) town of 2,000 apartments, and parks which cover nearly as much land again. The flats accommodated thousands of athletes during the Games, and were afterwards put to normal residential use.

Two 44-floor skyscrapers were also built, one for offices and one for a hotel and apartments. At their feet is a new marina (Port Olímpic), lined with cafés and restaurants.

Barceloneta ㉓

Map 5 B5. ⊗ *Barceloneta.*

BARCELONA'S fishing "village", which lies on a triangular tongue of land jutting into the sea just below the city centre, is renowned for its fish restaurants and port-side cafés.

Barceloneta was built by the architect and military engineer Juan Martín de Cermeño in 1753 to rehouse people made homeless by the construction,

just inland, of a large fortress, La Ciutadella *(see p150)*. The area was later inhabited largely by fishermen and workers.

Its last remaining warehouse, built by Elies Rogent in the 1880s, was remodelled in 1992 to become the Palau de Mar. This is a complex of bars, cafés and restaurants specializing in fish dishes. Upstairs there is a museum of Catalan history.

Barceloneta's short streets, laid out in a grid system, and the low, balconied houses have a friendly air and seem far removed from the city. In the small Plaça de la Barceloneta, at the centre of the district, is the Baroque church of Sant Miquel del Port, also designed by Cermeño. A market is often held in the square in front of it.

Port Vell ㉔

Map 5 A4. ⊗ *Barceloneta, Drassanes.* **Aquàrium** 🄲 *(93) 221 74 74.* ◯ *10am–8pm daily.* 📷

THE CITY'S NEW leisure port lies at the foot of the Ramblas, which is connected by a pedestrian jetty across to the yacht clubs on the far Moll d'Espanya (*moll* meaning quay or wharf). A swing bridge allows vessels to pass through. At the end of this quay is Maremagnum, a large complex of restaurants, shops and cinemas, and Europe's largest aquarium.

The Moll de la Fusta (Timber Wharf) includes red bridges inspired by Van Gogh's bridge at Arles. It is built on two levels – the upper level dotted with terrace cafés giving a good view over the port. Nearby is

the restaurant Gambrinus *(see p173)*, identified by a giant lobster designed by Alfredo Arribas and Javier Mariscal. At the end of the wharf stands *El Cap de Barcelona (Barcelona Head)*, a strikingly colourful, columnar, 20-m (66-ft) tall sculpture by American Pop artist Roy Lichtenstein.

The popular cable car passing dramatically over Port Vell from Montjuïc to Barceloneta was closed in 1995, pending a future decision on whether to rebuild it or demolish it.

Monument a Colom ㉕

Plaça del Portal de la Pau. **Map** 2 F4. 🄲 *(93) 302 52 24.* ⊗ *Drassanes.* ◯ *Oct–May: 10am–2pm, 3:30–6:30pm Tue–Sun; Jun–Sep: 9am–8:30pm daily.* 📷

THE COLUMBUS monument in the Portal de la Pau (the "Gate of Peace") was designed by Gaietà Buigas for the 1888 Universal Exhibition.

The 60-m (200-ft) monument – a cast iron column on a stone plinth – marks the spot where Columbus stepped ashore in 1493 after discovering America, bringing with him six Caribbean Indians. He was accorded a state welcome by the Catholic Monarchs in the Saló del Tinell *(see p142)*. The Indians' subsequent conversion to Christianity is commemorated in the cathedral *(see pp144–5)*.

A lift gives access to a viewing platform at the top of the monument. The bronze statue, pointing out to sea, was designed by Rafael Arché.

Fishing boat moored at the quayside of Barceloneta

A *golondrina* departing from the Plaça del Portal de la Pau

Golondrinas 26

Plaça del Portal de la Pau. **Map** 2 F5.
(93) 442 31 06. Drassanes.
Jun – Sep: 11am – 8pm daily; Oct –
May: 10am – 1pm Mon – Fri, 11am –
5.30pm Sat & Sun.

SIGHTSEEING TRIPS around
Barcelona's harbour can be made on small double-decker boats called *golondrinas* (literally "swallows"). They moor beside the steps of the Plaça del Portal de la Pau at the bottom of Las Ramblas.

Tours last around half an hour. The boats go out beneath the steep, castle-topped hill of Montjuïc towards the industrial port. They usually stop off at the breakwater, which reaches out to sea from Barceloneta, to allow passengers to disembark for a stroll.

An alternative, commentated, two-hour trip takes in the commercial port and beaches and stops off at the Port Olímpic.

Museu Marítim and Drassanes 27

Avinguda de les Drassanes. **Map** 2 F4.
(93) 301 18 71. Drassanes.
10am – 7pm Tue – Sun; 12 Oct,
1 Nov, 6 & 8 Dec: 10am – 2pm.
some public hols.

THE GREAT GALLEYS that made
Barcelona a major seafaring power were built in the sheds of the Drassanes (shipyards), which now house the maritime museum. These royal dry docks are the largest and most complete surviving medieval complex of their kind in

the world. They were founded in the mid-13th century, when dynastic marriages uniting the kingdoms of Sicily and Aragón meant that better maritime communications between the two became a priority. Three of the yards' four original corner towers survive.

Among the vessels to slip from the Drassanes' vaulted halls was the *Real*, flagship of Don Juan of Austria, Charles V's illegitimate son, who led the Christian fleet to victory against the Turks at Lepanto in 1571 *(see p55)*. The museum's showpiece is a full-scale replica decorated in red and gold.

The *Llibre del Consulat de Mar*, a book of nautical codes and practice, serves as a reminder that Catalonia was once the arbiter of maritime law in the Mediterranean. The expertise of its sailors is also evident in the museum's collection of pre-Columbian charts and maps, including one of 1439 which was used by the navigator Amerigo Vespucci.

Stained-glass window in the Museu Marítim

BARCELONA'S FIESTAS

La Mercè *(24 Sep)*. The patroness of Barcelona, Nostra Senyora de la Mercè (Our Lady of Mercy), whose church is near the port, is honoured for a week around 24 September with masses, concerts and dances. The biggest events are the *carrefoc* – a procession of people dressed as devils and monsters, illuminated by fireworks – and the *piro musical* – an impressive firework display with music held at the Font Màgica in Montjuïc.

Firework display during the fiesta of La Mercè

Els Tres Tombs *(17 Jan)*. Horsemen, dressed in top hats and tails, ride three times through the streets in honour of St Anthony, the patron saint of animals.
La Diada *(11 Sep)*. Catalonia's "national" day is an occasion for singing the Catalan anthem and separatist demonstrations.
Dia de Sant Ponç *(11 May)*. Stalls along Carrer Hospital sell herbs, honey and candied fruit on the day of the patron saint of beekeepers and herbalists.
Festa Major *(mid-Aug)*. Each district hosts its own *festa* in which streets compete to outdo each other in the inventiveness and beauty of their decorations. The most spectacular displays take place in the old district of Gràcia.

EIXAMPLE

BARCELONA CLAIMS to have the greatest collection of Art Nouveau buildings of any city in Europe. The style, known in Catalonia as Modernisme, flourished after 1854, when it was decided to pull down the medieval walls to allow the city to develop into what had previously been a construction-free military zone.

The designs of the civil engineer Ildefons Cerdà i Sunyer (1815–76) were chosen for the new expansion (eixample) inland. These plans called for a rigid grid system of streets, but at each intersection the corners were chamfered to allow the buildings there to overlook the junctions or squares. The few exceptions

Jesus of the Column,
Sagrada Família

to this grid system include the Diagonal, a main avenue running from the wealthy area of Pedralbes down to the sea, and the Hospital de la Santa Creu i de Sant Pau by Modernista architect Domènech i Montaner (1850–1923). He hated the grid system and deliberately angled the hospital to look down the diagonal Avinguda de Gaudí towards Antoni Gaudí's church of the Sagrada Família, the city's most spectacular Modernista building (see pp162–3). The wealth of Barcelona's commercial elite, and their passion for all things new, allowed them to give free rein to the age's most innovative architects in designing their residences as well as public buildings.

SIGHTS AT A GLANCE

Museums and Galleries
Fundació Antoni Tàpies ❷

Churches
Sagrada Família pp162–3 ❻

Modernista Buildings
Casa Milà, "La Pedrera" ❸
Casa Terrades, "Casa de les Punxes" ❹
Hospital de la Santa Creu i de Sant Pau ❺
Illa de la Discòrdia ❶

KEY

▢	Street-by-Street map *pp178–9*
Ⓜ	Metro station
🚆	Railway station
🚏	Main bus stop
🛈	Tourist information
P	Parking

GETTING THERE

Metro line 1 has stations at either end of the Passeig de Gràcia (Catalunya and Diagonal), and one in the middle, at the Illa de la Discòrdia (Passeig de Gràcia). Metro line 5 takes you straight to the Sagrada Família and Hospital de Sant Pau (a long walk from other sights).

0 metres	500
0 yards	500

◁ **Nativity façade of the Sagrada Família – the only façade to be more or less completed in Gaudí's lifetime**

Street-by-Street: Quadrat d'Or

THE HUNDRED OR SO city blocks centring on the Passeig de Gràcia are known as the Quadrat d'Or, "Golden Square", because they contain so many of Barcelona's best Modernista buildings *(see pp136–7)*. This was the area within the Eixample favoured by the wealthy bourgeoisie, who embraced the new artistic and architectural style with enthusiasm, not only for their residences, but also for commercial buildings. Most remarkable is the Illa de la Discòrdia, a single block containing houses by Modernisme's most illustrious exponents. Many interiors can be visited by the public, revealing a feast of stained glass, ceramics and ornamental ironwork.

Perfume bottle, Museu del Perfum

Diagonal Metro

Passeig de Gràcia, the Eixample's main avenue, is a showcase of highly original buildings and smart shops. The graceful street lamps are by Pere Falqués (1850–1916).

Vinçon home decor store *(see p183)*

RAMBLA DE CATALUNYA

PASSEIG DE GRÀCIA

Fundació Tàpies
Topped by Antoni Tàpies' wire sculpture Cloud and Chair, *this 1879 building by Domènech i Montaner houses a wide variety of Tàpies' paintings, graphics and sculptures* **2**

Casa Amatller

Museo del Perfum

Casa Ramon Mulleras

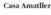

★ **Illa de la Discòrdia**
In this city block, four of Barcelona's most famous Modernista houses vie for attention. All were created between 1900 and 1910. This ornate tower graces the Casa Lleó Morera by Domènech i Montaner **1**

To Plaça de Catalunya

Casa Batlló

Casa Lleó Morera

Passeig de Gràcia Metro

Museu de la Música is housed in the Palau Baró de Quadras designed by Puig i Cadafalch in 1904. This carving adorns the doorway. The museum has displays of historical instruments collected from around the world.

LOCATOR MAP
See Street Finder map 3

AVINGUDA DIAGONAL

CARRER DE PAU CLARIS

CARRER DE PROVENÇA

Casa Thomas

CARRER DE MALLORCA

CARRER DE ROGER DE LLÚRIA

CARRER DEL BRUC

To Sagrada Família

ARRER DE VALÈNCIA

CARRER D'ARAGÓ

Palau Ramon de Montaner

Casa Terrades
Built in red brick with carved stone ornamentation, this 1905 house by Puig i Cadafalch echoes the Gothic buildings of northern Europe ❹

★ Casa Milà "La Pedrera"
Gaudí put all his architectural daring into this, his most famous house. The result is a remarkable wave-like façade and a roofscape of chimneys and vents resembling abstract sculptures ❸

| 0 metres | 100 |
| 0 yards | 100 |

KEY

– – – Suggested route

STAR SIGHTS

★ **Illa de la Discòrdia**

★ **Casa Milà "La Pedrera"**

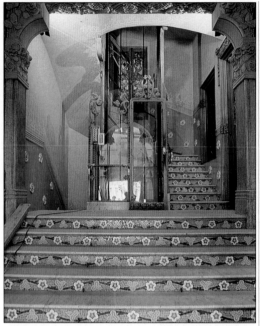

Sumptuous interior of the Casa Lleó Morera, Illa de la Discòrdia

Illa de la Discòrdia ❶

Passeig de Gràcia, between Carrer d'Aragó and Carrer del Consell de Cent. **Map** 3 A4. ⓜ Passeig de Gràcia.

THE MOST famous group of Modernista (see pp136–7) buildings in Barcelona amply illustrates the range of styles involved in the movement. The city block in which they stand has been dubbed the Illa de la Discòrdia, "Block of Discord", owing to the startling visual argument between them.

The three most famous houses, on Passeig de Gràcia, were remodelled in Modernista style from existing houses early in the 20th century, but named after their original owners.

No. 35 is Casa Lleó Morera (1902–6), the first residential work of Lluís Domènech i Montaner. The ground floor was gutted to create a shop in 1943, but the sumptuous Modernista interiors upstairs still exist and the first floor may in future be opened to the public.

Beyond the next two houses, one of which is a beauty shop containing a perfume museum,

is Casa Amatller, designed by Puig i Cadafalch in 1898. Its façade is a harmonious blend of styles, featuring Moorish and Gothic windows encased in iron grilles. The stepped gable roof is dotted with tiles. Inside the wrought-iron main doors is a fine stone staircase beneath a stained-glass roof. The building, now used by the Institut Amatller d'Art

Hispànic, has a beautiful wood-panelled library. Next door is Antoni Gaudí's Casa Batlló (1904–6). Its façade is typically liquid, with heavily tiled walls and curving iron balconies pierced with holes to look like masks or skulls. The hump-backed, scaly-looking roof is thought to represent a dragon, with St George (the patron saint of Catalonia) as a chimney. Step inside to see the blue-tiled entrance hall.

Fundació Antoni Tàpies ❷

Carrer d'Aragó 255. **Map** 3 A1. 📞 (93) 487 03 15. ⓜ Passeig de Gràcia. 🕐 11am–8pm Tue–Sun & public hols (Sun in Aug: 11am–3pm). ● 1 & 6 Jan, 25 & 26 Dec. 🚫 ♿

ANTONI TÀPIES, born in 1923, is Barcelona's best-known living artist. Inspired by Surrealism, his abstract work is executed in a variety of materials, including concrete and metal (see p156). It is not easy to appreciate at first, but the exhibits should help those interested obtain a clearer perspective, even if there are not enough here to gain a full understanding of the artist's work. They are housed in the first domestic building in Barcelona to be built with iron (1880), designed by Domènech i Montaner for his brother's publishing firm.

ANTONI GAUDÍ (1852–1926)

Born in Reus (Tarragona) into a family of artisans, Gaudí was the leading exponent of Catalan Modernisme. Following a stint as a blacksmith's apprentice, he studied at Barcelona's School of Architecture. Inspired by a nationalistic search for a romantic medieval past, his work was supremely original. His first major achievement was the Casa Vicens (1888) at No. 24 Carrer de les Carolines. But his most celebrated building is the extravagant church of the Sagrada Família (see pp162–3), to which he devoted his life from 1914. He gave all his money to the project and often went from house to house begging for more, until his death a few days after being run over by a tram.

Decorated chimney pot, Casa Vicens

◁ **Extraordinary sculptured and ceramic-encrusted chimneys of Gaudí's Casa Milà**

The rippled façade of Gaudí's apartment building, Casa Milà

Casa Milà ❸

Passeig de Gràcia 92. **Map** 3 B3. 📞
(93) 484 59 80. Ⓜ Diagonal.
Ⓒ Guided tours only: Tue–Sat 10am,
11am, noon, 1pm. Ⓒ public hols.

Usually called "la pedrera" ("the stone quarry"), the Casa Milà is Gaudí's greatest contribution to Barcelona's civic architecture, and his last work before he devoted himself entirely to the Sagrada Família (see pp162–3).

Built between 1906 and 1910, "La Pedrera" completely departed from the established construction principles of the time and, as a result, was ridiculed and strongly attacked by Barcelona's intellectuals.

Gaudí designed this corner apartment block, eight storeys high, around two circular courtyards. In the basement he incorporated the city's first underground car park. The intricate ironwork balconies, by Josep Maria Jujol, are like seaweed against the wave-like walls of white undressed stone. There are no straight walls anyhere in the building.

The Milà family had an apartment on the first floor. Regular guided tours from an office on the ground floor take in the extraordinary roof, where the multitude of sculpted air ducts and chimneys look so threatening they have been dubbed the espantabruixas, the witch-scarers.

Casa Terrades ❹

Avinguda Diagonal 416. **Map** 3 B3.
Ⓜ Diagonal. Ⓒ to public.

This free-standing, six-sided apartment block by Modernista architect Puig i Cadafalch gets its nickname, Casa de les Punxes (House of the Points), from the spires on its six corner turrets, which are shaped like witches' hats. It was built between 1903 and 1905 by converting three existing houses on the site and was Cadafalch's largest work. It is an eclectic mixture of medieval and

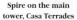

Spire on the main tower, Casa Terrades

Renaissance styles. The towers and gables are influenced in particular by north European Gothic architecture. However, the deeply carved, floral stone ornament of the exterior, in combination with red brick as the principal building material, are typically Modernista.

Hospital de la Santa Creu i de Sant Pau ❺

Carrer de Sant Antoni Maria Claret 167.
Map 4 F1. 📞 (93) 291 90 00. Ⓜ
Hospital de Sant Pau. **Grounds** Ⓒ
daily; write in advance for permission to
visit pavilions not in medical use. 🔲 📷

Lluís Domènech i Montaner began designing a new city hospital in 1902. Totally innovative in concept, his scheme consisted of 26 attractive Mudéjar-style pavilions set in large gardens, as he strongly disliked huge wards and believed that patients would recover better amid fresh air and trees. All the connecting corridors and service areas were hidden underground.

Also believing art and colour to be therapeutic, he decorated the pavilions profusely. The turreted roofs were tiled with ceramics, and the reception pavilion embellished with sculptures by Pau Gargallo and mosaic murals. The vast project was completed in 1930, after Domènech's death, by his son, Pere.

Statue of the Virgin, Hospital de la Santa Creu i de Sant Pau

Sagrada Família ❻

Europe's most unconventional church, the Temple Expiatori de la Sagrada Família, is an emblem of a city that likes to think of itself as individualistic. Crammed with symbolism inspired by nature and striving for originality, it is Gaudí's *(see pp136–7)* greatest work. In 1883, a year after work had begun on a Neo-Gothic church on the site, the task of completing it was given to Gaudí who changed everything, extemporizing as he went along. It became his life's work and he lived like a recluse on the site for 16 years. He is buried in the crypt. At his death only one tower on the Nativity façade had been completed, but several more have been finished to his original plans. After the Civil War, work resumed and continues today, financed by public subscription.

A carved whelk

Bell Towers
Eight of the 12 spires, one for each apostle, have been built. Each is topped by Venetian mosaics.

THE FINISHED CHURCH

Gaudí's initial ambitions have been scaled down over the years, but the design for the completion of the building remains impressive. Still to come is the central tower, which is to be encircled by four large towers representing the Evangelists. Four towers on the Glory (south) façade will match the existing four on the Passion (west) and Nativity (east) façades. An ambulatory – like an inside-out cloister – will run round the outside of the building.

Tower with lift

The apse was the first part of the church Gaudí completed. Stairs lead down from here to the crypt below.

The altar canopy, designed by Gaudí, is still waiting for the altar.

★ Passion Façade
This bleak façade was completed in the late 1980s by artist Josep Maria Subirachs. A controversial work, its sculpted figures are angular and often sinister.

Entrance to Crypt Museum

Main entrance

Spiral Staircases
Steep stone steps – 400 in each – allow access to the towers and upper galleries. Majestic views reward those who climb or take the lift.

VISITORS' CHECKLIST

Carrer de Mallorca 401. **Map** 4 E3.
📞 (93) 455 02 47. 🚇 Sagrada
Familia. 🚌 19, 34, 43, 50, 51, 54.
🕐 Apr–Aug: 9am–8pm daily;
Sep: 9am–7pm daily; Oct–Mar:
9am–6pm daily. ● 1 Jan, 25 Dec
(pm). 📷 ✝ 9am, 8:15pm Mon–
Sat; 9am, 10:30am, 11:45am,
1pm, 8:15pm Sun. ♿

Tower with lift

★ **Nativity Façade**
The most complete part of Gaudí's church, finished in 1904, has doorways which represent Faith, Hope and Charity. Scenes of the Nativity and Christ's childhood are embellished with symbolism, such as white doves, which represent the congregation.

★ **Crypt**
The crypt, where Gaudí is buried, was built by the original architect, Francesc de Paula Villar i Lozano, in 1882. This is where services are currently held. The lower floor contains a small museum, tracing the careers of both architects and the church's complicated history.

The final parts of the structure to be built will be the nave and the south (Glory) façade – which was originally planned as the main entrance. The finished building will be in the form of a Latin cross. A forest of intricately fluted pillars will support four galleries above the side aisles.

STAR FEATURES

★ Passion Façade

★ Nativity Façade

★ Crypt

MONTJUÏC

THE HILL OF MONTJUÏC, rising to 213 m (699 ft) above the commercial port on the south side of the city, is Barcelona's biggest recreation area. Its museums, art galleries, funfair and nightclubs make it a popular place in the evenings as well as during the day.

There was probably a Celt-iberian settlement here before the Romans built a temple to Jupiter on their Mons Jovis, which may have given Montjuïc its name – though another theory suggests that a Jewish cemetery on the hill inspired the name Mount of the Jews.

The absence of a water supply meant that there were few buildings on Montjuïc until the castle was erected on the top in 1640.

Statue, gardens of the Palau Nacional

The hill finally came into its own as the site of the 1929 International Fair. With great energy and flair, buildings were erected all over the north side, with the grand Avinguda de la Reina María Cristina, lined with huge exhibition halls, leading into it from the Plaça d'Espanya. In the middle of the avenue is the Font Màgica (Magic Fountain), which is sometimes illuminated in colour. Above it is the Palau Nacional, home of the city's great art collection. The Poble Espanyol is a crafts centre housed in copies of buildings from all over Spain. The last great surge of building on Montjuïc was for the 1992 Olympic Games, which have left Barcelona with inter-national-class sporting facilities.

SIGHTS AT A GLANCE

Historic Buildings
Castell de Montjuïc **7**

Modern Architecture
Estadi Olímpic de Montjuïc **8**
Pavelló Mies van der Rohe **4**

Museums and Galleries
Fundació Joan Miró **1**
Museu Arqueològic **2**
Museu Nacional d'Art de Catalunya **3**

Squares
Plaça d'Espanya **6**

Theme Parks
Poble Espanyol **5**

GETTING THERE

Apart from the exhibition halls near Espanya metro station, reaching most of Montjuïc's attractions on foot involves a steep climb. However, buses 13 and 61 will take you up the hill from Plaça d'Espanya. For the funfair and castle, take the funicular from metro Parallel, then the cable car. Both run from 11am–7:30/8pm every weekend, and daily in summer.

KEY

	Street-by-Street map *pp166–7*
Ⓜ	Metro station
🚡	Cable car station
🚠	Funicular railway station
P	Parking

0 metres   500
0 yards   500

◁ **Changing colours of the Font Màgica (Magic Fountain) on the grand avenue leading up to Montjuïc**

Street-by-Street: Montjuïc

MONTJUIC IS A SPECTACULAR vantage point from which to view the city. It has a wealth of art galleries and museums, as well as a funfair, and an open-air theatre adjoining a rose garden. The most interesting buildings lie around the Palau Nacional, where Europe's greatest Romanesque art collection is housed. Montjuïc is approached from the Plaça d'Espanya between brick pillars based on the campanile of St Mark's in Venice, which give a foretaste of the eclecticism of building styles. The Poble Espanyol illustrates the traditional architecture of Spain's regions, while the Fundació Joan Miró is boldly modern.

Pavelló Mies van der Rohe
This statue by Georg Kolbe (see p169) stands serenely in the steel, glass, stone and onyx pavilion built in the Bauhaus style as the German contribution to the 1929 International Exhibition ❹

★ Poble Espanyol
Containing replicas of buildings from many regions, this "village" provides a fascinating glimpse of vernacular styles ❺

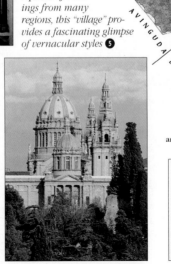

★ Museu Nacional d'Art de Catalunya
Displayed in the National Palace, the main building of the 1929 International Exhibition, is Europe's finest collection of early medieval frescoes. These were a great source of inspiration for Joan Miró (see p168) ❸

To Montjuïc castle and Olympic stadium

STAR SIGHTS

★ Poble Espanyol

★ Museu Nacional d'Art de Catalunya

★ Fundació Joan Miró

Fountains and cascades descend in terraces from the Palau Nacional. Below them is the Font Màgica (Magic Fountain). On summer evenings, from Thursday to Sunday, its jets are programmed to a multi-coloured music and light show. This marvel of water-and-electrical engineering was originally built by Carles Buigas (1898–1979) for the 1929 International Exhibition.

LOCATOR MAP
See Street Finder map 1

ça d'Espanya

 IUS I TAULET

Museu Etnològic displays artifacts from Oceania, Africa, Asia and Latin America.

AVINGUDA DE LA TÈCNICA

CARRER DE LLEIDA

PASSEIG DE LA SANTA MADRONA

PASSEIG DE LA SANTA MADRONA

PASSEIG DE LA SANTA MADRONA

Mercat de les Flors theatre *(see p185)*

Teatre Grec is an open-air theatre set among gardens.

AVINGUDA DE MIRAMAR

Museu Arqueològic
The museum displays important finds from prehistoric cultures in Catalonia and the Balearic Islands. The Dama de Ibiza, *a 4th-century sculpture, was found in Ibiza's Carthaginian necropolis (see p487)* ❷

★ **Fundació Joan Miró**
This tapestry by Joan Miró hangs in the centre he created for the study of modern art. In addition to Miró's works in various media, the modern building by Josep Lluís Sert is of architectural interest ❶

To funfair, Montjuïc castle and cable car

KEY

– – – Suggested route

0 metres   100

0 yards   100

Flame in Space and Naked Woman (1932) by Joan Miró

Fundació Joan Miró ❶

Parc de Montjuïc. **Map** 1 B3. (93) 329 19 08. Espanya, then bus 61. Jul–Sep: 10am–8pm Tue–Sat, Oct–Jun: 11am–7pm Tue, Wed, Fri & Sat, 11am–9:30pm Thu, 10:30am–2:30pm Sun & public hols.

THE SON OF A GOLDSMITH, Joan Miró (1893–1983) studied at the fine art school at La Llotja *(see p148)*. From 1919, he spent much of his time in Paris. Though opposed to Franco, he returned to Spain in 1940 and from then on lived mainly in Mallorca, where he died.

An admirer of primitive Catalan art and Gaudí's Modernisme *(see p136)*, Miró always remained a Catalan painter but invented and developed a Surrealistic style, with vivid colours and fantastical forms suggesting dream-like situations. During the 1950s he concentrated on ceramics.

In 1975, after the return of democracy to Spain *(see p64)*, his friend, the architect Josep Lluís Sert, designed the stark, white building to house a permanent collection of graphics, paintings, sculptures and tapestries lit by natural light. Miró himself donated the works and some of the best pieces on display include his *Barcelona Series* (1939–44), a set of 50 black-and-white lithographs. Periodic exhibitions of other artists' work are also held.

Museu Arqueològic ❷

Passeig Santa Madrona 39. **Map** 1 B3. (93) 423 21 49. Espanya, Poble Sec. 9:30am–1:30pm & 3:30–7pm Tue–Sat, 9am–2pm Sun. public hols. except Sun.

HOUSED IN the Renaissance-inspired 1929 Palace of Graphic Arts, the museum shows artifacts from prehistory to the Visigothic period (415–711 AD). Highlights are finds from the Greco-Roman town of Empúries *(see p206)*, Hellenistic Mallorcan jewels and Iberian silver treasure. There is also a splendid collection of Visigothic jewellery.

Museu Nacional d'Art de Catalunya ❸

Parc de Montjuïc. **Map** 1 A2. (93) 423 71 99. Espanya. 10am–7pm Tue–Sat, 10am–9pm Thu, 10am–2:30pm Sun.

THE AUSTERE Palau Nacional was built for the 1929 International Exhibition, but in 1934 it was used to house an art collection that has since become the most important in the city.

The museum includes what is probably the greatest display of Romanesque items in the world, centred around a series of magnificent 12th-century frescoes. These have been peeled from a number of Catalan Pyrenean churches and re-pasted on to replicas of the original vaulted ceilings and apses they decorated, to save them from plunder and the ravages of time. The most remarkable are the wall paintings from Santa Maria de Taüll *(see p201)* and from Sant Climent de Taüll *(see p20)*.

There is also an impressive Gothic collection, covering the whole of Spain but particularly good on Catalonia. Notable artists of the time are exhibited, including the 15th-century Spanish artists Lluís Dalmau and Jaume Huguet.

Other items include a large number of wooden and stone sculptures, and altarpieces. An outstanding example is the massive 14th-century *Altar to Our Lady* by the Serra brothers.

12th-century *Christ in Majesty*, **Museu Nacional d'Art de Catalunya**

Morning by Georg Kolbe (1877–1945), Pavelló Mies van der Rohe

Pavelló Mies van der Rohe ❹

Avinguda del Marqués de Comillas. **Map** 1 B2. ☎ (93) 423 40 16. Ⓜ *Espanya*. ◯ *Apr–Oct: 10am–8pm daily, Nov–Mar: 10am–6pm daily*. ♿

I F THE ELEGANTLY simple lines of the glass and polished stone German Pavilion look modern today, they must have shocked visitors to the International Exhibition in 1929. Designed by Ludwig Mies van der Rohe (1886–1969), director of the Avant-Garde Bauhaus school, it includes his famous *Barcelona Chair*. The building was demolished after the exhibition, but a replica was built on the centenary of his birth.

Poble Espanyol ❺

Avinguda del Marqués de Comillas. **Map** 1 A2. ☎ (93) 325 78 66. Ⓜ *Espanya*. ◯ *9am–2am Tue–Thu, 9am–3am Fri & Sat, 9am–midnight Sun*. ♿

T HE IDEA BEHIND the Poble Espanyol (Spanish Village) was to illustrate and display local Spanish architectural styles and crafts. It was laid out for the 1929 International Exhibition, but has proved to be enduringly popular.

Building styles from all over Spain are illustrated by 116 houses. These are arranged on streets radiating from a main square and were created by many well-known architects

and artists of the time. The village was refurbished at the end of the 1980s and is now a favourite place to visit for both tourists and native *Barcelonins*.

Resident artisans produce a wide range of crafts including hand-blown glass, ceramics, sculpture, Toledo damascene (*see p372*) and Catalan canvas sandals. The Torres de Ávila (*see p185*), which form the huge main entrance, have been converted into one of the city's most popular nightspots, with an interior by designers Alfredo Arribas and Javier Mariscal. There are also shops, cafés, bars and a children's theatre.

View from Palau Nacional down-hill towards the Plaça d'Espanya

Plaça d'Espanya ❻

Avinguda de la Gran Via de les Corts Catalanes. **Map** 1 B1. Ⓜ *Espanya*.

T HE FOUNTAIN in the middle of this road junction, the site of public gallows until they were transferred to Ciutadella in 1715, is by Josep Maria Jujol, one of Gaudí's followers. The sculptures are by Miquel Blay. The 1899 bullring to one side is by Font i Carreras, but Catalans have never taken to bullfighting and the arena is now used as a music venue.

On the Montjuïc side of the roundabout is the Avinguda de la Reina María Cristina. This is flanked by two 47-m (154-ft) high brick campaniles by Ramon Raventós, modelled on the belltowers of St Mark's in Venice and built as the entrance way to the 1929 International Exhibition. The avenue, lined with exhibition buildings, leads up to Carles Buigas's illuminated *Font Màgica* (Magic Fountain) in front of the Palau Nacional.

Castell de Montjuïc ❼

Parc de Montjuïc. **Map** 1 B5. ☎ (93) 329 86 13. Ⓜ *Paral·lel, then funicular & cable car*. **Museum** ◯ *9:30am–7:30pm Tue–Sun*. ♿

T HE WHOLE OF THE summit of Montjuïc is occupied by a huge, 18th-century castle with fabulous views over the port.

The first castle was built in 1640, but was destroyed by Felipe V in 1705. The present star-shaped fortress was built on the ruins for the Bourbon family. During the War it of Independence it was captured by French troops. After the Civil War it became a prison, in which the defeated Catalan leader Lluís Companys was executed in 1940.

The castle is now a military museum with an extensive display of ancient weaponry and models of Catalan castles.

Estadi Olímpic de Montjuïc ❽

Passeig Olímpic 17–19. **Map** 1 A3. ☎ (93) 426 20 89. Ⓜ *Espanya, Poble Sec*. ◯ *10am–6pm daily*. ♿

T HE NEO-CLASSICAL FAÇADE has been preserved from the original stadium, built by Pere Domènech i Roura for the 1936 "Alternative" Olympics. However, these were cancelled at the outbreak of the Civil War in 1936. The arena was re-fitted to increase its capacity to 70,000 for the 1992 Olympics.

Nearby are the steel-and-glass **Palau Sant Jordi** indoor stadium, by Japanese architect Irata Isozaki, and swimming pools by Ricardo Bofill.

Entrance to the refurbished 1992 Olympic Stadium

FURTHER AFIELD

THE RADICAL redevelopment of Barcelona's outskirts in the late 1980s and early 1990s gave it a wealth of new buildings, parks and squares. The city's main station, Sants, was rebuilt and the neighbouring Parc de l'Espanya Industrial and Parc Joan Miró were created, containing lakes, modern sculpture and futuristic architecture. The Parc de Clot, beyond the new national theatre *(see p184)*, is also of striking modern design. In the west of the city, where the streets start to climb steeply, are the historic royal palace and monastery of Pedralbes, and Gaudí's famous Parc Güell, dating from 1910. Beyond is the Serra de Collserola, the city's closest rural area. Two funiculars provide an exciting way of reaching its heights, which offer superb views of the city. Tibidabo, the highest point, with a funfair, the Neo-Gothic church of the Sagrat Cor and a modern steel-and-glass communications tower, is a favourite place among *Barcelonins* for a day out.

Parc Güell gateway signs

SIGHTS AT A GLANCE

Museums and Galleries
Museu de la Ciència ⑧
Museu del Futbol Club
 Barcelona ③

Historic Buildings
Monestir de Pedralbes ⑤
Palau Reial de Pedralbes ④

Modern Buildings
Torre de Collserola ⑥

Parks and Gardens
Parc de l'Espanya Industrial ②
Parc Güell ⑨
Parc de Joan Miró ①

Theme Parks
Tibidabo ⑦

| 0 metres | 500 |
| 0 yards | 500 |

KEY

	Street-by-Street map
	Built-up area
🚉	Railway station
🚠	Funicular railway station
━━	Motorway
━━	Major road
━━	Minor road

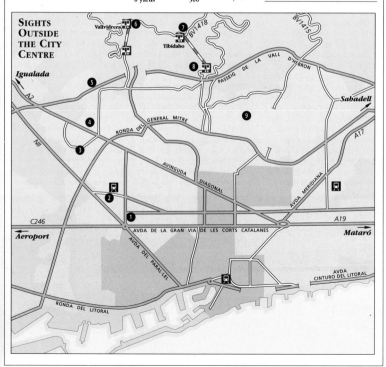

SIGHTS OUTSIDE THE CITY CENTRE

◁ **The Neo-Gothic Temple Expiatori del Sagrat Cor, dominating Barcelona from the summit of Tibidabo**

Dona i Ocell (1983) by Joan Miró in the Parc de Joan Miró

Parc de Joan Miró ❶

Carrer d'Aragó 1. 🚇 *Tarragona.*

BARCELONA'S 19th-century slaughterhouse *(escorxa-dor)* was transformed in the 1980s into this unusual park, hence its alternative name, Parc de l'Escorxador.

It is constructed on two levels, the lower of which is devoted to football pitches interspersed with landscaped sections of palms, pines, eucalyptus trees and flowers. The upper level is completely paved and is dominated by a magnificent 1983 sculpture by the Catalan artist Joan Miró *(see p168)* entitled *Dona i Ocell* (Woman and Bird). Standing 22 m (72 ft) high in the middle of a pool, its surface is coated with colourful pieces of glazed tile.

Parc de l'Espanya Industrial ❷

Plaça de Joan Peiró. 🚇 *Sants-Estació.*

THIS MODERN PARK, designed by the Basque architect Luis Peña Ganchegui, owes its name to the textile mill that used to stand on the 5-hectare (12-acre) site.

Laid out in 1986 as part of Barcelona's policy to provide more open spaces within the city, the park has canals and a rowing lake – with a Classical statue of Neptune at its centre. Tiers of steps rise around the lake like an amphitheatre and on one side a row of ten futuristic watchtowers dominates the entire area. Their only function is to serve as public viewing platforms and lamp standards.

Six contemporary sculptors are represented in the park, among them Andrés Nagel, whose huge metal dragon incorporates a children's slide.

Museu del Futbol Club Barcelona ❸

Avda de Aristides Maillol. 📞 *(93) 496 36 00.* 🚇 *Maria Cristina, Les Cortes.* ⏰ *Apr–Oct: 10am–1pm, 3–6pm Mon–Sat, 10am–2pm public hols; Nov–Mar: 10am–1pm, 3–6:30pm Tue–Fri, 10am–2pm Sat & Sun.* 📷 ♿

CAMP NOU, Europe's largest football stadium, is home to the city's famous football club, Barcelona FC (Barça, as it is known locally). Founded in 1899, it is one of the world's richest soccer clubs, and has more than 100,000 members.

The stadium is a magnificent, sweeping structure, built in 1957

Line of watchtowers in the Parc de l'Espanya Industrial

to a design by Francesc Mitjans. An extension was added in 1982 and it can now comfortably seat 98,000 fans, with standing room for 17,000 more.

The club's museum, which displays club memorabilia and trophies on two floors, and has a souvenir shop, is one of the most popular in Barcelona. There are also paintings and sculptures of famous club footballers commissioned for the Blau-grana Biennial, an exhibition held in celebration of the club in 1985 and 1987. *Blau-grana* (blue-burgundy) are the colours of Barça's strip. The club's flags were used as an expression of local nationalist feelings during the Franco dictatorship, when the Catalan flag was banned.

As well as hosting its own high-profile matches (mainly at weekends), Camp Nou also accommodates affiliated local soccer clubs and promotes other sports in its sports centre, ice rink and mini-stadium.

View across Camp Nou stadium, prestigious home of the Futbol Club Barcelona

Palau Reial de Pedralbes ❹

Avinguda Diagonal 686. 🅲 (93) 280 16 21. 🚇 Palau Reial. 🕐 10am–3pm Tue–Sun. 🔴 1 Jan, Good Fri, May, 24 Jun, 25 & 26 Dec. 🗐 ♿ 📷

THE PALACE OF PEDRALBES was once the main house on the estate of Count Eusebi Güell. In 1919 he offered it to the royal family to use when they visited Barcelona. The first visit was from Alfonso XIII in 1926, before which it was refurbished to be fit for a king. Visitors can still see the throne, supported by golden lions, that was created for him.

The building was opened to the public in 1937 and a decorative arts museum installed. Among the exhibits are items of period furniture brought here from other great houses in the city. A genealogical tree traces the 500-year dynasty of the count-kings of Barcelona, showing Catalonia's union by marriage with the kingdom of Aragón in 1137 *(see p217)*.

The palace also houses a ceramics museum, which has displays of historic Catalan and Moorish pottery and modern ceramics, including works by Miró and Picasso *(see p148)*.

The palace gardens are well laid out with small ponds and paths. Just behind the gardens, in Avinguda de Pedralbes, is the entrance to the original Güell estate. It is guarded by a black wrought-iron gate, its top forged into a great, open-jawed dragon, and two gate houses, all by Gaudí *(see pp136–7)*.

Madonna of Humility, **Monestir de Santa Maria de Pedralbes**

Monestir de Santa Maria de Pedralbes ❺

Baixada del Monestir 9. 🅲 (93) 203 92 82 (Monastery), (93) 280 14 34 (Thyssen-Bornemisza Collection). 🚇 Reina Elisenda. 🕐 10am–2pm Tue–Sun, 10am–5pm Sat. 🗐

APPROACHED through an arch in its ancient walls, the monastery of Pedralbes still retains the air of a lived-in enclosed community. This is heightened by the good state of preservation of its furnished cells, kitchens, infirmary and refectory. But the nuns of the Order of St Clare moved to an adjoining building in 1983. The monastery was founded in 1326 by Elisenda de Montcada de Piños, fourth wife of Jaime II of Catalonia and Aragón. Her alabaster tomb lies in the wall between the church and the cloister. On the church side her effigy is dressed in royal robes; on the other as a nun.

The most important room in the monastery is the Capella (chapel) de Sant Miquel, with murals of the *Passion* and the *Life of the Virgin*, both painted by Ferrer Bassa in 1346, when Elisenda's niece, Francesca Saportella, was abbess.

In 1989, some 60 paintings forming part of the Thyssen-Bornemisza Collection (most of which is in Madrid – *see pp278–9*) were donated to the monastery. They now hang in the former dormitory and are mainly religious in theme. The collection is strong in Italian and Spanish works, including examples by Fra Angelico, Tiepolo, Canaletto, Veronese, Velázquez and Zurbarán.

Torre de Collserola ❻

Carretera de Vallvidrera al Tibidabo. 🅲 (93) 211 79 42. 🚇 Avda del Tibidabo, then Tramvia Blau & Funicular. 🕐 Jan & Jul–15 Sep: 11am–7pm Tue–Sun; Feb–Apr: 11am–7pm Sat, Sun & Easter; May–Jun: 11am–8pm Wed–Sun & public hols. 🗐 ♿

IN A CITY that enjoys thrills, the ultimate ride is offered by the communications tower near Tibidabo mountain *(see p174)*. A glass-sided lift takes less than two minutes to reach the top of this 288-m (944-ft) tall structure standing on the summit of a 445-m (1,460-ft) hill – not a pleasant experience for those who fear heights.

The tower was designed by English architect Norman Foster for the 1992 Olympic Games. Needle-like in form, it is a tubular steel mast on a concrete pillar. There are 13 levels. The top one has an observatory with a powerful telescope, and a public viewing platform with a 360° view encompassing Barcelona, the sea and the mountain chain on which Tibidabo sits.

BARCELONA V REAL MADRID

FC Barcelona

Més que un club is the motto of Barcelona FC: "More than a club". More than anything else it has been a symbol of the struggle of Catalan nationalism against the central government in Madrid. To fail to win the league is one thing. To come in behind Real Madrid is a complete disaster. Each season the big question is which of the two teams will win the title. Under the Franco regime in a memorable episode in 1941, Barça won 3–0 at home. At the return match in Madrid, the crowd was so hostile that the police and referee "advised" Barça to prevent trouble. Demoralized by the intimidation, they lost 11–1. Loyalty is paramount: one Barça player who left to join Real Madrid received death threats.

Real Madrid

Merry-go-round, Tibidabo

Tibidabo ❼

Plaça del Tibidabo. (93) 211 79 42. 🚋 Avda Tibidabo, then Tramvia Blau & Funicular. **Funfair** ☐ May: noon–8pm Wed–Sun; Jun: noon–8pm Tue–Sun; Jul–mid-Sep: noon–10pm Tue–Sun; mid-Sep–Apr: noon–7pm weekends & public hols. ● 1 Apr, Nov. 🗝 **Temple del Sagrat Cor** ☐ 10am–7pm daily.

THE HEIGHTS OF TIBIDABO are reached by the Tramvia Blau (Blue Tram), Barcelona's one last surviving tram, and a funicular railway. The name, inspired by Tibidabo's views of the city, comes from the Latin *tibi dabo* (I shall give you) – a reference to the Temptation of Christ when Satan took him up a mountain and offered him the world spread at his feet.

The hugely popular Parc d'Atraccions (funfair, *see p185*) first opened in 1908. The rides were completely renovated in the 1980s. While the old ones retain their charm, the modern technology of the newer ones provides the latest in vertiginous experiences. Their hilltop location at 517 m (1,696 ft) adds to the thrill. Also in the park is the Museu d'Automates, displaying automated toys, juke boxes and gaming machines.

Tibidabo is crowned by the Temple Expiatori del Sagrat Cor (Church of the Sacred Heart), built with religious zeal but little taste by Enric Sagnier between 1902 and 1911. A lift takes you up to the feet of an enormous figure of Christ.

Just a short bus ride away is another viewpoint – the Torre de Collserola (*see p173*).

Museu de la Ciència ❽

Carrer Teodor Roviralta 55. (93) 212 60 50. 🚋 Avinguda del Tibidabo, then Tramvia Blau. ☐ 10am–8pm Tue–Sun. 🗝 ♿

THE CITY'S science museum provides some excellent hands-on experiences. Here you can test your senses and physical abilities and learn about world ecology. Separate floors are devoted to sound and light. There is a weather station, and a planetarium which stages 30-minute shows. Outside is a full-sized submarine, which you can enter through holes cut in the hull.

Parc Güell ❾

Carrer d'Olot. (93) 213 04 88. 🚇 Lesseps. ☐ 10am–8pm daily. ♿ 🚻

DESIGNATED a World Heritage Site by UNESCO, the Parc Güell is Antoni Gaudí's (*see pp136–7*) most colourful creation. He was commissioned in the 1890s by Count Eusebi Güell to design a garden city on 20 hectares (50 acres) of the family estate. In the event, little of the grand design for decorative public buildings and 60 houses among landscaped gardens became reality. What we see today was completed between 1910 and 1914, and the park opened in 1922.

Most atmospheric is the Room of a Hundred Columns, a cavernous covered market hall of 84 crooked pillars, which is brightened by glass and ceramic mosaics. Above it, reached by a flight of steps flanked by ceramic animals, is the Gran Plaça Circular, an open space with a snaking balcony of coloured mosaics, said to have the longest bench in the world. It was executed by Josep Jujol, one of Gaudí's chief collaborators. The view from here is panoramic.

The two mosaic-decorated pavilions at the entrance are by Gaudí, but the Casa-Museu Gaudí, a gingerbread-style house where Gaudí lived from 1906–26, was built by Francesc Berenguer. It contains drawings and furniture by Gaudí.

Mosaic-encrusted chimney by Gaudí at the entrance of the Parc Güell

BARCELONA STREET FINDER

THE MAP REFERENCES given with the sights, shops and entertainment venues described in the Barcelona section of the guide refer to the street maps on the following pages. Map references are also given for Barcelona hotels (see

pp543–5), and for bars and restaurants (see pp584–6). The schematic map below shows the area of Barcelona covered by the Street Finder. The symbols used for sights and other features and services are listed in the key at the foot of the page.

KEY TO STREET FINDER

◻ Major sight	🛥 Golondrina boarding point	✝ Church	
◻ Place of interest	🚡 Cable car	⊠ Post office	
◻ Other building	🚟 Funicular railway station	= Railway line	
➔ Main railway station	🚕 Taxi rank	→ One-way street	
🚋 Local (FF CC) railway station	P Parking	Pedestrianized street	
Ⓜ Metro station	ℹ Tourist information		
🚌 Main bus stop	✚ Hospital with casualty unit	**SCALE OF MAP PAGES**	
🚍 Coach station	🏛 Police station	0 metres 250	
		0 yards 250	

SHOPPING IN BARCELONA

CITY WITH impeccable style, Barcelona is where you'll find the best in Catalan, Spanish and international design. For those in search of fashion, a good place to begin a tour of Barcelona is on the streets around the Passeig de Gràcia, which make up the most important shopping area, and where crowds browse among the well-known fashion and design stores. In this area there are also many interesting

Wall tile outside La Manual Alpargatera

old shops such as food stores, herbalists and pharmacies – some displaying beautiful Modernista frontages. For those who enjoy the hustle and bustle of small crowded streets, the Barri Gòtic, in the heart of the city, has something for everyone. Particularly interesting are the antique dealers and the shops specializing in traditional crafts such as carnival masks, ceramics and handmade espadrilles.

Some of the beautifully displayed confectionery at Escribà

FOOD AND DRINK

BARCELONA's cake shops are sights in themselves and, with its displays of chocolate sculptures, no *pastisseria* is more enticing or spectacular than **Escribà**. Other food shops also have a great deal of character, none more so than **Colmado Quílez** in the Eixample. This wonderful old store stocks a huge range of hams, cheeses and preserves, in addition to a comprehensive selection of Spanish and foreign wines and spirits.

DEPARTMENT STORES AND GALERÍAS

THE BRANCH of **El Corte Inglés**, Spain's largest department store chain, on Plaça Catalunya, is a Barcelona landmark and a handy place to find everything under one roof, including plug adaptors and services like key-cutting. Other branches are located around the city. Barcelona's hypermarkets also sell a wide

range of goods. As they are on the outskirts of the city – south along the Gran Via towards the airport, and on the Avinguda Meridiana to the north – a car is the best way to reach them.

The fashion malls or *galerías*, built mostly during the affluent 1980s, are hugely popular. Both branches of **Bulevard Rosa**, on the Passeig de Gràcia and the Avinguda Diagonal, have hundreds of shops selling clothes and accessories. Also on the Avinguda Diagonal is **La Illa**, a large, lively shopping mall containing chain stores as well as specialist retailers.

FASHION

INTERNATIONAL fashion labels are found alongside clothes by young designers on and around the Passeig de Gràcia. **Adolfo Domínguez** stocks classically styled clothes for men and women; **Armand Basi** sells quality leisure and sportswear; and discount designer fashion is available at

Contribuciones. Many shops offer traditional, fine-quality tailoring skills and **Calzados E Solé**, which is situated in the Old Town, specializes in classic handmade shoes and boots.

SPECIALITY SHOPS

A WALK AROUND Barcelona can reveal a wonderful choice of shops selling traditional craft items and handmade goods that in most places have now been largely replaced by the production line. **La Caixa de Fang** has a good variety of Catalan and Spanish ceramics, among them traditional Catalan cooking pots and colourful tiles. **L'Estanc** has everything for the smoker, including the best Havana cigars. **La Manual Alpargatera** is an old shoe shop that specializes in Catalan-style espadrilles. These are handmade on the premises and come in all colours. The city's oldest shop, **Cereria Subirà** (*see pp140–41*), sells candles in every imaginable form.

Menswear department in Adolfo Domínguez

DESIGN, ART AND ANTIQUES

IF YOU ARE interested in modern design, or just looking for gifts, you should pay a visit to **Vinçon**, the city's most famous design emporium. Situated on the Passeig de Gràcia, it has everything for the home, including beautiful fabrics and furniture. A must is **BD-Ediciones de Diseño**, which has the feel of an art gallery. Housed in a building designed by Domènech i Montaner, the shop has furniture based on designs by Gaudí and Charles Rennie Mackintosh, and sells wonderful contemporary furniture and accessories.

Most of the commercial art galleries and print shops are found on Carrer Consell de

Mouthwatering fruit stalls in La Boqueria market

Cent, in the Eixample, while the Barri Gòtic – especially the Carrer de la Palla and Carrer del Pi – is the best place to browse around small but fascinating antique shops. As well as fine furniture and old dolls, **L'Arca de l'Avia** sells antique silks and lace, all of which are set out in pretty displays.

The stylishly sparse display of furniture at Vinçon

BOOKS AND NEWSPAPERS

MOST CITY-CENTRE news kiosks stock English-language newspapers, but the most comprehensive stock of foreign newspapers and magazines is in **Crisol**, which also sells books, videos, CDs and photographic equipment.

MARKETS

NO-ONE SHOULD miss the chance to look around **La Boqueria** on the Ramblas, one of the most spectacular food markets in Europe. It has every kind of food: fresh fruit, fine meats and all types of seafood. There is an antiques market in the Plaça del Pi on Thursdays. On Sunday mornings coin, stamp and book collectors set up stall in the Plaça Reial, and a craft market is held near the Sagrada Família. The city's traditional flea market, **Els Encants**, takes place on Mondays, Wednesdays, Fridays and Saturdays. It offers a variety of jewellery and clothes.

DIRECTORY

FOOD AND DRINK

Colmado Quilez
Rambla de Catalunya 63.
Map 3 A4.
 (93) 215 23 56.

Escribà Pastisseries
Gran Via de les Corts
Catalanes 546. **Map** 2 E1.
 (93) 454 75 35.

DEPARTMENT STORES AND GALERÍAS

Bulevard Rosa
Passeig de Gràcia 55.
Map 3 A4.
 (93) 309 06 50.

El Corte Inglés
Pl Catalunya 14. **Map** 5 B1.
 (93) 302 12 12.

La Illa
Avinguda Diagonal 557.
 (93) 444 00 00.

FASHION

Adolfo Domínguez
Passeig de Gràcia 89.
Map 3 A3.
 (93) 215 13 39.

Armand Basi
Centre Comercial
Maremàgnum, Moll
d'Espanya.
Map 5 A4.
 (93) 225 80 58.

Calzados E Solé
Carrer Ample 7.
Map 5 A3.
 (93) 301 69 84.

Contribuciones
Riera de Sant Miquel 30.
Map 3 A2.
 (93) 218 71 40.

SPECIALITY SHOPS

La Caixa de Fang
C/ Freneria 1. **Map** 5 B2.
 (93) 315 17 04.

Cereria Subirà
C/ Llibreteria 7. **Map** 5 B2.
 (93) 315 26 06.

L'Estanc
Via Laietana 4. **Map** 5 B3.
 (93) 310 10 34.

La Manual Alpargatera
C/ d'Avinyó 7. **Map** 5 A3.
 (93) 301 01 72.

DESIGN, ART AND ANTIQUES

L'Arca de l'Avia
Carrer dels Banys Nous 20.
Map 5 A2.
 (93) 302 15 98.

BD-Ediciones de Diseño
Carrer de Mallorca 291–3.
Map 3 B4.
 (93) 458 69 09.

Vinçon
Pg Gràcia 96. **Map** 3 B3.
 (93) 215 60 50.

BOOKS AND NEWSPAPERS

Crisol
Carrer Consell de Cent
341. **Map** 3 A4.
 (93) 215 31 21.

MARKETS

La Boqueria
Ramblas 100. **Map** 5 A2.

Els Encants
Plaça de les Glòries.
Map 4 F5.

ENTERTAINMENT IN BARCELONA

FEW CITIES CAN MATCH the vitality of Barcelona and nowhere is this more evident than in its live arts scene. The stunning Palau de la Música Catalana has keen and critical audiences. It regularly hosts some of the world's greatest classical musicians, including Montserrat Caballé and José Carreras, who are both *Barcelonins*. Equally dynamic are the many exciting

Busker in the Barri Gòtic

theatre and dance companies performing all year round at numerous indoor and outdoor venues.

Modern music fans are well catered for by any number of rock venues and live jazz and salsa clubs, not to mention the buskers on the Ramblas or in the squares of the Barri Gòtic. A tradition of old Barcelona that continues to thrive is its brash, glittering music halls.

The magnificent interior of the Palau de la Música Catalana

ENTERTAINMENT GUIDES

THE MOST COMPLETE guide to what's on each week in Barcelona is the *Guía del Ocio*, out every Thursday. It includes a cinema listings section. The Friday *El País* also has an entertainments supplement.

SEASONS AND TICKETS

THEATRE and concert seasons for the main venues run from September to June, with limited programmes at other times. In summer the city hosts the Festival del Grec, a showcase of international music, theatre and dance, in open-air venues such as the Teatre Grec in Montjuïc and the Plaça del Rei in the Barri Gòtic. There is also a varied menu of concerts during the Festa de la Mercé (*see p153*) in September.

The simplest way to get theatre and concert tickets is to buy them at the box office of the relevant venue, although tickets for many theatres can

also be bought from branches of the Caixa de Catalunya or La Caixa savings banks. Tickets for the Festival should be obtained from tourist offices.

CLASSICAL MUSIC

BARCELONA'S **Palau de la Música Catalana** (*see p149*) is one of the world's most beautiful concert halls. The Orquestra Simfònica de Barcelona performs there throughout the season.

Barcelona's status as the opera capital of Spain took a knock when the Liceu opera house burned down in 1994; but restoration is due to be completed in 1999. Meanwhile, opera-goers can see productions staged at the Palau de la Música Catalana and other theatres around the city. Check with tourist offices for details.

THEATRE AND DANCE

WORTH SEEING are Catalan contemporary theatre groups such as Els Comediants or La Cubana whose original

style combines theatre, music, mime and elements from traditional Mediterranean fiestas.

The **Mercat de les Flors** (*see p167*), a converted former flower market in Montjuïc, is an exciting theatre presenting quality productions of classic and modern plays in Catalan. The new **Teatre Nacional de Catalunya**, near the Plaza de Toros Monumental, is another showcase for Catalan drama.

Although classical ballet has suffered from a lack of venues since the loss of the Liceu, there are many contemporary dance companies and regular performances are staged at the Mercat de les Flors in Montjuïc.

MUSIC HALL

A STAGE SHOW that is camp and tacky with extremely vulgar jokes may not appeal to everyone, but the music halls along the Avinguda del Paral·lel take you back in time to the golden age of variety. The legendary 1920s **El Molino** (The Windmill) is still the most popular place for a noisy night out.

Outrageous stage show at one of Barcelona's many clubs

**Gambrinus bar and restaurant,
identified by its looming lobster**

CAFÉS, BARS AND CLUBS

AMONG BARCELONA'S most famous modern sights are the hi tech design bars built in the prosperous 1980s. The **Mirablau** looks over the city and **Gambrinus** *(see p152)* is at the harbour. The **Torres de Ávila**, in the Poble Espanyol *(see p169)*, is the height of post-modernism. **Otto Zutz** has live music. Less chic, but still fun, are the **Apolo**, and **La Paloma**, a fine dance hall complete with a 1904 interior where the paso doble rules.

Two of the best-known champagne and cocktail bars are in the old city: **Boadas** and **El Xampanyet**. The **Bar Velódromo** is a friendly Art Deco café. The cafés on the secluded Plaça del Sol in the Gràcia district are an ideal place for a quiet drink.

ROCK, JAZZ AND WORLD MUSIC

BIG NAMES like David Byrne and Paul McCartney have performed at **Zeleste**, while **La Boîte** has live folk and blues. In summer, festivals and open-air concerts are held around the city. Jazz venues include the **Harlem Jazz Club**, while Latin music fans can enjoy live salsa at **Antilla Cosmopolita**.

FUNFAIRS

IN SUMMER, Barcelona's giant funfairs open till the early hours and are crowded until closing time. **Tibidabo** *(see p174)* and the older **Montjuïc** fairgrounds are even more enjoyable if you go there by tram, funicular or cable car.

SPORTS

THE UNDOUBTED KINGS of sport in this city are **FC Barcelona**. They boast the largest football stadium in Europe, the Nou Camp *(see p173)*, and have a fanatical following. Barcelona also has a high-ranking basketball team.

Packed house at the gigantic Nou Camp stadium

DIRECTORY

CLASSICAL MUSIC

Palau de la Música Catalana
Carrer de Sant Francesc de Paula 2. **Map** 5 B1.
((93) 268 10 00.

THEATRE AND DANCE

Mercat de les Flors
Carrer de Lleida 59.
Map 1 B3.
((93) 426 18 75.

Teatre Nacional de Catalunya
Pl de les Artes. **Map** 4 F5.

MUSIC HALL

El Molino
Carrer de Vila i Vilà 99.
Map 2 E3.
((93) 441 63 83.

CAFÉS, BARS AND CLUBS

Gambrinus
Moll de la Fusta. **Map** 6 F4.
((93) 221 50 14.

Apolo
Carrer Nou de la Rambla 113.
Map 2 E3.
((93) 441 90 06.

Bar Velódromo
Carrer de Muntaner 213.
((93) 430 51 98.

Boadas
Carrer dels Tallers 1.
Map 5 A1.
((93) 318 95 92.

Mirablau
Plaça Doctor Andreu.
((93) 418 58 79.

Otto Zutz
Carrer de Lincoln 15.
Map 3 A1.
((93) 238 07 22.

La Paloma
C/ Tigre 27. **Map** 2 F1.
((93) 301 68 97.

Torres de Ávila
Poble Espanyol, Avinguda M de Comillas. **Map** 1 A1.
((93) 424 93 09.

El Xampanyet
Carrer Montcada 22.
Map 5 B2.
((93) 319 70 03.

ROCK, JAZZ AND WORLD MUSIC

Antilla Cosmopolita
Carrer de Muntaner 244.
((93) 200 77 14.

La Boîte
Avinguda Diagonal 477.
((93) 419 55 50.

Harlem Jazz Club
Carrer de la Comtessa de Sobradiel 8.
((93) 310 07 55.

Zeleste
Carrer de Almogàvers 122.
Map 6 F2.
((93) 309 12 04.

FUNFAIRS

Parc d'Atraccions de Montjuïc
Map 1 C4.
((93) 441 70 24.

Tibidabo
((93) 211 79 42.

SPORTS

FC Barcelona
Nou Camp, Avinguda Aristides Maillol.
((93) 496 36 00.

EASTERN
SPAIN

Introducing Eastern Spain

EASTERN SPAIN covers an extraordinary range of climates and landscapes, from the snowbound peaks of the Pyrenees in Aragón to the beaches of the Costa Blanca and Costa Cálida, popular for their winter warmth and sunshine. The region has a wealth of historical sights including ancient monasteries near Barcelona, magnificent Roman ruins in Tarragona, Mudéjar churches and towers in Aragón and the great cathedrals of Valencia and Murcia. Away from the busy coasts, the countryside is often attractive but little visited.

Zaragoza

ARAGON
(see pp216–31)

Teruel

Ordesa National Park (see pp222–3) *in the Pyrenees has some of the most dramatic mountain scenery in Spain. It makes excellent walking country.*

Zaragoza (see pp226–7) *has many striking churches, especially the cathedral, the Basílica de Nuestra Señora del Pilar, and the Mudéjar-style Iglesia de la Magdalena.*

**VALEN
AND MU**
(see pp232

Valen

Valencia (see pp240–43) *is Spain's third largest city. It has an old centre of narrow streets overlooked by venerable houses and monuments, such as El Miguelete, the cathedral's conspicuous bell tower. The city hosts a spectacular festival, Las Fallas, in March.*

Murcia cathedral (see p252), *built in the 14th century, has a Baroque façade and belfry, and two ornate side chapels – one in late-Gothic style and the other Renaissance. In Murcia, you can also visit an elegant 19th-century gentlemen's club, the Casino.*

Alic

| 0 kilometres | 50 |
| 0 miles | 50 |

Murcia

◁ **The 12th-century monastery at Gerri de la Sal in Catalonia**

The Costa Brava (see pp206–207), stretching south from the French border, is a mix of cliffs, wooded coves and pretty beaches. Lloret de Mar is the busiest, most popular tourist resort on the coast.

Poblet (see pp212–13), enclosed by triple walls, is one of the most interesting medieval Cistercian monasteries in Catalonia. It contains a royal pantheon with the carved tombs of six of the kings of Aragón.

Tarragona (see pp214–15) was one of the most important cities in Roman Spain. Among its remains are an amphitheatre and an aqueduct. A statue of Roger de Llúria, the great 13th-century Catalan naval commander, overlooks the beach.

The Costa Blanca (see pp248–51) is an attractive coast, as well as a popular holiday destination. Calp is overshadowed by a huge rock, the Penyal d'Ifach. In La Vila Joiosa, a line of houses has been painted in striking colours to make them visible to sailors at sea.

Regional Food: Eastern Spain

THE MEDITERRANEAN CUISINE of the east coast has been enriched by centuries of foreign influence, from the Romans and the Moors especially. Olives, rice, oranges, almonds and saffron are combined with produce from the sea and the mountains. The varied cooking of Catalonia embraces sweet and savoury combinations, fish stews, snails and several classic sauces, like spicy *romesco* made from red peppers, tomatoes and chillies. High-quality fruit and vegetables, such as ñora peppers, grow on the fertile coastal plains of Valencia and Murcia. Paella is the best known of the many rice dishes of these two regions. The cold, dry, mountain air of Aragón is ideal for curing hams.

Ñora peppers

Amanida *is a Catalan salad that combines vegetables with cured meat or cheese, or some kind of fish or shellfish.*

Oranges *are the main crop of Valencia and Alicante. These two provinces are the world's biggest orange exporters; they also grow three-quarters of Spain's lemons. The tangy Valencia orange is used mainly for its juice; the sweet navel orange, which is easier to peel, is usually grown for eating. Many varieties of satsuma and clementine are also grown.*

Parrillada de mariscos *is an assortment of shellfish grilled on a barbecue and served with allioli (garlic mayonnaise).*

Prawns

Saffron rice

Mussels

Suquet, *one of the famous fish and shellfish stews of Catalonia, is made with saffron, wine, tomatoes and potatoes.*

Peppers

Paella, *a Valencian rice dish known the world over, is cooked in a large, shallow, two-handled pan, traditionally over an open fire. Short-grain Spanish rice, flavoured and perfumed with saffron, is simmered with a variety of colourful ingredients: seafood, chicken, rabbit, pork, tomatoes, peppers, and fresh and dried beans.*

Fideus a la cassola *is a dish of fideus (a kind of noodle) with red peppers, pork chops or fillet, and sausages.*

Butifarra amb mongetes *is a traditional Catalan dish of grilled black sausage with dried white beans.*

Cochifrito, *a simple peasant dish from Aragón, is prepared from lamb fried with lemon, garlic and paprika.*

Pollo al ajillo *is chicken grilled with garlic. It is served with a white wine or sherry sauce made with the juices of the chicken.*

Pastel de carne, *a Murcian pie of Middle Eastern origin, consists of minced meat and chopped boiled eggs in a puff pastry case.*

Llagosta i pollastre *is a typical Catalan combination of lobster with chicken in a tomato and hazelnut sauce.*

Crema catalana *is a rich egg custard with a golden brown layer of grilled sugar on top. It is served very cold.*

Pear

Apple

Cherry

Orange

Pumpkin

Candied fruits (frutas escarchadas) *are a popular way of preserving the abundant produce of the region. In Aragón they are often chocolate coated.*

Almendras garrapiñadas

Torta imperial

Almond sweets, *like* almendras garrapiñadas *(almonds coated in a crunchy sugar) and* torta imperial *(containing toasted almonds), were introduced to Spain by the Moors. Turrón comes in two main varieties: one white and hard and studded with whole nuts; the other made from a soft paste of ground almonds.*

Butifarra blanca

Butifarra negra   Chorizo

Fuet

SAUSAGES

Catalan sausages, especially those from the mountain town of Vic, are renowned. The white *butifarra* sausage contains pork, tripe and pine nuts, while the black variety uses blood, pork belly and spices. Both can be grilled or served with beans. The region produces many types of cured sausage, such as the firm, finely textured *llangonisseta*, and the long, dry *fuet*. The coarser, scarlet-coloured chorizo, particularly beloved of Aragón and Murcia, contains paprika, and can be sliced finely and eaten with bread, perhaps as a tapa, or served in stew or soup.

Wines of Eastern Spain

SPAIN'S EASTERN SEABOARD offers a wide spread of wines of different styles. Catalonia deserves pride of place, and here the most important region is Penedès, home of *cava* (traditional-method sparkling wine) and some high quality still wine. In Aragón, Cariñena reds can be good, and Somontano, in the Pyrenees, has fine, international-style varietals. Valencia and Murcia provide large quantities of easy-drinking reds, whites and *rosados* (rosés). Most notable among these are the rosés of Utiel-Requena, the Valencian Moscatels and the strong, full-bodied reds made in Jumilla.

Cabernet Sauvignon vines

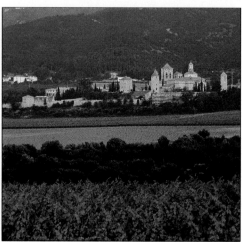

Monastery of Poblet and Las Murallas vineyards in Catalonia

Somontano has had remarkable success because of the COVISA company's cultivation of international grape varieties such as Chardonnay and Pinot Noir.

```
0 kilometres          100

0 miles          50
```

KEY FACTS ABOUT WINES OF EASTERN SPAIN

Location and Climate
The climate of Eastern Spain varies mainly with altitude – low-lying parts are hot and dry; it also gets hotter the further south you go. The wine regions of Catalonia have a Mediterranean climate along the coast, which becomes drier futher inland. The middle Penedès is a favoured location with a range of climates which suits many grape varieties. Somontano has a cooler, altitude-tempered climate. Valencia and Murcia can be, in contrast, unrelentingly hot.

Grape Varieties
The most common native red grape varieties planted in much of Eastern Spain are Garnacha, Tempranillo – which is called Ull de Llebre in Catalonia – Monastrell and Cariñena. Bobal makes both reds and, to a greater extent, rosés in Utiel-Requena. For whites, Catalonia has Parellada, Macabeo and Xarel·lo (the trio most commonly used for *cava*), while in Valencia, Merseguera and Moscatel predominate. In the regions furthest to the southeast, Airén and Pedro Ximénez are sometimes found. French grape varieties, such as Chardonnay, Merlot, Cabernet Sauvignon and Sauvignon Blanc, flourish in the regions of Penedès, Costers del Segre and Somontano.

Good Producers
Somontano: COVISA (Viñas del Vero), Viñedos del Altoaragón. *Alella:* Marqués de Alella, Parxet. *Penedès:* Codorníu, Conde de Caralt, Freixenet, Juvé y Camps, Masía Bach, Mont-Marçal, René Barbier, Miguel Torres. *Costers del Segre:* Castell del Remei, Raimat. *Priorato:* Cellers Scala Dei, Masía Barril. *Valencia:* Vicente Gandía. *Utiel-Requena:* C. Augusto Egli. *Alicante:* Gutiérrez de la Vega. *Jumilla:* Asensio Carcelén (Sol y Luna), Bodegas Vitivino.

CHARDONNAY

RAIMAT

Raimat is an estate near Lleida where the Raventós family produces a remarkable range of wines, such as a Chardonnay-based cava.

Barrel delivery in Cariñena, Aragón

TORRES.

Gran Coronas

Reserva 1985

Torres was one of the first Penedès firms to plant French grape varieties, like Cabernet Sauvignon.

KEY

☐	Campo de Borja, Calatayud and Cariñena
☐	Somontano
☐	Ampurdán-Costa Brava
☐	Alella
☐	Penedès
☐	Conca de Barberà
☐	Costers del Segre
☐	Tarragona and Terra Alta
☐	Priorato
☐	Valencia
☐	Utiel-Requena
☐	Alicante, Yecla and Jumilla

Utiel-Requena produces rosés as well as hearty reds, such as this one from Garnacha and Tempranillo grapes.

CASA LO ALTO

Jumilla's hilly vineyards are planted with the black Monastrell grape, which can produce highly concentrated, and sometimes sweet, reds.

SOL y LUNA

WINE REGIONS

Penedès, Catalonia's premier wine region produces a range of wines as well as *cava*, from delicate whites to beefy reds. Catalonia's smaller wine regions include Alella and Priorato. Two up-and-coming regions, situated inland, are Costers del Segre and Conca de Barberà. Aragón's leading wine region is Somantano, northeast of Zaragoza. Further south lie the extensive, bulk-producing vineyards of Valencia, Utiel-Requena, Alicante, and, in Murcia, Jumilla and Yecla.

Flowers of the Matorral

Yellow bee orchid

T HE MATORRAL, a scrubland rich in wild flowers, is the distinctive landscape of Spain's eastern Mediterranean coast. It is the result of centuries of woodland clearance, during which the native holm oak was felled for timber and to provide land for grazing and cultivation. Many colourful plants have adapted to the extremes of climate here. Most flower in spring, when hillsides are daubed with pink and white cistuses and yellow broom, and the air is perfumed by aromatic herbs such as rosemary, lavender and thyme. Buzzing insects feed on the abundance of nectar and pollen.

Spanish broom *is a small bush with yellow flowers on slender branches. The black seed pods split when dry, scattering the seeds on the ground.*

The century plant's flower stalk can reach 10 m (32 ft).

Rosemary

Jerusalem sage*, an attractive shrub which is often grown in gardens, has tall stems surrounded by bunches of showy yellow flowers. Its leaves are greyish-white and woolly.*

Rose garlic *has round clusters of violet or pink flowers at the end of a single stalk. It survives the summer as the bulb familiar to all cooks.*

FOREIGN INVADERS

Prickly pear in bloom

Several plants from the New World have managed to colonize the bare ground of the *matorral*. The prickly pear, thought to have been brought back by Christopher Columbus, produces a delicious fruit which can be picked only with thickly gloved hands. The rapidly growing century plant, a native of Mexico which has tough spiny leaves, sends up a tall flower shoot only when it is 10–15 years old, after which it dies.

Flowering shoots of the century plant

Common thyme *is a low-growing aromatic herb which is widely cultivated for use in the kitchen.*

The mirror orchid*, a small plant which grows on grassy sites, is easily distinguished from other orchids by the brilliant metallic blue patch inside the lip, fringed by brown hairs.*

Temp (°C)	Rainfall (mm)

J F M A M J J A S O N D

— Temperature   ▓ Rainfall

CLIMATE CHART

Most plants found in the *matorral* come into bloom in the warm, moist spring. The plants protect themselves from losing water during the dry summer heat with thick leaves or waxy secretions, or by storing moisture in bulbs or tubers.

WILDLIFE OF THE MATORRAL

The animals which live in the *matorral* are most often seen early in the morning, before the temperature is high. Countless insects fly from flower to flower, providing a source of food for birds. Smaller mammals, such as mice and voles, are active only at night when it is cooler and there are few predators around.

Holm oaks are very common in Eastern Spain. The leaves are tough and rubbery to prevent water loss.

The strawberry tree is an evergreen shrub with glossy serrated leaves. Its inedible strawberry-like fruit turns red when ripe.

Tree heather

Grey-leaved cistus, growing on sunny sites, has crumpled petals and bright yellow anthers.

Narrow-leaved cistus exudes a sticky aromatic gum used in perfumes.

Star clover is a low-growing annual whose fruit develops into a star-shaped seed head. Its flowers are often pale pink.

Ladder snakes feed on small mammals, birds and insects. The young are identified by a black pattern like the rungs of a ladder, but adults are marked with two simple stripes.

Scorpions hide under rocks or wood by day. When disturbed, the tail is curled quickly over the body in a threatening gesture. The sting, lethal to small animals, can cause some irritation to humans.

The Dartford warbler, a skulking bird which has a dark plumage and a cocked tail, sings melodiously during its mating display. Males are more vividly coloured than females.

The swallow-tail butterfly is one of the most conspicuous of the great many insects living in the matorral. *Bees, ants and grasshoppers are also extremely common.*

CATALONIA

LLEIDA · ANDORRA · GIRONA
BARCELONA PROVINCE · TARRAGONA

CATALONIA *is a proud nation-within-a-nation which was once, under the count-kings of Barcelona-Aragón, one of the Mediterranean's great sea powers. It has its own semi-autonomous regional government and its own language, Catalan, which has all but replaced Spanish in place names and on road signs throughout the region.*

The Romans first set foot on the Iberian Peninsula at Empúries on Catalonia's Costa Brava ("wild coast"). They left behind them great monuments, especially in and around Tarragona, the capital of their vast province of Tarraconensis. Later, Barcelona emerged as the region's capital, economically and culturally important enough to rival Madrid.

In the 1960s the Costa Brava became one of Europe's first mass package-holiday destinations. Although resorts such as Lloret de Mar continue to draw the crowds, former fishing villages such as Cadaqués remain relatively unspoiled on this naturally attractive coast.

Inland, there is a rich artistic heritage to be explored. Catalonia has several spectacular monasteries, especially Montserrat, its spiritual heart, and Poblet. There are also many medieval towns, such as Montblanc, Besalú and Girona – which contain a wealth of monuments and museums.

In the countryside there is a lot to seek out, from the wetland wildlife of the Río Ebro delta to the vineyards of Penedès (where most of Spain's sparkling wine is made). In the high Pyrenees rare butterflies brighten remote mountain valleys, and little hidden villages encircle exquisite Romanesque churches.

Fruit trees in blossom near Balaguer, in the province of Lleida

◁ A fisherman inspects his nets in Cadaqués on the Costa Brava

Exploring Catalonia

CATALONIA INCLUDES a long stretch of the Spanish Pyrenees, whose green, flower-filled valleys hide picturesque villages with Romanesque churches. The Parc Nacional d'Aigüestortes and Vall d'Aran are paradises for naturalists, while Baqueira-Beret offers skiers reliable snow. Sun-lovers can choose between the rugged Costa Brava or the long sandy stretches of the Costa Daurada. Tarragona is rich in Roman monuments. Inland are the monasteries of Poblet and Santes Creus and the well-known vineyards of Penedès.

Isolated houses in the countryside around La Seu d'Urgell

KEY

🟫 Motorway

▬ Major road

▭ Minor road

▬ Scenic route

〜 River

🌿 Viewpoint

GETTING AROUND

The motorway from France enters Eastern Spain at La Jonquera and, from Barcelona, follows the coast via Tarragona to Valencia. More motorways radiate from Barcelona. A tunnel near Puigcerdà has made the central Catalan Pyrenees easily accessible. Buses, more frequent in summer, connect most towns. The main north–south railway hugs the coast from Blanes south-wards. Other lines run from Barcelona through Vic, Lleida and Tortosa.

Pau, Toulouse

① VALL D'ARAN
VIELHA ②
③ BAQUEIRA-BERET
④
⑤ PARC NACIONAL D'AIGÜESTORTES
VALL DE BOÍ

LA SEU D'URGELL

TREMP

SOLSONA

② LLEIDA
Zaragoza

POBLET ②
MONTBLANC ②
SANTES C ②

TARRAGONA ③
CAMBRILS   SALOU ②
COSTA DAURADA

TORTOSA ③

②
DELTA DE L'EBRE
● SANT CARLES DE LA RÀPITA

Valencia

SEE ALSO

- *Where to Stay* pp545–7

- *Restaurants and Bars* pp586–8

Church on the
seafront of Sitges

Vineyards outside Gandesa, west of Tarragona

SIGHTS AT A GLANCE

The Vall d'Aran, surrounded by the snow-capped mountains of the Pyrenees

BUTTERFLIES OF THE VALL D'ARAN

A huge variety of butterflies and moths is found high in the mountains and valleys of the Pyrenees. In particular, the isolated Vall d'Aran is the home of several unique and rare subspecies. The best time of year to see the butterflies is between May and July.

Grizzled Skipper
(Pyrgus malvae)

Checkered Skipper
(Carterocephalus palaemon)

Clouded Apollo
(Parnassius mnemosyne)

Vall d'Aran ❶

Lleida. 🚍 *Vielha.* 🚶 *Vielha (973) 64 01 10.*

THIS VALLEY OF VALLEYS – *aran* means valley – is a beautiful 600-sq km (230-sq mile) haven of forests and flower-filled meadows, surrounded by towering mountain peaks.

The Vall d'Aran was formed by the Riu Garona, which rises in the area and flows out to France as the Garonne. With no proper link to the outside world until 1924, when a road was built over the Bonaigua Pass, the valley was cut off from the rest of Spain for most of the winter. Snow still blocks the narrow pass from November to April, but today access is easy through the Túnel de Vielha from El Pont de Suert.

The fact that the Vall d'Aran faces north means that it has a climate similar to that found on the Atlantic coast. Many rare wild flowers and butterflies flourish in the perfect conditions created by the damp breezes and shady slopes. It is also a noted habitat for many species of narcissus.

Tiny villages have grown up beside the Riu Garona, often around Romanesque churches, notably at **Bossòst**, **Salardú**, **Escunhau** and **Arties**. The valley is also ideal for outdoor sports such as skiing and is popular with walkers.

Vielha ❷

Lleida. 🚶 *2,300.* 🚍 🚶 *Carrer Sarriulera 10, (973) 64 01 10.* 🔄 *Thu.* 🎉 *Fiesta de Vielha (8 Sep).*

NOW A MODERN SKI RESORT, the capital of the Vall d'Aran preserves relics of its medieval past. The Romanesque church of **Sant Miquel** has an octagonal bell tower, a tall, pointed roof and a superb wooden 12th-century crucifix, the *Mig Aran Christ.* It once formed part of a larger carving, since lost, which represents the Descent from the Cross. The **Museu de la Vall d'Aran** is a museum devoted to Aranese history and folklore.

🏛 **Museu de la Vall d'Aran**
Carrer Major 26. 📞 *(973) 64 18 15.*
🕐 *Jul – mid-Sep: daily; mid-Sep – Jun: Tue – Sun.*
⬛ *public hols.* ♿ 📷

Mig Aran Christ (12th-century), Sant Miquel church, Vielha

Baqueira-Beret ❸

Lleida. 🏨 100. 🚗 ℹ️ *Baqueira,*
(973) 64 44 55. 🎭 *Romeria de*
Nuestra Señora de Montgarri (2 Jul).

THIS EXTENSIVE ski resort, one of the best in Spain, is popular with both the public and the Spanish royal family. There is reliable winter snow cover and a choice of over 40 pistes at altitudes from 1,520 m to 2,470 m (4,987 ft to 8,104 ft).

Baqueira and Beret were separate mountain villages before skiing became popular, but they have now merged to form a single resort. The Romans took full advantage of the thermal springs located here, which are nowadays appreciated by tired skiers.

Vall de Boí ❹

Lleida. 🚗 *La Pobla de Segur.*
🚌 *El Pont de Suert.* ℹ️ *Barruera,*
(973) 69 40 18.

THIS SMALL VALLEY on the edge of the Parc Nacional d'Aigüestortes is dotted with tiny villages, many of which are built around magnificent Catalan Romanesque churches.

Dating from the 11th and 12th centuries, these churches are distinguished by their tall belfries, such as the six-storey bell tower of the **Església de Santa Eulàlia** at Erill-la-Vall.

The two churches at Taüll, **Sant Climent** *(see p20)* and **Santa Maria**, have superb frescoes. Between 1919 and 1923 the originals were taken for safekeeping to the Museu Nacional d'Art de Catalunya in Barcelona *(see p168)* and replicas now stand in their place. You can climb the towers of Sant Climent for superb views of the surrounding countryside.

Other churches in the area worth visiting include those at **Coll**, for its fine ironwork, **Barruera**, and **Durro**, which has another massive bell tower.

At the head of the valley is the hamlet of **Caldes de Boí**, popular for its thermal springs and ski facilities. It is also a good base for exploring the Parc Nacional d'Aigüestortes, the entrance to which is only 5 km (3 miles) from here.

The tall belfry of Sant Climent church at Taüll in the Vall de Boí

Parc Nacional d'Aigüestortes ❺

Lleida. 🚗 *La Pobla de Segur.*
🚌 *El Pont de Suert, La Pobla de Segur.*
ℹ️ *Barruera, (973) 69 40 18.*

THE PRISTINE mountain scenery of Catalonia's only national park *(see pp26–7)* is among the most scenically spectacular in the Pyrenees.

Established in 1955, the park covers 10,230 hectares (25,280 acres). Its full title is Parc Nacional d'Aigüestortes i Estany de Sant Maurici, named after the lake *(estany)* of Sant Maurici in the east and the Aigüestortes (literally, twisted waters) area in the west. The main village is the mountain settlement of Espot, on the park's eastern edge. Dotted around the park are waterfalls and the sparkling, clear waters of around 150 lakes and tarns which, in an earlier era, were scoured by glaciers to depths of up to 50 m (164 ft).

The finest scenery is around Sant Maurici lake, which lies beneath the twin shards of the Sierra dels Encantats, (Mountains of the Enchanted). From here, there is a variety of walks, particularly along the string of lakes that lead north to the towering peaks of Agulles d'Amitges. To the south is the dramatic vista of Estany Negre, the highest and deepest tarn in the park.

Early summer in the lower valleys is marked by a mass of pink and red rhododendrons, while later in the year wild lilies bloom in the forests of fir, beech and silver birch.

The park is also home to a variety of wildlife. Chamois (also known as izards) live on the mountain screes and in the meadows, while beavers and otters can be spotted by the lakes. Golden eagles nest on mountain ledges, and grouse and capercaillie are found in the woods.

During the summer the park is popular with walkers, while in winter, the snow-covered mountains are ideal for cross-country skiing.

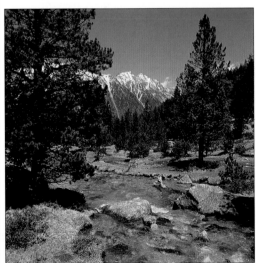

A crystal-clear stream, Parc Nacional d'Aigüestortes

THE CATALAN LANGUAGE

Catalonia's national emblem

Catalan has now fully recovered from the ban it suffered under Franco's dictatorship and has supplanted Castilian (Spanish) as the language in everyday use all over Catalonia. Spoken by more than eight million people, it is a Romance language akin to the Provençal of France. Previously it was suppressed by Felipe V in 1717 and only officially resurfaced in the 19th century, when the Jocs Florals (medieval poetry contests) were revived during the rebirth of Catalan literature. A leading figure of the movement was the poet Jacint Verdaguer (1845–1902).

Andorra ❻

Principality of Andorra. 🏘 58,000. 🚌 Andorra la Vella. 🛈 Pl de la Rotonda, Andorra la Vella, (07-376) 82 71 17.

ANDORRA OCCUPIES 464 sq km (179 sq miles) of the Pyrenees between France and Spain. In 1993, it became fully independent and held its first ever democratic elections. Since 1278, it had been an autonomous feudal state under the jurisdiction of the Spanish bishop of La Seu d'Urgell and the French Count of Foix (a title adopted by the President of France). These are still the ceremonial joint heads of state.

Andorra's official language is Catalan and its currency the peseta, though French and Castilian are also spoken and French francs are accepted.

For many years Andorra has been a tax-free paradise for shoppers, a fact reflected in the crowded shops and supermarkets of the capital **Andorra la Vella**. Les Escaldes (near the capital), as well as Sant Julià de Lòria and El Pas de la Casa, (the towns nearest the Spanish and French borders), have also become shopping centres.

Most visitors never see Andorra's rural charms, which match those of other parts of the Pyrenees. The region is excellent for walkers. One of the main routes leads to the **Cercle de Pessons**, a bowl of lakes in the east, and past Romanesque chapels such as **Sant Martí** at La Cortinada. In the north is the picturesque Sorteny valley where traditional farmhouses have been converted into snug restaurants.

La Seu d'Urgell ❼

Lleida. 🏘 11,000. 🚌 🛈 Parc del Segre, (973) 36 00 92. 🛒 Tue & Sat. 🎉 Fiesta Mayor (last week of Aug).

THIS ANCIENT Pyrenean town was made a bishopric by the Visigoths in the 6th century. Feuds between the bishops of Urgell and the Counts of Foix over land ownership led to the emergence of Andorra in the 13th century.

The 12th-century **cathedral** has a much venerated Romanesque statue of Santa Maria d'Urgell. The **Museu Diocesà** contains medieval works of art and manuscripts, including a 10th-century copy of St Beatus of Liébana's *Commentary on the Apocalypse* (see p106).

🏛 Museu Diocesà
Bisbe 1. 🕿 (973) 26 86 28. 🕙 Mon–Sat. ⬤ public hols. 🎫

Carving, La Seu d'Urgell cathedral

Puigcerdà ❽

Girona. 🏘 6,500. 🚌 🚏 🛈 Pl de l'Ajuntament, (972) 88 05 42. 🛒 Sun. 🎉 Fiesta del Lago (third Sun of Aug).

PUIG IS CATALAN for hill. Although Puigcerdà sits on a relatively small hill compared with the encircling mountains, which rise to 2,900 m (9,500 ft), it nevertheless has a fine view right down the beautiful Cerdanya valley, watered by the trout-filled Riu Segre.

Puigcerdà, very close to the French border, was founded in 1177 by Alfonso II as the capital of Cerdanya, an important agricultural region, which shares a past and its culture with the French Cerdagne. The Spanish enclave of **Llívia**, an attractive little town with a medieval pharmacy, lies 6 km (3.5 miles) inside France.

Cerdanya is the largest valley in the Pyrenees. At its edge is the nature reserve of **Cadí-Moixeró**, which has a population of alpine choughs.

Portal of Monestir de Santa Maria

Ripoll ❾

Girona. 🏘 12,000. 🚌 🚏 🛈 Plaça Abat Oliva, (972) 70 23 51. 🛒 Sat. 🎉 Sant Eudald (11–12 May).

ONCE A TINY mountain base from which raids against the Moors were made, Ripoll is now best known for the **Monestir de Santa Maria**, built in AD 888. The town has been called "the cradle of Catalonia" as the monastery was both the power base and cultural centre of Guifré el Pilós (Wilfred the Hairy), founder of the 500-year dynasty of the House of Barcelona. He is buried in the monastery.

In 1032, under Abbot Oliva, the huge west portal gained a superb series of intricate carvings, which are perhaps the finest Romanesque carvings in Spain. They depict historical and evangelical tales as well as biblical scenes. The two-storey cloister is the only other part of the original monastery to have survived wars and anti-clerical purges. The rest is a 19th-century reconstruction.

The medieval town of Besalú on the banks of the Riu Fluvià

Sant Joan de les Abadesses ⓿

Girona. 🏛 3,800. 🚌 🛈 Passeig Comte Guifré, (972) 72 05 99. 🚍 Sun. 📷 Fiesta Mayor (second week of Sep).

A FINE, 12th-century Gothic bridge arches over the Riu Ter to this unassuming market town, whose main attraction is its **monastery**.

Founded in AD 885, it was a gift from Guifré, first count of Barcelona, to his daughter, the first abbess. The peaceful church is unadorned except for a superb wooden calvary, *The Descent from the Cross*. Made in 1150, it looks almost modern; part of it, a thief, was burnt in the Civil War and replaced with such skill that it is hard to tell which section is new. The monastery's museum has a series of Baroque and Renaissance altarpieces.

12th-century calvary, Sant Joan de les Abadesses monastery

ENVIRONS: To the north is **Camprodon**, a small town full of grand houses, and shops selling local produce. The region is especially noted for its *llonganisses* (sausages).

Olot ⓫

Girona. 🏛 2,700. 🚌 🛈 Bisbe Lorenzana 15, (972) 26 01 41. 🚍 Mon. 📷 Corpus Christi (May/Jun), Fiesta del Tura (8 Sep).

T HIS SMALL MARKET TOWN is at the centre of a landscape pockmarked with the conical hills of extinct volcanoes. But it was an earthquake in 1474 which last disturbed the town, destroying its medieval past.

During the 18th century the town's textile industry spawned the "Olot School" of art: finished cotton fabrics were printed with drawings, and in 1783 the Public School of Drawing was founded.

Much of the school's work, which includes sculpted saints and paintings such as Joaquim Vayreda's *Les Falgueres*, is in the **Museu Comarcal de la Garrotxa**, housed in an 18th-century hospice. There are also pieces by *Modernista* sculptor Miquel Blay, whose damsels support the balcony at No. 38 Passeig Miquel Blay.

⛫ Museu Comarcal de la Garrotxa
Edifici Hospici 8. 📞 (972) 27 91 30. ⭕ Wed–Mon. 🌀 ⛁

Besalú ⓬

Girona. 🏛 2,100. 🚌 🛈 Plaça de la Llibertat 1, (972) 59 12 40. 🚍 Tue. 📷 Sant Vicenç (22 Jan), Fiesta Mayor (last weekend of Sep).

A MAGNIFICENT medieval town, with a striking approach across a fortified bridge over the Riu Fluvià, Besalú has two fine churches. These are the Romanesque **Sant Vicenç** and **Sant Pere**, the sole remnant of Besalú's Benedictine monastery. It was founded in AD 948, but pulled down in 1835 leaving a big, empty square.

In 1964 a **mikvah**, a ritual Jewish bath, was discovered by chance. It was built in 1264 and is one of only three of that period to survive in Europe. The tourist office has the keys to all the town's attractions.

To the south, the sky-blue lake of **Banyoles**, where the 1992 Olympic rowing contests were held, is ideal for picnics.

Sausage shop in the mountain town of Camprodon

GIRONA TOWN CENTRE

Banys Arabs ②
Cathedral ④
Centre Bonastruc Ça Porta ⑦
Església de Sant Feliu ③
Església de Sant Pere de
    Galligants ①
Museu d'Art ⑤
Museu d'Història
    de la Ciutat ⑥

KEY

P Parking

0 metres   250
0 yards   250

Girona ⑬

Girona. 🚶 75,000. ✈ 🚌 🚉 🛈
*Rambla de la Llibertat 1, (972) 22 65
75.* 🗓 *Tue, Sat.* 🎭 *El Pedal (last fortnight of Sep), San Narciso (29 Oct).*

THIS HANDSOME TOWN puts
on its best face beside the
Riu Onyar, where tall, pastel-
coloured buildings rise above
the water. Behind them, in
the old town, the Rambla de
la Llibertat is lined with busy
shops and street cafés.

The houses were built in the
19th century to replace sections of the city wall damaged
during a seven-month siege
by French troops in 1809. Most
of the rest of the ramparts, first
raised by the Romans, are still

intact and have been turned
into the **Passeig Arqueològic**
(Archaeological Walk), which
runs right around the city.

The starting point of the
walk is on the north side of
the town, near the **Església
de Sant Pere de Galligants**
(St Peter of the Cock Crows).
The church now houses the
city's archaeological collection.

From here a narrow street into the old part of town passes
through the north gate, where
huge Roman foundation stones
are still visible. They mark the
route of the Via Augusta, the
important road which originally ran from Tarragona to
Rome. The most popular place
of devotion for the people of
Girona is the **Església de**

Sant Feliu, which brims with
history. The church, begun in
the 14th century, was built
over the tombs of St Felix and
St Narcissus, both patrons of
the city. Next to the high altar
are eight Roman sarcophagi
embedded in the apse wall.

Despite their name, the
nearby **Banys Arabs** (Arab
Baths), lit by a fine octagonal
lantern, were built in the late
12th century, about 300 years
after the Moors had left.

🏛 Centre Bonastruc Ça
Porta

Carrer de Sant Llorenç. 📞 *(972) 21
67 61.* 🕐 *Tue–Sun.* 🎟
Amid the maze of alleyways
and steps in the old town is
the former, partially restored,
Jewish quarter of El Call. The
Centre Bonastruc Ça Porta
gives a history of Girona's
Jews, who were expelled in
the late 15th century after
being forced into a ghetto.

🔯 Cathedral
The style of Girona Cathedral's
solid west face is pure Catalan
Baroque, but the rest of the
building is Gothic. The single
nave, built in 1416 by Guillem
Bofill, is the widest Gothic
span in Christendom. Behind
the altar is a marble throne
known as "Charlemagne's
Chair" after the Frankish king

Painted houses crowded along the bank of the Riu Onyar in Girona

whose troops took Girona in 785. In the chancel is a 14th-century jewel-encrusted silver and enamel altarpiece, the best example in Catalonia. Among the fine Romanesque paintings and statues in the cathedral's museum are a 10th-century illuminated copy of St Beatus of Liébana's *Commentary on the Apocalypse*, and a 14th-century statue of the Catalan king, Pere the Ceremonious.

The collection's most famous item is a tapestry, called *The Creation*, decorated with lively figures. The rich colours of this large 11th- to 12th-century work are well preserved.

Tapestry of *The Creation*

🏛 Museu d'Art
Pujada de la Catedral 12. 📞 (972) 20 95 36. ◯ Tue–Sun. 🗲 ♿
This former episcopal palace is one of Catalonia's best art galleries, with items ranging from the Romanesque period to the 20th century. The many items from churches destroyed through war or neglect give an idea of the richness of church interiors long ago. Highlights are carvings and a silver-clad altar of the 10th century from the church at Sant Pere de Rodes. A 12th-century beam from Cruïlles is painted with humorous figures of monks.

🏛 Museu d'Història de la Ciutat
Carrer de la Força 27. 📞 (972) 22 22 29. ◯ Tue–Sun.
The city's history museum is housed in an 18th-century former convent. Parts of the convent's cemetery are pre-served, including the recesses where the bodies of members of the Capuchin Order were placed while decomposing. The collection includes scientific items and old *sardana* (*see p215*) instruments.

Figueres ⓮

Girona. 🏘 35,000. 🚉 🚌 🛈 *Plaça del Sol, (972) 50 31 55.* 🅰 *Thu.* 🎉 *Santa Cruz (3 May), San Pedro (29 Jun).*

FIGUERES is in the north of the Empordà (Ampurdán) region, the fertile plain that sweeps inland from the Gulf of Roses. Every Thursday, the market here fills with fruit and vegetables from the area.

The **Museu de Joguets** (Toy Museum) is housed on the top floor of the old Hotel de Paris, on the Rambla, Figueres' main street. Inside are exhibits from all over Catalonia. At the lower end of the Rambla is a statue of Narcís Monturiol i Estarriol (1819–85), claimed to be the inventor of the submarine.

A much better-known son of the town is Salvador Dalí, who founded the **Teatro-Museo Dalí** in 1974. The most visited museum in Spain after the Prado, it is an entertaining place occupying Figueras's old main theatre. Its roof has an eye-catching glass dome. Not all the work shown is by Dalí, and none of his best-known works are here. But the whole

***Rainy Taxi*, a monument in the garden of the Teatro-Museo Dalí**

place, ranging from *Rainy Taxi* – a black Cadillac being sprayed by a fountain – to the Mae West Room, with furnishings made to look like a huge face, is a monument to the man who, fittingly, is buried here.

🏛 Museu de Joguets
Rambla. 📞 (972) 50 45 85. ◯ Wed–Mon. ● Feb. 🗲
🏛 Teatro-Museo Dalí
Plaça Gala-Salvador Dalí. 📞 (972) 51 18 00. ◯ Tue–Sun. ● 1 Jan, 25 Dec. 🗲

THE ART OF DALÍ

Salvador Dalí e Domènech was born in Figueres in 1904 and mounted his first exhibition at the age of 15. After studying at the Escuela de Bellas Artes in Madrid, and dabbling with Cubism, Futurism and Metaphysical painting, the young artist embraced Surrealism in 1929, becoming the movement's best-known painter. Never far from controversy, the self-publicist Dalí became famous for his hallucinatory images – such as *Woman-Animal Symbiosis* – which he described as "hand-painted dream photographs". Dalí's career also included writing and film-making, and established him as one of the 20th century's greatest artists. He died in his home town in 1989.

Ceiling fresco in the Wind Palace Room, Teatro-Museo Dalí

Empúries ⓯

Girona. 🚌 *L'Escala.* 📞 *(972) 77 02 08.* 🕐 *daily.* 🎫 *for ruins.*

THE EXTENSIVE ruins of the Greco-Roman town of Empúries (Ampurias) occupy an imposing site beside the sea. Three separate settlements were built between the 7th and 3rd centuries BC: the old town (known to archaeologists as Palaiapolis); the new town (Neapolis), and the Roman town, which was founded by Julius Caesar in 49 BC.

The **old town** (Palaiapolis) was founded by the Greeks in 600 BC as a trading port. It was built on what was then a small offshore island, and is now the site of the tiny walled hamlet of Sant Martí de Empúries.

Around 550 BC this was re-placed by a larger colony on the shore – the new town – which the Greeks named Emporion ("trading place"). In 218 BC, the Romans landed at Empúries and built a city next to the new town. From here they began their subjugation of the peninsula *(see p46)*.

Excavations in the **Greek new town** have uncovered several temples, including one to Asklepios, the god of healing. On the main street are the remains of the agora (meeting place), and floor mosaics. A museum nearby exhibits some finds from the site, although the best are now in the Museu Arqueològic of Barcelona *(see p168)*. The extensive **Roman town** was located on the hill behind the museum. So far excavations have revealed the ruins of two villas and a forum.

An excavated Roman pillar in the ruins of Empúries

Looking south along the Costa Brava from Tossa de Mar

Cadaqués ⓰

Girona. 🏘 *2,000.* 🚌 ℹ️ *Carrer Cotxe 2, (972) 25 83 15.* 🕐 *Mon.* 🎉 *Santa Esperanza (18 Dec).*

THIS PRETTY, whitewashed resort, overlooked by the large Baroque **Església de Santa Maria**, is the most easterly in the country. In the 1960s it was dubbed "Spain's St Tropez", largely because of the young crowd which sought out Salvador Dalí in the nearby unspoiled creek of Portlligat.

The **Centre d'Art Perrot-Moore** contains fine examples of Dalí's work, some excellent Picassos, and a room dedicated to contemporary artists.

🏛 Centre d'Art Perrot-Moore

Carrer Vigilant 1. 📞 *(972) 25 82 31.* 🕐 *daily.* 🎫 ♿

Tossa de Mar ⓱

Girona. 🏘 *3,500.* 🚌 ℹ️ *Avinguda Pelegri 25, (972) 34 01 08.* 🕐 *Thu.* 🎉 *Fiesta de Verano (29 Jun).*

AT THE END of a tortuous corniche, the Roman town of Turissa is one of the prettiest places along the Costa Brava. Above the modern town is the **Vila Vella** (old town), a protected national monument. The medieval walls, which have three towers, enclose fishermen's cottages, a 14th-century church and countless bars.

Within the old town is the **Museu Municipal**. This collection of local archaeological finds and modern art includes

The Flying Violinist, by the 20th-century Russian artist Marc Chagall.

🏛 Museu Municipal

Plaça Roig y Soler. 📞 *(972) 34 07 09.* 🕐 *Tue–Sun.* 🌑 *25 Dec.* 🎫

Blanes ⓲

Girona. 🏘 *26,000.* 🚌 ℹ️ *Plaça de Catalunya 21, (972) 33 03 48.* 🚌 *Mon.* 🎉 *Santa Ana (24–6 Jul).*

THE WORKING PORT of Blanes has one of the longest beaches on the Costa Brava, but the highlight of the town is the **Jardí Botànic Mar i Murtra**. These fine gardens, designed by the German Karl Faust in 1928, are spectacularly sited above cliffs. There are 7,000 species of Mediterranean and tropical plants here, in particular African cacti.

🌿 Jardí Botànic Mar i Murtra

Passeig Karl Faust 10. 📞 *(972) 33 08 26.* 🕐 *daily.* 🌑 *Sat before Easter & 24 Dec.* 🎫

A few of the many species of cacti, Jardí Botànic Mar i Murtra

The Costa Brava

THE COSTA BRAVA ("wild coast") runs for some 200 km (125 miles) from Blanes northwards to the region of Empordà (Ampurdán), which borders France. It is a mix of pine-backed sandy coves, golden beaches and crowded, modern resorts. The busiest resorts – Lloret de Mar, Tossa de Mar and La Platja d'Aro – are to the south. Sant Feliu de Guíxols and Palamós are still working towns behind the summer rush. Just inland there are medieval villages to explore, such as Peralada, Peratallada and Pals. Wine, olives and fishing were the mainstays of the area before the tourists came in the 1960s.

Cadaqués retains an air of seclusion as it is accessible only by a steep road. It has an arty air and its small, stony beaches remain unspoiled and less crowded than others.

Roses lies at the head of a sweeping bay. Its sandy beach, the longest on the Costa Brava, has become a mecca for lovers of water sports.

L'Escala is a small resort, popular mainly with local tourists. It has fine beaches and a small port where fishing nets dry in the sun.

L'Estartit is a good base for the Illes Medes, a former pirates' lair, which now form a marine reserve with clear waters perfect for skin diving.

Begur is a hilltop town just inland. It has good views of the coast, and small coves are tucked at its feet.

Palamós is a working port with modern hotels to the south, and secluded beaches and coves lapped by clear water to the north.

Lafranc, a whitewashed resort, with a promenade leading to neighbouring Calella, is one of the coast's most pleasant resorts.

La Platja d'Aro's long and sandy beach is lined with modern hotel blocks. It is one of the most popular resorts on the coast.

Tossa de Mar has a golden beach and a small cove beneath the fortified old town.

0 kilometres   10

0 miles   5

Lloret de Mar has more hotels than anywhere else on the coast. But there are unspoiled beaches nearby, such as Santa Cristina.

Monestir de Montserrat ⑲

The "SERRATED MOUNTAIN" (*mont serrat*), its highest peak rising to 1,236 m (4,055 ft), is a magnificent setting for Catalonia's holiest place, the Monastery of Montserrat, which is surrounded by chapels and hermits' caves. The monastery was first mentioned in the 9th century, enlarged in the 11th century, and in 1409 became independent of Rome. In 1811, when the French attacked Catalonia in the War of Independence *(see p59)*, the monastery was destroyed and the monks killed. Rebuilt and repopulated in 1844, it was a beacon of Catalan culture during the Franco years. Today Benedictine monks live here.

A Benedictine monk

The Old Museum displays a collection of liturgical items brought from the Holy Land.

Plaça de Santa Maria
The focal points of the square are two wings of the Gothic cloister built in 1477. The modern monastery façade is by Françesc Folguera.

Plaça de la Creu   **Gothic cloister**

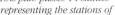

The New Museum has a collection of 19th- and 20th-century Catalan paintings and many Italian works.

The Way of the Cross
This path passes 14 statues representing the stations of the Cross. It begins near the Plaça de l'Abat Oliba.

View of Montserrat
The complex includes shops, cafés and a hotel. Funicular railways take visitors from the Plaça de la Creu to the Cova Santa and the hermitage of Sant Joan.

STAR FEATURES

★ **Basilica Façade**

★ **Black Virgin**

★ **Basilica Façade**
Agapit and Venanci Vallmitjana sculpted Christ and the apostles on the basilica's Neo-Renaissance façade. It was built in 1900 to replace the Plateresque façade of the original church, consecrated in 1592.

VISITORS' CHECKLIST

Montserrat (Barcelona province). ☎ (93) 835 02 51. 🚠 Aeri de Montserrat, then cable car. 🚌 from Barcelona. **Basilica** ◯ 9am–7:30pm Mon–Sat, 8am–7:30pm Sun. ✝ throughout the day, from 9am Mon–Fri, from 7:30am Sat, from 8am Sun & religious hols. & **Old Museum** ◯ 10:30am–2pm daily. ● 6–31 Jan. **New Museum** ◯ 3–6pm daily. ● 6–31 Jan. 📷 & ⊞

★ **Black Virgin**
La Moreneta looks down from behind the altar. Protected behind glass, her wooden orb protrudes for pilgrims to touch.

Basilica Interior
The sanctuary in the domed basilica is adorned by a richly enamelled altar and paintings by Catalan artists.

The Escolania is the famous choir of 50 boy choristers, who sing twice a day in the basilica.

Terminus for cable car from Aeri de Montserrat railway station

THE VIRGIN OF MONTSERRAT

The small wooden statue of La Moreneta (the dark one) is the soul of Montserrat. It is said to have been made by St Luke and brought here by St Peter in AD 50. Centuries later, the statue is believed to have been hidden from the Moors in the nearby Santa Cova (Holy Cave). Carbon dating suggests, however, that the statue was carved around the 12th century. In 1881 Montserrat's Black Virgin became patroness of Catalonia.

The blackened Virgin of Montserrat

Inner Courtyard
On one side of the courtyard is the baptistry (1902), with sculptures by Charles Collet. Pilgrims may approach the Virgin through a door to the right.

Vic ⑳

Barcelona. 🏠 30,000. 🚉 🚌 🛈
Plaça Major 1, (93) 886 20 91. 🛋
Tue & Sat. 🎪 *Mercat del Ram (Sat before Easter), Sant Miquel (5–15 Jul).*

MARKET DAYS – Tuesdays and Saturdays – are the best time to go to this small country town. This is when the excellent local sausages *(embotits)*, for which the area is renowned, are piled high in the large Gothic Plaça Major, along with other produce from the surrounding plains.

In the 3rd century BC Vic was the capital of an ancient Iberian tribe, the Ausetans. The town was then colonized by the Romans – the remains of a Roman temple survive today. Since the 6th century the town has been a bishop's see. In the 11th century, Abbot Oliva commissioned the El Cloquer tower, around which the cathedral was built in the 18th century. The interior of the cathedral is covered with vast murals by Josep Maria Sert (1876–1945). They are painted in reds and golds, and represent scenes from the Bible.

Adjacent to the cathedral is the **Museu Episcopal de Vic**, which has one of the best collections of Romanesque artifacts in Catalonia. Its large display of mainly religious art and relics includes bright, simple murals and wooden sculptures from rural churches. Also on display are 11th- and 12th-century frescoes and some superb altar frontals.

Cardona dominating the surrounding area from its hilltop site

🏛 **Museu Episcopal**
Plaça Bisbe Oliva. 🎫 *(93) 886 22 14.*
⭕ *daily.* 📷

Cardona ㉑

Barcelona. 🏠 6,200. 🚉 🛈 *Avinguda Rastrillo, (93) 869 27 98.* 🛋 *Sun.*
🎪 *Fiesta Mayor (second Sun of Sep).*

THE 13TH-CENTURY ruddy-stoned castle of the Dukes of Cardona, constables to the crown of Aragón, is set on the top of a hill. The castle was rebuilt in the 18th century and is now a luxurious parador *(see p534).* Beside the castle is an elegant early 11th-century church, the **Església de Sant Vicenç**, where the Dukes of Cardona are buried.

The castle gives views of the town below and of the Montanya de Sal (Salt Mountain), a huge salt deposit beside the Riu Cardener which has been mined since Roman times.

Twelfth-century altar frontal, Museu Episcopal de Vic

Solsona ㉒

Lleida. 🏠 6,500. 🚌 🛈 *Avinguda Pont, (973) 48 23 10.* 🛋 *Tue & Fri.*
🎪 *Carnival (late Feb); Corpus Christi (May/Jun); Fiesta Mayor (8–10 Sep).*

NINE TOWERS and three gateways remain of Solsona's moated fortifications. Inside the walls is an ancient town of noble mansions. The cathedral houses a beautiful black stone Virgin. The adjoining **Museu Diocesà i Comarcal** contains Romanesque paintings, and local archaeological finds.

🏛 **Museu Diocesà i Comarcal**
Plaça Palau 1. 🎫 *(973) 48 21 01.*
⭕ *Tue–Sun.* ⬤ *1 Jan & 25 Dec.* ♿

Lleida ㉓

Lleida. 🏠 120,000. 🚉 🚌 🛈
Avinguda de Madrid 36, (973) 27 09 97. 🛋 *Thu & Sat.* 🎪 *Sant Anastasi (11 May), Sant Miquel (29 Sep).*

DOMINATING Lleida (Lérida), the capital of Catalonia's only landlocked province, is **La Suda**, a large, ruined fort taken from the Moors in 1149. The old cathedral, **La Seu Vella**, founded in 1203, is situated within the walls of the fort, high above the town. It was transformed into barracks by Felipe V in 1707 but today, sadly, is desolate, the haunt of pigeons. It remains imposing, however, with magnificent Gothic windows in the cloister.

A lift descends from the Seu Vella to the Plaça de Sant Joan in the town below. This square is at the mid-point of a busy, pedestrianized shopping street that sweeps round the foot of the hill. The new cathedral is here, as are manorial buildings such as the reconstructed 13th-century town hall, the **Paeria**.

Poblet 24

See pp212–13.

Montblanc 25

Tarragona. 6,000. *Muralla Santa Tecla 24, (977) 86 12 32. Fri. Fiesta Mayor (8 Sep).*

THE MEDIEVAL grandeur of Montblanc lives on within its walls, which are considered to be Catalonia's finest piece of military architecture. At the **Sant Jordi** gate, St George allegedly slew the dragon. The **Museu Comarcal de la Conca de Barberà** has interesting displays on local crafts.

Museu Comarcal de la Conca de Barberà
Carrer Josa 6. *(977) 86 03 49. Tue–Sun.*

Santes Creus 26

Tarragona. 100. *Plaça de Sant Bernard, (977) 63 83 01. Sat & Sun. Sta Llúcia (13 Dec).*

HOME TO THE the prettiest of the "Cistercian triangle" monasteries is the tiny village of Santes Creus. The other

two, Vallbona de les Monges and Poblet (*see pp212–13*), are nearby. The **Monestir de Santes Creus** was founded in 1150 by Ramon Berenguer IV (*see p50*) during his reconquest of Catalonia. The Gothic cloisters are decorated with figurative sculptures, a style first permitted by Jaime II, who ruled from 1291 to 1327. His finely carved tomb, along with that of other nobles, is in the 12th-century church. The austerity of the interior is relieved by a beautiful rose window.

Monestir de Santes Creus
(977) 63 83 29. Tue–Sun.

Vilafranca del Penedès 27

Barcelona. 28,500. *Carrer Cort 14, (93) 892 03 58. Sat. Fiesta Mayor (29–31 Aug).*

THIS BUSY MARKET town is set in the heart of Catalonia's main wine-producing region (*see pp192–3*). The **Museu del Vi** (Wine Museum), in the 14th-century palace of the kings of Aragón, documents the long history of the area's wine trade. Local bodegas can be visited for wine tasting.

Eight km (5 miles) to the north is **Sant Sadurní**, the capital of Spain's sparkling wine, *cava* (*see pp576–7*).

Museu del Vi
Plaça Jaume I. *(93) 890 05 82. Tue–Sun.*

Anxaneta climbing to the top of a tower of casteller

CATALONIA'S FIESTAS

Human Towers (*various dates and locations*). The province of Tarragona is famous for its *castellers* festivals, where teams of men stand on each others' shoulders in an effort to build the highest human tower. Each tower, which can be up to seven storeys high, is topped by a small boy called the *anxaneta*. *Castellers* can be seen in action in many towns, especially Vilafranca del Penedès and Valls.

Dance of Death (*Maundy Thu*), Verges (Girona). Men dressed as skeletons perform a macabre dance.

St George's Day (*23 Apr*). Lovers give each other a rose and a book on the day of Catalonia's patron saint. The book is in memory of Cervantes, who died on this day in 1616.

La Patum (*Corpus Christi, May/Jun*), Berga (Barcelona province). Giants, devils and bizarre monsters parade through the town.

Midsummer's Eve (*23 Jun*). Celebrated all over Catalonia with bonfires and fireworks.

Monestir de Santes Creus, surrounded by poplar and hazel trees

Monestir de Poblet ㉔

THE MONASTERY OF SANTA MARIA DE POBLET is a haven of tranquillity and a resting place of kings. It was the first and most important of three sister monasteries, known as the "Cistercian triangle" *(see p211)*, that helped to consolidate power in Catalonia after it had been recaptured from the Moors by Ramon Berenguer IV. During the 1835 Carlist revolution, the abbey was plundered and seriously damaged by fire. Restoration of the impressive ruins, now largely complete, began in 1930 and monks returned in 1940.

The dormitory is reached by stairs from the church. The vast 87-m (285-ft) gallery dates from the 18th century. Half of it is still in use by the monks.

The 13th-century refectory is a vaulted hall with an octagonal fountain and a pulpit.

View of Poblet
The abbey, its buildings enclosed by fortified walls that have hardly changed since the Middle Ages, is in an isolated valley near the Riu Francolí's source.

Museum

Wine cellar

Library
The Gothic scriptorium was converted into a library in the 17th century, when the Duke of Cardona donated his book collection.

Former kitchen

Royal doorway   **Royal palace**

TIMELINE

1157 Founding of sister monastery at Vallbona de les Monges		*Royal tombs*		
	14th century Main cloister finished		**1812** Poblet desecrated by French troops	
1168 Santes Creus founded – third abbey in Cistercian triangle		**1479** Juan II, last king of Aragón, buried here		**1940** Monks return

1100	1300	1500	1700	1900

1196 Alfonso II is the first king to be buried here	**1336–87** Reign of Pere the Ceremonious, who designates Poblet a royal pantheon		**1953** Tombs reconstructed. Royal remains returned
1151 Poblet monastery founded by Ramon Berenguer IV		**1788–1808** Reign of Carlos IV, who has main reredos installed	**1835** Disentailment *(p59)* of monasteries. Poblet ravaged

Chapterhouse
This perfectly square room, with slender columns, has tiers of benches for the monks. It is paved with the tombstones of 11 abbots who died between 1393 and 1693.

Parlour cloister

San Esteban cloister

New sacristy

The Abbey Church, large and unadorned, with three naves, is a typical Cistercian building.

Baroque church façade

★ **Cloisters**
The evocative, vaulted cloisters were built in the 12th and 13th centuries and were the centre of monastic life. The capitals are beautifully decorated with carved scrollwork.

VISITORS' CHECKLIST

Off N240, 10 km (6 miles) from Montblanc. ☎ (977) 87 00 89. 🚌 L'Espluga de Francolí, then taxi. 🅿 🕐 10am–12:30pm, 3–5:30pm (6pm Jun–Sep) daily. ⬤ 25 Dec. 📷 ✝ 8am & 6pm Mon–Sat; 8:30am, 10am, 1pm & 6pm Sun. 🚫

★ **High Altar Reredos**
Behind the stone altar, supported by Romanesque columns, an impressive alabaster reredos fills the apse. It was carved by Damià Forment in 1527.

★ **Royal Tombs**
The tombs in the pantheon of kings were begun in 1359. In 1950 they were reconstructed by the sculptor Frederic Marès.

STAR FEATURES

★ High Altar Reredos

★ Royal Tombs

★ Cloisters

Palm trees lining the waterfront at Sitges

Sitges ❷❽

Barcelona. 🏘 *15,000.* 🚃 🚌 🏛
Carrer Sinia Morera 1, (93) 811 76 30.
🛒 *every other Thu.* 🎉 *Fiesta Mayor
(23–24 Aug).*

Lively bars line the seafront at Sitges which is popular with both locals and foreigners. Modernista artist Santiago Rusiñol (1861–1931) spent much time here. He bequeathed his eclectic collection of wrought-iron ceramics, sculptures and paintings to the **Museu Cau Ferrat**, which also has works by El Greco.

🏛 **Museu Cau Ferrat**
Carrer Fonollar. 📞 *(93) 894 03 64.*
☐ *Tue–Sun.* ● *public hols.* 🎟

Costa Daurada ❷❾

Tarragona. 🚃 🚌 *Calafell, San Vicente,
Salou.* 🏛 *Tarragona, (977) 23 34 15.*

The entire coast of Tarragona province is known as the Costa Daurada, the Golden Coast, because of its long, sandy beaches. **Vilanova i la Geltrú** and **El Vendrell** are two of the many ports along it that are still active. The **Museu Pau Casals** in El Vendrell is dedicated to the famous cellist.

Port Aventura, south of Tarragona, is one of Europe's largest theme parks. Its exotically-inspired attractions are named Mediterrània, México,

China, Polynesia and Wild West. **Salou** and **Cambrils** to the south are the liveliest resorts – the others are mostly low-key, family holiday places.

🏛 **Museu Pau Casals**
Avinguda Palfuriana 59–61. 📞 *(977)
68 34 68.* ☐ *Tue–Sun.* 🎟 ♿

🎢 **Port Aventura**
Autovía Salou–Vila-seca. 📞 *(977) 77
90 00.* ☐ *Apr–Oct.* 🎟 ♿

Tarragona ❸❶

Tarragona. 🏘 *75,000.* ✈ 🚃 🚌
🏛 *Carrer Fortuny 4, (977) 23 34 15.*
🛒 *Tue & Thu.* 🎉 *Santa Tecla (23 Sep).*

Tarragona is now a major industrial port with a large petrochemical industry, but it also preserves many remnants of its Roman past. It was then the capital of Tarraconensis. The Romans chose it as their base for the conquest of the peninsula, which began in the 3rd century BC *(see pp46–7).*

The avenue of Rambla Nova ends abruptly above the sea on the clifftop Balcó de Europa, from which the extensive ruins of the **Anfiteatro Romano** can be seen. Within them is the ruined 12th-century church of **Santa María del Miracle**.

Nearby is the Praetorium, a Roman tower that was converted into a palace in medieval times. It is sometimes known as the Castell de Pilato (named after Pontius Pilate), and it now houses the **Museu de la Romanitat**. This displays Roman and medieval finds, and gives access to the cavernous passageways of the excavated Roman circus, built

The remains of the Roman amphitheatre, Tarragona

in the 1st century AD. Adjoining the Praetorium is the **Museu Nacional Arqueològic,** containing the most important collection of Roman artifacts in Catalonia. It has a large collection of bronze implements, stone busts and beautiful mosaics, including the *Head of Medusa*.

Among the most impressive Roman remains in the city are the gigantic stones built into the Roman wall. An archaeological walk runs along a 1-km (1,100 yds) long stretch of the wall and its towers.

Behind it is the 12th-century **cathedral**, built on the site of a Roman temple to Jupiter and a subsequent Arab mosque. The structure evolved over many centuries, as seen from the harmonious blend of styles of the exterior. Inside is an alabaster altarpiece of St Tecla carved by Pere Johan in 1434. The large 13th-century cloister, which is filled with orange trees, has early Gothic vaulting, but the doorway is Romanesque in its geometric decoration.

In the west of town is a 3rd-to 6th-century Christian cemetery (ask about opening times in the archaeological museum). Some of the carved sarcophagi, in the site museum were originally used as pagan tombs.

ENVIRONS: The well-preserved **Aqüeducte de les Ferreres** lies just outside the city, next to the A7 motorway. (There is a lay-by for viewing.) This 2nd-century aqueduct was built to bring water to the city from the Riu Gaià, 30 km (19 miles) to the north. The **Arc de Berà**, a 1st-century triumphal arch on the Via Augusta, is 20 km (12 miles) northeast on the N340.

🏛 **Museu Nacional Arqueològic de Tarragona**
Plaça del Rei 5. 📞 *(977) 23 62 09.*
⭕ *Tue –Sun.* 🚫 ♿
🏛 **Museu de la Romanitat**
Plaça del Rei. 📞 *(977) 24 19 52.*
⭕ *Tue –Sun.* 🚫

Tortosa ③

Tarragona. 🏠 *30,000.* 🚉 *Plaça Bimil·lenari, (977) 51 08 22.* 🚌 *Mon.* 🎉 *Nuestra Señora de la Cinta (first week of Sep).*

A RUINED CASTLE and medieval walls are clues to Tortosa's historical importance. Sited at the lowest crossing point on the Riu Ebre (Río Ebro), it has been strategically significant since Iberian times. The Moors held the city from the 8th century until 1148. The old Moorish castle, known as La Zuda, is all that remains of their defences. It has now been renovated as a parador *(see p547)*. The Moors also built a mosque in 914. Its foundations were later used for the present cathedral, on which work began in 1347. Although it was not completed for two centuries, the style is pure Gothic.

Tortosa was badly damaged in 1938–39 during one of the fiercest battles of the Civil War *(see pp62–3)*, when the Ebre formed the front line between the opposing forces.

Ruins of the Palaeo-Christian Necropolis

Delta de L'Ebre ④

Tarragona. 🚉 *Aldea.* 🚌 *Deltebre, Aldea.* 🛈 *Deltebre (977) 48 96 79.*

T HE DELTA of the Riu Ebre is a prosperous rice-growing region and wildlife haven. Some 70 sq km (27 sq miles) have been turned into a nature reserve, the **Parc Natural del Delta de L'Ebre**. In Deltebre there is an information centre and an interesting **Eco-Museu**, with an aquarium containing species found in the delta.

The main towns in the area are **Amposta** and **Sant Carles de la Ràpita**, both of which serve as good bases for exploring the reserve.

The best sites for seeing the huge variety of wildlife are along the shore, from the Punta del Fangar in the north to the Punta de la Banya in the south. Everywhere is accessible by car except Illa de Buda. Flamingoes breed on this island and, along with other water birds such as black-winged stilts, herons and avocets, can be seen from tourist boats that leave from Riumar and Deltebre.

🏛 **Eco-Museu**
Carrer Martí Buera 22. 📞 *(977) 48 96 79.* ⭕ *daily.* ⬤ *25 Dec.* ♿

THE SARDANA

Catalonia's national dance is more complicated than it appears. The success of the Sardana depends on all of the dancers accurately counting the complicated short- and long-step skips and jumps, which accounts for their serious faces. Music is provided by a *cobla*, an 11-person band consisting of a leader playing a three-holed flute *(flabiol)* and a little drum *(tabal)*, five woodwind players and five brass players. When the music starts dancers join hands and form circles. The Sardana is performed during most local fiestas *(see p211)* and at special day-long gatherings called *aplecs*.

A group of Sardana dancers captured in stone

ARAGÓN

HUESCA · TERUEL · ZARAGOZA

STRETCHING ALMOST HALF *the length of Spain, and bisected by the Ebro, one of the country's longest rivers, Aragón takes in a wide variety of scenery, from the snow-capped summits of Ordesa National Park in the Pyrenees to the dry plains of the Spanish interior. This largely unsung and undervisited region contains magnificent Mudéjar architecture and many unspoiled medieval towns.*

From the 12th–15th centuries Aragón was a powerful kingdom, or, more accurately, a federation of states, including Catalonia. In its heyday, in the 13th century, its dominions stretched across the Mediterranean as far as Sicily. By his marriage to Isabel of Castile and León in 1469, Fernando II of Aragón paved the way for the unification of Spain.

After the Reconquest, Muslim architects and craftsmen were treated more tolerantly here than elsewhere, and they continued their work in the distinctive Mudéjar style, building with elaborate brickwork and patterned ceramic decoration. Their work can be seen in churches all over Aragón and there are outstanding examples in the cities of Teruel and the capital, Zaragoza, Spain's fifth largest city, which stands on the banks of the Ebro.

The highest peaks of the Pyrenees lie in Huesca province. Some of the region's finest sights are in the Pyrenean foothills, which are crossed by the Aragonese variation of the pilgrims' route to Santiago de Compostela. Probably the most spectacular of them is the monastery of San Juan de la Peña – half-concealed beneath a rock overhang – which was founded in the 9th century.

The climate of the region varies as much as the landscape: winters can be long and harsh and summers hot.

A view of the rooftops and medieval walls of Daroca

◁ Torla village church, on the edge of Ordesa National Park

Exploring Aragón

THE LANDSCAPES OF ARAGON range from the high Pyrenees, north of Huesca, through the desiccated terrain around Zaragoza to the forested hills of Teruel province. The cities of Teruel and Zaragoza have some of the most striking Mudéjar monuments in Spain. There are many small, picturesque preserved towns in the region. Ordesa National Park contains stunning mountain scenery, but it can only be visited fully after the snow melts in spring, and even then much of it has to be explored on foot. Pretty Los Valles offers less dramatic but

Stone carving, San Juan de la Peña equally enjoyable landscapes and is a popular tourist destination. Other attractive places include the impressively sited Castillo de Loarre and Monasterio de San Juan de la Peña, and the waterfalls of Monasterio de Piedra.

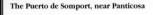

The Puerto de Somport, near Panticosa

SIGHTS AT A GLANCE

3 Lourdes
3 PUERTO DE SOMPORT

4 PARQUE NACIONAL DE ORDESA

N260

7 JACA

ONASTERIO DE SAN
UAN DE LA PEÑA

N260

UERO
10
CASTILLO
DE LOARRE

5 BENASQUE

N230

6 AINSA

11 HUESCA

12 ALQUÉZAR

N240

BARBASTRO

14 GRAUS
13 SANTUARIO DE
TORRECIUDAD

MONZÓN

Flumen

A129

A131

A230

SARIÑENA

A131

Cinca

N240

A140

Noguera Ribagorzana

Lleida

A2

N232

NII

BUJARALOZ

NII

FRAGA

A2

CHITE

HIJAR

N211

A223

N232

ALCAÑIZ

22

CASPE

A221

A225

N211

A225

VALDERROBRES **23**

CANTAVIEJA

RRA DE GUDAR

0 kilometres 20

0 miles   20

A RUBIELOS

GETTING AROUND

Zaragoza is linked by motorway to the Basque Country, Navarra, Madrid and Barcelona. Major roads link the region's main cities with each other, and Teruel with Valencia. Many minor roads have been improved and may be fast and uncongested in the flatter, central areas. But expect progress in the mountainous areas to be slowed down by herds of cattle, ice in winter or meltwater floods in spring. The principal railway lines run from Zaragoza to Madrid, Barcelona and Valencia. Coaches are infrequent, except between the main population centres. Zaragoza has a small international airport.

KEY

	Motorway
	Major road
	Minor road
	Scenic route
	River
☀	Viewpoint

lencia

Mudéjar tower of Tarazona cathedral

The town hall, Sos del Rey Católico

Sos del Rey Católico ❶

Zaragoza. 🏛 1,000. 🚗 🛈 Plaza de la Villa 1, (948) 88 80 65. 🚌 Fri. 🎉 San Esteban (third week of Aug).

FERNANDO OF ARAGON – the so-called "Catholic King" who married Isabel of Castile, thereby uniting Spain (see pp52–3) – was born in this small town in 1452, hence its distinguished royal name.

The **Palacio de Sada**, the king's reputed birthplace, with a beautiful inner courtyard, is among the town's grandest stone mansions. It stands in a small square amid a maze of narrow cobbled streets.

At the top of the town are the stumpy remnants of a castle and the **Iglesia de San Esteban**. The church's ancient font and carved capitals are noteworthy, as are the 13th-century frescoes in two of the crypt's apses. From both the castle and the church there are magnificent views over the surrounding hills.

The Gothic-arched **Lonja** (commodities exchange) and the 16th-century **town hall** (ayuntamiento) are located on the adjacent main square.

ENVIRONS: The "Cinco Villas" are five towns recognized by Felipe V for their loyalty during the War of the Spanish Succession (see p58). Sos del Rey Católico is the most appealing of these. The others are Ejea de los Caballeros, Tauste, Sábada and **Uncastillo**. This last town, 20 km (12 miles) to the southeast, has a fortress and a Romanesque church, the Iglesia de Santa María.

Los Valles ❷

Huesca. 🚉 Jaca. 🚌 from Jaca to Hecho. 🛈 Plaza Condes Xiquena, Hecho, (974) 37 53 29.

THE DELIGHTFUL VALLEYS of Ansó and Hecho, formed by the Veral and Aragón Subordán rivers respectively, were isolated until recently due to poor road links. Their villages have retained traditional customs and a local dialect called cheso, which is passed down from parents to children. Now the area's crafts and costumes have made it popular with tourists, especially in summer. The Pyrenean foothills and pine forests above the valleys are particularly good for walking, fishing and cross-country skiing.

Ansó lies in the prettiest valley, which becomes a shadowy gorge where the Río Veral and the road next to it squeeze between vertical crags and through rock tunnels. Many of its buildings have stone façades and steep, tiled roofs. In the Gothic church (16th century) there is a museum dedicated to local costume.

Hecho is host to an open-air festival of modern sculpture. Previous years' exhibits lie scattered around the village. The bucolic village of **Siresa**, which contains the 11th-century church of San Pedro, lies to the north of Hecho.

Puerto de Somport ❸

Huesca. 🚉 Somport. 🛈 Canfranc, (974) 37 30 29.

JUST INSIDE THE BORDER with France, the Somport Pass was for centuries a strategic crossing point for the Romans and Moors, and for medieval pilgrims en route to Santiago de Compostela (see pp78–9). Today the austere scenery is specked with holiday apartments built for skiing. **Astún** is modern and well organized, while **El Formigal**, to the east, is a stylish, purpose-built resort with long, gentle runs for beginners. Non-skiers can enjoy the scenery around the Panticosa gorge. **Sallent de Gállego** is popular for rock-climbing and fishing.

Steep, tiled roofs of Hecho, with a typical pepperpot chimney

Rough and craggy landscape around Benasque

Parque Nacional de Ordesa **4**

See pp222–3.

Benasque **5**

Huesca. **14** 1,100. **1** Calle de San Pedro, (974) 55 12 89. **2** Tue. **3** San Marcial (30 Jun–6 Jul).

TUCKED AWAY IN THE northeast corner of Aragón, at the head of the Esera valley, the village of Benasque presides over a ruggedly beautiful stretch of Pyrenean scenery. Although the village has expanded greatly to meet the holiday trade, a sympathetic use of wood and stone has resulted in buildings which complement the existing older houses. A stroll through the old centre filled with aristocratic mansions is a delight.

The most striking buildings in Benasque are the 13th-century **Iglesia de Santa María Mayor**, and the **Palacio de los Condes de Ribagorza**. The latter has a Renaissance façade.

Above the village rises the Maladeta massif. There are magnificent views from its ski slopes and hiking trails. Several local mountain peaks, including **Posets** and **Aneto**, exceed 3,000 m (9,800 ft).

ENVIRONS: For walkers, skiers and climbers, the area around Benasque has a great deal to offer, for all levels of ability.

The neighbouring resort of **Cerler** was developed with care from a rustic village into a popular base for skiing and other winter sports.

At Castejón de Sos, 15 km (9 miles) south of Benasque, the road passes through the **Congosto de Ventamillo**, a scenic rocky gorge.

Ainsa **6**

Huesca. **14** 1,000. **1** Cruce de Carreteras, (974) 51 00 03. **2** Tue. **3** San Sebastián (20 Jan).

THE CAPITAL of the kingdom of Sobrarbe in medieval times, Ainsa has retained its charm. The Plaza Mayor, a broad cobbled square, is surrounded by neat terraced arcades of brown stone. On one side stands the shapely belfry of the **Iglesia de Santa María** – consecrated in 1181 – and beyond, old streets lead up to the restored castle.

Jaca **7**

Huesca. **14** 14,000. **1** Avda Regimento de Galicia 2, (974) 36 00 98. **2** Fri. **3** La Victoria (first Fri of May), Santa Orosia (late Jun).

JACA DATES BACK as far as the 2nd century AD. In the 8th century the town bravely repulsed the Moors – an act which is commemorated in the festival of La Victoria – and in 1035 became the first capital of the kingdom of Aragón. Jaca's 11th-century **cathedral**, one of Spain's oldest, is much altered inside. Traces of its original splendour can be seen on the restored south porch and doorway, where carvings depict biblical scenes involving Isaac and David. The dim nave and chapels are decorated with ornate vaulting and sculpture. A museum of sacred art, in the cloisters, contains a collection of Romanesque and Gothic frescoes and sculptures from local churches. The streets that surround the cathedral form an attractive quarter.

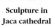

Sculpture in Jaca cathedral

Jaca's only other significant tourist sight is its 16th-century **citadel**, a fort decorated with corner turrets, on the edge of town. Today the town serves as a principal base for the Aragonese Pyrenees.

The arcaded main square of Ainsa with the Iglesia de Santa María

Parque Nacional de Ordesa ❹

Pirineo
Aragonés

Parque Nacional Ordesa y Monte Perdido

Valle de Ordesa →

← Valle de Bujaruelo

Signpost in Ordesa National Park

WITHIN ITS BORDERS the Parque Nacional de Ordesa y Monte Perdido combines all the most dramatic elements of Spain's Pyrenean scenery. At the heart of the park are four glacial canyons – the Ordesa, Añisclo, Pineta and Escuain valleys – which carve the great upland limestone massifs into spectacular cliffs and chasms. Most of the park is accessible only on foot: even then, snow during autumn and winter makes it inaccessible to all, except those with specialist climbing equipment. In high summer, however, the crowds testify to the park's well-earned reputation as a paradise for walkers and nature lovers alike.

Valle de Ordesa
The Río Arazas cuts through foreste limestone escarpments, providing some of Ordesa's most popular walk

Torla
This village, at the gateway to the park, huddles beneath the forbidding slopes of Mondarruego. With its core of cobbled streets and slate-roofed houses around the church, Torla is a popular base for visitors to Ordesa.

PYRENEAN WILDLIFE

Spanish Ibex

Ordesa is a spectacle of flora and fauna, with many of its species unique to the region. Trout streams rush along the valley floor, where slopes provide a mantle of various woodland harbouring all kinds of creatures, including otters, marmots and capercaillies (large grouse). On the slopes, flowers burst out before the snow melts, with gentians and orchids sheltering in crevices and edelweiss braving the most hostile crags. Higher up, the Pyrenean chamois is still fairly common; but the unique Ordesa ibex, or mountain goat, is now becoming scarce and is a protected species. The rocky pinnacles above are the domain of birds of prey.

Spring gentian (*Gentiana verna*)

El Taillón
Brecha Roland
3,144 m (10,315 ft)
Gruta de Casteret
Mondarruego
2,848 m (9,344 ft)
VALLE DE ORD
Cascada Torromboteral
SIERRA DE LAS C
Torla
BIESCAS
Broto
Oto
Sarvisé
Jalle
AINSA

0 kilometres 2
0 miles 2

KEY

Major road
Minor road
Footpath
Spanish/French border
National park boundary
ℹ Tourist information
Viewpoint

View from Parador de Bielsa
The parador (see p548), at the foot of Monte Perdido, looks out at stunning sheer rock faces streaked by waterfalls.

VISITORS' CHECKLIST

ℹ️ *Visitors' centre, 9 km (5.5 miles) north of Torla on road to Valle de Ordesa, (974) 24 33 61.*
🚌 *Change at Sabiñánigo for Torla.* 🚂 *Sabiñánigo.*

[map labels:]
Perdido
Parador de Bielsa
55 m
008 ft)
VALLE DE PINETA
Cinca
BIELSA
Refugio de Góriz
SIERRA DE LAS TUCAS
Cascada
Cola de Caballo
de Soaso
Vellos
CAÑON DE AÑISCLO
GARGANTA DE ESCUAIN
Revilla
Escuaín
BIELSA
Tella
Nerín
Bestué
Puértolas
Vellos

Cola de Caballo
The 70-m (230-ft) "Horse's Tail" waterfall makes a scenic stopping point near the northern end of the long hike around the Circo Soaso. It provides a taste of the spectacular scenery found along the route.

Hikers in Ordesa National Park

TIPS FOR WALKERS

Several well-marked trails follow the valleys and can be easily tackled by anyone reasonably fit, though walking boots are a must. The mountain routes may require climbing gear so check first with the visitors' centre and get a detailed map. Pyrenean weather changes rapidly – beware of ice and snow early and late in the season – but in case of need there are several *refugios*, which provide basic overnight shelter.

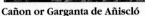

Cañon or Garganta de Añascló
A wide path leads along this beautiful, steep-sided gorge, following the wooded course of the turbulent Río Vellos through dramatic limestone scenery.

Royal
pantheon

Lower
church

Capilla de
San Victorián

Cloister

Residential
quarters

Upper church

Capilla
de San
Voto

Monasterio de San Juan de la Peña ❽

Huesca. 【 (974) 36 25 21. ◯ mid-
Oct – mid-Mar: Wed – Sun; mid-Mar –
mid-Oct: daily. ◐ public hols in winter.

SET UNDER a bulging rock, this monastery, founded in the 9th century, was an early guardian of the legendary Holy Grail *(see p240)*. In the 11th century it underwent reformation in Cluniac style, and was the first monastery to introduce the Latin Mass in Spain.

After a fire in the 17th century, was abandoned in favour of a newer one further up the hillside. This was later sacked by Napoleon's troops, although the Baroque façade survives.

The church of the old monastery is on two storeys. The lower one is a primitive rock-hewn crypt built in the early 10th century. The upper storey contains an 11th-century church with a simple triple

apse hollowed out of the side of the cliff. The well-preserved Romanesque pantheon contains the neatly stacked tombs of the early Aragonese kings. The exterior cloister is San Juan de la Peña's *pièce de résistance*, the capitals of its columns splendidly carved with biblical scenes.

Agüero ❾

Huesca. 🏠 169. 🚏 Plaza Mayor 1,
(974) 38 04 98. 🎆 San Roque
(15–19 Aug).

THE PICTURESQUE setting of this attractive village, clustered against a dramatic crag of eroded pudding stone, amply rewards a brief detour from the main road. The most important reason for visiting Agüero, however, is to see

the 12th-century **Iglesia de Santiago**. This Romanesque church is reached by a long stony track leading uphill just before the village.

The capitals of the columns in this unusual triple-naved building are carved with fantastical beasts as well as scenes from the life of Jesus and the Virgin Mary. The beautiful carvings on the doorway display biblical events, including scenes from the Epiphany

and Salome dancing ecstatically. The lively, large-eyed figures are attributed to the mason responsible for the superb carvings in the monastery at San Juan de la Peña.

Castillo de Loarre ❿

Loarre (Huesca). 【 (974) 38 26 27.
🚍 Ayerbe. 🚌 from Huesca.
◯ Tue – Sun. ◐ Dec.

THE RAMPARTS of this sturdy, imposing fortress stand out majestically above the road approaching from Ayerbe. It is so closely moulded around the contours of a rock that at night or in poor visibility it could be mistaken for a natural outcrop. On a clear day, the hilltop setting is stupendous, with magnificent views of the surrounding orchards and reservoirs of the Ebro plain. Inside the stout curtain walls

Village of Agüero, situated under a rocky crag

lies a complex founded in the 11th century on the site of a Roman castle. It was later re-modelled under Sancho I (Sancho Ramírez) of Aragón, who established a religious community here, placing the complex under the rule of the Order of St Augustine.

Within the castle walls is a Romanesque church which is decorated with alabaster windows, a chequered frieze and interesting carved column capitals. Its crypt contains the remains of St Demetrius.

Sentry paths, iron ladders and flights of steps ramble precariously around the castle's towers, dungeons and keep.

Huesca ⓫

Huesca. 👥 45,000. 🚉 🚌 🛈 Calle Coso Alto 23, (974) 22 57 78. 🗓 Mon, Tue & Thu. 🎉 San Vicente (22 Jan), San Lorenzo (9–15 Aug).

Altarpiece by Damià Forment, in Huesca cathedral

FOUNDED IN THE 1st century BC, the independent state of Osca (present-day Huesca) had a senate and an advanced education system. From the 8th century, the area grew into a Moorish stronghold. In 1096 it was captured by Peter of Aragón and was the region's capital until 1118, when the title passed to Zaragoza.

Huesca is now the provincial capital. The pleasant old town has a Gothic **cathedral**. The eroded west front is surmounted by an unusual wooden gallery in Mudéjar style. Above the nave is slender-ribbed star vaulting studded with golden bosses. The cathedral's best feature is an alabaster altarpiece by the master sculptor,

The formidable Castillo de Loarre looming above the surrounding area

Damià Forment. On the altarpiece, a series of energetic Crucifixion scenes in relief are highlighted by illumination.

Opposite the cathedral is the Renaissance **town hall** (*ayuntamiento*). Inside hangs *La Campana de Huesca*, a gory 19th-century painting depicting the town's most memorable event: the beheading of a group of troublesome nobles in the 12th century by order of King Ramiro II.

The massacre occurred in the Sala de la Campana of the 17th-century university. This now houses the superb **Museo Arqueológico Provincial**, containing archaeological finds and a collection of art, including Gothic frescoes and early Aragonese works.

🏛 Museo Arqueológico Provincial
Plaza de la Universidad. 📞 (974) 22 05 86. 🕙 Tue–Sun. ⬤ public hols. 🎟

Alquézar ⓬

Huesca. 👥 300. 🛈 Calle de la Iglesia, (974) 31 80 67. 🎉 San Sebastián (21 Jan).

THIS MOORISH VILLAGE attracts much attention because of its spectacular setting. Its main monument, the stately 16th-century **collegiate church**, dominates a hill jutting above the strange rock formations of the canyon of the Río Vero. Inside, the church's cloisters have capitals carved with biblical scenes. Next to it is the chapel built after Sancho I recaptured Alquézar from the Moors. Nearby are the ruined walls of the original alcazar, which gives the village its name.

Santuario de Torreciudad ⓭

Huesca. 📞 (974) 30 40 25. 🚌 to El Grado from Barbastro. 🕙 daily. ♿

THIS SHRINE was built in memory of the founder of the Catholic lay order of Opus Dei – José María Escrivá de Belaguer – who died in 1975. It occupies a high promontory, with picturesque views over the turquoise waters of the **Embalse de El Grado** at Torreciudad. The huge church is made of angular red brick in a stark, modern design.

Inside, the elaborate modern altarpiece of white marble, sheltering a glittering Romanesque Virgin, is in contrast to the bleak, functional nave.

ENVIRONS: The small town of **Barbastro**, which lies 20 km (12 miles) to the south, has an arcaded *plaza mayor* and a 16th-century cathedral with an altar by Damià Forment.

The ruins of Alquézar castle, rising above the village

Houses with frescoed façades on the Plaza de España, Graus

Graus **⓮**

Huesca. 👥 3,300. 🚌 ℹ️ Plaza de
España 15, (974) 54 00 02. 🚍 Mon.
🎉 Santo Cristo and San Vicente
(13–14 Sep).

CONCEALED IN THE HEART of
Graus's old town lies the
unusual **Plaza de España**, surrounded by brick arcades and
brightly frescoed half-timbered
houses. One of these was the
home of the infamous Tomás
de Torquemada, the Inquisitor
General (see p52). The old
quarter, with its narrow streets,
is best explored on foot. At
fiesta time, this small town is
a good place to see typical
Aragonese dancing.

ENVIRONS: About 20 km (12
miles) northeast, the hill village
of **Roda de Isábena** has the
smallest cathedral in Spain.
Dating from 1067, this striking
building has a 12th-century
cloister off which is a chapel
with 13th-century frescoes.
North of the village is the
picturesque Isábena valley.

Tarazona **⓯**

Zaragoza. 👥 11,000. 🚌 ℹ️ Calle
Iglesia 5, (976) 64 00 74. 🚍 every
other Thu. 🎉 San Agustín (28 Aug),
San Atilano (5 Oct).

MUDEJAR TOWERS stand high
above the earth-coloured,
mottled pantiles of this ancient
bishopric. On the outskirts of
the old town is the **cathedral**,
all turreted finials and pierced
brickwork with Moorish cloister tracery and Gothic tombs.
In the upper town on the

other side of the river, more
churches, in typical Mudéjar
style, can be found amid the
maze of narrow hilly streets.
More unusual perhaps are the
former bullring, now a circular
plaza enclosed by houses, and
the splendid Renaissance **town
hall** (ayuntamiento). The
town hall, built of golden
stone, has a façade carved with
mythical giants and a frieze
showing the fall of Granada
in 1492 (see pp52–3).

Monasterio de Veruela **⓰**

Vera de Moncayo (Zaragoza). 📞 (976)
64 90 25. 🚌 Vera de Moncayo.
⭕ daily. 🦽 ♿

THIS ISOLATED CISTERCIAN retreat, set in the green
Huecha valley near the Sierra
de Moncayo, is one of the
greatest monasteries in Aragón.
Founded in the 12th century
by French monks, the huge
abbey church has a mixture
of Romanesque and Gothic

features. Worn green and blue
Aragonese tiles line the floor
of its handsomely vaulted triple
nave. The well-preserved
cloisters sprout exuberantly
decorated beasts, heads of
human beings and foliage in
the Plateresque style (see p21).
The plain, dignified chambers
make a suitable venue for art
exhibitions in the summer.

ENVIRONS: In the hills to the
west the small **Parque Natural
de Moncayo** rises to a height
of 2,315 m (7,600 ft). Streams
race through the woodland
of this nature reserve, which
throngs with bird life. A tortuous potholed road leads to
a chapel at the highest point.

Zaragoza **⓱**

Zaragoza. 👥 600,000. ✈️ 🚌 🚆
ℹ️ Glorieta de Pío XII, (976) 39 35 37.
🚍 Wed, Sun. 🎉 San Valero (29 Jan),
Cincomarzada (5 Mar), San Jorge
(23 Apr), Virgen del Pilar (12 Oct).

A CELTIBERIAN settlement
called Salduba existed on
the site of the present city; but
it is from the Roman settlement
of Cesaraugusta that Zaragoza
takes its name. Its fortuitous
location on the fertile banks
of the Río Ebro ensured the
ascendancy of Zaragoza, now
Spain's fifth largest city and
the capital of Aragón.
Badly damaged during the
War of Independence (see
p58), the city was largely rebuilt but the old centre retains
a number of interesting buildings. Most of the city's main
sights are grouped around the
vast Plaza del Pilar. The most

Entrance and tower of the Monasterio de Veruela

impresssive of them is the **Basílica de Nuestra Señora del Pilar**, with its huge church sporting 11 brightly tiled cupolas. Inside, the Santa Capilla (Lady Chapel) by Ventura Rodríguez contains a small statue of the Virgin on a pillar amid a blaze of silver and flowers. Her long skirt-like *manta* is changed every day, and devout pilgrims pass behind the chapel to kiss an exposed section of the pillar.

Nearby, on the square, stand the **town hall** *(ayuntamiento)*, the Gothic-Plateresque **Lonja** (commodities exchange) and the **Palacio Episcopal**.

Occupying the east end of the square is Zaragoza's cathedral, **La Seo**, displaying a great mix of styles. Part of the exterior is faced with typical Mudéjar brick and ceramic decoration, and inside are a fine Gothic reredos and splendid Flemish tapestries.

Close by is the flamboyant Mudéjar bell tower of the **Iglesia de la Magdalena**, and remains of the Roman forum. Parts of the **Roman walls** can also be seen at the opposite side of the Plaza del Pilar, near the **Mercado de Lanuza**, a market with sinuous ironwork in Art Nouveau style.

Some of the cupolas of the Basílica de Nuestra Señora del Pilar

The **Museo Camón Aznar** exhibits the eclectic collection of a wealthy local art historian, whose special interest was Goya. The top floor contains a collection of his etchings. Many minor works by artists of other periods can be seen, as well as good contemporary art. The **Museo de Zaragoza** contains many paintings, as well as archaeological artifacts.

The **Museo Pablo Gargallo** is a showroom for the Aragonese sculptor after whom it is named, who was active at the beginning of the 20th century.

One of the most important monuments in Zaragoza lies on the busy road to Bilbao. The **Alfajería** is an enormous Moorish palace built in the 11th century. A courtyard of lacy arches surrounds a sunken garden and a small mosque.

🏛 **Museo Camón Aznar**
Calle Espoz y Mina 23. ☎ *(976) 39 73 28.* ⏰ *Tue–Sun.*
🏛 **Museo de Zaragoza**
Plaza de los Sitios 5. ☎ *(976) 22 21 81.* ⏰ *Tue–Sun.* ♿
🏛 **Museo Pablo Gargallo**
Plaza de San Felipe 3. ☎ *(976) 39 20 58.* ⏰ *Tue–Sun & public hols.* ♿

ZARAGOZA CITY CENTRE

Basílica de Nuestra Señora del Pilar ④
La Seo (Cathedral) ⑦
Lonja ⑥
Mercado de Lanuza ②
Museo Camón Aznar ⑤
Museo Pablo Gargallo ③
Palacio Episcopal ⑧
Roman walls ①

0 metres   150
0 yards   150

KEY

🅿 Parking
ℹ Tourist information
✝ Church

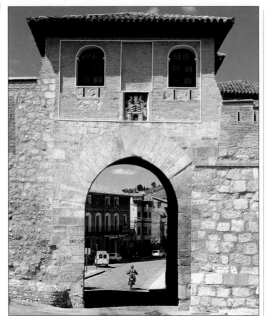

Gateway through the medieval walls of Daroca

Calatayud ⓲

Zaragoza. ⓜ 20,000. 🚉 🚌 🛈 Plaza el Fuerte, (976) 88 63 22. 🛒 Tue. 🎉 San Roque (14–17 Aug).

THE HUGE MOORISH FORTRESS and minaret-like church towers of Calatayud are visible far across the surrounding clay hills and fertile red plains. Only ruins are left of the 8th-century Arab castle of the ruler, Ayub, which gave the town its name (*Kalat Ayub* means castle of Ayub). The church of **Santa María la Mayor** has a Mudéjar tower and an elaborate façade in the Plateresque style.

The ruins of the Roman settlement of Bilbilis, birthplace of the poet Martial, are east of Calatayud, near Huérmeda.

Monasterio de Piedra ⓳

3 km (2 miles) south of Nuévalos. 📞 (976) 84 90 11. 🚉 Calatayud. 🚌 from Zaragoza. 🕐 daily. 🎫 ♿

FOUNDED BY Alfonso II of Aragón in 1195, this Cistercian monastery suffered damage in the 19th century and was subsequently rebuilt. Some of the original buildings survive, however, including the chapterhouse, refectory and hostel – all of which date back to the 13th century.

In the damp, blackened cellars, the monks once distilled strong potions of herbal liqueur in a large alembic. The kitchen was allegedly the first place in Europe where drinking chocolate, from Mexico, was prepared (*see p55*).

The park in which the monastery stands is a picturesque nature reserve full of grottoes and waterfalls. A hotel is now located in the old monastery buildings (*see p548*).

Daroca ⓴

Zaragoza. ⓜ 2,400. 🛈 Plaza de España 4, (976) 80 01 29. 🛒 Thu. 🎉 Santo Tomás (7 Mar).

AN IMPRESSIVE ARRAY of battlemented medieval walls stretches approximately 4 km (2 miles) around this old Moorish stronghold. Although parts of the walls have decayed, the 114 towers and fortified gateways are still a remarkable sight, particularly from the main road to Zaragoza.

The **Colegial de Santa María**, a church in the central square, houses the Holy Cloths from the Reconquest (*see pp50–51*). After a surprise attack by the Moors in 1239, priests celebrating Mass in the countryside hastily bundled the consecrated bread into the linen sheets used to cover the altar. When the cloths were unwrapped they were miraculously stained with blood.

ENVIRONS: The agricultural town of **Monreal del Campo**, 42 km (26 miles) south of Daroca, has a saffron museum. The backbreaking labour of harvesting the autumn crocus, formerly an important crop, is no longer profitable.

Fuendetodos ㉑

Zaragoza. ⓜ 180. 🛈 Calle Zuloaga, (976) 14 38 01. 🎉 San Roque (last Sat of May), San Bartolomé (24 Aug).

THIS SMALL VILLAGE was the birthplace of one of Spain's best-known artists of the late 18th and early 19th centuries,

Interior of Goya's cottage in Fuendetodos

Castle-parador above Alcañiz

Francisco de Goya. The **Casa-Museo de Goya** is a neat cottage said to be the painter's home. It has been restored and furnished in appropriate period style. On display are some of the artist's personal effects as well as engravings.

ENVIRONS: Lying 20 km (12 miles) east of Fuendetodos is **Belchite**, the site of one of the most horrific battles of the Spanish Civil War *(see pp62–3)*, for control of the strategic Ebro valley. Remains of the old, shell-torn town have been left tottering as a monument to the horrors of war.

In **Cariñena**, 25 km (16 miles) west of Fuendetodos, bodegas offer the opportunity to sample and buy the excellent, full-bodied red wine for which the region is justly renowned *(see pp192–3)*.

🏛 **Casa-Museo de Goya**
Calle Alfóndiga 3. 📞 (976) 14 38 30.
⭕ Tue–Sun. 📷

Alcañiz ㉒

Teruel. 🏘 *12,800.* 🚉 ℹ *Calle Mayor 1, (978) 83 12 13.* 🚌 *Tue.* 📷 *Fiestas Patronales (8–14 Sep).*

FROM A DISTANCE, two buildings rise above the town of Alcañiz. One is the **castle**, which was the headquarters of the Order of Calatrava in the 12th century. This historic building has been converted into a parador *(see p548)*. The keep, the Torre del Homenaje, has a collection of 14th-century frescoes depicting the conquest of Valencia by Jaime I.

The other building is the **Colegiata de Santa María**. This church, on the sloping Plaza de España, has a Gothic tower and a Baroque façade.

On the same square are the elegantly galleried **Lonja** (commodities exchange), with its lacy Gothic arches, and the **town hall** *(ayuntamiento)*, with one Mudéjar and one Renaissance façade.

FRANCISCO DE GOYA

Self-portrait by Goya

Born in Fuendetodos in 1746, Francisco de Goya specialized in designing cartoons for the tapestry industry *(see p296)* in his early life, and in decorating churches such as Zaragoza's Basílica del Pilar with vivacious frescoes. In 1799 he became painter to Carlos IV, and depicted the king and his wife María Luisa with unflattering accuracy *(see p29)*. The invasion of Madrid by Napoleon's troops in 1808 *(see pp58–9)* and its attendant horrors had a profound and lasting effect on Goya's temperament, and his later works are imbued with cynical despair and isolation. He died in Bordeaux in 1828.

ARAGÓN'S FIESTAS

Las Tamboradas *(Maundy Thursday and Good Friday)*, Teruel province. During Easter Week, brotherhoods of men wearing long black robes beat drums in mourning for Christ. Las Tamboradas begins with "the breaking of the hour" at midnight on Thursday in Híjar. The Tamborada in Calanda begins the following day at midday. The solemn drum rolls continue for several hours. Aching arms and bleeding hands are considered to be signs of religious devotion.

Young drummer in Las Tamboradas, Alcorija

Carnival *(Feb/Mar)*, Bielsa (Huesca). The protagonists of this fiesta, known as *Trangas*, have rams' horns on their heads, blackened faces and teeth made of potatoes. They are said to represent fertility.
Romería de Santa Orosia *(25 Jun)*, Yebra de Basa (Huesca). Pilgrims in folk costume carry St Orosia's skull to her shrine.
Día del Pilar *(12 Oct)*, Zaragoza. Aragón's distinctive folk dance, the *jota*, is performed everywhere during the city's festivities in honour of its patroness, the Virgin of the Pillar *(see p227)*. On the Día del Pilar there is a procession with cardboard giants, and a spectacular display of flowers dedicated to the Virgin.

Alcalá de la Selva castle, overlooking the town

Valderrobres ❷

Teruel. 🏚 *1,980.* 🛈 *Plaza de España 1, (978) 85 00 01.* 🚌 *Sat.* 🎪 *San Roque (15–19 Aug).*

JUST INSIDE Aragón's border with Catalonia, the delightful town of Valderrobres overlooks the shallow, trout-filled Río Matarrana. Dominating the town is the restored **castle**, which was formerly a palace for Aragonese royalty. Below it stands the imposing Gothic **Iglesia de Santa María la Mayor**, with an enorous rose window in Catalan Gothic style. The unusual arcaded plaza has a pleasing town hall *(ayuntamiento)* completed in the end of the 16th century.

ENVIRONS: To the south lies tiny **Mirambel**, a carefully restored medieval village surrounded by sturdy ramparts.

🏯 **Castillo de Valderrobres**
⬜ *Jul–Sep: Mon, Oct–Jun: Sat.* 📷

Sierra de Gúdar ❷

Teruel. 🚌 *Mora de Rubielos.* 🚌 *Alcalá de la Selva.* 🛈 *Plaza de la Iglesia 4, (978) 80 10 00.*

THIS RANGE OF HILLS, northeast of Teruel, is a region of pine woods and jagged limestone outcrops erupting from scrub-covered slopes. At 2,019 m (6,624 ft), **Peñarroya** is the highest point. Nearby Valdelinares, Aragón's third-highest village, is a ski station. From the access roads there are panoramic views of the hills. Especially noteworthy are the views from the towns of **Linares de Mora** and **Alcalá**

de la Selva, which has a castle set against a backdrop of rock faces. Its Baroque church, with shell motifs and twisted columns, shelters the shrine of the Virgen de la Vega.

Mora de Rubielos ❷

Teruel. 🏚 *1,400.* 🛈 *Plaza de la Villa 1, (978) 80 00 00.* 🚌 *Mon & Fri.* 🎪 *San Miguel (28 Sep–1 Oct).*

DOMINATED BY one of the best-preserved castles in Aragón, Mora de Rubielos has a medieval old town. Its fortified Gothic **collegiate church** has chapels decorated with *azulejos* from Manises, near Valencia. There is an elegant black fountain nearby which depicts dolphins playing.

ENVIRONS: Rubielos de Mora, lying 10 km (6 miles) to the southeast, is worth exploring simply for its well-preserved stone and timber buildings. Among the balconied houses is an Augustinian convent with a Gothic reredos.

Teruel ❷

Teruel. 🏚 *31,000.* 🚉 🚌 🛈 *Calle Tomás Nougués 1, (978) 60 22 79.* 🚌 *Thu.* 🎪 *Día del Mesón de las Tortillas (Tue of Easter week), La Vaquilla del Ángel (mid-Jul), Feria del Jamón (mid-Sep).*

THIS INDUSTRIAL TOWN has been the scene of much desperate fighting throughout the centuries. It began with the Romans, the first to capture and civilize Celtiberian Turba. During the Reconquest the town became a strategic frontier prize. In 1171 Alfonso II recaptured Teruel for Christian Spain, but many Muslims continued to live peacefully in the city, which they embellished with beautiful Mudéjar towers. The last mosque was closed only at the height of the Inquisition *(see p264)*, in 1502. More recently, during the terrible, freezing winter of 1937, the bitterest battle of the Civil War *(see pp62–3)* was fought here. There were many thousands of casualties.

The old quarter is home to the wedge-shaped Plaza del Torico, with a monument of a

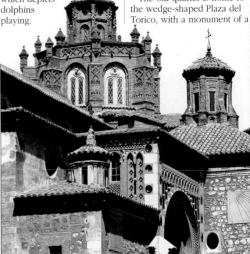

Tiled towers and rooftops of Teruel cathedral

Balconied café above Albarracín's main square

small bull, the city's emblem. Within walking distance lie the five remaining Mudéjar towers. Most striking are those of **San Salvador** and **San Martín**, both dating back to the 12th century. The latter has multi-patterned brickwork studded with blue and green ceramics.

Inside the **Iglesia de San Pedro** are the tombs of the famous Lovers of Teruel. The **cathedral** has more colourful Mudéjar work, including a lantern dome of glazed tiles, and a tower completed in the 17th century. The dazzling coffered ceiling is painted with lively scenes of medieval life.

The **Museo Provincial**, one of Aragón's best museums, is housed in an elegant mansion. It has a large collection of ceramics, testifying to an industry for which Teruel has long been known. North of the centre is the **Acueducto de los Arcos**, a 16th-century aqueduct.

🏛 Museo Provincial
Pl Fray Anselmo Polanco 3. **(** (978) 60 01 50. **☐** Tue – Sun. **◐** public hols.

Albarracín ㉗

Teruel. 🏘 1,200. **☐ 🛈** Calle de la Catedral 5 (978) 71 02 51. 🎪 Los Mayos (30 Apr–1 May), Patronales (13–15 Sep).

I T IS EASY TO SEE WHY this pic-turesque town earned the honour of an international award for historical preserva-tion. A dramatic cliff above the Río Guadalaviar is the perfect setting for this attractive cluster of mellow pink buildings.

Standing on a ridge behind the town are the defensive walls, interspersed with towers which date from Muslim times.

There is a good view of the town from below the **Palacio Episcopal** (Bishop's Palace). Inside the neighbouring 16th-century **cathedral**, which is topped by a belfry, there is a Renaissance carved wooden altarpiece depicting scenes from the life of St Peter. The treasury museum contains 16th-century Brussels tapestries and enamelled chalices.

Some of Albarracín's sturdy beamed and galleried houses have an unusual two-tier structure. The ground floor is limestone, and the overhanging upper storey is covered in rough coral-pink plasterwork.

Many have been restored to their medieval form. Just outside the town are the caves of Navazo and Callejón, with their prehistoric rock paintings. Reproductions can be seen in Teruel's Museo Provincial.

ENVIRONS: In the surrounding **Montes Universales**, which rise to 1,170 m (3,840 ft), is the source of the Tagus, one of Spain's longest rivers. From fertile cereal plains to crum-bling rocks, this area is a colourful mixture of poplars, junipers and thick pine woods, with poppies in spring. At **Cella**, northeast of Albarracín, the Río Jiloca has its source.

Rincón de Ademuz ㉘

Valencia. **☐** Ademuz. **🛈** Valencia, (96) 352 54 78.

T HIS REMOTE ENCLAVE south of Teruel officially belongs to the Comunidad Valenciana (see p233); but is effectively an island of territory, stranded between the borders of Aragón and Castilla-La Mancha. The area has not prospered in re-cent years – due to its isolated location – and many houses are abandoned. But it still has its own austere charm and some peaceful tracts of country scattered with red rocks.

THE LOVERS OF TERUEL

According to legend, in 13th-century Teruel two young people, Diego de Marcilla and Isabel de Segura, fell in love and wished to marry. She came from a wealthy family, but he was poor, and her parents forbade the match. Diego was given five years in which to make his fortune and establish a name for himself. At the end of this time he returned to Teruel, laden with wealth, only to find his bride-to-be already married to a local nobleman. Diego died of a broken heart and Isabel, full of despair at his death, died the following day.

Isabel de Segura   **Diego de Marcilla**

VALENCIA AND MURCIA

CASTELLÓN · VALENCIA · ALICANTE · MURCIA

TODAY, THE CENTRAL REGION *of Spain's eastern Mediterranean coast is an important holiday destination – the beaches of the Costa Blanca, the Costa del Azahar and the Costa Cálida draw millions of tourists annually. Centuries ago, Muslim settlers made these regions bloom, and the fertile fields and citrus groves of the coastal plains are still Spain's citrus orchard and market garden.*

These productive lands have been occupied for more than 50,000 years. The Greeks, Phoenicians, Carthaginians and Romans all settled here before the Moors arrived, trading the products of land and sea.

The provinces of Castellón, Valencia and Alicante (which make up the Comunidad Valenciana) were reconquered from the Moors by a Catalan army. The language these troops left behind them developed into a dialect, *valenciano*, which is widely spoken and increasingly seen on signposts. Murcia, to the south, is one of Spain's smallest autonomous regions.

The population is concentrated on the coast where the historic towns and cities of Valencia, Alicante and Cartagena have been joined by modern package holiday resorts, such as Benidorm and La Manga del Mar Menor. Inland, where tourism has barely reached, the landscape rises into the chains of mountains that stand between the coast and the plateau of Central Spain. The scenery inland ranges from picturesque valleys and hills in the Maestrat, in the north of Castellón, to the semi-desert terrain around Lorca in southern Murcia.

The warm climate encourages outdoor life and exuberant fiestas. Most famous of these are Las Fallas of Valencia; the mock battles between Moors and Christians staged in Alcoi; and the lavish, costumed Easter processions in Murcia and Lorca.

Hill terraces of olive and almond trees ascending the hillsides near Alcoi

◁ **The Penyal d'Ifach, rising directly out of the sea to tower above the Costa Blanca near Calp**

Exploring Valencia and Murcia

THE COASTS OF VALENCIA AND MURCIA are popular for seaside holidays and ideal for water sports almost all year round. Principal resorts include Benidorm, Benicassim and La Manga del Mar Menor. Some coastal towns such as Peñíscola, Gandia, Dénia, Alicante and Cartagena have charming old quarters, castles and other monuments well worth visiting. Close to the sea are several scenic nature reserves: the freshwater lagoon of L'Albufera, and, on the Costa Blanca, the saltpans of Santa Pola and the striking limestone crag of the Penyal d'Ifach.

Inland, the region offers excursions to such undiscovered beauty spots as El Maestrat and the mountains around Alcoi, as well as the undervisited historic towns of Xàtiva and Lorca. The two regional capitals, Valencia and Murcia, are both lively university cities with fine cathedrals and numerous museums.

Fishing nets strung out in the lagoon of L'Albufera

GETTING AROUND

The region's principal roads are the A7 motorway (toll-paying from Alicante northwards except for the Valencia bypass) and the N332 along the coast. Other major roads, most of which are dual carriageways, connect Valencia with Madrid (NIII), Murcia with Madrid (N301) and Valencia with Teruel and the north of Spain (N234). There are main rail lines from Alicante, Valencia and Murcia to Madrid, but the rest of the rail network is rather fragmented and buses are often quicker than trains. A scenic narrow-gauge railway line along the Costa Blanca connects Dénia to Alicante via Benidorm. The region's international airports are at Alicante and Valencia.

0 kilometres   25

0 miles   20

SEE ALSO

- *Where to Stay* pp549–51
- *Restaurants and Bars* pp590–92

CHELVA 9

ALTO TURIA

NIII   REQUENA

Madrid

N322

Xúquer

Madrid, Albacete

YECL

N344

Albacete   JUMILLA

Segura   N301

C334

CARAVACA DE LA CRUZ 33

C330   C415

Quipar

MURCIA 28   OR

N340

Sangonera

Granada   32 LORCA

N340   N332   MAR M

Almería   CARTAGENA 30

ÁGUILAS   COSTA CÁLIDA   31

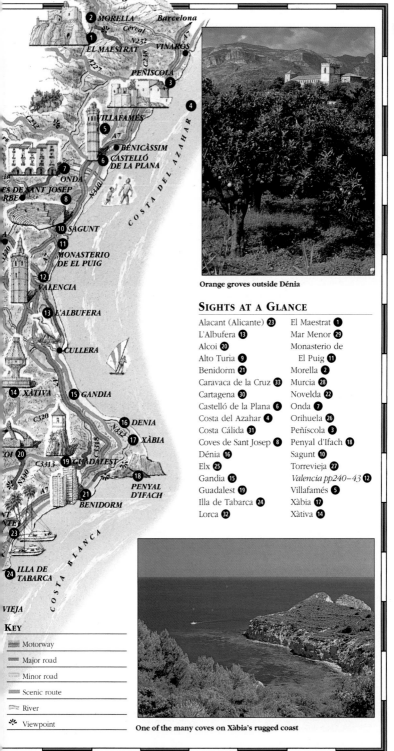

Orange groves outside Dénia

SIGHTS AT A GLANCE

One of the many coves on Xàbia's rugged coast

The unbroken medieval wall surrounding the historic hilltop town of Morella in El Maestrat

El Maestrat ❶

Castellón & Teruel. 🚇 Morella.
🛈 Morella, (964) 17 30 32.

CRUSADING WARLORDS of the Knights Templar and the Knights of Montesa – known as *maestres* (masters) – gave their name to this lonely upland region. To rule over this frontier land, which straddles the border between Valencia and Aragón, they built fortified settlements in dramatic defensive positions, often on rocky crags. The best preserved of them is **Morella**, the principal town. **Forcall**, not far from Morella, has two 16th-century mansions on its porticoed

The Torre de la Sacristía, in the restored village of Mirambel

square. To the south, the village of **Ares del Maestre** is spectacularly sited beneath a 1,318-m (4,300-ft) high rock.

Cantavieja is the most important town in the Aragonese part of El Maestrat (where it is known as El Maestrazgo). It has a handsome, arcaded square. The walled village of **Mirambel**, nearby, has been meticulously restored to its medieval condition.

There are several spooky but fascinating shrines to the Virgin in El Maestrat, notably the cave at **La Balma**, which is reached via a rocky ledge.

The scenery in most parts is striking: fertile valleys alternate with breathtaking cliffs and bare, flat-topped mountains overflown by eagles and vultures. Tourism is developing very slowly here: there are few places to stay and the roads can be windy and slow.

Morella ❷

Castellón. 🏚 2,900. 🚇 🛈 Plaza de San Miguel 3, (964) 17 30 32. 🚌 Sun.
📅 Sexeni (Aug, every six years).

BUILT ON a high, isolated outcrop and crowned by a ruined castle, Morella cuts a dramatic profile. Its unbroken medieval walls retain six gateways, which lead into a fan-shaped maze of streets and

steep, tapering alleys, many of which are shaded by the eaves of ancient houses. The main street is lined with shady porticoes. In the upper part of town is the **Basílica de Santa María la Mayor**. Its unique raised choirloft is reached by a finely carved spiral staircase.

EN ESTA CASA OBRO SAN VICENTE FERRER EL PROGIGIOSO ILAGRO DE LA RESURRECCION DE UN NIÑO QUE SU MADRE NAJENADA HABIA DESCUARTIZADO Y GUISADO Y SERVIO AL SANTO (1414)

MORELLA'S MIRACLE

A plaque on the wall of Morella's Calle de la Virgen marks the house in which St Vincent Ferrer is said to have performed a bizarre miracle in the early 15th century. A housewife, distraught at having no meat to offer the saint, cut up her son and put him in the cooking pot. When St Vincent discovered this, he reconstituted the boy – except for one of his little fingers, which his mother had eaten to see if the dish was sufficiently salted.

Peñíscola ❸

Castellón. 🏛 4,100. 🚌 ℹ️ Paseo Marítimo, (964) 48 02 08. 🗓 Mon. 🎪 Patronales (mid-Sep).

THE FORTIFIED OLD TOWN of Peñíscola clusters around the base of a castle built on a rocky promontory, surrounded on three sides by the sea. This labyrinth of narrow winding streets and white houses is enclosed by massive ramparts. These are entered by either the Fosch Gate – reached by a ramp from the Plaza del Caudillo – or through the San Pedro Gate, from the harbour.

The **Castell del Papa Luna** was built on the foundations of an Arab fortress in the late 13th century by the Knights Templar. Their cross is carved above the door. It later became the residence of the papal pretender Pedro de Luna, cardinal of Aragón. He was elected Pope Benedict XIII during the Great Schism that split the Catholic Church at the end of the 14th century. Although he was deposed by the Council of Constance in 1414, he continued to proclaim his right to the papacy until his death as a nonagenarian in 1423.

The uppermost battlements of the castle are false: they were built for a scene from the 1961 film El Cid. Modern Peñíscola has expanded beyond the old walls and is now a thriving holiday resort.

♦ **Castell del Papa Luna**
Calle Castillo. ☎ (964) 48 00 21. ⭕ daily. ⬤ 9 Sep, 6 & 25 Dec. 🎟

Sunset view of the beach and old town of Peñíscola

Costa del Azahar ❹

Castellón. 🚊 Castelló de la Plana. 🚌 Castelló de la Plana. ℹ️ Castelló de la Plana, (964) 22 10 00.

THE "ORANGE BLOSSOM COAST" of Castellón province is named after the dense citrus groves of the coastal plain. The two principal resorts are Benicassim, where handsome old villas have been supplemented by modern hotels and other tourist amenities, and Peñíscola. Alcossebre and Oropesa also have popular beaches. Vinaròs – the most northerly point – and Benicarló are key fishing ports supplying prawns and date-mussels to local restaurants.

Sculpture in the Casa del Batle

Villafamés ❺

Castellón. 🏛 1,400. 🚌 ℹ️ Plaza del Ayuntamiento 1, (964) 32 90 01. 🗓 Fri. 🎪 Patronales (mid-Aug).

THIS MEDIEVAL TOWN climbs from a flat plain along a rocky ridge to the restored round keep of its castle. The older, upper part of the town is a warren of sloping streets filled with sturdy houses.

A 15th-century mansion houses the **Casa del Batle**, a museum of contemporary art. The works on display, some of which are for sale, date from 1959 to the present.

🏛 **Casa del Batle**
Calle Diputación 20. ☎ (964) 32 91 52. ⭕ daily. 🎟

Castelló de la Plana's planetarium, close to the beach

Castelló de la Plana ❻

Castellón. 🏛 140,000. 🚌 🚊 ℹ️ Plaza María Agustina 5, (964) 22 10 00. 🗓 Mon. 🎪 Fiesta de la Magdalena (second week of Mar).

ORIGINALLY FOUNDED on high ground inland, the capital of Castellón province was relocated nearer to the coast in the 13th century.

The city centre, the Plaza Mayor, is bordered by the market, the town hall, the cathedral and **El Fadri**, a 58-m (190-ft) high octagonal bell tower erected in the 1590s.

The **Museo Provincial de Bellas Artes**, in an 18th-century house, contains a collection of artifacts dating from the middle Palaeolithic era, paintings from the 15th to the 20th centuries and modern ceramics from the region. Among the artworks is José de Ribera's Saint Jerome.

The **Convento de las Madres Capuchinas** has an important collection of paintings which are attributed to Francisco de Zurbarán.

In **El Planetario** there are demonstrations of the night sky, the solar system and the nearest stars. It also has exhibits on perception, holography and minerals.

🏛 **Museo Provincial de Bellas Artes**
Calle Balleros 25. ☎ (964) 35 97 11. ⭕ Mon–Sat.
🏛 **Convento de las Madres Capuchinas**
Calle Núñez de Arce 11. ☎ (964) 22 06 41. ⭕ daily. ♿
🏛 **El Planetario**
Paseo Marítimo 1, El Grao. ☎ (964) 28 25 84. ⭕ Jul–Aug: Tue–Sat, Oct–Jun: Tue–Sun. 🎟 ♿

Onda ●

Castellón. ⓘ 16,800. 🚆 🛈 Calle
Cervantes 10, (964) 77 18 40.
🔄 Thu. 🎉 Feria (last week of Oct).

ONDA, HOME to a thriving
ceramics industry, is
overlooked by a ruined **castle**,
which was known to its
Moorish founders as the
"Castle of the Three Hundred
Towers". The old quarter of
the town has some character,
especially the charming square
of **Plaza del Almudín**, with
its medieval porticoes.

But the main reason to visit
Onda is to take a look at the
Museo El Carmen, a natural
history museum belonging to
a Carmelite monastery just
outside the town.

The collection was begun
in 1952 by the monks for their
own private scientific study. It
was only opened to the public
a decade later. The clever use
of subdued lighting lends
dramatic effect to the 10,000
plant and animal specimens
which are exhibited over three
floors. Objects include large
stuffed animals placed in
naturalistic settings, butterflies
and other insects, shells, fossils,
minerals and grisly, preserved
anatomical specimens.

🏛 Museo El Carmen
Carretera de Tales. 📞 (964) 60 07 30.
🕐 Tue–Sun. 🖼

**Two butterfly exhibits in the
Museo El Carmen**

**Boat ride through the winding
Coves de Sant Josep**

Coves de Sant Josep ●

Vall d'Uixó (Castellón). 📞 (964) 69
05 76. 🚆 Vall d'Uixó. 🖼

THE CAVES OF St Joseph were
first explored in 1902. The
subterranean river that formed
them, and which still flows
through them, has been chart-
ed for almost 2.5 km (1.5
miles). However, its source
has not yet been discovered
and only part of this distance
can be explored on a visit.

Boats take visitors along the
serpentine course of the river.
You may have to duck to
avoid projections of rock on
the way. Here and there the
narrow caves open out into
large chambers such as the
Sala de los Murciélagos (Hall
of the Bats – the bats left
when the floodlights were
installed). The water reaches its
deepest point of 12 m (39 ft) in
the *Lago Azul* (Blue Lake). You
can explore a further 255 m
(837 ft) along the *Galería
Seca* (Dry Gallery) on foot.
The caves are often closed to
visitors after heavy rain.

Alto Turia ●

Valencia. 🚆 Chelva. 🛈 C234,
northwest of Tuéjar, (96) 163 50 84.

THE ATTRACTIVE WOODED HILLS
of the upper reaches of the
Río Turia in Valencia (Alto
Turia) are popular with hikers
and day-trippers. **Chelva**, the
main town, has an unusual
clock on its church which

shows not only the hour but
the day and month as well.
The town is overlooked by the
Pico del Remedio (1,054 m/
3,458 ft), from the summit of
which there is a fine panoramic
view of the region. In a valley
near Chelva, at the end of an
unsurfaced but drivable track,
are the remains of a Roman
aqueduct, **Peña Cortada**.

The most attractive and interesting village in Alto Turia is
Alpuente, situated above a dry
gorge. Between 1031 to 1089,
when it was captured by El
Cid *(see p352)*, Alpuente was
the capital of a small *taifa*, a
Moorish kingdom. In the 14th
century it was still important
enough for the kingdom of
Valencia's parliament to meet
here. The town hall is confined to a small tower over a
14th-century gateway, which
was later extended in the 16th
century by the addition of a
rectangular council chamber.

Requena, to the south is
Valencia's main wine town.
Further south, Valencia's other
principal river, the Xúquer
(Júcar), carves tremendous
gorges near Cortes de Pallas
on its way past the **Muela de
Cortes**. This massive, wild
plateau and nature reserve is
crossed by one small road
and a lonely dirt track.

LA TOMATINA

The highpoint of the annual
fiesta in Buñol (Valencia) is
a sticky food fight on the
last Wednesday of August,
which attracts thousands of
visitors dressed in their
worst clothes. Lorry loads of
ripe tomatoes are provided
by the town council for
participants to hurl at each
other. No one in range of
the combatants is spared:
foreigners and photo-
graphers are prized targets.

The battle originated in
1944. Some say it began
with a fight between friends.
Others say irreverent locals
pelted civic dignitaries with
tomatoes during a proces-
sion. Increasing national and
international press coverage
means that more people
attend, and more tomatoes
are thrown, every year.

Sagunt's ruined fortifications, added to by successive rulers of the town

Sagunt ⑩

Valencia. 🏛 60,000. 🚌 🚈 🛈 Pl
Cronista Chabret, (96) 266 22 13. 🚈
Wed. 🎭 Fiestas (mid-Jul–mid-Aug).

SITED NEAR THE JUNCTION of two Roman roads, Sagunt (Sagunto) played a crucial role in Spain's ancient history.

In 219 BC Hannibal, the Carthaginian commander in southern Spain, stormed and sacked Rome's ally Saguntum. All the inhabitants of the town were said to have died in the assault, the last throwing themselves on to bonfires rather than fall into the hands of Hannibal's troops. The incident sparked off the Second Punic War, a disaster for the Carthaginians, which ended with Rome's occupation of the peninsula *(see pp46–7)*.

The town still contains several reminders of the Roman occupation, including the 1st-century AD **Roman theatre**. Built out of limestone in a natural depression on the hillside above the town, it has been controversially restored by the regional government using modern materials. The theatre is now used as a venue for music, plays and Sagunt's annual theatre festival.

The ruins of the **castle**, sprawling along the crest of the hill above the modern-day town, mark the original site of Saguntum. Superimposed on each other are the excavated remains of various civilizations, including the Iberians, the Carthaginians, the Romans and the Moors. The ruins of the castle are divided into seven divisions, or plazas, the highest of them being La Ciudadela.

⚐ **Castillo de Sagúnt**
⬜ Tue–Sat. 🎭

Monasterio de El Puig ⑪

El Puig (Valencia). 📞 (96) 147 02 00.
🚌 El Puig. 🚈 El Puig. ⬜ daily.
⬤ Mon pm. 🎭 ✔

THIS MERCEDARIAN monastery was founded by King Jaime I of Aragón, who conquered Valencia from the Moors in the 13th century.

The monastery is now home to a collection of 240 paintings from between the 16th and 18th centuries and the Museo de la Imprenta y de la Obra Gráfica (Museum of Printing and Graphic Art). The museum commemorates the printing of the first book in Spain – thought to have been in Valencia in 1474 – and illustrates the development of the printing press. Exhibits include printers' blocks and a replica of the smallest book in the world.

Messy participants throwing tomatoes at each other in the annual fiesta of La Tomatina

Valencia ⑫

S PAIN'S THIRD LARGEST CITY is sited in the middle of the *huerta*: a fertile plain of orange groves and market gardens, which is one of Europe's most intensively farmed regions. With its warm coastal climate, Valencia is known for its exuberant outdoor living and nightlife. In March the city stages one of Spain's most spectacular fiestas, Las Fallas *(see p245)*, in which giant papier-mâché sculptures are burned in the streets. Modern Valencia is a centre for trade and manufacturing, notably ceramics. A ferry service connects the city with the Balearic Islands.

Flowers in honour of Valencia's patroness, Virgen de los Desamparados

Exploring Valencia

Valencia stands on the course of the Río Turia. The city centre and the crumbling old quarter of El Carmen are on the right bank. Most of the monuments are within walking distance of the Plaza del Ayuntamiento, the triangular main square which is presided over by the town hall.

The city was founded by the Romans in 138 BC and later conquered by the Moors. It was captured by El Cid *(see p352)* in 1096, retaken by the Moors, and finally recaptured by Jaime I, the Conqueror, in 1238, to become absorbed into the kingdom of Aragón.

The three finest buildings in Valencia were built during its economic and cultural heyday in the 14th and 15th centuries: the Torres de Serranos, a gateway that survived the demolition of the medieval walls in the 19th century, La Lonja and the cathedral.

🏛 Palau de la Generalitat

Plaza de la Virgen. 【 *(96) 386 61 00.* ☐ *by prior appointment only.*
This palace, which is now used by the Valencian regional government, was built in Gothic style between 1482 and 1579 but added to in the 17th and 20th centuries. It surrounds an enclosed stone patio from

which two staircases ascend to splendidly decorated rooms.

The larger of the two Salas Doradas (Golden Chambers), on the mezzanine level, has a multicoloured coffered ceiling and tiled floor. The walls of the parliament chamber are decorated with frescoes.

🔒 Basílica de la Virgen de los Desamparados

The ornately dressed statue of Valencia's patroness, the Virgin of the Helpless, stands above an altar in this 17th-century church, lavishly adorned with flowers and candles. She is honoured during Las Fallas by La Ofrenda ("the Offering"), a display of flowers in the square outside the church.

🔒 Cathedral

Built originally in 1262, the cathedral has been added to over the ages, and its three doorways are all in different styles. The oldest is the Romanesque Puerta del Palau but the main entrance is the 18th-century Baroque portal, the Puerta de los Hierros.

A unique court meets on Thursdays at midday in front of the other doorway, the Gothic Puerta de los Apóstoles. For an estimated 1,000 years, the Water Tribunal has settled disputes between farmers over the distribution of irrigation water in the *huerta*.

Inside the cathedral, a chapel holds an agate cup, claimed to be the Holy Grail. According to legend it arrived in Valencia from Jerusalem by way of San Juan de la Peña monastery in Aragón *(see p224)*.

The Miguelete, the cathedral's bell tower on Plaza de Zaragoza

The cathedral's 68-m (223-ft) high octagonal bell tower, the Miguelete, built between 1380 and 1420, is Valencia's main landmark. From its top there are fine views of the city.

La Lonja

Plaza del Mercado 31. ((96) 352 54 78. ◯ Tue–Sun.

An exquisite Late Gothic hall, built between 1482 and 1498 as a commodities exchange, La Lonja is now used for hosting cultural events such as concerts and exhibitions. The outside walls are decorated with gargoyles and a variety of other grotesque figures. The high ceiling of the transactions hall is formed by star-patterned vaulting which is supported on graceful spiral columns.

Mercado Central

Plaza del Mercado 6. ((96) 382 91 00. ◯ Mon–Sat.

This huge iron, glass and tile Art Nouveau building, with its parrot and swordfish weathervanes, opened in 1928 and is one of the largest and most attractive markets in Europe.

Ornate toilet sign outside Valencia's Mercado Central

Every morning its thousand or so stalls are filled with a bewildering variety of seafood, vegetables, fruit, spices and herbs.

Museo Nacional de Cerámica

González Martí Calle Rinconada García Sanchis. ((96) 351 63 92. ◯ Tue–Sat. ● 1 Jan, 19 Mar, 1 May, 6 & 25 Dec.

Spain's National Ceramics Museum is housed in the Baroque mansion of the Marqués de Dos Aguas, an 18th-century fantasy of coloured plasterwork. The doorway is surrounded by

VISITORS' CHECKLIST

Valencia. ⚐ 760,000. ✈ 8 km (5 miles) SW. ⬛ C/ Játiva 24, (96) 352 02 02. ⬛ Avda Menéndez Pidal 13, (96) 349 72 22. ⬛ Estación Marítima, (96) 367 07 04. ⓘ Ayuntamiento, (96) 352 54 78. ⬛ Mon–Sat. ⬛ Las Fallas (19 Mar), Corpus Christi (May/Jun).

an elaborate carving by Ignacio Vergara. The 5,000 exhibits include prehistoric, Greek and Roman ceramics, pieces by Picasso and a splendid traditional tiled Valencian kitchen.

Colegio del Patriarca

This seminary was built in the mid-16th century around a two-storey Renaissance courtyard. The walls and ceiling of the church are covered with frescoes by Bartolomé Matarana. During the Friday morning mass, the painting above the altar, *The Last Supper* by Francisco Ribalta, is lowered to reveal a painting of the crucifixion by an anonymous 15th-century German artist.

VALENCIA CITY CENTRE

Basílica de la Virgen de los Desamparados ②
Cathedral ③
Colegio del Patriarca ⑦
Estación del Norte ⑬
Instituto Valenciano de Arte Moderno (IVAM) ⑪
Jardines del Río Turia ⑧
La Lonja ④
Mercado Central ⑤
Museo Nacional de Cerámica ⑥
Museo de la Prehistoria ⑫
Museo San Pío V ⑨
Palau de la Generalitat ①
Torres de Serranos ⑩

KEY

Ⓜ Metro station

🅿 Parking

ⓘ Tourist information

✝ Church

0 metres   250
0 yards   250

The Palau de la Música, Valencia's prestigious concert hall

Beyond the Centre

The centre of the city is bordered by two wide avenues, the Gran Vía Marqués del Turia and the Gran Vía Ramón y Cajal. Beyond these lie the 19th-century suburbs laid out symmetrically on a grid plan.

The left bank of the river is dominated by the Avenida Blasco Ibáñez (named after a local novelist), running from the Jardines Reales towards the sea, 4 km (2.5 miles) from the centre. The best way to get around beyond the city centre is by the metro system, one line of which is a tramway to the beaches of El Cabañal and La Malvarrosa.

🌿 Jardines del Río Turia

Where once there was a river there is now a 5-km (3-mile) long strip of gardens, sports fields and playgrounds crossed by a dozen bridges. In a prominent position above the riverbed stands the Palau de la Música, an international-class concert hall built in the 1980s. The centrepiece of the nearby children's playground is the giant figure of Gulliver pinned to the ground and covered with steps and slides. Inside the figure there is a scale model of Valencia.

The best of Valencia's other public gardens stand near the banks of the river. The largest

of them, the Jardines Reales – known locally as Los Viveros – contain a small zoo. The intimate Italian-style Monforte Gardens are dotted with marble statues and filled with hibiscus and magnolia. The Jardín Botánico was created in 1802 by the botanist Antonio José Cavanilles. It is planted with 7,000 species of shrubs and trees, including many subtropical varieties.

🏛 Museo De Bellas Artes

Palacio San Pío V, Calle San Pío V 9.
📞 (96) 360 57 93. ⬜ Tue –Sun. ⬤ 1 Jan, Good Fri, 25 & 31 Dec.
An important collection of 2,000 paintings and statues dating from antiquity to the last century is housed in this former seminary, which was built between 1683 and 1744.

Valencian art dating from the 14th and 15th centuries is represented by a series of huge golden altarpieces. They are the work of Alcanyis, Pere Nicolau and Maestro de Bonastre. *The Passion* – a triptych by the Flemish painter Hieronymus Bosch hangs on the first floor, together with Velázquez's self-portrait and several works by El Greco, Murillo, Ribalta, Van Dyck and the local Renaissance painter Juan de Juanes.

On the top floor there are six paintings by Goya and pictures by three important

Valencian artists from the 19th and 20th centuries: Ignacio Pinazo, Joaquín Sorolla and Antonio Muñoz Degrain. A large collection of the latter's hallucinatory coloured paintings are gathered together in one room, among them the disturbing *Amor de Madre*.

♣ Torres de Serranos

Plaza de los Fueros.
Erected in 1238 as a triumphal arch in the city's walls, this gateway combines defensive and decorative features. Its two imposing towers are crowned with battlements and at the same time lightened by delicate Gothic tracery. Valencia's other surviving gateway is the 15th-century Torres de Quart,

Ecce Homo (16th century) by Juan de Juanes in the Museo San Pío V

The towering gateway of the Torres de Serranos

providing access to the city from the west. It is more functional in appearance than the Torres de Serranos and, although restored, it still bears the pockmarks of cannonfire – reminders of the War of Independence *(see p59)*.

⛫ Instituto Valenciano de Arte Moderno (IVAM)
Calle Guillem de Castro 118. **(** *(96) 386 30 00.* ⏰ *Tue–Sun.* 📷 🔥
The Valencian Institute of Modern Art is housed in two buildings. The Centro Julio González, built in the 1980s, has nine galleries including ones devoted to two artists from Valencia, Julio González, considered to be the father of 20th-century Spanish sculpture, and the painter Ignacio Pinazo. A well-preserved 13th-century Carmelite convent in the nearby Calle Museo has been converted into the Centro del Carmen, which is devoted to temporary exhibitions of contemporary works. The interior has been left bare, allowing the visitor to appreciate the mixture of architectural styles, including Gothic and Renaissance.

⛫ Museo Domingo Fletcher
Calle Corona 36. **(** *(96) 388 35 79.* ⏰ *Tue –Sun.*
Valencia's prehistory museum displays part of a unique collection of 5,000 Stone Age engravings of deer and horses made on limestone plaques that were found in the Cueva de Parpalló, in the hills above the coast near Gandia *(see p244)*. The neighbouring Museo de Etnología (Folk Museum), which shares the same opening hours, contains displays illustrating traditional rural village life.

🚉 Estación del Norte
Calle Játiva 24. **(** *(96) 352 02 02.* ⏰ *daily.*
Valencia's mainline railway station was built between 1907 and 1917 in a style inspired by Austrian Art Nouveau. Its twin white towers are adorned with bunches of sculpted oranges. Inside the building, the foyer and cafeteria are decorated with ceramic murals and stained glass depicting the life and crops of the *huerta* and L'Albufera *(see p244)*.

Art Nouveau-style column in the Estación del Norte

⛫ Museo del Gremio Artistas Falleros
Calle del Ninot 24. **(** *(96) 347 65 85.* ⏰ *daily.* 🔥
Up to 170 artists and craftsmen labour all year round in the *barrio* of Ciudad Fallera to build the elaborate papier-mâché sculptures that are burned during Las Fallas *(see p245)*. They sometimes show visitors around their workshops – except during their busiest period in the months leading up to March. Each year the best *ninots* (papier-mâché cartoon-like figures) are saved from the flames and put on display in this craft guild museum, along with posters, photographs and other memorabilia dating from 1902.

El Cabañal and La Malvarrosa Beaches
To the east of the city, the beaches of El Cabañal and La Malvarrosa are bordered by a broad and lively esplanade about 2 km (1.5 miles) long. Although these two former fishermen's districts were carelessly developed in the 1960s and '70s, they retain some quaint, traditional houses tiled on the outside to keep them cool in summer. The light of La Malvarrosa inspired the Impressionist painter Joaquín Sorolla *(see p295)*. The Paseo de Neptuno, near the port, is lined with restaurants, many of which specialize in paella.

ENVIRONS: The fertile and intensively farmed plain of the *huerta* is a raw of fields planted with artichokes and *chufas*, the raw ingredient of *horchata*. Here you can find a few surviving examples of Valencia's traditional farmhouse, the *barraca*, with its steeply pitched, thatched roof.

Manises, near the airport, is renowned for its ceramics, which are sold in shops and factories. There is also a ceramics museum.

VALENCIA'S SUMMER SPECIALITY

In summer, the bars and cafés of Valencia offer a thirst-quenching drink unique to the area. *Horchata*, a sweet, milky drink produced mainly in the nearby town of Alboraia, is made from *chufas* (earth almonds). It is served semi-frozen and usually eaten with *fartons* – soft, sweet bread sticks – or *rosquilletas* – crunchy biscuit sticks. The oldest *horchatería* in the city centre is Santa Catalina, off the Plaza de la Virgen.

Painted tiles showing woman serving *horchata*

Fishing boats on the shore of the freshwater lake, L'Albufera

L'Albufera ⑬

Valencia. 🚉 ℹ️ *Raco de l'Olla, (96) 162 73 45.*

A FRESHWATER LAKE situated on the coast just south of Valencia, L'Albufera is one of the prime wetland habitats for birds in Eastern Spain.

It is cut off from the sea by a wooded sandbar, the Dehesa, and fringed by a network of paddy fields which produce a third of Spain's rice.

L'Albufera is fed by the Río Turia and connected to the sea by three channels, which are fitted with sluice gates to control the water level. The lake reaches a maximum depth of 2.5 m (8 ft), and is gradually shrinking because of natural silting and the reclamation of land. In the Middle Ages the lake encompassed an area over ten times its present size.

Over 250 species of birds – including large numbers of egrets and herons – have been recorded in the lake's reed beds and marshy islands, the *matas*. L'Albufera was declared a nature reserve in 1986 to protect its birdlife. Many birds can be seen with binoculars from the shores of the lake.

A visitors' centre at Raco de l'Olla provides information on the ecology of lake, the paddy fields and the Dehesa.

Xàtiva ⑭

Valencia. 🚶 25,000. 🚉 🚌 ℹ️ *Calle Alameda de Jaime I 50, (96) 227 33 46.* 🔄 *Tue & Fri.* 🎭 *Las Fallas (third week of Mar).*

A LONG THE NARROW RIDGE of Mount Vernissa, above Xàtiva, run the ruins of a once-grand **castle** of 30 towers. It was largely destroyed by Felipe V in the War of the Spanish Succession *(see p58)*. Felipe also set fire to the town, which continues to wreak its revenge in an extraordinary way – by hanging Felipe's full-length portrait upside down in the **Museo Municipal**.

Until the attack, Xàtiva was the second town of the kingdom of Valencia. It is thought

Felipe V's full-length portrait hanging upside down in Xàtiva

to have been founded by the Phoenicians. Under the Moors it became prosperous, and in the 12th century it was the first European city to make paper.

Among the sights in the narrow streets and squares of the old town are a former hospital with a Plateresque façade, and a medieval fountain in the Plaça de la Trinidad.

The oldest church in Xàtiva is the **Ermita de San Feliú** (Chapel of St Felix) on the road up to the fortress. It dates from around 1269 and is hung with a number of 14th- to 16th-century icons.

♦ Castillo de Xàtiva
Subida del Castillo. 📞 *(96) 227 42 74.* ⭕ *Tue –Sun.*
🏛 Museo Municipal
Carrer de la Corretgeria 46. 📞 *(96) 227 65 97.* ⭕ *Tue–Sun.*

Gandia ⑮

Valencia. 🚶 53,000. 🚉 ℹ️ *Calle Marqués de Campo, (96) 287 77 88.* 🔄 *Sat.* 🎭 *Las Fallas (19 Mar).*

I N 1485, Rodrigo Borja (who became Pope Alexander VI) was granted the title of Duchy of Gandia. He founded the Borgia clan and, together with his son Cesare and daughter Lucretia, was later implicated in murder and debauchery.

Rodrigo's great-grandson later redeemed the family name by joining the Jesuit order. He was canonized as St Francis Borja by Pope Clement X in 1671.

The house in which he was born and lived, the **Palacio Ducal** (Duke's Palace), is now owned by the Jesuits. Its simple Gothic courtyard belies the richly decorated chambers within, especially the Baroque Golden Gallery. The small patio has a tiled floor depicting the four elements of earth, air, fire and water.

Palacio Ducal
Calle Santo Duque 1. (96) 287 12 03. Mon –Sat.

The ornate and gilded interior of the Palacio Ducal, Gandia

Denia ⑯

Alicante. 27,000. Plaza Oculista Buigues 9, (96) 642 23 67. Mon. Patronales (early Jul).

THIS TOWN was founded as a Greek colony. It takes its name from the Roman goddess Diana – a temple in her honour was excavated here. In the 11th century it became the capital of a short-lived Muslim kingdom, whose dominion extended from Andalusia to the Balearic Islands.

It is now a fishing port and holiday resort. The town centre spreads around the base of a low hill. A large **castle**, originally an Arab fortress, stands on its summit, overlooking the harbour. The entrance gateway, the Portal de la Vila, survives, though it was much altered in the 17th century.

The Palacio del Gobernador (Governor's House), within the castle, contains an archaeological museum which shows the development of Denia from 200 BC to the 18th century.

North of the harbour is the sandy beach of Las Marinas. To the south is the rocky and less developed Las Rotas beach, which is good for snorkelling.

Castillo de Denia
Calle San Francisco. (96) 642 06 56. daily.

Xàbia ⑰

Alicante. 17,000. Plaza de la Iglesia 4, (96) 579 43 56. Thu. Aduanas de Mar (first week of Sep).

PIRATES AND SMUGGLERS once took advantage of the hiding places afforded by the cliffs, caves, inlets and two rocky islands that make up Xàbia's attractive coastline.

The town centre is perched on a hill a short way inland, on the site of an Iberian walled settlement. Many of the buildings lining its streets are made from the local Tosca sandstone. The 16th-century **Iglesia de San Bartolomé** was fortified to serve its congregation as a refuge in times of invasion. It has openings over the door through which missiles could be dropped on to attackers.

The seafront is overlooked by ruined 17th- and 18th-century windmills. Because of council policy, Xàbia's beaches have been kept mercifully free of the high-rise apartment blocks that dominate many other Spanish resorts.

Entrance to the Gothic Iglesia de San Bartolomé in Xàbia

The ceremonial burning of Las Fallas on St Joseph's Day

VALENCIA AND MURCIA'S FIESTAS

Las Fallas *(19 Mar)*. Huge papier-mâché monuments *(fallas)* are erected in the crossroads and squares of Valencia around 15 March and ceremonially set alight on the night of the 19th, St Joseph's Day. Costing millions of pesetas each, the *fallas* depict satirical scenes and can take up to a year to build. During the fiesta, the city echoes to the sound of fire crackers.

Good Friday, Lorca (Murcia). The "blue" and "white" brotherhoods compete to outdo each other in pomp and finery during a grand procession of biblical characters.

Moors and Christians. *(22–4 Apr)*, Alcoi (Alicante). Two costumed armies march into the city, where they perform ceremonies and fight mock battles in commemoration of the Reconquest.

Bous en la Mar *(early Jul)*, Denia (Alicante). People dodge bulls on the quay until one or the other falls into the sea *(see p35)*.

Misteri d'Elx *(14–15 Aug)*, Elx (Alicante). This choral play, in the Iglesia de Santa María, has spectacular special effects.

La Tomatina *(last Wed of Aug)*, Buñol (Valencia). Thousands of participants pelt each other with ripe tomatoes *(see pp238–9)*.

The Costa Blanca

Less hectic than the Costa del Sol *(see pp448–9)* and with warmer winters than the Costa Brava *(see p207)*, the Costa Blanca occupies a prime stretch of Spain's Mediterranean coastline. Alicante, with its airport and mainline railway station, is the arrival and departure point for most tourists. Between Alicante and Altea there are long stretches of sandy beach which have been heavily built up with apartment blocks and hotels. North of Altea there are more fine beaches, but they are broken by cliffs and coves. South from Alicante, as far as the resort of Torrevieja, the scenery is drier and more barren, relieved only by the wooded sand dunes of Guardamar del Segura.

Gandia marks the southern end of the Costa de Valencia, whose extensive beaches of fine sand and shallow water are popular with the Spanish.

● Gandia

● Oliva

Dénia's Las Marinas beach is a flat, sandy strip lined by hotels. The rocky Les Rotes beach is good for snorkelling.

● Denia

● Xàbia

Xàbia's busiest beach is El Arenal. Most of the resort's coastline is punctuated by cliffs and coves.

Altea is a resort with an unspoiled, whitewashed old town on a hilltop. Beneath it is a long, shingle beach.

● Moraira

Calp

● Altea

Santa Pola is still a working fishing port, but its long, sandy beaches are very popular.

● Benidorm
La Vila Joiosa

Benidorm's liveliest beach, Levante, is considered to be one of the ten best beaches in the world. Poniente is further from the town centre.

● El Campello

● Platja de Sant Joan

Platja de Sant Joan has a long strip of seamless sand bordered by a road and a narrow-gauge railway, which gives easy access to the beach.

● Alacant (Alicante)

● Santa Pola
Illa de Tabarca

The Illa de Tabarca attracts daytrippers for its natural beauty and clear waters, good for snorkelling.

● Guardamar del Segura

Guardamar del Segura has one of the coast's least busy beaches. It is bordered by windswept sand dunes covered with aromatic pine woods.

Torrevieja

0 kilometres   25

0 miles   25

Torrevieja is a very popular package holiday resort with sweeping, sandy beaches to the south. It has been highly developed in recent years.

Alicante's city centre is served by the popular Postiguet beach. Nearby are vast, sandy beaches, such as La Albufereta and Sant Joan.

◁ **Entrance of the Moorish army, part of a festival to commemorate the Reconquest, Ontinyent, Valencia**

Penyal d'Ifach

Alicante. 🚉 Calp. 🚌 Calp. 🛈 Calp, (96) 583 69 20.

WHEN VIEWED from afar, the rocky outcrop of the Penyal d'Ifach seems to rise vertically out of the sea. One of the Costa Blanca's most dramatic sights, this 332-m (1,089-ft) tall block of limestone looks virtually unclimbable. However, a short tunnel, built in 1918, allows walkers access to the much gentler slopes on its seaward side.

Allow about two hours for the round trip, which starts at the visitors' centre above Calp harbour. It takes you up gentle slopes covered with juniper and fan palm, with the waves crashing below. As you climb, and at the exposed summit, there are spectacular views of a large stretch of the Costa Blanca. On a clear day you can see the hills of Ibiza (see p486).

The Penyal d'Ifach is also home to 300 types of wild plant, including several rare species. Migrating birds use it as a landmark, and the salt flats below it are an important habitat for them. The rock was privately owned until 1987, when the regional government acquired it and turned it into a nature reserve.

Situated below the rock is the Iberian town of Calp, renowned for its beaches, such as Levante and Les Bassetes.

The magnificent limestone rock Penyal d'Ifach

Guadalest ❶

Alicante. 🚶 170. 🛈 Plaza de San Gregorio 1, (96) 588 52 19. 🎉 Fiestas de los Jóvenes (6 Jun), Virgen de la Asunción (mid-Aug).

DESPITE DRAWING coach loads of day-trippers from Benidorm, the pretty mountain village of Castell de Guadalest remains relatively unspoiled. This is largely because its older part is accessible only on foot by a single entrance: a sloping tunnel cut into the rock on which the castle ruins and the church's distinctive belfry are precariously perched.

Guadalest was founded by the Moors, who carved the surrounding hillsides into terraces and planted them with crops. These are still irrigated by the original ditches constructed by the Moors. The village was badly damaged by earthquakes in 1644 and 1748.

From the main square, a flight of steps ascends to the **castle**, from which there are magnificent views of the surrounding mountains.

At the **Museo de Miniaturas** you can see a microscopic version of Leonardo da Vinci's *Last Supper*, painted on a grain of rice, Goya's *The Naked Maja* (see p283), painted on the wing of a fly, and a sculpture of a camel passing through the eye of a needle.

🏛 Museo de Miniaturas
Calle de la Iglesia 5. 📞 (96) 588 50 62. ⭕ daily. 📷

The belfry of Guadalest, perched on top of a rock

Alcoi ❷

Alicante. 🚶 65,000. 🚉 🚌 🛈 Plaza de España 1, (96) 554 52 11. 🎉 Moors and Christians (22–4 Apr).

SITED AT THE confluence of three rivers and surrounded by high mountains, Alcoi is an industrial city. But it is best known for its mock battles between Moors and Christians (see p245) and its *peladillas* – almonds coated in sugar.

On the slopes above it is **Font Roja** (the red spring), a nature reserve and shrine, marked by a towering statue of the Virgin Mary.

ENVIRONS: To the north of Alcoi is the **Sierra de Mariola**, a mountain range famed for its medicinal and culinary herbs. The best point of access is the village of **Agres**. A scenic route runs from the north of Agres to the summit of Mont Cabrer at 1,390 m (4,560 ft). It passes two ruined *neveras* – pits once used to store ice for preserving fish and meat.

The bullring of **Bocairent**, 10 km (6 miles) west of Agres, was carved out of rock in 1813. A nearby cliff is pockmarked with **Les Covetes dels Moros** ("the Moors' Caves"). Despite their name, the origin of these man-made caves is a mystery.

Benidorm ㉑

Alicante. 🏠 47,000. 🚌 🚊 ℹ️ *Calle Martínez Alejos 16, (96) 585 13 11.* 🗓️ *Wed, Sun.* 🎭 *Virgen del Carmen (16 Mar), Las Fallas (19 Mar).*

WITH FORESTS of skyscrapers overshadowing its two long beaches, this famous holiday resort is more reminiscent of Manhattan than the obscure fishing village it still was in the early 1950s.

Benidorm boasts more accommodation than any other resort on the Mediterranean, but its clientele has changed since the 1980s when its name was synonymous with "lager louts". A huge public park and open-air auditorium used for cultural events, the **Parque de l'Aigüera**, is emblematic of the facelift Benidorm has gone through in recent years. The town now attracts more elderly holidaymakers from the north of Spain than youths from England. Even so, the top attractions of this resort are still said to be sex, sun, night-clubs and "English" pubs.

A small park on a promontory between the Levante and Poniente beaches, called the **Balcón del Mediterráneo**, ends in a giant waterspout – a single-jet fountain. From here there is a panoramic view of most of Benidorm. A short way out to sea is the Illa de Benidorm, a wedge-shaped

Main staircase with floral lamp in the Casa Modernista, Novelda

island served by ferries from the harbour. The island is being converted into a nature reserve to protect its sea birds.

ENVIRONS: La Vila Joiosa (Villajoyosa), to the south, is much older than Benidorm. Its principal sight is a line of brightly painted houses that overhang the riverbed. They were painted in such vivid colours, it is said, so that their fishermen owners would be able to identify their homes when they were out at sea.

The older part of **Altea**, to the north of Benidorm, stands on a hill above modern beach-front developments. It is a delightful jumble of white houses, narrow streets and alleys, and long flights of steps arranged round a prominent, blue-domed church.

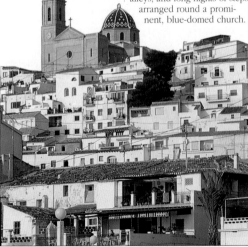
The old town of Altea, dominated by its domed church

Novelda ㉒

Alicante. 🏠 23,000. 🚌 🚊 ℹ️ *Plaza de España 1, (96) 560 03 77.* 🗓️ *Wed, Sat.* 🎭 *Santa María Magdalena (third week of Jul).*

THE INDUSTRIAL TOWN of Novelda is dominated by its many marble factories. But it is the exquisitely preserved Art Nouveau house, the **Casa Modernista**, that is of special interest. It was built in 1903 and rescued from demolition in 1975 by a local bank. The three-storey building is furnished in period style. There are few straight lines or functional shapes and almost every inch of wall-space has some floral or playful motif.

ENVIRONS: Villena town hall has a collection of Bronze Age gold objects, the **Tesoro de Villena** *(see pp44–5).*

🏛️ **Casa Modernista**
Calle Mayor 24. 📞 *(96) 560 02 37.* ⬤ *Sat & Sun.*
🏛️ **Tesoro de Villena**
Ayuntamiento. 📞 *(96) 580 11 50.* ⬤ *by prior arrangement.*

Alicante ㉓

Alicante. 🏠 270,000. ✈️ 🚌 🚊 ⛴️ ℹ️ *Explanada de España 2, (96) 520 00 00.* 🗓️ *Thu, Sat.* 🎭 *Hogueras (third week of Jun).*

A PORT AND SEASIDE resort built around a natural harbour, Alicante (Alacant) is the principal city of the Costa Blanca. Both the Greeks and Romans established settlements here. In the 8th century the Moors refounded the city under the shadow of Mount Benacantil. The summit of this hill is now occupied by the **Castillo de Santa Bárbara**, which dates mainly from the 16th century. From its top battlements there is a view over the whole city.

The focus of the city is the **Explanada de España**, a palm-lined promenade along the waterfront. The 18th-century Baroque **town hall** *(ayuntamiento)*, is worth seeing for the Salón Azul (Blue Room) with its mirrored gallery. A metal disc on the pink marble staircase is used as a

Yachts moored in Alicante harbour, beside the Explanada de España

reference point in measuring the sea level all around Spain. A local painter, Eusebio Sempere (1924–85), assembled the eclectic range of 20th-century art on display in the 17th-century **Casa de la Asegurada**. It includes paintings by Dalí, Miró, Picasso *(see pp28–9)* and Sempere himself.

🏰 **Castillo de Santa Bárbara**
Playa del Postiguet. 📞 *(96) 516 21 28.* ◯ *daily.* 📷 &

🏛 **Ayuntamiento**
Plaza del Ayuntamiento. 📞 *(96) 514 91 00.* ◯ *Mon–Sat by arrangement.*

🏛 **Casa de la Asegurada**
Plaza de Santa María 3. 📞 *(96) 514 94 69.* ◯ *Tue–Sun.*

Illa de Tabarca ㉔

Alicante. 🚢 *from Santa Pola/Alicante.*
ℹ *Santa Pola, (96) 669 22 76.*

T HE BEST POINT of departure for the Illa de Tabarca is Santa Pola. This small, flat island is divided into two parts: a stony, treeless area of level ground known as *el campo* (the countryside), and a walled settlement, which is entered through three monumental gateways. The settlement was laid out on a grid plan in the 18th century, on the orders of Carlos III, to prevent the island being used by pirates.

Tabarca is a popular place to swim or snorkel and it can get crowded in the summer.

Fish and salt have long been important to the economy of Santa Pola. A Roman fish salting works has been excavated here, and outside the town are some modern saltpans.

Elx ㉕

Alicante. 🏠 *200,000.* 🚆 🚌
ℹ *Parque Municipal, (96) 545 38 31.*
🗓 *Mon, Sat.* 🎉 *Virgen de la Asunción (second week of Aug).*

T HE FOREST of over 300,000 palm trees that surrounds Elx (Elche) on three sides is said to have been planted by the Phoenicians around 300 BC. Part of it has been enclosed as a private garden called the **Huerto del Cura**. Some of the palms – one with a trunk which has divided into eight branches – are dedicated to various notable people, such as the Empress Elizabeth of Austria, who visited here in 1894.

The first settlement in the area, around 5000 BC, was at La Alcudia, where a 5th-century BC Iberian stone bust of a priestess, *La Dama de Elche (see p44)*, was discovered in 1897. The original is in Madrid, but there are several replicas scattered around Elx.

The blue-domed Baroque church, the **Basílica de Santa María**, was built in the 17th century to house the **Misteri d'Elx** *(see p37)*. Next to it is **La Calahorra**, a Gothic tower, which is a surviving part of the city's defences.

A clock on the roof next to the town hall has two 16th-century mechanical figures, which strike the hours on bells.

🌴 **Huerto del Cura**
Porta de la Morera 49. 📞 *(96) 545 19 36.* ◯ *daily.* 📷 &

🏛 **La Calahorra**
Calle Uberna. 📞 *(96) 545 28 19.* ◯ *Tue–Sun.* 📷

Orihuela ㉖

Alicante. 🏠 *51,000.* 🚆 🚌 ℹ *Calle Francisco Die 25, (96) 530 27 47.*
🗓 *Tue.* 🎉 *La Reconquista (17 Jul).*

I N THE 15TH CENTURY Orihuela was prosperous enough for Fernando and Isabel to stop and collect men and money on their way to do battle against the Moors at Granada. The Gothic **cathedral**, with its Romanesque cloister, contains Velázquez's *The Temptation of St Thomas Aquinas*. Among the 18th-century processional floats displayed in the **Museo de Semana Santa** (Easter Week Museum) is one bearing a statue of a she-devil, *La Diablesa*.

🏛 **Museo de Semana Santa**
Calle Ballesteros Villanueva. 📞 *(96) 674 40 89.* ◯ *Mon–Sat.* 📷 &

La Diablesa, Orihuela

Torrevieja ㉗

Alicante. 🏠 *30,000.* ℹ *Plaza Capdepont, (96) 571 59 36.* 🗓 *Fri.*
🎉 *Habaneras (Aug).*

D URING THE 1980s, Torrevieja grew at a prodigious rate as thousands of Europeans purchased homes here. Before tourism, the town's source of income was sea salt. The salt works are the most productive in Europe and the second most important in the world.

Torrevieja stages a festival of *habaneras*, melodic songs originating in Cuba, brought back to Spain by salt exporters.

Capilla del Junterón, Murcia

Murcia 28

Murcia. 🏙 140,000. 🚗 🚉
ℹ️ Alejandro Seiquer 4, (968) 21
37 16. 🛍 Thu. 🎭 Semana Santa
(Easter Week).

A REGIONAL CAPITAL and university city on the River
Segura, Murcia was founded in
825 by the Moors, following
successful irrigation of the
surrounding fertile plain.

The centre of the modern
city is the 18th-century square,
La Glorieta. The pedestrianized Calle de la Trapería, linking the cathedral and the former marketplace (now the
Plaza Santo Domingo), is the
city's main street.

On it stands a gentlemen's
club founded in 1847, the
Casino (ask the doorman for
permission to look round). It is
entered through an Arab-style
patio, fashioned on the royal
chambers of the Alhambra. The
huge romantic ballroom has a
highly polished parquet floor
and is illuminated by five large
crystal chandeliers. A painting
covering the ceiling of the
ladies' cloakroom depicts the
goddess Selene.

Work on the **cathedral**
began in 1394 over the foundations of Murcia's central
mosque, and it was finally
consecrated in 1467. The large
tower was added much later
and constructed in stages from
the 16th to the 18th centuries.
The architect Jaime Bort built
the main, Baroque façade
between 1739 and 1754.

The cathedral's finest features
are two exquisitely ornate side
chapels. The first, the Capilla
de los Vélez, is in Late Gothic

style and was built between
1490 and 1507. The second,
the Renaissance Capilla del
Junterón, dates from the early
16th century.

The **cathedral museum**
displays grand Gothic altarpieces, a frieze from a Roman
sarcophagus and the third
largest monstrance in Spain.

Francisco Salzillo (1707–83),
one of Spain's greatest sculptors, was born in Murcia, and
a museum in the **Iglesia de
Jesús** (Church of Jesus)
exhibits nine of his *pasos* –
sculptures on platforms. These
are carried through the streets

Arab-style patio, Murcia Casino

of the city on Good Friday
morning. The figures are so
lifelike that a fellow sculptor
is said to have told the men
carrying a *paso*: "Put it down,
it will walk by itself".

ENVIRONS: The folk museum,
the **Museo de Tradiciones y
Artes Populares**, stands beside
a large water wheel – a 1955
copy in iron of the original

15th-century wooden wheel.
The three galleries display
agricultural and domestic
items, some of them 300 years
old. A traditional, thatched
Murcian farmhouse *(barraca)*
forms part of the museum.

🎰 **Casino**
Calle Trapería 18. 🅲 (968) 21 22 55.
🔲 daily, by permission. 🏷️
🏛 **Museo Etnológico de la
Huerta de Alcantarilla**
Carretera de Granada. 🅲 (968)
89 38 66. 🔲 Tue–Sun. 🚻

Mar Menor 29

Murcia. ✈️ San Javier. 🚉 from
Cartagena. 🚌 La Manga. ℹ️ La
Manga, (968) 14 18 12.

T HE ELONGATED, high-rise
holiday resort of La Manga,
built on a long, thin, sandy
strip, separates the Mediterranean and the Mar Menor,
literally "the Smaller Sea".

Really a large lagoon, the
sheltered Mar Menor can be
5°C (9°F) warmer than the
Mediterranean in summer. Its
high mineral concentrations
first drew rest-cure tourists in
the early 20th century. They
stayed at the older resorts of
Santiago de la Ribera and Los
Alcázares, which still have
pretty wooden jetties protruding from their beaches.

From Santiago de la Ribera
you can take a ferry to two of
the five islands in the Mar
Menor, the biggest of which is
called the Isla Mayor.

The old saltpans at Lo Pagán,
near San Pedro del Pinatar, are
now a nature reserve.

The resort of Los Alcázares on the edge of the Mar Menor

View of the domes and spires of Cartagena's town hall from the seafront

Cartagena ⓿

Murcia. 🏛 170,000. ✈ San Javier.
🚉 🚌 ⛴ ℹ Plaza Ayuntamiento,
(968) 50 64 83. 🗓 Wed. 🎭 Semana
Santa (Easter Week), Carthaginians
and Romans (23 Sep).

THE FIRST SETTLEMENT founded in the natural harbour of Cartagena was constructed in 223 BC by the Carthaginians, who called it *Quart Hadas* (New City). After conquering the city in 209 BC, the Romans renamed it *Carthago Nova* (New Carthage).

Although the city declined in importance in the Middle Ages, its prestige increased in the 18th century when it became a major naval base.

You can get an overview of the city from the park which surrounds the ruins of the **Castillo de la Concepción**, Cartagena's castle. On the quayside below is a prototype submarine designed by Isaac Peral in 1888. The city hall, opposite, marks the end of the Calle Mayor, a street overlooked by balconies and lined with handsome buildings. Excavations in the city include a Roman street and the **Muralla Bizantina** (Byzantine Wall), built between 589 and 590.

The **National Underwater Archaeology Museum** has an interesting collection of ancient Roman and Greek jars.

⋔ **Muralla Bizantina**
Calle Nueva. 📞 (968) 50 79 66.
◻ Tue–Sat.

🏛 **Museo Nacional de Arqueología Submarino**
Carretera Faro de Navidad. 📞 (968) 50 84 15. ◻ Tue–Sun. ♿

Costa Cálida ㉛

Murcia. 🚉 Cartagena. 🚌 Murcia.
ℹ Águilas, (968) 41 33 03.

THE MOST POPULAR RESORTS of Murcia's "Warm Coast" are around the Mar Menor. Between Cabo de Palos and Cabo Tinoso the few small beaches are dwarfed by cliffs and headlands. The resorts of the southern part of the coast are relatively quiet for Spain. There are several fine beaches at Puerto de Mazarrón; and at nearby Bolnuevo the wind has eroded soft rocks into strange shapes. The growing resort of Águilas marks the southern limit of the coast, at the border with Andalusia.

Lorca ㉜

Murcia. 🏛 70,000. 🚉 🚌
ℹ Palacio de Guevara, (968) 46 61 57.
🗓 Thu. 🎭 Semana Santa (Easter Week), Feria (3rd week Sep), Dia de San Clemente (23 Nov).

THE FERTILE FARMLAND around Lorca, Murcia's third most important town, is an oasis in one of the most arid areas of Europe. Lorca was an important staging post on the Via Heraclea, as witnessed by the Roman milepost standing in a corner of the Plaza San Vicente. During the wars between Moors and Christians in the 13th to 15th centuries, Lorca became a frontier town between Al Andalus and the Castilian territory of Murcia. Its castle dates from this era, although only two of its original 35 towers remain. After Granada fell the town lost its importance and, except for one surviving gateway, its walls were demolished.

The centre of the town, the Plaza de España, is lined with handsome stone buildings. One side is occupied by the **Colegiata de San Patricio** (Church of St Patrick), built between 1533 and 1704, the only church in Spain dedicated to the Irish saint. At the head of the square is the town hall. A former prison, it was built in two blocks between 1677 and 1739, and later connected by an arch that spans the street.

Caravaca de la Cruz ㉝

Murcia. 🏛 21,500. ℹ Plaza del Arco 1, (968) 70 20 00. 🗓 Mon.
🎭 Vera Cruz (May).

A TOWN OF ancient churches, Caravaca de la Cruz's fame lies in its castle which houses the **Santuario de la Vera Cruz** (Sanctuary of the True Cross). This is where a double-armed cross is said to have appeared miraculously in 1231 – 12 years before the town was seized by Christians. The highlight of the Vera Cruz fiesta is the Race of the Wine Horses, which commemorates the lifting of a Moorish siege of the castle. The Cross of Caravaca was dipped in wine which the thirsty defenders then drank and recovered their fighting strength.

ENVIRONS: Just to the north is the pretty village of **Moratalla**, an attractive jumble of steep streets and brightly painted houses lying beneath a 15th-century castle. The village is among the foothills of the range of mountains marking Murcia's western border. **Cehegín**, east of Caravaca, is a partially preserved medieval town.

Roman milepost topped by a statue of St Vincent, Lorca

MADRID

Introducing Madrid

S PAIN'S CAPITAL, a city of over three million people, is situated close to the geographical centre of the country, at the hub of both road and rail networks. Because of its distance from the sea and its altitude – 660 m (2,150 ft) – the city endures cold winters and hot summers, making spring and autumn the best times to visit. Madrid's attractions include three internationally famous art galleries, a royal palace, grand public squares and many museums filled with the treasures of Spain's history. The city is surrounded by its own small province, the Comunidad de Madrid, which takes in the Sierra de Guadarrama and one of Spain's most famous monuments, the palace of El Escorial.

The Palacio Real (see pp266–7) *the royal palace built by Spain's first Bourbon kings, dominates the western part of Old Madrid. Its lavishly decorated chambers include the throne room.*

The Plaza Mayor (see p263), *Old Madrid's great 17th-century square, has been a focal point of the city since the days when it was used as a public arena for bullfights, trials by the Inquisition and executions (see p264). An equestrian statue of Felipe III stands in the middle of the square.*

OLD MADRID
(see pp258–71)

MADRID PROVINCE
(see pp308–309)

El Escorial (see pp312–13), *the massive, architecturally austere monastery-palace built by Felipe II, has some sumptuous apartments decorated with great works of art. Marble sarcophagi in the octagonal Royal Pantheon contain the mortal remains of most Spanish monarchs.*

0 kilometres   25

0 miles   20

◁ **Sculpted fountain of the Goddess Cybele in the Plaza de Cibeles, with the main post office behind**

The Museo Thyssen-Bornemisza (see pp278–9), one of the most important privately assembled art collections in the world, was given to Spain in 1993. The 18th-century palace houses major works by Titian, Rubens, Goya, Van Gogh and Picasso.

BOURBON MADRID (see pp272–89)

The Plaza de Cibeles (see p276); one of the city's most impressive squares, is ringed by distinctive buildings, including the 19th-century Banco de España and Madrid's main post office, with sculptures on its white façade.

The Parque del Retiro (see p287) has leafy paths and avenues, and a boating lake overlooked by a majestic colonnade. It is an ideal place in which to relax between visits to the great art galleries and museums of Bourbon Madrid.

The Museo del Prado (see pp282–5) is one of the world's greatest art galleries. It has important collections of paintings by Velázquez and Goya, whose statue stands outside the main entrance.

| 0 metres | 500 |
| 0 yards | 500 |

The Centro de Arte Reina Sofía (see pp288–9), an outstanding museum of 20th-century art, is entered by highly original exterior glass lifts. Inside, the star exhibit is Guernica, Picasso's famous painting of the horrors of the Civil War.

Old Madrid

When Felipe II chose Madrid as his capital in 1561, it was a small Castilian town of little real significance. In the following years, it was to grow into the nerve centre of a mighty empire.

According to tradition, it was the Moorish chieftain Muhammad ben Abd al Rahman who established a fortress above the Río Manzanares. Magerit, as it was called in Arabic, fell to Alfonso VI of Castile between 1083 and 1086. Narrow streets with houses

Drawer designed for storing herbs, Palacio Real

and medieval churches began to grow up on the higher ground behind the old Arab alcazar, which was replaced by a Gothic palace in the 15th century.

When this burned down in 1734, it was replaced in turn by the present Bourbon palace, the Palacio Real.

The population had scarcely reached 20,000 when Madrid was chosen as capital, but by the end of the century it had more than trebled. The 16th-century city is known as the "Madrid de los Austrias", after the reigning Habsburg dynasty. During this period royal monasteries were endowed and churches and private palaces were built.

In the 17th century, the Plaza Mayor was added and the Puerta del Sol, the "Gate of the Sun", became the spiritual and geographical heart not only of Madrid but of all Spain.

Sights at a Glance

Historic Buildings
Palacio Real pp266–7 **9**

Museums and Galleries
Real Academia de
Bellas Artes **14**

Churches and Convents
Catedral de San Isidro **2**
Iglesia de San Nicolás **5**
Monasterio de las
Descalzas Reales **13**

Monasterio de la
Encarnación **10**
Nuestra Señora de la
Almudena **7**

Streets, Squares and Parks
Campo del Moro **8**
Gran Vía **12**
Plaza de España **11**
Plaza Mayor **4**
Plaza de Oriente **6**

Plaza de la Villa **3**
Puerta del Sol **1**

Getting There
The metro is the fastest and easiest way to get to Old Madrid. Take line 1 to Gran Vía or Sol; alternatively, lines 2, 3, 5, and 10 are also good for getting to the main sights. Useful buses include the 51, 52 and 150 to Puerta del Sol.

Key

■ Street-by-Street map pp260–61
Ⓜ Metro station
🚏 Main bus stop
ℹ Tourist information
🅿 Parking

0 metres 500
0 yards 500

◁ **Statue of Cervantes by Lorenzo Coullaut-Valera in the Plaza de España**

Street-by-Street: Old Madrid

Sᴛʀᴇᴛᴄʜɪɴɢ ꜰʀᴏᴍ ᴛʜᴇ ᴍᴇᴅɪᴇᴠᴀʟ Plaza de la Villa to the busy Puerta del Sol, the compact heart of Old Madrid is steeped in history and full of interesting sights. Trials by the Inquisition *(see p264)* and executions were once held in the Plaza Mayor. This porticoed square is Old Madrid's finest piece of architecture, a legacy of the Habsburgs *(see pp54–7)*. Other buildings of note are the Catedral de San Isidro and the Palacio de Santa Cruz. For a more relaxing way of enjoying Old Madrid, sit in one of the area's numerous cafés or browse among the stalls of the Mercado de San Miguel.

★ **Plaza Mayor**
This beautiful ... century square competes with t... Puerta del Sol ... the focus of Old... Madrid. The arcades at the ... of the three-stor... buildings are fi... with cafés and craft shops ❹

The Mercado de San Miguel is housed in a 19th-century building with wrought-iron columns. The market sells a variety of food and household goods.

To Palacio Real

CALLE MAYOR

PLAZA MORENAS

PLAZA DE LA VILLA

CALLE DE SACRAMENTO

CORDÓN

PUÑONROSTRO

Town hall *(ayuntamiento)*

Casa de Cisneros

Arco de Cuchilleros

★ **Plaza de la Villa**
The 15th-century Torre de los Lujanes is the oldest of several historic buildings standing on this square ❸

0 metres		10
0 yards		100

The Basílica Pontificia de San Miguel is an imposing 18th-century church with a beautiful façade and a graceful interior. It is one of very few churches in Spain inspired by the Italian Baroque style.

Sᴛᴀʀ Sɪɢʜᴛs

★ Plaza Mayor

★ Plaza de la Villa

★ Puerta del Sol

★ **Puerta del Sol**
With its shops and cafés, the Puerta del Sol is one of the city's liveliest areas. This sign for Tío Pepe, a brand of sherry, has become synonymous with the square ❶

LOCATOR MAP
See Street Finder map 2

Iglesia de San Ginés

Sol Metro

To Bourbon Madrid

CALLE DEL ARENAL

PUERTA DEL SOL

CALLE DE ALCALÁ

CALLE MAYOR

CALLE DE POSTAS

CALLE PAZ

CALLE DE CARRETAS

ESPOZ Y MINA

BARCELONA

PLAZA MAYOR

PLAZA PROVINCIA

PLAZA DE JACINTO BENAVENTE

SALVADOR

DUQUE DE RIVAS

CALLE DE LA COLEGIATA

Tirso de Molina Metro

The Palacio de Santa Cruz was built as the court prison in the 17th century. This Baroque *(see p21)* palace is now occupied by the Foreign Ministry.

Catedral de San Isidro
This was Madrid's provisional cathedral until La Almudena was completed (see p265). It is named after the city's patron, St Isidore, a local 12th-century farmer ❷

Kilometre Zero, the centre of Spain's road network, Puerta del Sol

Puerta del Sol ❶

Map 2 F3.   Ⓜ *Sol.*

NOISY WITH TRAFFIC, chatter and policemen's whistles, the Puerta del Sol or Gateway of the Sun makes a fitting centre for Madrid. This is one of the city's most popular meeting places, and huge crowds converge on this famous square on their way to the shops and sights in the old part of the city.

The square marks the site of the original eastern entrance to the city, once occupied by a gatehouse and castle. These disappeared long ago and in their place came a succession of churches. In the late 19th century the area was turned into a square and became the centre of café society.

Today the "square" is shaped like a half moon. Its straight southern side is occupied by an austere red-brick building, originally the city's post office, built in the 1760s under Carlos III. In 1847 it became the headquarters of the

The bronze bear and strawberry tree of Madrid, Puerta del Sol

Ministry of the Interior. In 1866 the clocktower, which gives the building much of its identity, was added. During the Franco regime *(see pp62–3)*, the police cells beneath the building were the site of many human rights abuses. In 1963, Julián Grimau, a member of the underground Communist party, allegedly fell from an upstairs window and miraculously survived, only to be executed shortly afterwards.

The building is now home to the regional government, the *Comunidad de Madrid,* and is the focus of many festive events. At midnight on New Year's Eve dense crowds fill the square and people swallow a grape on each stroke of the clock, a tradition supposed to bring good luck for the rest of the year. Outside the building, a symbol on the ground marks Kilometre Zero, considered the centre of Spain's huge road network.

The buildings opposite are arranged in a semicircle and contain modern shops and cafés. On the corner of Calle del Carmen is a bronze statue of the symbol of Madrid – a bear reaching for the fruit of a *madroño* (strawberry tree).

The Puerta del Sol has witnessed many important historical events. On 2 May 1808 the uprising against the occupying French forces began here, but the crowd, pitted against the well-armed French troops, was crushed *(see p59)*. In 1912 the liberal prime minister José Canalejas was assassinated in the square and, in 1931, the Second Republic *(see p61)* was proclaimed from the balcony of the Ministry of the Interior.

Catedral de San Isidro ❷

Calle de Toledo 37. **Map** 2 E4.
🄲 *(91) 369 20 37.* Ⓜ *La Latina.*
🄾 *8am–12:30pm, 6–8:45pm Mon–Sat, 8am–2:30pm, 5:45–8:45pm Sun.*

BUILT IN THE Baroque style *(see p21)* for the Jesuits in the mid-17th century, this twin-towered church served as Madrid's cathedral until La Almudena *(see p265)* was completed in 1993.

After Carlos III expelled the Jesuits from Spain in 1767 *(see p58)*, Ventura Rodríguez was commissioned to redesign the interior of the church. It was then re-dedicated to Madrid's patron saint, St Isidore, and two years later the saint's remains were moved here from the Iglesia de San Andrés. San Isidro was returned to the Jesuits during the reign of Fernando VII (1814–33).

Altar in the Catedral de San Isidro

Plaza de la Villa ❸

Map 2 D4. Ⓜ *Ópera, Sol.*

THE MUCH RESTORED and frequently remodelled Plaza de la Villa is one of the most atmospheric spots in Madrid. Some of the city's most historic secular buildings are situated around this square.

The oldest building is the early 15th-century Torre de los Lujanes, with its Gothic portal and Mudéjar-style horseshoe arches. François I of France was allegedly imprisoned in it following his defeat at the Battle of Pavia in 1525. The Casa de Cisneros was built in 1537 for the nephew

Portal of the Torre de los Lujanes

of Cardinal Cisneros, founder of the historic University of Alcalá *(see pp314–15)*. The main façade, on the Calle de Sacramento, is an excellent example of the Plateresque style *(see p21)*.

Linked to this building, by an enclosed bridge, is the town hall *(ayuntamiento)*. Designed in the 1640s by Juan Gómez de la Mora, architect of the Plaza Mayor, it exhibits the same combination of steep roofs with dormer windows, steeple-like towers at the corners and an austere façade of brick and stone. Before construction was finished – more than 50 years later – the building had acquired handsome Baroque doorways. A balcony was later added by Juan de Villanueva, the architect of the Prado *(see pp282–5)*, so that the Royal Family could watch Corpus Christi processions passing by.

Plaza Mayor ❹

Map 2 E4. Ⓜ *Sol.*

T HE PLAZA MAYOR forms a splendid rectangular square, all balconies and pinnacles, dormer windows and steep slate roofs. The square, with its theatrical atmosphere, is very Castilian in character. Much was expected to happen here and a great deal did – bullfights, executions, pageants and trials by the Inquisition *(see p264)* – all watched by crowds, often in the presence of the reigning king and queen.

The first great public scene was the beatification of Madrid's patron, St Isidore, in 1621. In the same year, the execution of Rodrigo Calderón, secretary to Felipe III, was held here. Although hated by the Madrid populace, Calderón bore himself with such dignity on the day of his death that the phrase "proud as Rodrigo on the scaffold" survives to this day. Perhaps the greatest occasion of all, however, was the arrival here – from Italy – of Carlos III in 1760.

The square was started in 1617 and built in just two years, replacing slum houses. Its architect, Juan Gómez de la Mora, was successor to Juan de Herrera, designer of Felipe II's austere monastery-palace, El Escorial *(see pp312–13)*. Mora echoed the style of his master, softening it slightly. The fanciest part of the arcaded construction is the Casa de la Panadería (bakery). Its façade, recently and crudely reinvented, is decorated with allegorical paintings.

The equestrian statue in the centre is of Felipe III, who ordered the square's construction. Started by the Italian Giovanni de Bologna and finished by his pupil Pietro Tacca in 1616, the statue was moved here in 1848 from the Casa de Campo *(see p292)*. Nowadays the square is lined with outdoor cafés, and is the venue for a collectors' market on Sundays *(see p305)*. The southern exit of the square leads into the Calle de Toledo towards the streets where the Rastro, Madrid's famous flea-market *(see p292)*, is held. A flight of steps in the south-west corner takes you under the Arco de Cuchilleros to the Calle de Cuchilleros, where there are a number of *mesones*, traditional restaurants.

Allegorical paintings on the Casa de la Panadería, Plaza Mayor

The Spanish Inquisition

THE SPANISH INQUISITION was set up by Fernando and Isabel in 1480 to create a single, monolithic Catholic ideology in Spain. Protestant heretics and alleged "false converts" to Catholicism from the Jewish and Muslim faiths were tried, to ensure the religious unity of the country. Beginning with a papal bull, the Inquisition was run like a court, presided over by the Inquisitor-General. However, the defendants were denied counsel, not told the charges facing them and tortured to obtain confessions. Punishment ranged from imprisonment to beheading, hanging or burning at the stake. A formidable system of control, it gave Spain's Protestant enemies a major propaganda weapon by contributing to the *Leyenda Negra* (Black Legend) which lasted, along with the Inquisition, into the 18th century.

Inquisition banner

A Protestant heretic appears before the royal family, his last chance to repent and convert.

A convicted defendant, forced to wear a red *sanbenito* robe, is led away to prison.

Those who have refused to confess are sentenced in public by day, and then executed before nightfall.

AUTO-DA-FÉ IN THE PLAZA MAYOR

This painting by Francisco Rizi (1683) depicts a trial, or *auto-da-fé* – literally, show of faith – held in Madrid's main square on 30 June 1680. Unlike papal inquisitions elsewhere in Europe, it was presided over by the reigning monarch, Carlos II, accompanied by his queen.

Torture *was widely used by the Inquisitors and their assistants to extract confessions from their victims. This early 19th-century German engraving shows a man being roasted on a wheel.*

The Procession of the Flagellants *(c.1812) by Goya shows the abiding influence of the Inquisition on the popular imagination. The penitents in the picture are wearing the tall conical hats of heretics tried by the Inquisition. These hats can still be seen in Easter Week processions (see p34) throughout Spain.*

Iglesia de San Nicolás ❺

Plaza de San Nicolás 1. **Map** 1 C3. 🚻
(91) 559 40 64. Ⓜ *Ópera.* ⬜ *9am–1:30pm, 5:30–8pm Mon, 9am–noon, 5:30–8pm Tue, 9–10am, 6:30–8pm Wed–Sat; 10am–2pm, 6:30–8pm Sun.*

THE FIRST MENTION of the church of San Nicolás is in a document of 1202. Its brick tower, with horseshoe arches, is the oldest surviving ecclesiastical structure in Madrid. It is thought to be 12th-century Mudéjar in style, and may have originally been the minaret of a Moorish mosque.

Plaza de Oriente ❻

Map 1 C3. Ⓜ *Ópera.*

DURING HIS DAYS as king of Spain, Joseph Bonaparte *(see p59)* carved out this stirrup-shaped space from the jumble of buildings to the east of the Palacio Real *(see pp266–7)*, providing the view of the palace enjoyed today.

The square was once an important meeting place for state occasions; kings, queens and dictators all made public appearances on the palace balcony facing the plaza. The many statues of early kings which stand here were originally intended for the palace roofline, but proved too heavy. The equestrian statue of Felipe IV in the centre of the square is by Italian sculptor Pietro

Equestrian statue of Felipe IV, by Pietro Tacca, Plaza de Oriente

View of Nuestra Señora de la Almudena and the Royal Palace

Tacca, and is based on drawings by Velázquez. Facing the palace, across the square, is the imposing Teatro Real, or Teatro de la Ópera, inaugurated in 1850 by Isabel II.

Nuestra Señora de la Almudena ❼

Calle de Bailén 8–10. **Map** 1 B3.
🚻 *(91) 542 22 00.* Ⓜ *Ópera.* ⬜ *10am–1:30pm, 6–7:30pm Mon–Sat, 10am–2:30 pm, 6–7:30pm Sun.* ♿

DEDICATED TO the city's patron, the cathedral of La Almudena was begun in 1879 and completed over a century later. Construction was slow – ceasing completely during the Civil War – and involved several architects. The cathedral's Neo-Gothic grey and white façade is similar to that of the Palacio Real, which stands opposite. The crypt houses a 16th-century image of the Virgen de la Almudena.

Further along the Calle Mayor is the site of excavations which have unearthed the remains of Moorish and medieval city walls.

Campo del Moro ❽

Map 1 A3. Ⓜ *Norte.* ⬜ *10:30am–8pm daily.*

THE CAMPO DEL MORO (the "Field of the Moor") is a pleasing park, rising steeply from the Río Manzanares to offer one of the finest views of the Palacio Real *(see pp266–7)*.

The park has a varied history. In 1109 a Moorish army, led by Ali ben Yusuf bivouacked here, hence the name. The park went on to become a jousting ground for Christian knights. In the late 19th century it was used as a lavish playground for royal children. Around the same time it was landscaped in what is described as English style, with winding paths, grass and woodland, fountains and statues. It was reopened to the public in 1931 under the Second Republic *(see p61)*, closed again under Franco, and not reopened until 1983. The Museo de Carruajes is situated in the lower part of the park, but is closed indefinitely. It houses official royal carriages and sedan chairs.

Palacio Real ❾

MADRID'S VAST AND LAVISH ROYAL PALACE was built to impress. The site, on a high bluff over the Rió Manzanares, had been occupied for centuries by a royal fortress, but after a fire in 1734, Felipe V commissioned a truly palatial replacement. Construction lasted 26 years, spanning the reign of two Bourbon monarchs, and much of the exuberant decor reflects the tastes of Carlos III and Carlos IV *(see p67)*. The palace was used by the royal family until the abdication of Alfonso XIII in 1931. The present king, Juan Carlos I, lives in the more modest Zarzuela Palace outside Madrid, but the Royal Palace is still used for state occasions.

Statue of Carlos III

★ Dining Room
This gallery was decorated in 1879. With its long table, ceiling paintings and superb tapestries, it evokes the grandeur of regal Bourbon entertaining.

★ Porcelain Room
The walls and ceiling of this room, built on the orders of Carlos III, are entirely covered in royal porcelain from the Buen Retiro factory. Most of the porcelain is green and white, and depicts cherubs and wreaths.

First floor

The Hall of Columns, once used for royal banquets, is decorated with 16th-century bronzes and Roman imperial busts.

★ Gasparini Rooms
Named after its Neapolitan designer, the Gasparini Room is decorated with lavish rococo chinoiserie. The adjacent antechamber, with painted ceiling and ornate chandelier, houses Goya's portrait of Carlos IV.

STAR FEATURES

★ Dining Room

★ Porcelain Room

★ Gasparini Rooms

★ Throne Room

Plaza de la Armería
The square in front of the main entrance is named after the palace's Royal Armoury. The outstanding collection of weaponry includes the suits of armour belonging to Charles V and Felipe II.

VISITORS' CHECKLIST

Calle de Bailén. **Map** 2 C3.
(91) 542 00 59. Ópera, Plaza de España. 3, 25, 33, 39, 148. Apr–Sep: 9am–6pm Mon–Sat, 9am–3pm Sun, public hols; Oct–Mar: 9:30am–5pm Mon–Sat, 9am–2pm Sun, public hols. once or twice a week for official functions.

Entrance Hall
A marble staircase by *abatini*, next to the statue of *arlos III* as a Roman emperor, leads to the main floor. The painted rococo ceiling by Giaquinto vividly depicts allegorical scenes.

Billiards room

Hall of the Halberdiers

Entrance

Pharmacy
This unique collection includes decorated Talavera pottery storage jars and herb drawers. The Pharmacy Museum has recipe books detailing medications prescribed for the royal family.

KEY TO FLOORPLAN

- Exhibition rooms
- Entrance rooms
- Carlos III rooms
- Chapel rooms
- Carlos IV rooms

Ticket office

Plaza de la Armería

Royal Armoury

★ Throne Room
The two gold and scarlet thrones here are exact reproductions of those of Charles V. The enormous mirrors were made in the royal glass factory of La Granja.

Entrance to the Monasterio de la Encarnación

Monasterio de la Encarnación ⑩

Plaza de la Encarnación 1. **Map** 1 C2.
📞 *(91) 547 05 10.* 🚇 *Ópera, Santo Domingo.* 🕐 *10:30am–12:30pm, 4–5:30pm Wed & Sat, 11am–2pm Sun.* 📷 ♿

STANDING in a delightful tree-shaded square, this tranquil Augustinian convent was founded in 1611 for Margaret of Austria, wife of Felipe III. The architect, Juan Gómez de la Mora, also built the Plaza Mayor *(see p263)* and the façade clearly reveals his work.

The interior of the convent, which is still inhabited by nuns, has the atmosphere of old Castile, with its blue and white Talavera tiles, wooden doors, exposed beams and portraits of royal benefactors.

Inside is a collection of 17th-century art, with paintings by José de Ribera and Vincente Carducho lining the walls. Polychrome wooden statues include *Christ at the Column*, by Gregorio Fernández.

The convent's main attraction is the reliquary chamber with a ceiling painted by Carducho. It is used to store the skulls and bones of saints. There is also a phial containing the dried blood of St Pantaleon. According to a popular myth, the blood liquefies each year on 27 July, the anniversary of the saint's death. Should the blood fail to liquefy, it is said that disaster will befall Madrid. The church,

rebuilt by Ventura Rodríguez after a fire in 1767, has paintings by Francisco Bayeu (Goya's brother-in-law) and frescoes by Luca Giordano.

Plaza de España ⑪

Map 1 C1. 🚇 *Plaza de España.*

ONE OF MADRID's busiest traffic intersections and most popular meeting places is the Plaza de España, which slopes down towards the Palacio Real *(see pp266–7)* and the Sabatini Gardens. In the 18th and 19th centuries the square was occupied by military barracks, built here because of the square's close proximity to the palace. However, further expansion of Madrid resulted in its being left as a public space.

The square acquired its present appearance during the Franco period *(see pp62–3)*, with the construction, on the northern side, of the massive Edificio de España in 1948. Across the square is the Torre de Madrid (1957), known as

La Jirafa (the Giraffe), which, for a while, was the tallest concrete structure in the world. The most attractive part of the square is its centre, occupied by a massive stone obelisk built in 1928. In front of it is a statue of the author Cervantes *(see p315)*. Below him, Don Quixote *(see pp376–7)* rides his horse Rocinante while the plump Sancho Panza trots alongside on his donkey. On the left-hand side is Dulcinea, Don Quixote's sweetheart.

Gran Vía ⑫

Map 2 D1. 🚇 *Plaza de España, Santo Domingo, Callao, Gran Vía.*

A MAIN TRAFFIC ARTERY of the modern city, the Gran Vía was inaugurated in 1910. Its construction spanned several decades and required the demolition of large numbers of run-down buildings and small lanes between the Calle de Alcalá and the Plaza de España. This somewhat hap-hazard road-building scheme soon became the subject of a

Stone obelisk with statue of Miguel de Cervantes, Plaza de España

◁ **Night-time traffic on the Gran Vía, seen from the Plaza de España**

One of the many 1930s buildings lining the Gran Vía

zarzuela – a comic opera – that most *Madrileño* of art forms *(see p306)*. Nowadays, the Gran Vía is at the centre of city life and, following a much needed restoration programme, has become an architectural showpiece.

The most interesting buildings are clustered at the Alcalá end, starting with the Corinthian columns, high level statuary and tiled dome of the Edificio Metrópolis *(see p274)*.

A temple with Art Nouveau mosaics on its upper levels crowns Number 1 Gran Vía. One feature of buildings at this end of the street is colonnaded galleries on the upper floors, imitating medieval Aragonese and Catalan architecture. Another is the fine wrought-iron balconies and carved stone details, such as the gargoyle-like caryatids at Number 12. This part of the Gran Vía has a number of old-world Spanish shops.

On the Red de San Luis, an intersection of four major roads, is the Telefónica building. As the first skyscraper to be erected in the capital – in 1929 – it caused a sensation. Beyond here, the Gran Vía becomes much more American in character, with cinemas, tourist shops and many cafés.

Opposite Callao metro station, on the corner of the Calle Jacometrezo, is another of Madrid's well-known buildings, the Art Deco Capitol cinema and bingo hall, which was built in the 1930s.

Monasterio de las Descalzas Reales ⓭

Plaza de las Descalzas 3. **Map** 2 E3.
☎ *(91) 542 00 59.* Ⓜ *Sol, Callao.*
◌ *10:30am–12:30pm, 4–5:30pm Tue–Thu & Sat, 10:30am–12:30pm Fri, 11am–1:30pm Sun.* 📷

M ADRID'S MOST notable religious building has a soothing, handsome exterior in red brick and granite. This is one of the rare surviving examples of 16th-century architecture in the city.

Around 1560 Felipe II's sister, Doña Juana, decided to convert the original medieval palace which stood here into a convent for nuns and women of the royal household. Her high rank, and that of her fellow nuns, accounts for the massive store of art and wealth of the Descalzas Reales (Royal Barefoot Sisters).

The richly painted stairway has a fresco of Felipe IV and his family looking downwards, as if from a balcony, and a fine ceiling by Claudio Coello and his pupils. It leads up to a small first-floor cloister, which is ringed with chapels containing works of art and precious objects relating to the lives of the former nuns. The main chapel contains the tomb of Doña Juana. The Gran Sala de Tapices contains several series

Decorated chapel, Monasterio de las Descalzas Reales

of tapestries, one woven in Brussels in 1627 for Felipe II's daughter, Isabel Clara Eugenia. Another, *The Triumph of the Eucharist*, is based on cartoons by Rubens. Major paintings on show include works by Brueghel the Elder, Titian, Zurbarán, Murillo and Ribera.

Fray Pedro Machado by Zurbarán

Real Academia de Bellas Artes ⓮

Calle de Alcalá 13. **Map** 3 A5.
☎ *(91) 532 15 46.* Ⓜ *Sevilla, Sol.*
◌ *9am–7pm Tue–Fri, 9am–2:30pm Sat–Mon & public hols.* 📷 ♿

F AMOUS FORMER STUDENTS of this arts academy, housed in an 18th-century building by Churriguera *(see p21)*, include Dalí and Picasso. Its art gallery displays a large selection of works, including excellent drawings by Raphael and Titian. A superb collection of old masters includes paintings by Rubens and Van Dyck. Spanish artists from the 16th to the 19th centuries are particularly well represented, with several magnificent works by Ribera, Murillo, El Greco and Velázquez. One of the highlights is Zurbarán's *Fray Pedro Machado*, typical of the artist's paintings of monks.

An entire room is devoted to Goya, a former director of the academy. On show here are his painting of a relaxed Manuel Godoy *(see p58)*, the *Burial of the Sardine (see p35)*, the grim *Madhouse*, and a self-portrait painted in 1815.

BOURBON MADRID

To the east of Old Madrid, there once lay an idyllic district of market gardens known as the Prado, the "Meadow". In the 16th century a monastery was built on this rising ground. The Habsburgs extended it to form a palace (see p287), of which only fragments now remain; the palace gardens are now the popular Parque del Retiro. The Bourbon monarchs,

especially Carlos III, chose this area to expand and embellish the city in the 18th century. Around the Paseo del Prado they built grand squares with fountains, a triumphal gateway, and what was to become the Museo del Prado, one of the world's greatest art galleries. A more recent addition to the area is the Centro de Arte Reina Sofía, a collection of modern Spanish art.

SIGHTS AT A GLANCE

Historic Buildings
Ateneo de Madrid ⑬
Café Gijón ⑮
Casa de Lope de Vega ⑩
Congreso de los Diputados ⑭
Estación de Atocha ㉑
Hotel Ritz ❶
Real Academia de la Historia ⑪
Teatro Español ⑫

Museums and Galleries
Centro de Arte Reina Sofía pp288–9 ㉒
Museo Arqueológico Nacional ⑱
Museo del Ejército ❼
Museo Nacional de Artes Decorativas ❻
Museo del Prado pp282–5 ❾
Museo Thyssen-Bornemisza pp278–9 ❸

Churches
Iglesia de San Jerónimo el Real ❽

Monuments
Puerta de Alcalá ❺

Streets, Squares and Parks
Calle de Serrano ⑰
Parque del Retiro ⑲
Plaza Cánovas del Castillo ❷
Plaza de Cibeles ❹
Plaza de Colón ⑯
Real Jardín Botánico ⑳

GETTING THERE
The metro is the fastest and easiest way to get to and around Bourbon Madrid. Lines 1, 2 and 4 serve all of the main sights. Useful buses include routes 14, 15 and 27 to the Plaza de Cibeles.

KEY
- Street-by-Street map pp272–3
- Ⓜ Metro station
- 🚉 Railway station
- Main bus stop
- 🛈 Tourist information
- Ⓟ Parking

0 metres 200
0 yards 200

◁ The expansive Parque del Retiro, which once formed the gardens of a Habsburg palace

Street-by-Street: Paseo del Prado

Façade of Banco de España

I N THE LATE 18TH CENTURY, before the museums and lavish hotels of Bourbon Madrid took shape, the Paseo del Prado was laid out and soon became a fashionable spot for strolling. Today the Paseo's main attraction lies in its museums and art galleries. Most notable are the Museo del Prado (just south of the Plaza Cánovas del Castillo) and the Museo Thyssen-Bornemisza, both displaying world famous collections of paintings. Among the grand monuments built under Carlos III are the Puerta de Alcalá and the Fuente de Cibeles, which stand in the middle of busy roundabouts.

The Paseo del Prado, based on the Piazza Navona in Rome, was built by Carlos III as a centre for the arts and sciences in Madrid.

Banco de Espana Metro

The Edificio Metrópolis *(see p271)*, on the corner of Gran Vía and Calle de Alcalá, was built in 1905. Its façade is distinctively Parisian.

Banco de España

CALLE DE ALCALÁ

VALDEIGLESIAS

BARQUILLO

CALLE DEL MARQUES

CALLE DE LOS MADRAZO

DE CUBAS

ZORRILLA

★ Museo Thyssen-Bornemisza
This excellent art collection occupies the Neo-Classical Villahermosa Palace, completed in 1806 ❸

PLAZA DE LAS CORTES

PLAZA CANOVAS DEL CASTILLO

Congreso de los Diputados
Spain's parliament witnessed the transition from dictatorship to democracy (see pp64–5) ⓮

STAR SIGHTS
★ Museo Thyssen-Bornemisza
★ Puerta de Alcalá
★ Plaza de Cibeles

Plaza de Canovas del Castillo
In the middle of this large square stands a sculpted fountain of the god Neptune in his chariot ❷

Hotel Palace

To Museo del Prado

0 metres	100
0 yards	100

★ Puerta de Alcalá
Sculpted from granite, this former gateway into the city is especially beautiful when floodlit at night ❺

Palacio de Comunicaciones

Palacio de Linares

LOCATOR MAP
See Street Finder maps 3–6

★ Plaza de Cibeles
A fountain with a statue of the Roman goddess Cybele stands in this square ❹

The Museo Nacional de Artes Decorativas
This museum, near the Retiro, was founded in 1912 as a showcase for Spanish ceramics and interior design ❻

Museo del Ejército
This huge collection of military memorabilia is housed in part of the former Retiro Palace ❼

Casón del Buen Retiro
(see p285)

Hotel Ritz
With its belle époque interior, the Ritz is one of the most elegant hotels in Spain ❶

The Monumento del Dos de Mayo commemorates the War of Independence against the French *(see p59).*

KEY

– – – Suggested route

Hotel Ritz ❶

Plaza de la Lealtad 5. **Map** 5 C1.
📞 *(91) 521 28 57.* Ⓜ *Banco de España.* Ⓩ ♿

A FEW MINUTES' walk from the Prado, this hotel is said to be Spain's most extravagant. It was commissioned in 1906 by Alfonso XIII, who was embarrassed at the lack of luxury accommodation in the city for his wedding guests.

The opulence of the Ritz *(see p553)* is reflected in its prices. Each of the 158 rooms is beautifully decorated in a different style, with carpets made by hand at the Real Fábrica de Tapices *(see p296)*.

At the start of the Civil War *(see pp62–3)* the hotel was converted into a hospital, and it was here that the Anarchist leader Buenaventura Durruti died of his wounds in 1936.

The Fuente de Neptuno

Plaza Cánovas del Castillo ❷

Map 5 C1. Ⓜ *Banco de España.*

THIS BUSY ROUNDABOUT is named after Antonio Cánovas del Castillo, one of the leading statesman of 19th-century Spain *(see p60)*, who was assassinated in 1897.

Dominating the plaza is the Fuente de Neptuno – a fountain with a statue depicting Neptune in his chariot, being pulled by two horses. The statue was designed in 1780 by Ventura Rodríguez as part of Carlos III's scheme to beautify eastern Madrid.

Visitors admiring the works of art in the Museo Thyssen-Bornemisza

Museo Thyssen-Bornemisza ❸

See pp278–9.

Plaza de Cibeles ❹

Map 3 C5. Ⓜ *Banco de España.* **Casa de América** 📞 *(91) 595 48 00.* ⏰ *11am–7pm Tue–Sat, 11am–2pm Sun.*

A S WELL AS BEING one of Madrid's best-known landmarks, the Plaza de Cibeles is also one of the most beautiful.

The Fuente de Cibeles stands in the middle of the busy traffic island at the junction of the Paseo del Prado and the Calle de Alcalá. This fine sculpted fountain is named after Cybele, the Graeco-Roman goddess of nature, and shows her sitting in her chariot, drawn by a pair of lions. Designed in the late 18th century by José Hermosilla and Ventura Rodríguez, it is considered a symbol of Madrid.

Around the square rise four important buildings, the most impressive of which is the main post office, the Palacio de Comunicaciones, mockingly known as "Our Lady of Communications". Its appearance – white, with high pinnacles – is often likened to a wedding cake. It was built between 1905 and 1917 on the site of former gardens.

On the northeast side of the square is the stone façade of the Palacio de Linares, built by the Marquis of Linares at the time of the second Bourbon restoration of 1875 *(see p60)*. At one time threatened with demolition, the palace was reprieved and converted into the Casa de América, and now displays a collection of paintings by Latin American artists. It is also used as a venue for theatrical performances and lectures.

In the northwest corner of the Plaza de Cibeles, surrounded by attractive gardens, is the heavily guarded Ministerio de Defensa, which is housed in the buildings of the former Palacio de Buenavista. The palace was commissioned by the Duchess of Alba in 1777 as a family residence, though its construction was twice delayed by fires.

Occupying a whole block on the opposite corner is the Banco de España, constructed between 1884 and 1891. Its design was inspired by the Venetian Renaissance style, with delicate ironwork adorning the roof and windows. Much-needed renovation work has returned the bank to its late 19th-century magnificence.

The Fuente de Cibeles, with the Banco de España in the background

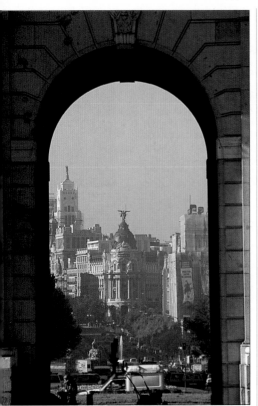

View through the central arch of the Puerta de Alcalá

Puerta de Alcalá ❺

Map 4 D5. Ⓜ *Retiro.*

THIS CEREMONIAL GATEWAY is the grandest of the monuments erected by Carlos III in his attempt to improve the looks of eastern Madrid. It was designed by Francesco Sabatini to replace a smaller Baroque gateway which had been built by Felipe III for the entry into Madrid of his wife, Margaret of Austria.

Construction of the gate began in 1769 and lasted nine years. It was built from granite in Neo-Classical style, with a lofty pediment and sculpted angels. It has five arches – three central and two outer rectangular ones.

Until the mid-19th century the gateway marked the city's easternmost boundary. It now stands in the busy Plaza de la Independencia, and is best seen when floodlit at night.

Museo Nacional de Artes Decorativas ❻

Calle de Montalbán 12. **Map** 4 D5.
🄲 *(91) 532 64 99.* Ⓜ *Retiro.*
🄾 *9am–3pm Tue–Fri, 10am–2pm Sat, Sun & public hols.* 🈂 ⛐

HOUSED IN A 19th-century palace overlooking the Parque del Retiro, the National Museum of Decorative Arts contains an interesting collection of furniture and *objets d'art*. The exhibits are mainly from Spain and date back as far as Phoenician times.

One of the finest exhibits on the museum's five floors is a kitchen, moved here from an 18th-century Valencian mansion. Its 1,500 tiles depict a domestic scene from the era. There are also some excellent ceramic pieces from Talavera de la Reina *(see p368)*, and a collection of jewellery and ornaments from the Far East.

Museo del Ejército ❼

Calle Méndez Núñez 1. **Map** 6 D1.
🄲 *(91) 522 89 77.* Ⓜ *Retiro.*
🄾 *10am–2pm Tue–Sun.* 🈂 ⛐

SPAIN'S ARMY MUSEUM occupies one of the remaining parts of the 17th-century Palacio del Buen Retiro. Individual rooms are dedicated to the military history of different periods and house a vast array of weapons, from Moorish times to the present day. The museum's grandest room, the Salón de Reinos, is named after the kingdoms which once made up Spain. These are depicted on the ceiling.

One of the highlights of the museum is the sword of El Cid – *La Tizona* – on display in the Sala de Armas. The tunic and sword of Boabdil, the last Moorish ruler of Granada *(see p52–3)*, are exhibited in the Sala Árabe.

In the Sala Colonial is a fragment of the cross which was planted in the ground by Columbus upon reaching the New World. In the same room is a piece of the tree under which Hernán Cortés sheltered during a rebellion by the Aztecs in Mexico *(see p54)*.

More recent events are illustrated by busts and flags from Spain's War of Independence *(see p59)*, in the Sala del Dos de Mayo. There are also several rooms devoted to the Spanish Civil War *(see pp62–3)*, as well as an entire room of tin soldiers.

The sword of El Cid, *La Tizona*, in the Museo del Ejército

Museo Thyssen-Bornemisza ❸

THIS MAGNIFICENT MUSEUM is based on the collection assembled by Baron Heinrich Thyssen-Bornemisza and his son, Hans Heinrich, the present baron. In 1992 it was installed in Madrid's 18th-century Villahermosa Palace, and was given to the nation the following year. From its beginnings in the 1920s, the collection was intended to illustrate the history of Western art, from Italian and Flemish primitives, through to 20th century Expressionism and Pop Art. The museum's outstanding collection, consisting of some 800 paintings, includes masterpieces by Titian, Goya, Van Gogh and Picasso, as well as works by lesser known artists. It is regarded by many critics as the most important privately assembled art collection in the world.

★ **Our Lady of the Dry Tree** *(c.1450)*
This tiny painted panel is by Bruges master Petrus Christus. The letter A hanging from the tree stands for "Ave Maria".

★ **Harlequin with a Mirror**
The figure of the harlequin was a frequent subject of Picasso's. The careful composition in this 1923 canvas, which is thought by some to represent the artist himself, is typical of Picasso's "Classical" period.

STAR PAINTINGS

★ **Our Lady of the Dry Tree** by Christus

★ **Harlequin with a Mirror** by Picasso

★ **The Toilet of Venus** by Rubens

GALLERY GUIDE

The galleries are arranged around a covered central courtyard, which rises the full height of the building. The top floor starts with early Italian art and goes through to the 17th-century. The first floor continues the story with 17th-century Dutch works and ends with German Express-ionism. The ground floor is dedicated to 20th-century paintings.

24
25
26
27
28
41
42
43
44
45
46
47
48

Hotel Room *(1931)*
Edward Hopper's painting is a study of urban isolation. The solitude is made less static by the suitcases and the train timetable on the woman's knee.

Portrait of Baron Thyssen-Bornemisz
This informal portrai the present baron, ag the background of a Watteau painting, wa painted by Lucian Fre between 1981 and 19

★ **The Toilet of Venus**
his reflection of ideal beauty was painted by the Flemish master Rubens after 1629, bowing his typically luscious use of colour and form.

VISITORS' CHECKLIST

Paseo del Prado 8. **Map** 5 C1.
(91) 369 01 51. Banco de España, Sevilla. 1, 2, 5, 9, 14, 15, 20. 10am–7pm Tue–Sun.

St Jerome in the Wilderness *(c.1575)*
Titian's work, painted when he was over 80, shows St Jerome as a penitent, meditating on Christ's Passion. In his later career, the artist strove for poetic rather than simply narrative effects.

St Casilda *(c.1630)*
Francisco de Zurbarán, best known for his depiction of monks in white habits, also painted saints. Here, the brilliant colours of St Casilda's robe stand out against the plain background.

Main entrance

KEY TO FLOORPLAN

- Ground floor
- First floor
- Second floor
- Non-exhibition space

Autumn Landscape in Oldenburg
Karl Schmidt-Rottluff was a member of the Brücke Expressionist group, founded in Dresden in 1905. He painted this north German landscape two years later.

Iglesia de San Jerónimo el Real ❽

Calle del Moreto 4. **Map** 6 D1. 📞 (91) 420 35 78. 🚇 Banco de España. 🕐 Oct–Jun: 8am–1:30pm, 5–8:30pm daily, (6–8:30pm Jul–Sep). ⬤ Easter Sat. ♿

BUILT IN THE 16TH century for Queen Isabel, but since remodelled, San Jerónimo is Madrid's royal church. From the 17th century it became virtually a part of the Retiro palace which once stood here (see p287). The church was

Castizos during San Isidro

MADRID'S FIESTAS

San Isidro (15 May). Madrid's great party around 15 May is in honour of St Isidore, the humble 12th-century farmworker who became the city's patron. With a *corrida* every day, this is Spain's biggest bullfighting event. Throughout the city there are also art exhibitions, open-air concerts and fireworks. Many people dress in Madrid's *castizo* folk costume for the occasion.
The Passion (Easter Saturday), Chinchón. A passion play is performed in the town's atmospheric arcaded Plaza Mayor.
Dos de Mayo (2 May). This four-day holiday marks the city's uprising against Napoleon's troops in 1808 (see p59).
New Year's Eve. The nation focuses on the Puerta del Sol (see p262) at midnight as crowds gather to swallow a grape on each chime of the clock.

originally attached to the Hieronymite monastery, which today stands beside it in ruins.

The church was the setting for the marriage of Alfonso XIII and Victoria Eugenia of Battenberg in 1906, and today it is a popular venue for high society weddings. King Juan Carlos I's coronation was held here in 1975.

Museo del Prado ❾

See pp282–5

Casa de Lope de Vega ❿

Calle de Cervantes 11. **Map** 5 B1. 📞 (91) 429 92 16. 🚇 Antón Martín. 🕐 9:30am–2pm Tue–Fri, 10am–1:30pm Sat. ⬤ public hols. 📷 🚫

FELIX LOPE DE VEGA, a leading Golden Age writer (see p30), moved into this sombre house in 1610. Here he wrote over two-thirds of his plays, thought to total almost 2,000.

Félix Lope de Vega

Meticulously restored in 1935 using some of Lope de Vega's own furniture, the house gives a great feeling of Castilian life in the early 17th century. A dark chapel with no external windows occupies the centre, separated from the writer's bedroom by only a barred window. The small garden at the rear, complete with the original well, is planted with the flowers and fruit trees mentioned by the writer in his works. He died here in 1635.

Statue of Goya in front of the Prado

Sunlit balcony of the magnificent Teatro Español

Real Academia de la Historia ⑪

Calle León 21. **Map** 5 A2. ☎ *(91) 429 06 11.* ⓜ *Antón Martín.* ◐ *4–7pm Mon–Fri with letter of introduction from your embassy.* 🚫

THE ROYAL ACADEMY of History is an austere brick building with stone trimmings, built by Juan de Villanueva in 1788. Its location, in the so-called Barrio de los Literatos (Writers' Quarter), is apt.

In 1898, the great intellectual and bibliophile, Marcelino Menéndez Pelayo, became director of the academy, living here until his death in 1912. The library, with more than 200,000 books and several important manuscripts, can be seen by arrangement.

Teatro Español ⑫

Calle del Príncipe 25. **Map** 5 A1. ☎ *(91) 429 62 97.* ⓜ *Sol.* ◐ *for performances from 7pm Tue–Sun.* 📷 ♿

DOMINATING the Plaza Santa Ana is the Teatro Español, one of Madrid's oldest and most beautiful theatres. From 1583 many of Spain's finest plays, by leading dramatists of the time such as Lope de Rueda, were first performed in the Corral del Príncipe which originally stood on this site. In 1802 this was replaced by the Teatro Español. The Neo-Classical façade, with pilasters and medallions, is by Juan de

Villanueva. Engraved on it are the names of great Spanish dramatists, including that of celebrated writer Federico García Lorca *(see p31).*

Ateneo de Madrid ⑬

Calle del Prado 21. **Map** 5 B1. ☎ *(91) 429 17 50.* ⓜ *Antón Martín, Sevilla.* ◐ *9am–1am Mon–Sat, 9am–10pm Sun & public hols.* 📷

FORMALLY FOUNDED IN 1835, this learned association has strongly liberal political leanings. It is similar to a gentlemen's club in atmosphere, with a grand stairway and panelled hall hung with the portraits of famous fellows. Closed down during past periods of repression and dictatorship, it is still a mainstay of liberal thought in Spain. Many leading Socialists are members of the Ateneo, along with writers and other intellectuals.

Carving on the façade of the Ateneo de Madrid

Congreso de los Diputados ⑭

Plaza de las Cortes. **Map** 5 B1. ☎ *(91) 390 60 00.* ⓜ *Sevilla.* ◐ *10am–12:30pm Sat and Mon–Fri by appointment.* 🚫 ♿

THIS IMPOSING YET attractive building is home to the Spanish parliament, the Cortes. Built in the mid-19th century on the site of a former convent, it is characterized by Classical columns, heavy pediments and guardian bronze lions. It was here, in 1981, that Colonel Tejero of the Civil Guard held the deputies at gunpoint on national television, as he tried to spark off a military coup *(see p64).* His failure was seen as an indication that democracy was now firmly established in Spain.

Bronze lion guarding the Cortes

Café Gijón ⑮

Paseo de Recoletos 21. **Map** 3 C4. ☎ *(91) 521 54 25.* ⓜ *Banco de España.* ◐ *9am–1:30am Sun–Fri, 9am–2am Sat & public hols.* ♿

MADRID'S CAFÉ LIFE *(see pp306–7)* was one of the most attractive features of the city from the turn of the 20th century, right up to outbreak of the Civil War. Of the many intellectuals' cafés which once thrived, only the Gijón survives. Today the café continues to attract a lively crowd of *literati.* With its cream-painted wrought-iron columns and black and white table tops, it is perhaps better known for its atmosphere than for its appearance.

Museo del Prado 𝟗

THE PRADO MUSEUM contains the world's greatest assembly of Spanish painting – especially works by Velázquez and Goya – ranging from the 12th to 19th centuries. It also houses impressive foreign collections, particularly of Italian and Flemish works. The Neo-Classical building was designed in 1785 by Juan de Villanueva on the orders of Carlos III. It opened as a museum in 1819 to display the royal collection of paintings, sculpture and decorative arts. The Casón del Buen Retiro, the Prado's annexe, has 19th- and 20th-century paintings and sculptures.

★ Velázquez Collection
The Triumph of Bacchus (1628), Velázquez's first portrayal of a mythological subject, shows the god of wine (Bacchus) with a group of drunkards.

The Adoration of the Shepherds *(1612–14)*
This dramatic work shows the elongated figures and swirling garments typical of El Greco's style. It was painted during his late Mannerist period for his own funerary chapel.

STAR EXHIBITS

★ Velázquez Collection

★ Goya Collection

The Annunciation
Fra Angelico's work of c.1430 is a high point of Italy's Early Renaissance, as illustrated by the detailed architectural setting and deep perspective of the interior.

The Garden of Delights *(c.1516)*
Hieronymus Bosch (El Bosco in Spanish), one of Felipe II's favourite artists, is especially well represented in the Prado. This enigmatic painting depicts paradise and hell.

Main entrance

GALLERY GUIDE
The best way to enter the Prado is through the Puerta de Goya, on Calle Felipe IV, which leads on to the first floor. The works are arranged in schools. The first floor is largely dedicated to the Spanish School, the ground floor to the Flemish.

First floor

Ground floor

VISITORS' CHECKLIST

Paseo del Prado. **Map** 5 C2.
(91) 420 28 36. Atocha, Banco de España. 6, 10, 14, 19, 27, 34, 37, 45. 9am–7pm Tue–Sat, 9am–2pm Sun & public hols. 1 Jan, Good Fri, 1 May, 25 Dec.
Casón del Buen Retiro: Calle de Alfonso XII 28. (91) 420 26 28. as above. one ticket covers both parts of museum.

★ Goya Collection
In The Clothed Maja *and* The Naked Maja *(both c.1800), Goya tackled the taboo subject of nudity, for which he was later accused of obscenity.*

The Three Graces *(c.1639)*
This was one of the last paintings by the Flemish master Rubens, and was part of the artist's personal collection. The three women dancing in a ring – the Graces – are the daughters of Zeus, and represent Love, Joy and Revelry.

The Martyrdom of St Philip *(c.1630)*
José de Ribera moved from his native Valencia to Naples as a young man. There he was influenced by Caravaggio's dramatic use of light and shadow, known as chiaroscuro, *as seen in this work.*

KEY TO FLOORPLAN

☐ Spanish painting
☐ Flemish and Dutch painting
☐ Italian painting
☐ French painting
☐ German painting
☐ Sculpture
☐ Temporary exhibitions
☐ Non-exhibition space

Exploring the Prado's Collection

THE IMPORTANCE OF THE PRADO is founded on its royal collections. The wealth of foreign art, including many of Europe's finest works, reflects the historical power of the Spanish crown *(see pp54–9)*. The Low Countries and parts of Italy were under Spanish domination for centuries. The 18th century was an era of French influence, following the Bourbon accession to the Spanish throne. The Prado is worthy of repeated visits, but if you go only once, see the Spanish works of the 17th century.

St Dominic of Silos Enthroned as Abbot (1474–7) by Bermejo

SPANISH PAINTING

RIGHT UP TO THE 19th century, Spanish painting focused on religious and royal themes. Although the limited subject matter was in some ways a restriction, it also offered a sharp focus that seems to have suited Spanish painters.

Spain's early medieval art is represented somewhat sketchily in the Prado but there are some examples such as the

anonymous mural paintings from the Holy Cross hermitage in Maderuelo, which show a Romanesque heaviness of line and forceful characterization.

Spanish Gothic art can be seen in the Prado in the works of Bartolomé Bermejo and Fernando Gallego. The sense of realism in their paintings was borrowed from Flemish masters of the time.

Renaissance features began to emerge in the works of painters such as Pedro de Berruguete, whose *Auto-da-fé* is both chilling and lively. *St Catherine*, by Fernando Yáñez de la Almedina, shows the influence of Leonardo da Vinci, for whom Yáñez probably worked while training in Italy.

What is often considered as a truly Spanish style – with its highly-wrought emotion and deepening sombreness – first started to emerge in the 16th century in the paintings of the Mannerists. This is evident in Pedro Machuca's fierce *Descent from the Cross* and in the Madonnas of Luis de Morales, "the Divine". The elongation of the human figure in Morales' work is carried to a greater extreme by Domenikos Theotocopoulos, better known as El Greco *(see p28)*. Although many of his masterpieces remain in his adopted town

Saturn Devouring One of his Sons (1820–23) by Francisco de Goya

of Toledo *(see p373)*, the Prado has an impressive collection, including *The Nobleman with his Hand on his Chest.*

The Golden Age *(see pp56–7)* was a particularly productive time for Spanish art. José de Ribera, who lived in (Spanish) Naples, followed Caravaggio in combining realism of character with the techniques of *chiaroscuro* and tenebrism. Another master who used this method was Francisco Ribalta, whose *Christ Embracing St Bernard* is here. Zurbarán, known for his still lifes and portraits of saints and monks, is also a notable presence in the Prado

This period, however, is best represented by the work of Diego Velázquez. As Spain's leading court painter from his late twenties until his death, he produced scenes of heightened realism, royal portraits, and religious and mythological paintings. Examples of all of these are displayed in the Prado. Perhaps his greatest work is *Las Meninas (see pp28–9)*.

Another great Spanish painter, Goya, revived Spanish art in the 18th century. He first specialized in cartoons for tapestries, then became a court painter. His work went on to embrace the horrors of war, as seen here in *The Third of May (see pp58–9)*, and culminated in a sombre series known as *The Black Painting.*

Still Life with Four Vessels (c.1658–64) by Francisco de Zurbarán

CASÓN DEL BUEN RETIRO

On the hill behind the Prado is its annexe, the Casón del Buen Retiro, once part of the Palacio del Buen Retiro *(see p287)*. Its exhibits include late 19th-century and early 20th-century works, as well as Neo-Classical and Romantic art, and paintings on historical themes. Some of the best paintings are by artists such as Mariano Fortuny, Santiago Rusiñol and the Impressionist Joaquín Sorolla *(see p295)*.

Children at the Beach (1910) by Joaquín Sorolla

FLEMISH AND DUTCH PAINTING

SPAIN'S LONG CONNECTION with the Low Countries *(see pp56–7)* led naturally to an intense admiration for the so-called Flemish primitives. Many exceptional works now hang in the Prado. *St Barbara*, by Robert Campin, has a quirky intimacy, and Rogier van der Weyden's *The Deposition* is an unquestioned masterpiece. Most notable of all, however, are Hieronymus Bosch's weird and eloquent inventions, which were collected by Felipe II. The Prado has some of his major paintings, including the *Temptation of St Anthony* and *The Haywain*. Works from the 16th century include the magnificent *Triumph of Death* by Brueghel the Elder. There are nearly 100 canvases by the 17th-century Flemish painter Peter Paul Rubens, of which the greatest is *The Adoration of the Magi*. The two most notable Dutch paintings on display are by Rembrandt: *Artemisia*, and a fine self-portrait.

The Deposition (c.1430) by Rogier van der Weyden

David Victorious over Goliath (c.1600) by Caravaggio

ITALIAN PAINTING

THE PRADO IS THE ENVY of many museums, not least for its vast collection of Italian paintings. Botticelli's dramatic wooden panels telling *The Story of Nastagio degli Onesti*, a vision of a knight forever condemned to hunt down and kill his own beloved, are a sinister high point. Raphael contributes the superb *Christ Falls on the Way to Calvary* and the sentimental *The Holy Family of the Lamb*.

Christ Washing the Disciples' Feet, by Tintoretto, is a profound masterpiece. Venetian masters Veronese and Titian are also very well represented. Titian served as court painter to Charles V, and few works express the drama of Habsburg rule so deeply as his sombre painting *The Emperor Charles V at Mühlberg*. Also on display are works by Giordano, Caravaggio and Tiepolo, master of Italian rococo.

FRENCH PAINTING

MARRIAGES BETWEEN French and Spanish royalty in the 17th century, culminating in the Bourbon accession to the throne in the 18th century, brought French art to Spain. The Prado has eight works attributed to Poussin, among them his serene *Parnassus* and *Landscape with St Jerome*. The magnificent *Landscape with the Embarkation of St Paula Romana at Ostia* is the best work here by Claude Lorrain. Among the 18th-century artists featured are Antoine Watteau and Jean Ranc. *Felipe V* is the work of the royal portraitist Louis-Michel van Loo.

GERMAN PAINTING

ALTHOUGH GERMAN ART is not especially well represented in the Prado, there are several paintings by Albrecht Dürer, such as his lively *Self-Portrait*, painted at the age of 26. Lucas Cranach also figures. Works by the late 18th-century painter Anton Raffael Mengs include portraits of Carlos III.

Floor mosaic in the Museo Arqueológico Nacional

Plaza de Colón ⑯

Map 4 D3. 🚇 Serrano, Colón.

THIS LARGE SQUARE, one of
Madrid's focal points, is
dedicated to Christopher
Columbus (Colón in Spanish).

It is overlooked by huge
tower blocks, built in the 1970s
to replace the 19th-century
mansions which stood here.

On the south side is a palace
housing the National Library
and Archaeological Museum.
The Post-Modernist sky-
scraper of the Heron Cor-
poration towers over the
square from the far side of
the Paseo de la Castellana.

The real feature of the
square, however, is the
pair of monuments dedi-
cated to the discoverer of
the Americas. The prettiest,
and oldest, is a Neo-Gothic
spire made in 1885, with
Columbus at its top, pointing west. Carved reliefs on
the plinth give highlights
of his discoveries. Across
the square is the second,
more modern monument
– a cluster of four large
concrete shapes inscribed
with quotations about
Columbus's journey to
America (see p53).

Constantly busy with
traffic, the plaza may
seem an unlikely venue
for cultural events. Be-
neath it, however, is an
extensive complex, the
Centro Cultural de la
Villa de Madrid, which
includes the city's mu-
nicipal art centre,

exhibition halls, lecture rooms,
a theatre and a café. The terminal for the bus which runs to
and from the airport (see p626)
is also located underground.

Calle de Serrano ⑰

Map 4 D4. 🚇 Serrano.

NAMED AFTER a 19th-century
politician, Madrid's smartest
shopping street runs north from
the Plaza de la Independencia
to the Plaza de la República
Argentina, in the district of
Salamanca. The street is
lined with shops (p304) –
many specializing in luxury
items – housed in old-
fashioned mansion-blocks.
Several of the country's top
designers, including Adolfo
Domínguez and Alfredo
Villalba, have boutiques
towards the north, near the
Museo Lázaro Galdiano
(see p295). Branches of the
Italian shops Versace and
Armani can be found on
the Calle de José Ortega y
Gasset. Lower down the
Calle de Serrano, towards
Serrano metro station, is a
branch of the British chain
store Marks & Spencer,
which has become
popular among Span-
iards and tourists
alike. On the Calle de
Claudio Coello, which
runs parallel with
Serrano, there are
several lavish antique
shops, in keeping
with the area's up-
market atmosphere.

**Statue of
Columbus, Plaza
de Colón**

Museo Arqueológico Nacional ⑱

Calle de Serrano 13. Map 4 D3.
📞 (91) 577 79 12. 🚇 Serrano.
🕐 9:30am–8:30pm Tue–Sat,
9:30am–2:30pm Sun. 🏫 ♿

WITH HUNDREDS of exhibits,
ranging from prehistoric
times to the 19th century, this
museum is one of Madrid's best.
Founded by Isabel II in 1867,
it consists mainly of material
uncovered during excavations
all over Spain, as well as pieces
from Egypt, Ancient Greece
and the Etruscan civilization.

The earliest finds – from the
prehistoric era – are arranged
in chronological order in the
basement. Highlights include
an exhibition on the ancient
civilization of El Argar in Andalusia (see p44), and a display
of jewellery uncovered at the
Roman settlement of Numantia,
near Soria (see p359).

The museum's ground floor
is largely devoted to the period
between Roman and Mudéjar
Spain. Iberian culture is also
represented on this floor, with
two notable sculptures – La
Dama de Elche (see p44) and
La Dama de Baza.

The Roman period is illustrated with some impressive
mosaics, including Monks and
Seasons, from Hellín (Albacete), and Bacchus and his
Train, from Zaragoza.

Outstanding pieces from the
Visigothic period include a
collection of 7th-century gold
votive crowns from Toledo
province, known as the Treasure of Guarrazar.

The Islamic era is represented
by pottery uncovered from
Medina Azahara in Andalusia
(see p453), as well as bronze
and metal objects.

Romanesque exhibits include
an ivory crucifix carved in 1063
for Fernando I of Castilla-León
and his Queen, Doña Sancha,
and the Madonna and Child
from Sahagún, considered a
masterpiece of Spanish art.

Steps outside the museum's
entrance lead underground to
an exact replica of the Altamira
caves in Cantabria (see p108)
– complete with their paintings
of the early Paleolithic era.

Parque del Retiro ⑲

Map 6 E1. 📞 *(91) 573 60 82.*
Ⓜ *Retiro, Ibiza, Atocha.* ♿

THE RETIRO PARK, in Madrid's smart Jerónimos district, takes its name from Felipe IV's royal palace complex, which once stood here. Nowadays, all that remains of the palace is the Casón del Buen Retiro *(see p285)* and the Museo del Ejército *(see p277)*.

Used privately by the royal family from 1632, the park became the scene of elaborate pageants, bullfights and mock naval battles. In the 18th century it was partially opened to the public, provided visitors were formally dressed, and in 1869 it was fully opened. Today, the Retiro remains one of the most popular places for relaxing in Madrid.

A short stroll from the park's northern entrance down the tree-lined avenue leads to the pleasure lake, where rowing boats can be hired. On one side of the lake is a half-moon colonnade in front of which an equestrian statue of Alfonso XII rides high on a column. Opposite, portrait painters and fortune-tellers ply their trade.

To the south of the lake are two attractive palaces. The Neo-Classical, red brick Palacio de Velázquez and the Palacio de Cristal (Crystal Palace) were built by Velázquez Bosco in 1887 as venues for exhibitions held during the same year.

Statue of Bourbon king Carlos III in the Real Jardín Botánico

Real Jardín Botánico ⑳

Plaza de Murillo 2. **Map** 6 D2.
📞 *(91) 420 30 17.* Ⓜ *Atocha.*
⭕ *10am–8pm daily.* 🎫 ♿

SOUTH OF the Prado *(see pp282–5)*, and a suitable place for resting after visiting the gallery, are the Royal Botanical Gardens. Inspired by Carlos III, they were designed in 1781 by botanist Gómez Ortega and Juan de Villanueva, the architect of the Prado.

Interest in the plants of South America and the Philippines took hold during the Spanish Enlightenment *(see p58)*, and the neatly laid out beds offer a huge variety of flora, ranging from trees and shrubs to medicinal plants and herbs.

Estación de Atocha ㉑

Plaza del Emperador Carlos V. **Map** 6 D4. 📞 *(91) 506 68 46.* Ⓜ *Atocha RENFE.* ⭕ *7am–11:30pm daily.* ♿

MADRID'S FIRST railway service, from Atocha to Aranjuez, was inaugurated in 1851. Forty years later Atocha station was replaced by a new building, which, in the 1980s, was given a modern extension. The older part of the station, built of glass and wrought iron, now houses a pleasant indoor palm garden. Adjoining it is the modern terminus for the high-speed AVE trains to Córdoba and Seville *(see p630)*.

The Ministerio de Agricultura, across the road, is a splendid late 19th-century building adorned with tiled corner domes and rooftop statuary.

Entrance of Madrid's Estación de Atocha, busy with travellers

Monument of Alfonso XII (1901), facing the Retiro's boating lake

Centro de Arte Reina Sofía ❷

THE HIGHLIGHT of this museum of 20th-century art is without doubt Picasso's *Guernica*. There are, however, other major works not to be missed, by influential artists including Miró and Picasso. The collection is housed in the former premises of Madrid's General Hospital, which was built in the late 18th century. Two exterior glass lifts were added in 1992 when the building was converted into the Art Centre. Although the interior is now a computer-controlled environment, it retains much of the atmosphere of the original building.

Portrait II *(1*
Joan Miró's b
enigmatic wo
shows elemen
Surrealism, d
being painted
than ten year
after the end
his true
Surrealist
period.

★ Woman in Blue *(1901)*
Picasso disowned this work after it won only an honourable mention in a national competition. Decades later it was located and acquired by the Spanish state.

Guernica

Landscape at Cadaqués
Salvador Dalí was born in Figueres in Catalonia. He became a frequent visitor to the town of Cadaqués, on the Costa Brava (see p207), where he painted this landscape in the summer of 1923.

Second floor

Accident
Alfonso Ponce de León's disturbing work, painted in 1936, prefigured his death in a car crash later that same year.

STAR EXHIBITS

★ **Woman in Blue**
by Picasso

★ **La Tertulia del Café de Pombo** by Solana

★ **Guernica** by Picasso

★ **La Tertulia del Café de Pombo** *(1920)*
José Gutiérrez Solana depicts a gathering of intellectuals (tertulia) *in a famous café in Madrid, which no longer exists.*

Glass lift

Entrance

Espíritu de los ájaros I *(1952)*
his work, by Basque
ulptor Eduardo Chillida, is made of forged
on mounted on stone. It is displayed on the
urth floor, along with more of his works.

VISITORS' CHECKLIST

Calle Santa Isabel 52. **Map** 5 C3.
(91) 467 50 62. Atocha.
6, 14, 18, 19, 27, 45, 55, 68.
10am–9pm Mon & Wed–Sat,
10am–2:30pm Sun. 1 Jan,
24, 25, 31 Dec & some public
hols. (free of charge on Sun).

GALLERY GUIDE

The permanent collection is on the second and fourth floors, arranged around an open courtyard. It traces art through the 20th century, from its beginnings to the present day. The second floor is dedicated to paintings from the earlier part of the century, with individual rooms allocated to significant artists such as Dalí, Miró and Picasso. The fourth floor continues with post-World War II to contemporary works, via movements such as Abstract Art, Pop Art and Minimal Art.

KEY TO FLOORPLAN

Exhibition space

Non-exhibition space

Visitors admiring *Guernica*

★ PICASSO'S GUERNICA

The most famous single work of the 20th century, this Civil War protest painting *(see pp62–3)* was commissioned by the Spanish Republican government in 1937 for a Paris exhibition. The artist found his inspiration in the mass air attack of the same year on the Basque town of Guernika-Lumo *(see p114)*, by German pilots flying for the Nationalist air force. The painting hung in a New York gallery until 1981, reflecting the artist's wish that it should not return to Spain until democracy was re-established. It was moved here from the Prado in 1992.

FURTHER AFIELD

S EVERAL OF MADRID's best sights, including some interesting but little-known museums, lie outside the city centre. The axis of modern Madrid is the Paseo de la Castellana, a long, wide avenue lined by skyscraper offices, and busy with traffic. A journey along it gives a glimpse of Madrid as Spain's commercial and administrative capital. La Castellana skirts the Barrio de Salamanca, an up-market district of stylish boutiques, named after the 19th-century aristocrat who built it, the Marquis de Salamanca.

The districts around Old Madrid, especially Malasaña and La Latina, offer a more typically authentic *Madrileño* atmosphere. On Sundays, some of the old streets are crowded with bargain-hunters at the sprawling second-hand market, El Rastro. If you need to escape from the bustle of the city for a while, west of Old Madrid, across the Río Manzanares, is Madrid's vast, green recreation ground, the Casa de Campo, with its pleasant pine woods, boating lake, amusement park and zoo.

Statue in Plaza de Cascorro

SIGHTS AT A GLANCE

Historic Buildings
Palacio de Liria **9**
Real Fábrica de Tapices **16**
Templo de Debod **6**

Churches and Convents
Ermita de San Antonio de la Florida **5**

Museums and Galleries
Museo de América **7**
Museo Cerralbo **8**
Museo Lázaro Galdiano **13**

Museo Municipal **11**
Museo Sorolla **12**

Streets, Squares and Parks
Casa de Campo **4**
La Latina **2**
Malasaña **10**
Paseo de la Castellana **14**
Plaza de la Paja **3**
Plaza de Toros de Las Ventas **15**
El Rastro **1**

0 kilometres   2

0 miles   1

KEY

	Main sightseeing area
	Parks and open spaces
🚉	Railway station
	Motorway
	Major road
	Minor road

SIGHTS OUTSIDE THE CITY CENTRE

◁ **Mudéjar arches and tilework on the exterior of the Plaza de Toros de Las Ventas**

El Rastro ❶

Calle Ribera de Curtidores. **Map** 2 E5. 🚇 *La Latina, Embajadores.* ⬜ *10am – 2pm Sun & public hols.*

Madrid's celebrated flea market *(see p305)*, established in the Middle Ages, has its hub in the Plaza de Cascorro and sprawls downhill towards the Río Manzanares. The main street is the Calle Ribera de Curtidores, or "Tanners' Riverbank", once the centre of the slaughterhouse and tanning industry.

Although some people claim that the Rastro has changed a great deal since its heyday during the 19th century, there are still plenty of *Madrileños*, as well as tourists, who shop here. They come in search of a bargain from the stalls which sell a huge range of wares – anything from new furniture to second-hand clothes. The wide range of goods and the lively crowds in the Rastro make it an ideal way to spend a Sunday morning.

The Calle de Embajadores is the market's other main street. It runs down past the dusty Baroque façade of the Iglesia de San Cayetano, designed by José Churriguera and Pedro de Ribera. Its interior has been restored since fire destroyed it during the Civil War.

Further along the street is the Real Fábrica de Tabacos (the Royal Tobacco Factory), begun as a state enterprise in 1809. Its female labour force has long had a reputation for taking an uncompromising, hard-line stance in industrial disputes.

Shoppers browsing around the Rastro flea market

La Latina ❷

Map 2 D5. 🚇 *La Latina, Lavapiés.*

The district of La Latina, together with the adjacent Lavapiés, is considered to be the heart of *castizo* Madrid. This term is used to describe the culture of the traditional working classes of Madrid – that of the true *Madrileño*.

La Latina runs along the city's southern hillside from the Plaza Puerta de Moros, southwards through the streets where the Rastro is held. To the east it merges with Lavapiés.
La Latina's steep streets are lined with tall, narrow houses, renovated to form an attractive neighbourhood. There are a number of old-fashioned bars around the Plaza de Tirso de Molina, although this square and the streets to the north of La Latina, around the Puerta del Sol, have sadly become notorious for petty crime.

Bottles of wine for sale in an old-style bar in Lavapiés

Plaza de la Paja ❸

Map 1 C4. 🚇 *La Latina.*

Once the focus of medieval Madrid, the area around the Plaza de la Paja – literally Straw Square – is still atmospheric. Despite its location, in a less than affluent district, many interesting buildings are located on the square.

Climbing upwards from the Calle de Segovia, a glimpse left along the Calle Príncipe Anglona yields a view of the Mudéjar-style brick tower of the Iglesia de San Pedro, dating

Interior of San Francisco el Grande

from the 14th century. Up past the fountain, the Plaza de la Paja ends with the harsh stone walls of the Capilla del Obispo, or Bishop's Chapel, belonging originally to the adjoining Palacio Vargas. The superb Plateresque altarpiece is by Francisco Giralte. Up to the left, the Baroque, cherub-covered dome of the Iglesia de San Andrés stands out.

Nearby is a small cluster of interlinked squares, ending in the Plaza Puerta de Moros, a reminder of the Muslim community which once occupied the area. From here, a right turn leads to the domed bulk of San Francisco el Grande, an impressive landmark. Inside the church is a collection of paintings by Goya and his brother-in-law Francisco Bayeu. The choirstalls were moved here from the monastery of El Paular *(see pp310–11)*.

Casa de Campo ❹

Avenida de Portugal. 📞 *(91) 463 63 34.* 🚇 *Batán, Lago, Norte.*

This former royal hunting ground, with pines and scrubland stretching over 1,740 ha (4,300 acres), lies in western Madrid. Its wide range of amenities make it a popular recreation area for *Madrileños*.

Attractions include a boating lake, a zoo, and an amusement park – the Parque de Atracciones *(see p307)* – with over 50 rides. Sports enthusiasts can make use of the swimming pool and jogging track. In the summer the park is also used as a venue for rock concerts.

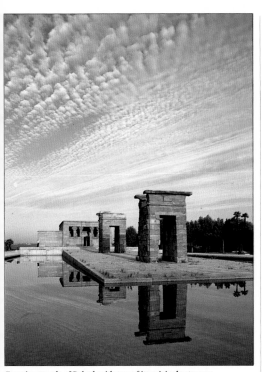

Egyptian temple of Debod, with two of its original gateways

Ermita de San Antonio de la Florida **5**

Glorieta San Antonio de la Florida 5.
((91) 542 07 22. **(M)** Norte
(Príncipe Pío). **(** 10am –2pm, 4 – 8pm
Tue – Fri, 10am – 2pm Sat & Sun.
(public hols. **(** **(** **(**

GOYA ENTHUSIASTS should not miss a visit to the Neo-Classical Ermita de San Antonio de la Florida, built during the reign of Carlos IV. The present church stands on the site of two previous ones, and is dedicated to St Anthony. It is named after the pasture-land of la Florida, on which the original church was built.

Goya took just four months, in 1798, to paint the cupola with an immense fresco. It depicts the resurrection of a murdered man who rises in order to prove the innocence of the falsely accused father of St Anthony. The characters in it are everyday people of the late 18th century: lurking, low-life types and lively *majas (see*

p283) – shrewd but elegant women. The fresco is considered by many art critics to be among Goya's finest works.

The tomb of the artist is housed in the chapel. His remains were brought here from Bordeaux, where he died in exile in 1828 *(see p229)*.

Templo de Debod **6**

Paseo de Pintor Rosales. **Map** 1 B1.
((91) 409 61 65. **(M)** Ventura
Rodríguez. **(** 10am –1pm
Sat & Sun; Jul–Sep: 10am –3pm
Tue – Fri; Oct–Jun: 10am–1pm,
4–7pm Tue – Fri. **(** public hols.

THE EGYPTIAN temple of Debod, built in the 4th century BC, was rescued from the area flooded by the Aswan Dam and given to Spain as a tribute to Spanish engineers involved in the project.

The temple is carved with shallow reliefs, and stands in a line with two of its original three gateways. They are situated on high ground above the Río Manzanares, in the gardens of the Parque del Oeste. From the park there are sweeping views over the Casa de Campo stretching to the Guadarrama mountains.

The park is the site of the former Montaña barracks, which were stormed by the populace at the start of the Civil War in 1936.

Further to the west, below the brow of the hill, there is an attractive rose garden.

Museo de América **7**

Avenida de los Reyes Católicos 6.
((91) 549 26 41. **(M)** Moncloa.
(10am –3pm Tue – Sat, 10am –
2:30pm Sun & public hols. **(** **(**

THIS HANDSOME MUSEUM houses a unique collection of artifacts related to Spain's colonization of parts of the Americas. Many of the exhibits, which range from prehistoric times to the present, were brought back to Europe by early explorers of the New World *(see pp54–5)*.

The collection is arranged on the first and second floors, and individual rooms are given a cultural theme such as society, communication and religion. There is documentation of the Atlantic voyages by the first explorers, and examples of the objects which they found.

The highlight of the museum is perhaps the rare Mayan *Códice Trocortesiano* (AD 1250–1500) from Mexico, a type of parchment illustrated with hieroglyphics of scenes from everyday life. Also worth seeing are the solid gold funereal ornaments from Colombia, the Treasure of the Quimbayas (AD 500–1000), and the collection of contemporary folk art from some of Spain's former American colonies.

Piece of the Treasure of the Quimbayas

Museo Cerralbo ⑧

Calle Ventura Rodríguez 17. **Map**
1 C1. ☎ *(91) 547 36 46.* Ⓜ *Plaza
de España, Ventura Rodríguez.* 🕙
*9:30am–2:30pm Tue–Sat, 10am–
2pm Sun.* ♿ ⌀

THIS 19TH-CENTURY mansion
near the Plaza de España
is a monument to Enrique de
Aguilera y Gamboa, the 17th
Marquis of Cerralbo. A com-
pulsive collector of art and
artifacts, he bequeathed his
lifetime's collection to the
nation in 1922, stipulating that
the exhibits be arranged
exactly as he left them. They
range from Iberian pottery to
18th-century marble busts.

One of the star exhibits is
El Greco's *The Ecstasy of Saint
Francis of Assisi.* There are
also lesser-known paintings
by Ribera, Zurbarán, Alonso
Cano and Goya, which hang
in the Picture Gallery.

The focal point of the main
floor is the ballroom, lavishly
decorated with mirrors. A large
collection of European and
Japanese weaponry is on display on this floor.

Palacio de Liria ⑨

Calle de la Princesa 20. ☎ *(91) 547
53 02.* Ⓜ *Ventura Rodríguez.* 🕙
write in advance for permission. ⌀

THE LAVISH but much
restored Palacio de Liria
was completed by Ventura
Rodríguez in 1780. Once the
residence of the Alba family,
and still owned by the
Duchess, it can be visited by
appointment only.

The palace houses the Albas'
outstanding collection of art,
and Flemish tapestries. There
are paintings by Titian, Rubens
and Rembrandt. Spanish art is
particularly well represented,
with major works by Goya,
such as his 1795 portrait of the
Duchess of Alba, as well as
examples of work by El Greco,
Zurbarán and Velázquez.

Behind the palace is the
Cuartel del Conde-Duque,
the former barracks of the
Count-Duke Olivares, Felipe
IV's minister. They were built
in 1720 by Pedro de Ribera,
who adorned them with a
Baroque façade. The barracks
now house a cultural centre.

Rooftops in the Malasaña district

Malasaña ⑩

Map 2 F1. Ⓜ *Tribunal, Bilbao.*

A FEELING OF the authentic
old Madrid pervades this
district of narrow, sloping
streets and tall houses. For
some years it was the centre
of the *movida*, the frenzied
nightlife which began after
the death of Franco.

A walk along the Calle San
Andrés leads to the Plaza del
Dos de Mayo. In the centre is
a monument to artillery officers
Daoiz and Velarde, who defended the barracks which
stood here at the time of the
uprising against the French in
1808 *(see p59).*

On Calle de la Puebla is the
Iglesia de San Antonio de los
Alemanes. The church was
founded by Felipe III in the
17th century as a hospital for
Portuguese immigrants, and
was later given over for use by
German émigrés. Inside, the
walls are decorated with 18th-
century frescoes by Giordano.

Museo Municipal ⑪

Calle de Fuencarral 78. **Map** 3 A3.
☎ *(91) 588 86 72.* Ⓜ *Tribunal.*
🕙 *9:30am–8pm Tue–Fri, 10am–2pm
Sat & Sun.* ● *public hols.* ♿

THE MUNICIPAL MUSEUM is
worth visiting just for its
majestic Baroque doorway
(see p21) by Pedro de Ribera,
arguably the finest in Madrid.
Housed in the former hospice
of St Ferdinand, the museum
was inaugurated in 1929. The

Main staircase of the exuberant Museo Cerralbo

basement is devoted to the city's archaeology, while upstairs is a series of bird's-eye views and maps showing how radically Madrid has been transformed over the years. Among them is Pedro Texeiro's map of 1656, thought to be the oldest of the city. There is also a meticulous model of Madrid, made in 1830 by León Gil de Palacio.

Modern exhibits include a reconstruction of the collage-filled study of Ramón Gómez de la Serna, a key figure of the famous literary gatherings in the Café de Pombo *(see p289)*. In the garden is the Baroque *Fuente de la Fama* (Fountain of Fame), also by Ribera.

Baroque façade of the Museo Municipal, by Pedro de Ribera

Museo Sorolla ⑫

Paseo del General Martínez Campos 37. 【 *(91) 310 15 84.* Ⓜ *Rubén Darío, Iglesia.* ◯ *10am–3pm Tue–Sat, 10am–2pm Sun.*

THE FORMER studio-mansion of Valencian Impressionist painter Joaquín Sorolla, now a museum housing his paintings, has been left virtually as it was when he died in 1923.

Although Sorolla is perhaps best known for his brilliantly lit Mediterranean beach scenes, the changing styles of his paintings are well represented in the museum, with examples of his gentle portraiture and a series of works representing people from different parts of Spain. Also on display are various objects amassed during the artist's lifetime, including Spanish tiles and ceramics. The

Sorolla's former studio in the Museo Sorolla

house, which was constructed in 1910, is surrounded by an Andalusian-style garden, designed by Sorolla himself.

Museo Lázaro Galdiano ⑬

Calle de Serrano 122. 【 *(91) 561 60 84.* Ⓜ *Núñez de Balboa.* ◯ *10am–2pm Tue–Sun.* 🖎 🗷

THIS IS ONE of the best art museums in the city. It is housed in the former mansion-home of the writer José Lázaro Galdiano, and consists of his private collection of fine and applied art, bequeathed to the nation in 1947. A colossal central hall, which rises through two floors,

Charles V's fob watch

dominates the mansion. The collection contains items of exceptional quality, ranging from a group of less familiar Goya portraits to a mass of fob watches, including a cross-shaped pocket-watch worn by Charles V when hunting. Among the most beautiful objects are a series of Limoges enamels, miniature sculptures, and *The Saviour*, a portrait attributed to Leonardo da Vinci.

The outstanding collection of art features paintings by English artists Constable, Turner, Gainsborough and Reynolds, as well as 17th-century works by Velázquez, Zurbarán, Ribera, Murillo and El Greco. The *Ecce Homo* is by Dutch painter Hieronymus Bosch.

Poster for Almodóvar's *Women on the Verge of a Nervous Breakdown*

LA MOVIDA

With Franco's death in 1975 came a new period of personal and artistic liberty. For the young, this was translated into the freedom to stay out late, drinking and sometimes sampling drugs. The phenomenon was known as *la movida*, "the action", and it was at its most intense in Madrid. Although analysts at the time saw it as having serious intellectual content, *la movida* has had few lasting cultural results, except for the emergence of satirical film director Pedro Almodóvar.

Torre de Picasso towering over the Paseo de la Castellana

Paseo de la Castellana ⑭

🚇 *Lima, Cuzco, Plaza de Castilla.*

THE BUSY TRAFFIC artery which cuts through eastern Madrid comprises several parts. Its southernmost portion – the Paseo del Prado *(see pp274–5)* – starts just north of the Estación de Atocha *(see p287)*. The oldest section of the road, it dates from the reign of Carlos III, who built it as part of his embellishment of eastern Madrid *(see p287)*. At the Plaza de Cibeles, the avenue becomes the handsome Paseo de Recoletos, which boasts fashionable cafés, including the Café Gijón *(see p281)*.

The Plaza de Colón marks the start of the Paseo de la Castellana, whose pavement cafés have become a focal point for young Madrid's social life. This northernmost section has several notable examples of modern architecture, including the huge grey Nuevos Ministerios building, completed under Franco. Further on, before reaching the Plaza de Lima, is the Torre de Picasso *(see p21)*, one of Spain's tallest buildings. East of the square is the Estadio Bernabéu, home of Real Madrid Football Club *(see p173)*. The building that dominates the Paseo, however, is the Puerta de Europa, locally known as "Torres Kio": twin glass blocks on either side of the road which have been built at an angle as if leaning toward each other.

Plaza de Toros de Las Ventas ⑮

Calle de Alcalá 237. 📞 *(91) 356 22 00.* 🚇 *Ventas.* ⏰ *for bullfights and concerts only.* **Museo Taurino** 📞 *(91) 725 18 57.* ⏰ *10am–1pm Tue–Fri & Sun.* ♿

WHATEVER your opinion of bullfighting, Las Ventas is undoubtedly one of the most beautiful bullrings in Spain. Built in 1929 in Neo-Mudéjar style, it replaced the city's original bullring which stood near the Puerta de Alcalá. With its horseshoe arches around the outer galleries and the elaborate tilework decoration, it makes an attractive venue for the *corridas* held during the bullfighting season, from May to October. The statues outside the bullring are monuments to two renowned Spanish bullfighters: Antonio Bienvenida and José Cubero.

Adjoining the bullring is the Museo Taurino. The museum contains an interesting and varied collection of bullfighting memorabilia, including portraits and sculptures of famous matadors, as well as the heads of several bulls killed during fights at Las Ventas. Visitors can examine close up the tools of the bullfighter's trade: capes and *banderillas* – sharp darts used to wound the bull *(see pp32–3)*. For some people, the gory highlight of the exhibition is the blood-drenched *traje de luces* worn by the legendary Manolete during his fateful bullfight at Linares

in Andalusia in 1947. Also on display is a costume which belonged to Juanita Cruz, a female bullfighter of the 1930s who was forced, in the face of prejudice, to leave Spain. In September and October, the bullring is used as a venue for a season of rock concerts.

Real Fábrica de Tapices ⑯

Calle Fuenterrabia 2. 📞 *(91) 551 34 00.* 🚇 *Menéndez Pelayo.* ⏰ *9am–12:30pm Mon–Fri.* ♿

FOUNDED BY Felipe V in 1721, the Royal Tapestry Factory is the sole survivor of several factories which were opened by the Bourbons *(see pp58–9)* during the 18th century. In 1889 the factory was relocated to this building just south of the Parque del Retiro.

Visitors can see the making of the carpets and tapestries by hand, a process which has changed little since the factory was established. Goya and his brother-in-law Francisco Bayeu created drawings, or cartoons, which were the inspiration for tapestries made for the royal family. Some of the cartoons are on display here; others can be seen in the Museo del Prado *(see pp282–5)*. Some of the tapestries can be seen at El Pardo *(see p314)* and at El Escorial *(see pp312–13)*. Nowadays one of the factory's main tasks is making and repairing the beautiful carpets decorating the Hotel Ritz *(see p276)*.

Plaza de Toros de Las Ventas, Madrid's beautiful bullring

MADRID STREET FINDER

THE MAP REFERENCES given with the sights, shops and entertainment venues described in the Madrid section of the guide refer to the street maps on the following pages. Map references are also given for Madrid hotels

(see pp552–4), and for bars and restaurants (pp592–4). The schematic map below shows the area of Madrid covered by the *Street Finder*. The symbols used for the sights and other features are listed in the key at the foot of the page.

KEY TO STREET FINDER

	Major sight		**P**	Parking		═══	Railway line
	Place of interest		**i**	Tourist information			One-way street
	Other building			Hospital with casualty unit			Pedestrianized street
	Railway station			Police station			
	Metro station			Church			
	Main bus stop			Convent or monastery			
	Coach station			Post office			

SCALE OF MAP PAGES

0 metres   250

0 yards   250

A **B** **C**

1
SEVILLA CALLE ARLABAN
PLAZA CANALEJAS
CARRERA DE SAN
CALLE DE LA CRUZ
CALLE POZO
CALLE NUÑEZ DE ARCE
PLAZA SANTA ANA
PLAZA DEL ANGEL
Teatro Español
Ateneo de Madrid
CALLE MANUEL FERNANDEZ Y GONZALEZ
Casa de Lope de Vega
VENTURA DE LA VEGA
CALLE
DE
JERONIMO
CALLE DE
ZORRILLA
Congreso de los Diputados
PLAZA DE LAS CORTES
MARQUES DE CUBAS
DEL PRADO
DUQUE DE MEDINACELI
SAN AGUSTIN
DE CERVANTES
SANTA CATALINA
Museo Thyssen-Bornemisza
Puente de Neptuno
PLAZA DE LA LEALTAD
Hotel Ritz
CALLE
PLAZA CANOVAS DEL CASTILLO
PASEO DEL

2
CALLE
PRINCIPE
ECHEGARAY
CALLE INFANTE
CALLE DE QUEVEDO
LEON
CALLE DE LAS
Real Academia de la Historia
PLAZA DE MATUTE
CAÑIZARES
CALLE DE LA MAGDALENA
CALLE DE LA CABEZA
CALLE ROSA
CALLE DEL OLMO
CALLE SAN SIMON
PLAZA ANTON MARTIN
Antón Martín
CALLE AMOR DE DIOS
SANTA POLONIA
CALLE SANTA MARIA
CALLE
MORATIN
PIE DORE
CALLE DUQUE FERNAN NUÑEZ
HUERTAS
LOPE DE VEGA
PLAZA JESUS
COSTANILLA DESAMPARADOS
PLAZA DE SAN JUAN
FUCAR
CALLE
VEGA
MAESTRO VILLARA
PLAZA PLATERIA MARTINEZ
VERONICA
SAN PEDRO
GOBERNADOR
ALMADEN
PASEO DEL

3
CALLE DEL OLIVAR
AVE MARIA
CALLE TORRECILLA DEL LEAL
CALLE TRES PECES
SAN CARLOS
CALLE ESPERANZA
CALLE PRIMAVERA
CALLE ESCUADRA
CALLE DE LA FE
CALLE BUENAVISTA
CALLE DE ZURITA
CALLE DE SALITRE
CALLE SAN COSME Y DAMIAN
CALLE DOCTOR PIGA
Lavapiés
PLAZA LAVAPIES
TRIBULETE
CALLE SAN EUGENIO
CALLE SAN ILDEFONSO
MARQUES DE TOCA
SANTA CALLE SANTA INES
CALLE DEL DOCTOR FOURQUET
SANTA
CALLE
HOSPITAL
DE
ATOCHA
CALLE DE SAN BLAS
CALLE DE CENICERO
DOCTOR MATA
SANCHEZ BUSTILLO
ISABEL
DOCTOR DRUMEN
Atocha RENFE
DOCTOR
Centro de Arte Reina Sofía

4
CALLE ESPINO
CALLE MIGUEL SERVET
CALLE DE VALENCIA
CALLE DE SOMBRERERIA
CALLE DEL DOCTOR FOURQUET
RONDA
DE
VALENCIA
RONDA DE VALENCIA
Embajadores
AMPARO
CALLE ALONSO BLANCO
CALLE DE MALLORCA
CALLE JOSE ANTONIO ARMONA
CALLE MARQUES LA VALDANA
ELCANO
SEBASTIAN
DE
ARGUMOSA
ATOCHA
DE
LA
CABEZA
CALLE TORTO
PIE TORTOSA
CALLE DELICIAS
VIZCAYA
CALLE
MU
ARGANZUELA

5
CALLE DE EMBAJADORES
CALLE
BERNARDINO
HERRERA
SEBASTIAN
CALLE PALOS DE LA FRONTERA
CALLE OBREGON
CALLE CARDENAL SOLIS
PASEO
SANTA
MARIA
CALLE
FRAY LUIS DE LEON
CALLE PALOS DE LA
CALLE BATALLA DE LA
CALLE MARTIN SOLER
Palos de la Frontera
Estación Sur de Autobuses
CALLE
DE
CANARIAS
CALLE
DE
SALADO
PEDRO UNANUE
CALLE DE LAS DELICIAS
Palos de la Frontera
FRONTERA
DE
PASEO DE LAS DELICIAS
PLAZA LUCA DE TENA
TARRAGONA
GLORIETA SANTA MARIA DE LA CABEZA
CALLE

A **B** **C**

DE   MENA

IX IXINGITY

MAURA

ONIO

MORETO

CALLE DE ALFONSO XII

PASEO   DE   LA   ARGENTINA

PUERTA DE
ESPAÑA

PASEO SALON DEL ESTANQUE

GTA DE LA
SARDANA

1

Museo del Ejército
CALLE MENDEZ NUÑEZ

Casón del
Buen Retiro

CASÓN DEL BUEN RETIRO

DEL

PASEO   PARTERRE

PASEO DEL PARAGUAY

PLAZA DE   PASEO DE VENEZUELA

HONDURAS

PALACIO DE
EXPOSICIONES

ACADEMIA

PUERTA DE
FELIPE IV

Iglesia de
San Jerónimo
el Real

CALLE DEL CASADO DEL ALISAL

PARQUE   DEL   RETIRO

LE

CALLE

ALBERTO   BOSCH

PASEO

SAN

PABLO

PALACIO DE
CRISTAL

ESPALTER

PUERTA DE MURILLO

PASEO DE LA REPUBLICA DE CUBA

2

EO

ROJAS   CLEMENTE

PASEO CELESTINO MUTIS

LA CHOPERA

REAL
JARDIN

BOTANICO

GLORIETA
DEL ANGEL
CAIDO

CLAUDIO MOYANO

PASEO   DEL   DUQUE   DE   FERNAN   NUÑEZ

ha

CALLE DE ALFONSO XII

PUERTA DEL
ANGEL CAIDO

VIVEROS
MUNICIPALES

3

Atocha
RENFE

OBSERVATORIO
ASTRONOMICO

CALLE POETA ESTEBAN VILLEGAS

CALLE DE ANDRES TORREJON

EO   INFANTA   ISABEL

CALLE DOCTOR VELASCO

Atocha ✕ II

CALLE LUIS CAMOENS

CALLE JUAN VALERA

Atocha

CALLE JUAN
BAUTISTA SACCHETTI

CALLE AGUSTIN QUEROL

JULIANA

AVENIDA   DE   LA   PASEO

CALLE JOSE
ARSELMO CLAVE

REINA

CRISTINA

n de
a

CIUDAD

DE

BARCELONA

CALLE FUENTERRABIA

4

P

P

Real Fábrica
de Tapices

CALLE VANDERGOTEN

Menéndez
Pelayo

CALLE NEBRIJA

MENDEZ

ALVARO

LACY

CALLE VARA DEL REY

CALLE   DE   TELLEZ

DELICIAS

AS

ANCORA

PJE ANCORA

5

DE

CANARIAS

SHOPPING IN MADRID

MADRID IS A CITY that offers the best of everything, from its handmade Spanish guitars to the latest designer clothes. That the city's shopping areas are quite well defined is an additional bonus. The elegant, up-market fashion stores are mostly concentrated in the Salamanca district and the latest in street fashion is available

Selection of Madrid's cakes

in the Chueca district, while most of the general clothes shops are situated in the city centre. There are food markets throughout the city, though the best speciality food and wine stores are to be found within Old Madrid. Not to be missed is the centuries-old Rastro *(see p292)* every Sunday, one of the greatest flea markets in the world.

FOOD AND DRINK

EVERY DISTRICT in Madrid has a food market with fresh meat, fish, fruit and vegetables. For gourmet specialities, take a walk around Old Madrid, where branches of the **Museo del Jamón** have enormous selections of the many different types of Spanish hams, cured sausages and cheeses. They also have bars and restaurants inside. A comprehensive stock of Spanish wines is sold in the beautiful **Mariano Madrueño**, which was established in 1895. North of Old Madrid is the

Horno San Onofre with its mouthwatering displays of cakes, breads and savouries, especially at Christmas.

DEPARTMENT STORES AND SHOPPING MALLS

THE DEPARTMENT STORE CHAIN, **El Corte Inglés**, has branches all over the city, selling clothes, foods and virtually everything else. They also offer services like photo-developing and shoe repairing.

Shopping malls have grown rapidly in Madrid in recent years and among the best are

the **Galería del Prado**, the **Jardín de Serrano** and **ABC Serrano**. For everything under one roof, go to the huge **La Vaguada** mall on the north side of the city. There are also several hypermarkets, mostly around the M30 ring road.

FASHION

A VARIED MIX of clothes stores are located around the Calle de Preciados in the centre of town, but the best-known Spanish and international fashion names are on the Calle de Serrano *(see p286)* and Calle Ortega y Gasset in the Salamanca district. **Ekseption** has a wide range of top designer labels, while the young, eccentric **Agatha Ruíz de la Prada** displays

On the catwalk in Madrid

her unique creations in a shop on a street off the west side of the Paseo de la Castellana.

The best place for clothes by young designers is the Chueca district, in and around the Calle del Almirante, with shops such as **Ararat**.

CRAFTS, DESIGN AND GIFTS

MADRID'S specialist craft shops are concentrated around the Plaza Mayor. They sell traditional craftwork like lace, embroidery and, at **Almoraima**, fans. **Arco de Cuchilleros** sells ceramics, leather and jewellery.

Two other districts, Huertas and Lavapiés, have many unusual old shops such as

The enticing frontage of the Museo del Jamón

Inside one of the many antique shops in the streets around the Rastro

Cerámica El Alfar for modern and traditional ceramics and Guitarrería F Manzanero for handmade guitars.

Among the best modern design shops is La Oca at the Puerta de Toledo, which has striking contemporary kitchen and household goods.

ART AND ANTIQUES

THE COMMERCIAL galleries and antiques shops of Madrid are conveniently grouped together. In the Salamanca district, especially along Calle de Claudio Coello, are some of the most exclusive antique shops. Cheaper and more unusual antiques can be found in the Huertas and La Latina districts, particularly around

the streets where the Rastro is held. Here, there are several arcades of small shops which open on weekdays, as well as during the Sunday market.

BOOKS AND NEWSPAPERS

THE GIANT French-owned FNAC book and video store has a good selection of books and magazines in English and other languages, and also a very efficient theatre and concert ticket desk. Booksellers is a good English-language bookshop.

The second hand bookstalls on the Calle Claudio Moyano, near the Parque del Retiro, are a permanent fixture. Here, rare volumes as well as cheap paperbacks can be acquired.

MARKETS

EACH SUNDAY thousands pack the long, narrow hill of Calle Ribera de Curtidores, centre of El Rastro market (see p292) which spreads over into the surrounding streets. At the top of the hill, in the Plaza de Cascorro, the stalls sell mostly clothes and jewellery, but elsewhere you can find just about anything.

The coin and stamp market, which is held every Sunday morning in the Plaza Mayor, is a little less hectic and also fascinating. There are also stalls selling second hand books and magazines, badges and other collectables.

Sunday morning in the busy Rastro flea market

DIRECTORY

FOOD AND DRINK

Horno San Onofre
Calle San Onofre 3.
Map 2 F2.
📞 (91) 532 90 60.

Mariano Madrueño
Calle Postigo de San Martín 3. **Map** 2 E2.
📞 (91) 521 19 55.

Museo del Jamón
Carrera de San Jerónimo 6.
Map 5 A1.
📞 (91) 521 03 46.

DEPARTMENT STORES AND SHOPPING MALLS

ABC Serrano
C/ Serrano 61. **Map** 4 E1.
📞 (91) 577 50 31.

Centro Comercial La Vaguada
Avenida Monforte de Lemos 36.
📞 (91) 730 10 00.

El Corte Inglés
C/ Preciados 3. **Map** 2 F3.
📞 (91) 379 80 00.

Galería del Prado
Plaza de las Cortes 7.
Map 5 B1.
📞 (91) 360 80 00.

Jardín de Serrano
Calle de Goya 6–8.
Map 4 E3.
📞 (91) 577 00 12.

FASHION

Agatha Ruíz de la Prada
Calle Marqués de Riscal 8.
Map 4 D1.
📞 (91) 310 44 83.

Ararat
Calle del Almirante 10.
Map 3 C4.
📞 (91) 531 81 56.

Ekseption
Calle de Velázquez 28.
Map 4 F3.
📞 (91) 577 43 53.

CRAFTS, DESIGN AND GIFTS

Almoraima
Plaza Mayor 12.
Map 2 E4.
📞 (91) 365 42 89.

Arco de Cuchilleros
Plaza Mayor 9.
Map 2 E4.
📞 (91) 365 26 80.

Cerámica El Alfar
Calle de Claudio Coello 112. **Map** 4 E2.
📞 (91) 411 35 87.

Guitarrería F Manzanero
Calle Santa Ana 12.
Map 2 D5.
📞 (91) 366 00 47.

La Oca
Ronda de Toledo 1.
📞 (91) 365 13 01.

BOOKS AND NEWSPAPERS

Booksellers
Calle José Abascal 48.
📞 (91) 442 79 59.

FNAC
C/ Preciados 28.
Map 2 E3.
📞 (91) 595 61 00.

MARKETS

El Rastro
Calle Ribera de Curtidores.
Map 2 E5.

ENTERTAINMENT IN MADRID

MADRID'S NIGHTLIFE is not for the faint-hearted. On a typical Saturday night the first stirrings of activity start in the cafés in the early evening, with the accent gradually shifting to tapas bars, restaurants and clubs; like the city's clamouring traffic, the revelling goes on through the night. Those with a slightly less frenetic evening

Flamenco guitarist in Parque del Retiro

in mind will find the best in all the Spanish arts – particularly flamenco and Madrid's own comic opera style, *zarzuela*. There is a good choice of classical music, and thriving jazz and rock circuits. Theatre lovers can choose between Spanish Golden Age classics, or modern mainstream and experimental drama.

Madrid's Teatro Real

ENTERTAINMENT GUIDES

THE BEST GUIDE to what's on currently in Madrid is the *Guía del Ocio*, which includes complete cinema listings and is on sale every Friday. Two daily newspapers have weekly entertainment supplements: *El Mundo*, on Thursday, and *El País*, on Friday.

SEASONS AND TICKETS

THE MAIN CONCERT and theatre seasons run from September to June. May's San Isidro fiesta *(see p280)* and the Festival de Otoño – from September to November – attract many top Spanish and international names in music, theatre and other arts – enquire at tourist offices for details.

The FNAC bookstore *(see p305)* sells concert and theatre tickets with little or no commission. State-funded theatres, like the **Auditorio Nacional** and **Teatro de la Zarzuela**, sell their own and each other's tickets. Bullfight and football tickets can be bought in advance at the **TEYCI** agency.

CLASSICAL MUSIC, DANCE AND ZARZUELA

THE TWO CONCERT HALLS of the **Auditorio Nacional** host a range of programmes each year by the Orquesta Nacional de España and international orchestras. Madrid's opera company is due to move into the **Teatro Real**, currently being restored.

The main dance company is the contemporary Compañía Nacional de Danza. **Teatro Albéniz** hosts dance performance as well as Madrid's own musical form, *zarzuela*, comic opera similar to operetta. There are productions at the **Teatro de la Zarzuela** and other theatres in summer.

THEATRE

MADRID'S MOST prestigious theatres are the **Teatro de la Comedia**, home to the Compañía Nacional de Teatro Clásico and its productions of Spanish Golden Age classics, and the **Teatro María Guerrero**, which presents modern drama in Spanish and

also hosts foreign productions. In addition, there is a thriving network of fringe venues, among the best of which is the frequently provocative **Teatro Alfil**. An enormous range of Spanish and international theatre talent, from established companies to radical new fringe groups, takes part in the annual Festival de Otoño.

FLAMENCO

ANDALUSIA MAY BE the home of flamenco *(see pp406–7)*, but Madrid is now where the best exponents are based. A club like **Casa Patas**, totally without amplification, perfectly catches the raw power of genuine flamenco guitar and *cante* singing at its finest. The **Café de Chinitas** is a good place to see spontaneous flamenco dancing.

CAFÉS, BARS AND CLUBS

MADRID'S BARS have a style of their own. The city has conserved many of its old grand cafés, which are wonderful places to sit and

Dancing the night away at the Joy Eslava dance club

Exterior of the historic Café Gijón

people-watch or chat. Of the literary cafés, the most famous is **Café Gijón** *(see p281)*.

A plush, popular club that attracts a lively young crowd is **Joy Eslava**, which doesn't hot up till well after midnight.

Wherever the night has been spent, an excellent way to finish is with a breakfast of *chocolate con churros (see p576)* at the **Chocolatería San Ginés**, just as the people of Madrid have been doing since it opened in 1894.

ROCK, JAZZ AND WORLD MUSIC

MAJOR INTERNATIONAL acts play regularly in Madrid's stadiums and sports halls, but **Sala Riviera** is a small, lively venue that has hosted acts such as Bob Dylan and The Cranberries. In summer there are open-air rock concerts in

the Casa de Campo's **Parque de Atracciones**. The **Café Central**, one of Europe's best jazz clubs, is near the Plaza Santa Ana, site of several good jazz and Latin music clubs, where you can see a live act, then dance the night away to the sinuous rhythms of salsa.

AMUSEMENTS

THE **Parque de Atracciones** funfair, in the Casa de Campo *(see p292)*, is popular with young and old. Modern water parks are also popular, and **Aqualung** is the most central of several in Madrid.

BULLFIGHTING AND FOOTBALL

BULLFIGHTING remains hugely popular in Madrid, and **Las Ventas** bullring *(see p296)*, the most important in Spain, holds *corridas* every Sunday from March to October. During the fiesta of San Isidro, in May, there are fights every day.

Real Madrid *(see p173)* are the local aristocrats of football and their Bernabéu stadium is one of the great theatres of the game. The ground of their rivals **Atlético de Madrid** is smaller and cheaper, and often has a better atmosphere.

Las Ventas bullring on the day of a bullfight

DIRECTORY	THEATRE	CAFÉS, BARS AND CLUBS	AMUSEMENTS
TICKETS	**Teatro Alfil** Calle del Pez 10. **Map** 2 E1. (91) 521 58 27.	**Café Gijón** Paseo de Recoletos 21. **Map** 3 C4. (91) 521 54 25.	**Aqualung** Paseo de la Ermita del Santo 40–48. (91) 526 43 92.
TEYCI Calle de Goya 7. **Map** 4 D3. (91) 576 45 32.	**Teatro de la Comedia** Calle del Príncipe 14. **Map** 5 A1.	**Chocolatería San Ginés** Pasadizo de San Ginés 5. **Map** 2 E3.	**Parque de Atracciones** Casa de Campo. (91) 463 29 00.
CLASSICAL MUSIC, DANCE AND ZARZUELA	(91) 521 49 31. **Teatro María Guerrero** Calle Tamayo y Baus 4.	(91) 365 65 46. **Joy Eslava** Calle del Arenal.	**BULLFIGHTING AND FOOTBALL**
Auditorio Nacional de Música C/ Príncipe de Vergara 146. (91) 337 01 00.	**Map** 3 C4. (91) 319 47 69. **FLAMENCO**	**Map** 2 E3. (91) 366 32 84. **ROCK, JAZZ AND WORLD MUSIC**	**Atlético de Madrid** Estadio Vicente Calderón, Paseo de la Virgen del Puerto 67. (91) 366 47 07.
Teatro Albéniz C/ Paz 11. **Map** 2 F4. (91) 531 83 11.	**Café de Chinitas** Calle Torija 7. **Map** 2 D2. (91) 547 15 02.	**Café Central** Pl del Ángel 10. **Map** 5 A1. (91) 369 41 43.	**Plaza Toros de Las Ventas** Calle de Alcalá 237. (91) 356 22 00.
Teatro Real Plaza de Isabel II. **Map** 2 D3.	**Casa Patas** Calle de Cañizares 10. **Map** 5 A2.	**Sala Riviera** Paseo de la Virgen del Puerto. **Map** 1 A4.	**Real Madrid** Estadio Santiago Bernabéu, Avenida de Concha Espina.
Teatro de la Zarzuela C/ Jovellanos 4. **Map** 3 B5. (91) 524 54 00.	(91) 369 04 96.	(91) 365 24 15.	(91) 344 00 52.

MADRID PROVINCE

MADRID PROVINCE (the Comunidad de Madrid) sits high on Spain's central plateau. There is plenty of superb scenery and good walking country in the sierras to the north, which are a refuge for city dwellers who go there to ski in winter or cool down during the torrid summers. In the western foothills of these mountains stands El Escorial, the royal palace-cum-monastery built by Felipe II, from which he ruled his empire. Close by is the Valle de los Caídos, the war monument erected by Franco. The smaller royal palace of El Pardo is on the outskirts of Madrid, and south of the city is the 18th-century summer palace of Aranjuez, set in lush parkland. Historic towns include Alcalá de Henares, which has a Renaissance university building, and Chinchón, where taverns cluster around a picturesque arcaded market square.

SIGHTS AT A GLANCE

Towns and Cities
Alcalá de Henares **9**
Buitrago del Lozoya **2**
Chinchón **10**
Manzanares el Real **7**

Historic Buildings
El Escorial pp312–13 **6**
Monasterio de Santa María de El Paular **3**
Palacio de El Pardo **8**

Palacio Real de Aranjuez **11**
Santa Cruz del Valle de los Caídos **5**

Mountain Ranges
Sierra Centro de Guadarrama **4**
Sierra Norte **1**

KEY

Madrid city

Madrid province

✈ Barajas Airport

Motorway

Major road

Minor road

Province boundary

0 kilometres   25
0 miles   20

SIGHTS IN MADRID PROVINCE

◁ Celebration of Mass in the church of the Monasterio de Santa María de El Paular

The village of Montejo de la Sierra in the Sierra Norte

Sierra Norte ❶

Madrid. 🚉 Montejo. 🛈 Calle Real 1, Montejo, (91) 869 70 58.

THE BLACK SLATE HAMLETS of the Sierra Norte, which were once known as the Sierra Pobre (Poor Sierra), are located in the most attractively rural part of Madrid province.

At **Montejo de la Sierra**, the largest village in the area, an information centre organizes riding, the rental of traditional houses (*see p531*), and visits to the nearby nature reserve of the **Hayedo de Montejo de la Sierra**. This is one of the most southern beech woods (*see p76*) in Europe, and a relic of a previous era, when climatic conditions here were more suitable for the beech. From Montejo, you can drive on to picturesque hamlets such as **La Hiruela** or **Puebla de la Sierra**, both of which are set in lovely walking country.

The drier southern hills slope down to the **Embalse de Puentes Viejas**, a reservoir where summer chalets cluster around artificial beaches. On the eastern edge of the sierra is the village of **Patones**, which is thought to have escaped invasion by the Moors and Napoleon's troops because of its isolated location.

Buitrago del Lozoya ❷

Madrid. 🏘 1,300. 🚉 🛈 Plaza de Picasso 1, (91) 868 00 56. 🏪 Sat. 🎉 La Asunción y San Roque (15 Aug).

PICTURESQUELY SITED above a meander in the Río Lozoya is the walled town of Buitrago del Lozoya. Founded by the Romans, it was fortified by the Arabs, and became an important market town in medieval times. The 14th-century Gothic-Mudéjar castle is in ruins, although the gatehouse, arches and stretches of the original Arab wall have survived. Today, the castle is used only as a venue for bullfights.

The old quarter, located within the walled enclosure, retains its charming atmosphere. The church of **Santa María del Castillo**, dating from the 15th century, has a beautiful Mudéjar tower and ceilings which were moved here from the old hospital. The **town hall** *(ayuntamiento)*, in the newer part of Buitrago, preserves a 16th-century processional cross. In the basement is the small **Museo Picasso**. The prints, drawings and ceramics on display were collected by the artist's friend and barber, Eugenio Arias, a native of Buitrago.

🏛 Museo Picasso
Plaza de Picasso 1. 🚇 (91) 868 00 56. 🔵 Tue.

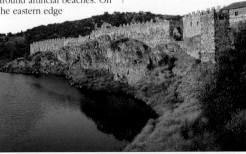

Altarpiece in the Monasterio de Santa María de El Paular

Monasterio de Santa María de El Paular ❸

Southwest of Rascafría on M604. 🚇 (91) 869 14 25. 🚉 Rascafría. 🕐 daily from noon. 🎟

FOUNDED IN 1390 as Castile's first Carthusian monastery, Santa María de El Paular stands on the site of a medieval royal hunting lodge. Although it is mainly Gothic in style, Plater-esque and Renaissance features were added later. The monastery was abandoned in 1836 when government minister Mendizábal ordered the sale of church goods *(see p59)*. It fell into disrepair until the state restored it in the 1950s. Today the complex comprises a working Benedictine monastery, a church and a private hotel *(see p554)*.

The church's delicate alabaster altarpiece, attributed to

Buitrago del Lozoya, standing next to the river

Flemish craftsmen, dates from
the 15th century. Its panels
depict scenes from the life of
Jesus. The lavish Baroque
camarín (chamber), behind
the altar, was designed by
Francisco de Hurtado in 1718.

Every Sunday, the monks
sing an hour-long Gregorian
chant in the church. If they
are not busy, they will show
you the cloister's Mudéjar brick
vaulting and double sun-clock.

The monastery is a good
starting point for exploring the
country towns of **Rascafría**
and **Lozoya** in the surrounding
Lozoya valley. To the southwest is the nature reserve of
Lagunas de Peñalara.

Sierra Centro de Guadarrama ④

Madrid. 🚉 *Puerto de Navacerrada,
Cercedilla.* 🚌 *Navacerrada, Cercedilla.*
ℹ️ *Navacerrada, (91) 856 00 06.*

T HE CENTRAL SECTION of the
Sierra de Guadarrama was
little visited until the 1920s,
when the area was first linked
by train to Madrid. Today, the
granite slopes are planted with
pines and specked by holiday
chalets. Villages such as
Navacerrada and **Cercedilla**
have grown into popular
resorts for skiing, mountain-
biking, rock-climbing and
horse riding. Walkers wanting
to enjoy the pure mountain
air can follow marked routes
from Navacerrada.

The **Valle de Fuenfría**, a
nature reserve of wild forests,
is best reached via Cercedilla.
It has a well-preserved stretch
of the original Roman road,
as well as several picnic spots
and marked walking routes.

The gigantic cross at Valle de los Caídos

Santa Cruz del Valle de los Caídos ⑤

North of El Escorial on M600. 📞
(91) 890 56 11. 🚌 *from El Escorial.*
🕐 *Tue–Sun.* ⚫ *some public hols.* 🎫

G ENERAL FRANCO had the
Holy Cross of the Valley
of the Fallen built as a memorial to those who died in the
Civil War *(see pp62–3)*. The

vast cross is located some
13 km (8 miles) north of El
Escorial *(see pp312–13)*, and
dominates the surrounding
countryside. Some Spaniards
find it too chilling – a symbol of
the dictatorship to be enjoyable, while for others its sheer
size is rewarding.

The cross is 150 m (490 ft)
high and rises above a basilica
carved 250 m (820 ft) deep
into the rock by Republican
prisoners of war. A number
of them are said to have died
in the 16-year project.

Next to the basilica's high
altar is the plain white tombstone of Franco, and, opposite,
that of José Antonio Primo de
Rivera, founder of the Falange
Española party. Another 40,000
coffins of soldiers from both
sides in the Civil War lie here
out of sight, including those
of two unidentified victims.

Visitors can take a lift up to
the arms of the cross, from
where there are magnificent
views over the pine forests.

Navacerrada pass in the Sierra de Guadarrama

El Escorial 6

FELIPE II'S IMPOSING GREY PALACE of San Lorenzo de El Escorial stands out against the foothills of the Sierra de Guadarrama to the northwest of Madrid. It was built between 1563 and 1584 in honour of St Lawrence, and its unornamented severity set a new architectural style which became one of the most influential in Spain. The interior was conceived as a mausoleum and contemplative retreat rather than a splendid residence. Its artistic wealth, which includes some of the most important works of art of the royal Habsburg collections, is concentrated in the museums, chapterhouses, church, royal pantheon and library. In contrast, the royal apartments are remarkably humble.

Fresco by Luca Giordano

★ Royal Pantheon
The funerary urns of Spanish monarchs line the marble mausoleum.

Main entrance

Bourbon Palace

Architectural Museum

Sala de Batallas

Patio de los Reyes

Entrance to Basilica only

Basilica
The highlight of this huge church, which is decorated only in parts, is the lavish altarpiece. The main chapel houses the cenotaphs of Felipe II and Charles V.

The Alfonso XII College was founded by monks in 1875 as a boarding school.

★ Library
This impressive array of 40,000 books incorporates Felipe II's personal collection. On display are precious manuscripts, including a poem by Alfonso X the Learned. The 16th-century ceiling frescoes are by Tibaldi.

STAR FEATURES
★ Royal Pantheon
★ Library
★ Museum of Art

The royal apartments, on the second floor of the palace, consist of Felipe II's modestly decorated living quarters. His bedroom opens directly on to the high altar of the basilica.

★ **Museum of Art**
Flemish, Italian and Spanish paintings hang in the museum, located on the first floor. One of the highlights is The Calvary, *by 15th-century Flemish artist Rogier van der Weyden.*

VISITORS' CHECKLIST

Paseo de Juan de Borbon Y Batemberg. **(** *(91) 890 59 02.*
(from Atocha or Chamartín.
(661, 664 from Moncloa. **(**
Apr–Sep: 10am–6pm Tue –Sun;
Oct–Mar: 10am–5pm Tue –Sun.
(public hols. **(** **(** *9:30am daily; 7pm, 8pm Sat & Sun.* **(** **(**

In the Patio de los Evangelistas is a temple by Herrera, adorned with statues of the Evangelists.

Chapterhouses
On display here is Charles V's portable altar. The ceiling frescoes depict monarchs and angels.

The monastery was founded in 1567, and has been run by Augustinian monks since 1885. It is closed to the public.

The Glory of the Spanish Monarchy by Luca Giordano
This beautiful fresco, above the main staircase, depicts Charles V and Felipe II, and scenes of the building of the monastery.

The Building of El Escorial
When chief architect Juan Bautista de Toledo died in 1567 he was replaced by Juan de Herrera, royal inspector of monuments. The plain architectural style of El Escorial is called desornamentado, *literally,* "unadorned".

Climber resting on a rock face of La Pedriza, near Manzanares el Real

Manzanares el Real ❼

Madrid. 🏛 *3,000.* 🚌 ℹ *Plaza del Pueblo 1, (91) 853 00 09.* 🚆 *Tue & Fri.* 🎉 *Fiesta de Verano (early Aug), Cristo de la Nave (14 Sep).*

FROM A DISTANCE, the skyline of Manzanares el Real is dominated by its restored 15th-century castle. Although the castle is equipped with some traditionally military features, such as double machicolations and turrets, it was used mainly as a residential palace by the Dukes of Infantado. Below the castle is a 16th-century church,

a Renaissance portico and fine capitals. Behind the town, bordering the foothills of the Sierra de Guadarrama, is **La Pedriza**, a mass of granite screes and ravines, very popular with climbers. It now forms part of an attractive nature reserve.

ENVIRONS: Colmenar Viejo, 12 km (7.5 miles) to the southeast of Manzanares, has a superb Gothic-Mudéjar church.

Palacio de El Pardo ❽

El Pardo, northwest of Madrid on N605. ☎ *(91) 376 15 00.* 🚌 *from Moncloa.* ⭕ *daily.* 📷

THIS ROYAL HUNTING lodge and palace, set in parkland just outside Madrid's city limits, boasts King Juan Carlos I and General Franco among its former residents. A guided tour takes visitors round the moated palace's original Habsburg wing and the identical 18th-century extension, designed by Francesco Sabatini.

The ornamental Bourbon interior is heavy with frescoes, gilt mouldings and tapestries, many of which were woven to designs by Goya *(see p296).* Today the palace is primarily used for accommodating visiting heads-of-state and for

entertaining royal guests. Surrounding the palace and the elegant 18th-century village of El Pardo is an enormous forest of holm oak. The area is popular for picnicking, and some game animals still run free.

Façade of Colegio de San Ildefonso in Alcalá de Henares

Alcalá de Henares ❾

Madrid. 🏛 *170,000.* 🚆 🚌 ℹ *Callejón Santa María, (91) 889 26 94.* 🚆 *Mon.* 🎉 *Feria de Alcalá (late Aug).*

AT THE HEART of a modern industrial town is one of Spain's most renowned university quarters. Founded in 1508 by Cardinal Cisneros, Alcalá's **university** became one of the

Lavish 18th-century tapestry inside the Palacio de El Pardo

foremost places of learning in 16th-century Europe. It was transferred to Madrid in the 19th century. Most of the original 40 colleges have since been destroyed, but the most historic one, **San Ildefonso**, survives. Former students include Golden Age playwright Lope de Vega *(see p280)*. In 1517 the university produced Europe's first polyglot bible, which had text in Latin, Greek, Hebrew and Chaldean.

Alcalá's other sights are the cathedral and the **Casa-Museo de Cervantes**, birthplace of the Golden Age author. It is now an interesting museum.

🏛 **Casa-Museo de Cervantes**
Calle Imagen 2. ☎ *(91) 889 96 54.* ◯ *Tue–Sun.* ● *public hols.*

Chinchón ❿

Madrid. 🏘 *4,200.* ☐ ❑ *Plaza Mayor 3, (91) 894 00 84.* ☐ *Sat.* 🎪 *Semana Santa (Easter Week), San Roque (12–18 Aug).*

CHINCHÓN IS arguably Madrid province's most picturesque town. The 16th-century, typically Castilian, porticoed **Plaza Mayor** has a splendidly theatrical air. It comes alive for the Easter passion play, acted out by the townspeople *(see p280)*, and during the August bullfights. The 16th-century church, perched above the square, has an altar painting by Goya, whose brother was a priest here. Just off the square is the 18th-century Augustinian monastery, which has been converted into a **parador**

Chinchón's unique porticoed Plaza Mayor

with a peaceful patio garden *(see p554)*. A ruined 15th-century castle is on a hill to the west of town. Although it is closed to the public, there are views of Chinchón and the countryside from outside it.

Chinchón is a popular weekend destination for *Madrileños*, who come here to sample the excellent chorizo and locally produced *anís (see p577)* in the town's many taverns.

Palacio Real de Aranjuez ⓫

Plaza de Parejas, Aranjuez. ☎ *(91) 891 07 40.* ☐ ☐ ◯ *Tue–Sun.* ● *some public hols.* 🈺 ♿

THE ROYAL SUMMER PALACE and gardens of Aranjuez grew up around a medieval hunting lodge standing beside a natural weir, the meeting point of the Tagus and Jarama rivers.

Today's palace of brick and white stone was built in the 18th century to replace the earlier Habsburg palace which burned down. A guided tour takes you through numerous Baroque rooms, among them the Chinese Porcelain Room,

the Hall of Mirrors and the Smoking Room, modelled on the Alhambra in Granada. It is worth visiting Aranjuez for the simple pleasure of walking in the 300 hectares (740 acres) of shady royal gardens which inspired Joaquín Rodrigo's *Concierto de Aranjuez*. The small Parterre Garden and the Island Garden, between the rivers, survive from the original 16th-century palace.

Between the palace and the River Tagus is the 18th-century Prince's Garden, decorated with sculptures, fountains and lofty trees from the Americas. In the garden is the Casa de Marinos (Sailors' House), a museum housing the launches once used by the royal family for trips along the river. At the far end of the garden is the Casa del Labrador (Labourer's Cottage), a decorative royal pavilion built by Carlos IV.

The town's restaurants are deservedly popular because of the exceptional quality of local produce, especially asparagus and strawberries. In summer, a 19th-century steam train, built to carry strawberries to the market in Madrid, runs between here and the capital.

MIGUEL DE CERVANTES

Miguel de Cervantes Saavedra, Spain's greatest literary figure *(see p30)*, was born in Alcalá de Henares in 1547. After fighting in the naval Battle of Lepanto (1571), he was held captive by the Turks for more than five years. In 1605, when he was almost 60 years old, the first of two parts of his comic masterpiece *Don Quixote (see p377)* was published to popular acclaim. He continued writing novels and plays until his death in Madrid on 23 April 1616, the same day that Shakespeare died.

Gardens surrounding the Royal Palace at Aranjuez

CENTRAL SPAIN

Introducing Central Spain

MUCH OF SPAIN'S VAST CENTRAL PLATEAU, the *meseta*, is covered with wheat fields or dry, dusty plains, but there are many attractive places to explore. Central Spain's mountains, gorges, forests and lakes are filled with wildlife. A deep sense of history permeates the towns and cities of the tableland, reflected in some stunning architecture: the Roman ruins of Mérida, the medieval mansions of Cáceres, the Gothic cathedrals of Burgos, León and Toledo, the Renaissance grandeur of Salamanca, and castles almost everywhere.

León Cathedral (see p336–7), an outstanding Gothic building, was completed during the 13th century. As well as many glorious windows of medieval glass, it has superb carved choir stalls depicting biblical scenes and everyday life.

León

CASTILLA Y LEÓN
(see pp328–59)

Zamora

Vallad

Salamanca (see pp340–43) is the site of some of the finest Renaissance and Plateresque architecture in Spain. Among the city's most notable buildings are the university, its façade a mass of carved detail; the old and new cathedrals (built side by side); and the handsome Plaza Mayor, built in warm golden sandstone.

Salamanca

Ávila

Cáceres

To

EXTREMADURA
(see pp382–95)

The Museo Nacional de Arte Romano in Mérida (see p392) houses Roman treasures. The city has a well-preserved Roman theatre.

Badajoz

0 kilometres   50

0 miles   50

◁ **Roofs and walls in the old part of Toledo**

Burgos Cathedral (see pp354–5) *is the work of some of the great medieval architects and artists, and it is full of treasures from all periods. This Baroque fresco of the coronation of the Virgin covers the domed ceiling of the sacristy.*

Segovia (see p346) *extends along a rocky spur that divides two rivers. The city's landmarks are the Alcázar (see pp326–7) – a castle with distinctive fairy-tale towers – and the Roman aqueduct, built in the 1st century AD, which towers 29 m (95 ft) above a busy urban square.*

Burgos

Soria

Madrid

Guadalajara

Cuenca's old town (see pp366–7) *was built on a ridge high above two gorges. One of the picturesque but precariously sited "Hanging Houses" is now home to a museum of abstract art.*

Cuenca

CASTILLA-LA MANCHA
(see pp360–81)

Toledo Cathedral (see pp374–5), *with its exuberant sculptured decoration, is a great medieval building in a city of monuments. Toledo's architectural wealth stems from a fusion of Jewish, Christian and Muslim cultures.*

Albacete

Regional Food: Central Spain

THE RESTAURANTS OF MADRID are a rich source of specialities from every Spanish region, along with superb fresh fish that is often on the table within a few hours of being caught. Game, such as wild boar, pheasant and partridge, is plentiful throughout Central Spain, but especially in Extremadura, where wild frog and tench are also eaten. Castilla y León and Castilla-La Mancha maintain a tradition of homely, robust cooking with a variety of warming one-pot pulse stews. The north also produces excellent bread, which is eaten with everything. Sausages and simple rabbit or pork dishes, spiced with cumin and garlic, are typical of Castilla-La Mancha; while Castilla y León is known for its suckling pig and milk-fed lamb, roasted whole in enormous bread ovens. Little cakes, such as Toledo's famous marzipans, are popular and many convents continue to make and sell their own.

Garlic

Patatas a la importancia *are egg-coated potatoes fried and then simmered in wine seasoned with onions and saffron.*

Saffron (azafrán) *comes from the purple autumn crocus, which has three deep red stigmas. Introduced by the Moors centuries ago, it is the world's most expensive spice because it must be picked by hand. The plains of La Mancha (see p376) yield Spain's highest quality saffron, which is sold in strands and date stamped. Saffron is soaked, crushed or toasted to add its taste and golden colour to a variety of dishes.*

Pollo al padre Pero, *a dish of Extremadura, is half a young chicken simmered in a spicy pepper and tomato sauce.*

Sopa de ajo *is a warming garlic soup which is thickened with bread. Poached egg and paprika are often added to it.*

Chickpeas

Chicken

Beef

Cabbage

Salt pork belly

Sausage

Cocido madrileño *is a widely available meat dish and every region has its own variation. It is essentially a slow-simmered stew of beef, chicken, ham and pork belly with chickpeas. Cabbage, chorizo and morcilla (black sausage) are also included. The broth is drunk first, as soup, and the rest often served as two further courses.*

Migas, *originally a shepherd's dish, is fried breadcrumbs. It is often served with fried peppers or, in Extremadura, with bacon.*

Perdiz con chocolate *is braised partridge with carrots and onions, served with a rich, dark, chocolate-tasting gravy.*

Pisto, *La Mancha's best dish, is Spain's version of ratatouille. It combines peppers, tomatoes, onions and courgettes.*

El frite, *from Extremadura, is a dish of fried lamb with garlic, onion and lemon, flavoured with the local paprika.*

Menestra de ternera *is a stew in which veal is simmered gently with young vegetables, such as carrots and peas.*

Cabrito al ajillo *is kid fried with onions and herbs. This savoury dish can also include pounded goat's liver.*

Sausages *are made in most of the villages of Extremadura and vary in their taste and appearance. Those made in Guijelo (including chorizo) and Montanchez are particularly good, as are the hams, cured loins and shoulders produced in Extremadura.*

Yemas *means yolks, which these sugary cakes resemble in their shape, colour and content. The best come from Ávila (see p344).*

Manchego, *made from sheep's milk on the plains of La Mancha, is widely regarded as Spain's greatest cheese. When fully mature it becomes very hard, similar to Parmesan. The texture and the taste vary depending on whether it is* fresco *(young),* curado *(over 13 weeks old) or* añejo *(at least 7 months old).*

Chickpeas

Lentils

Pinto beans

PULSES

An enormous variety of pulses, in all colours, shapes and sizes is grown on the plains of Castilla y León. The best pulses are expensive, and their names are legally protected. The best-known white beans are the *alubias blancas* of Barco de Ávila; the best chickpeas are grown in Fuentesauco; and the finest lentils come from La Armuña.

Wines of Central Spain

THE WINES OF CENTRAL SPAIN originate in either the small, high-quality regions of northwest Castilla y León or in the vast wine-producing plains of La Mancha and Valdepeñas. Ribera del Duero has become Spain's most fashionable red wine region, with its aromatic, rich yet fine reds made from Tinto Fino grapes (the local name for Tempranillo) and, more recently, lighter, fruity wines. Rueda makes a good white wine, made from the Verdejo grape. La Mancha and Valdepeñas both produce lots of simple white wine, and reds which can be mellow and fruity.

Harvesting Viura grapes at Rueda

Artesian well for irrigating vines in La Mancha

COLEGIATA
TINTO
1985

Toro makes the most powerful and fiery of all red wines from the ubiquitous Tempranillo grape.

Villafranca del Bierzo
Ponferrada • • Cacabel

N122

ZAMC
Duer

SALAMANC

N620

N630

KEY FACTS ABOUT WINES OF CENTRAL SPAIN

Location and Climate
Ribera del Duero, Rueda and Toro are all high-lying areas with extreme climates – very hot summer days combined with cool nights, and cold winters. The marked difference of temperature between day and night helps to preserve the acidity in the grapes. Both La Mancha and Valdepeñas are extremely hot and dry areas. In recent years, droughts have caused a severe shortage of grapes.

Grape Varieties
The Tempranillo grape – also known as Tinto Fino, Tinto del Toro and Cencibel – produces nearly all the best red wines of Central Spain. Cabernet Sauvignon is permitted in some regions; it is used in some Ribera del Duero wines and occasionally surfaces as a single varietal, as at the estate of the Marquis of Griñón in Méntrida. Verdejo, Viura and Sauvignon Blanc are used for white Rueda. The white Airén grape predominates in the vineyards of Valdepeñas and La Mancha.

Good Producers
Toro: Fariña (Gran Colegiata). **Rueda:** Álvarez y Diez, Los Curros, Marqués de Riscal, Sanz. **Ribera del Duero:** Alejandro Fernández (Pesquera), Boada, Hermanos Pérez Pascuas (Viña Pedrosa), Ismael Arroyo (Valsotillo), Vega Sicilia, Victor Balbás. *Méntrida:* Marqués de Griñón. **La Mancha:** Fermín Ayuso Roig (Estola), Vinícola de Castilla (Castillo de Alhambra). **Valdepeñas:** Casa de la Viña, Félix Solís, Luis Megía (Marqués de Gastañaga), Los Llanos.

Traditional earthenware *tinaj* still used for fermenting wine

0 kilometres 100

0 miles 50

Vineyard near Moral de Calatrava in Valdepeñas

Pesquera *is made by Alejandro Fernández, the second most notable producer in the Ribera del Duero region, after Vega Sicilia.*

KEY

- Bierzo
- Cigales
- Toro
- Rueda
- Ribera del Duero
- Vinos de Madrid
- Méntrida
- La Mancha
- Valdepeñas
- Almansa

Marqués de Griñón *is an intense Cabernet Sauvignon wine with a deep colour, made on a vast estate outside Toledo. Although officially a Vino de Mesa (see p577), its quality is as high as a DO wine.*

Señorío de los Llanos *is produced in Valdepeñas. Its fine reds – made from Cencibel (Tempranillo) and aged in oak – are of excellent value.*

WINE REGIONS

The wine regions of Ribera del Duero, Toro and Rueda, are situated on remote, high plateaus, straddling the Río Duero. To the northwest lies the isolated region of Bierzo, whose wines have more in common with neighbouring Valdeorras in Galicia. Some wine is produced around Madrid, and southwest of the capital is the largely undistinguished region of Méntrida. Most of Central Spain's wine is produced in La Mancha – the world's largest single wine region – and in the smaller enclave of Valdepeñas, which produces wines of a higher quality.

Birds of Central Spain

THE VAST AND VARIED wild habitats of Central Spain are home to the richest avifauna in the peninsula. White storks' nests are a common sight on the church towers and chimneypots of towns. Grebes, herons and shovelers can be seen in the marshlands; the distinctive hoopoe is often spotted in woods; and grasslands are the nesting grounds of bustards and cranes. The

Bee-eater mountains and high plains are the domain of birds of prey such as the imperial eagle, peregrine falcon and vultures. Deforestation, changing agricultural practices and hunting have all taken their toll in recent decades. Today, almost 160 bird species are the subject of conservation initiatives.

MIGRATION ROUTES

— Cranes

— Storks

— Raptors

— Wildfowl

MARSHLAND AND WET MEADOW

Wetlands, such as Lagunas de Ruidera *(see p379)*, on the edge of the plains of La Mancha, are vital feeding grounds for a wide range of waterfowl, some of which may remain in Spain throughout the year. Other migratory species use such sites as stopover points to feed, rest and build up enough energy to enable them to complete their journeys.

WOODLAND AND SCRUB

Habitats in areas of woodland, such as the Parque Nacional de Cabañeros *(see p369)*, and scrub support many species, such as rollers and woodpeckers, throughout the year. Food is plentiful and there are many places to roost and nest. Early in the morning is the best time for spotting some of the rarer species, such as the bluethroat.

Little egrets *are recognized by their snow white plumage and graceful slow flight. They feed largely on frogs, snails and small fish.*

Rollers *are commonly found in woodland, often nesting in tree stumps or holes left by woodpeckers. Their food includes grasshoppers, crickets and beetles.*

Shovelers *feed on the water surface with a characteristic shovelling motion. The male has brightly coloured plumage but the female is a dull brown.*

Hoopoes *can be easily identified by their striking plumage and by the crest which can be raised if the bird is alarmed. They feed on ground insects.*

STORKS

Both the white and the (much rarer) black stork breed in Spain. They can be recognized in flight by their slow, steady wingbeats and may occasionally be seen soaring on thermals, usually during migrations. During the breeding season they put on elaborate courtship displays, which involve "dancing", wing-beating and bill-clapping. Their large nests, made of branches and twigs and lined with grasses, are constructed on roofs, towers, spires and chimneypots, where they are easy to watch. They feed on insects, fish and amphibians. Stork populations are threatened by wetland reclamation and the use of pesticides.

Nesting on a monastery roof

The endangered black stork

GRASSLAND AND FIELD

Many of Spain's natural grasslands have been ploughed over to plant cereals and other crops. Remaining vestiges are rich in wild grasses and flowers and are vital habitats for species such as bustards and larks.

Cranes perform elegant courtship dances and are also stately birds in flight, their long necks extended to the limit. They are omnivores, feeding on amphibians, crustaceans, plants and insects.

Great bustards nest in shallow depressions formed in open grassland and cultivated fields. Spain is home to half of the world's population.

MOUNTAIN AND HIGH PLAIN

Some of Spain's most spectacular birds of prey live in mountain ranges, such as the Sierra de Gredos *(see p344)*, and the high plains of Central Spain. The broad wingspans of eagles and vultures allow them to soar on currents of warm air as they scan the ground below for prey and carrion.

Imperial eagles, with their vast wingspan of 2.25 m (7 ft), are extremely rare – only around 100 pairs are left in the whole of Spain.

Griffon vultures, a gregarious species, nest in trees and on rocky crags, often using the same place from year to year. Their broad wingspans can exceed 2 m (6 ft).

The Castles of Castile

Coca Castle *(see p347)*, a classic
Mudéjar design in brick

THE GREATEST CONCENTRATION
of Spain's 2,000 castles is in
Castile (now part of Castilla y
León), which derived its name
from the word *castillo*, or castle.
In the 10th and 11th centuries
this region was the battleground
between Moors and Christians.
Villages and towns were fortified
as protection against one side or
the other. Most of the surviving

**13th-century fresco of
the siege of a castle**

castles in Castile, however, were built as noble residences after the area had been reconquered and there
was no longer a military purpose for them. Fernando
and Isabel *(see pp52–3)* banned the building of new
castles at the end of the 15th century; many existing
ones were converted to domestic use.

Patio de armas
(courtyard)

**Bartizan
turrets**

**The Torre de
Juan II** contained
the dungeons.

La Mota Castle (see p348), *at Medina
del Campo, near Valladolid, was originally a Moorish castle but was rebuilt after
1440 and later became the property of
Fernando and Isabel. The square-
shaped Torre del Homenaje has twin
bartizan turrets at its corners and
machiolations beneath its battlements.
Great curtain walls surround the castle.*

The barbican, with the
coat of arms of the Catholic
Monarchs carved over the
gate, contains the portcullis
and guards' watchrooms.

Belmonte Castle (see p376) *was built
in the 15th century as the stronghold
of the quarrelsome Marquis of Villena,
Juan Pacheco. Late-Gothic in style, it
has a sophisticated, hexagonal ground
plan, with a triangular bailey.*

SEGOVIA ALCÁZAR

The plan of the royal castle of Segovia *(see p346)* is determined by the contours of the rocky outcrop on which it stands. Begun in the 12th century, the Alcázar was mostly built between 1410 and 1455. It had to be largely rebuilt following a fire in 1862. The fortress's formidable walls conceal several sumptuous apartments.

Torre del Homenaje has pointed turrets, atypical of Spanish castles.

Curtain wall

The King's Room, the most important room in the castle, is Gothic in style.

The Pine Cone Room gets its name from the golden pine cones on the ceiling.

The Galley Room

The Throne Room has ornate plasterwork and a Mudéjar ceiling.

TERMS USED IN THIS GUIDE

Alcazar: Castle or palace used as a royal residence.

Bartizan: A small turret which projects from the battlements of a tower above attackers.

Cross and orb loophole: Narrow slit, shaped to allow archers to shoot at various angles.

Curtain wall: Outer, windowless wall, often low enough for archers to fire over it from the keep and other towers.

Machicolation: A projection overhanging the wall beneath a battlement to allow boiling oil, missiles or human waste to be dropped on to the enemy.

Torre del Homenaje: The fortified tower or keep at the heart of a castle, often built to a square plan, in which the nobleman's family lived.

Peñafiel Castle (see p349) has been compared to a battleship because of its long, narrow shape. The site above the Duero valley has been defended since the 10th century, but the present castle is 15th-century.

THE CASTLES OF CASTILLA Y LEÓN

Some of Central Spain's finest surviving castles can be visited today. A few, such as Ciudad Rodrigo *(see p339)*, have been turned into luxurious paradors *(see pp534–5)*.

Torrelobatón · Valladolid · Peñaranda de Duero · Calatañazor · Zamora · Simancas · Peñafiel · Gomaz · Buen Amor · Coca · Cuéllar · Berlanga de Duero · La Mota · Pedraza · Salamanca · Turégano · Segovia · Arévalo · Ávila · MADRID · Ciudad Rodrigo

N630 · NV1 · N601 · N620 · N1 · N122 · Duero · N110 · Tormes

0 kilometres 100
0 miles 50

CASTILLA Y LEÓN

LEÓN · ZAMORA · SALAMANCA · ÁVILA · SEGOVIA
VALLADOLID · PALENCIA · BURGOS · SORIA

AWESOME EXPANSES OF OCHRE PLAINS *stretch to hills crowned with the castles that cover this vast region. Through Spain's history, these central provinces have had a major influence on its language, religion and culture. Their many historic cities preserve some of the country's most magnificent architectural sights.*

The territories of the two rival medieval kingdoms of Castile and León, occupying the northern half of the great plateau in the centre of Spain, now form the country's largest region, or *comunidad autónoma*.

Castile and León were first brought together under one crown in 1037 by Fernando I; but the union was not consolidated until the early 13th century. The kingdom of Castile and León was one of the driving forces of the Reconquest. El Cid, the legendary hero, was born near Burgos.

Wealth pouring in from the wool trade and the New World, reaching a peak in the 16th century, financed the many great artistic and architectural treasures that can be seen today in the cities of Castilla y León. Burgos has an exuberantly decorated Gothic cathedral. León cathedral is famous for its medieval stained glass. At the heart of the monumental city of Salamanca is the oldest university in the peninsula. Segovia's aqueduct is the largest Roman structure in Spain and its Alcázar is the country's most photographed castle. Ávila is surrounded by an unbroken wall, built by Christian forces against the Moors. In Valladolid, the regional capital, a superb collection of multicoloured sculpture is displayed in a magnificent 15th-century building.

Beyond the cities, in Castilla y León's varied countryside, there are many attractive small towns which preserve outstanding examples of the region's vernacular architecture.

Cereal fields and vineyards covering the fertile Tierra de Campos in Palencia province

◁ The battle-scarred castle of Calatañazor (Soria), site of a Christian victory against the Moors in 1002

Exploring Castilla y León

COVERING THE NORTHERN PART of Central Spain's vast tableland, Castilla y León has a huge variety of sights. Many – the university of Salamanca, the Alcázar and aqueduct of Segovia, the medieval walls of Ávila, the monastery at Santo Domingo de Silos, and the great cathedrals of Burgos and León – are well known. Other historic towns and villages worthy of a detour include Ciudad Rodrigo, Covarrubias, Pedraza de la Sierra and Zamora. This region also has great tracts of beautiful countryside, especially in the mountains of the Sierra de la Peña de Francia and the Sierra de Gredos.

SIGHTS AT A GLANCE

Tour

SEE ALSO

0 kilometres   50

0 miles   30

Map labels: Oviedo, N630, C63, EL BIERZO 1, CUEVAS DE VALPORQUERO 6, Lugo, VILLAFRANCA DEL BIERZO 2, A66, LEÓN 7, N536, PONFERRADA 3, ASTORGA 5, N601, N625, VALENCIA DE DON, C622, Bragança, PUEBLA DE SANABRIA 4, Embalse de Cernadilla, N525, BENAVENTE, N610, Tera, N631, N122, MEDINA DE RIOSECO, ZAMORA 8, TORO, Duero, TORDESILL, C527, N630, N620, Embalse de Almendra, Duero, MEDINA CA, Águeda, N620, SALAMANCA 11, ALBA DE TORMES, N501, Guarda, CIUDAD RODRIGO 9, SIERRA DE LA PEÑA DE FRANCIA 10, Embalse de Santa Teresa, Tormes, N110, BÉJAR, C526, Cáceres, SIERRA DE GREDOS 12, Tiétar

GETTING AROUND

Madrid makes a convenient springboard for touring in Castilla y León. The major cities of the region are connected by rail but the coach is often a quicker alternative. If you intend exploring rural areas or visiting small towns it is advisable to hire a car. There are few motorways and as a consequence main roads tend to be dominated by trucks. Minor roads, generally in good condition, are a more enjoyable way of seeing the countryside.

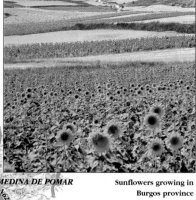

Sunflowers growing in Burgos province

KEY

▬▬▬	Motorway
▬▬▬	Major road
▭▭▭	Minor road
▬▬▬	Scenic route
◝◝	River
✳	Viewpoint

Santander

● CERVERA DE PISUERGA

25 AGUILAR DE CAMPOO

● MEDINA DE POMAR

FRIAS ●

Gasteiz (Vitoria)

26 BRIVIESCA

N120

N623

24 FRÓMISTA

28

BURGOS

N620

Arlanzón

N234

23 PALENCIA

LERMA **29**

C113

27 COVARRUBIAS

30 SANTO DOMINGO DE SILOS

Iruña (Pamplona)

N122

VALLADOLID

Duero

N122

31 PEÑARANDA DE DUERO

ARANDA DE DUERO

N603

33 SORIA

N234

AYLLON

EL BURGO DE OSMA

32

N122

C116

18 CASTILLO DE COCA

Zaragoza

ALO

17 ● HOCES DE DURATÓN

SEPÚLVEDA

C114

C101

16 PEDRAZA DE LA SIERRA

34 MEDINACELI /Madrid

SEGOVIA **15**

14 LA GRANJA DE SAN ILDEFONSO

N11

Madrid

N403

Toledo

Peñaranda de Duero castle

El Bierzo ❶

León. 🚆 *Ponferrada.* 🚌 *Ponferrada.*
ℹ️ *Ponferrada, (987) 42 42 36.*

THIS NORTHWESTERN region of
León province was at one
time the bed of an ancient
lake. Sheltered by hills from
the worst extremes of Central
Spain's climate, its sun-soaked,
alluvial soils make for fertile
orchards and vineyards. Over
the centuries, the area has also
yielded rich mineral pickings
including coal, iron and gold.
Many hiking routes and picnic spots are within reach of
the main towns of Ponferrada
and Villafranca del Bierzo.

In the eastern section, you
can trace the course of the old
Road to Santiago *(see pp78–9)*
through the **Montes de León**,
past the pilgrim church and
medieval bridge of Molinaseca.
Turning off the road at the remote village of Acebo you pass
through a deep valley where
there are signs pointing to the
Herrería de Compludo, a
fascinating water-powered
ironworks which dates from
the 7th century. The machinery is still in working order and
is demonstrated regularly.

The **Lago de Carucedo**, to
the southwest of Ponferrada,
is an ancient artificial lake. It
acted as a reservoir in Roman
times, a by-product of a vast
gold mining operation. Using
slave labour, millions of tonnes
of alluvium were washed from

A *palloza* in the Sierra de Ancares

the hills of Las Médulas by a
complex system of canals and
sluice gates. The ore was then
panned, and the gold dust collected on sheep's wool. It has
been estimated that more than
500 tonnes of precious metal
were extracted from the hills
between the 1st and 4th centuries AD. These ancient workings lie within a memorable
landscape of wind-eroded
crags, and hills pierced by tunnels and colonized by gnarled
chestnut trees. You can best
appreciate the area from a
viewpoint at Orellán, which is
reached via a rough, steep
track. **Las Médulas**, a village
south of Carucedo, is another
place to go for a fine view.

To the north of the NVI highway lies the Sierra de Ancares,
a wild region of rounded, slate
mountains marking the borders

of Galicia and Asturias. Part
of it now forms the **Reserva
Nacional de los Ancares
Leoneses**, an attractive nature
reserve. The heathland dotted
with oak and birch copses is
home to deer, wolves, brown
bears and capercaillies.

Several isolated villages high
in the hills contain *pallozas* –
primitive, pre-Roman stone
dwellings thatched with rye.
One of the most striking collections of these huts can be
found in the isolated village of
Campo del Agua, in the west.

🏛 **Herrería de Compludo**
Compludo. 📞 *(987) 45 91 66.*
🕐 *Tue–Sat.*

Villafranca del Bierzo ❷

León. 🏘 *2,700.* 🚌 ℹ️ *Plaza Mayor 1,
(987) 54 02 91.* 🛒 *Tue.* 🎭 *Winter
Fiesta (28 Jan), Fiesta del Cristo (14 Sep).*

EMBLAZONED MANSIONS line the
ancient streets of this delightful town on the Road to
Santiago. The solid, early 16th-
century, drum-towered castle
is still inhabited. Near the Plaza
Mayor a number of imposing
churches and convents compete for attention. Particularly
worth seeing are the fine sculptures adorning the north portal
of the simple, Romanesque
Iglesia de Santiago. At the
church's Puerta del Perdón
(Door of Mercy), pilgrims who

Craggy, tree-clad hills around the ancient gold workings near the village of Las Médulas

were too weak to make the final gruelling hike across the hills of Galicia could obtain dispensation. Visitors to the town can also sample the local speciality, cherries marinated in *aguardiente*, a spirit.

ENVIRONS: One of the finest views over El Bierzo is from **Corullón**, to the south. This pretty village with grey stone houses is set in a sunny location above the broad, fertile basin of the Río Sil where the vines of the Bierzo wine region flourish (*see pp74–5*). Two churches, the late 11th-century San Miguel and the restored, Romanesque San Esteban, are worth a visit. Down in the valley, the Benedictine monastery at **Carracedo del Monasterio** stands in ruined splendour. Founded in 990, it was at one time the most powerful religious community in El Bierzo.

Puerta del Perdón of Villafranca's Iglesia de Santiago

Ponferrada ❸

León. 🏘 60,000. 🚌 🚊 🏤 C/ Gil y Carrasco 4, (987) 42 42 36. 🛒 Wed & Sat. 🎉 Virgen de la Encina (7 Sep).

A MEDIEVAL BRIDGE reinforced with iron (*pons ferrata*), erected for the benefit of pilgrims on their way to Santiago de Compostela, gave this town its name. Today, prosperous from both iron and coal deposits, Ponferrada has expanded into a sizeable town.

Most of its attractions are confined to the small old quarter. Ponferrada's majestic **castle** was constructed between the

The imposing Templar castle of Ponferrada

12th and 14th centuries by the Knights Templar to protect pilgrims. During the Middle Ages it was one of the largest fortresses in northwest Spain.

Standing on the main square is the Baroque **town hall** (*ayuntamiento*). One entrance to the square is straddled by a tall clock-tower which sits above one of the gateways of the medieval wall. Nearby is the Renaissance **Basílica de la Virgen de la Encina**. The older **Iglesia de Santo Tomás de las Ollas** is hidden away in the town's village-like northern suburbs. Mozarabic, Romanesque and Baroque elements combine in the architecture of this simple church. The 10th-century apse has beautiful horseshoe arches. Ask at the nearest house for the key.

ENVIRONS: A pleasant drive through the idyllic **Valle de Silencio** (Valley of Silence), south of Ponferrada, follows a poplar-fringed stream past several bucolic villages. The last and most beautiful of these is **Peñalba de Santiago**, sheltering beneath an attractive ring of mountains. The 10th-century Mozarabic church of Santiago de Peñalba has horseshoe arches above its double portal.

Puebla de Sanabria ❹

Zamora. 🏘 1,800. 🚌 🏤 Plaza Mayor 1, (980) 62 00 02. 🚌 Fri. 🎉 Las Victorias (9 Sep).

T HIS ATTRACTIVE OLD village lies beyond the undulating broom and oak scrub of the Sierra de la Culebra. A steep cobbled street leads past stone and slate houses with huge, overhanging eaves and walls bearing coats of arms, to a hilltop church and castle.

The village has become the centre of a popular inland holiday resort based around the largest glacial lake in Spain, the **Lago de Sanabria**, now a nature reserve. Among the many activities available are fishing, walking and water sports.

Local touring routes beckon visitors to Ribadelago on the lakeshore, though the road to the quaint hill village of **San Martín de Castañeda** gives better views. There's a small visitors' centre for the nature reserve in San Martín's restored monastery. The village is so traditional that you may still see cattle yoked to wooden carts, and women dressed in black from head to toe.

The 12th-century church and 15th-century castle of Puebla de Sanabria

The nave of Astorga cathedral

Astorga **5**

León. ⚑ 13,500. 🚉 🚌 **ℹ** *Plaza de España.* 【 *(987) 61 68 38.* 🚍 *Tue.* 🎏 *Santa Marta (late Aug).*

THE ROMAN TOWN of Asturica Augusta was a strategic halt on the Vía de la Plata (Silver Road), a Roman road linking Andalusia and northwest Spain. Later it came to form a stage on the pilgrimage route to Santiago *(see pp78–9)*.

Soaring above the ramparts in the upper town are Astorga's two principal monuments, the cathedral and the Palacio Episcopal. The **cathedral** was built between the 15th and the 18th centuries and displays a variety of architectural styles ranging from its Gothic apse to the effusive Baroque of its two towers, which are carved with various biblical scenes. The gilt altarpiece by Gaspar Becerra is a masterpiece of the Spanish Renaissance. Among the many fine exhibits found in the cathedral's museum are the 10th-century carved casket of Alfonso III the Great, the jewelled Reliquary of the True Cross and a lavish silver monstrance which is studded with enormous emeralds.

Opposite the cathedral is a fairy-tale building of multiple turrets and quasi-Gothic windows. The unconventional **Palacio Episcopal** (Bishop's Palace) was designed at the end of the 19th century by Antoni Gaudí, the highly original Modernista architect *(see p160)*, for the incumbent bishop, a fellow Catalan, after a fire in 1887 had destroyed the previous building. Its bizarre appearance as well as its phenomenal cost so horrified the diocese that no subsequent bishops ever lived in it. Today it houses an assembly of medieval religious art devoted to the history of Astorga and the pilgrimage to Santiago. Roman relics, including coins and fragments of mosaics unearthed in the Plaza del Parque, are evidence of Astorga's importance as a Roman settlement. The palace's interior is decorated with Gaudí's splendid ceramic tiles and stained glass.

Reliquary of the True Cross

♛ **Palacio Episcopal**
Pl Eduardo de Castro. 【 *(987) 61 68 82.* ◻ *Mon–Sat.* ● *1 & 6 Jan.* 🎏

Cuevas de Valporquero **6**

Valporquero. 【 *(987) 29 21 89.* 🚌 *from León.* ◻ *Apr–May: Sat & Sun; Jun–Sep: daily; Oct–Nov: Fri–Sun.* 🎏

THIS COMPLEX OF limestone caves – technically a single cave with three separate entrances – is directly beneath the village of Valporquero de Torío in the northern part of León province. The caves were formed in the Miocene period between 5 and 25 million years ago. Severe weather conditions in the surrounding mountains make the water-sculpted caverns inaccessible between December and Easter. Less than half of the huge system, which stretches 3,100 m (10,200 ft) under the ground, is open to the public.

Guided tours take parties through an impressive series of galleries in which lighting picks out the beautiful limestone concretions. Iron and sulphur oxides have tinted the rocks many subtle shades of red, grey and black. The massive Gran Rotonda, covering an area of 5,600 sq m (18,350 sq ft) and reaching a height of 20 m (65 ft), is the most stunning cave in the complex.

As the interior is cold, and the surface often slippery to walk on, it is advisable to wear warm clothes and sturdy shoes.

Illuminated stalactites hanging from the roof of one of the chambers in the Cuevas de Valporquero

León ❼

eón. 🏛 150,000. 🚉 🚌 ℹ *Plaza
e la Regla 4, (987) 23 70 82.*
🌙 *Wed & Sat.* 🎭 *San Juan and San
edro (24–9 Jun), San Froilán (5 Oct).*

FOUNDED AS a camp for the
Romans' Seventh Legion,
León became the capital of a
kingdom in the Middle Ages.
As such it played a central
role in the early years of the
Reconquest *(see pp48–9)*.

The city's most important
building – apart from its great
cathedral *(see pp336–7)* – is
the **Basílica de San Isidoro**,
built into the Roman walls
which encircle the city. A separate entrance leads through
to the Romanesque **Panteón
Real** (Royal Pantheon), the
last resting place of more than
20 monarchs. It is superbly
decorated with carved capitals and 12th-century frescoes
illustrating a variety of biblical
and mythical subjects, as well
as scenes of medieval life.

The alleyways in the picturesque old quarter around the
Plaza Mayor are interspersed
with bars and cafés, decrepit
mansions and churches. Two
well-preserved palaces stand
near to the Plaza de Santo
Domingo: the **Casa de los
Guzmanes**, with its elegantly
arcaded Renaissance patio,
and Antoni Gaudí's unusually
restrained **Casa de Botines**
(which is now a bank).

The **Hostal de San Marcos**,
down beside the river, is a
prime example of Spanish

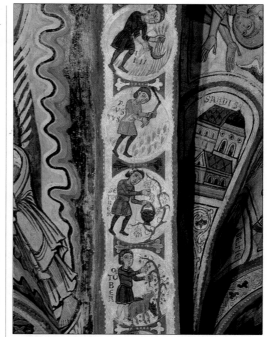
Frescoes in Basílica de San Isidoro showing medieval seasonal tasks

Renaissance architecture *(see
p21)*. It was founded during
the 12th century as a monastery to lodge travellers en route
to Santiago. The present building was begun in 1513 as the
headquarters of the Knights of
Santiago. The incredibly elaborate project continued into the
18th century, when a Baroque
pediment added a final flourish
to the beautiful Plateresque
façade studded with scallop
shells. The main hall has a fine
16th-century coffered ceiling.
A parador *(see p534)* now occupies the main part of the
Hostal de San Marcos. In the
vaulted galleries off the church
and cloister is the **Museo de
León**, whose many treasures
include a haunting little ivory
crucifix, the *Cristo de Carrizo*.

ENVIRONS: Around 30 km
(20 miles) east of León is the
**Iglesia de San Miguel de
Escalada**. Dating from the 10th
century, it is one of the finest
surviving churches built by the
Mozarabs – Christians influenced by the Moors. Notice
the Visigothic panels and the
exterior gallery of stately horseshoe arches resting on carved
capitals. At **Sahagún**, 70 km
(40 miles) southeast of León,
are the Mudéjar churches of
San Tirso and San Lorenzo,
with triple apses and belfries.
A colossal ruined castle overlooks the Río Esla beside
Valencia de Don Juan, 40 km
(25 miles) south of León.

🏛 **Museo de León**
Plaza de San Marcos. ☎ *(987) 24 50
61.* ◯ *Tue–Sun.* 🖊

THE MARAGATOS

Astorga is the principal town of
the Maragatos, an ethnic
group of unknown origin,
thought to be descended
from 8th-century Berber
invaders. By marrying
only among themselves,
they managed to preserve
their customs through the
centuries and keep them-
selves apart from the rest
of society. Although the
demise of their traditional
trade of mule-driving has
changed their way of life, the
Maragatos still keep to their
communities. Their costumes
can be seen during fiestas.

**Maragatos dressed in
traditional costume**

León Cathedral

THE MASTER BUILDERS of this Spanish Gothic cathedral *par excellence* *(see p20)* were inspired by French techniques of vaulting and buttressing. The present structure of golden sandstone, built on the site of three previous cathedrals, was begun in the mid-13th century and completed less than 100 years later. It combines a slender but very high nave with the huge panels of stained glass – on a variety of themes – which are the cathedral's most magnificent feature. Although it has survived for 700 years, today there is concern about air pollution, which in places is attacking the soft stone.

Carved detail from the choir

West Rose Window
This window, measuring 8 m (26 ft) in diameter, dates from the 13th century, making it one of the cathedral's oldest.

The 13th- to 14th-century cloister galleries are decorated with Gothic frescoes by Nicolás Francés.

Cathedral Museum
Pedro de Campaña's panel, The Adoration of the Magi, is one of the many magnificent treasures displayed in the museum.

Entrance

★ West Front
The three portals are decorated with 13th-century carvings. Those above the Portada del Juicio depict a scene from the Last Judgment, where the Blessed pass into paradise.

Inside the Cathedral

The plan of the building is a Latin cross. The tall nave is slender but long, measuring 90 m (295 ft) by 40 m (130 ft) at its widest. To appreciate the dazzling colours of the stained glass it is best to visit on a sunny day.

VISITORS' CHECKLIST

Plaza de Regla. ☎ *(987) 23 01 25.*
🕐 *Jul–Sep: 8:30am–2pm & 4–8pm; Oct–Jun: 8:30am–1:30pm & 4–7pm daily.* ✝ *9am & 6pm Mon–Fri, hourly Sat & Sun.* 🚫 ♿
Museum 🕐 *Jul–Sep: 9:30am–1pm Mon–Sat, 4–6:30pm Mon–Fri; Oct–Jun: 9:30am–12:30pm Mon–Sat, 4–6pm Mon–Fri.* 📷

The altarpiece includes five original panels by Gothic master Nicolás Francés.

Silver reliquary
Made in the 16th century by Enrique de Arfe, this ornate chest holds the mortals remains of the patron of León, St Froilan.

The Capilla de la Virgen Blanca contains an original Gothic sculpture of the Virgin smiling. A copy stands by the west door.

The choir has two tiers of 15th-century stalls. Behind it is the carved and gilded retrochoir, in the shape of a triumphal arch.

★ Stained Glass
The windows, covering an area of 1,800 sq metres (19,350 sq ft), are the highlight of the cathedral.

STAR FEATURES

★ **West Front**

★ **Stained Glass**

LEÓN'S STAINED GLASS

León cathedral's great glory is its magnificent glasswork. The 125 large windows and 57 smaller, round ones date from every century from the 13th to the 20th.
They cover an enormous range of subjects, from mythical beasts to plants. Many depict saints and characters from biblical stories.

Window with plant motif

Some of the windows reveal fascinating details about medieval life: *La Cacería*, in the north wall, depicts a typical hunting scene, while the rose window in the Capilla del Nacimiento shows pilgrims worshipping at the tomb of St James in Santiago de Compostela in Galicia *(see pp88–9)*.

A large window in the south wall

Zamora **8**

Zamora. **🏛** 65,000. **🚉 🚌 🛈** *Calle de Santa Clara 20, (980) 53 18 45.* **🚢** *Tue.* **🎉** *Semana Santa (Easter Week), San Pedro (29 Jun).*

L ITTLE REMAINS of Zamora's past as an important strategic frontier town. In Roman times, it was on the Vía de la Plata *(see p334)*, and during the Reconquest was fought over fiercely. The city has now expanded far beyond its original boundaries, but the old quarter contains a wealth of Romanesque churches.

The ruins of the **city walls**, built by Alfonso III in 893, are pierced by the Postigo de la Traición (Traitor's Gate), where Sancho II was betrayed and stabbed to death in 1072. The **parador** *(see p557)* is housed in a former palace with a Renaissance courtyard adorned with coats of arms.

Two other palaces, the **Casa de los Momos** and the **Casa del Cordón**, have ornately carved façades and windows.

Zamora's most important monument is its unique **cathedral**, a 12th-century structure built in Romanesque style but with a number of later Gothic additions. The building's most eye-catching feature is its striking, scaly, hemispherical dome. Inside, there are superb iron grilles and Mudéjar pulpits surround Rodrigo Alemán's 15th-century choir stalls. The

Peaceful gardens of the Colegiata de Santa María in Toro

allegorical carvings of nuns and monks on the misericords and armrests were once considered risqué. The museum, off the sober cloisters, displays an important collection of 15th-century Flemish tapestries known as the *Black Tapestries*. These illustrate classical and military scenes.

Nearby, several churches exhibit features characteristic of Zamora's architectural style, notably multi-lobed arches and heavily carved portals. The best are the 12th-century **Iglesia de San Ildefonso** and the **Iglesia de la Magdalena**.

Another reason for visiting Zamora is for its lively Easter Week celebrations, when elaborate *pasos* (sculpted floats) are paraded through the streets. During the rest of the year the *pasos* can be admired in the **Museo de Semana Santa**.

ENVIRONS: The 7th-century Visigothic church of **San Pedro de la Nave**, 12 km (7.5 miles) northwest of Zamora, has charming carvings adorning its

Sierra de la Peña de Francia **10**

T HESE ATTRACTIVE schist hills buttress the western edges of the Sierra de Gredos *(see p344)*. Narrow roads wind their way through picturesque chestnut, olive and almond groves, and quaint rural villages of wood and stone. The highest point of the range is La Peña de Francia, which, at 1,732 m (5,700 ft), is easily recognizable from miles around. The views from the peak, and from the roads leading up to it, offer a breathtaking panorama of the surrounding empty plains and rolling hills.

La Peña de Francia ①
Crowning the peak is a windswept Dominican monastery sheltering a blackened, Byzantine-style statue of the Virgin and Child.

La Alberca ②
This pretty and much-visited village sells local honey, hams and handicrafts. On 15 August each year it celebrates the Assumption with a traditional mystery play performed in costume.

CIUDAD RODRIG

SA 202

SA 201

CORIA

| 0 kilometres | 5 |
| 0 miles | 5 |

KEY

▭▭ Tour route

= Other roads

☆ Viewpoint

Las Batuecas ③
The road from La Alberca careers do into a green valley the monastery whe Luis Buñuel made film *Tierra sin Par (Land without Bre*

The unmistakable peak of La Peña de Francia

Fish-scale tiling on dome of Zamora cathedral

capitals and friezes. **Toro**, 33 km (21 miles) east of Zamora, is at the heart of a wine region *(see pp322–3)*. The highlights of its **Colegiata de Santa María** are the west portal, and, inside, a fine Hispano-Flemish painting, *La Virgen de la Mosca* (The Virgin and the Fly). In 1476, the forces of Isabel I *(see pp52–3)* secured a crucial victory over the Portuguese at Toro, confirming her succession to the throne of Castile.

Ciudad Rodrigo 9

Salamanca. 🕍 16,000. 🚌 🚆 🚹
Plaza de Amayuelas 5, (923) 46 05
61. 🚍 Tue. 🎭 San Sebastián (20
Jan), Romería de San Blas (3 Feb),
La Charrada (Sat before Easter).

DESPITE ITS LONELY setting – stranded on the country's western marches miles from anywhere – this lovely old town is well worth a detour. Its frontier location inevitably gave rise to fortification, and its robust 14th-century castle is now an atmospheric **parador** *(see p555)* with good views over the Río Agueda. The prosperous 15th and 16th centuries were Ciudad Rodrigo's heyday. In 1812, during the War of Independence *(see pp58–9)*, the city, then occupied by the French, was besieged for 11 days before falling to the Duke of Wellington's forces.

The golden stone buildings within the ramparts are delightful. The main monument is the **cathedral**, whose belfry still bears the marks of shellfire from the siege. The exterior has a shapely curved balustrade and accomplished portal carvings. Inside, it is worth seeing the cloisters (in a variety of architectural styles) and the choir stalls, carved with lively scenes by Rodrigo Alemán. The main attraction of the adjacent **Capilla de Cerralbo** (Cerralbo Chapel) is a Ribera altarpiece. Off the chapel's south side is the quiet, arcaded Plaza del Buen Alcalde.

Miranda del Castañar ④
The narrow streets of this pretty, fortified village are lined with ancient houses with wide eaves.

SALAMANCA

Santibáñez de la Sierra

Cristóbal

Cepeda

Sotoserrano

Béjar ⑤
This textile town is strung out along a ridge at the foot of the Sierra de Béjar. From the approach road, 19th-century factories and mills can be seen.

SALAMANCA

La Calzada

TIPS FOR DRIVERS

Tour length: 72 km (45 miles).
Stopping-off points: Candelario, Miranda del Castañar and La Alberca all have good eating places, and are renowned for their hams and sausages. In summer, refreshments are available from the hospedería (inn) in La Peña's monastery.

Candelario ⑥
The steep, cobbled streets are lined with deep channels and stormgates to cope with the spring melt-water from the surrounding mountains and flash floods.

PLASENCIA

Street-by-Street: Salamanca ⓫

Shell detail, façade of the Casa de las Conchas

THE GREAT UNIVERSITY CITY of Salamanca is Spain's finest showcase of Renaissance and Plateresque architecture. Founded as an Iberian settlement in pre-Roman times, the city fell to Hannibal in 217 BC. Preeminent among its artists and master craftsmen of later years were the Churriguera brothers *(see p21)*. Their work can be seen in many of Salamanca's golden stone buildings, notably in the Plaza Mayor. Other major sights are the two cathedrals and the 13th-century university, one of Europe's oldest and most distinguished.

The Casa de las Conchas is easily identifiable from the stone scallop shells that stud its walls. It is now a library.

The Palacio de Monterrey is a Renaissance mansion.

★ Universidad
In the centre of the university's elaborate façade is this medallion, carved in relief, which depicts the Catholic Monarchs.

★ Catedral Vieja and Catedral Nueva
Despite being in different architectural styles, the adjoining old and new cathedrals blend well together. This richly coloured altarpiece painted in 1445 is in the old cathedral.

Puente Romano
The Roman bridge across the Río Tormes, built in the 1st century AD, retains 15 of its original 26 arches. It provides an excellent view of the city.

STAR SIGHTS

★ Universidad

★ Catedral Vieja and Catedral Nueva

★ Plaza Mayor

0 metres 100
0 yards 100

Museo Art Nouveau y Art Deco

KEY

– – – Suggested route

★ Plaza Mayor
This 18th-century square is one of Spain's largest and grandest. On the east side is the Royal Pavilion, decorated with a bust of Felipe V, who built the square.

VISITORS' CHECKLIST

Salamanca. 180,000. 6 km (3.5 miles) east. Paseo de la Estación, (923) 12 02 02. Avda de Filiberto Villalobos 71, (923) 23 67 17. Plaza Mayor 14, (923) 21 83 42. Sun. San Juan de Sahagún (12 Jun), Virgen de la Vega (8 Sep).

Iglesia de San Martín

PLAZA MAYOR

The **Palacio de Fonseca** was built in 1538 by Alonso de Fonseca.

Torre del Clavero
This 15th-century tower still has its original turrets. They are adorned with the coats of arms of its founders, and Mudéjar trelliswork.

Iglesia-Convento de San Esteban
The Plateresque façade of the church is carved with delicate relief. Above the door is a frieze decorated with medallions and coats of arms.

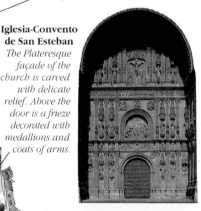

CALLE DE SAN PABLO

CALLE DEL CONSUELO

PLAZA DEL CONCILIO DE TRENTO

ARROYO SANTO DOMINGO

R ESPERABÉ

Convento de las Dueñas
Sculptures on the capitals of the beautiful two-storey cloister show demons, skulls and tormented faces, which contrast with serene carvings of the Virgin.

Exploring Salamanca

The majority of Salamanca's monuments are located inside the city centre, which is compact enough to explore on foot. The university, the Plaza Mayor, and the old and new cathedrals are all unmissable.

🏛 Catedral Vieja and Catedral Nueva

Unusually, the 16th-century new cathedral did not replace the old, but was constructed beside it. It is in a mix of architectural styles, being mainly Gothic, with Renaissance and Baroque additions. The west front has elaborate Late Gothic stonework, and a central panel carved with religious scenes.

The 12th- to 13th-century Romanesque old cathedral is entered through the new one. The highlight is a wonderful altarpiece of 53 panels, painted in lustrous colours by Nicolás Florentino. It frames a statue of Salamanca's patron saint, the 12th-century Virgen de la Vega, which was crafted in Limoges enamel. In the vault above it is a fresco depicting scenes from the Last Judgment, which is also by Florentino.

The 13th-century Capilla de Anaya (Anaya Chapel) contains the superb 15th-century alabaster tomb of Diego de Anaya, an archbishop of Salamanca.

Façade of Salamanca University, on the Patio de las Escuelas

🏛 Universidad

Patio de las Escuelas 1. **(** (923) 29 44 00. ⬜ daily. ● 25 Dec. 🈲

Salamanca's historic university was founded by Alfonso IX of León in 1218. The extravagant 16th-century façade of the Patio de las Escuelas (Schools Square) is a perfect example of the Plateresque style (see p21). Opposite is a statue of Fray Luis de León, who taught theology at the university. Inside, his former lecture room is preserved in its original style. Off the Patio de las Escuelas is the Escuelas Menores building, which houses a huge zodiac fresco, The Salamanca Sky.

🏛 Plaza Mayor

This magnificent square was built by Felipe V to thank the city for its support during the War of the Spanish Succession (see p58). Designed by the Churriguera brothers (see p21) in 1729 and completed in 1755, it was once used for bullfights, but nowadays is a delightful place to stroll or shop. Within the harmonious blend of arcaded buildings and cafés are the Baroque town hall and, opposite, the Royal Pavilion, from where the royal family used to watch events in the square. The Plaza Mayor is built of warm golden sandstone, and is especially resplendent at dusk.

Royal Pavilion in Salamanca's beautiful Plaza Mayor

🏛 Iglesia-Convento de San Esteban

The 16th-century church of this Dominican monastery is particularly interesting for its superb ornamented façade. The relief on the central panel, completed by Juan Antonio Ceroni in 1610, depicts the stoning of St Stephen, to whom the monastery is dedicated. Above this is a frieze, delicately carved with figures of children and horses.

The interior of the large single-nave church is equally stunning. The ornate altarpiece, of twisted gilt columns decorated with vines, is the work of José Churriguera and dates from 1693. Below it is one of Claudio Coello's last paintings, another representation of the martyrdom of St Stephen.

The double-galleried Claustro de los Reyes, completed in Plateresque style in 1591, has capitals which are carved with the heads of the prophets.

Salamanca's double cathedral, towering over the city

Sculpted shells on the walls of the Casa de las Conchas

♦ Casa de las Conchas
Calle de la Compañía 2. ☎ (923) 26 93 17. ○ Mon–Sat.
The name of this mansion – House of the Shells – derives from the golden stone scallop shells that cover most of its walls. The shells are a symbol of the Order of Santiago, one of whose knights, Rodrigo Maldonado, built the mansion at the beginning of the 16th century. He also adorned the building with his family's coat of arms. It is now a library.

♦ Convento de las Dueñas
Plaza del Concilio de Trento.
☎ (923) 21 54 42. ○ daily.
The main feature of this Dominican convent, which stands opposite San Esteban, is its Renaissance double cloister, whose tranquil gardens seem strangely at odds with the grotesques carved on the capitals. The cloister also preserves a tiled Moorish arch.

♦ Museo Art Nouveau y Art Deco
Calle Gibraltar 14. ☎ (923) 12 14 25. ○ Tue–Sun.
This important art collection, housed in a 19th-century building, includes paintings, jewellery and furniture from all over Europe. Individual rooms are devoted to porcelain and Limoges enamel, and stained-glass work by Lalique.

♦ Palacio de Fonseca
Calle Fonseca 4. ☎ (923) 29 45 70. ○ daily.
The patio of this Renaissance palace has a first-floor arcade on huge pedestals. Today it houses the council offices.

♦ Convento de las Úrsulas
Calle de las Úrsulas 2. ☎ (923) 21 98 77. ○ Mon–Sat.
In the church of this convent is the superbly carved tomb of its founder, Alonso de Fonseca, the powerful 16th-century Archbishop of Santiago. The museum includes fine paintings by Luis de Morales.

♦ Casa de las Muertes
Calle Bordadores. ● to public.
The House of the Dead takes its name from the small skulls that embellish its façade. Grotesques and other figures also feature, and there is a cornice decorated with cherubs. The façade, designed by Diego de Siloé in 1513, is a wonderfully accomplished example of the early Plateresque style.

The adjacent house is where author and philosopher Miguel de Unamuno died in 1936. The Casa-Museo de Unamuno, next door to the university, contains information about his life.

Skull carving on the façade of the Casa de las Muertes

♦ Colegio de los Irlandeses
Calle de Fonseca 4. ☎ (923) 29 45 70. ○ daily.
Also known as the Colegio del Arzobispo, this college was founded by the Archbishop of Toledo in 1521 as a seminary for Irish priests. It has an Italianate courtyard and a chapel with a Plateresque doorway.

♦ Torre del Clavero
Plaza de Colón.
The tower is the last vestige of a palace that once stood here. It was built around 1480 and is named after a former resident, the key warden *(clavero)* of the Order of Alcántara.

The octagonal Torre del Clavero

ENVIRONS: To the northwest of the city, the course of the Río Tormes leads through the fortified old town of **Ledesma**, across lonely countryside to the Arribas del Duero, a series of massive reservoirs near to the Portuguese border.

Dominating the town of **Alba de Tormes**, 20 km (12 miles) east of Salamanca, is the Torre de la Armería, the only remaining part of the castle of the Dukes of Alba. St Teresa of Ávila *(see p345)* is buried in the town. Pilgrims flock to the Iglesia-Convento de las Madres Carmelitas, which she founded in 1571, and where the saint's remains are now kept.

The castle of **Buen Amor**, 26 km (16 miles) to the north of Salamanca, was founded in 1227. Later, it was converted into a palace and used as a residence by the Catholic Monarchs while fighting against Juana la Beltraneja *(see p52)*.

Sierra de Gredos ⑫

Ávila. 🚌 Hoyos del Espino.
ℹ️ Hoyos del Espino, (920) 34 90 07.

THIS GREAT mountain range, west of Madrid, has abundant wildlife, especially ibex and birds of prey. Some parts have been developed to cater for weekenders who come skiing, fishing, hunting or hiking. Tourism here isn't a recent phenomenon – Spain's first parador opened in Gredos in 1928 (see p556). Despite this, there are many traditional villages off the beaten track.

The slopes on the south side of the range, extending into Extremadura, are fertile and sheltered, with pinewoods, and apple and olive trees. The austere northern slopes, in contrast, have a covering of thin scrub and are scattered with granite boulders.

A single main road, the N502, crosses the centre of the range via the Puerto del Pico, a pass at 1,352 m (4,435 ft), leading to Arenas de San Pedro, the largest town of the Sierra de Gredos. On this road is the castle of **Mombeltrán**, built at the end of the 14th century.

Near Ramacastañas, south of the town of Arenas de San Pedro, are the limestone caverns of the **Cuevas del Águila**.

The sierra's highest summit, the Pico Almanzor (2,592 m, 8,500 ft) dominates the west. Around it lies the **Reserva Nacional de Gredos**, protecting the mountain's wildlife.

The Toros de Guisando near El Tiemblo in the Sierra de Gredos

Near El Tiemblo, in the east, stand the **Toros de Guisando**, four stone statues resembling bulls, believed to be of Celtiberian origin (see pp44–5).

Ávila ⑬

Ávila. 👥 50,000. 🚉 🚌 ℹ️ Plaza de la Catedral 4, (920) 21 13 87. 📅 Fri. 🎉 Summer Fiesta (mid-Jul), Santa Teresa (15 Oct).

AT 1,131 M (3,710 FT) above sea level, Ávila de los Caballeros ("of the Knights") is the highest provincial capital in Spain. In winter access roads can be blocked with snow, and at night the temperature plummets. The centre of the city is encircled by the finest-preserved **medieval walls** in Europe. One of the best views of the walls is from Los Cuatro Postes (Four Posts) on the road to Salamanca. This is the place where the young St Teresa,

Tuna in Ávila

who had run away from home, was caught by her uncle. Built in the 11th century, the walls are over 2 km (1 mile) long. They are punctuated by 88 sturdy turrets, on which storks can be seen nesting in season. The ground falls away very steeply from the walls on three sides, making the city practically impregnable. The east side, however, is relatively flat, and therefore had to be fortified more heavily. The oldest sections of the wall are here. They are guarded by the most impressive of the city's nine gateways, the **Puerta de San Vicente**. The apse of the **cathedral** also forms part of the walls. The cathedral's warlike (and unfinished) exterior, decorated with beasts and scaly wild men, is an unusual design. The interior is a mixture of Romanesque and Gothic styles

The superbly preserved 11th-century walls, punctuated with 88 cylindrical towers, which encircle Ávila

using an unusual mottled red and white stone. Finer points to note are the carvings on the retrochoir and, in the apse, the tomb of a 15th-century bishop known as El Tostado, "the Tanned One", because of his dark complexion.

Many churches and convents in Ávila are linked to St Teresa, who was born in the city. The **Convento de Santa Teresa** was built on the site of her home within the walls and she also lived for more than 20 years in the **Monasterio de la Encarnación** outside the walls. There is even a local sweetmeat, *yemas de Santa Teresa*, named after the saint.

The **Iglesia de San Vicente**, also located just outside the eastern walls, is Ávila's most important Romanesque church, distinguished by its ornamented belfry. It was begun in the 12th century but has some Gothic features which were added later. The west door-

Cloisters of the Real Monasterio de Santo Tomás in Ávila

way is often compared to the Pórtico da Gloria of Santiago cathedral (*see p88*). Inside, the carved tomb of St Vincent and his sisters depicts their hideous martyrdom in graphic detail. Another Romanesque-Gothic church worth seeing is the **Iglesia de San Pedro.**

Some way from the centre is the **Real Monasterio de Santo Tomás**, with three cloisters. The middle one, carved with the yoke and arrow emblem of the Catholic Monarchs, is the most beautiful. The last cloister leads to a museum displaying chalices and processional crosses. The church contains the tomb of Prince Juan, the only son of Fernando and Isabel. In the sacristy lies another historic figure: Tomás de Torquemada, head of the Inquisition (*see p52*).

In Ávila, you may see groups of *tunas* – students dressed in traditional costume walking the town's streets while singing songs and playing guitars.

Beautiful gardens and palace of San Ildefonso

La Granja de San Ildefonso ⓮

Segovia. ▐ (921) 47 00 19.
🚌 from Madrid or Segovia.
◯ Tue–Sun. 📷 ✔

THIS SUMPTUOUS royal pleasure palace is set against the backdrop of the Sierra de Guadarrama mountains. It stands on the site of a hunting lodge built by Enrique IV during the 15th century.

In 1720, Felipe V embarked on a project to recreate fond childhood memories of his grandfather Louis XIV's glorious court at Versailles. A succession of different artists and architects contributed to the rich furnishings inside and the splendid gardens without.

Many rooms were damaged in a fire in 1918. Although they were sumptuously restored, the interior never quite regained its original splendour.

A guided tour meanders through countless impressive salons decorated with ornate *objets d'art* and Classical frescoes against settings of marble, gilt and velvet. Huge glittering chandeliers, produced in the local crystal factory, hang from the ceiling. In the private apartments there are superb court tapestries. The church is fittingly adorned in lavish high Baroque style, and the Royal Mausoleum contains the tomb of Felipe V and his queen.

In the gardens, stately chestnut trees, clipped hedges and statues frame a complex series of pools. On some summer afternoons spectacular fountains are set in motion.

ST TERESA OF JESUS

Teresa de Cepeda y Ahumada (1515–82) was one of the Catholic Church's greatest mystics and reformers. When aged just seven, she ran away from home in the hope of achieving martyrdom at the hands of the Moors, only to be recaptured by her uncle on the outskirts of the city. She became a nun at 19 but rebelled against her order. From 1562, when she founded her first convent, she travelled around Spain with her disciple, St John of the Cross, founding more convents for the followers of her order, the Barefoot Carmelites. Her remains are in Alba de Tormes near Salamanca (*see p343*).

Statue of St Teresa in the cathedral museum

SEGOVIA CITY CENTRE

Alcázar ⑦
Aqueduct ②
Casa de los Picos ③
Cathedral ⑥
Iglesia de San Esteban ⑤

Iglesia de San Juan
  de los Caballeros ①
Iglesia de San Martín ④

KEY

P Parking

i Tourist information

† Church

⌂ Convent or monastery

Segovia ⑮

Segovia. 56,000. Plaza Mayor 10, (921) 46 03 34. Thu. San Juan (24 Jun), San Pedro (29 Jun), San Frutos (25 Oct).

SEGOVIA IS THE MOST spectacularly sited city in Spain. The old town is set high on a rocky spur and surrounded by the Río Eresma and Río Clamores. It is often compared to a ship – the Alcázar on its sharp crag forming the prow, the pinnacles of the cathedral rising like masts, and the aqueduct trailing behind like a rudder. The view from the valley below at sunset is magical.

The **aqueduct**, in use until the late 19th century, was built at the end of the 1st century AD by the Romans, who turned ancient Segobriga into an important military base.

The **cathedral**, dating from 1525 and consecrated in 1678, is the last great Gothic church in Spain. It was built to replace the old cathedral, which was destroyed in 1520 during the revolt of the Castilian towns *(see p54)*. The cloister, however, survived and was rebuilt on the new site. The pinnacles, flying buttresses, tower and dome form an impressive silhouette, while the interior is

light and elegantly vaulted. Graceful ironwork grilles enclose the side chapels. The chapterhouse museum, with a coffered ceiling, houses 17th-century Brussels tapestries.

At the city's western end is the **Alcázar** *(see pp326–7)*. Rising sheer above crags with a multitude of gabled roofs, turrets and crenellations, it appears like the archetypal fairy-tale castle. Although there has been a fortress here since the Middle Ages, the present building is mostly a fanciful reconstruction following a fire in 1862. It contains a museum

of weaponry and a series of elaborately decorated rooms.

Notable churches in Segovia include the Romanesque **San Juan de los Caballeros**, which has an outstanding sculptured portico, **San Esteban** with a striking five-storey tower, and **San Martín** with its beautiful arcades and capitals. Just inside the city walls is the **Casa de los Picos**, a mansion whose unique façade is adorned with diamond-shaped stones.

ENVIRONS: The vast palace of **Riofrío**, 11 km (7 miles) to the southwest, is set in a deer park.

The imposing Gothic cathedral of Segovia

SEGOVIA'S AQUEDUCT

Water channel

Slots used to support blocks of ashlar

Arches reach a maximum height of 29 m (95 ft).

Water from the Río Frío flowed into the city, filtered through a series of tanks along the way.

Two tiers of arches – a total of 728 m (2,400 ft) in length – were needed to cope with the ground's gradient.

In this niche a statue of the Virgin Mary replaces an earlier inscription relating to the founding of the aqueduct.

Segovia's distinctive Alcázar, towering over the city

It was built as a hunting lodge by Felipe V's widow, Isabel Farnese, in 1752, and has richly decorated rooms. It also houses a hunting museum.

♠ **Alcázar de Segovia**
Plaza del Alcázar. 📞 (921) 46 07 59. ⬜ daily. ⬤ 1 Jan, 25 Dec. 📷 ♿
♛ **Palacio de Riofrío**
📞 (921) 47 00 19. ⬜ Tue–Sun. 📷

Pedraza de la Sierra ⑯

Segovia. 🏠 400. 🛈 Plaza Mayor 2, (921) 50 98 17. 🎊 Nuestra Señora la Virgen del Carrascal (8 Sep).

THE ARISTOCRATIC little town of Pedraza de la Sierra is perched high over rolling countryside. Within its medieval walls, old streets lead past mansions, emblazoned with coats of arms, to the porticoed **Plaza Mayor** (see p23). The huge, austere **castle**, standing on a rocky outcrop, was the home of local artist Ignacio

Zuloaga (1870–1945). The castle museum shows some of his works. At weekends, *Madrileños* flock to Pedraza's restaurants for roast lunches.

ENVIRONS: The main sight at **Turégano**, 30 km (19 miles) north, is a large hilltop castle which incorporates the 15th-century Iglesia de San Miguel.

Sepúlveda ⑰

Segovia. 🏠 1,050. 🛈 Plaza del Trigo 3, (921) 54 00 95. 🎪 Wed. 🎊 Patronales (last week of Aug).

SPECTACULARLY SITED on a slope above the Río Duratón, this picturesque town offers views of the Sierra de Guadarrama. Parts of its medieval walls and castle survive. Of its several Romanesque churches, the **Iglesia del Salvador**, behind the main square, is purely 11th century and is notable for possessing one of the oldest side doors in Spain (1093).

ENVIRONS: Winding through a canyon haunted by griffon vultures is the Río Duratón, 7 km (4 miles) west of Sepúlveda. This area of striking beauty has been designated a natural park, the **Parque Natural de las Hoces del Duratón**.
Ayllón, 45 km (28 miles) northeast of Sepúlveda, has an arcaded main square and the Plateresque (see p21) Palacio de Juan de Contreras of 1497.
The Iberian and Roman ruins at **Tiermes**, 28 km (17 miles) further southeast, have been partially excavated, and finds can be seen in Soria's Museo Numantino (see p359).

Castillo de Coca ⑱

Coca (Segovia). 📞 (921) 58 60 62. 🚌 from Segovia. ⬜ Wed–Mon. 📷

BUILT IN THE late 15th century for the influential Fonseca family, Coca castle (see p326) is one of Castilla y León's most memorable fortresses. It was used more as a residential palace than a defensive castle, although its multiplicity of turrets and battlements are a fine example of Mudéjar military architecture. Built of thin, rose-tinted bricks, it is a complex moated structure comprising three concentric walls which surround a massive keep. The castle is now a forestry school, which has a display of Romanesque woodcarvings.

ENVIRONS: The 14th-century castle of **Arévalo**, 26 km (16 miles) southwest, is where Isabel I spent her childhood. The porticoed Plaza de la Villa is surrounded by a number of attractive half-timbered houses.

Massive keep of the 15th-century Castillo de Coca

Medina del Campo ⑲

Valladolid. 🏠 20,000. 🚉 🚌
🛈 Plaza Mayor 27, (983) 81 13 57.
🗓 Sun. 🎪 San Antolín (2–8 Sep).

MEDINA BECAME wealthy in medieval times on the proceeds of huge sheep fairs and is still an important agricultural centre today. The vast brick Gothic-Mudejár **Castillo de la Mota** (see p326), on its outskirts, was built in 1440 by the powerful Fonseca family. However, the town transferred the castle's ownership to the Crown in 1475. Isabel I and her daughter Juana "la Loca" ("the Mad") both stayed here. Later, it served as a prison – Cesare Borja, one of its more celebrated inmates, was incarcerated here from 1506–08. In a corner of the Plaza Mayor stands the modest house (built over an arch) where Isabel died in 1504; her statue presides over the square.

Castillo de la Mota at Medina del Campo

ENVIRONS: Towering over the plains, some 25 km (16 miles) to the south of Medina del Campo, are the walls of **Madrigal de las Altas Torres**. In 1451 Isabel was born here in a palace that later became the Monasterio de las Agustinas in 1527.

Statue of Isabel, Medina del Campo

♣ **Castillo de la Mota**
Avda Castillo de la Mota. ▐ (983) 80 10 24. ◻ daily. ● public hols.

Tordesillas ⑳

Valladolid. 🏠 10,000. 🚉 🛈 Plaza Mayor, (983) 77 06 54. 🗓 Tue. 🎪 Semana de la Peña (16–22 Sep).

THIS PLEASANT TOWN is where the historic treaty between Spain and Portugal was signed in 1494, dividing the lands of the New World (see p53). A fateful oversight by the Spanish map makers left the immense prize of Brazil to Portugal.

The town's main sight is the **Convento de Santa Clara**. It was constructed by Alfonso XI in 1350 and converted by his son Pedro the Cruel into a residence for his mistress, María de Padilla. Pining for her native Andalusia, she had the convent decorated with fine Moorish arches, baths and tiles. Most impressive are the patio and the main chapel. There is a display of royal musical instruments, including the portable organ of Juana "la Loca". After the death of her husband, Juana spent 46 years in semi-confinement here until her own death in 1555. In the old quarter, the **Iglesia de San Antolín** is a sculpture museum.

🏛 **Convento de Santa Clara**
▐ (983) 77 00 71. ◻ Tue–Sun. 🎟
🏛 **Iglesia de San Antolín**
Calle Postigo. ▐ (983) 77 05 25.
◻ Apr–Oct: Tue–Sun, Nov–Mar: phone for opening times.

Moorish patio in the Convento de Santa Clara, Tordesillas

Valladolid ㉑

Valladolid. 🏠 350,000. 🚉 🚌 🛈
Plaza de Zorrilla 3, (983) 35 18 01.
🗓 Sun. 🎪 San Pedro Regalado (13 May), San Mateo (21–9 Sep).

THE ARABIC CITY of Belad-Walid (meaning "Land of the Governor") is located at the confluence of the Río Esgueva and Río Pisuerga. Although it has become sprawling and industrialized, Valladolid has some of Spain's best Renaissance art and architecture.

Fernando and Isabel (see pp52–3) were married in the Palacio Vivero in 1469 and, following the completion of the Reconquest in 1492, they made Valladolid their capital. Less spectacularly, Columbus died here, alone and forgotten, in 1506. In 1527 Felipe II was born in the Palacio de los Pimentel. José Zorrilla, who popularized the legendary Don Juan in his 1844 play (see p31), was also born in the city.

The city's university dates from the 15th century. The Baroque façade (see p21) was begun in 1715 by Narciso Tomé, who later created the remarkable Transparente of Toledo cathedral (see p375).

The **Iglesia de San Pablo** has a spectacular façade, embellished with angels and coats of arms in Plateresque style. Among the other noteworthy churches are **Santa María la Antigua**, with its slim Romanesque belfry, and the **Iglesia**

de Las Angustias, where Juan de Juni's fine sculpture of the Virgen de los Cuchillos (Virgin of the Knives) is on display.

♕ Casa de Cervantes

Calle Rastro 7. █ *(983) 30 88 10.* ◯ *Tue–Sun.* ◉ *public hols.*
The Golden Age author of *Don Quixote (see p30)* lived in this simple house with white-washed walls for the last years of his life. The rooms have been thoroughly restored and contain some of Cervantes' original furnishings and fittings.

🔒 Cathedral

Calle Arribas 1. █ *(983) 30 43 62.*
Work started on the unfinished cathedral in 1580 by Felipe II's favourite architect, Juan de Herrera, but gradually lost momentum over the centuries. Churrigueresque *(see p21)* flourishes on the façade are in contrast to the sombre, square-pillared interior, whose only redeeming flamboyance is a Juan de Juni altarpiece. The Museo Diocesano inside, however, contains some fine pieces of religious art and sculpture.

🏛 Museo Nacional de Escultura

Cadenas de S Gregorio 1. █ *(983) 25 03 75.* ◯ *Tue–Sat.* ◉ *public hols.* 📷
The art collection of the Museo Nacional de Escultura is located in the beautiful Colegio de San Gregorio. The display consists mainly of multicoloured wooden religious sculptures from the 13th–18th centuries. It is Europe's most distinguished collection of such works. They include examples by many of

Berruguete's *Natividad,* in Museo Nacional de Escultura, Valladolid

the masters of the Spanish Renaissance, including Juan de Juni's emotive depiction of the burial of Christ and *Recumbent Christ* by Gregorio Fernández. An Alonso Berruguete altarpiece, and walnut choir stalls by Diego de Siloé and other artists, are among the other fine works to be found here.

The building itself is worthy of attention, particularly the Plateresque *(see p21)* staircase, the chapel by Juan Güas, and the superb patio of twisted columns and delicate basket arches. The façade is an astonishing example of Isabelline *(see p20)* sculpture, portraying a bewildering mêlée of naked children scrambling about in thorn trees, hairy wild men, and strange birds and beasts. It is attributed mainly to Gil de Siloé and Simon of Cologne.

🏛 Museo Oriental

Paseo de los Filipinos 7. █ *(983) 30 69 00.* ◯ *daily.* 📷
Beyond the Parque de Campo Grande is this small but interesting museum. The Museo Oriental is housed in the Real Colegio de los Agustinos Filipinos, a grandiose Neo-Classical Augustinian college, and contains an important collection of curios and art brought from China and the Philippines by missionaries.

ENVIRONS: The moated grey castle that dominates the village of **Simancas,** 11 km (7 miles) southwest of Valladolid, was converted by Charles V into Spain's national archive.

The Visigothic church in the village of **Wamba,** 15 km (9 miles) to the west, contains the tomb of King Recceswinth.

An unusual long, narrow 14th-century castle on a ridge overlooks the wine town of **Peñafiel,** 60 km (40 miles) east of Valladolid *(see p327).*

Medina de Rioseco **㉒**

Valladolid. 🏘 *4,900.* 🚉 ℹ *Plaza Mayor, (983) 70 08 25.* 🚌 *Wed.* 🎉 *San Juan (24–9 Jun).*

D URING THE MIDDLE AGES this town, like Medina del Campo, grew wealthy from the profitable wool trade. These riches enabled it to commission leading artists, mainly of the Valladolid school, to decorate its churches. The dazzling star vaulting and superb woodwork of the **Iglesia de Santa María de Mediavilla,** near the centre of town, are evidence of this. Inside, the Benavente Chapel is a *tour de force,* with a colourful stucco ceiling by Jerónimo del Corral (1554), and an altarpiece by Juan de Juni. The enormous monstrance (1585) in the treasury is by Antonio de Arfe.

The interior of the **Iglesia de Santiago** is equally stunning, with a triple altarpiece by the Churriguera brothers of Salamanca *(see p21).*

The ancient buildings on Medina de Rioseco's main street, the Calle de la Rúa, are supported on wooden pillars, forming shady porticoes.

Façade of Colegio de San Gregorio, Valladolid

Altarpiece by Juan de Juni, Iglesia de Santa María de Mediavilla

CASTILLA Y LEÓN'S FIESTAS

El Colacho *(Sun after Corpus Christi, May/Jun),* Castrillo de Murcia (Burgos). Babies born during the previous 12 months are dressed in their best Sunday clothes and laid on mattresses in the streets. Crowds of people, including the anxious parents, watch as *El Colacho* – a man dressed in a bright red and yellow costume – jumps over the babies in order to free them from illnesses, especially hernias. He is said to represent the devil fleeing from the sight of the Eucharist. This ritual is thought to have originated in 1621.

El Colacho jumping over babies in Castrillo de Murcia

St Agatha's Day *(Sun closest to 5 Feb),* Zamarramala (Segovia). Every year two women are elected as mayoresses to run the village on the day of St Agatha, patron saint of married women. They ceremonially burn a stuffed figure representing a man.
Good Friday, Valladolid. The procession of 28 multicoloured sculptures which depict various scenes of the Passion is one of the most spectacular in Spain.
Fire-walking *(23 Jun),* San Pedro Manrique (Soria). Men, some carrying people on their backs, walk barefoot over burning embers. It is said that only local people can do this without being burned.

The beautiful carved retrochoir of Palencia cathedral

Palencia ㉓

Palencia. 🏘 79,000. 🚊 🚌
🛈 Calle Mayor 105, (979) 74 00 68.
📅 Tue, Wed & Thu. 🎉 Virgen de la Calle (2 Feb), San Antolín (2 Sep).

I N MEDIEVAL TIMES, Palencia was a royal residence and the site of Spain's first university, founded in 1208. The city gradually diminished in importance following its involvement in the failed revolt of the Castilian towns of 1520 *(see p54).*

Although Palencia has since expanded considerably on profits from coal and wheat, its centre, by the old stone bridge over the Río Carrión, remains almost village-like.

The city's main sight is the **cathedral**, known as *La Bella Desconocida* (the Unknown Beauty). It is especially worth a visit for its superb works of art, many the result of Bishop Fonseca's generous patronage. The retrochoir, exquisitely sculpted by Gil de Siloé and Simon of Cologne, and the two altarpieces, are also noteworthy. The altarpiece above the high altar was carved by Philippe de Bigarny early in the 16th century. The inset panels are by Juan de Flandes, Isabel I's court painter. Behind the high altar is the Chapel of the Holy Sacrament, with an altarpiece dating from 1529 by Valmaseda. In this chapel, high on a ledge to the left, is the colourful tomb of Doña Urraca of Navarra. Below the retrochoir, a Plateresque *(see p21)* staircase leads down to the fine Visigothic crypt.

ENVIRONS: Baños de Cerrato, 12 km (7 miles) to the south, contains the tiny Visigothic Iglesia de San Juan Bautista. Founded in 661, it is alleged to be the oldest intact church in Spain. Typical Visigothic carved capitals and horseshoe arches decorate the interior.

Frómista ㉔

Palencia. 🏘 1,000. 🛈 Plaza de Tui, (979) 81 00 01. 📅 Fri. 🎉 Patrón de Frómista (week after Easter), Virgen del Otero (8 Sep).

T HIS TOWN on the Road to Santiago de Compostela *(see pp78–9)* is the site of one of Spain's purest Romanesque churches. The **Iglesia de San Martín** is the highlight of the town, partly due to an energetic restoration in 1904. Decadent additions were swept away, leaving the church, dating from 1066, entirely Romanesque in style. The presence of Pagan and Roman motifs suggest it may have pre-Christian origins.

ENVIRONS: Carrión de los Condes, 20 km (12 miles) to the northwest, is also on the Road to Santiago. The frieze on the door of the Iglesia de Santiago depicts not religious figures but local artisans. There are carvings of bulls on the façade of the 12th-century Iglesia de Santa María del Camino. The Convento de San Zoilo has a Gothic cloister and offers simple accommodation.

Located at **Gañinas,** 20 km (12 miles) to the northwest (just south of Saldaña), is the well-preserved Roman villa,

Interior of the Iglesia de San Juan Bautista at Baños de Cerrato

Posada of the Monasterio de Santa María la Real, Aguilar de Campoo

La Olmeda. It has a number of impressive mosaics, including a hunting scene with lions and tigers. Finds from the villa are displayed in the archaeological museum located in the Iglesia de San Pedro in Saldaña.

⋔ Villa Romana La Olmeda
Pedrosa de la Vega. ◯ Tue–Sun.
⬤ 22 Dec–31 Jan. 🎫 ticket also covers archaeological museum.

Aguilar de Campoo ㉕

Palencia. 🏠 7,000. 🚌 🛈 Calle Modesto la Fuente 1, (979) 12 20 05. 🚌 Tue. 🎊 San Pedro (29 Jun).

Sɪᴛᴜᴀᴛᴇᴅ ʙᴇᴛᴡᴇᴇɴ the parched plains of Central Spain and the lush green foothills of the Cantabrian Mountains is the old fortified town of Aguilar de Campoo. At one end of its ancient porticoed main square is the impressive bell tower of the **Colegiata de San Miguel**. In this church is a mausoleum containing the tomb of the Marquises of Aguilar.

Among the other places of interest include the **Ermita de Santa Cecilia**, near the castle, and the restored Romanesque-Gothic **Monasterio de Santa María la Real**, on the outskirts of town, which has a small, friendly *posada* (inn), ideal for a night's stay *(see p555)*.

Environs: Six km (4 miles) south, at **Olleros de Pisuerga**, is a church built in a cave. From the parador at **Cervera de Pisuerga**, 25 km (15 miles) northwest of Aguilar, there are stunning views, and tours of the **Reserva Nacional de Fuentes Carrionas**. This is a rugged region of mountain lakes overlooked by Fuentes Carrionas, a 2,487-m (8,159-ft) summit, and other peaks.

Briviesca ㉖

Burgos. 🏠 6,100. 🚌 🚌 🛈 Calle Marqués de Torre Soto 8, (947) 59 18 18. 🚌 Sat. 🎊 Feria de San José (19 Mar), Santa Casilda (9 May).

Tʜɪs ʟɪᴛᴛʟᴇ ᴡᴀʟʟᴇᴅ ᴛᴏᴡɴ, in the northeast of Burgos province, has an arcaded main square and several dignified mansions. The best known of its churches is the **Convento de Santa Clara**, with its 16th-century walnut reredos carved with religious scenes. In 1388 Juan I of Aragón created the title Príncipe de Asturias for his son, Enrique, in the town. The Santuario de Santa Casilda, situated outside Briviesca, has a collection of votive objects.

Environs: Oña, 25 km (15 miles) north, is an attractive town. Its former Benedictine monastery of San Salvador was founded in 1011.

Overlooking a fertile valley, 20 km (12 miles) further northeast, is the little hilltop town of **Frías**. Its craggy castle overlooks cobbled streets lined with many pretty old houses. Crossing the Río Ebro is a fortified medieval bridge, which still has its central gate tower.

At **Medina de Pomar**, 30 km (20 miles) north of Oña, is a 15th-century castle, once the seat of the Velasco family. Inside are the ruins of a palace with Mudéjar stucco decoration and Arabic inscriptions.

The medieval bridge over the Río Ebro at Frías, with its central gate tower

Flemish triptych inside the collegiate church in Covarrubias

Covarrubias ㉗

Burgos. 🏠 600. 🚌 🚶 Calle Doña Urraca 2, (947) 40 30 51. 🗓 Tue. 🎉 San Cosme and San Damián (26–7 Sep).

NAMED AFTER the reddish caves on its outskirts, the delightful town of Covarrubias stands on the banks of the Río Arlanza. Medieval walls surround the charming old centre with its arcaded half-timbered houses (see p22). The distinguished **collegiate church** gives an inkling of the historical importance of Covarrubias, for here is the tomb of Fernán González, first independent Count of Castile, and one of great figures in Castilian history. By uniting several fiefs in battles against the Moors in the 10th century, he set in motion the rise in Castilian power that ensured the resulting kingdom of Castile would play a leading role in the unification of Spain. The church museum in the sacristy contains treasures, notably a Flemish triptych of the Adoration of the Magi, attributed to Gil de Siloé, and a 17th-century organ.

ENVIRONS: A short distance east along the Río Arlanza lies the ruins of the 11th-century Romanesque monastery of **San Pedro de Arlanza**. At **Quintanilla de las Viñas**, 24 km (15 miles) north of Covarrubias, is a ruined 7th-century Visigothic church. The reliefs on the columns of the triumphal arch are remarkable, depicting sun and moon symbols that may be pagan.

Burgos ㉘

Burgos. 🏠 106,000. ✈ 🚌 🚶 Plaza de Alonso Martínez 7, (947) 20 31 25. 🗓 Wed & Sun. 🎉 San Lesmes (30 Jan), San Pedro and San Pablo (30 Jun).

FOUNDED IN 884, Burgos has played a significant political and military role in Spanish history. It was the capital of the united kingdoms of Castile and León from 1073 until losing that honour to Valladolid after the fall of Granada in 1492 (see pp52–3). During the 15th and 16th centuries, like many Castilian towns, Burgos grew wealthy from the wool trade and used its riches to finance most of the great art and architecture which can be seen in the city today. Less auspiciously, Franco chose Burgos as his headquarters during the Civil War (see pp62–3).

The city's strategic location on the main Madrid–France highway and on the route to Santiago (see pp78–9) ensure many visitors; but even without this Burgos would justify a long detour. Despite its size and extremes of climate, it is one of most agreeable provincial capitals in Castilla y León.

Approach via the bridge of Santa María, which leads into the old quarter through the **Arco de Santa María**, a gateway carved with statues of various local worthies. The main bridge into the city, however, is the Puente de San Pablo, where a statue commemorates the city's hero, El Cid. Not far

from the bridge stands the **Casa del Cordón**, a 15th-century palace (now a bank) which has a Franciscan cord motif carved over the portal. A plaque declares that this is the spot where the Catholic Monarchs welcomed Columbus on his return, in 1497, from the second of his famous voyages to the Americas.

The lacy, steel-grey spires of the **cathedral** (see pp354–5) are a prominent landmark from almost anywhere in the city. On the rising ground behind it stands the **Iglesia de San Nicolás**, whose main feature is a superb altarpiece by Simon of Cologne (1505). The crowded carvings vividly depict a number of scenes from the life of St Nicholas. Other churches worth visiting are the **Iglesia de San Lorenzo**, with its superb Baroque ceiling, and the **Iglesia de San Esteban**, which has a museum of altarpieces. The **Iglesia de Santa Águeda**, is the place where El Cid made King Alfonso VI swear that he

The Arco de Santa María in Burgos, adorned with statues and turrets

EL CID (1043–99)

Rodrigo Díaz de Vivar was born into a noble family in Vivar del Cid, north of Burgos, in 1043. He served Fernando I, but was banished from Castile after becoming embroiled in the fratricidal squabbles of the king's sons, Sancho II and Alfonso VI. He switched allegiance to fight for the Moors, then changed side again, capturing Valencia for the Christians in 1094, ruling the city until his death. For his heroism he was named El Cid, from the Arabic Sidi (Lord). He was a charismatic man of great courage, but it was an anonymous poem, El Cantar del Mío Cid, in 1180, that immortalized him as a romantic hero of the Reconquest (see pp50–51). The tombs of El Cid and his wife, Jimena, are in Burgos cathedral.

Statue of El Cid in Vivar del Cid

BURGOS CITY CENTRE

Arco de Santa María ⑥
Casa del Cordón ⑦
Cathedral ④
Iglesia de San
  Esteban ①
Iglesia de San
  Lorenzo ⑤
Iglesia de San
  Nicolás ②
Iglesia de Santa
  Águeda ③
Museo de
  Burgos ⑧

KEY

🚍 Coach station

🅿 Parking

ℹ Tourist information

✝ Church

0 metres   150
0 yards   150

---

played no part in the murder of his elder brother, King Sancho II *(see p338).*

Across the river, the palace of the Casa de Miranda houses the archaeological section of the **Museo de Burgos,** with finds from the Roman city of Clunia. Nearby, the Casa de Angulo contains the Fine Arts section, whose prize exhibits are Juan de Padilla's tomb by Gil de Siloé, and a Moorish casket in enamelled ivory.

Two religious houses, on the outskirts of Burgos, are worth visiting. Just west of the city is the **Real Monasterio de las**

Sculpted tomb of Juan de Padilla by Gil de Siloé, in Casa de Angulo

Huelgas, a Cistercian convent founded in 1187 by Alfonso VIII. It was lavishly endowed and soon achieved great prestige, accepting only the most distinguished nuns. One of the most interesting parts is the Museo de Ricas Telas, a textile museum containing ancient fabrics from the convent's many royal tombs. Another highlight is the Gothic cloister of San Fernando, decorated with Moorish designs of peacocks and stars. In the Capilla de Santiago is a curious articulated wooden figure of St James holding a sword, with which, according to tradition, royal princes were dubbed Knights of Santiago.

To the east of Burgos is the **Cartuja de Miraflores**, a Carthusian monastery founded during the 15th century. The church includes two of Spain's most notable tombs, attributed to Gil de Siloé. One holds the bodies of Juan II and Isabel of Portugal (the parents of Isabel the Catholic); the other contains that of her brother, Prince Alfonso. Equally spectacular is the multicoloured altarpiece by Gil de Siloé, allegedly gilded with the first consignment of gold brought back to Spain from the New World.

Polychrome altarpiece by Gil de Siloé, in Cartuja de Miraflores

🏛 **Museo de Burgos**
Calle Calera 23. 📞 (947) 26 58 75.
🕐 *Tue–Sun.* 📷 ⚕

🏠 **Real Monasterio de las Huelgas**
Calle de las Huelgas. 📞 (947) 20 16 30. 🕐 *Tue–Sun.* ⚕

🏠 **Cartuja de Miraflores**
Ctra de San Pedro Cardeña. 🕐 *daily.*

ENVIRONS: Ten km (6 miles) southeast of Burgos is the **Monasterio de San Pedro de Cardeña.** El Cid led his family to safety here while he rode into exile after King Alfonso VI had banished him from the territory of Castile.

Burgos Cathedral

SPAIN'S THIRD-LARGEST CATHEDRAL was founded in 1221 by Bishop Mauricio under Fernando III. The groundplan – a Latin cross – measures 84 m (92 yds) by 59 m (65 yds). Its construction was carried out in several stages over three centuries and involved many of the greatest artists and architects in Europe. The style is almost entirely Gothic, and shows influences from Germany, France, and the Low Countries. First to be built were the nave and cloisters, while the intricate, crocketed spires and the richly decorated side chapels are mostly later work. The architects cleverly adapted the cathedral to its sloping site, incorporating stairways inside and out.

Christ at the Column, by Diego de Siloé

West Front
The lacy, steel-grey spires soar above a sculpted balustrade depicting Castile's early kings.

★ Golden Staircase
This elegant Renaissance staircase by Diego de Siloé (1523) links the nave with the Puerta Alta (kept locked) at street level.

Lantern

Tomb of El Cid

STAR FEATURES

★ Golden Staircase

★ Constable's Chapel

★ Transept Crossing

Capilla de Santa Tecla

Puerta de Santa María (main entrance)

Capilla de Santa Ana
The altarpiece (1492) in this chapel is by the sculptor Gil de Siloé. The central panel shows the Virgin with St Joachim.

Capilla de la Presentación (1519–24) is a funerary chapel with a star-shaped, traceried vault.

Retrochoir
Several of the reliefs around the chancel were carved by Philippe de Bigarny. This expressive scene, which was completed in 1498, depicts the road to Calvary.

VISITORS' CHECKLIST

Plaza de San Fernando. ☎ (947) 20 47 12. ⊙ 9:30am–1pm, 4–7pm daily. ✝ 9am, 10am, 11am, 7:30pm Sun–Fri, 7:30pm, 8:30pm Sat. 🚫 ♿ 🎦

Capilla de San Juan Bautista and museum

★ **Constable's Chapel**
The tomb of the High Constable of Castile and his wife lies beneath the openwork vault of this chapel of 1517.

Sacristy *(1765)*
The sacristy was rebuilt in Baroque style, with an exuberant plasterwork vault and rococo altars

Capilla de la Visitación

Puerta de la Coronería
The tympanum of this portal of 1230 shows Christ flanked by the Evangelists. Statues of the apostles sit below.

Capilla del Santisímo Cristo

★ **Transept Crossing**
The magnificent star-ribbed central dome, begun in 1539, rises on four huge pillars. It is decorated with effigies of prophets and saints. Beneath it is the tomb of El Cid and his wife.

Lerma 🕮

Burgos. 🏛 2,600. 🚊 🚌 ℹ️ Calle Audiencia 6, (947) 17 01 43. 🚌 Wed. 🎪 Nuestra Señora (8–9 Sep).

THE GRANDIOSE APPEARANCE of this town is largely due to the ambition of the notorious first Duke of Lerma (see p56), Felipe III's corrupt favourite and minister from 1598–1618. He misused vast quantities of Spain's new-found wealth on new buildings in his home town – all strictly Classical in style, in accordance with prevailing fashion. At the top of the town, the haughty **Palacio Ducal**, built in 1605 as his residence, contrasts strikingly with the agreeable jumble of earlier houses leading down to the medieval gateway.

There are good views over the Río Arlanza from the archways near to the **Convento de Santa Clara** and also from the **Colegiata de San Pedro** church, which has a bronze statue of the Duke's uncle.

The narrow, sloping streets of the old town of Lerma

Cloisters of the Monasterio de Santo Domingo de Silos

Monasterio de Santo Domingo de Silos 🕮

Santo Domingo de Silos (Burgos). 📞 (947) 39 00 68. 🚌 from Burgos. ◐ daily. ✝️ 9am, 7pm & 9:30pm.

ST DOMINIC gave his name to the monastery that he rebuilt in 1042 over the ruins of a Visigothic abbey destroyed by the Moors. It is a place of spiritual and artistic pilgrimage, and its tranquil setting has inspired countless poets.

Others come to admire the beautiful Romanesque cloisters, whose capitals are sculpted in a great variety of designs, both symbolistic and realistic, many showing fantastic beasts. The carvings on the corner piers depict various scenes from the Bible and the ceilings are coffered in Moorish style. The body of St Dominic rests in a sarcophagus, supported by

three Romanesque lions, in the north gallery. The old pharmacy, just off the cloister, has a display of jars from Talavera de la Reina (see p368).

The Benedictine community holds regular services in Gregorian chant in the Neo-Classical church by Ventura Rodríguez. The monastery offers accommodation for male guests.

ENVIRONS: Just to the southwest lies the **Garganta de la Yecla** (Yecla Gorge), where a path leads down to a narrow fissure cut by the river. To the northeast are the peaks and wildlife reserve of the **Sierra de la Demanda**, extending over the border into La Rioja.

The 15th-century castle of Peñaranda de Duero

Peñaranda de Duero 🕮

Burgos. 🏛 600. 🚌 ℹ️ Calle Real 1, (947) 55 20 68. 🚌 Wed. 🎪 Santiago (25 Jul), Virgen de la Asunción (15 Aug).

THE CASTLE OF Peñaranda was built during the Reconquest (see pp50–51) by the Castilians, who had driven the Moors back south of the Río Duero. From its hilltop site, there are views down to one of the most charming villages in old Castile, where pantiled houses cluster around a huge church. The main square is lined with porticoed, timber-framed buildings and the superb Renaissance **Palacio de los Condes de Miranda**. Framing its main doorway are various heraldic devices, and inside is a patio which has double galleries

GREGORIAN PLAINCHANT

At regular intervals throughout the day, the monks of Santo Domingo de Silos sing services in plainchant, an unaccompanied singing of Latin texts in unison. The origins of chant date back to the beginnings of Christianity, but it was Pope Gregory I (590–604) who codified this manner of worship. It is an ancient and austere form of music which has found a new appeal with modern audiences. In 1994 a recording of the monks became a surprise hit all over the world.

Manuscript for an 11th-century Gregorian chant

◁ View from the castle over the church and town of Peñaranda, on the Río Duero

Curtain walls and drum towers of Berlanga de Duero castle

and fine decorated ceilings. On Calle de la Botica, off the square, is a 17th-century pharmacy displaying antique blue and white apothecary jars.

ENVIRONS: In the old quarter of **Aranda de Duero**, 20 km (12 miles) to the west, is a notable church, the **Iglesia de Santa María**, with an elaborate Isabelline façade (see p20).

🏛 **Palacio de Avellaneda**
Plaza de Peñaranda.
📞 (947) 55 20 13. ⬜ Tue–Sun.

El Burgo de Osma ❷

Soria. 🏘 5,000. 🚹 Plaza Mayor 9, (975) 34 01 07. 🔄 Sat. 🎉 Virgen del Espino and San Roque (14–19 Aug).

THE MOST INTERESTING sight in this attractive village is the **cathedral**. Although it is mostly Gothic (dating from 1232), with Renaissance additions, the tall tower is Baroque (1739). Its treasures include a Juan de Juni altarpiece, a white marble pulpit and the tomb of the founder, San Pedro de Osma. The museum contains a valuable collection of illuminated manuscripts and codices.

Porticoed buildings line the streets and the Plaza Mayor, and storks nest on the Baroque Hospital de San Agustín.

ENVIRONS: Overlooking the Río Duero at **Gormaz**, 15 km (9.5 miles) south, is a massive castle with 28 towers. There are also mighty medieval fortresses at **Berlanga de Duero**, 12 km (7.5 miles) further to the

southeast, and at **Calatañazor**, 25 km (15.5 miles) northeast of El Burgo de Osma, near to the place where the Moorish leader al Mansur was killed in battle in 1002 (see p49).

Soria ❸

Soria. 🏘 33,000. 🚹 Plaza Ramón y Cajal, (975) 21 20 52. 🔄 Thu. 🎉 San Juan (late Jun), San Saturio (2 Oct).

CASTILLA Y LEON'S smallest provincial capital stands on the banks of the Río Duero. Soria's stylish, modern parador (see p557) is named after the poet Antonio Machado (1875–1939, see p31), who wrote in praise of the town and the surrounding plains. Many of the older buildings are gone, but notable among these remaining are the imposing russet **Palacio de los Condes de Gómara**, and the handsome **Concatedral de San Pedro**, both built in the 16th-century.

The **Museo Numantino**, opposite the municipal gardens, displays a variety of finds from the nearby Roman ruins

of Numantia and Tiermes (see p347). Across the Duero is the ruined monastery of **San Juan de Duero**, with a 13th-century cloister of interlacing arches.

ENVIRONS: North of Soria are the ruins of **Numantia**. The Celtiberian inhabitants endured a year-long Roman siege in 133 BC before defiantly burning the town and themselves (see p46). To the northwest is the Sierra de Urbión, a range of pine-clad hills with a lake, the **Laguna Negra de Urbión**.

🏛 **Museo Numantino**
Paseo de Espolón. 📞 (975) 22 13 97.
⬜ Tue–Sun. 🎫 ♿

Medinaceli ❹

Soria. 🏘 1,500. 🚉 🚹 Plaza Mayor 2, (975) 73 41 76. 🎉 Julián de San Agustín (28 Aug), Cuerpos Santos (13 Nov).

ONLY A triumphal arch remains of Roman Ocilis, perched on a high ridge over the Río Jalón. Built in the 2nd or 3rd century AD, it is the only one in Spain with three arches. It has been adopted as the symbol for ancient monuments on Spanish road signs.

ENVIRONS: Lying just to the east are the red cliffs of the Jalón gorges. On the Madrid–Burgos road is the Cistercian monastery of **Santa María de Huerta**, founded in 1179. Its glories include a 13th-century Gothic cloister and the superb, crypt-like Monks' Refectory.

🏛 **Monasterio de Santa María de Huerta**
📞 (975) 32 70 02. ⬜ daily. 🎫 ♿

Decorative arches in the cloister of the monastery of San Juan de Duero

CASTILLA-LA MANCHA

GUADALAJARA · CUENCA · TOLEDO · ALBACETE · CIUDAD REAL

L A MANCHA'S EMPTY BEAUTY, *its windmills and medieval castles, silhouetted above the sienna plains, was immortalized by Cervantes in Don Quixote's epic adventures. Its brilliantly sunlit, wide horizons are one of the classic images of Spain. This scarcely visited region has great, scenic mountain ranges, dramatic gorges and the two monument-filled cities of Toledo and Cuenca.*

You will always find a castle nearby in this region – as the name Castilla suggests. Most were built in the 9th–12th centuries, when the region was a battleground between Christians and Moors. Others mark the 14th- and 15th-century frontiers between the kingdoms of Aragón and Castile. Sigüenza, Belmonte, Alarcón Molina de Aragón and Calatrava La Nueva are among the most impressive.

Toledo, which was the capital of Visigothic Spain, is an outstanding museum city. Its rich architectural and artistic heritage derives from a coalescence of Muslim, Christian and Jewish cultures with medieval and Renaissance ideas and influences.

Cuenca is another attractive city. Its old town is perched above converging gorges; on two sides it spills down steep hillsides. Villanueva de los Infantes, Chinchilla, Alcaraz and Almagro are towns of character built between the 16th and 18th centuries. Ocaña and Tembleque each has a splendid *plaza mayor* (main square).

La Mancha's plains are brightened by natural features of great beauty in its two national parks – the Tablas de Daimiel, and Cabañeros, within the Montes de Toledo. Rimming the plains are beautiful upland areas: the olive groves of the Alcarria; Cuenca's limestone mountains; and the peaks of the Sierra de Alcaraz. The wine region of La Mancha is the world's largest expanse of vineyards. Around Consuegra and Albacete fields turn mauve in autumn as the valuable saffron crocus blooms.

Windmills above Campo de Criptana on the plains of La Mancha

◁ Old houses in Cuenca, a city dramatically located over two gorges

Exploring Castilla-La Mancha

THE HISTORIC CITY OF TOLEDO is Castilla-La Mancha's major tourist destination. Less crowded towns with historical charm include Almagro, Oropesa, Alcaraz and Guadalajara. At Sigüenza, Calatrava, Belmonte and Alarcón there are medieval castles, reminders of the region's eventful past. Some towns on the plains of La Mancha, such as El Toboso and Campo de Criptana, are associated with the adventures of Don Quixote *(see p377)*. The wooded uplands of the Serranía de Cuenca, the Alcarria and the Sierra de Alcaraz provide picturesque scenic routes. A haven for bird lovers is the wetland nature reserve of the Tablas de Daimiel.

The village of Alcalá del Júcar

SIGHTS AT A GLANCE

SEE ALSO

Cattle grazing on the isolated
plains of La Mancha

GETTING AROUND

Castilla-La Mancha is best explored by car as it is well-endowed with a network of motorways radiating outwards from Madrid. These are the N401 to Toledo, the NII to Sigüenza, the NIII to Albacete, the NIV to Valdepeñas, and the NV to Oropesa. The region is also served by the high-speed AVE train which runs between Madrid and Seville, stopping at Ciudad Real. Otherwise, public transport is infrequent and slow. Albacete and Toledo have domestic airports.

KEY

▬▬	Motorway
▬▬	Major road
▭▭	Minor road
▬▬	Scenic route
≈	River
☀	Viewpoint

The tranquil Montes de Toledo

0 kilometres   50

0 miles   30

Atienza **❶**

Guadalajara. 🏘 *500.* 🛈 *Plaza de España 11, (949) 39 90 01.* 🚌 *Fri.* 🎪 *La Caballada (May/Jun).*

R ISING HIGH above the valley it once protected, Atienza contains vestiges of its medieval past. Crowning the hill are a ruined 12th-century castle. The arcaded Plaza Mayor and the Plaza del Trigo are joined by an original gateway. The **Museo de San Gil**, a religious art museum, is in the church of the same name. The **Iglesia de Santa María del Rey**, at the foot of the hill, displays a Baroque altarpiece.

ENVIRONS: **Campisábalos**, to the west, has an outstanding 12th-century Romanesque church. The **Hayedo de Tejera Negra**, further west, is a nature reserve of beech woods.

🏛 **Museo de San Gil**
Calle General Franco. ☎ *(949) 39 90 14.* ◯ *Sep–Jun: Sat & Sun; Jul–Aug: daily.* 📷

Sigüenza **❷**

Guadalajara. 🏘 *5,000.* 🚊 🛈 *Plaza Mayor 1, (949) 39 32 51.* 🚌 *Sat.* 🎪 *San Juan (24 Jun), San Roque (15 Aug).*

D OMINATING the hillside town of Sigüenza is its impressive castle-parador *(see p559).* The **cathedral**, in the old town, is Romanesque, with later additions, such as the Gothic-Plateresque cloisters. In one of the chapels is the Tomb of El Doncel, built for Martín Vázquez de Arce, Isabel

Semi-recumbent figure of El Doncel on his tomb in Sigüenza cathedral

of Castile's page *(see p52).* He was killed in battle against the Moors in 1486. The sacristy has a beautiful ceiling carved with flowers and cherubs, by Alonso de Covarrubias.

Molina de Aragón **❸**

Guadalajara. 🏘 *3,000.* 🛈 *Calle del Carmen 1, (949) 83 24 53.* 🚌 *Thu.* 🎪 *Día del Carmen (16 Jul), Ferias (30 Aug–5 Sep).*

M OLINA'S ATTRACTIVE medieval quarter is at the foot of a hill next to the Río Gallo. The town was disputed during the Reconquest and then captured from the Moors by Alfonso I of Aragón in 1129. Many monuments were destroyed during the War of Independence *(see p59),* but the 11th-century hilltop castle preserves six original towers. It is possible to visit the newly restored Romanesque **Iglesia de Santa Clara**.

ENVIRONS: West of Molina is the chapel of the **Virgen de la Hoz**, set in a beautiful rustred ravine. Further southwest is a nature reserve, the **Parque Natural del Alto Tajo**.

Arab ramparts above Molina de Aragón's old town

La Alcarria **❹**

Guadalajara. 🚊 *Guadalajara.* 🛈 *Guadalajara, (949) 22 06 98.*

T HIS VAST STRETCH of undulating olive groves and fields east of Guadalajara is still evocative of Camilo José Cela's *(see p31)* classic book *Journey to the Alcarria.* Driving through the rolling hills dotted with small villages, it seems that little has changed since this account of the hardship of Spanish rural life was written in the 1940s.

Towards the centre of the Alcarria are three immense, adjoining reservoirs called the **Mar de Castilla** (Sea of

Olive groves in La Alcarria in the province of Guadalajara

Castile). The first reservoir was built in 1946, and holiday homes have subsequently sprung up close to the shores and on the outskirts of villages.

Historic **Pastrana**, which is situated 40 km (25 miles) southeast of Guadalajara, is one of the most attractive towns in the Alcarria. It grew up around a mansion, the **Palacio Mendoza**, and by the 17th century had become larger and more affluent than Guadalajara. The **Iglesia de la Asunción** contains four 15th-century Flemish tapestries and a painting by El Greco.

Brihuega, 30 km (19 miles) northeast of Guadalajara, has a pleasant old centre.

Guadalajara **❺**

Guadalajara. 🚶 60,000. 🚋 🚌 ❚
Plaza Mayor 7, (949) 22 06 98. 🏬 Tue,
Sat. 🎭 Virgen de la Antigua (Sep).

G UADALAJARA'S HISTORY is largely lost within the modern city, although traces of its Renaissance splendour survive. The **Palacio de los Duques del Infantado**, built between the 14th and 17th centuries by the powerful Mendoza dynasty, is an outstanding example of Gothic-Mudéjar architecture *(see p20)*. The main façade and the two-storey patio are adorned with delicate carving. Following Civil War bombing, the palace was restored and now houses the Museo Provincial. Among the churches in the town is the **Iglesia de Santiago**, with a

Detail of the façade of the Palacio de los Duques del Infantado

Gothic-Plateresque chapel by Alonso de Covarrubias. The 15th-century **Iglesia de San Francisco** is home to the mausoleum of the Mendoza family. The cathedral is built on the site of a mosque.

ENVIRONS: At **Lupiana**, 11 km (7 miles) east of Guadalajara, is the two-storey Monasterio de San Bartolomé, which was founded in the 14th century.

🏛 Palacio de los Duques del Infantado
Avenida del Infantado del Ejército.
❚ (949) 21 33 01. ☐ daily. 🎟

Serranía de Cuenca **❻**

Cuenca. 🚋 Cuenca. ❚ Cuenca,
(969) 23 21 19.

T O THE NORTH AND EAST of Cuenca stretches the vast *serranía*, a mountainous area of forests and pastures dissected by deep gorges. Its two most popular beauty spots are the **Ciudad Encantada**

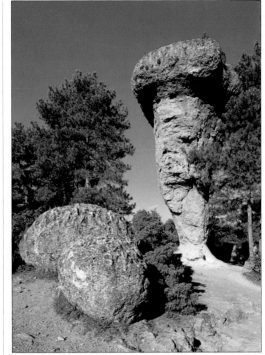

Sculpted rock figures in Ciudad Encantada

(Enchanted City), where the limestone has been eroded into spectacular shapes, and the moss-clad waterfalls and rock pools of the **Nacimiento del Río Cuervo** (Source of the River Cuervo).

The main river flowing through the area, the Júcar, carves a gorge near Villalba de la Sierra. The viewpoint of the **Ventana del Diablo** gives the best view of the gorge.

Between Beteta and Priego (known for its pottery and canework), to the north, is another spectacular river canyon, the **Hoz de Beteta**, where the Río Guadiela has cut its way through the surrounding cliffs. There are good views from the convent of **San Miguel de las Victorias**. A small road leads to the 18th-century royal spa of **Solán de Cabras**

In the emptier eastern and southern tracts is **Cañete**, a pretty fortified old town with a parish church displaying 16th-century paintings. To the southeast of Cañete are the eerie ridgetop ruins of the abandoned town of **Moya**.

Street-by-Street: Cuenca 🍷

Cuenca's picturesque old town sits astride a steeply sided spur which drops precipitously on either side to the deep gorges of the Júcar and Huécar rivers. Around the Moorish town's narrow, winding streets grew the Gothic and Renaissance city, its monuments built with with the profits of the wool and textile trade. The main sight is the cathedral, one of the most original works of Spanish Gothic, with Anglo-Norman influences. One of the picturesque Hanging Houses, which jut out over the Huécar ravine, has been converted into the excellent Museum of Abstract Art.

The Plaza de la Merced buildings contrast with the modern Museo de Ciencia (Science Museum) nearby.

Museo de Ciencia

Torre de Mangana
This ruined lookout tower at the top of the town is all that remains of an Arab fortress. There are wonderful panoramic views from the top.

CALLE DE SANTA MARIA

CALLE DE ALFONSO VIII

CALLE MOSEN DIEGO DE VALERA

| 0 metres | 50 |
| 0 yards | 50 |

Ayuntamiento

Museo Arqueológico
The collection, covering prehistory up to the 17th century, includes an excellent exhibition on Roman Cuenca.

KEY

– – – Suggested route

★ Museo de Arte Abstracto
Spain's abstract art museum is inside one of the Hanging Houses. It contains works by the movement's leading artists, including Antoni Tàpies and Eduardo Chillida.

Plaza Mayor
This café-lined, arcaded square is in the heart of the old town. The 18th-century Baroque town hall (ayuntamiento), built over arches, stands at the south end.

VISITORS' CHECKLIST

Cuenca. 40,000. Calle Mariano Catalina, (969) 22 07 20. Calle Fermín Caballero 20, (969) 22 70 87. Plaza Mayor 1, (969) 23 21 19. Tue. Semana Santa (Easter Week). **Museo Diocesano** Tue–Sun. **Museo de Arte Abstracto** Tue–Sun. **Museo Arqueológico** Tue–Sun.

The Iglesia de San Miguel, perched over the Júcar gorge, was built in the Gothic style. It has a beautiful Mudéjar ceiling.

SEVERO CATALINA

PLAZA MAYOR

CALLE DE SAN PEDRO

CALLE DE JULIÁN ROMERO

O VALERO

To Parador de Cuenca

Museo Diocesano
The cathedral's treasures, which are housed in the Palacio Episcopal, include paintings by El Greco.

★ Cathedral
Highlights of the 12th to 16th-century building are the decorated altar, chapterhouse and the side chapels.

★ Hanging Houses
The 14th-century beamed Casas Colgadas were once used as a summer residence for the royal family.

STAR SIGHTS

★ **Museo de Arte Abstracto**

★ **Hanging Houses**

★ **Cathedral**

Remains of a Roman building in Segóbriga

Segóbriga **⓿**

Saelices (Cuenca). **[** (969) 13 20 64. **◯** Tue –Sun. **Museum ◐** public hols, 24, 25 & 31 Dec. 🎫 ♿

THE SMALL RUINED Roman city of Segóbriga, near the town of Saelices, is located in open, unspoiled countryside close to the Madrid–Valencia motorway. The Romans who lived here exploited the surrounding area, growing cereals, felling timber and mining minerals.

Many parts of the city can be explored. The 3rd-century theatre – which has a capacity of 2,000 people – is sometimes used for dramatic performances today. Segóbriga also had a necropolis, an amphitheatre, a temple to Diana and public baths. The quarries which supplied the stone to build the city can also be seen.

Nearby, there is a small museum containing some of the site's finds, although the best statues are in Cuenca's Museo Arqueológico (see p366).

Monasterio de Uclés **❾**

Uclés (Cuenca). **[** (969) 13 50 58. **◯** 9am – dusk daily. 🎫

THE SMALL VILLAGE OF Uclés, to the south of the Alcarria, is dominated by its impressive castle-monastery, nicknamed "El Escorial de La Mancha" for the similarity of its church's profile to that of El Escorial (see pp312–13). Originally an impregnable medieval fortress, Uclés became the monastery seat of the Order of Santiago from 1174, because of its cen-

tral geographical location. The austere building you see today, used as a seminary school, is mainly Renaissance, but overlaid with ornamental Baroque detail. Among its attractive features are a magnificent carved wooden ceiling and staircase.

Illescas **❿**

Toledo. 🏠 7,500. 🚉 🛈 Plaza Mayor 1, (925) 51 10 51. 🗓 Thu. 🎉 Fiesta de Milagro (11 Mar), Fiesta Patronal (31 Aug).

JUST OFF THE Madrid–Toledo motorway, Illescas was the summer location for Felipe II's court. While there is little to see of its old town, the 16th-century **Hospital de la Caridad**, next to the Iglesia de la Asunción (which is easily identified by its Mudéjar tower), is important for its art collection. The hospital has five outstanding late El Grecos

Ceramics in Talavera workshop

(see p373) hanging in its 16th-century interior. The subjects of three of these are the Nativity, the Annunciation and the Coronation of the Virgin.

🏠 **Hospital de la Caridad** Calle Cardenal Cisneros 2. **[** (925) 54 00 35. **◯** daily. 🎫 ♿

Talavera de la Reina **⓫**

Toledo. 🏠 80,000. 🚉 🚌 🛈 Avenida del Principe 23, (925) 82 53 22. 🗓 Wed. 🎉 Virgen del Prado (24 May), San Mateo (27 Sep).

A RUINED 15TH-CENTURY bridge across the Tagus marks the entrance to the old part of this busy market town, famous for its ceramics. From the bridge you can walk past the surviving section of the Roman and medieval wall to the **collegiate church**. This is the largest of the town's four Gothic-Mudéjar churches and is notable for its fine rose window.

Talavera's ceramic workshops are on the western edge of town. They still produce the blue and yellow *azulejos* (tiles) which have been a trademark of the town since the 16th century; but nowadays they also make domestic and decorative objects.

A good selection of the town's *azulejos* can be seen in the large **Ermita del Virgen del Prado** by the river. Many of the interior walls have superb 16th- to 20th-century tile friezes of religious scenes.

Part of a frieze of tiles in Talavera's Ermita del Virgen del Prado

Traditional embroidery work in Lagartera, near Oropesa

Oropesa ⑫

Toledo. ⚥ 2,900. 🚉 🚌 Plaza del Navarro 9, (925) 43 00 02. 🎭 Virgen de Peñitas (8–9 Sep), Beato Alonso de Orozco (19 Sep).

Oropesa's medieval and Renaissance splendour as one of Toledo's satellite communities has left a charming old quarter at the centre of today's small farming town. A circular Ruta Monumental starts from the massive, mainly 15th-century **castle** on the top of the hill. A Renaissance extension – thought to be the work of Juan de Herrera, co-architect of El Escorial (see pp312–13) – was added to the castle in the 16th-century by the wealthy and influential Álvarez family. A large part of the castle has been converted into a parador (see p559).

The Ruta Monumental continues around the town, taking in a number of churches, convents, a small ceramics museum and the town hall which presides over the main square.

Environs: The area around Oropesa is excellent for buying handicrafts. **Lagartera**, just to the west of the town, is famous for the embroidery and lacework by the women in the village and **El Puente del Arzobispo**, 12 km (7 miles) south of Oropesa, is a good source of painted ceramics and esparto (grass-weaving) work. **Ciudad de Vascos**, further southeast, is a ruined 10th-century Arab city in splendid countryside around Azután.

Montes de Toledo ⑬

Toledo. 🚉 San Martín de Montalbán. 🚌 Toledo, (925) 22 08 43.

To the southwest of Toledo a range of low mountains sweeps towards Extremadura. In medieval times the Montes de Toledo were owned by bishops and the kings. They cover an area of approximately 1,000 sq km (386 sq miles).

The attractive new nature reserve of the **Parque Nacional de Cabañeros** (see pp26–7) encloses a sizeable area of woodland and pastures used for grazing sheep. The easiest access to the park is from **Pueblo Nuevo del Bullaque**. From here it is possible to make four-hour guided trips in Landrovers, during which you may spot wild boar, deer and imperial eagles. In the pasturelands stand chozos, conical refuges for shepherds and their families.

In the eastern foothills of the Montes de Toledo is **Orgaz**, with a parish church which contains works by El Greco. Nearby villages, such as **Los Yébenes** and **Ventas con Peña Aguilera**, are known for their leather goods and restaurants serving game.

On the plains stands the small church of **Santa María de Melque**, believed to date back to the 8th century. Close by is the Templar castle of **Montalbán**, a vast but ruined 12th-century fortress. Nearer to Toledo, at **Guadamur**, there is another handsome castle.

A chozo (shepherd's cabin) in the Parque Nacional de Cabañeros

---

CASTILLA-LA MANCHA'S FIESTAS

La Endiablada (2–3 Feb) Almonacid del Marquesado (Cuenca). At the start of the two-day-long "Fiesta of the Bewitched", men and boys, gaudily dressed as "devils", with cowbells strapped to their backs, gather in the house of their leader, the Diablo Mayor. They accompany the images of the Virgen de la Candelaria (Virgin of Candlemas) and St Blaise in procession. As the devils dance alongside the floats bearing the saints' images, they ring their bells loudly and incessantly.

One of the so-called "devils" in La Endiablada fiesta

Romería del Cristo del Sahúco (Pentecost, May/Jun), Peñas de San Pedro (Albacete). A cross-shaped coffin bearing a figure of Christ is carried 15 km (9 miles) here from its shrine by men dressed in white.

La Caballada (Pentecost), Atienza (Guadalajara). Horsemen follow the route across country taken by the 12th-century muleteers of Atienza, who are said to have saved the boy King Alfonso VIII of Castile from his uncle, Fernando II.

Corpus Christi (May/Jun), Toledo. One of Spain's most dramatic Corpus Christi (see p34) processions. The cathedral monstrance (see p374) is paraded in the streets.

Street-by-Street: Toledo ⓮

Damascene work, typical of Toledo

PICTURESQUELY SITED on a hill above the River Tagus is the historic centre of Toledo. Behind the old walls lies much evidence of the city's rich history. The Romans built a fortress on the site of the present-day Alcázar.
The Visigoths made Toledo their capital in the 6th century AD, and left behind several churches. In the Middle Ages, Toledo was a melting pot of Christian, Muslim and Jewish cultures, and it was during this period that the city's most outstanding monument – its cathedral – was built. In the 16th century the painter El Greco came to live in Toledo, and today the city is home to many of his works.

The Iglesia de San Román, of Visigothic origin, now contains a museum relating the city's past under the Visigoths.

Puerta de Valmardón

| 0 metres | | 100 |
| 0 yards | | 100 |

CARDENAL LORENZANA

CALLE DE SAN ROMÁN

CALLE DE ALFONSO X

CALLE DE ALFONSO XII

CALLE DE LA TRINIDAD

★ Iglesia de Santo Tomé
This church, with a beautiful Mudéjar tower, houses El Greco's masterpiece, The Burial of the Count of Orgaz (see p28).

To Sinagoga de Santa María la Blanca and Monasterio de San Juan de los Reyes

To Sinagoga del Tránsito and Casa-Museo de El Greco

Archbishop's Palace

Taller del Moro
Once used as a workshop by craftsmen building the cathedral, this Mudéjar palace now houses a museum of Mudéjar ceramics and tiles.

STAR SIGHTS

- ★ Iglesia de Santo Tomé
- ★ Museo de Santa Cruz
- ★ Cathedral

Puerta del
as a double
ish arch and
two towers.

Ermita del Cristo de la Luz
This small mosque, the city's only remaining Muslim building, dates from around AD 1000.

To tourist information,
Estación de Autobuses,
and Estación de RENFE

VISITORS' CHECKLIST

Toledo. 65,000.
Paseo de la Estación, (925) 22
30 99. *Avenida de Castilla-La Mancha 3*, (925) 21 58 50.
Puerta de Bisagra, (925) 22
08 43. Tue. *Corpus Christi (May/Jun), Virgen del Sagrario, (15 Aug)*. **Iglesia de San Román** Tue–Sun. **Taller del Moro** Tue–Sun.

The Plaza de Zocodover is named after the market which was held here in Moorish times. It is still the city's main square, with many cafés and shops.

FILERITOS

PLAZA DE ZOCODOVER

CALLE DEL COMERCIO

CUESTA DE CARLOS V

★ **Museo de Santa Cruz**
The city's main fine arts collection includes several tapestries from Flanders. Among them is this 15th-century zodiac tapestry, with well-preserved rich colours.

RAMÓN PARRO

SIXTO

L CISNEROS

KEY

– – – Suggested route

★ **Cathedral**
Built on the site of a Visigothic cathedral and a mosque, this impressive structure is one of the largest cathedrals in Christendom (see pp374–5). The Flamboyant Gothic high altar reredos (1504) is the work of several artists.

Alcázar
Outside the fortress is this monument, in memory of the Nationalists who died here in a 70-day siege during the Civil War.

Toledo cathedral rising above the rooftops of the medieval part of the city

Exploring Toledo

Toledo is easily reached from Madrid by rail, bus or car, and is then best explored on foot. To visit all the main sights you need at least two days, but it is possible to walk around the medieval and Jewish quarters in a long morning. To avoid the heavy crowds, go midweek and stay for a night, when the city is at its most atmospheric.

♠ Alcázar

Cuesta del Alcázar. 【 (925) 22 30 38. ◯ *Tue – Sun.* 🖼

Charles V's fortified palace stands on the site of former Roman, Visigothic and Muslim fortresses. Its severe square profile suffered damage by fire three times before being almost completely destroyed in 1936 when the Nationalists survived a 70-day siege by the Republicans. Restoration followed the original plans and the building now houses an army museum. The siege headquarters have been preserved as a monument to Nationalist heroism. Much is made of an alleged telephone conversation between the besieged Colonel Moscardó and his son, held by the Republicans and threatened with death unless his father surrendered. The Colonel refused, and his son was later killed, though not necessarily as a direct result of his father's refusal to capitulate.

🏛 Museo de Santa Cruz

Calle Cervantes 3. 【 (925) 22 10 36. ◯ *daily.* 🖼

This museum is housed in a 16th-century hospital founded by Cardinal Mendoza. The building has some outstanding Renaissance architectural features, including the main doorway, staircase and cloister. The four main wings, laid out in the shape of a Greek cross, are dedicated to the fine arts. The collection is especially strong in medieval and Renaissance tapestries, paintings and sculptures. There are also works by El Greco, including one of his last paintings, *The Assumption* (1613), still in its original altarpiece. Decorative

The Assumption by El Greco (1613) in the Museo de Santa Cruz

arts on display include two typically Toledan crafts: armour and damascened swords, made by inlaying blackened steel with gold wire. Damascene work, such as plates and jewellery (as well as swords), is still produced in the city.

♠ Iglesia de Santo Tomé

Plaza del Conde 1. 【 (925) 21 02 09 ◯ *daily.* 🖼

Visitors come to Santo Tomé mainly to admire El Greco's masterpiece, *The Burial of the Count of Orgaz (see p28).* An important patron of the church the Count paid for much of the 14th-century building that stands today. The painting, commissioned in his memory by a parish priest, depicts the miraculous appearance of St Augustine and St Stephen at his burial, to raise his body to heaven. It has never been moved from the setting for which it was painted, nor restored. Nevertheless, it is remarkable for its contrast of glowing and sombre colours. In the foreground, allegedly, are the artist himself and his son (both looking out) as well as Cervantes. The church itsel is thought to date back to the 12th century, and its tower is one of the best examples of Mudéjar architecture in the city

Nearby is the **Pastelería Santo Tomé**, a good place to buy locally made marzipan.

⊞ Sinagoga de Santa María la Blanca

Calle de los Reyes Católicos 4.
⏺ *(925) 22 72 57.* ⭘ *daily.* 🈂

The oldest and largest of the city's eight original synagogues, this monument dates back to the 12th century. In 1405 it was taken over as a church by the military-religious Order of Calatrava. Restoration has returned it as far as possible to its original beauty – finely carved stone capitals and wall panels stand out against plain white horseshoe arches and plasterwork. In the main chapel is a Plateresque altarpiece. In 1391 a massacre of Jews took place on this site, a turning point after years of religious tolerance in the city.

Mudéjar arches in the Sinagoga de Santa María la Blanca

⊞ Sinagoga del Tránsito

Calle Samuel Leví. ⏺ *(925) 22 36 65.*
⭘ *Tue–Sun.* 🈂

The most elaborate Mudéjar interior in the city is hidden behind the deceptively humble façade of this former synagogue, built in the 14th century by Samuel Ha-Leví, the Jewish treasurer to Pedro the Cruel. The interlaced frieze of the lofty prayer hall harmoniously fuses Islamic, Gothic and Hebrew geometric motifs below a wonderful coffered ceiling.

Adjoining the synagogue is an interesting museum dedicated to Sephardi (Spanish Jewish) culture. The manuscripts, tombstones, wedding costumes and sacred objects of worship date from both before and after the Jews' expulsion from Spain at the end of the 15th century *(see p53)*.

Ornate ceiling in the Monasterio de San Juan de los Reyes

⛪ Monasterio de San Juan de los Reyes

Calle de los Reyes Católicos 21.
⏺ *(925) 22 38 02.* ⭘ *daily.* 🈂 ♿

A wonderful mixture of architectural styles, this monastery was commissioned by the Catholic Monarchs in honour of their victory over the Portuguese at the battle of Toro in 1476 *(see p339)*. Originally, it was intended to be their burial place, but they were actually laid to rest in Granada *(see p462)*. Largely the work of Juan Güas, the church's main Isabelline structure was completed in 1492. Although it was badly damaged by Napoleon's troops in 1808 *(see p59)*, it has been restored to its original splendour. It retains superb features such as a Gothic cloister (1510) – unique in the city – which has a beautiful multi-coloured Mudéjar ceiling. Near to the church is a stretch of the Jewish quarter's original wall.

🏛 Casa-Museo de El Greco

Calle Samuel Leví. ⏺ *(925) 22 40 46.* ⭘ *Tue–Sun.* 🈂

It is not clear whether El Greco actually lived in or simply near to this house in the heart of the Jewish quarter, which has been turned into a museum containing an important collection of his works. Canvases on display include *View of Toledo*, a detailed depiction of the city at the time, and the superb series *Christ and the Apostles*. Underneath the museum, on the ground floor, is a domestic chapel with a fine Mudéjar ceiling and a collection of art by painters of the Toledan School, such as Luis Tristán, a student of El Greco.

⛪ Iglesia de Santiago del Arrabal

This is one of Toledo's most beautiful Mudéjar monuments. It can be easily identified by its tower, reminiscent of a minaret, which is said to date back to the 12th-century Reconquest *(see pp50–51)*. The church, which was built slightly later, has a beautiful woodwork ceiling. The ornate Mudéjar pulpit and Plateresque altarpiece stand out against the otherwise plain Mudéjar interior.

⊞ Puerta Antigua de Bisagra

When Alfonso VI conquered Toledo in 1085, he entered it through this gateway, alongside El Cid. It is the only gateway in the city to have kept its original 10th-century military architecture. The huge towers are topped by a 12th-century Arab gatehouse.

EL GRECO

Born in Crete in 1541, El Greco ("the Greek") came to Toledo in 1577 to paint the altarpiece in the convent of Santo Domingo el Antiguo. Enchanted by the city, he stayed here, painting religious portraits and altarpieces for other churches. Although El Greco was trained in Italy and influenced by masters such as Tintoretto, his works are closely identified with the city where he settled. He died in Toledo in 1614.

Domenikos Theotocopoulos, better known as El Greco

Toledo Cathedral

THE SPLENDOUR OF TOLEDO'S massive cathedral reflects its history as the spiritual heart of the Spanish church and the seat of the Primate of all Spain. Still today, the Mozarabic Mass, which dates back to Visigothic times, is said here by papal permission. The present cathedral was built on the site of a 7th-century church. Work began in 1226 and spanned three centuries, until the completion of the last vaults in 1493. This long period of construction explains the cathedral's mixture of styles: pure French Gothic – complete with flying buttresses – on the exterior; with Spanish decorative styles, such as Mudéjar and Plateresque work, used in the interior.

Sacristy
El Greco's The Denuding of Christ, *above the marble altar, was painted especially for the cathedral. Also here are works by Titian, Van Dyck and Goya.*

The Cloister, on two storeys, was built in the 14th century on the site of the old Jewish market.

View of Toledo Cathedral
Dominating the city skyline is the Gothic tower at the west end of the nave. The best view of the cathedral, and the city, is from the parador (see p560).

The belfry in the tower contains a heavy bell known as *La Gorda* ("the Fat One").

The Puerta de Mollete, on the west façade, is the main entrance to the cathedral. From this door, *mollete*, or soft bread, was distributed to the poor.

★ Monstrance
In the Treasury is the 16th-century Gothic silver monstrance, over 3 m (10 ft) high. It is carried through the streets of Toledo during the Corpus Christi celebrations (see p369).

STAR FEATURES

★ Monstrance

★ Transparente

★ High Altar Reredos

★ Choir

★ Transparente
This Baroque altarpiece of marble, jasper and bronze, by Narciso Tomé, is illuminated by an ornate skylight. It stands out from the mainly Gothic interior.

VISITORS' CHECKLIST

Calle Arco Palacio 2. ☎ (925) 22
22 41. ◯ Jun–Sep: 7:45am–
1pm & 3:30–7:30pm daily, Oct–
May: 7:45am–1pm & 3:30–
6:30pm daily. ✝ 9am, 11am,
3pm, 6pm, 7pm daily (and noon
& 1pm Sun). **Choir, Treasury,
Sacristy and Chapterhouse**
◯ Jun–Sep: 10:30am–1pm &
3:30–7:30pm daily (Oct–May:
until 6:30pm). ⊘ ♿

Capilla de Santiago

The Capilla de San Ildefonso contains the superb Plateresque tomb of bishop Alonso Carrillo de Albornoz.

Chapterhouse
Above 16th-century frescoes by Juan de Borgoña is this multicoloured Mudéjar ceiling, unique in the city.

Puerta de los Leones

★ High Altar Reredos
The polychrome reredos, one of the most beautiful in Spain, depicts scenes from Christ's life.

The Puerta del Pardón, or Door of Mercy, has a tympanum decorated with religious characters.

The Capilla Mozárabe has a beautiful Renaissance ironwork grille, carved by Juan Francés in 1524.

★ Choir
The carvings on the wooden lower stalls depict scenes of the fall of Granada. The alabaster upper ones show figures from the Old Testament.

Windmills on the ridge above Consuegra, overlooking the plains of La Mancha

Tembleque ⓯

Toledo. 🏘 *2,500.* 🚌 *Plaza Mayor 1, (925) 14 55 25.* 🚍 *Wed.* 🎉 *Jesús de Nazareno (late Aug).*

THE WELL-PRESERVED timbered Plaza Mayor *(see p23)* at Tembleque dates from the 17th century. It is decorated with the red cross of the Knights Hospitallers, the military order which once ruled the town.

ENVIRONS: Ocaña, 30 km (20 miles) north of Tembleque, centres on the enormous yet elegant, late 18th-century brick *plaza mayor.* It is of the largest squares in Spain, after those in Madrid and Salamanca.

Consuegra ⓰

Toledo. 🏘 *9,600.* 🚌 🚍 *Molino de Viento Volero, (925) 47 57 31.* 🚍 *Sat.* 🎉 *La Rosa de Azafrán (late Oct).*

CONSUEGRA'S ELEVEN windmills *(see p23)* and ruined castle stand on a ridge above the town, overlooking the plains of La Mancha. One windmill has working machinery which is set in motion every year during the town's festival to celebrate the autumn harvest of a colourful local crop: saffron *(see p320).* During the fiesta, pickers compete to see who can strip petals from the saffron crocus the fastest.

ENVIRONS: About 4 km (2.5 miles) along the road to **Urda** is a ruined Roman dam. An old restaurant *(see p598)* at **Puerto Lápice**, off the NIV 20 km (13 miles) south of Consuegra, claims to be the inn in which Don Quixote was "knighted" by the indulgent landlord.

Campo de Criptana ⓱

Ciudad Real. 🏘 *14,500.* 🚌 🚍 🛈 *Calle Barbero 1, (926) 56 22 31.* 🚍 *Tue.* 🎉 *Virgen de Criptana (17 Apr).*

THE REMAINING TEN windmills of what was originally La Mancha's largest collection – 32 – stand on a hillcrest above wheat plains. Three date back to the 16th century and have their original machinery intact. One windmill is the tourist information office. Another four contain museums of local life.

ENVIRONS: More windmills stand above nearby **Alcázar de San Juan** and **Mota del Cuervo**, a good place to buy *queso Manchego*, La Mancha sheep's cheese *(see p321).*

El Toboso ⓲

Toledo. 🏘 *2,200.* 🛈 *Plaza de Juan Carlos I, (925) 19 73 75.* 🚍 *Wed.* 🎉 *San Agustín (27–30 Aug).*

OF ALL THE villages of La Mancha claiming links to Don Quixote, El Toboso has the clearest ties. It was chosen by Cervantes as the birthplace of Dulcinea, Don Quixote's sweetheart. The **Casa de Dulcinea**, the home of Doña Ana Martínez Zarco, on whom the character of Dulcinea was allegedly based, has been refurbished for visitors in its original 16th-century style.

The village was considered to be of such cultural importance that the French army is said to have refused to attack it during the War of Independence *(see pp58–9).*

🏛 **Casa de Dulcinea**
📞 *(925) 19 72 88.* ⏰ *Tue–Sun.* 📷

Belmonte ⓳

Cuenca. 🏘 *2,600.* 🚌 🛈 *Plaza del Caudillo 1, (967) 17 00 08.* 🚍 *Mon.* 🎉 *San Bartolomé (late Aug), Virgen de Gracia (second week of Sep).*

BELMONTE'S MAGNIFICENT 15th-century **castle** *(see p326)* is one of the best preserved in the region. It was built by Juan Pacheco, Marquis of Villena, after Enrique IV gave him the town in 1456. Inside it has decorative carved coffered ceilings, and Mudéjar plasterwork. The **collegiate church** is especially

Belmonte's splendid 15th-century castle

remarkable for its richly decorated chapels and Gothic choir stalls, which were brought here from Cuenca cathedral *(see p367)*. There is also outstanding ironwork, a Renaissance reredos and the font at which the Golden Age poet Fray Luis de León (1527–91), was baptized.

ENVIRONS: Two villages near Belmonte also flourished under the Marquis of Villena. The church at **Villaescusa de Haro**, 6 km (4 miles) to the northeast, has an outstanding 16th-century reredos. **San Clemente**, some 40 km (25 miles) further southeast, clusters around two near-perfect Renaissance squares. There is a Gothic alabaster cross in the Iglesia de Santiago Apóstol.

🏰 **Castillo de Belmonte**
⬜ *daily.* 🖼️

The castle of Alarcón, which has been converted into a parador

Alarcón ⓴

Cuenca. 🏘️ *230.* ℹ️ *Plaza Infante Don Juan Manuel 1, (969) 33 03 54.* 📅 *Cristo de la Fé (14 Sep).*

PERFECTLY PRESERVED, the fortified village of Alarcón guards a narrow loop of the Río Júcar from on top of a rock. As you drive through its defences, you may have the impression of entering a film-set for a medieval epic.

The village dates back to the 8th century. It became a key military base for the Reconquest *(see pp50–51)* and was recaptured from the Moors by Alfonso VIII in 1184 following a nine-month siege. It was later acquired by the Marquis

of Villena. Alarcón has dramatic walls and three defensive precincts. The small, triangular **castle**, high above the river, has been turned into a parador *(see p558)*, preserving much of its medieval atmosphere.

Two churches in the village are worth visiting. The **Iglesia de Santa María** is a lovely Renaissance church, with a fine portico and an altarpiece attributed to the Berruguete school. The nearby **Iglesia de Santísima Trinidad** is in Plateresque style *(see p21)*.

Alcalá del Júcar ㉑

Albacete. 🏘️ *200.* ℹ️ *Calle Pósito 1, (967) 47 30 01.* 📅 *Sun (Apr–Oct).* 📅 *San Lorenzo (7–15 Aug).*

WHERE THE RÍO JÚCAR runs through the chalk hills to the northeast of Albacete, it cuts a deep, winding gorge,

The chalk cliffs of Alcalá del Júcar, honeycombed with tunnels

the Hoz de Júcar, along which you can drive for a stretch of 40 km (25 miles). Alcalá del Júcar is dramatically sited on the side of a spur of rock jutting out into the gorge. The town is a warren of steep alleys and flights of steps. At the top of the town, below the castle, houses have been extended by digging caves into the soft rock. Some of these have been transformed into tunnels cut from one side of the spur to the other.

ENVIRONS: To the west, the gorge runs past fertile orchards to the Baroque **Ermita de San Lorenzo**. Further on is the picturesque village of **Jorquera**, which was an independent state for a brief period during the Middle Ages, refusing to be ruled by the crown. It retains its Arab walls. A collection of shields is on display in the Casa del Corregidor.

DON QUIXOTE'S LA MANCHA

Cervantes *(see p315)* doesn't specify where his hero was born but several places are mentioned in the novel. Don Quixote is knighted in an inn in Puerto Lápice, believing it to be a castle. His sweetheart, Dulcinea, lives in El Toboso. The windmills he tilts at, imagining them to be giants, are thought to be those at Campo de Criptana. Another adventure takes place in the Cueva de Montesinos *(see p379)*.

Illustration from a 19th-century edition of *Don Quixote*

Albacete ❷

Albacete. 🏠 160,000. ✈ 🚆 🚌 🖈
Calle del Tinte 2, (967) 58 05 22. 🖴
Tue. 🎇 Virgen de los Llanos (8 Sep).

DESPITE BEING LABELLED one of Spain's least interesting cities, this provincial capital is not without its attractions. The main one is the excellent **Museo Provincial**, which has exhibits ranging from Iberian sculptures and unique Roman amber and ivory dolls to 20th-century paintings. The city's **cathedral**, begun in 1515, has a Renaissance altarpiece.

Albacete is also renowned for its daggers and jackknives, which have been crafted here since Muslim times, and the agricultural and trade fair, held each September.

🏛 Museo Provincial
Parque Abelardo Sánchez. 📞 (967) 22 83 07. 🗓 daily. 🏷 ♿

Restored castle of Almansa, overlooking the town

ENVIRONS: Chinchilla de Monte Aragón, 12 km (7 miles) to the southeast, has a well-preserved old quarter around a main square. Above the town is the picturesque shell of its 15th-century castle.

Almansa, 70 km (43 miles) further east, is dominated by another imposing castle, which is of Moorish origin.

Alcaraz ❷

Albacete. 🏠 1,900. 🖈 Plaza Mayor 1, (967) 38 00 02. 🖴 Wed. 🎇 Rosario de Cortes (1 May), Feria (4–9 Sep).

AN IMPORTANT ARAB and Christian stronghold, Alcaraz's military power waned after the Reconquest but its economy flourished around its (now defunct) carpet-making industry.

Standing in the attractive Renaissance Plaza Mayor are the "twin towers" of **Tardón** and **Trinidad**, and an 18th-century commodity exchange,

Sierra de Alcaraz ❷

WHERE THE SIERRAS of Segura and Alcaraz push northwards into the southeastern plains of La Mancha, they form spectacular mountains, broken up by dramatic gorges and fertile valleys. The source of the Río Mundo is a favourite beauty spot. Nearby Riópar, perched on the side of the mountain, has a 15th-century parish church. Among the less-explored villages, Letur, Ayna, Yeste and Liétor are especially picturesque. Their narrow, winding streets and craft traditions clearly reflect their Muslim origins.

Source of the Río Mundo ⑤
The river begins as a waterfall, inside the Cueva de Los Chorros, and tumbles down a dramatic cliff face into a bubbling spring at the bottom.

0 kilometres   5

0 miles   5

KEY

🚃 Tour route

= Other roads

🔆 Viewpoint

Yeste ④
The village of Yeste, which stands at the foot of the Sierra de Ardal, is crowned by a hilltop Arab castle. It was reconquered under Fernando III, and was later ruled by the Order of Santiago.

the **Lonja del Corregidor**, with Plateresque decoration. The square is surrounded by lively, narrow streets with traditional houses. On the outskirts of the town are the castle ruins and the one surviving arch of a Gothic aqueduct. Alcaraz also makes a good base for touring the sierras of Alcaraz and Segura.

The twin towers of Tardón and Trinidad on Alcaraz's main square

Lagunas de Ruidera ㉕

Cuidad Real. 🚌 *Ossa de Montiel.* ℹ️ *Ruidera, (926) 52 81 16.*

ONCE NICKNAMED "The Mirrors of La Mancha", the 16 interconnected lakes which make up the Parque Natural de las Lagunas de Ruidera stretch for 20 km (12 miles) through a valley. They allegedly take their name from a story in *Don Quixote (see p377)* in which a certain Mistress Ruidera, her daughters and her nieces, are said to have been turned into lakes by a magician.

Although La Mancha's falling water table has led to a decline in the amount of water in the lakes, they are still worth visiting for their wealth of wildlife, which includes great and little bustards, herons and many types of duck. The wildlife has recently come under threat due to the increasing number of tourists, and the development

One of the lakes in the Parque Natural de las Lagunas de Ruidera

of holiday chalets on the lakes' shores. In Ruidera village there is an information centre for the park. Near one of the lakes, the Laguna de San Pedro, is the **Cueva de Montesinos**, a deep, explorable cave which is the setting for an episode in *Don Quixote*.

To the northwest, the lakes link up with the Embalse de Peñarroya reservoir, which is overlooked by a castle.

Ayna ①
The village of Ayna is set deep in a gorge of the Río Mundo. There are spectacular views over the countryside from the Mirador del Diablo.

Foothills of the Sierra de Alcaraz

Liétor ②
Worth visiting in this small hillside village are the Gothic Ermita de Belén and the Iglesia de Santiago, with a *trompe l'oeil* altarpiece.

TIPS FOR DRIVERS

Tour length: 280 km (175 miles).
Stopping-off points: All of these villages have bars and restaurants. Alternatively, there are numerous places along the way to stop for a picnic.

Letur ③
With its pretty whitewashed Jewish quarter, this is perhaps the most picturesque village in the area.

Villanueva de los Infantes ❷

Ciudad Real. 🏘 6,000. 🚌
ℹ Plaza Mayor 3, (926) 36 00 24.
🗓 Fri. 🎪 Ferias (late Aug), Virgen de Antigua (8 Sep), Santo Tomás (18 Sep).

VILLANUEVA'S OLD TOWN, which centres on the graceful Neo-Classical Plaza Mayor, is one of the most attractive in La Mancha. Many buildings on the square have wooden balconies and arcades. Also on the square is the **Iglesia de San Andrés**, which has a Renaissance façade. Inside are a Baroque altarpiece and organ, as well as the now empty tomb of the Golden Age author Francisco de Quevedo. He lived and died in the **Convento de los Domínicos**.

ENVIRONS: The village of **San Carlos del Valle**, 16 km (10 miles) to the northwest, has a perfectly preserved 18th-century square and galleried houses built of rust-red stone.

Valdepeñas ❷

Ciudad Real. 🏘 26,000. 🚌 🚍 ℹ
Pl de España, (926) 31 25 52. 🗓 Thu.
🎪 Grape Harvest (first week of Sep).

VALDEPEÑAS is the capital of La Mancha's vast wine region, the world's largest expanse of vineyards, producing vast quantities of red wine (see pp192–3). This largely modern town comes alive for its September wine festival. In the network of older streets around the café-lined Plaza de España are the **Iglesia de la Asunción** and the municipal museum.

Valdepeñas has over 30 bodegas which can be visited. One of them, **Bodega Museo**, has some of the few remaining traditional cellars, with huge earthenware jars, *tinajas*.

🍷 **Bodega Museo**
Calle El Caisto 102. 📞 (926) 31 28 49.
🕐 daily.

Courtyard of the Palacio del Viso in Viso del Marqués

Viso del Marqués ❷

Ciudad Real. 🏘 3,300. 🚌 ℹ Plaza de la Dretania 8, (926) 33 60 01. 🗓 Tue. 🎪 San Andrés (second Sun of May), Feria (24–8 Jul).

THE SMALL VILLAGE of Viso del Marqués in La Mancha is the unlikely setting of the **Palacio del Viso**, a grand Renaissance building. This mansion was commissioned in 1564 by the Marquis of Santa Cruz, the admiral of the fleet which defeated the Turks at Lepanto in 1571 (see p55). One of the main features of the house is a Classical patio. Inside, the principal rooms have been decorated with Italian frescoes.

ENVIRONS: About 25 km (16 miles) to the northeast of Viso del Marqués is Spain's oldest bullring at **Las Virtudes**. Square and galleried, it was built in 1641 next to a 14th-century church, which has a Churrigueresque altarpiece.

🏛 **Palacio del Viso**
Plaza del Pradillo 12. 📞 (926) 33 60 08. 🕐 Tue–Sun.

Calatrava la Nueva ❷

Carretera de Calzada de Calatrava.
📞 (926) 69 31 19. 🕐 Tue–Sun.

MAGNIFICENT in its isolated hilltop setting, the ruined castle-monastery of Calatrava la Nueva is reached by a stretch of original medieval road.

The castle was founded in 1217 by the Knights of Calatrava, Spain's first military-religious order (see p50), to be used as their headquarters. The complex is of huge proportions, with a double patio and a church with a triple nave. The church has been restored and is illuminated by a beautiful rose window above the entrance.

Expanse of vineyards near Valdepeñas

Calatrava la Nueva castle, dominating the plains of La Mancha

After the Reconquest, the building continued to be used as a monastery until it was abandoned in 1802 following earthquake damage.

Opposite the castle are the ruins of a Muslim frontier fortress, **Salvatierra**, which was captured from the Moors by the Order of Calatrava in the 12th century.

Almagro ㉚

Ciudad Real. 🏘 *10,000.* 🚉 🚌
🛈 *Calle Bernardas 2, (926) 86 07 17.*
🗓 *Wed.* 🎉 *Virgen de las Nieves (5 Aug), San Bartolomé (25 Aug).*

ALMAGRO was disputed during the Reconquest, until the Order of Calatrava captured it and built the castle of Calatrava la Nueva to the southwest of the town. The rich architectural heritage of the atmospheric old town is partly the legacy of the Fugger brothers, the Habsburgs' bankers who settled in nearby Almadén during the 16th century.

The town's main attraction is its colonnaded stone plaza, with characteristic enclosed, green balconies. On one side is a unique 17th-century courtyard-theatre – the **Corral de Comedias** – the site of a drama festival which is held every August in honour of St Bartholomew.

Other monuments worth seeing include the Fuggers' Renaissance warehouse and former university, and also the parador *(see p558)*.

ENVIRONS: To the northwest is **Ciudad Real**, founded by Alfonso X the Learned in 1255. Among its sights are the cathedral, the Iglesia de San Pedro, and the Mudéjar gateway, the Puerta de Toledo.

Raised walkway in the Parque Nacional de Las Tablas de Daimiel

Tablas de Daimiel ㉛

Ciudad Real. 🚉 *Daimiel.* 🛈 *Daimiel, (926) 69 31 18.*

THE MARSHY WETLANDS of the Tablas de Daimiel, northeast of Ciudad Real, are the feeding and nesting grounds of a huge range of aquatic and migratory birds. Despite being national parkland since 1973, they have become an ecological *cause célèbre* due to the growing threat from the area's lowering water table. This has affected the area's wildlife in recent years.

One corner of the park is open to the public, with walking routes to islets and observation towers. Breeding birds here include great crested grebes and mallards. Otters and red foxes are among the mammals which have traditionally inhabited the park.

Valle de Alcudia ㉜

Ciudad Real. 🚉 *Fuencaliente.*
🛈 *Ciudad Real, (926) 47 00 01.*

ALCUDIA'S LUSH lowlands, which border the Sierra Morena foothills to the south, are among central Spain's most unspoiled countryside. The area is used largely as pasture land. In late autumn it starts to fill up with sheep, whose milk is used to make the excellent farmhouse cheese for which the valley is known.

The mountain village of **Fuencaliente** has thermal baths that open in the summer. Further north, **Almadén** is the site of a large mercury mine. **Chillón**, to the northwest, has a late Gothic church.

Small isolated farmhouse in the fertile Valle de Alcudia

EXTREMADURA

CÁCERES · BADAJOZ

O F ALL THE SPANISH REGIONS, *far-flung Extremadura – "the land beyond the River Douro" – is the most remote from the modern world. Green sierras run southwards through rolling hills strewn with boulders. Forests and reservoirs shelter rare wildlife. The towns, with their atmospheric old quarters, have a romantic, slow-paced charm. In winter, storks nest on their spires and chimneys.*

The finest monuments in Extremadura are the ruins of ancient settlements scattered across the region. Many are exceptionally well preserved. Some of Spain's finest Roman architecture is to be seen in Mérida, capital of the Roman province of Lusitania, which has an aqueduct and a magnificent theatre. Other Classical remains dot the countryside – notably a Tartessan temple at Cancho Ruano and a Roman bridge at Alcántara. Smaller finds are displayed in Badajoz museum.

Modern development has bypassed the old town of Cáceres, whose ancient walls, winding streets and nobles' mansions are still marvellously intact. Trujillo, Zafra and Jerez de los Caballeros have medieval and Renaissance quarters; and there are small, splendidly decorated cathedrals in Plasencia, Coria and Badajoz. The castles and stout walls of Alburquerque and Olivenza mark frontiers embattled through history. Many cathedrals and monasteries were built in the troubled times during and after the Reconquest by the large military-religious orders which then governed the region for the crown.

Extremadura was the birthplace of many conquistadors and emigrants to the New World; the riches they found there financed a surge of building. Guadalupe monastery, in the eastern hills, is the most splendid monument to the region's New World ties.

View over the rooftops of the historic town of Cáceres

◁ An old stone cross in the woods near Yuste, a Hieronymite monastery founded in 1404

Exploring Extremadura

EXTREMADURA IS IDEAL for nature lovers and those who want to get off the beaten track to discover the old Spain. It offers beautiful driving and walking country in its northern sierras and valleys, and exceptional wildlife in Monfragüe Natural Park. Some of the best Roman ruins in Spain can be found throughout Extremadura, especially in the regional capital, Mérida. The walled old town of Cáceres, with its well-preserved Jewish quarter, and the monasteries of Guadalupe and Yuste, are other historic sights not to be missed. To the south, the Templar towns in the Sierra Morena, such as Jerez de los Caballeros, have fine old buildings, while the small, historic towns of Coria, Zafra and Llerena all make charming bases for excursions.

SIGHTS AT A GLANCE

Orchards near Hervás in the
Valle del Ambroz

Cattle grazing in the fields near Cáceres

Ávila
Segovia
TORNAVACAS

MONASTERIO
DE YUSTE
6

ENCIA

TALAYUELA

Tiétar

C511

NV

Madrid

Embalse de Valdecañas

RQUE NATURAL
MONFRAGÜE

Tajo

TRUJILLO

8 GUADALUPE

Madrid

C401

LOGROSÁN

Embalse
de Cíjara

N502

C711

Embalse de
García de Sola

HERRERA DEL DUQUE

N430

N430

VILLANUEVA
DE LA SERENA

Embalse de Orellana

C413

Ciudad Real

N502

Embalse de la Serena

Zújar

CANCHO RUANO
17

C420

Zújar

Córdoba

AZUAGA

kilometres 25

miles 15

KEY

Motorway

Major road

Minor road

Scenic route

River

Viewpoint

SEE ALSO

• *Where to Stay* pp560–61

• *Restaurants and Bars* pp598–600

GETTING AROUND

Extremadura is not very well connected by air or rail services. Badajoz has the only (domestic) airport in the region, while the region's main rail link is the line from Madrid to Cáceres, Mérida and Badajoz. It is generally much more convenient to travel by car, the principal road routes being the NV motorway from Navalmoral to Badajoz and the N630 between Plasencia and Mérida. Coach services are infrequent, and in many areas, such as the northern sierras, they are non-existent.

Roman bridge crossing the Río Guadiana at Mérida

Beehives, a common sight in Las Hurdes

Las Hurdes ❶

Cáceres. 🚉 Pinofranqueado, Caminomorisco, Nuñomoral.
🛈 Pinofranqueado, (927) 67 41 81.

LAS HURDES' slate mountains, goats and beehives were memorably caught in the 1932 Luis Buñuel film, *Tierra sin Pan* (*Land without Bread*). The area's legendary poverty disappeared with the arrival of roads in the 1950s, but the black slopes, riverbeds and hill terraces remain.

From Pinofranqueado or Vegas de Coria, roads climb past picturesque "black" villages like Batequilla, Fragosa, and El Gasco, which sits under an extinct volcano. The more developed **Lower Hurdes** area, crossed by the Río Hurdano and the main access route (C512), is dotted with camp sites and restaurants serving traditional cuisine.

Sierra de Gata ❷

Cáceres. 🚉 Cáceres. 🛈 Moraleja, (927) 51 50 75.

THERE ARE 40 hamlets in the Sierra de Gata, scattered between olive groves, orchards and fields. The area has retained its old-fashioned rural charm by conserving hunters' paths for woodland walking, and its local crafts, most notably lace-making. In the lowland towns of Valverde de Fresno and Acebo, the local dialect, *chapurriau*, is still spoken. On the higher slopes, **Eljas**, **Gata** and **Villamiel** have ruins of medieval fortresses. The old granite houses have carved family crests on the front and distinctive outside staircases.

Coat of arms on a house front in Acebo

Hervás ❸

Cáceres. 🚹 4,000. 🛈 Plaza de González Fiori 6, (927) 48 10 45.
🚌 Sat. 🎉 Nuestra Señora de la Asunción (14–17 Aug).

SITTING AT THE TOP of the wide Valle del Ambroz, Hervás is known for its medieval Jewish quarter, with its whitewashed houses. The tiny streets, dotted with taverns and craft workshops, slope down towards the Río Ambroz. Just off the main plaza is the **Museo Pérez Comendador-Leroux**, named after the town's noted 20th-century sculptor, whose work is exhibited here.

The next town up towards the Béjar pass is **Baños de Montemayor**, whose name comes from its sulphurous baths, which date back to Roman times. These were revived in the early 1900s and are open to the public in summer. At **Caparra**, southwest of Hervás, a triumphal arch stands on the Roman road, the Vía de la Plata (*see p334*).

🏛 **Museo Pérez Comendador-Leroux**
Calle Asensio Nelia 5. 🇨 (927) 48 16 55. 🕐 Tue–Sun. ⬤ public hols.

Traditional lace-making in one of the villages of the Sierra de Gata

Ancient wall and olive groves in the Valle del Ambroz

Coria ❹

Cáceres. ⚑ 11,600. 🚌 🛈 *Avenida de Extremadura 39, (927) 50 13 51.* 🗓 *Thu.* 🎉 *Día de la Virgen (week after Easter), San Juan (24 Jun).*

CORIA'S WALLED old town, perched above the Río Alagón, boasts a Gothic-Renaissance **cathedral** with rich Plateresque carving, and the 16th-century **Convento de la Madre de Dios**, which has a fine Renaissance cloister.

Forming part of the town walls, which are a Muslim and medieval patchwork, are an impressive castle tower, and four gates, two of which date back to Roman times. The gates are closed during the fiesta of San Juan in June for night-time bull-running. Situated below the old town is the **Puente Seco**, a Roman bridge over the river.

Plasencia ❺

Cáceres. ⚑ 40,000. 🚌 🚉 🛈 *Calle del Rey 8, (927) 42 21 59.* 🗓 *Tue.* 🎉 *Ferias (8–11 Jun).*

PLASENCIA'S golden-grey walls, rising above a curve in the banks of the Río Jerte, tell of the town's past as a military bastion. Nowadays Plasencia is best known for its Tuesday market, dating back to the 12th century, which is held in the main square.

A short walk away are the town's two cathedrals, which are built back-to-back. The 16th-century **Catedral Nueva** has a Baroque organ and carved wooden choir stalls. The Romanesque **Catedral Vieja**, next to it, has a museum with works by Ribera, and a late 14th-century Bible.

The nearby **Museo Etnográfico y Textil**, housed in a 14th-century hospital, has displays of crafts and costumes.

The rest of the Jerte valley has pockets of outstanding beauty, such as the **Garganta de los Infiernos**, a nature reserve with dramatic, rushing waterfalls.

🏛 **Museo Etnográfico y Textil**
Calle Trujillo 17. 📞 *(927) 42 18 43.* ⏰ *Wed–Sun.*

Monasterio de Yuste ❻

Cuacos de Yuste (Cáceres). 📞 *(927) 17 21 30.* ⏰ *daily.* 🎟

THE HIERONYMITE monastery of Yuste, where Charles V *(see p55)* retired from public life in 1556 and died two years later, is remarkable for its simplicity and its lovely setting in the wooded valley of La Vera.

The church's Gothic and Plateresque cloisters and the austere palace are open to visitors. Just below it is **Cuacos de Yuste**, the most unspoiled of La Vera's old villages, where peppers, for making paprika, hang outside the houses.

Paprika peppers hanging up around a door in Cuacos de Yuste

A *Carantoña*, during the fiesta of St Sebastian, Acehuche

EXTREMADURA'S FIESTAS

Encamisá *(16 Jan),* Navalvillar de Pela (Badajoz). Riders on horseback parade around town, where bonfires are set alight for the occasion.
Carantoñas *(20 Jan),* Acehuche (Cáceres). During the fiesta of St Sebastian, the *Carantoñas* take to the streets of the town dressed up in animal skins, with their faces covered by grotesque masks designed to make them look terrifying. They represent the wild beasts which are said to have left the saint unharmed.
Pero Palo *(Carnival Feb/Mar),* Villanueva de la Vera (Cáceres). In this ancient ritual a wooden figure dressed in a suit and representing the devil is paraded around the streets and then destroyed – except for the head, which is reused the year after.
Los Empalaos *(Maundy Thursday),* Valverde de la Vera (Cáceres). Men do penance by walking in procession through the town with their arms outstretched and bound to small tree trunks.
Los Escobazos *(7 Dec),* Jarandilla de la Vera (Cáceres). At night, the town is illuminated by bonfires in the streets, and torches are made from burning brooms.

Parque Natural de Monfragüe **❼**

Cáceres. ⬛ *Villareal de San Carlos.* ℹ
Villareal de San Carlos, (927) 45 51 04.

T O THE SOUTH of Plasencia, rolling hills drop from scrubby peaks through wild olive, cork and holm oak woods to the dammed Tagus and Tiétar river valleys. In 1979, some 500 sq km (200 sq miles) of these hills were granted natural park status in order to safeguard the area's outstandingly varied wildlife species, which includes a large proportion of Spain's protected bird species *(see pp324–5)*.

The many species of bird which breed here include the black-winged kite, black vulture and, most notably, the black stork, as well as more

Birdwatchers in the Parque Natural de Monfragüe

common aquatic species on and near the water. Mammals living here include the lynx, red deer and wild boar. At **Villareal de San Carlos**, a hamlet founded in the 18th century, there is parking and an information centre which gives out maps of walks. An ideal time to visit the park is September, when many migrating birds stop off here.

Guadalupe **❽**

Cáceres. 🏘 *2,500.* ⬛ ℹ *Plaza de Santa María de Guadalupe 1, (927) 15 41 28.* ⬛ *Wed.* 🎎 *San Blas (3 Feb), Cruz de Mayo (first Sun of May).*

T HIS VILLAGE grew around the magnificent Hieronymite **Monasterio de Guadalupe**, founded in 1340. In the main square there are shops that sell handmade ceramics and beaten copper cauldrons, both traditional monastic crafts, now made as souvenirs.

The turreted towers of the monastery, which is set in a deep wooded valley, help give it a fairy-tale air. According to legend, a shepherd found a charred wooden image of the Virgin Mary here in the early 14th century. The monastery grew to splendour under royal patronage, acquiring schools of

grammar and medicine, three hospitals, an important pharmacy and one of the largest libraries in Spain.

Adjoining the monastery is a 16th-century *hospedería* (guest house) where royalty once stayed. This is now a hotel run by the monks *(see p560)*. The old hospital has been converted into a parador. In the car park is a plaque commemorating Spain's first human dissection, which took place here in 1402.

By the time the New World was discovered, the monastery was very important and in 1496 was the site of the baptism of some of the first native Caribbeans brought to Europe by Columbus *(see pp52–3)*.

The monastery was sacked by Napoleon in 1808 but was refounded by Franciscans a century later. Today it is still a

major centre of Catholicism, visited every year by thousands of pilgrims from around the Spanish-speaking world.

Guided tours (in Spanish only) begin in the museums of illuminated manuscripts, embroidered vestments and fine art. They continue to the choir and the magnificent Baroque sacristy, nicknamed "the Spanish Sistine Chapel", because of Zurbarán's portraits of monks hanging on the highly decorated walls. For many, the chance to touch or kiss the tiny Virgin's dress in the *camarín* (chamber) behind the altar is the highlight of the tour. Finally, you can linger in the 16th-century Gothic cloister which has two tiers of horse-shoe arches around an ornate central pavilion. The church, with a magnificent 16th-century iron grille partly forged from the chains of freed slaves, may be visited separately.

ENVIRONS: The surrounding **Villuercas** and **Los Ibores** sierras, where herbs were once picked for the monastery pharmacy, have good woodland walks. The road south also gives access to the pasture lands of **La Serena**, a vital breeding ground for birds of the steppe *(see pp324–5)*, and the huge reservoir of **Cíjara**, surrounded by a game reserve.

Monasterio de Guadalupe, overlooking the town

Trujillo ❾

Cáceres. 🏠 9,000. 🚌 ℹ️ *Plaza Mayor, (927) 32 26 77.* 🚍 *Thu.* 🧀 *Feria del Queso (Apr/May), San Miguel (Sep).*

WHEN THE PLAZA MAYOR of the medieval hilltop town of Trujillo is floodlit at night, it is one of the most beautiful squares in Spain. By day, there is much to visit, including the **Iglesia de Santa María la Mayor**, on one of the town's winding streets, which contains various sarcophagi.

At the top of the hill there is an Islamic fortress, which defended the town against the Christian advance during the Reconquest *(see pp50–51)*, but in 1232 it was retaken by the forces of Fernando III. Trujillo was the birthplace of

Statue of Francisco Pizarro in Trujillo's main square

several conquistadors, most notably Francisco Pizarro, who conquered Peru *(see p54)*, of whom there is a statue in the main square. His brother, Hernando Pizarro, founded

the **Palacio del Marqués de la Conquista**, one of several palaces and convents built with New World wealth. It has an elaborate corner window with carved stone heads of the Pizarro brothers and their Inca wives. The beautiful 16th-century **Palacio de Orellana-Pizarro** was built by Francisco de Orellana, the explorer of Ecuador and the Amazon. It has a fine Plateresque patio.

Once a year, in late April or early May, gourmets descend on the town for its renowned week-long cheese fair.

🏛️ **Palacio del Marqués de la Conquista**
Plaza Mayor. ⏰ *daily.*
🏛️ **Palacio de Orellana-Pizarro**
Plaza de Don Juan Tena. 📞 *(927) 32 11 62.* ⏰ *daily.*

The Virgin of Guadalupe, her face blackened by smoke from smouldering lamps, is worshipped by pilgrims from around the world. She is kept in the camarín, *and dressed up for feast days. On her lap sits the infant Jesus.*

Gothic cloister

Embroidery museum

Painting and sculpture museum

Church

The chapterhouse has 87 illuminated manuscripts by the monks of Guadalupe.

The sacristy contains Zurbarán's Father Gonzalo de Illescas at Work.

Street-by-Street: Cáceres ⓪

A FTER ALFONSO IX OF LEON conquered Cáceres in 1227, its growing prosperity as a free trade town attracted merchants, and later aristocracy, to settle here. They rivalled each other with stately homes and palaces fortified by watchtowers, most of which Isabel and Fernando, the reigning monarchs *(see pp52–3)*, ordered to be demolished in 1476 to halt the continual jostling for power. Today's serene Renaissance town dates from the late 15th and 16th centuries, after which economic decline set in. Untouched by the wars of the 19th and 20th centuries, Cáceres became Spain's first listed heritage city in 1949.

★ **Casa de los Golfines de Abajo**
The ornamental façade of this 15th-century mansion displays the shield of one of the town's leading families, the Golfines.

Casa y Torre de Carvajal
This typical Renaissance mansion has a 13th-century round Arab tower and a peaceful garden with a patio.

PLAZA DE SANTA MARÍA

To tourist information

★ **Iglesia de Santa María**
Facing the Palacio Episcopal, this Gothic-Renaissance church has a beautiful cedarwood reredos and a 15th-century crucifix – the Cristo Negro *(Black Christ).*

Arco de la Estrella
This low-arched gateway was built by Manuel Churriguera in 1726. It leads through the city walls from the Plaza Mayor into the old town and is flanked by a 15th-century watchtower.

```
0 metres          50
0 yards           50
```

KEY

– – – Suggested route

Barrio de San Antonio

This quaint old Jewish quarter, with narrow streets of whitewashed houses restored to their original condition, takes its name from the nearby hermitage of St Anthony.

VISITORS' CHECKLIST

Cáceres. 90,000. Avenida de Alemania, (927) 23 50 61. Avenida de Alemania, (927) 23 25 50. Plaza Mayor 37, (927) 24 63 47. Wed. Las Candelas (Feb), San Jorge (23 Apr). **Museo Provincial** Tue–Sun.

★ Museo Provincial

Housed in the Casa de las Veletas, this museum has contemporary art and archaeology from the region.

The Convento de San Pablo sells delicious *yemas* (candied egg yolks) made by the nuns.

Casa y Torre de la Cigüeña
The slender, battlemented tower of the House of the Stork was allowed to remain after 1476 because of the owner's loyalty to Isabel. It is now owned by the army.

The Iglesia de San Mateo, built between the 14th and 17th centuries, is one of Cáceres' earliest churches.

Casa del Sol (Casa de los Solis)
The façade of this elegant Renaissance building, once home of the Solis family, is emblazoned with a sun (sol) motif.

STAR SIGHTS

★ **Casa de los Golfines de Abajo**

★ **Iglesia de Santa María**

★ **Museo Provincial**

Arroyo de la Luz ⑪

Cáceres. 🏠 *6,900.* 🚌 🛈 *Plaza de la Constitución 16, (927) 27 00 02.* 🔼 *Thu.* 🎭 *Día de la Patrona (Easter Mon).*

THE SMALL TOWN of Arroyo de la Luz is home to one of the artistic masterpieces of Extremadura. Its **Iglesia de la Asunción**, completed in 1565, contains a spectacular altarpiece which incorporates 20 paintings by the mystical religious painter Luis de Morales.

ENVIRONS: The area has a large population of white storks *(see p325)*. Nearby **Malpartida** is home to the largest colony, whose nests adorn the church roof. There are some good picnic spots in the surrounding countryside.

Alterpiece in the Iglesia de la Asunción, Arroyo de la Luz

Alcántara ⑫

Cáceres. 🏠 *1,900.* 🚌 🛈 *Plaza de España 1, (927) 39 01 27.* 🔼 *Tue.* 🎭 *Feria (15–17 Apr), San Pedro (19 Oct).*

ALCÁNTARA has two important sights. One is the drystone **Roman bridge**, 71 m (233 ft) above the Tagus river, which has an honorary arch and a temple. The other is the ruined **Convento de San Benito**. This was built as the headquarters of the Knights of the Order of Alcántara, during the 16th century, and was sacked by Napoleon. Its surviving treasures are in the **Iglesia de Santa María de Almocóvar**.

Walls of the 16th-century Convento de San Benito, Alcántara

Valencia de Alcántara ⑬

Cáceres. 🏠 *6,000.* 🚌 🚌 🛈 *Calle de Hernan Cortes, (927) 58 03 44.* 🔼 *Mon.* 🎭 *Día de los Mayos (1 May).*

THE GOTHIC QUARTER of this hilltop frontier town is given an elegant air by its fountains and shady orange trees. The **Castillo de Buena Piedra**, which was built by the Knights of the Order of Alcántara, now houses a youth hostel. On the outskirts of the town are more than 40 dolmens, or megalithic burial sites.

ENVIRONS: Alburquerque, to the southeast, is sited on a rocky outcrop with a magnificent panoramic view from the ramparts and keep of its castle. Below is the walled old town and the 15th-century Iglesia de Santa María del Mercado.

Mérida ⑭

Badajoz. 🏠 *60,000.* 🚌 🚌 🛈 *Avenida José Álvarez y Saenz de Buruaga, (924) 31 53 53.* 🔼 *Tue.* 🎭 *Fiestas Patronales (10 Dec).*

FOUNDED BY AUGUSTUS in 25 BC, Augusta Emerita grew into the cultural and economic capital of Rome's westernmost province, Lusitania, but lost its eminence under the Moors. Though a small city, Mérida, the capital of Extremadura, has many fine Roman monuments.

The best approach is from the west of town, via the modern suspension bridge over the Río Guadiana, bringing you to the original entrance of the Roman city and Arab fortress.

The city's centrepiece is the **Roman theatre** *(see pp46–7)*. One of the best preserved Roman theatres anywhere, it is still used in summer for the city's drama festival and is part of a larger site with an **amphitheatre** *(anfiteatro)* and gardens. Nearby are the remains of a Roman house, the **Casa del Anfiteatro**, where there are underground galleries and large areas of well-preserved mosaics.

Opposite stands Rafael Moneo's stunning red-brick **Museo Nacional de Arte Romano**. The semicircular arches of its main hall are built to the same height as the city's Los Milagros aqueduct. Off this hall, which features sculptures from the Roman theatre, there are three galleries exhibiting ceramics, mosaics, coins and statuary. There is also an excavated Roman street. Near

Megalithic tomb on the outskirts of Valencia de Alcántara

Mérida's well-preserved Roman theatre, still used as a venue for classical drama

the museum are several other monuments, namely two villas with fine mosaics, and a racecourse (closed for excavation).

A chapel in front of the 3rd century **Iglesia de Santa Eulalia** is dedicated to the child saint who was martyred on this site in Roman times. Towards the centre of the town are the **Templo de Diana** (1st century AD), with tall, fluted columns,

Sculpture of **Emperor Augustus**

and the **Arco de Trajano**. The **Museo de Arte Visigodo** (Museum of Visigothic Art) is in the Convento de Santa Clara, which is situated off the main square. From the huge **Puente de Guadiana** there is a good view of the massive walls of the **Alcazaba**, one of Spain's oldest Moorish buildings (AD 835), whose precinct includes towers, a cistern and more Roman ruins. To the

east of the town stands the **Casa del Mithraeo**, also known as the Casa Romana, with its Pompeiian-style frescoes and superb mosaics.

The magnificent, ruined Los Milagros aqueduct, with its granite and brick arches, are off the N630 towards Cáceres.

🏛 **Museo de Arte Visigodo**
Calle Santa Julia. 📞 *(924) 30 01 06.* ◯ *Tue–Sun.* ● *public hols.*
🏛 **Museo Nacional de Arte Romano**
Calle José Ramón Mélida. 📞 *(924) 31 16 90.* ◯ *Tue–Sun.* 🎫 ♿

MERIDA TOWN CENTRE

Alcazaba ⑦
Amphitheatre ④
Arco de Trajano ⑩
Casa del Anfiteatro ③
Casa del Mithraeo ⑥
Iglesia de Santa Eulalia ①
Museo de Arte Visigodo ⑨
Museo Nacional de Arte Romano ②
Puente de Guadiana ⑧
Roman theatre ⑤
Templo de Diana ⑪

KEY

🚉 Railway station
ℹ Tourist information
✚ Church

0 metres 250
0 yards 250

Badajoz ⓯

Badajoz. 🏠 100,000. ✈ 🚆 🚌
ℹ Plaza de la Libertad 3, (924) 22 27
63. 🚌 Tue & Sun. 🎉 Feria (24 Jun).

BADAJOZ is a plain, modern
city, though it retains traces
of its former importance. It was
a major city under the Moors
but the plundering resulting
from centuries of conflicts with
Portugal, and most recently
the Civil War, robbed Badajoz
of its former splendour.

The Alcazaba now houses
the **Museo Arqueológico**,
which has over 15,000 pieces
from around the province, as
far back as Paleolithic times.
Nearby is the medieval cathedral, with a stunning tiled
cloister and rich interior.

🏛 **Museo Arqueológico**
Pl José Álvarez y Saenz de Buruaga. 📞
(924) 22 23 14. ⏱ Tue–Sun. 🎟 ♿

Olivenza ⓰

Badajoz. 🏠 8,000. 🚌 ℹ Plaza de
España, (924) 49 01 51. 🚌 Sat.
🎉 Muñecas de San Juan (23 Jun).

APORTUGUESE ENCLAVE until
1801, Olivenza has a
colourful hybrid character.
Within the walled town are
the medieval castle, housing
the **Museo Municipal**, a
museum of rural life, and
three churches. **Santa María
del Castillo** has a wonderfully naive family tree of the
Virgin Mary. **Santa María
Magdalena**, with its glorious
spiralling columns, is a fine
example of the 16th-century
Portuguese Manueline style.

Interior of Santa María Magdalena
church, Olivenza

The 16th-century **Santa Casa
de Misericordia** is unmissable
for its blue and white tiled
friezes. In one, God is shown
offering a coat to Adam and
Eve as he banishes them from
the Garden of Eden.

Off the main square is the
Pastelería Fuentes, which
sells técula mécula, a custard
cake it has patented.

🏛 **Museo Municipal**
Plaza de Santamaría. 📞 (924) 49
02 22. ⏱ Tue–Sun. ♿

Cancho Ruano ⓱

Zalamea de la Serena. 📞 (924) 78
00 32. ⏱ daily.

THIS SANCTUARY-PALACE, which
is thought to have been
built under the civilization of
Tartessus (see p45), was discovered in 1978. Excavations
on this small but unique site
have revealed a moated temple
that was rebuilt three times –

many of the walls and slate
floors are still intact. Each
temple was constructed on a
grander scale than the previous one and then burned in
the face of invasion during
the 6th century BC.

Most of the artifacts unearthed, including jewellery, ceramics and furniture, are on
display in the archaeological
museum at Badajoz.

ENVIRONS: A Roman funereal
monument stands next to the
church in nearby **Zalamea de
la Serena**. The town comes
alive during the September
fiestas, when the townsfolk
act out the classic 17th-century
play, The Mayor of Zalamea,
by Calderón de la Barca (see
p30), which was supposedly
based on a local character.
Shops in the town also sell
torta de la Serena, a cheese
made of sheep's milk.

Remains of the Tartessan
sanctuary at Cancho Ruano

Zafra ⓲

Badajoz. 🏠 15,000. 🚆 🚌
ℹ Plaza de España 30, (924) 55 10 36.
🚌 Fri. 🎉 San Miguel (2–8 Oct).

AT THE HEART of this graceful
town, nicknamed "little
Seville" because of its similarity
to the capital of Andalusia,
are two arcaded squares. The
Plaza Grande, the larger of the
two, is the site of the **Iglesia
de la Candelaria**, which has a
Zurbarán altarpiece. Converging on it is the older, 15th-
century **Plaza Chica**, which
used to be the marketplace.
Situated on the nearby Calle

The colourful tiled cloister in the cathedral of Badajoz

Altarpiece by Zurbarán in the Iglesia de la Candelaria at Zafra

Sevilla is the 15th-century Convento de Santa Clara and the **Alcázar de los Duques de Feria**, which is now a parador *(see p561)* with a marble court-yard by Juan de Herrera.

ENVIRONS: Some 25 km (16 miles) to the south, in **Fuente de Cantos**, is the house in which the painter Francisco de Zurbarán was born in 1598.

Jerez de los Caballeros ⑲

Badajoz. 🏠 10,500. 🚌 🚹 Plaza de la Alcazaba, (924) 73 00 11. 🚍 Wed. 🎉 Feria del Jamón (3–5 May), San Bartolomé (24 Aug).

THE HILLSIDE PROFILE of Jerez, which is broken by three Baroque church towers, is one of the most picturesque in Extremadura. This small town is also historically important – Vasco Núñez de Balboa, who discovered the Pacific, was born here. In the **castle**, now

laid out as gardens, knights of the Order of Knights Templar were beheaded in the Torre Sangrienta (Bloody Tower) in 1312. The old quarters of the town grew up around three churches: **San Bartolomé**, its façade studded with glazed ceramics; **San Miguel**, whose brick tower dominates the Plaza de España; and **Santa María de la Encarnación**.

ENVIRONS: Fregenal de la Sierra, 25 km (16 miles) to the south, is an attractive old town with a bullring.

Llerena ⑳

Badajoz. 🏠 6,000. 🚌 🚌 🚹 Plaza de España 1, (924) 87 00 68. 🚍 Thu. 🎉 Nuestra Señora de la Granada (1–15 Aug), San Miguel (late Sep).

EXTREMADURA's southeastern gateway to Andalusia, the town of Llerena, is a mixture of Mudéjar and Baroque build-ings. In the pretty main square,

which is lined with palm trees, stands the arcaded, whitewash-and-brick church of **Nuestra Señora de la Granada**, its sumptuous interior reflecting its former importance as a seat of the Inquisition *(see p264)*. At one end of the square is a fountain designed by Zurbarán, who lived in the town for 13 years. Also worth seeing is the 16th-century **Convento de Santa Clara**, on a street leading out of the main square.

ENVIRONS: At **Azuaga**, 30 km (20 miles) east of Llerena, is the Iglesia de la Consolación, which contains Renaissance and Mudéjar tiles.

Tentudía ㉑

Badajoz. 🚌 Calera de León. 🚹 Calera de León, (924) 584 101.

WHERE THE SIERRA MORENA runs into Andalusia, fortified towns and churches founded by the medieval military orders stand among the wooded hills of Tentudía. Here, on a hilltop, stands the tiny **Monasterio de Tentudía**. Founded in the 13th century by the Order of Santiago, the monastery contains a superb Mudéjar cloister, and reredos with Seville *azulejos* (tiles).

At **Calera de León**, just 6 km (4 miles) north of Tentudía, there is a magnificent, partly ruined, Renaissance convent, which was also founded by the Order of Santiago. The convent has a Gothic church and a two-storey cloister.

Bullring at Fregenal de la Sierra

SOUTHERN SPAIN

Southern Spain at a Glance

O NE LARGE REGION – Andalusia – extends across the south of Spain. Its landscape varies from the deserts of Almería in the east, to the wetlands of Doñana National Park in the west; and from the snow-capped peaks of the Sierra Nevada to the beaches of the Costa del Sol. Three inland cities between them share the greatest of Spain's Moorish monuments: Granada, Córdoba and Seville, the capital, which stands on the banks of the Río Guadalquivir. Andalusia has many other historic towns as well as attractive, whitewashed villages, important nature reserves and the sherry producing vineyards around Jerez de la Frontera.

Córdoba's Mezquita (see pp456–70) *has a remarkable forest of arches in its interior and an exquisitely decorated* mihrab *(prayer niche) facing Mecca.*

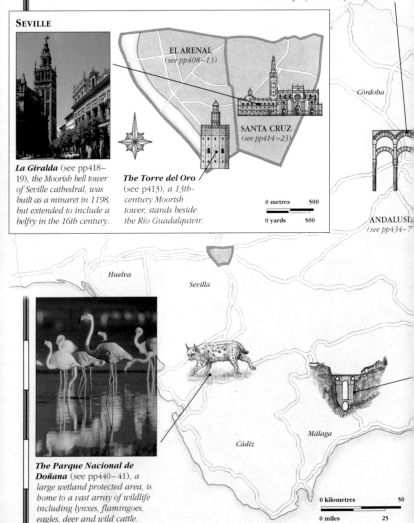

SEVILLE

EL ARENAL
(see pp408–13)

SANTA CRUZ
(see pp414–23)

Córdoba

ANDALUSI
(see pp434–7)

| 0 metres | 500 |
| 0 yards | 500 |

La Giralda (see pp418–19), *the Moorish bell tower of Seville cathedral, was built as a minaret in 1198, but extended to include a belfry in the 16th century.*

The Torre del Oro (see p413), *a 13th-century Moorish tower, stands beside the Río Guadalquivir.*

Huelva

Sevilla

Cádiz

Málaga

The Parque Nacional de Doñana (see pp440–41), *a large wetland protected area, is home to a vast array of wildlife including lynxes, flamingoes, eagles, deer and wild cattle.*

| 0 kilometres | 50 |
| 0 miles | 25 |

◁ **Whitewashed houses with red-tiled roofs in Montefrío, near Granada**

Above the city of Granada rises the famous Alhambra (see pp466–7). *The austere exterior of this great Moorish fortress-palace, built under the Nasrid dynasty, gives no hint of the sumptuous halls and enchanting courtyards and gardens contained within it.*

The town hall (see p474), *or ayuntamiento, in the historic town of Baeza was built in the early Spanish Renaissance style, called Plateresque. Great attention to detail is displayed in the carving of this pillar at the entrance.*

Jaén

Granada

Almería

The Puente Nuevo (see p446), *a bridge built in the 18th century, spans the deep Tajo gorge, which divides the old white town of Ronda from its newer districts.*

The Cabo de Gata nature reserve (see p477) *is an area of steep cliffs and secluded coves, with a stretch of seabed that is rich in marine flora and fauna.*

Regional Food: Southern Spain

THE ARAB PRESENCE made a lasting impact on the cuisine of Southern Spain. Rice, lemons, oranges, olives and vines were introduced, as well as many new vegetables and spices. Typical today are barbecued meats, sauces flavoured with cumin or saffron and sweets made from crushed almonds. Tomatoes and peppers are much used. Local sherry vinegars are used for dressing salads. The region is famous for its grilled fish, especially sardines, and deep-fried *calamares* (squid). Quality ham and pork are used widely in sausages; and in the mountains, stews of tripe or chickpeas are common fare. Tapas *(see pp574–5)* were invented in Andalusia and a wide variety of them is still served throughout the region.

Old sherry vinegar

Cachorreñas *is a fish soup from Cádiz. It is made with bread, and often clams, and flavoured with bitter orange peel.*

Olives and olive oil *have been an important product of Andalusia since Roman times. Today, a third of Europe's olive oil is made here. Fruity green extra virgin oil comes from the olive mills of Baena and the Sierra de Segura. The many types of table olives include fat* gordales, *small green* manzanillas *and stuffed olives.*
Aceitunas aliñadas *are marinated, cracked olives.*

Olive oil and olives

Fritura de pescado *is a typical dish from Málaga and Cádiz, where squid and fish are served with wedges of fresh lemon.*

Red pepper

Cold gazpacho soup

Fideos a la malagueña *is a variation on paella made with the local spaghetti (instead of rice), shellfish and peppers.*

Croutons

Cucumber

Gazpacho *is a chilled raw soup that is made by pounding bread and garlic with tomatoes, cucumber and peppers. Olive oil makes it creamy and vinegar gives it a refreshing tang. It is usually garnished with diced vegetables and croutons.*

Pescado a la sal *is fish baked whole in a crust of salt. It is often eaten accompanied by garlic mayonnaise or parsley sauce.*

Habas a la rondeña, *broad beans with cured ham, are so well known they are often called "Spanish-style" beans.*

Rabo de toro *is bull's tail braised with vegetables and red wine – one of the best dishes to employ bull's meat.*

Ternera con alcachofas, *a traditional Cordoban dish, combines veal and artichoke hearts in a Montilla wine sauce.*

Huevos a la flamenca *is a simple gypsy meal of eggs baked in small dishes with vegetables. Chorizo is often included.*

Tocino de cielo *is the most luscious of the custard and caramel desserts; the name means "heavenly bacon".*

Biscuits *include roscones or rings, round cinnamon- and almond-flavoured* mantecados *and soft fried* empanadillas.

FRUITS

Everything grows in the south, the market garden of Europe. Crops include strawberries, apples and pears as well as oranges and lemons. Tropical fruit is grown too, and Spain is also known for its melons. Figs grow wild, while the city of Granada owes its name to the locally grown pomegranate.

Figs

Oranges

Melon

Persimmons

Pomegranates

Strawberries

Jamón serrano

Chorizo

Morcilla

Salchichón

HAMS AND SAUSAGES

Some of the best *jamón serrano* (cured ham) comes from the mountains of Andalusia, in particular from Jabugo *(see p438)* and Trevélez *(see p460)*. Cooking sausages include paprika-flavoured chorizos and black *morcillas*, made using blood and spices. Cured sausages like chorizo and *salchichones* are often sliced and served as tapas.

Wines of Southern Spain

ANDALUSIA IS A LAND of fortified wines, and the best of these is *Jerez* (sherry). Andalusians drink the light, dry fino and manzanilla styles of sherry as wines (they only have 15.5 per cent alcohol) – always chilled, and often as an accompaniment to tapas *(see pp576–7)*. The longer-aged, richer, yet still dry styles of amontillado and oloroso sherry go well with the cured *jamón serrano (see p574)*. Other wines include fino, which may or may not be fortified, and Madeira-like Málaga.

González Byass logo

Working the soil in Jerez

Tío Pepe *is one of the finos of Jerez, which are noted for their bouquet of flor (yeast), pale colour and appetizing finish.*

WINE REGIONS

The Jerez wine region covers the chalky downs between the towns of Jerez, Sanlúcar and El Puerto de Santa María. South of the Montilla-Moriles region are Málaga's vineyards, which have been reduced by urban development.

Montilla, softer in style than sherry, can make an excellent partner for Andalusia's regional cuisine.

Manzanilla *is matured only in the town of Sanlúcar de Barrameda, which is situated where the Guadalquivir river meets the Atlantic Ocean. Like fino, it is bone dry, but has a distinctive salty tang.*

0 kilometres   50

0 miles   25

KEY

- Condado de Huelva
- Jerez-Xérès-Sherry
- Montilla-Moriles
- Málaga

KEY FACTS ABOUT WINES OF SOUTHERN SPAIN

Location and Climate
The Jerez region has one of the sunniest climates in Europe – summer heat tempered by ocean breezes. The best type of soil is white, chalky *albariza*. In Montilla it is more clayey.

Grape Varieties
The best dry sherry is produced from the Palomino grape. Pedro Ximénez is used for the sweeter styles and is the main grape in Montilla and Málaga. Moscatel is also grown in Málaga.

Good Producers
Condado de Huelva: Manuel Sauci Salas (Riodiel), A.Villarán (Pedro Ximénez Villarán). *Jerez:* Barbadillo (Solear), Blázquez (Carta Blanca), Caballero (Puerto), Garvey (San Patricio), González Byass (Alfonso, Tío Pepe), Hidalgo (La Gitana, Napoleón), Lustau, Osborne (Quinta), Pedro Domecq (La Ina), Sandeman. *Montilla-Moriles:* Alvear (C.B., Festival), Gracia Hermanos, Pérez Barquero, Tomás García. *Málaga:* Scholtz Hermanos, López Hermanos.

HOW SHERRY IS MADE

Sherry is mixed from two principal grape varieties: Palomino, which makes a drier, more delicate sherry; and Pedro Ximénez, which is made into a fuller, sweeter type of sherry.

Grape-drying is only required for Pedro Ximénez grapes. They are laid on esparto mats to shrivel in the sun, concentrating the sugar.

Crusher and de-stemmer

Grape-picking takes place during the first three weeks in September. Palomino grapes are taken to the presses quickly to ensure freshness.

Grape-pressing and de-stalking, in cylindrical stainless steel vats, is usually done at night to avoid the searing Andalusian heat.

Fermentation vat in steel

Flor, a yeast, may form on the exposed surface of young wine in the fermentation vat, preventing oxidization and adding a delicate taste. If flor develops, the wine is a fino.

Fortification is the addition of pure grape spirit, raising the level of alcohol from around 11 per cent by volume to around 18 per cent for olorosos, and 15.5 per cent for finos.

The solera system

The youngest **solera** contains new wine.

Sherry for bottling is taken from the oldest *solera* on the bottom row.

The finished product

The solera system assures that the qualities of a sherry remain constant. The wine from the youngest solera is mixed with the older in the barrels below and as a result takes on its character.

Moorish Architecture

THE FIRST SIGNIFICANT PERIOD of Moorish architecture arrived with the Cordoban Caliphate. The Mezquita was extended lavishly during this period and possesses all the enduring features of the Moorish style: arches, stucco work and ornamental use of calligraphy. Later, the Almohads imported a purer Islamic style, as can be seen in La Giralda *(see p418–9)*. The Nasrids built the superbly crafted Alhambra *(see p466–7)* while the Mudéjares *(see p51)* used their skill to create beautiful Moorish-style buildings such as the Palacio Pedro I in Seville's Reales Alcázares *(see pp422–3)*.

Reflections *in water, combined with an overall play of light, were central to Moorish architecture.*

Moorish domes *were frequently unadorned on the outside. Inside, an intricate lattice of stone ribs supported the dome's weight. Like this one in the Mezquita* (see pp456–7), *they were inlaid with multi-coloured mosaics featuring stylized flowers.*

Defensive walls

Moorish gardens were often arranged around gently rippling pools and channels.

DEVELOPMENT OF MOORISH ARCHITECTURE

Pre-Caliphal era 710–929	Caliphal era 929–1031	Almoravid and Almohad era 1091–1248	Nasrid era 1238–1492
	1031–91 *Taifa* period *(see p50)*		**c.1350** Alhambra palace

700	800	900	1000	1100	1200	1300	1400

785 Mezquita in Córdoba begun

1184 La Giralda in Seville begun

c.1350 Palacio Pedro I

936 Medina Azahara near Córdoba begun

Mudéjar era, after c.1215

Azulejos (see p420), gla. tiles, often adorned walls geometric patterns, as here the Reales Alcázares (p42

MOORISH ARCHES

The Moorish arch was developed from the horseshoe arch that the Visigoths used in the construction of churches. The Moors modified it and used it as the basis of great architectural endeavours, such as the Mezquita. Subsequent arches show more sophisticated ornamentation and the slow demise of the basic horseshoe shape.

Caliphal arch, Medina Azahara *(see p453)*

Almohad arch, Reales Alcázares *(see p422)*

Mudéjar arch, Reales Alcázares *(see p422)*

Nasrid arch, the Alhambra *(see p466)*

MOORISH PALACE

The palaces of the Moors were designed with gracious living, culture and learning in mind. The imaginary palace here shows how space, light, water and ornamentation were combined to harmonious effect.

Arcaded galleries provided shade around courtyards.

Clay tiles

Entrance halls were complex to confuse unwanted visitors.

Moorish baths made use of steam and hot water. Like Roman baths, they often had underfloor heating.

Elaborate stucco work typifies the Nasrid style of architecture. The Sala de los Abencerrajes in the Alhambra (see p467) was built using only the simplest materials, but it is nevertheless widely regarded as one of the most outstanding monuments of the period of the Moorish occupation.

Water cooled the Moors' elegant courtyards and served a contemplative purpose, as here in the Patio de los Leones in the Alhambra (see p467).

Flamenco, the Soul of Andalusia

Seville feria poster 1953

MORE THAN JUST A DANCE, flamenco is a forceful artistic expression of the sorrows and joys of life. Although it has interpreters all over Spain and even the world, it is a uniquely Andalusian art form, traditionally performed by gypsies. There are many styles of *cante* (song) from different parts of Andalusia, but no strict choreography – dancers improvise from basic movements, following the rhythm of the guitar and their feelings. Flamenco was neglected in the 1960s and 1970s, but recent years have seen a revival of serious interest in traditional styles and the development of exciting new forms.

Sevillanas, *a folk dance that strongly influenced flamenco, is danced by Andalusians in their bars and homes.*

At a *tablao* (flamenco club) there will be at least four people on stage, including the hand clapper.

The origins of flamenco are hard to trace. Gypsies may have been the main creators of the art, mixing their own Indian-influenced culture with existing Moorish and Andalusian folklore, and with Jewish and Christian music. There were gypsies in Andalusia by the early Middle Ages, but only in the 18th century did flamenco begin to develop into its present form.

THE SPANISH GUITAR

The guitar has a major role in flamenco, traditionally accompanying the singer. The flamenco guitar developed from the modern classical guitar, which evolved in Spain in the 19th century. Flamenco guitars have a lighter, shallower construction and a thickened plate below the soundhole, used to tap rhythms. Today, flamenco guitarists often perform solo. One of the greatest, Paco de Lucía, began by accompanying singers and dancers, before making his debut as a soloist in 1968. His inventive style, which combines traditional playing with Latin, jazz and rock elements, has influenced many musicians outside the realm of flamenco, such as the group Ketama, who play flamenco-blues.

Classical guitar

Expert guitarist Paco de Lucía

Singing *is an integral part of flamenco and the singer often performs solo. Camarón de la Isla (1952–92), a gypsy born near Cádiz, was among the most famous contemporary* cantaores *(flamenco singers). He began as a singer of expressive* cante jondo *(literally, "deep songs"), from which he developed his own, rock-influenced style. He has inspired many singers.*

WHERE TO ENJOY FLAMENCO

Most of the leading performers are based in Madrid (see p306). In Granada, Sacromonte's caves (p465) are an exciting venue. In Seville, the Barrio de Santa Cruz (pp414–23) has good tablaos.

La Chanca *is a* bailaora *(female dancer) who is renowned for her fiery and forceful movements. Cristina Hoyos, another dancer famous for her highly polished personal style, leads her own flamenco dance company, which received world-wide acclaim in the 1980s.*

The proud yet graceful posture of the *bailaora* is suggestive of a restrained passion.

A harsh, vibrating voice is typical of the singer.

Traditional polka-dot dress

The bailaor *(male dancer) plays a less important role than the* bailaora. *However, many have achieved fame, including Antonio Canales. He has introduced a new beat through his original foot movements.*

THE FLAMENCO TABLAO

These days it is rare to come across spontaneous dancing at a *tablao,* but if dancers and singers are inspired, an impressive show usually results. Artists performing with *duende* ("magic spirit") will hear appreciative *olés* from the audience.

FLAMENCO RHYTHM

The unmistakable rhythm of flamenco is created by the guitar. Just as important, however, is the beat created by hand-clapping and by the dancer's feet in high-heeled shoes. The *bailaoras* may also beat a rhythm with castanets; Lucero Tena (born in 1939) became famous for her solos on castanets. Graceful hand movements are used to express the dancer's feelings of the moment – whether pain, sorrow, or happiness. Like the movements of the rest of the body, they are not choreographed, and the styles used vary from person to person.

Castanets made of wood

Flamenco hand movements, always improvised

Plaza
de
Toros
de

SEVILLA

PROPIEDAD DE LA REAL MAESTRANZA DE CABALLERIA · Empresa PAGES

(FUERA DE ABONO)

GRANDIOSA NOVILLADA CON PICADORES

DOMINGO

18

SEPTIEMBRE 1994

ORGANIZADA PARA LA MUTUALIDAD BENEFICA DE LOS EMPLEADOS DE LA PLAZA DE TOROS

6 ESCOGIDOS NOVILLOS 6

JANDILLA

PARA LOS NOVILLEROS

ADOLFO DE LOS REYES
de Alcalá de Guadaira, Sevilla

LUIS REINOSO
"EL CARTUJANO"
de La Puebla de la Calzada (Badajoz), triunfador de las novilladas de promoción 1994, con salida por
la Puerta del Príncipe, que vuelve a la Maestranza para debutar con picadores. Y

GREGORIO BRAVO
de Alcalá del Río (Sevilla), que hará su debut con picadores.

LA NOVILLADA DARA COMIENZO A LAS 7 DE LA TARDE

GIN RIVES

GIN RIVES

EL ARENAL

Torre del Oro shown
on 20th-century tiles

BOUNDED BY the Río Guadalquivir and guarded by the 13th-century Torre del Oro, El Arenal used to be a district of munitions stores and shipyards. Today this quarter is dominated by the dazzling white bullring, the Plaza de Toros de la Maestranza, where the Sevillians have been staging *corridas* for more than two centuries. The many bars and bodegas in the neighbouring streets are especially busy during the summer bullfighting season.

Once central to the city's life, the influence of the Guadalquivir declined as it silted up during the 17th century. By then El Arenal had become a notorious underworld haunt clinging to the city walls. The river was converted into a canal in the early 20th century but restored to its former navigable glory in time for Expo '92. The east bank was transformed into a tree-lined promenade with excellent views of Triana and La Isla de la Cartuja across the water *(see p428)*.

The Hospital de la Caridad testifies to the city's continuing love affair with the Baroque. Its church is filled with famous paintings by Murillo, and the story of the Seville School is told in the immaculately restored Museo de Bellas Artes further north. The city's stunning collection of art includes great works by Zurbarán, Murillo and Valdés Leal.

SIGHTS AT A GLANCE

Historic Buildings
Hospital de la Caridad ❹
Plaza de Toros de la
    Maestranza ❸
Torre del Oro ❺

Museums
Museo de Bellas Artes ❶

Churches
Iglesia de la Magdalena ❷

GETTING THERE

This area is well served by the orange Tussam buses. Take the C4, which runs along the Paseo de Colón. Alternatively, use one of the numerous routes to Plaza Nueva.

KEY

	Street-by-Street map *See pp410–11*
	Coach station
	Main bus stop
	Parking

0 metres   500
0 yards   500

◁ Pasting up an advertisement for a bullfight on the walls of the Plaza de Toros de la Maestranza

Street-by-Street: El Arenal

ONCE HOME TO THE PORT of Seville, El Arenal also housed the ammunition works and the artillery headquarters. Now its atmosphere is set by the city's bullring, the majestic Plaza de Toros de la Maestranza. During the bullfighting season *(see p412)* the area's bars and restaurants are packed, but for the rest of the year El Arenal's backstreets re-

Statue of Carmen

main quiet. The riverfront is dominated by one of Seville's best-known monuments, the Moorish Torre del Oro, while the long, tree-lined promenade beside the Paseo de Cristóbal Colón is perfect for a slow, romantic walk along the Guadalquivir.

★ **Plaza de Toros de la Maestranza**
Seville's 18th-century bullring, one [of] Spain's oldest, has a Baroque façade in white and ochre ❸

CALLE DE ADRIANO

Carmen
(see p427),
sculpted in bronze, stands opposite the bullring.

CALLE ANTONIA DÍAZ

PASEO DE CRISTÓBAL COLÓN

Paseo Alcalde Marqués de Contadero

The Teatro de la Maestranza, a show-piece theatre and opera house, was opened in 1991. Home of the Orquesta Sinfónica de Sevilla, the theatre also features international opera and dance companies.

STAR SIGHTS

★ **Plaza de Toros de la Maestranza**

★ **Hospital de la Caridad**

★ **Torre del Oro**

The Guadalquivir used to cause catastrophic inundations. Following floods in 1947 a barrage was constructed. Today, tourists enjoy peaceful boat trips, starting from the Torre del Oro.

El Buzo ("The Diver") is one of many traditional tapas bars and *freidurías* on or just off Calle Arfe. Nearby is Mesón Sevilla Jabugo I, a bar where jamón ibérico (*see p438*) is served.

LOCATOR MAP
See Street Finder map 3

El Postigo is an arts and crafts market.

GARCÍA VINUESA

ARFE

To the Cathedral

El Torno, in the secluded Plaza de Cabildo, sells sweets made in a convent.

AVENIDA DE LA CONSTITUCIÓN

DE MAYO

TOMÁS DE IBARRA

TEMPRADO

★ Hospital de la Caridad
The walls of this Baroque hospital church are hung with fine paintings by Bartolomé Esteban Murillo and Juan de Valdés Leal **④**

To Reales Alcázares

Maestranza de Artillería

CALLE SANTANDER

Bodegón Torre del Oro (*see p600*)

0 metres	75
0 yards	75

KEY

- - - Suggested route

★ Torre del Oro
Built in the 13th century to protect the port, this crenellated Moorish tower now houses a small maritime museum **⑤**

Madonna and Child in the Baroque Iglesia de la Magdalena

Museo de Bellas Artes ❶

Plaza del Museo 9. **Map** 1 B5. *(95) 422 07 90.* 43, C3. 9am–3pm Tue–Sun (also 4–7pm during temporary exhibitions; phone to check).

T HE CONVENTO de la Merced Calzada has been restored to create one of the best art museums in Spain. Completed in 1612 by Juan de Oviedo, the building is designed around three patios which today are adorned with trees, flowers and some fine *azulejos (see p420).* The Patio Mayor is the largest of these, remodelled by the architect Leonardo de Figueroa in 1724. The convent church is notable for its Baroque domed ceiling, painted by Domingo Martínez.

The museum's collection of Spanish art and sculpture, from the medieval to the modern, focuses on the work of Seville School artists. Among the star attractions is *La Servilleta*, a Virgin and Child (1665–8), which is said to be painted on a napkin *(servilleta).* One of Murillo's most popular works, it may be seen in the restored convent church. The boisterous *La Inmaculada* (1672) by Juan de Valdés Leal is on display in a gallery devoted to the artist's forceful religious

San Jerónimo Penitente in the Museo de Bellas Artes

paintings. The museum also contains several fine works by Zurbarán including *San Hugo en el Refectorio* (1655), which was painted for the monastery at La Cartuja *(see p428).*

Iglesia de la Magdalena ❷

Calle San Pablo 10. **Map** 3 B1. *(95) 422 96 03.* 43. 7:30–11am, 6:30–9pm Mon–Fri, 7:30am–1pm Sat & Sun.

T HIS IMMENSE BAROQUE church by Leonardo de Figueroa, completed in 1709, is gradually being restored to its former glory. In its southwest corner stands the Capilla de la Quinta Angustia, a Mudéjar chapel with three cupolas. This chapel survived from an earlier church where the great Seville School painter Batolomé Murillo was baptized in 1618. The font that was used for his baptism is now in the baptistry of the present building. The church's west front is topped by a belfry which is painted in vivid colours.

Among the religious works in the church are a painting by Francisco de Zurbarán, *St Dominic in Soria*, housed in the Capilla Sacramental (to the right of the south door), and frescoes by Lucas Valdés over the sanctuary. On the wall of the north transept there is a cautionary fresco of a medieval *auto-da-fé (see p264).*

Plaza de Toros de la Maestranza ❸

Paseo de Cristóbal Colón. **Map** 3 B2. *(95) 422 45 77.* C4. 10am–1:30pm Mon–Sat.

S EVILLE'S FAMOUS bullring, built between 1761–1881, is arguably the most magnificent in Spain and well worth a visit.

The arcaded arena holds up to 14,000 spectators. Guided tours of this immense building start from the main entrance on Paseo de Cristóbal Colón. On the west side is the Puerta del Príncipe (Prince's Gate), through which the triumphant matadors are carried aloft by admirers from the crowd.

Just beyond the *enfermería* (emergency hospital) is a museum of portraits, posters and costumes, including a purple cape painted by Pablo Picasso. The tour continues on to the chapel where matadors pray for success, and then to the stables where the horses of the *picadores* (lance-carrying horsemen) are kept.

The bullfighting season starts with the April fair and continues intermittently until October. Most *corridas* take place on Sunday evenings. Tickets can be bought from the *taquilla* (booking office) at the bullring.

Next door to the Plaza de Toros, and echoing its circular bulk, is the Teatro de la Maestranza. Seville's austere opera house and theatre, designed by Luis Marín de Terán and Aurelio de Pozo, opened in 1991. Fragments of ironwork from the 19th-century ammunition works that first occupied the site adorn the river façade.

Arcaded arena of the Plaza de Toros de la Maestranza, begun in 1761

Finis Gloriae Mundi by Juan de Valdés Leal in the Hospital de la Caridad

Hospital de la Caridad ❹

Calle Temprado 3. **Map** 3 B2. 📞 *(95) 422 32 32.* 🚌 *C4.* 🕐 *10am–1pm, 4:30–6:30pm Mon–Sat.* ⚫ *public hols.* 📷 🚫

THIS CHARITY HOSPITAL was founded in 1674 and it is still used today as a sanctuary for elderly and infirm people. In the gardens stands a statue of its benefactor, Miguel de Mañara, whose dissolute life before he joined a brotherhood is said to have inspired the story of Don Juan. The façade of the hospital church, with its whitewashed walls, reddish stonework and framed *azulejos*, provides a glorious example of Sevillian Baroque.

Inside are two square patios decorated with plants, 18th-century Dutch tiles, and fine fountains with Italian statues depicting Charity and Mercy. At their northern end a passage to the right leads to another patio, containing a 13th-century arch which survives from the city's shipyards. Here, too, a bust of Mañara stands amid pretty rose bushes.

Inside the church there are a number of original canvases by some of the leading painters of the 17th century, despite the fact that some of its greatest artworks were looted by Marshal Soult during the Napoleonic occupation of 1808–14 *(see p58).*

Directly above the entrance is the ghoulish *Finis Gloriae Mundi* (The End of the World's Glory) by Juan de Valdés Leal, and opposite hangs his morbid *In Ictu Oculi* (In the Blink of an Eye). Many of the other works that can be seen are by Murillo, including *St John of God Carrying a Sick Man* and portraits of the Child Jesus and *St John the Baptist as a Boy.*

Torre del Oro ❺

Paseo de Cristóbal Colón. **Map** 3 B2. 📞 *(95) 422 24 19.* 🚌 *C4.* 🕐 *10am–2pm Tue–Fri, 11am–2pm Sat & Sun.* ⚫ *Aug & public hols.* 📷 🚫

IN MOORISH SEVILLE the Tower of Gold formed part of the walled defences, linking up with the Reales Alcázares *(see pp422–3).* It was built as a defensive lookout in 1220, with a companion tower on the opposite riverbank. A mighty metal chain was stretched between the two to prevent hostile ships from sailing upriver. The turret was not added until 1760. The gold referred to in its name may be the gilded *azulejos* that once clad its walls, or treasures from the Americas unloaded here. The tower has had many uses: a gunpowder store, a chapel, a prison and port offices. Now, as the Museo Marítimo, it exhibits maritime maps and antiques.

The Torre del Oro, built by the Almohads

SEVILLE'S FIESTAS

April Fair *(two weeks after Easter).* Life in the city moves over the river to the fairground for a week. Here, members of clubs, trade unions and neighbourhood groups meet in numerous *casetas* (entertainment booths) to drink and dance all night to the infectious, non-stop rhythm of *sevillanas.* (Access to booths may be limited to private parties.) Every day, from around 1pm, elegant, traditionally dressed riders on horseback and mantilla-crowned women in open carriages show off their finery in parades. During the afternoons, bullfights are often staged in the Maestranza bullring.

Float in Holy Week procession

Holy Week *(Mar/Apr).* Over 100 gilded *pasos* (floats bearing religious images) are borne through the streets between Palm Sunday and Easter Day. Singers in the crowds often spontaneously burst into *saetas,* fragments of song in praise of Christ or the Virgin. Emotions are high in the early hours of Good Friday as the images of the Virgen de la Macarena and the Virgen de la Esperanza de Triana emerge from their churches.
Corpus Christi *(May/Jun).* The *Seises,* boys dressed in Baroque costume, dance before the main altar of the cathedral *(see p419).*

SANTA CRUZ

EVILLE'S OLD JEWISH QUARTER, the Barrio de Santa Cruz, is a warren of white alleyways and patios that has long been the most picturesque corner of the city. Many of the best-known sights are located here: the cavernous Gothic cathedral with its landmark tower, La Giralda; the splendid Reales Alcázares, with the royal palaces and lush gardens of Pedro I and Carlos V; and the Archivo de Indias, whose documents tell of Spain's exploration and conquest of the Americas.

Spreading northeast from these great monuments is an enchanting maze of whitewashed streets. The Golden Age artist Bartolomé Esteban

Murillo lived here in the 17th century, while his contemporary, Juan de Valdés Leal, decorated the Hospital de los Venerables with superb Baroque frescoes.

Further north is one of Seville's favourite shopping streets, the Calle de las Sierpes. The market squares around it, such as the charming Plaza del Salvador, provided backdrops for some of the stories of Cervantes. Nearby, the ornate façades and interiors of the Ayuntamiento (town hall) and the Casa de Pilatos, a gem of Andalusian architecture, testify to the great wealth that flowed into the city from the New World during the 16th century, much of it spent on art.

Ornate streetlamp, Plaza del Triunfo

SIGHTS AT A GLANCE

Historic Buildings
Archivo de Indias **6**
Ayuntamiento **2**
Casa de Pilatos **4**
Hospital de los Venerables **5**
Reales Alcázares pp422–3 **7**

Churches
Cathedral and La Giralda pp418–19 **1**

Streets and Plazas
Calle de las Sierpes **3**

GETTING THERE

This area is well served by orange Tussam buses. Take any of routes 21, 22, 23, 25, 26, 30, 31, 33, 34, 40, 41 or 42 to reach the Avenida de la Constitución, convenient for most of the sights. *Circular* C3 or C4 will take you instead to the Puerta de Jerez.

KEY

Street-by-Street map *(pp416–17)*

i Tourist information

0 metres 400

0 yards 400

◁ **La Giralda seen from the gardens of the Reales Alcázares**

Street-by-Street: Santa Cruz

Window grille, Santa Cruz

THE MAZE of narrow streets to the east of Seville cathedral and the Reales Alcázares represents Seville at its most romantic and compact. As well as the expected souvenir shops, tapas bars and strolling guitarists, there are plenty of picturesque alleys, hidden plazas and flower-decked patios to reward the casual wanderer. Once a Jewish ghetto, its re-stored buildings, with characteristic window grilles, are now a harmonious mix of up-market residences and tourist accommodation. Good bars and restaurants make the area well worth an evening visit.

Plaza Virgen de los Reyes is often lined by horse-drawn carriages. In the centre of the square is an early 20th-century fountain by José Lafita.

Palacio Arzobispal, the 18th-century Archbishop's Palace, is still used by Seville's clergy.

AVENIDA DE LA CONSTITUCIÓN

M

ROMERO

★ Cathedral and La Giralda
This huge Gothic cathedral and its Moorish bell tower are Seville's most popular sights ❶

Convento de la Encarnación

SANTO TOMAS

MIGUEL MAÑARA

Archivo de Indias
Built in the 16th century as a merchants' exchange, the Archive of the Indies now houses documents relating to the Spanish colonization of the Americas ❻

Museo de Arte Contemporáneo

Plaza del Triunfo has a Baroque colum celebrating the city's survival of the great earthquake of 1755. the centre is a mo statue of the Virgi Mary (Immaculate Conception).

Calle Mateos Gago is shaded by orange trees and filled with souvenir shops, cafés and tapas bars. Bar Giralda at No. 2, whose vaults are the remains of a Moorish bath house, is popular for its wide variety of tapas.

LOCATOR MAP
See Street Finder maps 3–4

Plaza Santa Cruz is adorned by an ornate iron cross from 1692.

MESON DEL MORO

ODRIGO CARO

XIMENEZ ENCISO

SANTA TERESA

JAMERDANA

REINOSO

LOPE DE RUEDA

PLAZA

STA CRUZ

GLORIA

JUSTINO DE NEVE

PL. DOÑA ELVIRA

SUSONA

PIMIENTA

CALLEJON DEL AGUA

VIDA

★ **Hospital de los Venerables**
The 17th-century home for elderly priests has a splendidly restored Baroque church ⑤

Callejón del Agua is a whitewashed alleyway offering glimpses into enchanting plant-filled patios. It is called "Water Street" because it was once a water conduit to the Reales Alcázares.

0 metres 50

0 yards 50

★ **Reales Alcázares**
Seville's Royal Palaces are a rewarding combination of exquisite Mudéjar (see pp422–3) craftsmanship, regal grandeur and landscaped gardens ⑦

KEY

– – – Suggested route

STAR SIGHTS

★ **Cathedral and La Giralda**

★ **Hospital de los Venerables**

★ **Reales Alcázares**

Seville Cathedral and La Giralda ❶

16th-century stained glass

S EVILLE'S CATHEDRAL occupies the site of a great mosque built by the Almohads *(see p50)* in the late 12th century. La Giralda, its bell tower, and the Patio de los Naranjos are a legacy of this Moorish structure. Work on the Christian cathedral, the largest in Europe, began in 1401 and took just over a century to complete. As well as enjoying its Gothic immensity and the works of art in its chapels and sacristy, visitors can climb La Giralda for stunning views over the city.

★ La Giralda
The Moorish bell tower is crowned with a 16th-century bronze portraying Faith. This weathervane (giraldillo) has given La Giralda its name.

Entrance

★ Patio de los Naranjos
In Moorish times worshippers would wash their hands and feet in the fountain under the orange trees before praying.

THE RISE OF LA GIRALDA

The tower was built as a minaret in 1198. In the 14th century the bronze spheres at its top were replaced by Christian symbols. A new belfry was planned in 1557, but built to a more ornate design by Hernán Ruiz in 1568.

1198   1400   1557 (plan)   1568

Puerta del Perdón

Roman pillars
brought from Itálica *(see p452)* surround the cathedral steps.

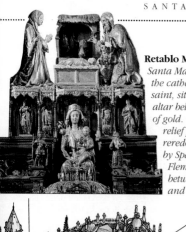

Retablo Mayor
*Santa María de la Sede,
the cathedral's patron
saint, sits at the high
altar below a waterfall
of gold. The 44 gilded
relief panels of the
reredos were carved
by Spanish and
Flemish sculptors
between 1482
and 1564.*

VISITORS' CHECKLIST

Plaza Virgen de los Reyes.
Map 3 C2. ☎ *(95) 456 33 21.*
🚌 *21, 22, 23, 31, 33, 40.*
Cathedral ⬜ *11am–5pm
Mon–Sat; 2–4pm Sun.* 📷 ✝
*9am, 10am, noon, 5pm Mon–
Sat; 11am, noon, 1pm Sun.* ♿
La Giralda ⬜ *11am–5pm
Mon–Sat; 10am–4pm Sun.*

**The Sacristía
Mayor** houses
many works of
art, including
paintings by
Murillo.

★ **Capilla Mayor**
*Monumental iron grilles
forged in 1518–32
enclose the main
chapel, which is
dominated by the
overwhelming
Retablo Mayor.*

**The Tomb of
Columbus** dates from
the 1890s. His coffin
is carried by bearers
representing the king-
doms of Castile, León,
Aragón and Navarra *(see p50).*

**Puerta
del Bautismo**

Iglesia del Sagrario,
a large 17th-century
chapel, is now used
as a parish church.

STAR FEATURES

★ **La Giralda**

★ **Patio de los
Naranjos**

★ **Capilla Mayor**

Puerta de la Asunción
*Though Gothic in style, this portal
was not completed until 1833. A
stone relief of the Assumption of the
Virgin decorates the tympanum.*

Genoese fountain in the Mudéjar Patio Principal of the Casa de Pilatos

Ayuntamiento ❷

Plaza Nueva 1. **Map** 3 C1. ((95) 459
01 01. 🚍 21, 30. ○ 5:30–7:30pm
Tue & Wed (entry with passport). 🗐

S EVILLE'S CITY HALL stands
between the Plaza de San
Francisco, where *autos-da-fé*
(public trials of heretics) were
held, and the Plaza Nueva.

The building was completed
between 1527 and 1534. The
side bordering the Plaza de
San Francisco is a fine example
of the ornate Plateresque style
(see p21) favoured by the
architect Diego de Riaño. The
west front, meanwhile, is part
of a Neo-Classical extension
built in 1891. Richly sculpted
ceilings survive in the vestibule
and in the lower Casa Consistorial (Council Meeting Room).
This contains Velázquez's
*Imposition of the Chasuble on
St Ildefonso*. The upper Casa
Consistorial has a dazzling
coffered ceiling and paintings
by Zurbarán and Valdés Leal.

Calle de las Sierpes ❸

Map 3 C1. 🚍 21, 30. **Casa de la
Condesa Lebrija** ((95) 421 81 83.
○ 5–7pm Mon & Fri.

S EVILLE'S MAIN pedestrianized
shopping promenade, the
"Street of the Snakes", runs
north from the Plaza de San
Francisco. Long-established
stores selling hats, fans and
traditional *mantillas* (lace
headdresses) stand alongside
clothes and souvenir shops.
The parallel streets of Cuna
and Tetuán also offer some
enjoyable window-shopping.

About half way up the street
walking north, Calle Jovellanos
to the left leads to the 17th-
century Capillita de San José.
Further on, at the junction
with Calle Pedro Caravaca, is
the anachronistic, upholstered
world of the Real Círculo de
Labradores, a private men's
club founded in 1856.

Opposite – with its entrance
in Calle Cuna – is a 15th-
century private mansion, the
Casa de la Condesa Lebrija.
Among the Lebrija family's
countless Roman treasures on
display on the ground floor is
a mosaic from the ruins of
nearby Itálica *(see p452)*.

Right at the end of the street,
take the opportunity to buy a
cake in La Campana, Seville's
best-known *pastelería*.

Casa de Pilatos ❹

Plaza de Pilatos 1. **Map** 4 D1. ((95)
422 52 98. 🚍 C3, C4. ○ **Ground
floor** 9am–8pm. **First floor** 10am–
2pm, 4–6pm. 🗐 🗐 🖰 ground floor.

E NRAPTURED BY by the architectural and decorative
wonders of High Renaissance
Italy and the Holy Land, the
first Marquess of Tarifa built
the Casa de Pilatos. It was so
called because it was thought
to resemble Pontius Pilate's
home in Jerusalem. Today it
is the residence of the Dukes
of Medinaceli and is still one
of the finest palaces in Seville.

Visitors enter it through a
marble portal, commissioned
by the Marquess in 1529 from
Genoese craftsmen. Across the
arcaded Apeadero (carriage
yard) is the Patio Principal.
This courtyard is essentially
Mudéjar *(see p51)* in style and
decorated with *azulejos* and
intricate plasterwork. In its
corners are three Roman
statues, depicting Minerva, a
dancing muse and Ceres, and
a Greek statue of Athena,
which dates from the 5th
century BC. In its centre is a
fountain which was imported
from Genoa. To the right,
through the Salón del Pretorio
with its coffered ceiling and
marquetry, is the Corredor de

AZULEJOS

Colourful *azulejos*, glazed ceramic tiles, are
a striking feature of Seville. The craft was
introduced to Spain by the Moors, who created
fantastic mosaics in sophisticated geometric patterns
for palace walls – the word *azulejo* derives from the Arabic
for "little stone". New techniques were introduced in the
16th century and later mass production extended their use
to decorative signs, shop façades and advertising hoardings.

Azulejo billboard for Studebaker Motor Cars (1924), Calle Tetuán

Fresco by Juan de Valdés Leal in the Hospital de los Venerables

Zaquizamí. The antiquities on display in adjacent rooms include a bas-relief of *Leda and the Swan* and two Roman reliefs commemorating the Battle of Actium of 31 BC.

Coming back to the Patio Principal, you turn right into the Salón de Descanso de los Jueces. Beyond is a rib-vaulted Gothic chapel, with Mudéjar plasterwork walls and ceiling. On the altar is a copy of a 4th-century sculpture in the Vatican, *The Good Shepherd*. Left through the Gabinete de Pilatos, with its small central fountain, is the Jardín Grande.

Returning once more to the main patio, behind the statue of Ceres, a tiled staircase leads to the upper floor. It is roofed with a wonderful *media naranja* (half orange) cupola built in 1537. There are Mudéjar ceilings in some rooms, which are filled with family portraits, antiques and furniture.

Hospital de los Venerables ❺

Plaza de los Venerables 8. **Map** 3 C2.
📞 (95) 456 26 96. 🚌 C3, C4.
🕐 10am – 2pm, 4–8pm daily. 🚫 ✓

SET IN THE HEART of the Barrio de Santa Cruz, this home for elderly priests was begun in 1675 and completed around 20 years later by Leonardo de Figueroa. It has recently been restored as a cultural centre by FOCUS (Fundación Fondo de Cultura de Sevilla).

Stairs from the central, rose-coloured, sunken patio lead to the upper floors, which, along with the infirmary and cellar, are used as exhibition galleries.

A separate guided tour visits the Hospital church, a showcase of Baroque splendours, with frescoes by both Juan de Valdés Leal and his son Lucas Valdés. Other highlights of the church include sculptures of St Peter and St Ferdinand by Pedro Roldán, flanking the east door; and *The Apotheosis of St Ferdinand* by Lucas Valdés, top centre in the reredos of the main altar. Its frieze (inscribed in Greek) recommends that visitors should "Fear God and Honour the Priest".

In the sacristy, the ceiling has an effective *trompe l'oeil* depicting *The Triumph of the Cross* by Juan de Valdés Leal.

Archivo de Indias ❻

Avda de la Constitución. **Map** 3 C2.
📞 (95) 421 12 34. 🚌 C3, C4, 21, 26, 31, 33, 34, 40. 🕐 10am – 1pm Mon–Fri (research 8am–3pm). 🚫

THE ARCHIVE of the Indies illustrates Seville's pre-eminent role in the colonization and exploitation of the New World. Built between 1584–98 to designs by Juan de Herrera, co-architect of El Escorial *(see pp312–13)*, it was originally a *lonja* (exchange), where merchants traded. In 1785, Carlos III had all Spanish documents relating to the "Indies" collected under one roof. Among the archive's 86 million handwritten pages and 8,000 maps and drawings are letters from Columbus, Cortés, and Cervantes and the extensive correspondence of Felipe II. Some documents are now stored on CD-ROM.

Upstairs, the library rooms contain regularly changing displays of drawings, maps and facsimile documents.

Façade of the Archivo de Indias by Juan de Herrera

Reales Alcázares 🄐

IN 1364 PEDRO I ordered the construction of a royal residence within the palaces which had been built by the city's Almohad *(see p50)* rulers. Within two years, craftsmen from Granada and Toledo had created a jewel box of Mudéjar patios and halls, the Palacio Pedro I, now at the heart of Seville's Reales Alcázares. Later monarchs added their own distinguishing marks: Isabel I *(see p52)* dispatched navigators to explore the New World from her Casa de la Contratación, while Carlos I (the Holy Roman Emperor Charles V – *see p54*) had grandiose, richly decorated apartments built.

Mudéjar stucco

Jardín de Troya

Gardens of the Alcázares
Laid out with terraces, fountains and pavilions, these gardens provide a delightful refuge from the heat and bustle of Seville.

★ Charles V Rooms
Vast tapestries and lively 16th-century azulejos *decorate the vaulted halls of the apartments and chapel of Charles V.*

Patio del Crucero lies above the old baths.

PLAN OF THE REALES ALCÁZARES

The complex has been the home of Spanish kings for almost seven centuries. The palace's upper floor is used by the royal family today.

KEY

☐ Area illustrated above

☐ Gardens

★ Patio de las Doncellas
The Patio of the Maidens boasts plasterwork by the top craftsmen of Granada.

★ Salón de Embajadores
Built in 1427, the dazzling dome of the Ambassadors' Hall is of carved and gilded, interlaced wood.

VISITORS' CHECKLIST

Patio de Banderas. **Map** 3 C2.
(95) 422 71 63. C3, C4, 21, 22, 23, 25, 26, 30, 31, 33, 34, 40, 41, 42. 10:30am–5pm Tue–Sat, 10am–1pm Sun.

Horseshoe Arches
Azulejos *and complex plasterwork decorate the Ambassadors' Hall, which has three symmetrically arranged, ornate archways, each with three horseshoe arches.*

Casa de la Contratación

The Patio de la Montería was where the court met before hunting expeditions.

The façade of the Palacio Pedro I is a prime example of Mudéjar style.

Puerta del León (entrance)

Patio de las Muñecas
The Patio of the Dolls and its surrounding bedrooms formed the domestic heart of the palace. It derives its name from two tiny faces on one of its arches.

Patio del Yeso
The Patio of Plaster, a garden with flower beds and a water channel, retains features of the earlier, 12th-century Almohad Alcázar.

STAR FEATURES

★ Charles V Rooms

★ Patio de las Doncellas

★ Salón de Embajadores

FURTHER AFIELD

THE NORTH OF Seville, La Macarena, is a characterful mix of decaying Baroque and Mudéjar churches, and old-style tapas bars. The place to visit here is the Basílica de la Macarena, a shrine to Seville's much-venerated Virgen de la Esperanza Macarena. Among the many convents and churches in the area, the Convento de Santa Paula offers a rare opportunity to peep behind the walls of an enclosed community.

The area south of the city is dominated by the extensive, leafy Parque María Luisa. A large part of the park originally formed the grounds of the Baroque Palacio de San Telmo. Many of the historic buildings in the park were erected for the Ibero-American Exposition of 1929. The grand five-star Hotel Alfonso XIII

Roman column, Alameda de Hércules

and the crescent-shaped Plaza de España are the most striking legacies of this upsurge of Andalusian pride. Nearby is the Royal Tobacco Factory, forever associated with the fictional gypsy heroine Carmen, who toiled in its sultry halls. Today, it is part of the Universidad, Seville's university.

There is more to see across the river from the city centre. With its cobbled streets and shops selling ceramics, the Triana quarter retains the feel of old Seville. In the 15th century a Carthusian monastery, the Monasterio de Santa María de las Cuevas, was built north of Triana. Columbus resided there and, largely due to this connection, the area around it, the Isla de la Cartuja, was chosen as the site for Expo '92. Today the site is being developed as cultural and educational theme parks.

SIGHTS AT A GLANCE

Historic Buildings
Palacio de San Telmo ❹
Universidad ❺

Churches and Convents
Basílica de la Macarena ❶
Convento de Santa Paula ❷
Iglesia de San Pedro ❸

Historic Areas
Isla de la Cartuja ❽
Parque María Luisa ❻
Triana ❼

0 kilometres   1
0 miles   0.5

KEY

- City centre
- Parks and open spaces
- 🚉 Railway station
- Major road
- Minor road

◁ **Pabellón de Andalucía, built on the Isla de la Cartuja for Expo '92**

St John the Baptist by Montañés
in the Convento de Santa Paula

Basílica de la Macarena ●

Calle Macarena. **Map** 2 D3.
[*(95) 437 01 95.* ▦ *C1, C2, 2, 10.*
○ *9:30am–12:30pm, 5–7pm daily.*
Treasury ○ *9am–1pm, 5–9pm daily.*

T HE BASILICA de la Macarena
was built in 1949 in the
Neo-Baroque style by Gómez
Millán as a new home for the
much-loved Virgen de la
Esperanza Macarena. It butts
on to the 13th-century Iglesia
de San Gil, where the image
was housed until a fire in 1936.

The image of the Virgin,
standing above the main altar
amid waterfalls of gold and
silver, has been attributed to
Luisa Roldán (1656–1703), the
most talented female artist of
the Seville School. The wall-
paintings, by Rafael Rodríguez
Hernández, date from 1982.

The Virgin's magnificent processional gowns and jewels are
among the exhibits displayed
in the museum in the Treasury.

Convento de Santa Paula ●

Calle Santa Paula 11. **Map** 2 E5.
[*(95) 442 13 07.* ▦ *10, 11.* ○
9:30am–1pm, 4:30–6:30pm daily.

F OUNDED IN 1475, Santa Paula
is still a working convent
and home to 40 nuns. You can
visit the museum, which consists of two galleries filled with
religious artifacts and paintings,

and buy jams and marmalades,
made by the nuns, from a
room near the exit. The nave
of the convent church has an
elaborately carved wooden
roof, dating from 1623. Among
the statues in the church are
St John the Evangelist and St
John the Baptist, both the work
of Juan Martínez Montañés.

Iglesia de San Pedro ●

Calle Doña María Coronel 1. **Map**
2 D5. [*(95) 421 68 58.* ▦ *10,
11, 24.* ○ *7–10pm Mon–Sat, 9am–
noon, 7–8pm Sun.*

D IEGO VELAZQUEZ, the Golden
Age painter *(see p28)*, was
baptized in this church in 1599.
It is built in a typically Sevillian mix of architectural styles.
Mudéjar elements survive in
the lobed brickwork of its
tower, which is surmounted by
a Baroque *(see p21)* belfry. The
principal portal – facing the
Plaza de San Pedro – is also
Baroque, and was added by
Diego de Quesada in 1613.

The poorly lit interior has a
Mudéjar wooden ceiling and
west door. The vault of one of
its chapels is decorated with
exquisite geometric patterns
of interlacing bricks.

Behind the church, in Calle
Doña María Coronel, cakes
and biscuits are sold from a
revolving drum in the wall of
the 14th-century Convento de
Santa Inés. Fronting its restored church is an arcaded
patio, which is decorated with
17th-century frescoes by
Francisco de Herrera.

**Modern tilework adorning the
front of the Iglesia de San Pedro**

Palacio de San Telmo ●

Avenida de Roma. **Map** 3 C3. [*(95)
459 75 05.* ▦ *C3, C4, 5, 34.* ○ *by
appointment only.* ⊘

T HIS IMPOSING PALACE, named
after the patron saint of
navigators, was built in 1682
as a university to train ships'
pilots, navigators and high-
ranking officers. In 1849 the
palace became the residence
of the Dukes of Monpensier
and until 1893 its vast grounds
included what is now the
Parque María Luisa. Today it
is the presidential headquarters
of the Junta de Andalucía (the
regional government).

The most striking feature of
the Palacio de San Telmo is the

Parque María Luisa ●

Map 4 D4. ▦ *C1, C2, 30, 31, 33,
34, 70, 72.* ♿ **Museo Arqueológico**
[*(95) 423 24 01.* ○ *9am–2pm
Tue–Sun.* ▨ ⊘ ♿ **Museo de
Artes y Costumbres Populares**
[*(95) 423 25 76.* ○ *9am–2:30pm
Tue–Sun.* ▨ ⊘ ♿

P RINCESS MARIA LUISA
donated part of the
grounds of the Palacio
de San Telmo to the city
for this park in 1893.
It was landscaped by

Plaza de España
was built in a
theatrical style by
Aníbal González.

The Glorieta de Bécquer
is an arbour with sculpted
figures depicting the phases
of love – a tribute to poet
Gustavo Adolfo Bécquer.

exuberant Churrigueresque portal designed by Leonardo de Figueroa, and completed in 1734. Surrounding the Ionic columns are allegorical figures representing the Sciences and Arts. St Telmo, holding a ship and charts, is flanked by the sword-bearing St Ferdinand and St Hermenegildo, with a cross. On the north façade is ranged a row of sculptures of Sevillian celebrities, added by Susillo in 1895. Among them are artists such as Montañés, Murillo and Velázquez.

Opposite is Seville's most famous hotel, the Alfonso XIII, dating from the 1920s. Its centrepiece is a grand patio with a fountain and orange trees. Non-residents are welcome to visit the bar and the restaurant.

Universidad ❺

Calle San Fernando 4. **Map** 3 C3.
📞 (95) 455 10 00. 🚌 C3, C4, 5, 25, 26, 34. 🕐 8am–8:30pm Mon–Fri.
⬤ public hols.

THE FORMER Real Fábrica de Tabacos (Royal Tobacco Factory) is now part of Seville University. In the 19th century, three-quarters of Europe's cigars were manufactured here, rolled by 10,000 *cigarreras* (female cigar-makers). It was these hot-blooded *cigarreras* who inspired French author Mérimée to create his famous gypsy heroine, *Carmen*.

Built in 1728–71, the factory complex is the largest building in Spain after El Escorial *(see pp312–13)* near Madrid.

Baroque fountain in one of the patios in the Universidad

The moat and watchtowers are evidence of the importance given to protecting the king's lucrative tobacco monopoly.

Jean Forestier, director of the Bois de Boulogne in Paris, who created a leafy setting for the 1929 Ibero-American Exposition. The most dazzling legacies of this extravaganza are the Plaza de España, decorated with regional scenes painted on ceramic tiles, and the Plaza de América, both the work of Aníbal González.

On the latter, in the Pabellón Mudéjar, the Museo de Artes y Costumbres Populares displays traditional Andalusian folk arts. Nearby, the Neo-Renaissance Pabellón de las Bellas Artes houses the provincial Museo Arqueológico. Among the exhibits devoted to the Roman era are statues and fragments found at Itálica *(see p452)*.

Fuente de los Leones

Plaza de América

Museo Arqueológico

Pabellón Real

The Isleta de los Patos sits in a lake graced by ducks and swans.

Museo de Artes y Costumbres Populares

Decorative tiles at Cerámica Santa Ana, a popular ceramics shop in Triana

Triana ❼

Map 3 A2. [tram] .C3, 40, 43.

THIS CLOSE-KNIT AREA, named after the Roman Emperor Trajan, was once Seville's gypsy quarter. Triana remains a traditional working-class district, with compact, flower-filled streets and a tangibly independent atmosphere. For centuries it has been famous for its potteries. The best-known of its ceramics shops today is Cerámica Santa Ana at No. 31 Calle San Jorge.

A good way to approach Triana is across the Puente de Isabel II, leading to the Plaza del Altozano. This square has glass-fronted, wrought-iron balconies called *miradores*. Nearby is one of the characteristic streets of the area, the Calle Rodrigo de Triana, with its houses painted in white and ochre. It is named after the Andalusian sailor who was first to sight the shores of the New World on Columbus's momentous voyage of 1492.

The Iglesia de Santa Ana, founded in the 13th century and splendidly renovated, is Triana's most popular church. In the baptistry is the Gypsy Font, which is believed to pass on the gift of flamenco song to the children of the faithful.

Isla de la Cartuja ❽

Map 1 B2. [tel] (95) 448 06 11. [bus] C1, C2, C3, C4, E5. **Monasterio de Santa María de las Cuevas** ☐ Apr–Sep: 11am–9pm Tue–Sun, Oct–Mar: 11am–7pm Tue–Sun. 🖾 🔥 **Pabellón de la Navegación** [tel] (95) 446 00 89. ☐ 10am–1pm, 5–8pm Tue–Sun. 🖾 🔥

THE ISLA DE LA CARTUJA was the site of Expo '92 (see pp64–5). Since then, large-scale redevelopment has been gradually transforming it into a complex of exhibition halls, museums and leisure areas.

The 15th-century Carthusian Monasterio de Santa María de las Cuevas, inhabited by monks until 1836, is at the heart of the area. Columbus stayed and worked here, and his body lay buried in the crypt of its church, the Capilla Santa Ana, between 1507 and 1542. The monastery was restored as a central exhibit for Expo '92.

By the river, south of the monastery, is the Pabellón de la Navegación, a maritime museum, and a replica of the Nao Victoria, a 16th-century ship. Nearby is the high-tech Omnimax Cinema, whose specially created films about the earth, explorers and space travel were among the most popular of the exhibits of Expo '92. Films are projected on an immense, semicircular screen, 24 m (80 ft) in diameter.

The centrepiece of Expo, the Lago de España, is to be turned into a mock ocean with islands and galleon battles, as part of a new theme park.

Tours around La Cartuja can be arranged. Contact the tourist office for further information.

Main entrance of the Carthusian Monasterio de Santa María de las Cuevas, founded in 1400

SEVILLE STREET FINDER

THE MAP REFERENCES given with the sights described in the Seville section of the guide refer to the maps on the following pages. Map references are also given for Seville hotels (see pp561–2) and restaurants (pp600–601). The schematic map below shows the area of Seville covered by the *Street Finder*. The symbols used for the sights and other features are listed in the key at the foot of the page.

KEY TO STREET FINDER

Major sight	**P** Parking	— One-way street
Place of interest	**i** Tourist information	Pedestrianized street
Other building	**✚** Hospital with casualty unit	
🚆 Railway station	**🚓** Police station	
🚌 Main bus stop	**✝** Church	
🚍 Coach station	**✚** Convent or monastery	
⛴ River bus boarding point	**⊠** Post office	**SCALE OF MAP PAGES**
🚕 Taxi rank	**═** Railway line	

0 kilometres 1

0 miles 0.5

0 metres 250

0 yards 250

ANDALUSIA

HUELVA · CÁDIZ · MÁLAGA · GIBRALTAR · SEVILLA
CÓRDOBA · GRANADA · JAÉN · ALMERÍA

ANDALUSIA IS WHERE *all Spain's stereotypes meet. Bullfighters, beaches, flamenco, white villages, cave houses, gaudy fiestas, religious processions, tapas and sherry are all here in abundance. But each is part of a larger whole, which includes great art and architecture, nature reserves and an easy-going way of life.*

The eight provinces of Andalusia stretch across Southern Spain from the deserts of Almería to the Portuguese border. One of Spain's longest rivers, the Guadalquivir, bisects the region. Andalusia is linked to the central tableland by a pass, the Desfiladero de Despeñaperros. The highest peaks on the Spanish mainland are in Andalusia's Sierra Nevada.

Successive invaders left their mark on Andalusia. The Romans built cities in this southern province, which they called Baetica, among them Córdoba, its capital, and the well-preserved Itálica near Seville. It was in Andalusia that the Moors lingered longest and left their greatest buildings – Córdoba's Mezquita and the splendid palace of the Alhambra in Granada. Inevitably, perhaps, the most visited places are the great cities and the busy Costa del Sol, with Gibraltar, a geographical and historical oddity, at its western end. But there are many attractions tucked into other corners of the region. Many of the sights of Huelva province, bordering Portugal, are associated with Christopher Columbus, who set sail from here in 1492. Film directors have put to good use the atmospheric landscapes of Almería's arid interior, which are reminiscent of the Wild West or Arabia. Discreetly concealed among the countless olive groves that cover Jaén province, but not to be missed, are Andalusia's two lovely Renaissance towns, Úbeda and Baeza.

The city of Jaén surrounded by olive groves, seen from the Castillo de Santa Catalina

◁ Doorway into the *mihrab* (prayer niche) in the Mezquita at Córdoba

Exploring Andalusia

A NDALUSIA IS SPAIN'S MOST VARIED region. It offers dramatic
desert scenery at Tabernas, water sports on the Costa del
Sol, skiing in the Sierra Nevada and sherry tasting in Jerez. Of
the many nature reserves, the vast, watery Doñana teems with
birdlife, while Cazorla is a rugged limestone massif. Granada
and Córdoba are unmissable for their Moorish heritage;
Úbeda and Baeza are Renaissance gems; and Ronda
is one of dozens of superb white towns.

KEY

▬▬	Motorway
▬▬	Major road
▬▬	Minor road
▬▬	Scenic route
➰	River
☼	Viewpoint

The smart marina at Sotogrande

GETTING AROUND

Andalusia has a modern motorway network, with the
principal NIV from Madrid following the Guadalquivir
valley to Córdoba, Seville and Cádiz. The fast AVE train
links Seville and Córdoba with Madrid. Though most other
large towns are on the rail network, services may be infrequent. Coaches cover most of the region, but journeys
can be slow. A car is essential for exploring remoter areas.
The main airports are Málaga, Seville, Jerez and Gibraltar.

0 kilometres   25

0 miles   25

SEE ALSO

• *Where to Stay* pp563–67

• *Restaurants and Bars* pp601–605

Singers in festive spirit at a village christening

SIGHTS AT A GLANCE

The famed *jamón ibérico* hanging in a bar in Jabugo, Sierra de Aracena

Sierra de Aracena ❶

Huelva. 🚉 *El Repilado.* 🚌 *Aracena.*
🛈 *Aracena, (959) 12 83 55.*

THIS WILD MOUNTAIN RANGE is one of the most remote and least visited corners of Andalusia. On the hillside above its main town, Aracena, are the ruins of a Moorish fort. The hill is pitted with caverns and in one of these, the **Gruta de las Maravillas**, is a lake in a chamber hung with many stalactites.

The village of **Jabugo** is famed for the tastiest cured ham in Spain, *jamón ibérico*, or *pata negra (see p 401)*.

Bronze jug, Museo Provincial, Huelva

Off the C421 are the giant opencast mines at Minas de Riotinto, where iron, copper and silver have been exploited since Phoenician times. The **Museo Minero** in the village traces the history of the Rio Tinto Company.

🏕 **Gruta de las Maravillas**
Calle San José. ☎ *(959) 12 83 55.*
🔘 *daily.* 🄯
🏛 **Museo Minero**
Plaza del Museo. ☎ *(959) 59 00 25.*
🔘 *Tue–Sun.* 🄯

Huelva ❷

Huelva. 👥 *142,000.* 🚉 🚌 🛈
Avda Alemania 12, (959) 25 74 03.
🄯 *Fri.* 🎉 *Las Colombinas (3 Aug).*

FOUNDED AS ONUBA by the Phoenicians, Huelva had its grandest days as a Roman port. It was almost wiped out in the great Lisbon earthquake of 1755. It is an industrial city today, sprawling around the quayside on the Río Odiel.

Columbus's departure for the New World *(see p52)* from Palos de la Frontera, across the Río Odiel estuary, is celebrated in the exhibits of the excellent **Museo Provincial**, which also charts the history of the Riotinto mines. To the east of the centre, the Barrio Reina Victoria is a bizarre example of English mock-Tudor suburban bungalows built by the Rio Tinto Company for its workers in the early 20th century. South of the town, at Punta del Sebo, the Monumento a Colón, a rather bleak statue of Columbus created by Gertrude Vanderbilt Whitney in 1929, dominates the Odiel estuary.

ENVIRONS: There are three resorts with sandy beaches near Huelva: **Punta Umbria**, on a promontory next to the bird-rich wetlands of the Marismas del Odiel; **Isla Cristina**, which is also an important fishing port and has excellent seafood restaurants; and **Mazagón** with miles of windswept dunes.

The hilly region east of Huelva known as **El Condado** produces several of Andalusia's finest wines, and Bollullos del Condado has the largest wine cooperative in the region. **Niebla**, nearby, has a Roman bridge. The town walls and 12th-century **Castillo de los Guzmanes** are both Moorish.

🏛 **Museo Provincial**
Alameda Sundheim 13. ☎ *(959) 25 93 00.* 🔘 *Tue –Sat.* 🄯
🏰 **Castillo de los Guzmanes**
C/ Castillo, Niebla. ☎ *(959) 36 22 70.*
🔘 *Mon–Sat. Phone to arrange visit.*

Monasterio de la Rábida ❸

Huelva. 🚌 *from Palos de la Frontera.*
☎ *(959) 35 04 11.* 🔘 *Tue–Sun.* 🄯

FOUR KILOMETRES (2.5 miles) to the north of Palos de la Frontera is the Franciscan **Monasterio de la Rábida**, founded in the 15th century.

In 1491, a dejected Columbus sought refuge here after his plans to sail west to find the East Indies had been rejected by the Catholic Monarchs. Its prior, Juan Pérez, fatefully used his considerable influence as Queen Isabella's confessor to reverse the royal decision.

Inside, frescoes painted by Daniel Vásquez Díaz in 1930 glorify the explorer's life and discoveries. Also worth seeing are the Mudéjar cloisters, the flower-filled gardens and the beamed chapterhouse.

Frescoes depicting the life of Columbus at the Monasterio de la Rábida

Palos de la Frontera ❹

Huelva. 🏘 *7,000.* 🚉 ℹ *C/ Rábida 3, (959) 35 08 51.* 🚌 *Sat.* 🎉 *Virgen de Santa María de la Rábida (3 & 16 Aug).*

COLUMBUS PUT TO SEA on 3 August 1492 from Palos, the home town of his two captains, the brothers Martín and Vicente Pinzón. Martín's former home, the **Casa Museo de Martín Alonso Pinzón**, is now a small museum of exploration, and his statue stands in the main square.

The 15th-century **Iglesia de San Jorge** has a fine portal, through which Columbus left after hearing Mass before leaving to board his caravel, the *Santa María*. The pier is now forlornly silted up.

ENVIRONS: In the beautiful white town of **Moguer** are treasures such as the 16th-century hermitage of Nuestra Señora de Montemayor, and the Neo-Classical town hall *(ayuntamiento).* The **Convento de Santa Clara** and the Monasterio de San Francisco have pretty cloisters.

🏛 **Casa Museo de Martín Alonso Pinzón**
Calle Colón 28. 📞 *(959) 35 01 99.* ⏰ *Tue –Sun.*
⛪ **Convento de Santa Clara**
Plaza de las Monjas. 📞 *(959) 37 01 07.* ⏰ *Tue –Sat.* ● *public hols.* 🎫

El Rocío ❺

Huelva. 🏘 *1,200.* 🚉 ℹ *Avda de la Canaliega, (959) 44 26 84.* 🚌 *Tue.* 🎉 *Romeria (May/Jun).*

BORDERING the wetlands of the Parque Nacional de Doñana *(see pp440–41)*, El Rocío is famous for its annual *romería*, which sees almost a million people converge on the village. Many of the pilgrims travel from distant parts of Spain, some on gaudily decorated ox-carts, to visit the **Iglesia de Nuestra Señora del Rocío**. A statue of the Virgin in the church is believed to have performed miraculous healings since 1280. Early on the Monday morning, men from Almonte fight to carry the statue in procession, and the crowd clambers on to the float to touch the image.

ANDALUSIA'S FIESTAS

Crowds following the image of the Virgin at El Rocío

Carnival *(Feb/Mar)*, Cádiz. The whole city puts on fancy dress for one of Europe's largest and most colourful carnivals. Groups of singers practise for many months to perform ditties satirizing current fashions, celebrities and politicians.
Romería de la Virgen de la Cabeza *(last Sun in Apr)*, Andújar (Jaén). A mass pilgrimage to a lonely sanctuary in the Sierra Morena.
Día de la Cruz *(first week in May)*, Granada and Córdoba. Neighbourhood groups compete to create the most colourful crosses adorned with flowers on squares and street corners.
Córdoba Patio Fiesta *(mid-May).* Flower-decked patios in old Córdoba are opened to the public with displays of flamenco.
El Rocío *(May/Jun).* More than 70 brotherhoods of pilgrims arrive at the village of El Rocío to pay homage to the Virgen del Rocío.
Columbus Festival *(late Jul/early Aug)*, Huelva. This celebration of Columbus's voyage is dedicated to the native music and dance of a different Latin American country every year.
Exaltación al Río Guadalquivir *(mid-Aug)*, Sanlúcar de la Barrameda (Cádiz). Horses are raced on the beach at the mouth of the Río Guadalquivir.

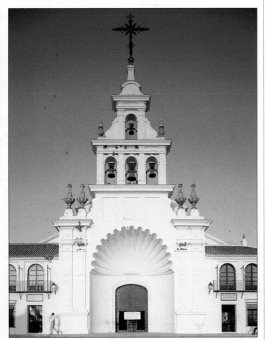

Iglesia de Nuestra Señora del Rocío, El Rocío

Parque Nacional de Doñana **❻**

Doñana NATIONAL PARK is ranked among Europe's greatest wetlands. Together with its adjoining protected areas, the park covers in excess of 75,000 hectares (185,000 acres) of marshes and sand dunes. The area used to be a hunting ground (coto) belonging to the Dukes of Medina Sidonia. As the land was never suitable for human settlers, wildlife was able to flourish. In 1969, this large area became officially protected. In addition to a wealth of endemic species, thousands of migratory birds stop over in winter when the marshes become flooded again, after months of drought.

Bird-spotting from boat on the Guadalquivir

Shrub Vegetation
Backing the sand dunes is a thick carpet of lavender, rock rose and other low shrubs.

La Rocina
El Acebrón
El Rocío
H312
El Acebuche
Matalascañas
Palacio de Doñana
Laguna de Santa Ol
Monte de Doñana

Umbrella Pine
This species of pine tree (Pinus pinea) *thrives in the wide dune belt, putting roots deep into the sand. The trees may get buried beneath the dunes.*

Coastal Dunes
Softly rounded, white dunes, up to 30 m (100 ft) high, fringe the park's coastal edge. The dunes, ribbed by prevailing winds off the Atlantic, shift constantly.

Monte de Doñana, the wooded area behind the sand dunes, provides shelter for lynx, deer and boar.

The Interior
The number of visitors to the park's interior is strictly controlled to ensure minimal environmental impact. The only way to view the wildlife here is on officially guided day tours.

KEY

▨	Marshes
▨	Dunes
•••	National park boundary
•••	Protected area
▬	Road
✿	Viewpoint
ℹ	Tourist information
P	Parking
🚌	Coach stop

Deer

Fallow deer (Dama dama) *and larger red deer* (Cervus elaphus) *roam the park. Stags engage in fierce contests in late summer as they prepare for breeding.*

VISITORS' CHECKLIST

Huelva & Sevilla. **Marginal areas**
🔲 *daily.* ● *1 Jan, 6 Jan, Pentecost, 25 Dec.* 🛈 **La Rocina** 📞 *(959) 44 23 40.* 🛈 **Palacio del Acebrón**: *exhibition "Man and Doñana".* 🛈 **El Acebuche**: *reception, audiovisual exhibition, café and shop.* 📞 *(959) 44 87 11.*
Self-guided footpaths:
La Rocina and Charco de la Boca (90 min); El Acebrón from Palacio del Acebrón (45 min); Laguna del Acebuche from Acebuche (45 min). **Inner park areas**
🔲 *May–Sep: Mon–Sat; Oct–Apr: Tue–Sun. Visit by guided tour only. Jeeps leave from El Acebuche at 8:30am & 5pm. Bookings* 📞 *(959) 43 04 32.* 🈂️

Wild cattle use the marshes as water holes.

Río Guadiamar

Marisma de Iznalcázar

Marisma Gallega

Río Guadalquivir

Sanlúcar de Barrameda

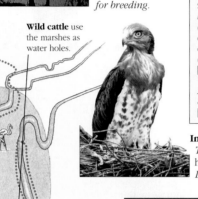

Imperial Eagle

The imperial eagle (Aquila heliaca adalberti) *is one of Doñana's rarest birds.*

Greater Flamingo

During the winter months, the salty lakes and marshes provide the beautiful, pink greater flamingo (Phoenicopterus ruber) *with crustaceans, its main diet.*

THE LYNX'S LAST REFUGE

The lynx is one of Europe's rarest mammals. In Doñana about 60 pairs of Spanish lynx *(Lynx pardellus)* have found a refuge. They have yellow-brown fur with dark brown spots and pointed ears with black tufts. Research is under way into this shy, nocturnal animal, which tends to stay hidden in scrub. It feeds mainly on rabbits and ducks, but might catch an unguarded fawn.

The elusive lynx, only glimpsed with patience

0 kilometres   5

0 miles   5

Sanlúcar de Barrameda ❼

Cádiz. 🏠 55,000. 🚌 ℹ️ Calzada del Ejército, (956) 36 61 10. 🚋 Wed. 🎉 Exaltación al Río Guadalquivir and horse races (mid-Aug).

A FISHING PORT at the mouth of the Río Guadalquivir, Sanlúcar is overlooked by a Moorish **castle**. This was the departure point for Columbus's third voyage in 1498 and also for Magellan's 1519 expedition to circumnavigate the globe.

Sanlúcar is best-known for its light, dry manzanilla sherry made by, among other producers, **Bodegas Barbadillo**. Boats from the quay take visitors across the river to the Parque Nacional de Doñana (see pp440–41).

ENVIRONS: Chipiona, along the coast, is a lively little resort town with an excellent beach. The walled town of **Lebrija**, inland, enjoys views over vineyards. Its Iglesia Santa María de la Oliva is a reconsecrated 12th-century Almohad mosque.

🍷 **Bodegas Barbadillo**
C/ Luis de Eguilaz 11. 📞 (956) 36 08 94. 🔘 Thu (by appointment). ♿

Entrance to the Barbadillo bodega in Sanlúcar de Barrameda

Jerez de la Frontera ❽

Cádiz. 🏠 190,000. ✈️ 🚌 🚏 ℹ️ Alameda Cristina 7, (956) 33 11 50. 🚋 Mon. 🎉 Grape Harvest (Sep).

J EREZ IS THE CAPITAL of sherry production (see pp402–403) and many bodegas can be visited. Among the well-known names are **González Byass** and **Pedro Domecq**.

The city is also famous for its **Real Escuela Andaluza de Arte Ecuestre**, a school of equestrian skills. There are public dressage displays on Thursdays. If you visit on another day you may be able to watch the horses being trained.

The **Museo de Relojes**, nearby, has one of the largest clock collections in Europe. On the Plaza de San Juan, the 18th-century **Palacio de Penmartín** houses the Centro Andaluz de Flamenco, where exhibitions give a good introduction to this music and dance tradition (see pp406–407). The partially restored, 11th-century **Alcázar** encompasses a well-preserved mosque, now a church. Just to the north is the **cathedral**, whose most interesting exhibit, The Sleeping Girl by Zurbarán, is in the sacristy.

ENVIRONS: The port of **El Puerto de Santa María** exports great quantities of sherry. Here, too, several bodegas can be visited including **Osborne** and **Terry**. The town also has a 13th-century castle and one of the largest and most famous bullrings in Spain.

🐴 **Real Escuela Andaluza de Arte Ecuestre**
Avda de Abrantes. 📞 (956) 31 11 11. 🔘 Mon–Fri. ● public hols. 📷 ♿
🏛️ **Museo de Relojes**
Calle Cervantes. 📞 (956) 18 21 00. 🔘 Mon–Sat. ● public hols. 📷 ♿
🐴 **Palacio de Penmartín**
Plaza de San Juan 1. 📞 (956) 34 92 65. 🔘 Mon–Fri. ● public hols.
🏰 **Alcázar**
Alameda Vieja. 🔘 Mon–Sat. ● public hols. ♿
🍷 **Sherry Bodegas**
🔘 phone in advance for tour times.
González Byass, C/ Manuel María González 12, Jerez. 📞 (956) 34 00 00.
Pedro Domecq, C/ San Ildefonso 3, Jerez. 📞 (956) 15 15 00. **Sandeman,** C/ Pizarro 10, Jerez. 📞 (956) 30 11 04. **Osborne,** C/ de los Moros, Puerto de Santa María. 📞 (956) 85 52 11.
Terry, C/ Santísima Trinidad, Puerto de Santa María. 📞 (956) 48 30 00.

Real Escuela Andaluza de Arte Ecuestre, Jerez de la Frontera

Cádiz

Egyptian mask, Museo de Cádiz

Jutting out of the Bay of Cádiz, and almost entirely surrounded by water, Cádiz lays claim to being Europe's oldest city. Legend names Hercules as its founder, although history credits the Phoenicians with establishing the town of Gadir in 1100 BC. Occupied by the Carthaginians, Romans and Moors in turn, the city also prospered after the Reconquest *(see pp50–51)* on wealth taken from the New World. In 1587 Sir Francis Drake sacked the city in the first of many British attacks in the war for world trade. In 1812 Cádiz briefly became Spain's capital when the nation's first constitution was declared here *(see p59)*.

VISITORS' CHECKLIST

Cádiz. 🛉 155,000. 🚂 Plaza de Sevilla, (956) 25 43 01. 🚌 Plaza de la Hispanidad, (956) 21 17 63. 🛈 Calle Calderón de la Barca 1, (956) 21 13 13. 🖪 Mon. 🎭 Carnival (Feb/Mar), Día de la Patrona (7 Oct).

Zurbarán's *Saint Bruno in Ecstasy*, in the Museo de Cádiz

Exploring Cádiz
The joy of visiting Cádiz is to wander along the waterfront with its well-tended gardens and open squares before exploring the old town, which is full of narrow alleys full of market and street life.

The pride of the city is its Carnival *(see p439)* – a riotous explosion of festivities, fancy dress, singing and drinking.

✛ Catedral
Known as the Catedral Nueva (New Cathedral) because it was built over the site of an older one, this Baroque and Neo-Classical church, with its dome of golden yellow tiles, is one of Spain's largest. Its carved stalls came from a Carthusian monastery. In the crypt is the tomb of the composer Manuel de Falla (1876–1946), a native of Cádiz. The cathedral's treasures are stored in the adjacent museum.

🏛 Museo de Cádiz
Plaza de Mina. 🖀 (956) 21 22 81. ◘ Tue–Sun. ◖ public hols. ♿ On the ground floor of this spacious museum there are archaeological exhibits charting the history of Cádiz, including Phoenician stone sarcophagi and statues of Roman emperors. Upstairs is one of the largest art galleries in Andalusia, displaying works by Rubens, Zurbarán and Murillo, as well as paintings by contemporary Spanish artists. On the third floor is a collection of puppets made for village fiestas. Some more recent ones satirize current political figures.

✛ Oratorio de San Felipe Neri
This 18th-century church has been a shrine to liberalism since 1812. In that year, as Napoleon tightened his grip on Spain during the War of Independence *(see pp58–9)*, a provisional government assembled here to try to lay the foundations of Spain's first constitutional monarchy. The liberal constitution it declared was bold but ineffectual.

CÁDIZ CATHEDRAL

The cupola was built between 1812 and 1838 by Juan Daura, the last in a long line of architects of this cathedral.

Baroque vaults

The presbytery altar was partly sponsored by Isabel II *(see p67)*.

Neo-Classical tower

Neo-Classical façade

Fishing boats at the resort of Zahara de los Atunes on the Costa de la Luz

Costa de la Luz 🔟

Málaga. 🚇 Cádiz. 🚇 Cádiz, Tarifa.
🛈 Cádiz, (956) 24 01 61.

THE COSTA DE LA LUZ (Coast of Light) between Cádiz and Tarifa, at Spain's southernmost tip, is an unspoiled, windswept stretch of coast characterized by strong, pure light – the source of its name. From the Sierra del Cabrito, to the west of Algeciras, it is often possible to see the outline of Tangier and the parched Moroccan landscape below the purple-tinged Rif mountains across the narrow Strait of Gibraltar.

Tarifa is named after an 8th-century Moorish commander, Tarif ben Maluk, who landed there with his forces during the Moorish conquest *(see pp48–9)*. Later, Tarifa and its 10th-century castle were defended by the legendary hero, Guzmán, during a siege by the Moors in 1292.

Tarifa has since become the windsurfing capital of Europe. The breezes that blow on to this coast also drive the numerous wind turbines visible in the hills above Tarifa.

Off the N340, at the end of a long, narrow road which strikes out across a wilderness of cacti, sunflowers and lone cork trees, is **Zahara de los Atunes**, a modest holiday resort with a few hotels. **Conil de la Frontera**, to the west, is busier and more built up.

The English admiral, Nelson, defeated a Spanish and French fleet off **Cabo de Trafalgar** in 1805, but died in the battle.

A Tour Around the Pueblos Blancos 🔢

INSTEAD OF SETTLING on Andalusia's plains, where they would have fallen prey to bandits, some Andalusians chose to live in fortified hilltop towns and villages. These are known as *pueblos blancos* (white towns) because they are whitewashed in the Moorish tradition *(see p22)*. They are working agricultural towns today, but touring them will reveal a host of references to the past.

Jimena de la Frontera ⑨
Set amid hills, where wild bulls graze among cork and olive trees, this town has a ruined Moorish castle.

Ubrique ②
Nestling at the foot of the Sierra de Ubrique, this *pueblo* is known for its flourishing leather industry.

SEVILLA

CÁDIZ,
JEREZ

Arcos de la Frontera ①

Embalse
los Huron...

Charco de
los Hurones

C344

CA521

Majaceite

CA503

KEY

━━ Tour route

═══ Other roads

TIPS FOR DRIVERS

Tour length: 205 km (127 miles).
Stopping-off points: There are places to stay and eat at all of these pueblos, but Ronda has the widest range of hotels (see p566) and restaurants (see p605). Arcos has a parador (see p563).

Gaucín ⑧
From here there are unsurpassed vistas over the Mediterranean, the Atlantic, the Rock of Gibraltar and across the strait to the Rif mountains of North Africa.

La Sauceda

0 kilometres   10

0 miles   5

Arcos de la Frontera ⑪

Cádiz. 🚶 30,000. 🚌 ℹ️ *Plaza del Cabildo, (956) 70 22 64.*
🚪 *Fri.* 🎉 *Velada de Nuestra Señora de las Nieves (4–6 Aug).*

A LTHOUGH LEGEND has it that a son of Noah founded Arcos it is more probable that it was the Iberians. It gained the name Arcobriga in the Roman era and, under the Caliphate of Córdoba *(see p48)*, became the Moorish stronghold of Medina Arkosh. It is an archetypal white town, with a labyrinthine old quarter twisting up to a ruined castle.

On the Plaza de España, at the top of the town, are the **parador** *(see p563)* and the **Iglesia de Santa María de la Asunción**, a Late Gothic-Mudéjar building noted for its choir stalls and altarpiece. The huge, Gothic **Iglesia de San Pedro**, perched on the edge of a cliff formed by the Río Guadalete, is a striking building. Nearby is the **Palacio del Mayorazgo**, which has an ornate Renaissance façade. The **town hall** *(ayuntamiento)* has a fine Mudéjar ceiling.

ENVIRONS: In the 15th-century the Guzmán family was granted the dukedom of **Medina Sidonia**, a white town atop a conical hill, southwest of Arcos de la Frontera. The family grew wealthy from its investments in the Americas and, as a result, Medina Sidonia became one of the most important ducal seats in Spain. The Gothic Iglesia de Santa María la Coronada is the town's finest building. It contains a notable collection of Renaissance religious art.

Iglesia de Santa María de la Asunción in Arcos de la Frontera

🏛️ **Palacio del Mayorazgo**
C/ San Pedro 2. 📞 *(956) 70 30 13.*
⭕ *Mon–Fri.* ⚫ *public hols.* ♿
🏛️ **Ayuntamiento**
Plaza del Cabildo. 📞 *(956) 70 00 02.*
⭕ *by permission.* ⚫ *public hols.*

Zahara de la Sierra ③
Fanning out below a castle ruin, this fine *pueblo blanco* has been declared a national monument.

COSTA DEL SOL

Grazalema ④
This village in the Sierra de Grazalema has the highest rainfall in Spain.

Ronda la Vieja ⑤
Significant remains of the Roman town of Acinipo, including a theatre, can be visited.

Setenil ⑥
Some of the streets of this unusual white town, which climbs up the sides of a gorge, are covered by rock overhangs. The gorge was carved out of volcanic tufa rock by the Río Trejo.

Ronda ⑦
(see pp446–7)

Street-by-Street: Ronda **⑬**

Plate hand-painted in Ronda

O NE OF THE MOST spectacularly located cities in Spain, Ronda sits on a massive rocky outcrop, straddling a precipitous limestone cleft. Because of its impregnable position this town was one of the last Moorish bastions, finally falling to the Christians in 1485. On the south side perches a classic Moorish *pueblo blanco (see pp444–5)* of cobbled alleys, window grilles and dazzling whitewash – most historic sights are in this part of the town. Located in El Mercadillo, the newer town, is one of the oldest bullrings in Spain.

★ Puente Nuevo
An impressive feat of 18th-century civil engineering, the "New Bridge" over the 100-m (330-ft) deep Tajo gorge joins old and new Ronda.

Convento de Santo Domingo was the local headquarters of the Inquisition *(see p264).*

To El Mercadillo, Plaza de Toros, parador (see p566) and tourist information

Casa del Rey Moro
From this 18th-century mansion, built on the foundations of a Moorish palace, 365 steps lead down to the river.

Mirador El Campillo (viewpoint)

SANTO DOMINGO

CALLE ARMIÑAN

TENORIO

PLAZA DEL CAMPILLO

0 metres 75
0 yards 75

★ Palacio Mondragón
Much of this palace was rebuilt following the Reconquest (see pp50–51), but its arcaded patio is adorned with original Moorish mosaics and plasterwork.

STAR SIGHTS
★ Puente Nuevo
★ Palacio Mondragón

Palacio del Marqués de Salvatierra
Bizarre images of biblical scenes and South American Indians embellish the façade of this palace, built in Renaissance style in the 18th century.

To Puente Viejo, Baños Árabes

Santa María la Mayor
A minaret and a Muslim prayer niche survive from the 13th-century mosque which once stood on the site of this church.

Minarete San Sebastián is a remnant of a 14th-century mosque.

MARQUÉS DE SALVATIERRA

CARMEN

ESCALERA

ARMIÑÁN

PLAZA DUQUESA DE PARCENT

VISITORS' CHECKLIST

Málaga. 🏠 40,000. 🚌 Avenida de Andalucía, (95) 287 16 73. 🚆 Plaza Concesión García Redondo, (95) 287 22 62. 🛈 Plaza de España 1, (95) 287 12 72. 🛒 Sun. 🎉 Virgen de la Paz (24 Jan), Semana Santa (Easter Week), Feria de la Primavera (21 May), Feria de Pedro Romero (Sep). **Casa del Rey Moro** 🌑 to the public. **Palacio del Marqués de Salvatierra** ⬜ Mon–Wed, Fri, Sat. 🌑 25 Jul–15 Sep. 📷 ♿ **Palacio Mondragón** ⬜ daily. 📷 ♿ **Plaza de Toros and Museo Taurino** ⬜ daily. 📷 ♿

Ayuntamiento
The town hall was remodelled in the 20th century and incorporates parts of older buildings. It has a two-tier arcaded façade and Mudéjar ceiling.

KEY
— — — Suggested route

BULLFIGHTING AT RONDA

Ronda's Plaza de Toros is the spiritual home of bullfighting. Inaugurated in 1785, it is one of the oldest, most important bullrings in Spain. In September, aficionados travel from all over the country for the singular atmosphere of the Corrida Goyesca and millions watch it on television. It is the dream of every aspiring matador to fight at Ronda. The classic Ronda style (more severe than the exuberant School of Seville) was developed by Pedro Romero. Born in 1754, he is widely considered to be the father of modern bullfighting.

Romero, who killed over 6,000 bulls

Algeciras ⓮

Cádiz. 🅟 150,000. 🅓 🅘 Calle
Juan de la Cierva, (956) 57 26 36.
🅣 Tue. 🅡 Feria Real (24 Jun–2 Jul).

FROM THE INDUSTRIAL city of
Algeciras, there are spectacular views of Gibraltar, 14 km
(9 miles) away across its bay.
The city is a major fishing port
and Europe's main gateway for
ferries to North Africa, especially Tangier and Spain's
territories of Ceuta and Melilla.

Gibraltar ⓯

British Crown Colony. 🅟 30,000. 🅓
🅘 Gibraltar Tourist Board, Duke of Kent
House, Cathedral Square, (9567) 749 50.
🅣 Wed–Fri–Sat 🅡 Nat Day (10 Sep).

THE HIGH, ROCKY headland of
Gibraltar was signed over
to Britain "in perpetuity" at the
Treaty of Utrecht in 1713 (see
p58). Today, about 4 million
people, mostly intent on duty-
free shopping, stream across the
border every year from La Línea
de la Concepción in Spain.

Among the chief sights of
Gibraltar are those testifying to
its strategic military importance
over the centuries. Half way up

**St Michael's Cave. During World
War II it served as a hospital.**

the famous Rock are an 8th-
century Moorish castle, whose
keep is still used as a prison,
and 80 km (50 miles) of **siege
tunnels** housing storerooms
and barracks. **St Michael's
Cave**, which served as a hospital during World War II, is now
used for classical concerts.

The **Apes' Den**, near Europa
Point, Gibraltar's southernmost
tip, is home to the tailless apes.
Legend says that the British will
keep the Rock only as long as
the apes remain there, despite
the machinations of politicans.

A cable car takes visitors to
the **Top of the Rock** at 450 m
(1,475 ft). **Gibraltar Museum**
charts the colony's history.

🎪 **The Keep, Siege Tunnels,
St Michael's Cave, Apes' Den**
Upper Rock Area. 🅒 (9567) 424 00.
🅞 daily. 🅞 1 Jan, 25 Dec. 🅦
🏛 **Gibraltar Museum**
18 Bombhouse Lane. 🅒 (9567) 742
89. 🅞 Mon–Sat. 🅞 public hols. 🅦

The Costa del Sol

THANKS TO ITS AVERAGE of 300 days' sunshine
a year and its varied coastline, the Costa
del Sol, between Gibraltar and Málaga, offers
a full range of beach-based holidays and water
sports. Complementing the sophistication and
luxury of Marbella are many other popular
resorts aimed at the mass market. More than
30 of Europe's finest golf courses lie just inland.

Puerto Banús is Marbella'
ostentatious marina. The
expensive shops, restaura
and glittering nightlife refle
the wealth of its clientele.

Estepona's quiet evenings
make it popular with families
with young children. Behind
the big hotels are old squares
shaded by orange trees.

San Pedro de Alcánta

Puerto

Estepona

• Sotogrande

Marina at Sotogrande
is an exclusive resort of
luxury villas. The
marina is fronted by
good seafood
restaurants.

San Roque

Algeciras •

Gibraltar

Tarifa

**San Pedro de
Alcántara** is a quiet
resort with a modern
marina and smart
holiday developments.

Yachts and motorboats in the exclusive marina of Marbella – the summer home of the international jet set

Marbella 🔟

Málaga. 🏘 80,000. 🚆 🛈 *Glorieta de la Fontanilla, (95) 277 14 42.* 🕓 *Mon.* 🎪 *San Bernabé (11 Jun).*

MARBELLA IS ONE of Europe's most exclusive holiday resorts, frequented by royalty and film stars. In winter, the major attraction is the golf. Among the delights of the old town, with its spotlessly clean alleys, squares, and smart shops and restaurants, is the **Iglesia de Nuestra Señora de la Encarnación**. Some of Picasso's least-known work can be seen in the **Museo de Grabado Contemporáneo**.

Taking part in the nightlife means bringing a full wallet; luckily the beaches – Babaloo, Victor's, Don Carlos, Cabopino and Las Dunas – are free.

🏛 Museo de Grabado Contemporáneo
C/ Hospital Bazan. 📞 *(95) 282 50 35.* 🕓 *Mon – Fri.* ⬤ *public hols.* 🗺

Marbella is the Costa del Sol's most stylish resort. The Playa de Don Carlos is considered the best of its 29 beaches.

Málaga

Rincón de la Victoria

Torremolinos

Rincón de la Victoria is an unspoiled family beach, famous for its spit-roasted sardines.

Benalmádena Costa

Fuengirola

Cabopino

Cabopino, on a not-too-crowded stretch of coast, is a wide, sandy nudist beach beside a modern marina.

Benalmádena Costa caters almost exclusively for package holidays. Behind the rather rocky beaches and very large marina is a plethora of tourist attractions.

Torremolinos, a high-rise holiday metropolis, is less brash than it used to be. Huge sums have been spent on new squares, a promenade, green spaces, and improving the beach with millions of tonnes of golden sand.

Fuengirola still has an active fishing port – as these boxes of fresh fish suggest – although it is better known today as a package-holiday resort with a chiefly British clientele. It has a spectacular backdrop of steep, ochre mountains.

0 kilometres 10

0 miles 10

The main façade of Málaga's
cathedral, consecrated in 1588

Málaga ⑰

Málaga. 🏘 *600,000*. ✈ 🚂 🚌
🛈 *Pasaje de Chinitas 4, (95) 221
34 45*. 🚢 *Sun*. 🎭 *Carnival (Feb/Mar),
Feria (second Sat–third Sun of Aug)*.

MÁLAGA, the second largest
city in Andalusia, is today
a thriving port, just as it was
in Phoenician times (when it
was known as Malaca), and
again under the Romans and
then the Moors. It also flourished during the 19th century,
when sweet Málaga wine *(see
p402)* was one of Europe's
most popular drinks – until
phylloxera ravaged the area's
vineyards in 1876.

The **cathedral** was begun
in 1528 by Diego de Siloé, but
it is a bizarre mix of styles. The
half-built second tower, abandoned in 1765 when funds
ran out, gave the cathedral its
nickname: La Manquita ("the
one-armed one").

Málaga's **Museo de Bellas
Artes** has paintings by Ribera,
Murillo, Zurbarán and Morales
and some childhood sketches
by Pablo Picasso. The **Casa
Natal de Picasso**, where the
painter spent his early years,
is now the headquarters of
the Picasso Foundation.

Málaga's vast **Alcazaba** *(see
p49)* was built between the
8th–11th centuries. There is a
partially excavated Roman
amphitheatre by its entrance,
but the real attraction is the
display of Phoenician, Roman
and Moorish artifacts in the
Museo Arqueológico.

On the hill directly behind
the Alcazaba are the ruins of
the **Castillo de Gibralfaro**, a
14th-century Moorish castle.

ENVIRONS: In the beautiful
hills to the north and east of
Málaga is the **Parque Natural
de los Montes de Málaga**.
Wildlife, such as eagles and
wild boars, thrive here amid
the scent of lavender and wild
herbs. Walkers can follow a
number of scenic marked trails.
Going north on the C345 you
can also visit a small preserved winery of the 1840s.

🏛 **Museo de Bellas Artes**
Calle San Agustín 8. 📞 *(95) 221
83 82*. 🕐 *Tue–Sun*. 🏷
⚓ **Alcazaba and Museo
Arqueológico**
Calle Alcazabilla. 📞 *(95) 221 60 05*.
🕐 *Tue–Sun*. 🏷

Garganta del Chorro ⑱

Málaga. 🚂 *El Chorro*. 🚌 *Parque
Ardeles*. 🛈 *Avenida de la Constitución,
Álora, (95) 249 83 80*.

UP THE FERTILE Guadalhorce
valley, just beyond the
village of El Chorro, is one of
the geographical wonders of

Andalusia. The Garganta del
Chorro is an immense chasm,
180 m (590 ft) deep and in
places only 10 m (30 ft) wide,
cut by the river through a limestone mountain. Downstream,
a hydroelectric plant detracts
from the wildness of the place.

From the village, for a true
sense of the gorge's dizzying
dimensions, take the **Camino
del Rey**, a catwalk clinging to
the rock face and leading to a
bridge across the gorge.

ENVIRONS: Álora, a classic
white town *(see pp444–5)*
with a ruined Moorish hilltop
castle and an 18th-century
church, lies 12 km (7 miles)
down the valley.

Along the twisting MA441
from Álora is the village of
Carratraca. In the 19th and
early 20th centuries, Europe's
highest society travelled here
for the healing powers of the
sulphurous springs. These
days, Carratraca has a faded
glory – water still gushes out
at 700 litres (155 gal) a minute
and the outdoor baths remain
open, but they are little used.

The Garganta del Chorro, rising high above the Guadalhorce river

Weathered limestone formations in El Torcal

El Torcal ⑲

Málaga. 🚗 *Antequera*. 🚌 *Antequera*. ℹ️ *Antequera, (95) 270 25 05.*

A MASSIVE EXPOSED HUMP of limestone upland, which has been slowly weathered into bizarre rock formations and caves, the Parque Natural del Torcal is very popular with hikers. Footpaths lead from a visitors' centre in the middle. Walks of up to two hours are marked by yellow arrows; longer walks by red.

The park is also a pleasure for natural historians, with fox and weasel populations, and colonies of eagles, hawks and vultures. It also protects rare plants and flowers, among them species of wild orchid.

Antequera ⑳

Málaga. 🏠 40,000. 🚌 🚆 ℹ️ *Pl San Sebastián 7, (95) 270 25 05.* 🛒 *Sun.* 🎉 *Ferias (end May & mid-Aug).*

THIS BUSY MARKET TOWN was strategically important first as Roman Anticaria and later as a Moorish border fortress defending Granada.

Of its many churches, the **Iglesia de Nuestra Señora del Carmen**, with its vast Baroque altarpiece, is not to be missed. At the opposite end of the town is the 19th-century **Plaza de Toros**, with a museum of bullfighting.

The hilltop **castle** was built in the 13th century on the site of a Roman fort. Visitors can walk round the castle walls by approaching through the 16th-century Arco de los Gigantes.

There are excellent views of Antequera from the Torre del Papabellotas on the best-preserved part of the wall.

In the town below, the 18th-century **Palacio de Nájera** is the setting for the Municipal Museum, the star exhibit of which is a splendid Roman bronze statue of a boy.

The massive **dolmens**, just outside the town, are thought to be the burial chambers of tribal leaders and date from around 2500–2000 BC.

ENVIRONS: Laguna de la Fuente de Piedra, north of Antequera, teems with bird life, including huge flocks of flamingos, which arrive to breed after wintering in West Africa. A road off the N334 leads to a lakeside viewing point. There is a visitors' centre in Fuente de Piedra village. To the east, also off the N334, is **Archidona**, worth a stop to admire its extraordinary, 18th-century, octagonal Plaza

The triumphal, 16th-century Arco de los Gigantes, Antequera

Ochavada built in French style, but which also incorporates traditional Andalusian features.

🎫 **Plaza de Toros**
Carretera de Sevilla. 📞 *(95) 270 26 76.* 🕐 *Tue–Sun.* **Museo Taurino** 🕐 *Sat, Sun, public hols.*
🏛️ **Palacio de Nájera**
Coso Viejo. 📞 *(95) 270 40 51.* 🕐 *Tue–Sun.* 🌐 *public hols.* 📷 ♿

Osuna ㉑

Sevilla. 🏠 17,500. 🚆 🚌 ℹ️ *Casa de Cultura, Calle Sevilla 22, (95) 481 22 58.* 🛒 *Mon.* 🎉 *San Alcadio (12 Jan), Virgen de la Consolación (8 Sep).*

Palacio del Marqués de la Gomera, in Osuna, completed in 1770

OSUNA was once a key Roman garrison town. It rose again to prominence in the 16th century under the Dukes of Osuna, who wielded immense power. In the 1530s they founded the **Colegiata de Santa María**, a grand church with a Baroque reredos and paintings by José de Ribera. This was followed in 1548 by the **University**, a rather severe building with a beautiful patio. Some fine mansions, among them the **Palacio del Marqués de la Gomera**, also reflect the town's former glory.

ENVIRONS: To the east lies **Estepa**, whose modern-day fame rests on its biscuits – *polvorones* and *mantecados* (*see p401*). The Iglesia del Carmen has a black and white, Baroque façade.

Tomb of Servilia in the Roman necropolis in Carmona

Carmona ㉒

Sevilla. 🚶 25,000. 🚐 🚌 ℹ️ *Arco de la Puerta de Sevilla, (95) 419 09 55.* 🚢 *Mon & Thu.* 🎭 *Feria (May), Fiestas Patronales (8–16 Sep).*

CARMONA IS THE FIRST major town east of Seville on the NIV, its old quarter built on a hill above the sprawling suburbs on the plain. Beyond the **Puerta de Sevilla**, a gateway in the Moorish city walls, is a dense cluster of mansions, Mudéjar churches, squares and winding, cobbled streets.

The Plaza de San Fernando has a feeling of grandeur which is characterized by the Renaissance façade of the old **Ayuntamiento**. The present town hall, set just off the square, dates from the 18th century; in its courtyard are some Roman mosaics. Close by is the **Iglesia de Santa María la Mayor**. Built in the 15th century over a mosque, whose patio still survives, this is the finest of Carmona's churches.

Dominating the town are the ruins of the **Alcázar del Rey Pedro**, once a palace of Pedro I, known as Pedro the Cruel. Parts of it now form a parador *(see p563).*

Just outside Carmona is the **Necrópolis Romana**, the extensive remains of a Roman burial ground. A site museum displays some of the items found in the graves, including statues, glass and jewellery.

♖ Ayuntamiento
Calle Salvador 2. 📞 *(95) 414 00 11.* 🚢 *Mon–Sat.* 🌑 *public hols.*

⛪ Necrópolis Romana
Avenida Jorge Bonsor 9. 📞 *(95) 414 08 11.* 🚢 *Tue–Sun.* 🌑 *public hols.*

Itálica ㉓

Sevilla. 📞 *(95) 599 73 76.* 🚌 *from Sevilla.* 🚢 *Tue–Sun* 🎟️

ITALICA WAS FOUNDED in 206 BC by Scipio Africanus. One of the earliest Roman cities in Hispania *(see pp46–7),* it grew to be one of the most important during the 2nd and 3rd centuries AD. Emperors Trajan and Hadrian were both born in the city and the latter, who reigned from 138–117 BC, added marble temples and other grand buildings. Archaeologists have speculated that the changing course of the Río Guadalquivir may have led to Itálica's subsequent demise during Moorish times.

Roman mosaic from Itálica

Next to the vast but crumbling **amphitheatre**, which once seated 25,000 people, is a display of finds from the site. More treasures are displayed in the Museo Arqueológico in Seville *(see p427).*

Visitors are free to wander among the traces of Itálica's streets and admire the mosaic floors of villas. However, little remains of the city's temples or of its baths as most of the stone and marble has been plundered over the centuries. Some better-preserved Roman remains, including baths and a theatre, can be seen in the village of **Santiponce**, just outside of the site.

Sierra Morena ㉔

Sevilla and Córdoba. 🚉 *Estación de Cazalla y Constantina.* 🚌 *Constantina, Cazalla.* ℹ️ *El Robledo, (95) 588 15 97.*

THE SIERRE MORENA, clad in oak and pine woods, runs across the north of the provinces of Sevilla and Córdoba. It forms a natural frontier between Andalusia and the plains of neighbouring Extremadura and La Mancha. Smaller sierras (ranges of hills) within the Sierra Morena chain are also named individually.

Fuente Obejuna, north of Córdoba, was immortalized by Lope de Vega *(see p280)* in his play about an uprising in 1476 against a local overlord. The Iglesia de San Juan Bautista in **Hinojosa del Duque** is a vast church in both Gothic and Renaissance styles. **Belalcázar** is dominated by the huge tower of a ruined 15th-century castle dominates. Storks nest on the church towers of the plateau of **Valle de los Pedroches**, east of Belalcázar.

Cazalla de la Sierra, the main town of the sierra north of Seville, is cosmopolitan, and popular with young *Sevillanos* at weekends. A unique, pungent concoction of cherry liqueur and aniseed, Liquor de Guindas, is produced here.

Constantina, to the east, is more peaceful and has superb views across the countryside.

A cow grazing in the pastures of the Sierra Morena north of Seville

Palma del Río ㉕

Córdoba. 🏠 19,000. 🚉 🚌
🛈 Casa de Cultura, Calle Gracia 15,
(957) 71 02 45. 🕑 Tue. 🎭 Ferias
(19–21 May & 18–20 Aug).

THE ROMANS sited a strategic settlement here, on the road between Córdoba and Itálica, almost 2,000 years ago. The remains of the 12th-century city walls are a reminder of the town's frontier days under the Almohads *(see p50).*

The **Iglesia de la Asunción**, a Baroque church, dates from the 18th century. The **Monasterio de San Francisco** is now a hotel *(see p566),* and guests can eat dinner in the 15th-century refectory of the Franciscan monks. Palma del Río is the home town of El Cordobés, one of Spain's most famous matadors. His biography, *Or I'll Dress You in Mourning,* paints a vivid picture of life in the town and of the days of desperate hardship which followed the end of the Civil War.

Bell tower, la Asunción

ENVIRONS: One of the most dramatic silhouettes in Southern Spain breaks the skyline of **Almodóvar del Río.** The Moorish castle – parts of it dating from the 8th century – stands on a hilltop overlooking the whitewashed town and fields of cotton.

♣ **Castillo de Almodóvar del Río**
📞 (957) 63 51 16. 🕑 daily for guided tours only.

Écija ㉖

Sevilla. 🏠 38,000. 🚉 🛈 Plaza de España 1, (95) 590 02 40. 🕑 Thu. 🎭 Feria (21–4 Sep).

ÉCIJA IS NICKNAMED "the frying pan of Andalusia" owing to its famously torrid climate. In the searing heat, the palm trees on the Plaza de España provide some blissful shade.

This is an ideal place to sit and observe daily life passing by, and is also where people come to stroll in the evening.

Écija has eleven Baroque church steeples. Many of them are adorned with gleaming *azulejos (see p420),* and when seen together they make a very impressive sight. The most florid of these is the **Iglesia de Santa María**, which overlooks the Plaza de España. The **Iglesia de San Juan**, with its exquisite, brightly coloured bell tower, is a very close rival.

The façade of the **Palacio de Peñaflor** is also in the Baroque style. Its pink marble doorway is topped by twisted columns, while an attractive wrought-iron balcony runs along the whole front façade.

🏛 **Palacio de Peñaflor**
Calle Caballeros. 📞 (95) 483 02 73. 🕑 daily (courtyard only).

Medina Azahara ㉗

Córdoba. 📞 (957) 32 91 30. 🚌 Córdoba. 🕑 Tue–Sun. 🎟 🛗

THIS ONCE-GLORIOUS palace was built in the 10th century for Caliph Abd al Rahman III, who named it after his favourite wife, Azahara. He spared no expense in its construction, employing more than 15,000 mules, 4,000 camels and 10,000 workers to bring build-

Detail of wood carving in the main hall of Medina Azahara

ing materials from North Africa and other parts of Andalusia.

The palace is built on three levels and includes a mosque, the caliph's residence and fine gardens *(see pp404–405).* Marble, ebony, jasper and alabaster once adorned its many halls, and it is believed that shimmering pools of quicksilver added lustre.

Unfortunately, the glory was short-lived. The palace was sacked by Berber invaders in 1010 and over subsequent centuries it was ransacked for its building materials. Now, the ruins give only glimpses of its former splendour – a Moorish main hall, for instance, decorated with marble carvings, still with its fine ceiling of carved wood. The palace is currently being restored, but so far progress has been slow.

Trompe l'oeil on the ornate Baroque façade of the Palacio de Peñaflor, Écija

Street-by-Street: Córdoba ㉘

Statue of Maimónides

THE HEART OF CORDOBA is the old Jewish quarter, situated to the west of the Mezquita's towering walls. A walk around this area gives the sensation that little has changed since the 10th century when this was one of the greatest cities in the Western world. Wrought ironwork decorates cobbled streets too narrow for cars, where silversmiths create fine jewellery in their workshops. Most of the chief sights are here, while modern city life takes place some blocks north, around the Plaza de Tendillas. To the east of this square is the Plaza de la Corredera, a 17th-century arcaded square with a daily market.

Sinagoga
Hebrew script covers the walls of this 14th-century synagogue. Spain's only other synagogues are in Toledo (see p373).

Museo Taurino
A replica of the tomb of the famous torero, Manolete, and the hide of the bull that killed him (see p33) are the star exhibits in this museum of bullfighting.

The Capilla de San Bartolomé, in Mudéjar style, is decorated with elaborate plasterwork.

★ Alcázar de los Reyes Cristianos
Water terraces and fountains add to the tranquil atmosphere of the gardens belonging to the palace-fortress of the Catholic Monarchs (see pp52–3), built in the 14th century.

KEY

‒ ‒ ‒ Suggested route

STAR SIGHTS

★ Alcázar de los Reyes Cristianos

★ Mezquita

The **Callejón de las Flores** brims with colourful geraniums, which contrast with the whitewashed walls of this alley, leading to a tiny square.

VISITORS' CHECKLIST

Córdoba. 305,000. Avda de América, (957) 40 02 02. Avda Medina Azahara 29, (957) 23 64 74. Palacio de Congresos, Calle Torrijos 10, (957) 47 12 35. daily. Semana Santa (Easter Week), Cruces de Mayo (1–4 May), Festival de los Patios (5–11 May), Feria (late May). **Sinagoga** Tue–Sun. **Museo Taurino** Tue–Sun. **Alcázar de los Reyes Cristianos** Tue–Sun.

The Palacio Episcopal now houses the tourist office.

Moorish bronze stag from Medina Azahara, Museo Arqueológico

Exploring Córdoba

Córdoba lies on a sharp bend in the Río Guadalquivir, which is spanned by a Roman bridge linking the 14th-century Torre de la Calahorra and the old town. One of the most atmospheric squares in Andalusia is the Plaza de los Capuchinos. With its haunting stone calvary surrounded by wrought-iron lamps, it is particularly evocative when seen by moonlight.

🏛 Museo de Bellas Artes

Plaza del Potro 1. (957) 47 33 45. Tue–Sun.
Exhibits in a former charity hospital include sculptures by local artist Mateo Inurria (1867–1924) and works by Valdés Leal, Zurbarán and Murillo of the Seville School.

🏛 Museo Arqueológico

Plaza Jerónimo Páez 7. (957) 47 40 11. Tue–Sun.
Located in a Renaissance mansion, displays include Roman mosaics, pottery and relief carvings, and impressive finds from the Moorish era.

🏛 Palacio de Viana

Plaza Don Gome 2. (957) 48 01 34. Thu–Tue. 1–15 June.
Furniture, tapestries, paintings and porcelain are displayed in the 17th-century former home of the Viana family. There are twelve beautiful patios.

🏛 Museo Romero de Torres

Plaza del Potro 1. (957) 49 19 09. Tue–Sun.
Julio Romero de Torres (1874–1930), who was born in this house, captured the soul of Córdoba in his paintings.

Puerta del Puente

The Puente Romano spans the Río Guadalquivir and is still supported by its original Roman foundations.

★ **Mezquita**
The mighty walls of the Great Mosque (see pp456–7) hide delicate arches, pillars and a dazzling mihrab.

0 metres   100

0 yards   100

Córdoba: the Mezquita

CORDOBA'S GREAT MOSQUE, dating back 12 centuries, embodied the power of Islam on the Iberian peninsula. Abd al Rahman I *(see p48)* built the original mosque between 785 and 787. The building evolved over the centuries, blending many architectural forms. In the 10th century al Hakam II made some of the most lavish additions, including the elaborate *mihrab* (prayer niche) and the *maqsura* (caliph's enclosure). During the 16th century a cathedral was built in the heart of the reconsecrated mosque, part of which was destroyed.

Patio de los Naranjos
Orange trees grow in the courtyard where the faithful washed before prayer.

Torre del Alminar
This bell tower, 93 m (305 ft) high, is built on the site of the original minaret. Steep steps lead to the top for a fine view of the city.

The Puerta del Perdón is a Mudéjar-style entrance gate, built during Christian rule in 1377. Penitents were pardoned here.

Puerta de San Esteban is set in a section of wall from an earlier Visigothic church.

EXPANSION OF THE MEZQUITA

Abd al Rahman I built the original mosque. Extensions were added by Abd al Rahman II, al Hakam II and al Mansur.

KEY TO ADDITIONS

☐ Mosque of Abd al Rahman I

☐ Extension by Abd al Rahman II

☐ Extension by al Hakam II

☐ Extension by al Mansur

☐ Patio de los Naranjos

STAR FEATURES

★ Mihrab

★ Capilla de Villaviciosa

★ Arches and Pillars

Cathedral
Part of the mosque was destroyed to accommodate the cathedral, started in 1523. Featuring an Italianate dome, it was designed chiefly by members of the Hernán Ruiz family.

VISITORS' CHECKLIST

Calle Torrijos. ☎ (957) 47 05 12. ◯ 10am–6pm Mon–Sat; 3:30–5:30pm Sun (Apr–Sep: until 7pm daily). ✝ 8am & 9am Mon–Fri; 8pm & 9pm Sat; 9am, 10:30am, 11:30am, noon, 12:30pm & 1pm Sun.

The cathedral choir has Churrigueresque stalls carved by Pedro Duque Cornejo in 1758.

Capilla Mayor

Capilla Real

★ **Arches and Pillars**
More than 850 columns of granite, jasper and marble support the roof, creating a dazzling visual effect. Many were taken from Roman and Visigothic buildings.

★ **Mihrab**
This prayer niche, richly ornamented, held a gilt copy of the Koran. The worn flagstones indicate where pilgrims circled it seven times on their knees.

★ **Capilla de Villaviciosa**
The first Christian chapel was built in the mosque in 1371 by Mudéjar (see p51) craftsmen. Its multi-lobed arches are stunning.

Baroque statuary in the Fuente del Rey at Priego de Córdoba

Montilla 29

Córdoba. 🏛 *24,000.* 🚉 🏛 **ℹ** *C/ Padre Miguel Molina, (957) 65 41 94.* 🛍 *Fri.* 🎉 *Grape Harvest (late Aug).*

M ONTILLA IS THE CENTRE of an important wine region that produces an excellent smooth white fino *(see p402).* Unlike sherry, it is not fortified with alcohol. Several bodegas, including **Alvear** and **Pérez Barquero**, will show visitors around by prior arrangement.

The Mudéjar **Convento de Santa Clara** dates from 1512. The town library is in the **Casa del Inca**, so named because Garcilaso de la Vega, who wrote about the Incas, lived there in the 16th century.

ENVIRONS: Aguilar, 13 km (8 miles) to the south, has the unusual, eight-sided Plaza de San José (built in 1810) and several seigneurial houses.

Baena, 40 km (25 miles) to the west of Montilla, is famous for its olive oil since Roman times. On the Plaza de la Constitución stands the Casa del Monte, an arcaded mansion dating from the 18th century. During Easter Week thousands of costumed drummers take to the streets.

🍷 **Bodega Alvear**
Avda María Auxiliadora 1. **【** *(957) 65 28 00.* 🕐 *Mon–Fri.* 🌑 *public hols.*
🍷 **Bodega Pérez Barquero**
Avda de Andalucía 27. **【** *(957) 65 05 00.* 🕐 *Mon–Fri.* 🌑 *public hols.*

Priego de Córdoba 30

Córdoba. 🏛 *22,000.* 🚌 **ℹ** *Calle del Río 33, (957) 70 06 25.* 🛍 *Sat.* 🎉 *Feria Real (1–6 Sep).*

P RIEGO DE CORDOBA'S claim to be the capital of Cordoban Baroque is borne out by the dazzling work of carvers, iron-workers and gilders in the many houses, and especially churches, built with wealth generated by a prosperous 18th-century silk industry.

A restored Moorish fortress stands in the whitewashed medieval quarter, the **Barrio de la Villa**. Close by is the outstanding **Iglesia de la Asunción**, converted from Gothic to Baroque style by Jerónimo Sánchez de Rueda. Its *pièce de résistance* is the sacristy, created in 1784 by local artist Francisco Javier Pedrajas. The main altar is Plater-esque *(see p21).*

At midnight every Saturday the brother-hood of another Baroque church, the **Iglesia de la Aurora**, parades the streets singing songs in praise of the Virgin.

Silk merchants built many of the imposing mansions that follow the curve around the Calle del Río. At the end of the street is the Baroque **Fuente del Rey** (The King's Fountain). Some 139 spouts splash water into three basins which are adorned with exuberant statuary.

La Asunción, Priego de Córdoba

ENVIRONS: Zuheros, perched on a crag in the limestone hills northwest of Priego, is one of Andalusia's prettiest villages. **Rute**, to the southwest, is known for its *anís (see p577).*

Alcalá la Real, in the low-lands east of Priego, is over-looked by the hilltop ruins of a castle and a church. There are two handsome Renaissance buildings on its central square: the Fuente de Carlos V and the Palacio Abacia.

Montefrío 31

Granada. 🏛 *8,500.* 🚌 **ℹ** *Plaza España 7, (958) 33 61 36.* 🛍 *Mon.* 🎉 *Fiesta patronal (14–18 Aug).*

T HE APPROACH to Montefrío from the south offers won-derful views of its tiled roof-tops and pretty whitewashed houses running up to a steep crag. This arche-typal Andalusian town is topped by the remains of its Moorish fortifications and the 16th-century Gothic **Iglesia de la Villa**, attributed to Diego de Siloé. In the centre of town is the Neo-Classical **Iglesia de la Encar-nación**, identifiable by its large dome. The architect Ventura Rodríguez (1717–85) is credited with its design. The town is known for its chorizo.

ENVIRONS: Santa Fé was built by the Catholic Monarchs at the end of the 15th century. Their army camped here while

Barrels of Montilla, the sherry-like wine from the town of the same name

The castle overlooking the resort of Almuñécar on the Costa Tropical

laying siege to Granada, and this was the site of the formal surrender of the Moors in 1492 *(see pp52–3)*. A Moor's severed head, carved in stone, adorns the spire of the parish church.

Sited above a gorge, **Alhama de Granada** was named Al hamma (hot springs) by the Moors. Their baths, close to the spot where the hot water gushes from the ground just outside town, can be seen in the Hotel Balneario.

Loja, on the Río Genil, near Los Infiernos gorge, is known as "the city of water" because of its spring-fed fountains.

Nerja **32**

Málaga. 🏛 15,000. 🚉 🛈 *Calle Puerta del Mar 2, (95) 252 15 31.* 🚌 *Tue.* 🎭 *Feria (8–12 Oct).*

THIS WELL-ESTABLISHED resort, built on a cliff above sandy coves, lies at the foot of the beautiful Sierra de Almijara. There are sweeping views up and down the coast from the rocky promontory known as **El Balcón de Europa** (the Balcony of Europe). Along it runs a promenade lined with cafés and restaurants.

East of the town are the **Cuevas de Nerja**, a series of vast caverns which were discovered in 1959. Wall paintings found here are believed to be about 20,000 years old. Only a few of the many cathedral-sized chambers are open to public view. One of these has been converted into an impressive auditorium which has a capacity of several hundred people. Concerts are held here in the summer.

ENVIRONS: In **Vélez-Málaga**, the ruins of the Fortaleza de Belén, a Moorish fortress set dramatically on a rocky outcrop, dominates the medieval Barrio de San Sebastián.

🖼 **Cuevas de Nerja**
Carretera de las Cuevas de Nerja.
🆑 *(95) 252 95 20.* ⭕ *daily.* 🎟

Almuñécar **33**

Granada. 🏛 20,500. 🚉 🛈 *Avda Europa, (958) 63 11 25.* 🚌 *Fri.* 🎭 *Virgen de la Antigua (15 Aug).*

ALMUÑÉCAR LIES on the Costa Tropical, so named because its climate allows the cultivation of exotic fruit. Just inland, mountains rise to more than 2,000 m (6,560 ft). The Phoenicians founded the first settlement here, called Sexi, and the Romans constructed an aqueduct, the remains of which can be seen today. Almuñécar is now a holiday resort, and apartment blocks fringe its beaches.

Above the old town is the **castle**, which was built by the Moors and altered in the 16th century. Below it is the **Parque Ornitológico** (comprising an aviary and botanic gardens) and the ruins of a Roman fish-salting factory. The **Museo Arqueológico** displays a variety of Phoenician artifacts.

ENVIRONS: The ancient white town of **Salobreña** is set amid fields of sugar cane. Narrow streets lead up a hill, first fortified by the Phoenicians, to the restored Arab castle. There are fine views of the Sierra Nevada *(see p461)* from here. Modern developments now line part of Salobreña's beach.

🦜 **Parque Ornitológico**
Plaza de Abderraman. 🆑 *(958) 63 54 75.* ⭕ *daily.* 🎟
🏛 **Museo Arqueológico**
Cueva 7 Palacios. ⭕ *Mon–Sat.* 🎟
♖ **Castillo de Salobreña**
Calle Castillo. ⭕ *daily.* 🎟

One of the succession of sandy coves that make up the resort of Nerja

The majestic peaks of the Sierra Nevada towering, in places, to over 3,000 m (9,800 ft) above sea level

Lanjarón ❸

Granada. 🏠 24,000. 🚌 🛈 *Plaza de la Constitución 29, (958) 77 00 02.* 🗓 *Tue & Fri.* 🎎 *San Juan (24 Jun).*

SCORES OF CLEAR, SNOW-FED springs bubble from the slopes of the Sierra Nevada; their abundance at Lanjarón, on the southern side of this great range of mountains, has given the town a long history as a health spa. From June to October, visitors flock to take the waters for arthritic, dietary and nervous ailments. Bottled water from Lanjarón is sold all over the country.

A major festival begins on the night of 23 June and ends in an uproarious water battle in the early hours of 24 June, the Día de San Juan. Every-

one in the streets gets doused.

The town is on the threshold of Las Alpujarras, a scenic upland area of dramatic landscapes, where steep, terraced hillsides and deep-cut valleys conceal remote, whitewashed villages. Roads to and from Lanjarón wind slowly and dizzily around the slopes.

A Tour of Las Alpujarras ❸

THE FERTILE, UPLAND VALLEYS of Las Alpujarras, clothed with chestnut, walnut and poplar trees, lie on the southern slopes of the Sierra Nevada. The architecture of the quaint white villages which cling to the hillsides – compact clusters of irregularly shaped houses with tall chimneys sprouting from flat, grey roofs – is unique in Spain. Local specialities are ham cured in the cold, dry air of Trevélez and brightly coloured, handwoven rugs.

Trevélez ④
Trevélez, in the shadow of Mulhacér Spain's highest mountain, is famous for its cured ham.

Poqueira Valley ②
Capileira, Bubión and Pampaneira are three villages typical of Las Alpujarras in this pretty river valley.

Orgiva ①
This is the largest town of the region, with a Baroque church in the main street and a lively Thursday market.

Fuente Agria ③
People come to this spring to drink the iron-rich, naturally carbonated waters.

Laujar de Andarax ⊛

Almería. 🏛 *1,900.* 🚆 ℹ *Almería, (950) 25 11 35.* 🛒 *3 & 17 of each month.* 🎉 *San Vicente (22 Jan), Virgen de la Salud (19 Sep).*

LAUJAR, IN THE ARID foothills of the Sierra Nevada looks southwards across the Andarax valley towards the Sierra de Gádor.

According to legend, Laujar de Andarax was founded by one of the grandsons of Noah. In the 16th century, Abén Humeya, leader of the greatest Morisco rebellion *(see p55)*, made his base here. The revolt was cruelly crushed by Christian troops and Abén Humeya was murdered by his own treacherous followers.

Inside Laujar's 17th-century church, **La Encarnación**, is a statue of the Virgin by Alonso Cano. Next to the Baroque **town hall** *(ayuntamiento)* is a fountain inscribed with some lines written by Francisco Villespesa, a dramatist and poet who was born in Laujar in 1877: *"Six fountains has my pueblo/He who drinks their waters/ will never forget them/so heavenly is their taste."*

Painting, Iglesia de la Encarnación

El Nacimiento, a park to the east of Laujar, is a suitable place to have a picnic. You can accompany it with one of the area's hearty red wines. **Ohanes**, above the Andarax valley further to the east, is an attractive hill town of steep streets and whitewashed houses known for its crops of table grapes.

Sierra Nevada ⊛

Granada. 🚆 *from Granada.* ℹ *Plaza de Andalucía, Monachil, (958) 30 12 30.*

FOURTEEN PEAKS more than 3,000 m (9,800 ft) high crown the heights of the Sierra Nevada. The snow lingers until July and begins falling again in late autumn. One of Europe's highest roads, the GR411, runs past **Solynieve**, an expanding ski resort at 2,100 m (6,890 ft), and skirts the two highest peaks, **Pico Veleta** at 3,398 m (11,149 ft) and **Mulhacén** at 3,482 m (11,420 ft).

The Sierra's closeness to the Mediterranean and its altitude account for the great diversity of the indigenous flora and fauna found on its slopes – the latter including golden eagles and some rare butterflies.

There are several mountain refuges for the use of serious hikers and climbers.

Yegen ⑥
A plaque marks the house where Gerald Brenan, the author of *South from Granada*, lived in the 1920s.

Puerto de la Ragua ⑧
This pass, which leads across the mountains to Guadix, is nearly 2,000 m (6,560 ft) high and is often snowbound in winter.

Válor ⑦
Abén Humeya, leader of a rebellion by Moriscos in the 16th century, was born here. A commemorative battle between Moors and Christians is staged each year in mid-September.

Cádiar ⑤
Free wine is traditionally on tap during the village's October fiesta.

KEY

〰️ Tour route

— Other roads

▲ Mountain peak

0 kilometres   5

0 miles   5

TIPS FOR DRIVERS

Tour length: 85 km (56 miles).
Stopping-off points: There are bars and restaurants in Orgiva, Capileira, Bubión (see p602) and Trevélez. Orgiva, Bubión and Trevélez have good hotels (see pp563–7). Orgiva is the last petrol stop before Cádiar.

Granada ㊳

Stone relief, Museo Arqueológico

THE GUITARIST ANDRES SEGOVIA (1893–1987) described Granada as a "place of dreams, where the Lord put the seed of music in my soul". It was first occupied by the Moors in the 8th century, and its golden period came during the rule of the Nasrid dynasty *(see p51)* from 1238 to 1492, when artisans, merchants, scholars and scientists all contributed to the city's international reputation as a centre for culture. Under Christian rule, following its fall to the Catholic Monarchs in 1492 and the expulsion of the Moors *(see pp52–3)*, the city blossomed in Renaissance splendour. There was a period of decline in the 19th century, but Granada has recently been the subject of renewed interest and efforts are being made to restore parts of it to their past glory.

Entrance to the Moorish *mihrab* in the Palacio de la Madraza

Façade of Granada cathedral

Exploring Granada

The old city centre around the cathedral is a maze of narrow one-way streets. It contains the Alcaicería – a reconstruction of a Moorish bazaar that burned down in 1843. Granada's two main squares are the Plaza Bib-Rambla, near the cathedral, and the Plaza Nueva. From the latter, Cuesta de Gomérez leads up to the city's two principal monuments: the Alhambra and the Generalife. On a hill opposite is the Albaicín district.

Churches well worth a visit are the Iglesia de San Juan de Dios, almost overwhelming in its wealth of Baroque decoration, and the Renaissance Iglesia de San Jerónimo.

🛉 Cathedral

On the orders of the Catholic Monarchs, work on the cathedral began in 1523 to plans in a Gothic style by Enrique de Egas. It continued under the Renaissance maestro, Diego de Siloé, who also designed the façade and the magnificent, circular Capilla Mayor. Under its dome, windows of 16th-century glass depict Juan del Campo's *The Passion*. The west front was designed by the Baroque artist Alonso Cano, who was born in the city. His grave and many of his works can be seen in the cathedral.

🛉 Capilla Real

The Royal Chapel was built for the Catholic Monarchs between 1506 and 1521 by Enrique de Egas. A magnificent *reja* (grille) by Maestro Bartolomé de Jaén encloses the high altar and the Carrara marble figures of Fernando and Isabel, their daughter Juana la Loca (the Mad) and her husband Felipe el Hermoso (the Fair). Their coffins are in the crypt. In the sacristy there are art treasures, including paintings by Botticelli and Van der Weyden, as well as Isabel's crown, Fernando's sword and their army banners.

🛕 Palacio de la Madraza

Calle Oficios 14. 📞 *(958) 22 34 47.* ⭕ *Sep–Jul: Mon–Fri.* ♿
Originally an Arab university, this building later became the city hall. The façade dates from the 18th century. Inside is a Moorish hall with a finely decorated *mihrab* (prayer niche).

🛕 Corral del Carbón

Calle Mariana Pineda. 📞 *(958) 22 59 90.* ⭕ *Mon–Sat.* ♿
This galleried courtyard, formerly a storehouse and inn for merchants, is a unique relic of the Moorish era. In Christian times it was a venue for theatrical performances; it later became a coal exchange. Today it houses craft shops and the main tourist office.

🛕 Casa de los Tiros

Calle Cementerio Santa Escolástica 3. 📞 *(958) 22 10 72.* ⭕ *to the public.*
This fortress-like palace was built in Mudéjar style in the 16th century. It originally belonged to the family that was awarded the Generalife after the fall of Granada. Among

Grille by Maestro Bartolomé de Jaén enclosing the altar of the Capilla Real

Cupola in the sanctuary of the Monasterio de la Cartuja

their possessions was a sword that had belonged to Boabdil. This is carved on the façade, along with statues of Mercury, Hector, Hercules, Theseus and Jason. The building owes its name to the muskets that project from its battlements: *tiro,* in Spanish, meaning shot.

⚜ Alhambra and Generalife
See pp466–7.

⚜ El Bañuelo
Carrera del Darro 31. 【 (958) 22 23 39. ◯ Tue–Sat. ● public hols.
These brick-vaulted Arab baths were built in the 11th century. The columns are topped by reused Visigothic and Roman capitals as well as Arab ones.

🏛 Museo Arqueológico
Carrera del Darro 41. 【 (958) 22 56 40. ◯ Tue–Sun. ● public hols.

VISITORS' CHECKLIST

Granada. 👥 262,000. ✈ 17 km (10.5 miles) southeast of city. 🚉 Avenida de los Andaluces, (958) 27 12 72. 🚌 Camino de Ronda, (958) 25 13 58. 🛈 Corral del Carbón, C/ Mariana Pineda, (958) 22 59 90. 🗓 Sun. 🎭 Semana Santa (Easter Week), Día de la Cruz (3 May), Corpus Christi (May/Jun).

This museum occupies the Casa de Castril, a Renaissance mansion with a Plateresque *(see p21)* portal. It displays Iberian, Phoenician and Roman finds from Granada province.

⛪ Monasterio de la Cartuja
A Christian warrior called El Gran Capitán founded this monastery outside Granada in 1516. There is a dazzling cupola by Antonio Palomino, and an extravagant Churrigueresque *(see p21)* sacristy by Luis de Arévalo and Luis Caballo.

GRANADA CITY CENTRE

Alhambra ⑥
El Bañuelo ⑦
Capilla Real ②
Casa de los Tiros ⑤
Cathedral ①
Corral del Carbón ④
Museo Arqueológico ⑧
Palacio de la Madraza ③

0 metres 250
0 yards 250

KEY

| See pp464–5
🅿 Parking
🛈 Tourist information
🕇 Church
⚜ Convent or monastery

Street-by-Street: the Albaicín

Ornate plaque on a house in the Albaicín

T HIS CORNER OF THE CITY, clinging to the hillside opposite the Alhambra, is where one feels closest to Granada's Moorish ancestry. A fortress was first built here in the 13th century and there were once over 30 mosques. Most of the city's churches were built over their sites. Along the cobbled alleys stand *cármenes*, villas with Moorish decoration and gardens, secluded from the world by their high walls. In the jasmine-scented air of evening, take a walk up to the Mirador de San Nicolás. The view over the maze of roof-tops of the Alhambra glowing in the sunset is magical.

Street in the Albaicín
Steep and sinuous, the Albaicín's streets are truly labyrinthine. Many street names start with Cuesta, *meaning slope.*

Real Chancillería
Built in 1530 by the Catholic Monarchs, the Royal Chancery has a beautiful Renaissance façade.

CALLE SAN
CALLE ACEITUNEROS
CÁRCEL ALTA
AIRE
PISAS
CARRERA DEL DARRO
SANTA A
PLAZA SANTA ANA

0 metres   50
0 yards   50

Casa de los Pisa, belonging to the Knights Hospitallers, displays works of art – some depicting St John of God, who died here in 1550.

STAR SIGHTS

★ Iglesia de Santa Ana

★ Museo Arqueológico

★ El Bañuelo

★ Iglesia de Santa Ana
At the end of the Plaza Nueva stands this 16th-century brick church in Mudéjar style. It has an elegant Plateresque portal and, inside, a coffered ceiling.

★ **Museo Arqueológico**
The ornate Plateresque carvings on the museum's façade include this relief of two shields. They show heraldic devices of the Nasrid kings of Granada, who were defeated by the Catholic Monarchs in 1492 (see pp52–3).

Carrera del Darro
The road along the Río Darro leads past crumbling bridges and the fine façades of ancient buildings, now all restored.

To Mirador de San Nicolás

KEY
- - - - Suggested route

CALLE ZAFRA

CALLE GLORIA

CARRETERA DEL SANTÍSIMO

DE LOS REYES

PLAZA CONCEPCIÓN

CARNERO

BAÑUELO

CONCEPCIÓN

CARRERA DEL DARRO

→ To Sacromonte

RÍO DARRO

The Convento de Santa Catalina was founded in 1521.

★ **El Bañuelo**
Star-shaped openings in the vaults let light into these well-preserved Moorish baths, which were built in the 11th century.

SACROMONTE

Granada's gypsies formerly lived in the caves honeycombing this hillside. In the past, travellers would go there to enjoy spontaneous outbursts of flamenco. Today, virtually all the gypsies have moved away, but touristy flamenco shows of variable quality are still performed here in the evenings *(see pp406–407)*. Sitting at the very top of the hill is the Abadía del Sacromonte, a Benedictine monastery. The ashes of St Cecilio, Granada's patron saint, are kept inside.

Gypsies dancing flamenco, 19th century

The Alhambra

A MAGICAL USE of space, light, water and decoration characterizes this most sensual piece of architecture. It was built under Ismail I, Yusuf I and Muhammad V, caliphs when the Nasrid dynasty *(see pp50–51)* ruled Granada. Seeking to belie an image of waning power, they created their idea of paradise on Earth. Modest materials were used (plaster, timber and tiles), but they were superbly worked. Although the Alhambra suffered pillage and decay, including an attempt by Napoleon's troops to blow it up, in recent times it has undergone extensive restoration and its delicate craftsmanship still dazzles the eye.

Sala de la Barca

★ Salón de Embajadores
The ceiling of this sumptuous throne room, built from 1334 to 1354, represents the seven heavens of the Muslim cosmos.

★ Patio de Arrayanes
This pool, set amid myrtle hedges and graceful arcades, reflects light into the surrounding halls.

Patio de Machuca

Entrance

PLAN OF THE ALHAMBRA

To the Generalife

Main gate

The Alhambra complex includes the Casas Reales, the 13th-century Alcazaba, the 16th-century Palace of Charles V, and the Generalife *(see p468)*, which is located just off the map.

KEY

- Casas Reales (shown above)
- Palace of Charles V
- Alcazaba
- Park
- Other buildings

Patio del Mexuar
This council chamber, completed in 1365, was where the reigning sultan listened to the petitions of his subjects and held meetings with his ministers.

Palacio del Partal

A pavilion with an arched portico and a tower is all that remains of this palace, the oldest building in the Alhambra.

VISITORS' CHECKLIST

For the Alhambra and Generalife.
📞 *(958) 22 04 45.* **Group reservations** 📞 *(958) 22 09 12.*
🚌 *2.* 🕐 *summer: 9am–8pm Mon–Sat, 9am–6pm Sun; winter: 9am–6pm daily.* **Last adm:** *15 minutes before closing time.*
Night visits: *summer: 10pm–midnight Tue, Thu & Sat; winter: 8–10pm Sat.* ♿ 📷 🍴

Washington Irving's apartments

Baños Reales

Jardín de Lindaraja

Sala de las Dos Hermanas, with its honeycomb dome, is regarded as the ultimate example of Spanish Islamic architecture.

Puerta de la Rawda

Sala de los Reyes

This great banqueting hall was used to hold extravagant parties and feasts. Beautiful ceiling paintings on leather, from the 14th century, depict tales of hunting and chivalry.

★ Sala de los Abencerrajes

This hall takes its name from a noble family, who were rivals of Boabdil (see pp52–3). According to legend, he had them massacred while they attended a banquet here. The geometrical ceiling pattern was inspired by Pythagoras's theorem.

The Palace of Charles V (1526) houses a collection of Spanish-Islamic art, whose highlight is the Alhambra vase *(see p48).*

★ Patio de los Leones

Built by Muhammad V, this patio is lined with arcades supported by 124 slender marble columns. At its centre, a fountain rests on 12 stocky, marble lions.

STAR FEATURES

★ Salón de Embajadores

★ Patio de Arrayanes

★ Sala de los Abencerrajes

★ Patio de los Leones

Granada: Generalife

FROM THE ALHAMBRA'S northern side, a footpath leads to the Generalife, the country estate of the Nasrid kings. Here, they could escape from palace intrigues and enjoy tranquillity high above the city, a little closer to heaven. The name Generalife, or Yannat al Arif, has various interpretations, perhaps the most pleasing being "the garden of lofty paradise". The gardens, begun in the 13th century, have been modified over the years. They originally contained orchards and pastures. The Generalife provides a magical setting for Granada's annual music and dance festival *(see p37)*.

The Patio de la Acequia is an enclosed oriental garden built round a long central pool. Rows of water jets on either side make graceful arches above it.

Sala Regia

Jardines Altos (Upper Gardens)

The Escalera del Agua is a staircase with water flowing gently down it.

The Patio de los Cipreses, otherwise known as the Patio de la Sultana, was the secret meeting place for Zoraya, wife of the Sultan Abu-l-Hasan, and her lover, the chief of the Abencerrajes.

Entrance

The Patio de Polo was the courtyard where palace visitors, arriving on horseback, would tether their steeds.

The Patio del Generalife lies just before the entrance to the Generalife. The walk from the Alhambra to the Generalife gardens passes first through the Jardines Bajos (lower gardens), before crossing this Moorish patio with its characteristically geometric pool.

The forbidding exterior of the castle above Lacalahorra

Castillo de Lacalahorra ③⑨

Lacalahorra (Granada). ☎ (958) 67 70 98. ☐ Guadix. ☐ Wed.

GRIM, IMMENSELY THICK walls and stout, cylindrical corner towers protect the castle on a hill above the village of Lacalahorra. It was Rodrigo de Mendoza, son of Cardinal Mendoza, who ordered the castle to be built for his bride. The work was carried out between 1509 and 1512 by Italian architects and craftsmen. Inside is an ornate, two-storeyed, arcaded Renaissance courtyard with pillars and a staircase carved from Carrara marble.

Guadix ④⓪

Granada. ☒ 20,000. ☐ ☐ ☐ Ctra de Granada, (958) 66 26 65. ☐ Sat. ☒ Fiesta & Feria (31 Aug –5 Sep).

THE TROGLODYTE QUARTER, with 2,000 caves that have been inhabited for centuries, is the town's most remarkable sight. The **Cueva-Museo** (cave museum) shows how people live underground.

The **cathedral** was begun in 1594 by Diego de Siloé and finished, by Gaspar Cayón and Vicente de Acero, between 1701 and 1796. Relics of San Torcuato, who founded Spain's first Christian bishopric, are kept in the cathedral museum.

Near the Moorish **Alcazaba**, dating from the 10th and 11th centuries, is the Mudéjar-style **Iglesia de Santiago**, a church with a fine coffered ceiling. The 16th-century **Palacio de Peñaflor** is being restored.

fl Cueva-Museo
Plaza de la Ermita Nueva. ● Sun. 🗝

Jaén ④①

☒ 100,000. ☐ ☐ ☐ Calle Arquitecto Berges 1, (953) 22 27 37. ☐ Thu. ☒ Nuestra Señora de la Capilla (11 Jun), San Lucas (Oct), Romería de Santa Catalina (25 Nov).

THE MOORS called Jaen *Geen* – meaning "way station of caravans" – because of its strategic site on the road beween Andalusia and Castile. Their hilltop fortress was rebuilt as the **Castillo de Santa Catalina** after it was captured by King Fernando III in 1246. Part of it is now a parador *(see p565).*

Andrés de Vandelvira, who was responsible for many of Úbeda's fine buildings *(see pp472–3)*, designed Jaén's **cathedral** in the 16th century. Later additions include the two 17th-century towers that now flank the west front.

An old mansion, the **Palacio Villardompardo**, houses a museum of arts and crafts, and also gives access to the **Baños Árabes**, the 11th-century baths of Ali, a Moorish chieftain. These have horseshoe arches, ceilings with small, star-shaped windows and two ceramic vats in which bathers once immersed themselves. Tucked away in an alley is the **Capilla de**

San Andrés, a Mudéjar chapel founded in the 16th century by Gutiérrez González who, as treasurer to Pope Leo X, was endowed with extensive privileges. A gilded iron screen by Maestro Bartolomé de Jaen is the highlight of the chapel.

The **Real Monasterio de Santa Clara** was founded in the 13th century and has a lovely cloister dating from the late 16th century. Its church, which has a coffered ceiling, contains a bamboo image of Christ made in Ecuador.

The **Museo Provincial** displays Roman mosaics and sculptures, and Iberian, Greek and Roman ceramics.

Horseshoe arches supporting the dome at the Baños Árabes, Jaén

♣ Castillo de Santa Catalina
Carretera al Castillo.
☎ (953) 23 00 00. ● Wed.
☷ Palacio Villardompardo
Plaza Santa Luisa de Marillac.
☎ (953) 23 62 92. ☐ Tue –Sun.
● public hols.
fl Museo Provincial
Po de la Estación 27. ☎ (953) 25 03 20. ☐ Tue –Sun. ● public hols.

Whitewashed cave dwellings in the troglodyte quarter of Guadix

Roman bridge spanning the Guadalquivir at Andújar

Andújar ⓐ

Jaén. 🏠 35,000. 🚌 🚉 🛈 Plaza de España 1, (953) 50 12 50. 🚌 Tue. 🎭 Romería (last Sun of April).

ANDÚJAR IS KNOWN FOR its olive oil and its pottery. It stands on the site of an Iberian town, Iliturgi, which was destroyed in the Punic Wars (see p46) by Scipio. The Roman conquerors built the 15-arched bridge spanning the Río Guadalquivir.

In the central square is the Gothic **Iglesia de San Miguel**, with paintings by Alonso Cano. The **Iglesia de Santa María la Mayor** has a Renaissance façade and a Mudéjar tower. Inside it is El Greco's *Christ in the Garden of Olives* (c.1605). A pilgrimage takes place to the nearby **Santuario de la Virgen de la Cabeza** in April.

ENVIRONS: The mighty fortress of **Baños de la Encina** has 15 towers and ramparts built by Caliph Al Hakam II in AD 967. Further north, the road and railway between Madrid and Andalusia squeeze through a spectacular gorge in the eastern reaches of the Sierra Morena, the **Desfiladero de Despeñaperros**.

Baeza ⓐ

See pp474–5.

Úbeda ⓐ

Jaén. 🏠 34,000. 🚌 🚉 🛈 Plaza del Ayuntamiento, (953) 75 08 97. 🚌 Fri. 🎭 San Miguel (28 Sep–4 Oct).

ÚBEDA IS A SHOWCASE of Renaissance magnificence, thanks to the patronage of some of Spain's most influential men of the 16th century. These included such dignitaries as Francisco de los Cobos, secretary of state, and his great-nephew, Juan Vázquez de Molina, who gave his name to Úbeda's most historic square. Surrounded by elegant palaces and churches, it is undoubtedly the jewel in Úbeda's crown. The old town is contained within city walls that were first raised by the Moors in 852.

Created on the orders of the Bishop of Jaén around 1562, the colossal former **Hospital de Santiago** was designed by Andrés de Vandelvira, who was credited with refining the Spanish Renaissance style to give it its more austere characteristics. The façade is flanked by square towers, one topped with a distinctive blue-and-white tiled spire. Today the building is a conference centre.

ÚBEDA CITY CENTRE

Capilla del Salvador ④
Hospital de Santiago ①
Iglesia de San Pablo ③
Museo Arqueológico ②
Palacio de las Cadenas ⑥
Parador de Úbeda ⑤
Santa María de los
    Reales Alcázares ⑦

KEY

🚌 Coach station

🛈 Tourist information

✝ Church

⛪ Convent or monastery

0 metres 250
0 yards 250

◁ **Fields of poppies and olive groves south of Andújar in the province of Jáen**

Laguna de Valdeazores in the Parque Nacional de Cazorla

Sited in the 15th-century Casa Mudéjar, the **Museo Arqueológico** exhibits artifacts from Neolithic to Moorish times.

The **Iglesia de San Pablo** has a 13th-century apse and a beautiful 16th-century chapel by Vandelvira. It is surmounted by a Plateresque tower that was completed in 1537.

A monument to the poet and mystic St John of the Cross (1549–91) stands in the **Plaza de Vázquez de Molina**. The **Capilla del Salvador**, on the square, was designed by three 16th-century architects – Diego de Siloé, Andrés de Vandelvira and Esteban Jamete – as the personal chapel of Francisco de los Cobos. Behind it stand Cobos' palace, with a Renaissance façade, and the Hospital de los Honrados Viejos (Hospital of the Honoured Elders), looking on to the Plaza de Santa Lucía. From here, the Redonda de Miradores follows the line of the city walls and offers views of the countryside.

The Plaza Vazquez de Molina also holds Úbeda's **parador** (see p567). Built in the 16th century, but much altered in the 17th, it was the residence of Fernando Ortega Salido, dean of Málaga and chaplain of the Capilla del Salvador.

Úbeda's town hall and tourist office occupy the **Palacio de las Cadenas**, a mansion built for Vázquez de Molina by Vandelvira. It gets its name from the iron chains (cadenas) once attached to the columns supporting the main doorway.

Also on the square are the church of **Santa María de los Reales Alcázares**, which

dates mainly from the 13th-century, and the **Cárcel del Obispo** (Bishop's Jail), where nuns who had been punished by the bishop were confined.

🏛 **Museo Arqueológico**
Casa Mudéjar, Calle Cervantes 6.
[(953) 75 37 02. ☐ Tue–Sun. &
🏥 **Hospital de Santiago**
Calle Obispo Cobos 2. [(953) 75 08 42. ☐ daily.

Capilla del Salvador, Úbeda, one of Spain's finest Renaissance churches

Parque Natural de Cazorla ㊺

Jaén. 🚌 Cazorla. 🛈 Carretera del Tranco km 17, (953) 72 01 15.

FIRST-TIME VISITORS are amazed by the spectacular scenery of this 214,336-ha (529,409-acre) nature reserve with thickly wooded mountains rising to peaks of 2,000 m (6,500 ft) and varied, abundant wildlife.

Access to the Parque Natural de Cazorla, Segura y Las Villas is via the town of Cazorla. Its imposing Moorish **Castillo de la Yedra** houses a folklore museum. From Cazorla, the road winds upwards beneath the much-photographed remains of the clifftop castle at **La Iruela**. After crossing a pass it drops down to a crossroads (El Empalme del Valle) in the thickly wooded valley of the Río Gualalquivir. Roads from here lead to the source of the river and to the peaceful modern parador (see p564).

The main road through the park follows the river. The information centre at Torre del Vinagre is 17 km (10.5 miles) from the crossroads.

ENVIRONS: There is a well-restored Moorish castle at **Segura de la Sierra**, 30 km (19 miles) from the reserve's northern edge. Below it is an unusual rock-hewn bullring.

♣ **Castillo de la Yedra**
[(953) 71 00 39. ☐ Tue–Sat.
● public hols. 📷

CAZORLA'S WILDLIFE

More than 100 bird species live in this nature reserve, some very rare, such as the golden eagle and the griffon vulture. Cazorla is the only habitat in Spain, apart from the Pyrenees, where the lammergeier lives. Mammals in the park include the otter – active at dawn and dusk – mouflon and wild boar, and a small remaining population of Spanish ibex. The red deer was reintroduced in 1952. Among the flora supported by the limestone geology is the indigenous *Viola cazorlensis*.

Wild boar foraging for roots, insects and small mammals

Street-by-Street: Baeza

Coat of arms,
Casa del Pópulo

NESTLING AMID the olive groves that characterize much of Jaén province, beautiful Baeza is a small town, unusually rich in Renaissance architecture. Called Beatia by the Romans and later the capital of a Moorish fiefdom, Baeza is portrayed as a "royal nest of hawks" on its coat of arms. It was conquered by Fernando III in 1226 – the first town in Andalusia to be definitively won back from the Moors – and was then settled by Castilian knights. An era of medieval splendour followed, reaching a climax in the 16th century, when Andrés de Vandelvira's splendid buildings were erected. In the early 20th century, Antonio Machado, one of his generation's greatest poets, lived here.

★ **Palacio de Jabalquinto**
An Isabelline-style (see p20) façade, flanked by elaborate, rounded buttresses, fronts this splendid Gothic palace.

Antigua Universidad
From 1542 until 1825, this Renaissance and Baroque building was one of Spain's first universities.

Torre de los Aliatares is a 1,000-year-old tower built by the Moors.

To Úbeda

Ayuntamiento
Formerly a jail and a courthouse, the town hall is a dignified Plateresque structure (see p21). The coats of arms of Felipe II, Juan de Borja and of the town of Baeza adorn its upper façade.

La Alhóndiga, the old corn exchange, has impressive triple-tier arches running along its front.

Casas Consistoriales Bajas

★ **Cathedral**
*The impressive
cathedral was
rebuilt by Andrés de
Vandelvira in 1567.
The Capilla
Sagrario has a
choir screen by
Bartolomé de Jaén.*

VISITORS' CHECKLIST

Jaén. 🏚 19,000. 🚆 Linares-
Baeza 13 km (8 miles), (953) 65
02 02. 🚌 Avenida Alcalde
Puche Pardo, (953) 74 04 68.
🛈 Plaza del Pópulo, (953) 74 04
44. 🛒 Tue. 🎉 Semana Santa
(Easter), Feria (mid-Aug), Romería
de la Yedra (early Sep).

Fuente de Santa María
*Architect-sculptor Ginés
Martínez of Baeza designed
this fountain in the form of
a triumphal arch. It was
completed in 1564.*

**Antigua
Carnicería** is the
16th-century former
slaughterhouse.

**Puerta de Jaén y
Arco de Villalar**
*This gateway in the city
ramparts is adjoined by
an arch erected in 1521
to appease Carlos I (see
p54) after a rebellion.*

| 0 metres | 75 |
| 0 yards | 75 |

KEY

🛈 Tourist information

– – – Suggested route

STAR SIGHTS

★ **Palacio de
Jabalquinto**

★ **Cathedral**

★ **Plaza del Pópulo**

★ **Plaza del Pópulo**
*The Casa del Pópulo, a fine Plateresque palace,
now the tourist office, overlooks this square. In
its centre is the Fuente de los Leones, a fountain
with an Ibero-Roman statue flanked by lions.*

Renaissance castle overlooking the village of Vélez Blanco

Vélez Blanco ㊻

Almería. 🏘 *2,400.* 🚌 *Vélez Rubio.* 🛈 *Ayuntamiento, Calle Corredera 38, (950) 41 50 01.* 🚌 *Wed.* 🎭 *Cristo de la Yedra (second Sun of Aug).*

DOMINATING THIS pleasant village is the mighty **Castillo de Vélez Blanco**. It was built between 1506 and 1513 by the first Marquis de Los Vélez. The castle's rich Renaissance interiors are now displayed in the Metropolitan Museum in New York, but there is a reconstruction of one of the original patios.

Just outside Vélez Blanco, the **Cueva de los Letreros** contains paintings from c.4000 BC. One depicts the Indalo, a figure holding a rainbow and believed to be a deity with magical powers, now adopted as the symbol of Almería.

🏚 **Cueva de los Letreros**
🚪 *daily.*

Mojácar ㊼

Almería. 🏘 *3,800.* 🚌 🛈 *Plaza Nueva, (950) 47 51 62.* 🚌 *Wed, Sun.* 🎭 *Moors and Christians (second weekend of Jul), San Agustin (28 Aug).*

FROM A DISTANCE, Mojácar shimmers like the mirage of a Moorish citadel, its white houses cascading over a lofty ridge, 2 km (1.2 miles) inland from long, sandy beaches.

Following the Civil War *(see pp62–3)*, the village fell into ruin as most of its inhabitants emigrated, but in the 1960s it was discovered by tourists, which gave rise to a new era of prosperity. The old gateway in the walls still remains, but otherwise the village has been completely rebuilt and holiday complexes have grown up along the nearby beaches. The coast south from Mojácar is among the least built up in Spain, with only small resorts and villages along its length.

Tabernas ㊽

Almería. 🏘 *3,100.* 🚌 🛈 *Ayuntamiento, Plaza del Pueblo 1, (950) 36 50 02.* 🚌 *Wed.* 🎭 *Virgen de las Angustias (11–15 Aug).*

TABERNAS IS SET in Europe's only desert. The town's Moorish fortress dominates the harsh surrounding scenery of cactus-dotted, rugged, eroded hills and dried-out riverbeds, which has provided the setting for many classic spaghetti westerns, such as *A Fistful of Dollars*. Two film sets can be visited: **Mini-Hollywood** and

Texas Hollywood, 1.5 km (1 mile) and 4 km (2.5 miles) from Tabernas respectively.

Not far from town is a solar energy research centre, where hundreds of heliostats follow the course of southern Andalusia's powerful sun.

ENVIRONS: Sorbas sits on the edge of the deep chasm of the Río de Aguas. It has two notable buildings: the 16th-century Iglesia de Santa María and a 17th-century mansion said to have been a summer retreat for the Duke of Alba.

Nearby is the karst scenery, honeycombed with hundreds of cave systems, of the **Yesos de Sorbas** nature reserve. Permission to explore them is required from Andalusia's environmental department.

🎬 **Mini-Hollywood**
Carretera N340. 📞 *(950) 36 52 36.* 🚪 *daily.* ● *Mon in winter.* 🏷
🎬 **Texas Hollywood**
Carretera N340, Tabernas. 📞 *(950) 16 54 58.* 🚪 *daily.* 🏷

Desert landscape around Tabernas, reminiscent of the Wild West

Still from *For a Few Dollars More* by Sergio Leone

SPAGHETTI WESTERNS

Two Wild West towns lie off the N340 highway west of Tabernas. Here, visitors can re-enact classic film scenes or watch stunt men performing bank hold-ups and saloon brawls. The *poblados del oeste* were built during the 1960s and early 1970s when low costs and eternal sunshine made Almería the ideal location for spaghetti westerns. Sergio Leone, director of *The Good, the Bad and the Ugly*, built a ranch here and film-sets sprang up in the desert. Local gypsies played Indians and Mexicans. The deserts and Arizona-style badlands are still used for television commercials and series, and by film directors such as Steven Spielberg.

The 10th-century Alcazaba, which dominates Almería's old town

Almería ㊾

Almería. 🏠 170,000. 🚉 🚌 🛈 Parque Nicolás Salmerón 11, (950) 27 43 55. 🖼 Tue, Fri & Sat. 🎉 Feria (last week of Aug), Winter Fiesta (Dec–early Jan).

A LMERÍA's colossal **Alcazaba**, dating from AD 995, is the largest fortress built by the Moors in Spain. The huge structure bears witness to the city's golden age, when it was an important port under the Caliphate of Córdoba *(see pp48–9)*. The Moorish city, known as Al Mariyat (Mirror of the Sea), exported mainly brocade, silk and cotton.

During the Reconquest, the Alcazaba withstood two major sieges before eventually falling to the armies of the Catholic Monarchs *(see pp52–3)* in 1489. The royal coat of arms can be seen on the Torre del Homenaje, built during their reign. The Alcazaba also has a Mudéjar chapel and gardens.

Adjacent to the Alcazaba is the old fishermen's and gypsy quarter of **La Chanca**, where some families live in caves with brightly painted façades and modern interiors. On Mondays a lively street market is held. Although this district is picturesque, it is also desperately poor and it is unwise to walk around here alone or at night with valuables.

Berber pirates from North Africa often raided Almería. Consequently, the **cathedral** looks almost more like a castle than a place of worship, with its four towers, thick walls and small windows. The site was originally occupied by a mosque. This was converted into a church, but in 1522 the

building was destroyed in an earthquake. Work on the present building began in 1524 under the direction of Diego de Siloé, who designed the nave and high altar in Gothic style. The Renaissance façade and the carved walnut choir stalls are by Juan de Orea.

Brightly coloured entrance to a gypsy cave in La Chanca district

Traces of Moorish Almería's most important mosque can be seen in the **Templo San Juan**. The **Plaza Vieja** is an attractive 17th-century arcaded square. On one side is the **town hall** *(ayuntamiento)*, a flamboyant building with a cream and pink façade dating from 1899.

ENVIRONS: One of Europe's most important examples of a Copper Age settlement lies at **Los Millares**, near Gádor, 17 km (10.5 miles) to the north of Almería. As many as 2,000 people may have occupied the site around 2500 BC.

♟ Alcazaba
Calle Almanzor. 【 (950) 27 16 17. 🕐 daily. ● 1 Jan, 25 Dec. 🎟
⋒ Los Millares
Carretera Santa Fé de Mondújar. 【 (950) 23 50 10. 🕐 Tue–Sun.

Parque Natural de Cabo de Gata ㊿

Almería. 🚌 San José. 🛈 Almería–Cabo de Gata road, (950) 16 04 35.

T OWERING CLIFFS of volcanic rock, sand dunes, salt flats and secluded coves characterize the 29,000-ha (71,700-acre) Parque Natural de Cabo de Gata. Within its confines are a few fishing villages, and the small resort of San José, on a fine sandy bay. A lighthouse stands at the dramatic end of the *cabo* (cape), which can be reached by road from the village of Cabo de Gata. The park includes a stretch of seabed 2 km (2,200 yards) wide and the marine flora and fauna protected within it attract scuba divers and snorkellers.

The dunes and saltpans between the cape and the Playa de San Miguel are a habitat for thorny jujube trees. Thousands of migrating birds stop here en route to and from Africa and among the 170 or so bird species recorded here are flamingoes, avocets, griffon vultures and Dupont's larks.

ENVIRONS: Set amid an oasis of citrus trees on the edge of the harsh Sierra de Alhamilla, **Níjar's** fame stems from the colourful pottery and the hand-woven *jarapas* – blankets and rugs – that are made here. The barren plain between Níjar and the sea has been brought under intensive cultivation using vast plastic greenhouses to conserve the scarce water.

The dramatic, dark volcanic rocks at Cabo de Gata, east of Almería

SPAIN'S
ISLANDS

Introducing Spain's Islands

S PAIN'S TWO GROUPS OF ISLANDS lie in separate seas –
the Balearics in the Mediterranean and the Canaries
in the Atlantic, off the African coast. Both are popular
package-tour destinations blessed with warm climates,
good beaches and clear waters. But each has more to
offer than high-rise hotels, fast-food restaurants and
discos. The Balearics have white villages, wooded
hills, caves and prehistoric monuments, while the
extraordinary volcanic landscapes of the Canaries are
unlike any other part of Spain. Four of Spain's national
parks *(see pp26–7)* are in the Canary Islands.

Ibiza (see pp486–8) *is the liveliest
of the Balearic Islands. Ibiza town
and Sant Antoni are the main tourist
centres, offering good nightlife and
excellent beaches.*

Eivissa
(Ibiza)

Formentera

CANARY ISLANDS
(See pp504–27)

La Palma

La Gomera

El Hierro

Tenerife

Tenerife (see pp510–
15), *the largest of the
Canary Islands, is fertile
in the north but arid in
the south. The volcanic
summit of Mount Teide
dominates the island.
Tenerife's beaches are
black but many have
been improved with
white sand imported
from the Sahara Desert.*

0 kilometres   50

0 miles   25

◁ **Vines growing in the volcanic soil of Lanzarote, protected by drystone walls**

In Menorca (see pp498–503) *tourism has developed more slowly than in Mallorca and Ibiza, and the island has largely avoided being over-commercialized. Scattered across the countryside are the ruins of unique Bronze Age buildings.*

BALEARIC ISLANDS
(See pp482–503)

Menorca

Mallorca

0 kilometres 50

0 miles 25

Mallorca (see pp490–97), *best known for its beaches, has caves and other natural features to explore. The most spectacular of the island's historic sights is the great Gothic cathedral in Palma, which rises above the boats moored in the old harbour.*

Lanzarote (see pp524–6) *is the most attractive of the Canary Islands, even though the landscape is strikingly bare. White houses contrast starkly with black volcanic fields. The most dramatic attraction is Timanfaya National Park, including the Montañas del Fuego.*

Lanzarote

Fuerteventura

ɪ Canaria

Gran Canaria (see p518–21) *centres on a symmetrical volcanic cone. The capital city of Las Palmas has some interesting museums and monuments. In contrast, the sprawling Maspalomas, on the south coast, is the biggest holiday resort in Spain.*

THE BALEARIC ISLANDS

IBIZA · FORMENTERA · MALLORCA · MENORCA

CHIC RESORTS *and attractive coves and beaches, combined with a climate which is hot but never uncomfortably so, have made tourism the mainstay of life along the coasts of the Balearic Islands. Inland, there is peace and quiet in abundance, and a great variety of sights to seek out: wooded hills, pretty white villages, monasteries, country churches, caves and prehistoric monuments.*

Standing at a crossroads in the Mediterranean, the Balearic Islands have been plundered or colonized in turn by Phoenicians, Greeks, Carthaginians, Romans, Moors and Turks. In the 13th century Catalan settlers brought their language, a dialect of which is widely spoken today.

The islands can justifiably claim to cater for all tastes: from sun-seekers on package holidays, for whom the larger resorts serve as brash fun factories, to jet-setters and film stars, who head for luxurious but discreet hideaways in the hills. The largest island, where tourism has been established the longest, is Mallorca. A massive Gothic cathedral stands near the waterfront of Palma, the capital. Menorca's green countryside is dotted with prehistoric monuments and its towns full of noble, historic mansions. The coast of Ibiza is notched by innumerable rocky coves. The island's hilly interior is characterized by brilliant white farmhouses and robust churches. On Formentera, small and relatively undeveloped, the pace of life is slow. The islets surrounding the four principal islands are mainly uninhabited; one of them, Cabrera (off Mallorca), is a national park.

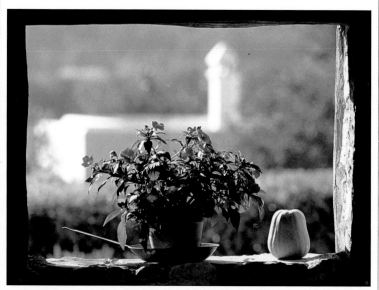

View through the window of one of Ibiza's traditional, whitewashed farmhouses

◁ The massive, heavily buttressed cathedral overlooking Palma de Mallorca's harbour

Exploring the Balearics

THOUGH THE BALEARIC ISLANDS are often associated with high-density, inexpensive package tourism, they offer enough variety to satisfy everyone's tastes. For those unattracted by the bustle of the coastal resorts and their beautiful beaches, the countryside and the old towns of Palma, Ibiza, Maó and Ciutadella are relatively undisturbed. Mallorca is by far the most culturally rich of the Balearics, with its distinguished collection of modern and traditional galleries, and interesting museums. Menorca is strong on Neolithic remains and neo-colonial architecture, while Ibiza is for lovers of clear, painterly light and rustic peasant houses; it also has some of the wildest nightclubs in Europe. Formentera – for many, the most alluring island – has crystal water, white sand, a pure, parched landscape and total tranquillity.

Poblat des Pescadors in the tourist village of Binibeca

MALLORCA

SOLLÉ
VALLDEMOSSA
LA GRANJA 8
ANDRATX 7
PAL
CAPOCOR

Early-morning mist on the waters of Port de Pollença in Menorca

0 kilometres   25

0 miles   15

IBIZA
ELS AMUNTS
SANT MIQUEL 4
SANT ANTONI 1
SANT JOSEP 2
3
EIVISSA (IBIZA)
5 SANTA EULARIA

FORMENTERA
6

GETTING AROUND

Nearly all foreign visitors to the Balearics arrive by plane: Mallorca, Menorca and Ibiza have connections to major European cities as well as Madrid, Barcelona and Valencia. Aviaco airline flies to most other Spanish cities out of Son Sant Joan airport in Palma. Another way of arriving is by boat from Barcelona, Valencia, Alicante or Dénia. Between the islands there are regular ferry services, run by Transmediterránea and Flebasa. Mallorca is the only island with rail services, which run between Palma and Inca, and between Palma and Sóller. Roads vary from excellent to poor, depending on how far you stray from the tourist trail. The best way to get around the islands is by car, except on Formentera, where the ideal mode of transport is the bicycle.

SIGHTS AT A GLANCE

A peaceful stroll on the sands of
Ibiza's Sant Miquel beach

SEE ALSO

- *Where to Stay* pp568–9

- *Restaurants and Bars* pp605–607

KEY

▬	Motorway
▬	Major road
▬	Minor road
▬	Scenic route
～	River
☀	Viewpoint

The rocky coast around the Coves d'Artá in Mallorca

Ibiza

THIS SMALL ISLAND, the nearest of the Balearics to the coast of Spain, was unknown and untouched by tourism until the 1960s, when it suddenly appeared in Europe's holiday brochures along with Benidorm and Torremolinos. There is still a curious, indefinable magic about Ibiza (Eivissa) and the island has not entirely lost its character. The countryside, particularly in the north, is a rural patchwork of groves of almonds, olives and figs, and wooded hills. Ibiza town retains the air of a 1950s Spanish provincial borough. At once package-tour paradise, hippie hideout and glamour hot spot, this is one of the Mediterranean's mythical destinations.

An Ibizan shepherdess

The bustling harbour of the resort of Sant Antoni

Sant Antoni ❶

Baleares. 🚶 14,500. 🚌 🚢
ℹ️ Passeig de Ses Fonts, (971) 34 33 63. 📅 Sant Antoni (17 Jan), Sant Bartolomé (24 Aug).

IBIZA'S SECOND TOWN, Sant Antoni was known by the Romans as Portus Magnus because of its large natural harbour. Formerly a tiny fishing village situated on an immaculate bay, it has turned into a sprawling and exuberant resort. Although it was once notoriously over-commercialized, the town has recently undergone a dramatic facelift. Nevertheless, the 14th-century parish church of Sant Antoni is practically marooned in a sea of modern high-rise hotels.

To the north of Sant Antoni, on the road to Cala Salada, is the chapel of **Santa Agnès**, an unusual early Christian temple (not to be confused with the village of the same name). When this catacomb-like chapel was discovered, in 1907, it contained Moorish weapons and fragments of pottery.

Sant Josep ❷

Baleares. 🚶 12,000. ℹ️ Carrer Pedro Escanellas 33–9, (971) 80 01 25.
📅 Sant Josep (19 Mar).

THE VILLAGE of Sant Josep, the administrative centre of southwest Ibiza, lies in the shadow of Ibiza's highest mountain. At 475 m (1,560 ft), Sa Talaiassa offers a panorama of all Ibiza, including the islet of **Es Vedrá**, rising from the

The salt lakes of Ses Salines, a haven for many bird species

sea like a rough-cut pyramid. For the most accessible view of this enormous rock, take the coastal road to the sandy cove of Cala d'Hort where there are a number of good restaurants and a quiet beach.

ENVIRONS: Before tourism, salt was Ibiza's main industry, most of it coming from the salt flats at **Ses Salines** in the southeast corner of the island. Mainland Spain is the chief consumer of this salt, but much goes to the Faroe Islands and Scandinavia for salting fish. It is loaded on to ships at Ibiza's southern-most port, La Canal. Ses Salines is also an important refuge for birds, including the flamingo. **Es Cavallet**, 3 km (2 miles) east, is an unspoiled stretch of soft, white sand.

Ibiza ❸

Baleares. 🚶 75,000. ✈️ 🚌 🚢
ℹ️ Paseo Vara del Rey 13, (971) 30 19 00. 🛒 Mon–Sat (summer only).
📅 Sant Antoni Abat (17 Jan), San Juan Bautista (24 Jun).

THE OLD QUARTER of Ibiza (Eivissa), known also as Dalt Vila, or upper town, is a miniature citadel guarding the mouth of the almost circular bay. The **Portal de ses Taules**, a magnificent gateway in the north wall of the 16th-century fortifications, carries the finely carved coat of arms of the kingdom of Aragón, to which the Balearic Islands belonged in the Middle Ages (see p217). Outside the walls is the 16th-century **Església de Santo Domingo** with its three red-tiled domes. The Baroque interior, with its barrel-vaulted ceiling and frescoed walls, has been restored to its former glory. Works of art by Erwin Bechtold, Barry Flanagan and other artists connected with Ibiza are on display in the **Museu d'Art Contemporani**, just inside the Portal de ses Taules. Crowning the whole Dalt Vila, and visible for miles around, is the **cathedral**, a 13th-century Catalan Gothic building with 18th-century additions. The cathedral's Museo de la Sacristia houses assorted works of art.

Under the Carthaginians, the soil of Ibiza was considered holy. The citizens of Carthage deemed it an honour to be buried in the **Necropolis of Puig d'es Molins**, thought to contain over 4,000 graves.

The crossroads village of **Jesús**, 3 km (2 miles) north, is well worth a visit for its pretty 16th-century church.

A backstreet in the Sa Penya district of Ibiza town

A view across the port toward Ibiza's upper town

Originally built as part of a Franciscan monastery, it has arguably the finest work of art in the Balearics, a 16th-century altarpiece by Rodrigo de Osona the Younger.

🏛 **Museu d'Art Contemporani**
C/ Ronda Narces Puget. ☎ (971) 30 27 23. ☐ Mon–Sat. ⬤ public hols. 🈲
⋔ **Necropolis of Puig d'es Molins**
Via Romana 31. ☎ (971) 30 17 71. ⬤ Mon. 🈲

Els Amunts ➍

Baleares. 🚌 Sant Miquel. ℹ Santa Eulària d'es Riu, (971) 33 07 28.

Els amunts is the local name for the uplands of northern Ibiza, which stretch from Sant Antoni on the west coast to Sant Vicenç in the northeast. Though hardly a mountain range – Es Fornás is the highest point, at a mere 450 m

(1,480 ft) – the area's inaccessibility has kept it unspoiled. There are few special sights here, apart from the landscape: pine-clad hills sheltering fertile valleys whose rich red soil is planted with olive, almond and fig trees, and the occasional vineyard. Tourist enclaves are also scarce – except for a handful of small resorts, such as Port de Sant Miquel, Portinatx and Sant Vicenç. Inland, villages like Sant Joan and Santa Agnès offer an insight into Ibiza's quiet, rural past.

The architectural highpoints of northern Ibiza are several beautiful white churches, like the one in **Sant Miquel** which, in summer, is host to a weekly display of Ibizan folk dancing. Outside Sant Llorenç is the tranquil, fortified hamlet of **Balàfia**, which has flat-roofed houses, tiny whitewashed alleys, and a watchtower that was used as a fortress during raids by the Turks.

IBIZA'S HOTTEST SPOTS

Ibiza's reputation for extraordinary nightlife is largely justified. The main action takes place in two areas: the Calle de la Virgen in the old harbour district, with its bars, fashion boutiques and restaurants; and the mega-discos out of town – Ku, Pachá, Amnesia and Es Paradis. When the last of these is closing, at about 7am, the wildest club of them all, Space, is only just opening its doors. Ibiza has long been a magnet for the rich and famous. Celebrities seem to have become more elusive of late, but a few well-known faces can often be glimpsed dining in the restaurant Las Dos Lunas, and taking the rays the next day on the beach at Ses Salines.

Nightclubbers enjoying a bubble bath at Amnesia

One of the many beautiful beaches along the unspoiled shores of the island of Formentera

Santa Eulària ❺

Baleares. 🏠 *5,000.* 🚍 🚢 **ℹ** *Carrer Mariano Riquer Wallis 4, (971) 33 07 28.* 🚍 *Wed.* 🎭 *Es Cana (15 Aug).*

DESPITE CATERING for tourism, the town of Santa Eulària d'es Riu (Santa Eulalia del Río), situated on the island's only river, has managed to hold on to its character far more than many other Spanish resorts.

The 16th-century church, with its pretty covered courtyard, and the surrounding old town, were built on the top of a little hill, the **Puig de Missa**, because this site was more easily defended in times of war than the shore below.

Adjacent to the church is the **Museu Etnològic**, a folk museum, which is housed in an ancient but tastefully adapted Ibizan farmhouse. Included in the exhibits (labelled in Catalan only) are traditional costumes, farming implements, toys and

The domed roof of Santa Eulària's 16th-century church

an olive press. A fascinating collection of old photographs reveals the drastic and irreversible changes Ibiza has suffered over the last 50 years.

🏛 Museu Etnològic
Puig de Missa. **📞** *(971) 33 28 45.* ⚫ *Mon.*

Formentera ❻

Baleares. 🚢 *from Ibiza.* **ℹ** *La Savina, (971) 32 20 57.*

AN HOUR'S BOAT RIDE from Ibiza harbour will bring you to this largely unspoiled island where the waters are blue and the way of life slow.

From the small port of La Savina, where the boat docks, there are buses to other parts of the island. As the service is limited, it is more advisable to hire a car, moped or bicycle from one of the shops nearby.

Sant Francesc, Formentera's tiny capital, is situated 3 km (2 miles) from La Savina. Most of the island's amenities are in this town, plus a pretty church (built in 1729), in the main square, and a folk museum.

From Sant Francesc, a bumpy minor road leads for 9 km (6 miles) southwards, ending at Cap de Barbaria, the site of an 18th-century defensive tower and a lighthouse.

Formentera is entirely flat, apart from the small plateau of **La Mola**, which takes up the whole eastern end of the island. From the fishing port of Es Caló the road winds up-

wards past the Restaurante Es Mirador, with its panoramic view of western Formentera, to the village of Nostra Senyora del Pilar on top of the plateau. About 3 km (2 miles) to the east is a lighthouse, Far de la Mola, sited on the highest point of the island. Nearby stands a monument to Jules Verne (1828–1905), who used Formentera for the setting of one of his novels, *Hector Servadac.*

Although there are many purple road signs indicating places of cultural interest on Formentera, most lead only to disappointment. But one sight well worth seeking out is the megalithic sepulchre of **Ca Na Costa** (1800–1600 BC) near Sant Francesc, the only one of its kind in the Balearics. This monument, a circle of upright stone slabs, pre-dates the Carthaginians *(see pp45–6).*

However, the island's great strength is not its history and culture, but its landscape, which has a spare and delicate beauty and some of the Mediterranean's last unspoiled shorelines. The finest beaches are, arguably, Migjorn, Tramuntana, and Cala Saona, all southwest of Sant Francesc. Illetes and Llevant are two beautiful beaches on either side of a long sandy spit in the far north of the island. If the water is calm you can wade through it from the Pas d'es Trocadors (where Illetes and Llevant meet) to the island of **Espalmador** – with its natural springs, superb beaches and lighthouse – which lies between Formentera and Ibiza.

Regional Food: The Balearic Islands

TRADITIONAL FOOD is being rediscovered in the Balearics. It varies from island to island but reflects the cuisine of Catalonia, with its combinations of sweet and savoury, and nuts and dried fruit. Pork is a main ingredient, and vegetable dishes and soups are also typical

Mayonnaise

fare. Menorca's capital, Maó, lays claim to the invention of mayonnaise, which is often served with succulent fish and shellfish. Mallorca is the home of the savoury *sobrassada (see p493)*, a delicious spicy sausage, and the sweet pastry known as *ensaimada*.

Huevos a la sollerica *are fried eggs served on top of smooth, red* sobrassada *sausage, served with a pea sauce.*

Langosta a la parrilla *partners spiny lobster with the local mayonnaise, which is made with eggs and olive oil.*

Berenjenas rellenas *are aubergines stuffed with onions, herbs and bread. Tomatoes and pork are also often added.*

Tumbet, *made in a brown earthenware* greixera *or casserole, combines layers of peppers and tomato with potato.*

Coca de trampó *is a pizza-style dish, topped with a selection of fresh vegetables, especially onions and peppers.*

Ensaimada *is a spiral-shaped yeast bun from Mallorca, and can be eaten either for breakfast or as a tea-time snack.*

DRINKS

While in Menorca 200 years ago, sailors from the English navy introduced the islanders to the potent drink of gin with lemon. A highly perfumed gin is still made on the island. A large selection of herb and other liqueurs is made in the Balearics, including *palo,* flavoured with crushed almond shells. The Balearics produce few wines. The main wine region, a *denominación de origen (see p576),* is around Binissalem in Mallorca, and produces mainly light whites and rosés. There are several red Mallorcan wines, which are best drunk young. The most popular Spanish drinks from the mainland, such as *anis,* brandy, beer and sangria *(see p577),* are available everywhere in the Balearics.

Herb liqueur

Almond liqueur

Gin

Mallorca

MALLORCA IS OFTEN LIKENED TO A CONTINENT rather than simply an island. Its varied nature never fails to astonish, whether you are looking for landscape, culture or just entertainment. No other European island has a wider range of scenery, from the fertile plains of central Mallorca to the almost alpine peaks of the Tramuntana. The island's mild climate and lovely beaches have made it one of Spain's foremost package tour destinations but there is a wealth of culture, too, evident in sights like Palma Cathedral (*see pp496–7*). Mallorca's appeal lies also in its charm as a living, working island: the cereal and fruit crops of the central plains, and the vineyards around Binissalem are vital to the island's economy.

Terraced orange grove in the Sierra Tramuntana

Andratx ❼

Baleares. 🏘 *7,000.* 🚌 ℹ *Plaça Miguel Moner 1, (971) 67 10 01.* 🛒 *Wed.* 🎎 *San Pedro (29 Jun), La Virgen de Carmen (16 Jul).*

THIS SMALL TOWN lies amid a valley of almond groves in the shadow of Puig de Galatzó, which rises to 1,026 m (3,366 ft). With its ochre and white shuttered houses and the old watchtowers perched high on a hill above the town, Andratx is a very pretty place.

The road southwest leads down to **Port d'Andratx** 5 km (3 miles) away. Here, in an almost totally enclosed bay, expensive yachts are moored in rows along the harbour and luxury holiday homes pepper the surrounding hillsides. In the past, Port d'Andratx's main role was as the fishing port and harbour for Andratx, but since the early 1960s it has gradually been transformed into an exclusive holiday resort for the rich and famous. When visiting Port d'Andratx, it is a good idea to leave all thoughts of the real Mallorca behind and simply enjoy it for what it is – a chic and affluent resort.

La Granja ❽

Esporles. ℂ *(971) 61 00 32.* 🚌 ⭕ *daily.* 🎞 ♿

LA GRANJA is a pivate estate, or *possessió*, near the little country town of Esporles. Formerly a Cistercian convent, it is now the property of the Seguí family, who have opened their largely unspoiled 18th-century house to the public as a kind of living museum of traditional Mallorca. Peacocks roam the gardens, salt cod and hams hang in the kitchen, *The Marriage of Figaro* plays in the ballroom, and the slight air of chaos just adds to the charm of the place.

Valldemossa ❾

Baleares. 🏘 *1,500.* 🚌 ℹ *Jardin de la Cartuja, (971) 61 20 02.* 🛒 *Sun.* 🎎 *Santa Catalina Tomas (28 Jul), San Bartolomé (24 Aug).*

THIS PLEASANT mountain town will forever be linked with the name of George Sand, the French novelist who stayed here during the winter of 1838–9 and later wrote unflatteringly of the island and its people in *Un Hiver à Majorque*. Dearer to Mallorcans is the Polish composer and pianist Frédéric Chopin (1810–49) who stayed with Sand at the **Real Cartuja de Jesús de Nazaret**. "Chopin's cell", off the monastery's main courtyard, is where

Bust of Frédéric Chopin at Valldemossa

a few of his works were written, and it still houses the piano on which he composed.

A few doors away is a 17th-century pharmacy displaying outlandish medicinal preparations such as "powdered nails of the beast". In the cloisters is a contemporary art museum with works by Tàpies, Hartung and Miró, and the Mallorcan artist Juli Ramis (1909–90). There is also a series of Picasso illustrations titled *The Burial of the Count of Orgaz*, inspired by the El Greco painting of the same name (*see p28*).

🏛 **Real Cartuja de Jesús de Nazaret**
Plaça de la Cartuja de Valldemossa.
ℂ *(971) 61 21 06.* ⬤ *Sun.* 🎞 ♿

A view across the harbour of Port d'Andratx

Alfàbia

Off C711. ☎ (971) 61 31 23.
🚌 tour bus from Palma. ⬤ Sun. 📷

VERY FEW *possessions* in Mallorca are open to the public, which makes Alfàbia all the more worth visiting. The house and garden are an ex-cellent example of a typical Mallorcan aristocratic estate and exude an unmistakably Moorish atmosphere. Very little remains of the original 14th-century architecture, so it is well worth looking out for the Mudéjar inscription on the ceil-ing of the entrance hall and the Hispano-Arabic fountains and pergola. The garden is a sump-tuous 19th-century creation, making imaginative use of shade and the play of water.

Sóller ⑪

Baleares. 🏠 11,000. 🚉 🚌 🅸
Plaça Constitució 1, (971) 63 02 00.
🗓 Sat. 🎏 second Sun of May.

SÓLLER IS A LITTLE TOWN grown fat on the produce of its olive groves and orchards, which climb up the slopes of the Sierra Tramuntana. In the 19th century Sóller traded its oranges and wine for French goods, and the town retains a faintly Gallic, bourgeois feel.

One of Sóller's best-known features is its delightfully old-fashioned narrow-gauge rail-way, complete with quaint wooden carriages. The town, whose station is in the Plaça d'Espanya, lies on a scenic route between Palma and the fishing village of Port de Sóller 5 km (3 miles) to the west.

ENVIRONS: From Sóller a road winds southwards along the spectacular west coast to **Deià** (Deyá). This village was once the home of Robert Graves (1895–1985), the English poet and novelist, who came to live here in 1929. His simple tombstone can be seen in the small cemetery. The **Museu Arqueològic**, curated by the archaeologist William Waldren, offers a glimpse into prehistoric Mallorca. Outside the village is **Son Marroig**, the estate of Austrian Archduke Ludwig

Houses and trees crowded together on the hillside of Deià

Salvator (1847–1915), who documented the Balearics in a series of books included in a display of his possessions on the first floor.

🏛 Museu Arqueològic
Es Clot Deià. ☎ (971) 63 90 01.
🕐 Apr–Oct: Tue–Sun. 📷 🅰

Statue of La Moreneta at the Monasteri de Lluc

Monasteri de Lluc ⑫

Lluc. 🚌 from Palma. ☎ (971) 51 70 25. 🕐 daily. 📷 museum only. 🅰

HIGH IN THE MOUNTAINS of the Sierra Tramuntana, in the remote village of Lluc, is an institution regarded by many as the spiritual heart of Mallorca. The Monasteri de Lluc was built mainly in the 17th and 18th centuries on the site of an ancient shrine. The monastery's Baroque church, with its imposing façade,

contains the stone image of La Moreneta, the Black Virgin of Lluc, supposedly found by a young shepherd boy on a nearby hilltop in the 13th century. Along the Camí dels Misteris, the paved walkway up to this hilltop, there are some bronze bas-reliefs by the Catalan architect and designer Antoni Gaudí *(see pp136–7)*. Just off the main Plaça dels Pelegrins are a café and bar, a pharmacy and a shop selling a variety of local handicrafts, wines and foods. The museum, situated on the first floor, in-cludes Mallorcan paintings and medieval manuscripts. The monastery incorporates a guest house *(see p568)*.

From Lluc, 13 km (8 miles) of tortuous road winds through the hills and descends towards the coast, ending at the beauti-ful rocky bay of **Sa Calobra**. From here, it is just 5 minutes' walk further up the coast to the Torrent de Pareis, a deep gorge opening into the sea.

Sheer cliff face rising out of the sea at Sa Calobra

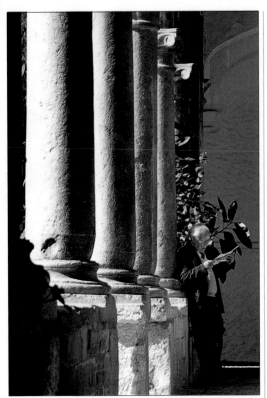

The cloisters of the Convent de Santo Domingo in Pollença

Pollença ⑬

Baleares. 🏘 12,000. 🚌 🛈 Ctra de Formentor, Port de Pollença, (971) 86 54 67. 🚢 Sun. 🎎 Sant Antoni (17 Jan).

ALTHOUGH POLLENÇA has become one of Mallorca's most popular tourist spots, it still appears unspoiled. The town, with its ochre-coloured stone houses and winding lanes, is picturesquely sited on the edge of fertile farmland. The Plaça Major, with its bars frequented mainly by locals, has an old-world atmosphere.

Pollença has fine churches, including the elegant 18th-century **Parròquia de Nostra Senyora dels Angels** and the Convent de Santo Domingo, which contains the **Museu Municipal**, with its displays on local archaeology. This convent also holds Pollença's Music Festival every August. A chapel perched on the top of a hill, **El Calvari**, is reached either by road or a torturous climb of 365 steps. On the altar there is a charming Gothic Christ, carved in wood.

ENVIRONS: **Alcúdia**, 10 km (6 miles) to the east, is surrounded by 14th-century walls pierced by two majestic gateways. Near the town centre is the **Museu Monogràfic de Pollença**, which exhibits statues, jewellery and other remains found in the Roman settlement of Pollentia, 1.5 km (1 mile) south of Alcúdia.

🏛 **Museu Municipal**
Carrer Santo Domingo. 📞 (971) 53 00 15. 🕐 Tue, Thu & Sun.
🏛 **Museu Monogràfic de Pollença**
Centro Cultural de Pollença Carrer Gillen Cifre de Colonya 33. 📞 (971) 53 00 15. 🕐 Tue, Thu & Sun. 🎎 ♿

Palma de Mallorca ⑭

See pp494–7.

Puig de Randa ⑮

8 km (5 miles) northeast of Llucmajor. 🚌 to Llucmajor, then taxi. 🛈 El Arenal, (971) 44 04 14.

IN THE MIDDLE of a fertile plain called the *pla* rises a mini-mountain 543 m (1,780 ft) high, the Puig de Randa. It is said that Mallorca's greatest son, the 14th-century theologian and mystic Ramon Llull, came to a hermitage on this mountain to meditate and write his religious treatise, *Ars Magna*. On the way up Puig de Randa there are two small monasteries, the 14th-century Santuari de Sant Honorat and the Santuari de Nostra Senyora de Gràcia. The latter, built on a ledge under an overhanging cliff, contains a 15th-century chapel with fine Valencian tiles inside, and offers an open view of the *pla*.

On the mountain top is the **Santuari de Cura**, built to commemorate Llull's time on the *puig*, and largely devoted to the study of his work. Its central courtyard is built in the typical beige stone of Mallorca. A small museum, housed in a 16th-century former school off the courtyard, contains some of Llull's manuscripts.

The philosopher Ramon Llull

Capocorb Vell ⑯

14 km (9 miles) south of Llucmajor. 📞 (971) 66 16 26. 🚌 from El Arenal. 🕐 Fri–Wed. 🎎

MALLORCA is not as rich in megalithic remains as Menorca, but this *talaiotic* village (*see p503*) in the stony flatlands of the southern coast is worth seeing – particularly on a quiet day when you can wander among the stones in peace. The settlement, which dates back to around 1000 BC, originally consisted of five *talaiots* (stone tower-like structures with timbered roofs) and 28 smaller dwellings. Little is known about its inhabitants and the uses for some of the rooms inside the buildings, such as the tiny underground gallery. Too small for living in, this room may have been used to perform magic rituals.

Part of the charm of this place lies in its surroundings among fields of fruit trees and dry stone walls, a setting that somehow complements the ruins. Apart from a snack bar nearby, the site remains mercifully undeveloped.

One of the *talaiots* of Capocorb Vell

Cabrera ⑰

Baleares. 🚢 from Colònia Sant Jordi. 🛈 Carrer Doctor Barraquer 5, Colònia Sant Jordi, (971) 65 60 73.

FROM THE BEACHES of Es Trenc and Sa Ràpita, on the south coast of Mallorca, Cabrera looms on the horizon. The largest island in an archipelago of the same name, it lies 18 km (11 miles) from the most southerly point of Mallorca. Cabrera is home to several rare plants, reptiles and seabirds, such as Eleonora's falcon. The waters around it are important for their marine life. All this has resulted in the archipelago being declared a national park *(see pp26–7)*. For centuries Cabrera was used as a military base and it was never colonized. On it stands a 14th-century castle.

A street in Felanitx

Felanitx ⑱

Baleares. 👥 9,000. 🚌 🛈 Plaça Constitució 1, (971) 58 00 51. 🛒 Sun. 🎉 Sant Joan Pelós (24 Jun).

THIS BUSTLING agricultural town is the birthplace of Renaissance architect Guillem Sagrera (1380–1456) and the 20th-century painter Miquel Barceló. Felanitx is visited mainly for three reasons: the imposing façade of the 13th-century church, the **Esglesia de Sant Miquel**; its *sobrassada de porc negre* (a spiced raw sausage made from the meat of the local black pig) and its lively religious fiestas including Sant Joan Pelós *(see p499)*.

About 5 km (3 miles) southeast is the **Castell de Santueri**, founded by the Moors but rebuilt in the 14th century by the kings of Aragón, who ruled Mallorca. Though a ruin, it is worth the detour for the views to the east and south from its vantage point, 400 m (1,300 ft) above the plain.

Coves del Drac ⑲

1.5 km (1 mile) south of Porto Cristo. 🚌 from Porto Cristo. 📞 (971) 82 07 53. 🕐 daily. ⚫ 1 Jan, 25 Dec. 🎫

MALLORCA has innumerable caves, ranging from mere holes in the ground to cathedral-like halls. The four vast chambers of the **Coves del Drac** are reached by a steep flight of steps, at the bottom of which is the beautifully lit cave known as "Diana's Bath". Another chamber holds the large underground lake, Martel, which is 39 m (128 ft) below ground level and is 177 m (580 ft) long. A boat trip on this lake is an unforgettable experience. Equally dramatic are the two remaining caves, imaginatively named "The Theatre of the Fairies" and "The Enchanted City".

ENVIRONS: The **Coves dels Hams** is so called because some of its stalactites are shaped like hooks – *hams* in Mallorcan. The caves are 500 m (1,640 ft) long and contain the "Sea of Venice", an underground lake on which musicians sail in a small boat.

The entrance to the **Coves d'Artá**, near Capdepera, is 40 m (130 ft) above sea level and affords a wonderful view. The caves' main attraction is a stalagmite 22 m (72 ft) high.

🎫 **Coves dels Hams**
11 km (7 miles) from Manacor towards Porto Cristo. 📞 (971) 82 09 88. 🕐 daily. ⚫ 1 Jan, 25 Dec. 🎫
🎫 **Coves d'Artá**
Canyamel, nr Capdepera. 📞 (971) 84 12 93. 🕐 daily. ⚫ 1 Jan, 25 Dec. 🎫

The dramatically lit stalactites of the Coves d'Artá

Street-by-Street: Palma ⑭

Forn des Teatre pastry shop

O N AN ISLAND whose name has become synonymous with mass tourism, Palma surprises by its cultural richness. Under the Moors it was already a prosperous town of fountains and cool courtyards. After he had conquered it in 1229, Jaime I wrote, "It seemed to me . . . the most beautiful city we had ever seen". Signs of Palma's past wealth are still evident in the sumptuous churches, grand public buildings and fine private mansions that crowd the old town. The hub of the city is the old-fashioned Passeig des Born, whose cafés invite you to try one of Mallorca's specialities, the *ensaimada*, a spiral of pastry dusted with icing sugar.

The Forn des Teatre is an old pastry shop noted for its *ensaimadas* and *gató* (almond cake).

The Fundació la Caixa, once the Gran Hotel, is now a cultural centre.

Palau de l'Almudaina
This once-royal Moorish palace now houses a museum, whose highlights include the chapel of Santa Ana, with its Romanesque portal, and the Gothic tinell or salon.

STAR SIGHTS

★ **Cathedral**

★ **Basílica de Sant Francesc**

La Llotja is a beautiful 14th-century stock exchange with tall windows and delicate tracery.

PLAÇA REI JOAN CARLES

PASSEIG DES BORN

CARRER UNIÓ

CARRER J

CARRER DE PALAU REIAL

CARRER DE SAN

CARRER MIR

AVINGUDA D'ANTONI MAURA

To Castell de Bellver and Fundació Pilar i Joan Miró

★ **Cathedral**
Built of golden limestone quarried from Santanyi, Palma's huge Gothic cathedral stands in a dramatic location near the waterfront.

Parc de la Mar

KEY

– – – Suggested route

VISITORS' CHECKLIST

Baleares. 🏙 305,000. ✈ 11 km
(7 miles) east. 🚉 Plaça Espanya,
(971) 75 20 51. 🚌 Plaça Espanya.
⛴ Muelle de Peraires, (971) 40
50 14. 🛈 Plaça Major 3, (971)
71 22 16. 🛍 Sat. 🎎 San
Sebastià (20 Jan). **Museu de
Mallorca** ⬜ Tue–Sun. 🏛 **Banys
Àrabs** ⬜ daily. 🏛 **Museu
Diocesà** ⬜ daily. 🏛 **Palau de
l'Almudaina** ⬜ Mon–Sat. 🏛

Estació de RENFE and ació de Autobuses

Plaça del Marqués de Palmer

0 metres   100
0 yards   100

A view along the circular walls of the Castell de Bellver

★ **Basílica de Sant Francesc**
The church and cloister of St Francis are in a refined Gothic style with a Baroque altarpiece and rose window.

The Museu Diocesà, housed in the Bishop's Palace, has a collection of religious artifacts.

Museu de Mallorca
The museum has displays on local history, art and architecture, including this statue of an ancient warrior.

Banys Àrabs
The 10th-century baths, with their well-preserved arches, are a remnant of the Balearic Islands' Moorish culture.

♟ Castell de Bellver
West side of Palma Bay. ☎ (971) 73
06 57. ⬜ daily.
About 2.5 km (1.5 miles) from the city centre, standing 113 m (370 ft) above sea level, is Palma's Gothic castle. It was commissioned by Jaime II during the short-lived Kingdom of Mallorca (1276–1349) as a summer residence, but soon after became a prison, and remained as such until 1915. The castle, situated on a wooded hill overlooking the bay of Palma, is of an unusual circular design.
Three of its towers are set into the main castle wall; the other is set apart from it, but linked by a high walkway. From some angles the castle looks more decorative than defensive: witness the cloister of delicate arches that rings the central courtyard.

🏛 Fundació Pilar i Joan Miró
Carrer Joan de Saridakis 29. ☎ (971)
70 14 20. ⬜ Mon.
When Joan Miró died in 1982, his wife took on the task of converting his former studio and home into an art centre. The building – christened "the Alabaster Fortress" by the Spanish press – is a stunning example of modern architecture designed by Navarrese architect Rafael Moneo. It incorporates Miró's original studio (complete with unfinished paintings), a permanent collection of the painter's work, a shop, a library and an auditorium.

Palma Cathedral

ACCORDING TO LEGEND, when Jaime I of Aragón was caught in a storm on his way to conquer Mallorca in 1229, he vowed that if God led him to safety he would build a great church in His honour. In the following years the old mosque of Medina Mayurqa was torn down and architect Guillem Sagrera (1380–1456) drew up plans for a new cathedral. In 1587 the last stone was added to the soaring vaults. Over subsequent years the cathedral has been rebuilt, notably early this century when the interior was remodelled by Antoni Gaudí *(see pp136–7)*. Today Palma Cathedral, or Sa Seu, as Mallorcans call it, is one of the most breathtaking buildings in Spain, combining vast scale with typically Gothic elegance *(see p20)*.

Bell Tower
This robust tower was built in 1389 and houses nine bells, the largest of which is known as Aloi, meaning "praise".

Palma Cathedral
One of the best-sited cathedrals anywhere, it is spectacularly poised high on the sea wall, above what was once Palma's harbour.

STAR FEATURES

★ **Great Rose Window**

★ **Baldachino**

19th-century tower

Entrance to cathedral museum

Portal Major

Flying buttresses

Cathedral Museum
One of the highlights of the beautifully displayed collection in the Old Chapterhouse is a 15th-century reliquary of the True Cross which is encrusted with jewels and precious metals.

★ **Great Rose Window**
The largest of seven rose windows looks down from above the High Altar like a gigantic eye. Built in 1370 with stained glass added in the 16th century, the window has a diameter of over 11 m (36 ft).

VISITORS' CHECKLIST

Carrer Palau Reial 29. (971) 72 31 30. Apr–Oct: 10am–6pm Mon–Fri; Nov–Mar: 10am–3pm Mon–Fri, 10am–2pm Sat. public hols. 9am, 7pm daily (Oct–Mar: 9am, 5:30pm Mon–Fri; 9am, 7pm Sat, Sun).

The Great Organ was built with a Neo-Gothic case in 1795, and restored in 1993 by Gabriel Blancafort.

Capella de la Trinitat
This tiny chapel was built in 1329 as the mausoleum of Jaime II and III of Aragón. It contains their alabaster tombs.

The Capella Reial, or Royal Chapel, was redesigned by Antoni Gaudí between 1904 and 1914.

Bishop's Throne
Built in 1269 and made of Carrara marble, the chair is embedded in a Gothic vaulted niche.

Choir stalls

Portal del Mirador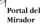

Nave
The magnificent ceiling, 44 m (144 ft) high, is held up by 14 slender pillars. At over 19 m (62 ft) wide, it is one of the broadest naves in the world.

★ **Baldachino**
Gaudí's bizarre wrought-iron canopy above the altar incorporates lamps, tapestries and a multi-coloured crucifix.

Menorca

MENORCA IS THE BALEARIC ISLAND furthest from the main-land and it is set apart from the rest of the country in many other ways. The coastline of Menorca is, argu-ably, more unspoiled than in any other part of Spain. Its countryside remains largely green and pleasant with cows roaming the meadows. The old towns of Maó – the island's capital – and Ciutadella are filled with noble, historic buildings and beautiful squares. Menorca also has abundant reminders of its more distant history: the island boasts a spectacular hoard of Bronze Age stone structures, which provide an invaluable insight into its prehistoric past. The Menorcans are often more inclined to drink the locally brewed gin *(ginebra)* than the wine which is favoured elsewhere in Spain.

Fishermen mending their nets in Ciutadella's harbour

The peaceful seafront of Ciutadella at twilight

Ciutadella **20**

Baleares. 🏛 *22,000.* 🚗 🚲 ℹ️ *Plaça de la Catedral, (971) 38 26 93.* 🔄 *Fri & Sat.* 🎉 *Sant Joan (24 Jun).*

THE KEY DATE in the history of Ciutadella is 1558. In that year the Turks, under Barba-rossa, entered and decimated the city, consigning 3,495 of its citizens to the slave markets of Constantinople. Of Ciutadella's main public buildings, only the fine Catalan Gothic **Església Catedral de Menorca** man-aged to survive this fearsome onslaught in more or less its original condition, only later to be stripped of all its paint-ings, ornaments and other treasures by Republican ex-tremists during the Civil War.

The nearby **Plaça des Born** was built as a parade ground for Moorish troops and from 1558 was gradually rebuilt in Renaissance style. Today it is one of Spain's most impressive squares, containing pleasant cafés and bordered by shady palm trees. At the centre of the Plaça des Born is an obelisk which commemorates the "Any de sa Desgràcia" (Year of Misfortune), when the Turks

The historic Plaça des Born in the centre of Ciutadella

invaded the city. Around the square are the Gothic-style **town hall** *(ajuntament)*, the late 19th-century **Teatre Municipal des Born**, and a series of aristocratic mansions with Italianesque façades, the grandest of which is the early 19th-century **Palau de Torre-Saura**. From the northern end of the Plaça des Born there is a fine view over Ciutadella's small sheltered harbour.

If you walk up the Carrer Major des Born past the cathedral, you come to **Ses Voltes**, an alley lined on both sides by whitewashed arches. Turn right along the Carrer des Seminari for the Baroque **Església dels Socors** and the **Museu Diocesà** with its displays of ecclesiastical para-phernalia. In the narrow streets of the old town there are many impressive palaces, but only the early 19th-century **Palau Salort**, on the Carrer Major des Born, is open to the public. The delightful Art Nouveau **market** (1895), its ironwork painted in smart municipal dark green, stands nearby.

The peace of Ciutadella is disturbed every June by the Festa de Sant Joan, an enter-taining and spectacular ritual of horsemanship. During the festival the local gin *(ginebra)* is drunk copiously and the city grinds to a halt for a week.

🏛 **Museu Diocesà**
Seminari 5. 📞 *(971) 71 40 63.* ⏱ *daily.* 📷

🏛 **Palau Salort**
Carrer Major del Born 9. 📞 *(971) 38 00 56.* ⏱ *May–Oct: daily.* 📷

Ferreries ㉑

Baleares. 🏠 *3,800.* 🚉 🛈 *Carrer Sant Bartomeu 55, (971) 37 30 03.* 🗓 *Tue, Fri, Sat.* 🎪 *Sant Bartomeu (23–5 Aug).*

FERRERIES LIES in between Maó and Ciutadella and sprang up when a road was built to connect the two towns. Today Ferreries is an attractive village of white houses, built against the slope of a hill. The simple church, Sant Bartomeu, dates from 1770.

The bay of **Santa Galdana**, 10 km (6 miles) to the south, is even prettier. You can take a pleasant walk from beach inland through the fertile river-bed of Barranc d'Algendar.

Courtyard in the Santuari del Toro

Es Mercadal ㉒

Baleares. 🏠 *2,500.* 🚉 🛈 *Carrer Major 16, (971) 37 50 02.* 🗓 *Sun.* 🎪 *Sant Martí (third Sun of Jul).*

ES MERCADAL is a small country town – one of the three, with Alaior and Ferreries, that are strung out along the main road from Maó to Ciutadella.

The town is unremarkable in itself, but within reach of it are three places of interest.

El Toro, 3 km (2 miles) to the east, is Menorca's highest mountain, at 350 m (1,150 ft). It is also the spiritual heart of the island and at its summit is the Santuari del Toro, built in 1670, which is run by nuns.

About 10 km (6 miles) north of Es Mercadal, the fishing village of **Fornells** transforms itself every summer into an outpost of St Tropez. In the harbour, smart yachts jostle with fishing boats, and jet-set Spaniards crowd into the Bar Palma. Fornells' main culinary speciality is the *caldereta de llagosta* (lobster casserole), but the quality varies and the prices can be high.

The road-cum-dirt track to the **Cap de Cavalleria**, 13 km (8 miles) north of Es Mercadal, passes through one of the Balearics' finest landscapes. Cavalleria is a rocky promon-tory, whipped by the tramon-tana wind from the north. It juts out into a choppy sea which, in winter, looks more like the North Atlantic than the Mediterranean. At the western edge of the peninsula are the remains of Sanitja, a Phoenician village mentioned by Pliny in the 1st century AD. The road leads to a headland, with a lighthouse and cliffs 90 m (295 ft) high, where peregrine falcons, sea eagles and kites ride the wind.

Further west along the coast is a string of fine, unspoiled beaches, though with difficult access: Cala Pregonda, Cala del Pilar and La Vall d'Algaiarens are three of the most beautiful.

Horse rearing in the fiesta of Sant Lluís

THE BALEARIC ISLANDS' FIESTAS

Sant Antoni Abat *(17 Jan),* Mallorca. This fiesta is celebrated with parades and the blessing of animals all over Mallorca and in Sant Antoni in Ibiza.

Sant Joan *(24 Jun),* Ciutadella (Menorca). The horse plays a major part in Menorca's festivals. In the streets and squares of Ciutadella on 24 June, the Day of St John the Baptist, elegantly dressed riders put their horses through ritualized medieval man-oeuvres. The fiesta reaches a climax when the horses rear up on their hind legs and the jubilant crowds swarm around them try-ing to hold them up with their hands. Similarly, the annual fiesta in Sant Lluís, which takes place at the end of August, sees many of the locals taking to the streets on horseback.

Sant Joan Pelós *(24 Jun),* Felanitx (Mallorca). As part of this fiesta, a man is dressed in sheepskins to represent John the Baptist.

Romeria de Sant Marçal *(30 Jun),* Sa Cabeneta (Mallorca). A feature of this fiesta is a market selling *siurells*, primitive Mallorcan whistles.

Our Lady of the Sea *(16 Jul),* Formentera. The island's main fiesta honours the Virgen del Carmen, patroness of fishermen, with a flotilla of fishing boats.

A quiet stretch of beach at Santa Galdana

The steep hillside of Maó running up from the harbour

Maó ㉓

Baleares. 🏛 23,000. 🚗 🚉 ⛴ 🛈
Plaça de S'Esplanada, (971) 36 37 90.
🚌 Tue, Sat. 🎉 Fiestas de Gracia (7–8
Sep), Fiesta de Sant Antoni (17 Jan).

THE QUIETLY ELEGANT town of
Maó has lent its Spanish
name, Mahón, to mayonnaise
(see p489). It was occupied
by the British three times during the 18th century. The legacy of past colonial rule can be
seen in sober Georgian town
houses, with their dark green
shutters and sash windows.

Maó's harbour is one of the
finest in the Mediterranean.
Taking the street leading from
the port to the upper town,
the S-shaped Costa de Ses
Voltes, you come to the 18th-
century **Església del Carme**,
a former Carmelite church
whose cool white cloister now
houses an attractive fruit and
vegetable market. Behind the
market is Maó's only museum,
the **Col·lecció Hernández**
Mora, which houses Menorcan
art and antiques. The nearby
Plaça Constitució is overlooked
by the church of Santa Maria,
which has a huge and well-
preserved organ, built in 1810.
Next door is the **town hall**
(ajuntament) with its Neo-
Classical façade, into which is
mounted the famous clock
donated by Sir Richard Kane
(1660–1736), the first British
governor of Menorca,

Located at the end of the
Carrer Isabel II is the **Església**
de Sant Francesc, with an
intriguing Romanesque doorway and Baroque façade. The
church houses the Museu de
Menorca (currently undergoing
refurbishment). Two minutes'
walk south of here will take
you to Maó's main square, the
Plaça de S'Esplanada, behind
which is the **Ateneu Científic**
Lliterat Artistic, a centre of
Menorca-related culture and
learning. Inside are collections
of local ceramics and maps,
and a library. It is advisable

to obtain permission before
looking around. On the north
side of the harbour is a mansion known as **Sant Antoni**
or the Golden Farm. As Maó's
finest example of Palladian
architecture, it has an arched
façade, painted plum red, with
white arches, in the traditional
Menorcan style. The British
admiral, Nelson, is thought to
have stayed here. The house
has a collection of Nelson
memorabilia and a fine library
but is closed to the public.

🏛 **Col·lecció Hernández**
Mora
Plaza Miranda 5, Claustre del Carme 5.
📞 (971) 35 05 97. 🕐 Mon–Sat. 🔲
🏛 **Ateneu Científic Lliterat**
Artistic
C/ Conde de Cifuentes 25. 📞 (971)
36 05 53. 🔲 Sun, public hols.

Cales Coves ㉔

Baleares. 🚉 Sant Climent. 📞 Maó,
(971) 36 37 90.

ON EITHER SIDE of a pretty
bay can be found Cales
Coves – the site of Neolithic
dwellings of up to 9 m (30 ft)
in length, hollowed out of the
rock face. The caves, thought
to have been inhabited since
prehistoric times, are today
occupied by a community of
people seeking an alternative
lifestyle. Some of the caves
have front doors, chimneys
and even butane cookers.

About 8 km (5 miles) west,
along the coast, lies Binibeca,
a tourist village built in a style
sympathetic to old Menorca.
The jumble of white houses
and tiny streets of the Poblat
de Pescadors, an imitation
fishing village, have the look
of the genuine article.

Modern sculpture outside one of
the dwellings at Cales Coves

◁ **The clear blue waters of Cala Turqueta in Menorca**

Ancient Menorca

Menorca is exceptionally rich in prehistoric remains – the island has been described as an immense open-air museum. The majority of the sites are the work of the "talaiotic" people who lived between 2000–1000 BC and are named after the *talaiots* or huge stone towers that characterize the Menorcan landscape. There are hundreds of these Bronze Age villages and structures dotted around the island. Usually open to the public and free of charge, these sites provide an invaluable insight into the ancient inhabitants of the Balearics.

Huge *talaiot* amid the settlement of Trepucó

DIFFERENT STRUCTURES

The ancient stone structures scattered around the countryside of Menorca and, to a lesser extent, Mallorca can be placed into three main categories: *taulas, talaiots* and *navetas*.

 Taulas *are two slabs of rock, one placed on top of the other, in a "T" formation. Suggestions as to their possible function range from a sacrificial altar to a roof support.*

 Talaiots *are circular or square buildings that may have been used as meeting places and dwellings.*

 Navetas *are shaped like upturned boats and apparently had a dual role as dwellings and burial quarters. At least ten of these remain in Menorca.*

Spectacular *taula* at Talatí de Dalt, standing 3 m (10 ft) high

Menorca has an estimated 1,600 megalithic sites, and the most interesting of these are shown here. Talaiotic remains are found all over the island, usually in rural settings, though most are in the flatter and more fertile south.

Cala Morell

Fornells

Ciutadella
Naveta d'es Tudons   Torrellafuda
Torretrencada   Ferreries   Es Mercadal

Alaior

Torralba d'en Salord
Torre d'en Gaumés   Talatí de Dalt   Maó
Trepucó

Sant Lluís

0 kilometres   10

0 miles   5

THE CANARY ISLANDS

La Palma · El Hierro · La Gomera · Tenerife
Gran Canaria · Fuerteventura · Lanzarote

P OISED ON THE EDGE OF THE TROPICS *west of Morocco, the Canaries enjoy a generous supply of sunshine, pleasantly tempered by the trade winds. Their scenery ranges from lava desert to primeval forest and from sand dunes to volcanic peaks. The old towns on the main islands have colonial centres, full of character.*

Seven islands and half a dozen islets make up the Canary archipelago. They are the tips of hundreds of volcanoes that first erupted from the sea bed 14 million years ago. Teneguía on La Palma last erupted in 1971.

In the 14th and 15th centuries, when navigators discovered the islands and claimed them for Spain, they were inhabited by the Guanches, who practised a stone culture. Sadly, little evidence of them remains.

Today the islands are divided into two provinces. The four western isles, making up the province of Santa Cruz de Tenerife, are all mountainous; Tenerife's colossal dormant volcano, Mount Teide, casts the world's biggest sea-shadow. La Palma, El Hierro and La Gomera, where Columbus stayed on his voyages, are all small, unspoiled islands, not yet developed for mass tourism.

The eastern islands belong to the province of Las Palmas. Rocky, forested Gran Canaria is the biggest island and its capital, Las Palmas, is a charming colonial town. Lanzarote, by contrast, is flat, with lunar landscapes, while Fuerteventura has long, virgin beaches.

Protected area of sand dunes at Maspalomas, next to busy Playa del Inglés, Gran Canaria

◁ La Rambla banana plantation on the north coast of the island of Tenerife

Exploring the Western Islands

TENERIFE HAS THE WIDEST RANGE of holiday attractions of any of the Canary Islands. The province of Santa Cruz de Tenerife also includes the three tiny westerly islands of La Palma, La Gomera and El Hierro, which are scarcely developed for tourism and have no large resorts. Gradually, more visitors are discovering these peaceful, green havens. If you enjoy walking, wildlife and mountain scenery, visit one of these hideaways. All three islands have comfortable hotels, including paradors. But compared with Gran Canaria and the eastern islands, there are fewer sandy beaches here, and little organized entertainment or sightseeing.

Las Teresitas artificial beach, Santa Cruz de Tenerife

SIGHTS AT A GLANCE

Candelaria **8**
Los Cristianos **4**
La Gomera **3**
El Hierro **2**
La Laguna **9**
Montes de Anaga **10**
La Orotava **7**
La Palma **1**
Parque Nacional del Teide
pp514–15 **5**
Puerto de la Cruz **6**
Santa Cruz de Tenerife **11**

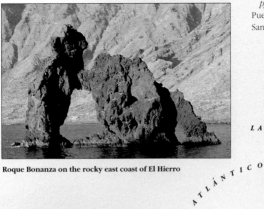

Roque Bonanza on the rocky east coast of El Hierro

KEY

	Motorway
	Major road
	Minor road
	Scenic route
	River
⚹	Viewpoint

Terraced hillside, maximizing cultivation in the lush green Valle Gran Rey, in western La Gomera

GETTING AROUND

From mainland Spain there are flights *(see p628)* and ferries *(see p629)* to the Canary Islands. Transport to the small islands is mainly from Tenerife. La Gomera is easily reached by ferry (90 mins) or hydrofoil (40 mins) from Los Cristianos. Small airports on La Palma and El Hierro are served by regular flights from Tenerife's northern airport of Los Rodeos. Unless you take an organized coach trip, a car is essential to see the island scenery. Roads are improving, but great care is needed for mountain driving.

MONTES DE ANAGA ⑩

TENERIFE

LA LAGUNA ⑨

SANTA CRUZ DE TENERIFE ⑪

PUERTO DE LA CRUZ ⑥

LA OROTAVA ⑦ TF5

BUENAVISTA DEL NORTE

CANDELARIA ⑧

C820

C821

C823

C822

PARQUE NACIONAL DEL TEIDE ⑤

VILAFLOR

C821

GRANADILLA DE ABONA

C822

TF1

④ LOS CRISTIANOS

0 kilometres   25

0 miles   10

SEE ALSO

The wild landscape of Punta de Teno in western Tenerife

La Palma ❶

Santa Cruz de Tenerife. ✈ ⛴ *Santa Cruz de la Palma.* 🛈 *Calle O'Daly 22, Santa Cruz de la Palma, (922) 41 21 06.*

Rᴇᴀᴄʜɪɴɢ ᴀɴ ᴀʟᴛɪᴛᴜᴅᴇ of 2,426 m (7,959 ft) on a land base of less than 728 sq km (280 sq miles), La Palma is the world's steepest island. It lies on the northwestern tip of the archipelago and has a cool, moist climate and lush vegetation. The mountainous interior of the island is covered with forests of indigenous pine, laurel and giant fern.

The centre of the island is dominated by **La Caldera de Taburiente**, a volcano's massive crater, more than 8 km (5 miles) wide. National park status *(see pp26–7)* is an indication of its botanical and geological importance. The International Astrophysics Observatory crowns the summit. A couple of adventurously engineered roads traverse La

The Parque Nacional de la Caldera de Taburiente, La Palma

Palma's dizzy heights, offering spectacular views of the craters of La Cumbrecita and Roque de los Muchachos.

Santa Cruz de la Palma, the island's main town and port, is an elegant place of old houses with balconies, some fine churches and several 16th-century buildings. In the cobbled street behind the sea-front, Calle O'Daly (named after an Irish banana trader), are the Iglesia de San Salvador, boasting a Mudéjar coffered ceiling, and the town hall *(ayuntamiento)*, which is housed in a cardinal's palace. A full-sized cement replica of the *Santa María*, Columbus's flagship, stands at the end of the Plaza Alameda.

The tortuous mountain road southwest of Santa Cruz winds over Las Cumbres mountains via Breña Alta to **El Paso** in the centre of the island. A relatively sizeable community, the village is known for its silk production and hand-rolled cigars.

Pastel façades and delicate wooden balconies in Santa Cruz, La Palma

Among the almond terraces and vineyards of southern La Palma, solidified lava from the Teneguia volcano is a reminder of its recent activity *(see p527)*.

Craters on El Hierro, Spain's most western territory

El Hierro ❷

Santa Cruz de Tenerife. ✈ ⛴ *Puerto de Estaca.* 🛈 *Calle Licenciado Bueno 3, Valverde, (922) 55 03 02.*

Dᴜᴇ ᴛᴏ ᴀ ᴅᴇᴀʀᴛʜ of sandy beaches, El Hierro has escaped the tourist invasions experienced by other islands. Instead it has caught the attentions of naturalists. Its hilly landscape and unusual fauna and flora are part of its appeal. El Hierro is the smallest of the Canaries, and the territory furthest west of the mainland; consequently it is the last place in Spain where the sun sets.

Valverde, the island's capital, stands inland at 600 m (2,000 ft) above sea level. Canary pines and peculiarly twisted

---

LA GOMERA'S WHISTLE LANGUAGE

The problems of communication posed by La Gomera's rugged terrain produced an unusual language, known as El Silbo. This system of piercing whistles probably developed because its sounds carry across the great distances from one valley to the next. Its origins are mysterious, but it was allegedly invented by the Guanches *(see p523)*. Few young Gomerans have any use for El Silbo today, and the language would probably be dead if it were not for the demonstrations of it still held for interested visitors at the parador, and in the restaurant at Las Rosas.

El Silbo practised on La Gomera

juniper trees cover El Hierro's mountainous interior, best seen from the many footpaths and scenic viewpoints along the roads. A ridge of woodland, curving east-west across the island, marks the edge of a volcano. The crater forms a fertile depression known as El Golfo.

In the far west is the **Ermita de los Reyes**, a place of pilgrimage and the starting point of the island's biggest fiesta, held in July every four years.

The turquoise seas off the south coast are popular with skin-divers, who base themselves in the small fishing village of **La Restinga**.

La Gomera ❸

Santa Cruz de Tenerife. 🚢 🏫 *Calle Real 4, San Sebastián de la Gomera, (922) 14 01 47.*

As yet LA GOMERA has no airport, but it is the most accessible and visited of the smaller western islands, only 40 minutes by hydrofoil from Los Cristianos on Tenerife (90 minutes by ferry). Many people come to La Gomera for a day only, taking a coach trip to get around about half of it. Others hire a car and explore independently: a scenic but exhausting drive for a single day as the terrain is intensely buckled, and the central plateau is deeply scored by dramatic ravines. Driving across these gorges involves negotiating countless dizzying hairpin bends.

The best way to enjoy the island is to stay awhile and

Terraced hillsides in the fertile Valle Gran Rey, La Gomera

explore it at leisure, preferably doing some walking. On a fine day, La Gomera's scenery is glorious. Rock pinnacles jut above steep slopes studded with ferns while terraced hillsides glow with palms and flowering creepers. The best section, the **Parque Nacional de Garajonay**, is a UNESCO World Heritage Site.

San Sebastián, La Gomera's main town and ferry terminal, is situated on the east coast, a scattering of white buildings around a small beach. Among its sights are some places associated with Columbus *(see pp54–5)*, who topped up

his water supplies here before setting out on his adventurous voyages. A well in the customs house bears the grand words "With this water America was baptized". According to legend he also prayed in the Iglesia de la Asunción, and stayed at a local house.

Beyond the arid hills to the south lies **Playa de Santiago**, the island's only real resort, which has a grey pebble beach. **Valle Gran Rey**, in the far west, is a fertile valley of palms and staircase terraces. These days it is colonized by foreigners attempting alternative lifestyles. In the north, tiny roads weave a tortuous course around several pretty villages, plunging at intervals to small, stony beaches. **Las Rosas** is a popular stop-off for coach parties, who can enjoy the visitors' centre and a restaurant with a panoramic view.

The road towards the coast from Las Rosas leads through the town of **Vallehermoso**, dwarfed by the huge **Roque de Cano**, which is an impressive mass of solidified lava. Just off the north coast stands **Los Órganos**, a fascinating rock formation of crystallized basalt columns resembling the pipes of an organ.

Juniper trees on El Hierro, twisted and bent by the wind

Tenerife

IN THE LANGUAGE of its aboriginal Guanche inhabitants, Tenerife means "Snowy Mountain", a tribute to its most striking geographical feature, the dormant volcano of Mount Teide, Spain's highest peak. The largest of the Canary Islands, Tenerife is a roughly triangular landmass rising steeply on all sides towards the cloud-capped summit that divides it into two distinct climatic zones: damp and lushly vegetated in the north, sunny and arid in the south. Tenerife offers a more varied range of attractions than any of the other Canary Islands, including its spectacular volcanic scenery, water sports and a vibrant atmosphere after dark. Its beaches, however, have unenticing black sand and are rather poor for swimming. The main resorts are crowded with high-rise hotels and apartments, offering nightlife but little peace and quiet.

Bananas in northern Tenerife

Los Cristianos **4**

Santa Cruz de Tenerife. 🏠 20,000.
🚌 ⛴ 🛈 Calle General Franco,
(922) 75 71 37. 🚌 Sun. 🎪 Fiesta
del Carmen (first Sun of Sep).

THE OLD FISHING VILLAGE of Los Cristianos, on Tenerife's south coast, has grown into a town spreading out along the foot of barren hills. Ferries and hydrofoils make regular trips from its little port to La Gomera (see p509).

To the north lies the modern expanse of **Playa de las Américas**, Tenerife's largest development. It offers visitors a cheerful, relaxed, undemanding cocktail of sun and fun.

A brief sortie inland leads to the much older town of **Adeje** and to the **Barranco del Infierno**, a wild gorge with an attractive waterfall (two hours' walk from Adeje).

Along the coast to the east, the **Costa del Silencio** is a pleasant contrast to most of the other large resorts, with

its less imposing bungalow developments surrounding fishing villages. El Abrigo has lively, bustling fish restaurants lining its small harbour.

Further east, **El Médano** shelters below an ancient volcanic cone. Its two beaches are popular with windsurfers.

Parque Nacional del Teide **5**

See pp514–15.

Puerto de la Cruz **6**

Santa Cruz de Tenerife. 🏠 30,000.
🚌 🛈 Plaza de la Iglesia, (922) 38
60 00. 🚌 Tue, Thu & Sat. 🎪 Fiesta
del Carmen (second Sun of Jul).

PUERTO DE LA CRUZ, the oldest resort in the Canaries, first sprang to prominence in 1706, when a volcanic eruption obliterated Tenerife's principal port of Garachico. Puerto de

la Cruz took its place, later becoming popular with genteel English convalescents. The older buildings, concentrated around the Plaza del Charco de los Camerones and the Puerto Pesquero, give the town much of its present character.

The beautiful Lago Martiánez lido, designed by the Lanzarote architect César Manrique (see p524), compensates for a lack of good beaches with its sea water pools, palms and fountains. Other local attractions include the Botanical Gardens, founded in 1788, which display over 1,000 different species.

Outside town, the **Bananera El Guanche** plantation has an exhibition on bananas and other tropical crops. **Icod de los Vinos**, a short drive west, attracts crowds for its spectacular ancient dragon tree.

🌴 **Bananera El Guanche**
Carretera Botánico, La Orotava.
📞 (922) 33 18 53. ☐ daily. 🎫 ♿

(see p509).

THE DRAGON TREE

The Canary Islands have many unusual plants, but the dragon tree (Dracaena draco) is one of the strangest. This primitive creature looks a little like a giant cactus, with swollen branches that sprout multiple tufts of spiky leaves. When cut, the trunk exudes a reddish sap once believed to have magical and medicinal properties. Dragon trees form no annual rings, so their age is a mystery. Some are thought to be thousands of years old. The most venerable surviving specimen can be seen at Icod de los Vinos.

The landscaped Lago Martiánez lido, Puerto de la Cruz

La Orotava 🔟

Santa Cruz de Tenerife. 🔺 40,000.
🚏 ℹ️ Santa Cruz de Tenerife, (922)
33 00 50. 🎭 Carnival (Feb/Mar),
Corpus Christi (May/Jun).

A SHORT distance from Puerto de la Cruz, in the fertile hills above the Orotava valley, La Orotava makes a popular excursion. The old part of this historic town clusters around the large **Iglesia de Nuestra Señora de la Concepción**. This domed Baroque building with twin towers was built in the late 18th century to replace an earlier church that was destroyed in earthquakes at the beginning of that century.

In the surrounding streets and squares are numerous old churches, convents and grand houses with elaborately carved wooden balconies. The **Casas de los Balcones** and **Casa del Turista** both have pretty interior courtyards that are open to the public.

Nuestra Señora de la Candelaria, patron saint of the Canary Islands

Candelaria 🔟

Santa Cruz de Tenerife. 🔺 12,000.
🚆 ℹ️ Calle Antón Guanche 1, (922)
50 04 15. 🚌 Sat, Sun. 🎭 Nuestra
Señora de la Candelaria (14–15 Aug).

THIS COASTAL TOWN is famous for its shrine to **Nuestra Señora de la Candelaria**, the Canary Islands' patron saint, whose image is surrounded by flowers and candles in a modern church in the main square. This gaudy Virgin, supposedly washed ashore in

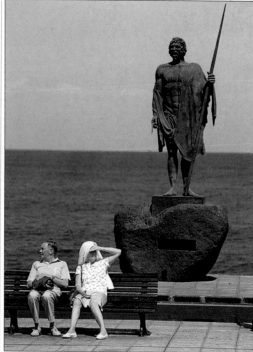

Statue of a Guanche chief on the seafront of Candelaria

pagan times, was venerated before Christianity reached the island. In 1826 a tidal wave returned her to the sea, but a replica draws pilgrims to worship here every August. Outside, stone effigies of Guanche chiefs line the sea wall.

La Laguna 🔟

Santa Cruz de Tenerife. 🔺 130,000.
🚏 ℹ️ Calle Carrera 1, (922) 60 11 00.
🚌 daily. 🎭 San Benito (15 Jul).

A BUSTLING university town and former island capital, La Laguna is the second largest settlement on Tenerife.

In its old quarter, best explored on foot, there are many atmospheric squares, historic buildings and several good museums. Most of the sights lie between the bell-towered **Iglesia de Nuestra Señora de la Concepción**, dating from 1502, and the Plaza del Adelantado, on which stand the town hall, a convent (with a fine, traditional balcony) and the elegant **Palacio de Nava**.

Montes de Anaga 🔟

Santa Cruz de Tenerife. 🚌 Santa Cruz
de Tenerife, La Laguna.

THE RUGGED MOUNTAINS north of Santa Cruz are kept green and lush by a cool, wet climate. They abound with a wide variety of interesting birds and plants, including cactuses, laurels and tree heathers. Walking the mountain trails is very popular, and maps showing many of the best paths are readily available from the tourist office. A steep road with marker posts climbs up from the village of San Andrés by the beautiful but artificial beach of Las Teresitas. On clear days there are marvellous vistas along the paths, especially from the view points of Pico del Inglés and Bailadero.

Winding down through the laurel forests of Monte de las Mercedes and the colourful valley of Tejina you reach **Tacoronte** with its interesting churches, an ethnographic museum and a bodega, where you can sample local wines.

THE CANARY ISLANDS' FIESTAS

Carnival *(Feb/Mar)*, Santa Cruz de Tenerife. One of Europe's biggest carnivals, this grand street party is a lavish spectacle of extravagant costumes and Latin American dance music to rival that of Rio de Janeiro. For years under the Franco regime, Carnival was suppressed for its irreverent frivolity. It begins with the election of a queen of the festivities and builds up to a climax on Shrove Tuesday when there is a large procession. The "funeral" of an enormous mock sardine takes place on Ash Wednesday. Carnival is also celebrated on the islands of Lanzarote and Gran Canaria.

Revellers in Carnival outfits on Tenerife

Corpus Christi *(May/Jun)*, La Orotava (Tenerife). The streets of the town are filled with flower carpets in striking patterns, while the Plaza del Ayuntamiento is covered in copies of works of art, formed from coloured volcanic sands. **Descent of the Virgin of the Snows** *(Jul, every five years: 2000, 2005)* Santa Cruz de La Palma. **Romería de la Virgen de la Candelaria** *(15 Aug)*, Candelaria (Tenerife). Pilgrims come here in their thousands to venerate the Canary Islands' patroness. **Fiesta del Charco** *(7–11 Sep)*, San Nicolás de Tolentino (Gran Canaria). People leap into a large saltwater pond to catch mullet.

Large ships moored at the busy port of Santa Cruz de Tenerife

Santa Cruz de Tenerife ⓫

Santa Cruz de Tenerife. 🏯 200,000.
🚌 ⛴ 🛈 Plaza de España 1, (922) 60
55 92. 🚗 Sun. 🎭 Carnival (Feb/Mar),
Día de la Cruz (3 May), Nuestra Señora
del Carmen (16 Jul).

Tenerife's capital city is an important regional port, with a deep-water harbour suitable for large ships. Its most attractive beach, **Las Teresitas**, lies 8 km (5 miles) to the north. Completely artificial, it was created by importing millions of tonnes of golden Saharan sand and building a protective reef just offshore. Shaded by palms, backed by mountains and so far devoid of concrete hotel developments, the result improves on anything nature has bestowed on Tenerife.

Santa Cruz can boast many handsome historic buildings. The hub of the town is around the **Plaza de España**, situated near the harbour. Just off it is the Calle de Castillo, the main shopping street. Its two most noteworthy churches are the **Iglesia de Nuestra Señora de la Concepción**, with parts dating from 1500, and Baroque **Iglesia de San Francisco**.

Particularly interesting is the **Museo Arqueológico**, located in the Palacio Insular, where Guanche mummies grin in glass cases. Inside the museum you can also see the cannon which is alleged to have removed the arm of the British admiral Nelson during an unsuccessful raid on the city at the end of the 18th century.

Other attractions include the **Museo de Bellas Artes** which features old masters as well as modern works. Many of its paintings focus on local events and landscapes. Contemporary sculptures adorn the **Parque Municipal García Sanabria**, a pleasant park with shady paths, laid out in 1926.

In the morning, visit the **Mercado de Nuestra Señora de África**, which combines a bazaar with a food market. Outside stalls sell mostly domestic goods; those inside offer an eclectic mix of live chickens, herbs, spices and cut flowers. Santa Cruz is especially worth a visit during its flamboyant annual carnival.

🏛 **Museo Arqueológico**
Calle Fuentes Morales. 📞 (922) 21
30 00. 🕐 Tue–Sun. 🚫 ♿
🏛 **Museo de Bellas Artes**
Calle José Murphy 12. 📞 (922) 24
43 58. 🕐 Mon–Fri.

The artificial beach of Las Teresitas in Santa Cruz

Regional Food: The Canary Islands

ALTHOUGH SOMETIMES hard to find, there is a regional cuisine in the Canaries. It combines elements of Guanche cooking with ingredients originally from other continents, such as sweetcorn and bananas. A climate of eternal spring provides a wealth of other fruit and vegetables. The sea supplies many colourful fish, like the purple and yellow *vieja* or bass which is eaten with *mojo*, a

Sweetcorn

pounded sauce that varies in its ingredients and colour depending on whether coriander or paprika is used. Many dishes are served with wrinkled *papas arrugadas* (jacket potatoes cooked in heavily salted water). *Gofio* is a Guanche cornmeal which is made into porridge and used to thicken stews and to make bread. Desserts include *bienmesabe,* a sweet cream of almonds, egg yolk and cinnamon.

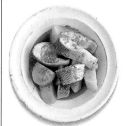

Sancocho, *parboiled fish best made with* sama, *a type of bass, is often served with sweet and plain potatoes.*

Sama frita con mojo verde *is fried fish served with a sauce blended from garlic, coriander and vinegar.*

Potaje de berros, *a thick soup, contains watercress, pork ribs, corn on the cob, potatoes, beans and cumin.*

Conejo al salmorejo, *an appetizing stew made with rabbit and tomato, is best eaten with* papas arrugadas.

Arroz con verduras *is a colourful mixture of rice with chopped peppers, sweetcorn and tomatoes.*

Puchero *is the local saffron-flavoured stew, made with chorizo sausage, beans, chickpeas and potatoes.*

Canary bananas *are the sweet La Gomera variety, small and aromatic. They are made into fritters and tarts; or served with rice and eggs, or meat sauce. Other fruits available are guava, mango and papaya.*

Dark Canary rum

DRINKS

In the early 17th century the Canary Islands were renowned for their amber-coloured Malvasía wine, which is rich, sweet and highly alcoholic. The best of it is made on Lanzarote. Less potent red and white wines are produced in the Tacoronte-Acentejo region of Tenerife. The Canary Islands also offer a selection of locally made spirits, most notable of which is the excellent white and dark rum *(ron).* Other drinks include liqueurs flavoured with coffee, orange or bananas, and a rough *coñac* (brandy).

Parque Nacional del Teide ❺

TOWERING OVER TENERIFE, Mount Teide, surrounded by a wild volcanic landscape, is an awesome sight. Millions of years ago a much larger adjacent cone exploded, leaving behind the devastation of Las Cañadas, a 16-km (10-mile) wide crater, and the smaller volcano, Teide, on its northern edge. Today volcanic material forms a wilderness of weathered, mineral-tinted rocks, ash beds and lava streams. A single road crosses the plateau of Las Cañadas, passing a parador, cable car station, and visitors' centre. Follow the marked paths to see the best of this unique, protected area.

Volcanic Landscapes
The eight-minute cable car ride leaves you 160 m (525 ft) short of Teide's summit. A path through volcanic rubble gives unforgettable views.

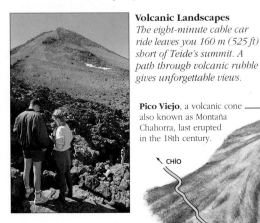

Pico del Teide, which is still volcanically active, is Spain's highest summit.

PICO DEL T
PICO D[_]18[_
3,718 m
(12,198 ft)

PICO VIEJO
PICO VIEJO
3,414 m

3,414 m
(11,200 ft)

Pico Viejo, a volcanic cone also known as Montaña Chahorra, last erupted in the 18th century.

CHÍO

0 kilometres   2

0 miles   1

KEY

═══ Road

──── Track

– – – Footpath

Mirador de Chío

R O Q U E S
D E   G A R C Í A

Mirador de La Ruleta

C823

L L A N O   D E   U C A N C A

Mirador de Boca Tauce

VILAFLOR

C821   Mi de

Los Roques de García
These flamboyantly shaped lava rocks near the parador are some of the most photographed in the whole park. The rocks of Los Azulejos, nearby, glitter blue-green because of the copper deposits within them.

WILD FLOWERS

The inhospitable badlands of Las Cañadas are inhabited by some rare and beautiful plants. Many of these are unique to the Canary Islands. Most striking is the tall *Echium wildprettii*, a kind of viper's bugloss, whose red spires reach 2 m (6 ft) in early summer. Other common plants include Teide broom, the distinctive Californian poppy, and a unique species of violet. The best time of year for flower-spotting is May to June. Displays housed in the visitors' centre will help identify them. Don't take any plants away with you: all vegetation within the park is strictly protected and must not be uprooted or picked.

La Caldera de Las Cañadas

A rim of fractured crags forms a pie-crust edge to the sides of this enormous caldera – a wide volcanic crater (see p527). *Now collapsed and intensely eroded, the perimeter of the caldera measures 45 km (28 miles).*

VISITORS' CHECKLIST

(922) 29 01 29. 342 & 348 from Puerto de la Cruz.
***El Portillo Visitors' Centre & cable car** (to NE of park on C821).*
9am–4pm daily.

At El Portillo Visitors' Centre, a video film and exhibition chart the origins of the park.

SANTA CRUZ DE TENERIFE

P i El Portillo

gio de Altavista

C821

Mirador de San José

Mirador del Tabonal Negro

LAS CAÑADAS

or de as del

Las Cañadas
The flat expanses of the seven cañadas *(small sandy plateaux) were created by the collapse of ancient craters. Several colourful plants have managed to colonize this dusty, barren wasteland.*

Parador
The recently refurbished Parador de Cañadas del Teide (see p571) *is set in the midst of the surreal scenery, and makes an excellent base for those who want to explore the park thoroughly.*

ary mustard *(...ymbrium ...rgaenum)*

Teide ...allflower *(...Erysium ...parium)*

Teide violet *(Viola cheiranthifolia)*

Teide viper's bugloss *(Echium wildprettii)*

Exploring the Eastern Islands

THE EASTERN PROVINCE of the Canary Islands – Las Palmas – comprises the islands of Gran Canaria, Lanzarote and Fuerteventura. All feature unusual and spectacular scenery, plenty of sunshine and excellent sandy beaches, but each has a very different atmosphere. Gran Canaria boasts the only really large town, Las Palmas, which is also the administrative centre for the eastern islands. It also offers the biggest resort, Maspalomas, with its Playa del Inglés, which has an unabashed package-holiday feel. As a contrast, the long, white beaches of Fuerteventura have been left fairly undeveloped and it is still possible to find privacy among their sand dunes. Lanzarote has fine beaches too, while its interior is dominated by an eerie volcanic landscape which makes for great excursions.

Corralejo's beach, in the north of Fuerteventura

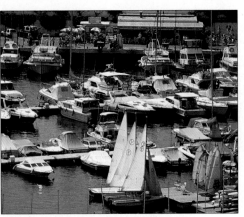

The marina at Puerto Rico, in southern Gran Canaria

GETTING AROUND

Most people travel from mainland Spain to the eastern islands by air *(see p628)*. The alternative is a long sea crossing from Cádiz *(see p629)*. There are flights between all the islands, except La Gomera, which has no airport. There are also regular inter-island ferries. Taxis and public transport are fine within resorts, but expensive over long distances. Cars can be hired on all the islands, usually at airports or ferry terminals. The main roads are well-surfaced and fast on the flatter sections, though traffic in Gran Canaria can be heavy in places. A four-wheel drive jeep is advisable to reach some remoter beaches.

GRAN CANARIA

AGAETE 15

17 LAS PALMAS DE GRAN CANARIA

TAFIRA 16

C810

18 CRUZ DE TEJEDA

SAN NICOLÁS DE TOLENTINO

C810

SANTA LUCÍA   C815   AGUIMES

PUERTO DE MOGÁN 12

GC1

13 PUERTO RICO

14 MASPALOMAS

ATLÁNTICO

0 kilometres   25

0 miles   10

SIGHTS AT A GLANCE

KEY

▬▬	Motorway
▬▬	Major road
▬▬	Minor road
▬▬	Scenic route
~~	River
❖	Viewpoint

SEE ALSO

- *Where to Stay* pp570–71

- *Restaurants and Bars*
  pp608–609

Volcanoes of Montañas de Fuego in Parque Nacional de Timanfaya, Lanzarote

Gran Canaria

GRAN CANARIA IS THE MOST POPULAR of the Canary Islands, with over 1.5 million holiday-makers visiting it each year. The island offers a surprising range of scenery, climate, resorts and attractions within its compact bounds. Winding roads follow the steep, ruggedly beautiful terrain which rises to a symmetrical cone at the centre of the island. Las Palmas, Gran Canaria's capital and port, is the largest city in the Canaries, and Maspalomas/Playa del Inglés, in the south, is one of the biggest resorts in Spain. Both tourist meccas are packed with high-rise hotels and villa complexes, but not far away there is some marvellous scenery to discover.

Farmer and donkey

Holiday-makers on the golden sands of Puerto Rico beach

Puerto de Mogán ⑫

Las Palmas. 680. ℹ Calle General Franco, (928) 56 91 00. Fri. Virgen del Carmen (Jul).

SITUATED AT THE END of the verdant valley of Mogán, this is one of Gran Canaria's most appealing and successful developments - an idyll to many visitors after the brash concrete of Playa del Inglés. Based around a small fishing port, it consists of a village-like complex of pretty, white, creeper-covered houses and a similarly designed hotel built around a marina. Boutiques, bars and restaurants add an ambience without any of the accompanying rowdiness.

The sandy beach, sheltered between the cliffs, is scarcely big enough for all visitors; a car is recommended to reach more facilities at Maspalomas. Ferries provide a leisurely way to get to nearby resorts.

Sun worshippers in Puerto Rico

Puerto Rico ⑬

Las Palmas. 1,500. ℹ Centro Comercial de Puerto Rico, (928) 56 00 29. María de Auxiliadora (May).

THE BARREN CLIFFS west of Maspalomas now sprout apartment complexes at every turn. Puerto Rico is an over-developed resort, but has one of the more attractive beaches on the island, a firm crescent of imported sand supplemented by lidos and excellent water sports facilities. It is a great place to learn sailing, diving and windsurfing, or just to lie back, relax and soak up the ultraviolet – Puerto Rico enjoys the best sunshine record in the whole of Spain.

Maspalomas ⑭

Las Palmas. 36,000. ℹ Avda de España, (928) 14 06 64. Wed & Sat. San Bartolomé (24 Aug).

WHEN THE FAST motorway from Las Palmas airport first tips you into this bewildering mega-resort, it seems like a homogeneous blur, but gradually three separate communities emerge. **San Agustín**, which is the furthest east, is restrained and sedate compared with the others. It has a series of beaches of dark sand, attractively sheltered by low cliffs and landscaped promenades, and a casino.

The next exit off the coastal highway leads to **Playa del Inglés**, the largest and liveliest resort, a triangle of land jutting into a huge belt of golden sand. Developed from the end of the 1950s, the area is built up with giant blocks of flats linked by a maze of roads. Many hotels lack sea views, though most have spacious grounds with swimming pools. At night the area pulsates with

Floral arches decorating a street of apartments in Puerto de Mogán

bright disco lights and flashing neon. There are more than 300 restaurants and over 50 discos in this resort alone.

West of Playa del Inglés the beach undulates into the **Dunas de Maspalomas**. A relieving contrast to the hectic surrounding resorts, these dunes form a nature reserve protected from further development. The western edge of the dunes (marked by a lighthouse) is occupied by a cluster of luxury hotels. Just behind the dunes lies a golf course encircled by bungalow estates.

Everything is laid on for the package holiday: water sports, excursions, fast food. Relief from beach fatigue comes with go-karts, camel safaris and funfairs. Best of these include **Palmitos Park**, with exotic birds in subtropical gardens; and **Sioux City**, a funpacked Western theme park.

Palmitos Park
Barranco de los Palmitos. (928) 14 11 58. daily.

Sioux City
Cañón del Águila. (928) 76 25 73. Tue–Sun.

Agaete ⑮

Las Palmas. 5,000. Calle Antonio de Armas 1, (928) 89 80 02. Fiesta de la Rama (4 Aug).

THE CLOUDIER northern side of the island is far greener and lusher than the arid south, and banana plantations take up most of the coastal slopes. Agaete, on the northwest coast, a pretty scatter of white houses around a striking rocky bay,

The rocky shore and steep cliffs of the northeast coast near Agaete

is growing into a small resort. Every August, Agaete holds the Fiesta de la Rama, a Guanche *(see p523)* rain-making ritual which dates from long before the arrival of the Spanish. An animated procession of villagers bearing green branches heads from the hills above the town down to the coast and into the sea. The villagers beat the water to summon the rain.

Sights in Agaete include the little **Ermita de las Nieves**, containing a fine 16th-century Flemish triptych and model sailing ships, and the **Huerto de las Flores**, a botanical garden. Ask for the key to the garden at the town hall, which is located on the same street.

ENVIRONS: A brief detour inland up along the Barranco de Agaete takes you through a fertile valley of papaya, mango and citrus trees. North of Agaete are the towns of Guía and Gáldar. Though there is little to see here, both parish churches do contain examples of the religious statuary of the celebrated 18th-century sculptor, José Luján Pérez.

Nearby, towards the north coast, lies the **Cenobio de Valerón**. One of the most dramatic of the local Guanche sights, this cliff-face is pockmarked with nearly 300 caves beneath a basalt arch. These are believed to have been hideaways for Guanche priestesses, communal grainstores and refuges from attack.

Huerto de las Flores
Calle Huertas. daily.

Miles of wind-sculptured sand: the dunes at Maspalomas

Tafira ⑯

Las Palmas. 🏘 *23,000.* 🚌
ℹ️ *Jardín Canario, (928) 35 36 04.*
🎊 *San Francisco (Oct).*

THE HILLS SOUTHWEST of Las
Palmas have long been
desirable residential locations.
A colonial air still wafts around
Tafira's patrician villas. The
Jardín Canario, a botanical
garden founded in 1952, is
the main reason for a visit.
Plants from all of the Canary
Islands can be studied in their
own, recreated habitats.

Near La Atalaya lies one of
Gran Canaria's most impressive
natural sights – the **Caldera
de la Bandama**. This is a
huge volcanic crater 1,000 m
(3,300 ft) wide, best seen
from the Mirador de Bandama
where you gaze down into
the green depression about
200 m (660 ft) deep. Some of
the inhabited caves in the
Barranco de Guayadeque, a
valley of reddish rocks to the
south, were dug in the late
15th century. A few of them
have electricity.

🌸 **Jardín Canario**
Carretera del Centro, Tafira.
📞 *(928) 35 36 04.* ⭕ *daily.*

Las Palmas de Gran Canaria ⑰

Las Palmas. 🏘 *350,000.* 🚌 ⛴
ℹ️ *Parque de Santa Catalina, (928)
26 46 23.* 🎊 *Carnival (Feb/Mar).*

LAS PALMAS IS THE LARGEST city
in the Canary Islands. A
bustling seaport and industrial
city, it sees 1,000 ships docking

Palm trees in a natural setting in the Jardín Canario, Tafira

each month. Las Palmas has
faded somewhat from the days
when wealthy convalescents
flocked here in winter and
glamorous liners called in on
transatlantic voyages. But it
remains a vibrant place to visit.

Las Palmas is a sprawling city
built around an isthmus
and its layout can be
confusing. The modern
commercial shipping area,
Puerto de la Luz, takes
up the eastern side of the
isthmus, which leads to the
former island of La Isleta,
a sailors' and military
quarter. On the other side
of the isthmus is the
crowded **Playa de las
Canteras**, a 3-km
(2-mile) long stretch
of golden beach. The
promenade behind has
been built up with bars,
restaurants and hotels.

The town centre stretches
along the coast from the isthmus. For a pleasant scenic tour,
begin in the **Parque Santa
Catalina**, near the port. This
is a popular, shady square of

Bronze dog at
Plaza Santa Ana

cafés and newspaper kiosks.
In the leafy residential quarter
of Ciudad Jardín is the Parque
Doramas and the traditional
casino hotel of Santa Catalina.

The **Pueblo Canario** is a
tourist enclave where visitors
can watch folk dancing, and
browse in the craft shops
and the small art gallery.
All this can be viewed
from above by walking
uphill towards the
Altavista district and the
Paseo Cornisa.

At the end of town is
the Barrio Vegueta, an
atmospheric quarter
which dates back to the
Spanish conquest. At
its heart stands the
**Catedral de Santa
Ana**, begun in 1500.
The adjacent **Museo
Diocesano de Arte
Sacro** contains works
of religious art. The square in
front is guarded by Canarian
dogs in bronze.

Nearby, the **Casa de Colón**
is a 15th-century governor's
residence where Columbus
stayed. A museum dedicated
to his voyages displays charts,
models and diary extracts.

Early history can be seen in
the **Museo Canario,** which
contains Guanche mummies,
skulls, pottery and jewellery.

🏛 **Museo Diocesano de
Arte Sacro**
Calle Espíritu Santo 20. 📞 *(928) 31
49 89.* ⭕ *Mon–Sat.* 🎫
⚰️ **Casa de Colón**
Calle Colón. 📞 *(928) 31 23 84.*
⭕ *daily.*
🏛 **Museo Canario**
Calle Doctor Chil 25. 📞 *(928) 31
56 00.* ⭕ *daily.* 🎫

The Casa de Colón museum, Las Palmas, dedicated to Columbus

Tour of Cruz de Tejeda ⑱

GRAN CANARIA'S mountainous interior makes for an ideal day tour, from any part of the island. Choose a fine day or the views may be obscured. The route from Maspalomas leads through dry ravines of bare rock and cacti, becoming more fertile with altitude. Roads near the central highlands snake steeply through shattered, tawny crags, past caves and pretty villages to panoramic viewpoints from which you can see Mount Teide *(see pp514–15)* on Tenerife. On the north side, the slopes are much lusher, growing citrus fruits and eucalyptus trees.

White farmhouses en route to Teror

Artenara ②
One of the inhabited caves in this town houses a little church. Another has been converted into an unusual restaurant, the Mesón de la Silla.

Teror ①
This charming old town has many well-preserved, typical Canary Islands houses. Its church, Nuestra Señora del Pino, is dedicated to Gran Canaria's patron saint.

Cruz de Tejeda ③
In this restaurant-only parador *(see p608)* you can eat Canary Islands specialities while enjoying magnificent mountain views.

Pico de las Nieves ⑤
A meteorological station crowns Gran Canaria's highest peak. At 1,949 m (6,395 ft), it is often chilly up here and it sometimes snows, so take extra clothing.

Vallesceo

Lanzarote

LAS PALMAS

C814

C817 ①

GC110

Cuevas Corcho

PINAR DE TAMADABA ②

GC110

Tejeda

C811

C811

Ayacata

C815

MASPALOMAS

TELDE

⑤

④

KEY

━━━ Tour route

═══ Other roads

❈ Viewpoint

🅿 Parador

0 kilometres   2

0 miles   1

Roque Nublo ④
This 60-m (195-ft) high jagged spike of basalt tops a 1,700-m (5,578-ft) peak. Together with nearby Roque Bentayga, it was sacred to the Guanches. It's a stiff climb to the summit.

TIPS FOR DRIVERS

Length: 35–45 km (22–28 miles).
Stopping-off points: popular lunch spots are Mesón de la Silla cave-restaurant in Artenara and Cruz de Tejeda parador.
Note: roads can be narrow with few passing places; sudden patches of cloud or mist may loom without warning.

Fuerteventura

L YING JUST 100 KM (60 MILES) off the Atlantic coast of
Morocco, leaf-shaped Fuerteventura is continually
battered by coastal winds. It is the second largest of the
Canary Islands after Tenerife, and the most sparsely
populated: its 30,000 inhabitants are outnumbered by
goats. The island used to be densely wooded, but
European settlers cut down the timber for shipbuilding;
the dry climate and the goats have since reduced the
vegetation to parched scrub. It is so dry that water has to
be shipped over from the mainland. The only significant
revenue is tourism, but the tourist industry is still in its
infancy compared with the other main islands. However,
visitors are increasing in number as thousands of sun-
worshippers flock to more than 150 splendid beaches.
The island is popular with water sports fans and naturists.

**A herd of goats near the airport
on Fuerteventura**

Península de Jandía ⑲

Las Palmas. 🚌 Costa Calma, Morro
Jable. ⛴ (jetfoil) from Gran Canaria.
ℹ️ Centro Comercial, Jandía Beach
Local 88, (928) 54 07 76.

E XCELLENT BEACHES of pale
sand fringe the elongated
Jandía peninsula in the south
of Fuerteventura. A string of
urbanizaciones (apartment
complexes) now takes up
much of the peninsula's sheltered east coast (Sotavento).
  Costa Calma, a burgeoning
cluster of modern complexes,
offers the most interesting
beaches with long stretches of
fine sand interrupted by low
cliffs and coves. **Morro Jable**,
a fishing village now swamped
by new developments, lies at
the southern end of a vast,
glittering strand. Beyond Morro
Jable, the access road dwindles
away into a potholed track
leading towards the lonely
lighthouse at Punta de Jandía.
  Expanses of deserted sand,
accessible only by four-wheel
drive vehicle, line the westerly,
windward coast (Barlovento)
– too exposed for all but the
hardiest beach lovers. Some
of the island's best subtropical
marine life can be found in
this area, however, making it
popular with skin divers.
  During World War II, Jandía
belonged to a German entre-
preneur. It was out of bounds
to locals and acquired its own
mystique. Even today, rumours
of spies, submarines and secret
Nazi bases still circulate.

Betancuria ⑳

Las Palmas. 🚶 600. 🚌 ℹ️ Calle
Amador Rodríguez 6, (928) 87 80 92.
🎉 San Buenaventura (14 Jul).

I NLAND, rugged peaks of
extinct volcanoes, separated
by wide plains, present a scene
of austere grandeur. Scattered,
stark villages and obsolete
windmills occupy the lowlands
which are occasionally fertile
enough to nurture a few crops
or palm trees. Beyond, devoid
of vegetation, the hills form
stark outlines. From a distance
they appear brown and grey,
but close up the rocks glow
with an astonishing range of
mauves, pinks and ochres.
The richness of colour in this
interior wilderness is at its

**The gilded interior of the Iglesia
Santa María in Betancuria**

most striking at sunset, when
a leisurely drive can reveal
some breathtaking scenes.
  Betancuria, built on a small
volcano in the centre of the
island, is named after Jean de
Béthencourt, Fuerteventura's
15th-century conqueror, who
moved his capital inland to
thwart pirates. Nestling in the
mountains, this peaceful oasis
is now the island's prettiest
village. The **Iglesia de Santa
María** contains gilded altars,
decorated beams and sacred
relics. Ask for the key at the
caretaker's house nearby. The
Museo Arqueológico houses
many local artifacts.

ENVIRONS: To the south, the
village of **Pájara** boasts a 17th-
century church with a curiously
decorated doorway. Its design
of serpents and strange beasts
is believed to be of Aztec influence. Inside, the twin aisles
both contain statues: one of a
radiant Madonna and Child in
white and silver, the other a
Virgen de los Dolores in black.
  La Oliva, to the north, was
the site of the Spanish military
headquarters until the 19th
century. The Casa de los
Coroneles (House of the
Colonels) is a faded yellow
mansion with a grand façade
and hundreds of windows.
Inside it has coffered ceilings.
The fortified church and the
arts centre displaying works
of Canary Islands artists are
also worth a visit.

🏛 **Museo Arqueológico**
Calle Fuentes Morales. 【 (922) 21
30 00. ◯ Tue–Sun. 🈲 ♿

Caleta de Fustes ㉑

Las Palmas. 🏘 *2,600.* 🚌 ℹ *Caleta Dorada, El Castillo, (928) 16 32 86.* 🎭 *Dia del Carmen (16 Jul).*

Ｓουτη of Puerto del Rosario, about halfway down the eastern coast of the island, lies Caleta de Fustes. This attractive and tasteful group of low-rise, self-catering holiday centres surrounds a horseshoe bay of soft, gently shelving sand. The largest complex, El Castillo, takes its name from an 18th-century watchtower situated by the harbour.

There are many water sports facilities, including diving and windsurfing schools, as well as the Pueblo Majorero, an attractive "village" of shops and restaurants around a central plaza near the beach. These features make Caleta de Fustes one of Fuerteventura's most relaxed and pleasant resorts, popular with all nationalities.

Fishing boats on a beach on the Isla de Lobos, near Corralejo

Puerto del Rosario ㉒

Las Palmas. 🏘 *14,000.* 🚌 🚐 🚢 ℹ *Calle Primero de Mayo 37, (928) 85 14 00.* 🎭 *El Rosario (7 Oct).*

Ｆuerteventura's commercial and administrative capital was founded in 1797. It was originally known as Puerto de Cabras (Goats' Harbour), after a nearby gorge that was once used for watering goats, but was rechristened to smarten up its image in 1957. As Puerto del Rosario is the only large port on Fuerteventura, it is the base for inter-island ferries and a busy fishing industry. The town is also enlivened by the presence of the Spanish Foreign Legion, which occupies large barracks here.

Corralejo ㉓

Las Palmas. 🏘 *4,000.* 🚢 ℹ *Plaza Pública, (928) 86 62 35.* 🛒 *Mon, Tue, Thu, Fri.* 🎭 *Dia del Carmen (16 Jul).*

Ｔhis much-expanded fishing village is now (together with the Jandía peninsula) one of the island's two most important resorts. Its main attraction is a belt of glorious sand dunes stretching to the south, resembling the Sahara in places, and protected as a nature reserve. This designation arrived too late, however, to prevent the construction of two obtrusive hotels right on the beach.

The rest of the resort, mostly consisting of apartments, spills out haphazardly from the town centre. The port area is lively, with busy fish restaurants and an efficient ferry service to Lanzarote, 40 minutes away.

Offshore is the tiny Isla de los Lobos, named after the once abundant monk seals *(lobos marinos).* Today, scuba divers, snorkellers, sport fishers and surfers claim the clear waters. Glass-bottomed cruise boats take less adventurous excursionists to the island for barbecues and swimming trips.

The Guanches

When Europeans first arrived in the Canary Islands in the late 14th century, they discovered a tall, white-skinned race, who lived in caves and later in small settlements around the edges of barren lava fields. Guanche was the name of one tribe on Tenerife, but it came to be used as the European name for all the indigenous tribes on the islands, and it is the one that has remained. The origins of the Guanches are still unclear, but it is probable that they arrived on the islands in the 1st or 2nd century BC from Berber North Africa. Within 100 years of European arrival the Guanches had been subdued and virtually exterminated by the ruthless conquistadors. Very few traces of their culture remain today.

Reminders of the Guanches can be seen in many places in the Canaries. Specimens of their mummified dead, as well as baskets and stone and bone artifacts, are on display in several museums and there are statues of chiefs in Candelaria (see p511) on Tenerife.

Guanche bowl for preparing *gofio (see p513)*

A Guanche basket

Lanzarote

THE EASTERNMOST and fourth largest of the Canary Islands is virtually treeless and has a permanent water shortage. Yet many visitors rate Lanzarote the most attractive of all the islands for the vivid shapes and contrasting colours of its volcanic landscapes. Despite low rainfall, carefully tended crops flourish in its black volcanic soil. Locals pride themselves on the way their island has been preserved from the worst effects of tourism; there are no garish billboards, overhead cables or high-rise buildings. Its present day image owes much to the artist César Manrique. Touring the spectacular volcanic Timanfaya National Park is a favourite trip.

Wind turbines harnessing Lanzarote's winds for power

Playa Blanca ❷

Las Palmas. 🏃 4,000. 🚌 ⛴
ℹ Plaza de los Remedios 1, Yaiza, (928) 83 02 50. 🚌 Wed. 🎪
Nuestra Señora del Carmen (Jul).

THE FISHING VILLAGE origins of this resort are readily apparent around its harbour. Although it has expanded in recent years, Playa Blanca remains an agreeably family-oriented place with some character. It has plenty of cafés and restaurants, shops and bars, and several large hotels. However, the buildings are well dispersed and the resort is rarely noisy at night. Visitors converge here not for nightlife or contrived entertainment, but for relaxing beach holidays. There are one or two good stretches of sand near to the town, but the most enticing lie hidden around the rocky headlands to the east, where the clear, warm sea laps into rocky coves, and clothes seem superfluous. **Playa Papagayo** is the best known of these, but a diligent search will probably gain you one all to yourself. A four-wheel drive vehicle is advisable to negotiate the narrow, unsurfaced roads which lead to these beaches.

Parque Nacional de Timanfaya ❷⑤

Las Palmas. ℹ Calle García Escámez 157, Arrecife, (928) 80 15 00.
🚌 from Arrecife. 🕐 daily. 🎟

FROM 1730–36, a series of volcanic eruptions took place on Lanzarote. Eleven villages were buried in lava, which eventually spread over 200 sq km (77 sq miles) of Lanzarote's most fertile land. Miraculously, no one was killed, though many islanders subsequently emigrated.

Today, the volcanoes that once devastated Lanzarote provide one of its most lucrative and enigmatic attractions, aptly known as the **Montañas de Fuego** (Fire Mountains). They are part of the Parque Nacional de Timanfaya, established in 1974 to protect a fascinating and important geological record. The entrance to the park lies just north of the small village of Yaiza. Here you can pause and take a 15-minute camel ride up the volcanic slopes for wonderful views across the park. Afterwards, you pay the entrance fee and drive through haunting scenery of dark, barren lava cinders

Las Coloradas beach near Playa Blanca in southern Lanzarote

CÉSAR MANRIQUE (1920–92)

Local hero César Manrique trained as a painter, and spent time in mainland Spain and New York before returning to Lanzarote in 1968. He campaigned for traditional and environmentally friendly development on the island for the remaining part of his life, setting strict building height limits and colour requirements. Dozens of tourist sites throughout the Canaries benefited from his talents and enthusiasm.

César Manrique in 1992

Camel rides from Yaiza across the Montañas de Fuego

topped by brooding red-black volcano cones. Finally, you will reach **Islote de Hilario**. You can park at El Diablo panoramic restaurant. From here, buses take visitors for exhilarating hour-long tours of the desolate, lunar-like landscapes.

Afterwards, back at Islote de Hilario, guides will provide graphic demonstrations that this volcano is not extinct but only dormant: brushwood pushed into a crevice bursts instantly into a ball of flame, while water poured into a sunken pipe shoots out in a scorching jet of steam.

The road from Yaiza to the coast leads to the **Salinas de Janubio** where salt is extracted from an old volcano crater. Nearby are the boiling springs of **Los Hervideros** and further north, at **El Golfo**, an eerie emerald-coloured lagoon.

Puerto del Carmen 26

Las Palmas. 9,000. *Calle San Antonio 4, (928) 83 36 75. Nuestra Señora del Carmen (Jul).*

MORE THAN 60 PER CENT of Lanzarote's tourists stay in this large resort, which now stretches several kilometres along the seafront. The coastal road carves its way relentlessly through a solid slab of holiday infrastructure: car hire offices, banks, bureaux de change, shops, bars, restaurants and discos. Behind the roadside arcades lie countless white villas, apartments and hotels.

Though dense, the buildings are pleasantly designed and unoppressive. All have easy access to a long golden beach, Playa Blanca, which in places

is very wide. Another beach nearby is Playa de los Pocillos. The original village lies west of the port, away from the hustle and bustle of the resort.

Fishing boat in Arrecife port

Arrecife 27

Las Palmas. 30,000. *Parque Municipal, (928) 80 15 17. Sat. San Ginés (25 Aug).*

ARRECIFE, with its modern buildings and lively streets, is the commercial and administrative centre of the island. Despite its modern trappings, the capital retains much of its old charm, with palm-lined promenades, a fine beach and two small, historic forts. The **Castillo de San Gabriel**, located on a small offshore island accessible by bridge, houses a museum of archaeology. The 18th-century **Castillo de San José**, now a museum of contemporary art, was renovated by César Manrique, and one of his paintings is on display here.

Castillo de San Gabriel
Arrecife. (928) 80 28 84. Mon–Fri.
Castillo de San José
Puerto de Naos. (928) 81 23 21. daily. 1 Jan, 24 Dec.

Costa Teguise 28

4 km (6 miles) north of Arrecife. *Arrecife, (928) 80 15 17.*

THIS RESORT, largely financed by a mining conglomerate, has transformed the arid, low-lying terrain north of Arrecife into an extensive cluster of timeshare accommodation, leisure clubs and luxury hotels. The contrast between old town Teguise, Lanzarote's former capital, and the exclusive, new Costa Teguise is striking. Fake greenery and suburban lamps line access boulevards amid barren ashlands. Neat white villas line a series of small sandy beaches. The high level of investment has succeeded in attracting some of its intended jet-set clientele. King Juan Carlos also has a villa here.

Umbrellas on the beach, Puerto del Carmen

Iglesia de San Miguel on the main square in Teguise

Teguise ㉙

Las Palmas. 🏘 *9,000.* 🚌 🛈 *Plaza General Franco 1, (928) 84 50 72.* 🛒 *Sun.* 🎉 *Día del Carmen (16 Jul), Las Nieves (5 Aug).*

Teguise, the island's capital until 1852, is a well-kept, old-fashioned town with wide, cobbled streets and patrician houses grouped around the **Iglesia de San Miguel**. The best time to visit is on a Sunday, when there is a lively handicrafts market and folk dancing. Just outside Teguise, the castle of Santa Bárbara contains the **Museo del Emigrante Canario**, which tells the story of Canarian emigrants to South America.

Environs: To see more of inland Lanzarote, follow the central road south of Teguise, through the strange farmland of **La Geria**. Black volcanic ash has been scooped into protective, crescent-shaped pits which trap moisture to enable vines and other crops to flourish. **Mozaga**, one of the main

villages in the area, is a major centre of wine production. On the roadside near Mozaga is the *Monumento al Campesino*, Manrique's *(see p524)* striking modern sculpture dedicated to Lanzarote's farmers.

Halfway between Teguise and Arrecife is the **Fundación César Manrique**. The fascinating former home of the artist incorporates five lava caves. It contains some of his own work and his collection of contemporary art.

🏛 **Museo del Emigrante Canario**
Montaña de Guanapay. 📞 *(928) 84 50 74.* 🕐 *daily.*

🏛 **Fundación César Manrique**
Taro de Tahíche. 📞 *(928) 84 31 38.* 🕐 *daily.*

Haría ㉚

Las Palmas. 🏘 *3,000.* 🚌 🛈 *Plaza de la Constitución 1, (928) 83 52 51.* 🎉 *San Juan (24 Jun).*

Palm trees and white, cube-shaped houses distinguish this picturesque village. It acts as a gateway to excursions round the northern tip of the island. The road to the north gives memorable views over exposed cliffs, and the 609-m (2,000-ft) high Monte Corona.

Environs: From Manrique's **Mirador del Río** you can see La Graciosa, and the northernmost of the Canary Islands, Alegranza. **Orzola** is a delightful fishing village providing fish lunches as well as boat trips to La Graciosa. To the south are the Mala prickly pear plantations, where cochineal (crimson dye) is extracted

from the insects which feed on the plants. Nearby is the **Jardín de Cactus**, a well-stocked cactus garden, which has a smart restaurant, again designed by Manrique.

🔭 **Mirador del Río**
Haría. 📞 *(928) 64 43 18.* 🕐 *daily.*

🌵 **Jardín de Cactus**
Guatiza. 📞 *(928) 52 93 97.* 🕐 *daily.*

Landscaped pool on top of the caves of Jameos del Agua

Jameos del Agua ㉛

Las Palmas. 📞 *(928) 83 50 10.* 🕐 *daily.* 📷

An eruption of the Monte Corona volcano formed the Jameos del Agua lava caves on Lanzarote's northeast coast. In 1965–8, these were landscaped by César Manrique into an imaginative subterranean complex containing a restaurant, nightclub, a swimming pool edged by palm trees, and gardens of oleander and cacti. Steps lead to a shallow seawater lagoon where a rare species of blind white crab, unique to Lanzarote, glows softly in the dim light. An exhibition on volcanology and Canarian flora and fauna also deserves a look. Folk-dancing evenings are regularly held in this unusual setting.

Environs: Another popular attraction is the nearby **Cueva de los Verdes**, a tube of solidifed lava stretching 6 km (4 miles) underground. Guided tours of the caves are available.

🔭 **Cueva de los Verdes**
Haría. 📞 *(928) 17 32 20.* 🕐 *daily.* 📷

Volcanic ash swept into crescent-shaped pits for farming, La Geria

Volcanic Islands

THE VOLCANIC ACTIVITY which formed the Canary Islands has created a variety of scenery, from distinctive lava formations to enormous volcanoes crowned by huge, gaping craters. The islands are all at different stages in their evolution. Tenerife, Lanzarote, El Hierro and La Palma are still volcanically active; dramatic displays of flames and steam can be seen in Lanzarote's Montañas de Fuego *(see p524)*. The last eruption was on La Palma in 1971.

Origin of the Islands
The Canaries are situated above faults in the earth's crust, which is always thinner under the oceans than under the continents. When magma (molten rock) rises through these cracks volcanoes are formed.

Atlantic Ocean — Transform fault — Atlas Fault
Canary Islands
Thin oceanic crust
Upper mantle
Africa
Dense lower mantle — Thick continental crust — Continental mantle between crust and earth's core

EVOLUTION OF THE CANARY ISLANDS

Fissures — Feeder dikes — Basalt lava flows — Crust — Mantle — Magma chamber

1 ***Lanzarote, El Hierro and La Palma*** are wide, gently sloping shield volcanoes standing on the sea floor. All of them are composed of basalt formed by a hot, dense magma. The flexible crust is pressed down by the weight of the islands.

Caldera — Shallow magma chamber

2 ***An explosive eruption*** can empty the magma chamber, leaving the roof unsupported. This collapses under the weight of the volcano above to form a depression, or caldera, such as Las Cañadas on Tenerife. There are thick lava flows during this stage of the island's evolution.

Sea level — Exposed solidified magma chamber

3 ***If eruptions cease*** a volcano will be eroded by the action of the sea, and by wind and rain. Gran Canaria's main volcano is in the early stages of erosion, while the volcano on Fuerteventura has already been deeply eroded, exposing chambers of solidified magma.

Rope lava near La Restinga, El Hierro

Pico Viejo crater, next to Mount Teide, Tenerife *(see p514)*

TRAVELLERS'
NEEDS

WHERE TO STAY

Logo for a luxury five-star hotel

MEDIEVAL CASTLES turned into luxury hotels and mansions converted into youth hostels typify the variety of places to stay in Spain. The tourists who sustain Spain's economy have almost 10,000 establishments to choose from, offering around 1 million beds. Suites in once-royal palaces are at the top of the scale. Then there are luxury beach hotels on the Costa del Sol and in the Balearic and the Canary islands. Visitors can also stay on remote farms, or in villas and old houses let for self-catering. For budget travel there are pensions, family-run *casas rurales* and guest houses, camp sites, and refuges with stunning views for mountaineers. Some of the best hotels in all these categories and in every style and price range are listed on pages 536–71.

Hotel de la Reconquista, Oviedo, an 18th-century mansion *(see p539)*

HOTEL GRADING AND FACILITIES

ALL OF SPAIN'S hotels are classified into categories and awarded stars by the country's regional tourist authorities. Hotels (indicated by an H on a blue plaque near the hotel door) are awarded from one to five stars. Hostals (Hs) and pensions (P) offer fewer comforts but are correspondingly cheaper than hotels.

Spain's star-rating system reflects the number and range of facilities available – whether the hotel has air conditioning, for instance, or a lift – rather than the quality of service.

Most hotels have restaurants that are open to non-residents. Although hotel-residencias (HR) and hostal-residencias (HsR) do not have dining rooms, some serve breakfast. Among Spain's largest hotel chains are **Grupo Sol-Meliá**, **Grupo Riu**, **NH** and **TRYP**. Many large tour operators book rooms in Spain's best hotels.

PARADORS

PARADORS are government-run hotels, classified from three to five stars. Spain's first parador opened in the Sierra de Gredos in 1928 *(see p556)*; there is now a wide network of them on the mainland and the islands. They are located close together so that there is never more than a day's drive to the nearest one. The best are in former royal hunting lodges, monasteries, castles and other monuments; some modern paradors have been purpose-built, often in spectacular scenery or in towns of historic interest *(see pp534–5)*.

A parador is not necessarily the best hotel in town, but it can be counted on to deliver a predictably high level of comfort. The bedrooms are usually spacious and comfortable, and are furnished in a way that varies little from parador to parador.

If you plan to tour in high season or to stay in the smaller paradors, it is wise to reserve a room. The paradors may be booked through the **Central de Reservas** in Madrid or through their London agent, **Keytel International**.

PRICES

SPANISH LAW requires all hotel managements to display their prices behind reception and in every room. As a rule, the higher a hotel's star-rating, the more you pay. Rates for a double room can be as little as 3,000 pesetas a night for a cheap one-star hostal; a five-star hotel will cost more than 20,000 pesetas a night, but a room price higher than 30,000 pesetas a night is exceptional.

Prices usually vary according to room, region and season. A suite or a very spacious room, or one with a view, a balcony or other special feature, may cost more than average. Rural and suburban hotels are generally less expensive than those in the city centre.

All the prices given on pages 536–71 are based on mid-season or high-season rates. High season

Jaén's parador, a modern extension of the medieval castle *(see p565)*

◁ **Madrileños** enjoying afternoon sunshine, drinks and conversation in the Plaza Mayor generally covers July and August, but in some areas it runs from April to October and in the Canary Islands the winter is high season.

Many of Spain's city hotels charge especially inflated rates for their rooms during major fiestas, such as the April Fair in Seville *(see p413)*, Los Sanfermines in Pamplona *(see p128)*, Carnival in Santa Cruz de Tenerife and Easter Week *(see p34)* in many places.

Most hotels quote prices per room and meal prices per person without including VAT *(IVA)*, which is currently 7 per cent in most of Spain, but 4 per cent in the Canary Islands.

The glass-domed foyer of the Palace Hotel, Madrid *(see p553)*

BOOKING AND CHECK-IN

OFF-SEASON IN RURAL or small towns you are unlikely to need to book ahead; but if you plan to travel in high season or want to stay in a particular hotel, you should reserve a room by phone or through a travel agent. You will need to reserve if you want a special room: one with a double bed (twin beds are the norm); on the ground floor; away from a noisy main road; or a room with a balcony or a view.

The resort hotels often close from autumn to spring. Before you travel, it is always advisable to check that your preferred hotels will be open at that time of year.

You will not normally be asked for a deposit when you book a hotel room. However, a deposit of 20–25 per cent

may be requested if you book during a peak period or for a stay of more than a few nights. Send it by credit card or giro in Spain and by credit card or banker's draft from outside the country. If you have to cancel, do so at least a week before the booking date or you may lose all or some of the deposit.

Most hotels will honour a booking only until 8pm unless business is poor. If you are delayed, call the hotel to assure them you are coming and to tell them when to expect you.

When you check in you will be asked for your passport or identity card to comply with Spanish police regulations. It will normally be returned to you promptly as soon as your details have been copied.

You are expected to check out of your room by noon on the last day of your stay, or to pay for another night.

PAYING

HOTELS THAT ACCEPT credit cards are listed on pages 536–71. In some large, busy hotels you may be asked to sign a blank credit card pay slip on arrival. Under Spanish law it is fraudulent to ask you to do this; you should refuse.

Eurocheques are accepted in some hotels, but personal cheques are not accepted in Spanish hotels, even if backed by a cheque guarantee card or drawn on a Spanish bank. Many people pay cash and in some cheap hotels this may be the only payment accepted.

Around 200–300 pesetas is the usual tip for all hotel staff.

The pretty beach of Melia Salinas Hotel, Lanzarote *(see p571)*

CASAS RURALES

CASAS RURALES are country houses whose owners accept a few visitors, usually in high season. They are most numerous in Asturias, Navarra, Aragón and Catalonia (where they are called *cases de pagès*). They are becoming common in Galicia and Cantabria (where they are called *casas de labranza*), and in Andalusia.

Casas rurales range in style from stately manor houses to small, isolated farms. Some offer bed and breakfast; some an evening meal or full board. Most are self-catering.

Do not expect hotel service or a long list of facilities in a *casa rural*. You may, however, be given a friendly welcome and good home cooking, all at a very affordable price.

Book *casas rurales* directly or through regional associations: **Central de Reservas de Casas Rurales** in Navarra; **RAAR** in Andalusia; **Rutastur** in Asturias; **TURAL** in Aragón; and **Turisvert** in Catalonia.

El Nacimiento, Turre, a charming Andalusian *casa rural* *(see p567)*

SELF-CATERING

Villas and holiday flats let by the week are plentiful along the Spanish coasts. In scenic areas of the countryside there are many *casas rurales* (farm and village houses) for rent by the day. To obtain information about the *casas rurales*, contact their regional organizations *(see p531)*. They also take bookings. **The Individual Traveller's Spain** and **Secret Spain** are two UK organizations that act as agents for owners of holiday houses and flats in Spain. Some other organizations and owners of holiday homes advertise in the travel sections of UK Sunday newspapers. Tour operators offer a range of self-catering accommodation.

The prices for self-catering accommodation vary according to the location, the nature of the property and the season. A four-person villa with a pool can cost under 40,000 pesetas for a week if it is inland; and 160,000 pesetas a week or more if it is on the coast.

An apartment hotel is a new type of accommodation; in Andalusia it is called a *villa turística*. Half hotel, half holiday flats, it gives guests a choice between self-catering (all rooms have a kitchen) or eating in the hotel restaurant. Holiday villages are similar, often catering for specialist interests. One example is the village of Ainsa in the mountain sports region of Aragón *(see p547)*, which offers a mix of camping and hostel accommodation, with restaurants and bars.

Typical holiday villas in Lanzarote's Puerto del Carmen, the Canary Islands

YOUTH HOSTELS AND MOUNTAIN REFUGES

To use the network of *albergues juveniles* (youth hostels) in Spain you need to show a YHA (Youth Hostel Association) card from your country or an international card, which you can buy from any hostel. Prices per person for bed and breakfast are lower than hotel prices.

Youth hostels can be booked directly or through the **Red Española de Albergues Juveniles** (Spanish Network of Youth Hostels). Despite the name, there is no age limit.

Mountaineers heading for the more remote areas may use the *refugios* (refuges). These are shelters with a dormitory, cooking facilities and heating. Some are huts with about six bunks; others are mountain houses with up to 50 beds.

The *refugios* are marked on large-scale maps of mountain areas and national parks. They are administered by the regional mountaineering associations and usually owned by clubs. The **Federación Española de Montañismo** and the local tourist offices will supply their addresses.

La Oliva monastery, Navarra *(see p126)*, welcomes paying guests

MONASTERIES AND CONVENTS

If you have a taste for peace and austerity you may enjoy a night in one of Spain's 150 religious houses where guests are welcome. Most belong to the Benedictine and the Cistercian orders. Room prices are inexpensive. They are not hotels, however; you have to book ahead by writing or by phone; and few have private telephones or television. The guests may be asked to tidy their rooms, observe the same strict mealtimes as the monks or nuns and to help with the washing up. Some convents admit only women and some monasteries only men.

Youth hostel in rustic style on the edge of Cazorla nature reserve, Jaén

CAMP SITES

THERE ARE more than 600 camp sites scattered across Spain. Most of them are on the coasts, but there are also some outside the major cities and in the most popular areas of countryside. Most sites have electricity and running water; some also have launderettes, playgrounds, restaurants, shops, a swimming pool and other amenities.

It is sensible to carry a camping carnet with you. This can be used instead of a passport to check in at sites and it covers you for third-party insurance. Carnets are issued in the UK by the AA, RAC and **The Camping and Caravanning Club**.

Every year, the *Guía Oficial de Campings* is published by Turespaña. Information about camp sites is available from the **Federación Española de Empresarios de Campings y Ciudades de Vacaciones** (Spanish Camp Site and Holiday Camp Federation), which also takes bookings. In Spain, camping is only permitted on official sites.

Sign for a camp site

DISABLED TRAVELLERS

HOTEL MANAGERS will advise on access for people in wheelchairs, and the staff will help, but few hotels are well equipped for disabled guests, although some of the youth hostels are. **Servi-COCEMFE** (the Confederación Coordinadora Estatal de Minusválidos Físicos de España) runs a hotel in Madrid for disabled people's groups. Servi-COCEMFE and Viajes 2000 *(see p613)* advise on hotels for guests with special needs. A UK charity, **Holiday Care Service**, produces a fact sheet on Spain. **IHD** (International Help for the Disabled), which is based in France, will arrange transport, hotels and other help for visitors to the Costa del Sol and Mallorca.

View from the Cabina Verónica mountain refuge, Picos de Europa

FURTHER INFORMATION

THE GUIA OFICIAL DE HOTELES is published every spring by Turespaña. It is sold in Spanish bookshops and news-stands and can be consulted in Spanish tourist offices. It lists every pension, hostal and hotel in Spain and gives their star-rating, their prices and a resumé of their facilities.

Each *comunidad autónoma* distributes a list of the hotels and other accommodation in its area via the tourist offices.

(see p613)

DIRECTORY

HOTEL CHAINS

Grupo Riu
📞 *(971) 49 08 21.*
FAX *(971) 74 38 98.*

Grupo Sol-Meliá
📞 *(91) 571 16 16.*
FAX *(91) 571 49 96.*

NH
📞 *(93) 253 35 00.*
FAX *(93) 417 00 48.*

TRYP
📞 *(91) 315 32 46.*
FAX *(91) 314 31 56.*

PARADORS

Central de Reservas
Calle Requena 3,
28013 Madrid.
📞 *(91) 516 66 66.*
FAX *(91) 516 66 57.*

Keytel International
402 Edgware Road,
London W2 1ED.
📞 *(0171) 402 8182 in UK.*
FAX *(0171) 724 9503in UK.*

SELF-CATERING AND BED AND BREAKFAST

Central de Reservas de Casas Rurales
Calle Espoz y Mina 15,
31002 Pamplona
(Navarra).
📞 *(948) 22 93 28.*
FAX *(948) 21 20 59.*

The Individual Traveller's Spain
Bignor, Pulborough,
West Sussex
RH20 1QD.
📞 *(01798) 869485 in UK.*

RAAR
Apartado 2035,
04080 Almería.
📞 *(950) 26 50 18.*
FAX *(950) 27 04 31.*

Rutastur
Apartado 29, Llanes,
33500 (Asturias).
📞 *(98) 540 12 43.*
FAX *(98) 540 25 41.*

Secret Spain
Model Farm, Rattlesden,
Suffolk IP30 0SY.
📞 *(01449) 737850 in UK.*

TURAL
22471 Laspaules (Aragón).
📞 *(& FAX) (974) 55 40 11.*

Turisvert
Plaça Sant Josep Oriol 4,
08002 Barcelona.
📞 *(93) 412 69 84.*
FAX *(93) 317 30 05.*

YOUTH HOSTELS

Red Española de Albergues Juveniles
C/ José Ortega y Gasset 71,
28006 Madrid.
📞 *(91) 347 77 00.*
FAX *(91) 401 81 60.*

MOUNTAIN REFUGES

Federación de Montañismo
C/ Alberto Aguilera 3,
28015 Madrid.
📞 *(91) 445 13 82.*
FAX *(91) 445 14 38.*

CAMPING

The Camping and Caravanning Club
📞 *(01203) 422024 in UK.*
FAX *(01203) 694886 in UK.*

Federación de Empresarios de Campings
C/ San Bernardo 97–9,
28015 Madrid.
📞 *(91) 448 12 34.*
FAX *(91) 448 12 67.*

DISABLED TRAVELLERS

Holiday Care Service
📞 *(01293) 774535 in UK.*
FAX *(01293) 784647 in UK.*

IHD (France)
📞 *(33) 94 81 61 51.*
FAX *(33) 94 81 61 43.*

Servi-COCEMFE
Calle Eugenio Salazar 2,
28002 Madrid.
📞 *(91) 413 80 01.*
FAX *(91) 416 99 99.*

FURTHER INFORMATION

Spanish Tourist Office
57 St James's Street,
London SW1A 1LD.
📞 *(0171) 499 0901.*
FAX *(0171) 629 4257.*

Spotify's Best: Paradors

PARADOR IS AN OLD SPANISH WORD for a lodging place for travellers of respectable rank. In the late 1920s a national network of state-run hotels called paradors was established. Many of the nearly 90 paradors are converted castles, palaces or monasteries, although some have been purpose-built in strategic tourist locations. They are generally well signposted and the prices are comparable with other luxury hotels. All offer a high degree of comfort and service, and have restaurants which offer regional cuisine.

Hotel de los Reyes Católicos, *one of the sights of Santiago de Compostela (see p86), may be the world's oldest hotel. It was founded as a hospital in 1499 (see p537).*

Hotel de los Reyes Católicos

Parador de León *is housed in the Hostal San Marcos, one of Spain's finest Renaissance buildings (see p21). The main hall has a magnificent coffered ceiling (see p556).*

Parador de León

Parador de Guadalupe is a 16th-century former hospice for pilgrims. It stands beside a famous monastery in Extremadura *(see p560).*

Parador de Guadalupe

Parador de Arcos de la Frontera *is situated in one of the archetypal* pueblos blancos *(white towns). Its wide, semicircular terrace offers panoramic views of the Moorish castle, the Guadalete river and the rolling farmland beyond (see p563).*

Parador de Arcos de la Frontera

Parador de Granada

Parador de Granada *is a captivating 15th-century convent built in the beautiful gardens of the Alhambra at the instruction of the Catholic Monarchs. Antique Spanish furniture fills the halls and rooms of this atmospheric parador, and an old roofless chapel forms a patio. Advance booking is essential (see p565).*

Parador de Sigüenza, *a massive hilltop castle enclosing a large courtyard, was formerly a Visigothic, then a Moorish, fortress. It is approached from the historic town below by a steep cobbled street* (see p559).

Parador de Viella is set in the spectacular Vall d'Arán and surrounded by high peaks. There is ample opportunity for outdoor activity, from skiing to hunting and fishing *(see p547)*.

Parador de Viella

Parador de Sigüenza

Parador de Alcañiz

Parador de Cuenca

Parador de Alcañiz *is located in a castle-monastery built by the Knights of Calatrava in the 12th century. Despite its imposing size, the parador has only 12 rooms. The cloister is now a peaceful garden* (see p548).

| 0 kilometres | 200 |
| 0 miles | 100 |

Parador de Cuenca is housed in the converted 16th-century convent of San Pablo. It enjoys magnificent views of the attractive old town *(see p558)*.

Parador de Cañadas del Teide *is a recently refurbished parador situated in the Mount Teide National Park* (see pp514–15) *on Tenerife. From its terraces there are views of the volcanic landscape* (see p571).

THE CANARY ISLANDS

Choosing a Hotel

T HE HOTELS in this guide have been selected across a
wide price range for excellent facilities and location.
Many also have a highly recommended restaurant. The
chart lists hotels by region, starting in the north; colour-
coded thumb tabs indicate the regions covered on each
page. For more details on restaurants see pages 578–609.

	CREDIT CARDS	NUMBER OF ROOMS	PRIVATE PARKING	SWIMMING POOL	GARDEN OR TERRACE
GALICIA					
ALFOZ: *Pazo Galea.* ℗℗ Castro de Ouro, 27776 (Lugo). ☎ *(982) 55 83 23.* FAX *(982) 55 83 23.* A 19th-century *pazo* (Galician manor house) with a splendid garden. The bedrooms are simple and modern. The owners, a Galician family, operate an original fulling mill and a flour mill as a tourist attraction. 🛏	MC V	5		●	
BAIONA: *Villa Sol.* ℗℗ C/ Palos de la Frontera 12, 36300 (Pontevedra). ☎ *(986) 35 56 91.* FAX *(986) 35 67 02.* A family-run hotel in an old country house decorated with antiques. Children are not admitted during the high season. 🛏	MC V	6	■		
BAIONA: *Parador de Baiona.* ℗℗℗℗ Carretera de Baiona, 36300 (Pontevedra). ☎ *(986) 35 50 00.* FAX *(986) 35 50 76.* This parador, built in the style of an old manor house or *pazo*, is located within the walls of Monterreal castle. 🛏 📺	AE DC MC V	124	■	●	■
BRIÓN: *Pousada de Rosalía.* ℗ Calle Soiglexia, Los Ángeles, 15280 (A Coruña). ☎ *(981) 88 75 80.* FAX *(981) 88 75 57.* A country house hotel, stone-built and surrounding a cloister. It offers simple accommodation not far from the coast and Santiago de Compostela. There are barbecues by the pool in summer. 🛏 📺	AE DC MC V	37	■	●	■
CAMBADOS: *Parador de Cambados.* ℗℗℗ Paseo de Cervantes, 36630 (Pontevedra). ☎ *(986) 54 22 50.* FAX *(986) 54 20 68.* This parador, on an estuary of the Rías Baixas, occupies a handsome *pazo* built round a large courtyard garden where drinks are served. Galician specialities and local wines are served in the restaurant. 🛏 📺	AE DC MC V	63	■		■
CERVO: *Pousada O'Almacén.* ℗ Carretera de Sargadelos 2, 27891 (Lugo). ☎ *(982) 55 78 36.* FAX *(982) 55 78 36.* A restored 18th-century building, once a food store for neighbouring hamlets. The best bedrooms look on to the Río Xunco. 🛏 📺	DC MC V	7	■		
CORNIDE: *Casa Grande de Cornide.* ℗℗℗ Calo, Teo, 15886 (A Coruña). ☎ *(981) 80 55 99.* FAX *(981) 80 57 51.* A welcoming small bed and breakfast hotel in a renovated house near Santiago de Compostela. It has a library and a garden with two traditional *hórreos* (granaries) and an 18th-century dovecote. 🛏 📺	AE DC MC V	7	■	●	■
A CORUÑA: *Ciudad de La Coruña.* ℗℗℗ Paseo de Adormideras, 15002. ☎ *(981) 21 21 00.* FAX *(981) 22 46 10.* A hotel with views over A Coruña bay, and a beach nearby. It has spacious, modern bedrooms and gym and spa facilities. 🛏 📺	AE DC MC V	132	■	●	■
A ESTRADA: *Pazo de Leira Herminia.* ℗ Calle Carballeira 6, Nigoi, 36684 (Pontevedra). ☎ *(986) 57 32 00.* FAX *(986) 57 32 00.* A quiet, cosy hotel offering bed and breakfast in a restored, stone-built country house near the source of the Río Liñares. It is a convenient base for visits to the Rías Baixas. 🛏		4	■	●	■
FERROL: *Parador de Ferrol.* ℗℗ C/ Almirante Fernández Martín, 15401 (A Coruña). ☎ *(981) 35 67 20.* FAX *(981) 35 67 21.* This spacious parador in the town centre is surrounded by gardens. It is decorated with nautical memorabilia of Ferrol's seafaring past. The bedroom windows look out over the harbour. 🛏 📺	AE DC MC V	38	■		■
A GUARDA: *Convento de San Benito.* ℗℗ Plaza de San Benito, 36780 (Pontevedra). ☎ *(986) 61 11 66.* FAX *(986) 61 15 17.* A converted 16th-century convent in which the nuns' cells have been transformed into bedrooms for the guests. They surround a small cloister with a palm tree and a stone fountain. 🛏 📺	AE DC MC V	24	■		

| Price categories for a standard double room per night, with tax, breakfast and service included:
ℙ under 8,000 ptas
ℙℙ 8,000–12,000 ptas
ℙℙℙ 12,000–16,000 ptas
ℙℙℙℙ 16,000–20,000 ptas
ℙℙℙℙℙ over 20,000 ptas | **CREDIT CARDS**
Indicates which credit cards are accepted: *AE* American Express; *DC* Diners Club; *MC* Master Card/Access; *V* Visa
PARKING
Parking provided by the hotel in a private car park or a private garage on the hotel site or very close by. Some hotels charge for use of private parking facilities.
SWIMMING POOL
Hotel pool outdoors unless otherwise stated.
GARDEN
Hotel with garden, courtyard or terrace, often providing tables for eating outdoors. |

	CREDIT CARDS	NUMBER OF ROOMS	PRIVATE PARKING	SWIMMING POOL	GARDEN OR TERRACE
NEDA: *Pazo da Merced.* ℙℙℙ Pazo da Merced, 15510 (A Coruña). ☎ (981) 38 29 00. FAX (981) 38 01 04. A restored, 17th-century stone manor house with its own chapel, at the head of the Ría de Ferrol. 🚗 📺	AE DC MC	5	■	●	■
POBRA DE TRIVES: *Pazo Casa Grande.* ℙℙ Calle Marqués de Trives 17, 32780 (Ourense). ☎ (988) 33 20 66. A *pousada* (small hotel) in an 18th-century stone manor, with a coat of arms on its central tower. Antiques and old paintings decorate the cosy interior. There is a chapel with a magnificent reredos. 🚗 📺	AE DC MC V	7	■		■
PONTEVEDRA: *Parador de Pontevedra.* ℙℙℙℙ Calle Barón 19, 36002. ☎ (986) 85 58 00. FAX (986) 85 21 95. An elegant parador in a stately manor in the old town. The decor incorporates antiques, gilt mirrors, chandeliers and tapestries. 🚗 📺	AE DC MC V	47	■		■
RIBEIRA: *Fonteclara.* ℙℙ C/ Sta Marina de Ribeira 6, 36685 (Pontevedra). ☎ (986) 57 32 09. FAX (981) 36 49 99. An old Galician country house of great character, peacefully located in the valley of the Río Ulloa. Visitors are offered bed and breakfast, and a sitting room with an open fireplace. 🚗 ♿	V	8	■	●	■
SANTIAGO DE COMPOSTELA: *Hogar San Francisco.* ℙℙ C/ Campillo de San Francisco 3, 15702 (A Coruña). ☎ (981) 58 16 00. FAX (981) 57 19 16. A hotel near the cathedral in what was a school for Franciscan friars, with the dining room occupying the former refectory. The bedrooms are simple but bright. 🚗	AE MC V	70			
SANTIAGO DE COMPOSTELA: *Reyes Católicos.* ℙℙℙℙℙ Praza do Obradoiro 1, 15705 (A Coruña). ☎ (981) 58 22 00. FAX (981) 56 30 94. Built under the Catholic Monarchs for poor pilgrims, this 16th-century parador is one of the world's grandest hotels *(see p86)*. It is built round four arcaded patios with fountains. 🚗 📺 ♿	AE DC MC V	136	■		■
O SAVIÑAO: *Torre de Vilariño.* ℙ Calle Fión 47, 27548 (Lugo). ☎ (982) 45 22 60. FAX (982) 45 22 60. A 17th-century inn converted into a hotel offering bed and breakfast, mainly to tourists following the so-called "Route of the Romanesque". The owners serve food and wine they make themselves. 🚗 📺	DC V	9	■	●	■
SISÁN-CAMBADOS: *Pazo Carrasqueira.* ℙℙ Calle Carrasqueira, 36638 (Pontevedra). ☎ (986) 71 00 32. FAX (986) 71 00 32. A guest house in a rural mansion, with a carved granite staircase and cosy bedrooms on the top floor. Fish, seafood, and Albariño wine (produced on the estate) are served in the dining room. 🚗 📺	AE MC V	9	■		■
A TOXA: *Gran Hotel de La Toja.* ℙℙℙℙ O Grove, 36991 (Pontevedra). ☎ (986) 73 00 25. FAX (986) 73 00 26. This mansion, built at the end of the 19th century on an island planted with palm and pine trees, is reached from the mainland by an iron bridge. The hotel has a ballroom and a health and fitness centre. 🚗 📺	AE DC V	198	■	●	■
TUI: *Parador de Tui.* ℙℙℙ Avenida de Portugal, 36700 (Pontevedra). ☎ (986) 60 03 09. FAX (986) 60 21 63. The public and guest rooms have superb views over the town of Tui and across the Río Miño, which forms the frontier with Portugal. Local dishes on the menu include eels and oysters. 🚗 📺 ♿	AE DC MC V	34	■	●	■
VERÍN: *Parador de Verín.* ℙℙℙ Monterrei, 32600 (Ourense). ☎ (988) 41 00 75. FAX (988) 41 20 17. Verín's parador is on a hilltop, surrounded by lawns and trees, with views across a valley to the medieval castle of Monterrei. Vineyards in the valley supply wines for the hotel restaurant. 🚗 📺	AE DC MC	23	■	●	■

Price categories for a standard double room per night, with tax, breakfast and service included:

Ⓟ under 8,000 ptas
ⓅⓅ 8,000–12,000 ptas
ⓅⓅⓅ 12,000–16,000 ptas
ⓅⓅⓅⓅ 16,000–20,000 ptas
ⓅⓅⓅⓅⓅ over 20,000 ptas

CREDIT CARDS
Indicates which credit cards are accepted: *AE* American Express; *DC* Diners Club; *MC* Master Card/Access; *V* Visa
PARKING
Parking provided by the hotel in a private car park or a private garage on the hotel site or very close by. Some hotels charge for use of private parking facilities.
SWIMMING POOL
Hotel pool outdoors unless otherwise stated.
GARDEN
Hotel with garden, courtyard or terrace, often providing tables for eating outdoors.

	CREDIT CARDS	NUMBER OF ROOMS	PRIVATE PARKING	SWIMMING POOL	GARDEN OR TERRACE
VILAGARCÍA DE AROUSA: *Pazo O'Rial.* ⓅⓅⓅ Calle El Rial 1, 36600 (Pontevedra). 📞 *(986) 50 70 11.* FAX *(986) 50 16 76.* Wooden beams, tiled floors and stone walls preserve the character of this old manor; cushions and fine fabrics give comfort. 🛏 TV	AE DC MC V	60	■	●	■
VILLALBA: *Parador de Villalba.* ⓅⓅⓅⓅ Valeriano Valdesuso, 27800 (Lugo). 📞 *(982) 51 00 11.* FAX *(982) 51 00 90.* A tiny parador in a medieval octagonal tower with thick walls and narrow windows, entered by a drawbridge. Booking is essential. 🛏 TV	AE DC MC V	6	■		■
VILLALONGA: *Pazo El Revel.* ⓅⓅⓅ Camino de la Iglesia 15, 36990 (Pontevedra). 📞 *(986) 74 30 00.* FAX *(986) 74 33 90.* A 17th-century manor house, its façade overgrown with creepers. It has peaceful formal gardens and a colonnaded terrace. 🛏 TV	MC V	22	■	●	■

ASTURIAS AND CANTABRIA

	CREDIT CARDS	NUMBER OF ROOMS	PRIVATE PARKING	SWIMMING POOL	GARDEN OR TERRACE
CANGAS DE ONÍS: *Aultre Naray.* ⓅⓅ Peruyes, 33547 (Asturias). 📞 *(98) 584 08 08.* FAX *(98) 584 08 48.* There are mountain views from this country house hotel in one of Northern Spain's least-known corners. Every bedroom is different. 🛏 TV	AE MC V	10	■		■
CASTROPOL: *Palacete Peñalba.* ⓅⓅ C/ El Cotarelo, Figueras, 33794 (Asturias). 📞 *(98) 563 61 25.* FAX *(98) 563 62 47.* This hotel in an Art Nouveau mansion built in 1912 by a Gaudí acolyte has oval balconies, curved staircases and its original furniture. 🛏 TV	AE DC MC V	13	■		
COLOMBRES: *La Casona de Villanueva.* ⓅⓅ Villanueva, Ribadedeva, 33590 (Asturias). 📞 *(98) 541 25 90.* FAX *(942) 541 25 14.* An 18th-century village house, carefully restored in the traditional style, with a peaceful atmosphere. Children under five are not admitted. 🛏	MC V	8	■		■
COLOMBRES: *Mirador de La Franca.* ⓅⓅ Playa de La Franca, Ribadedeva, 33590 (Asturias). 📞 *(98) 541 21 45.* FAX *(98) 541 21 53.* There are magnificent views from the lounge and restaurant of this hotel in a rocky cove set back from La Franca beach. The waters of the bay are safe for water sports and underwater fishing. 🛏 TV	AE DC MC V	50	■		■
COMILLAS: *Casal del Castro.* ⓅⓅ Calle San Jerónimo, 39520 (Cantabria). 📞 *(942) 72 00 36.* A large, 17th-century house decorated and furnished with antiques. It is on the edge of the town, not far from excellent beaches. 🛏 TV	DC MC V	45	■		■
COSGAYA: *Hotel del Oso.* ⓅⓅ Ctra Potes–Fuente Dé, 39539 (Cantabria). 📞 *(942) 73 30 18.* FAX *(942) 73 30 36.* Surrounded by the mountains of the eastern Picos de Europa, this is a comfortable hotel, very popular with foreign tourists. 🛏	AE DC MC V	17	■	●	■
ESCALANTE: *San Román de Escalante.* ⓅⓅⓅⓅ Ctra Escalante–Castillo, 39795 (Cantabria). 📞 *(942) 67 77 45.* FAX *(942) 67 76 43.* A hotel in an exquisitely decorated 17th-century house overlooking trees and meadows. Beside it is a Romanesque chapel. 🛏 ▤ TV ♿	AE DC MC V	9	■		■
FUENTE DÉ: *Parador de Fuente Dé.* ⓅⓅ Fuente Dé, 39588 (Cantabria). 📞 *(942) 73 66 51.* FAX *(942) 73 66 54.* This modern building at the foot of the Picos de Europa cable car has pleasant bedrooms and long galleries with huge windows. It is an ideal base for fishing or walking in the mountains. 🛏 TV ♿	AE DC MC V	78	■		■
GIJÓN: *La Casona de Jovellanos.* ⓅⓅⓅ Plaza de Jovellanos 1, 33201 (Asturias). 📞 *(98) 534 20 24.* FAX *(98) 535 61 51.* A small hotel in an 18th-century building overlooking a little square in the old part of the city, and near the San Lorenzo beach. 🛏 TV	AE MC V	16			■

GIJÓN: *Parador Molino Viejo.* ℗℗℗℗ AE DC V — 40
Parque de Isabel la Católica, 33203 (Asturias). (*(98) 537 05 11.* FAX *(98) 537 02 33.*
A parador in a corner of one of Spain's prettiest parks, in a converted
windmill of a type common in Gijón from the 15th to the 18th century.
The old watercourse is preserved in the grounds. 🛏 ▤ TV 🛗

LIÉRGANES: *Posada del Sauce.* ℗℗℗ AE MC V — 50
C/ José Antonio 25, 39722 (Cantabria). (*(942) 52 80 23.* FAX *(942) 52 81 17.*
This is an imposing 19th-century mountain house in a beautiful village.
It has a covered swimming pool, but the bedrooms are rather small. 🛏

LLANES: *Gran Hotel Paraiso.* ℗℗ AE DC MC V — 30
Calle Pidal 2, 33500 (Asturias). (*(98) 540 19 71.* FAX *(98) 540 25 90.*
White marble floors, antique furniture and a grand piano in the lounge
contribute to the kitsch atmosphere of this hotel. It overlooks one of
the town's busiest streets, so book a parking space in advance. 🛏 ▤ TV

LLANES: *La Posada de Babel.* ℗℗ MC V — 8
La Pereda, 33509 (Asturias). (*(98) 540 25 25.* FAX *(98) 540 25 25.*
The spectacular Picos de Europa tower above this small, family-run
hotel. It is partly modern, but has huge, traditional fireplaces and one
bedroom is a converted *hórreo* (old grain store). 🛏 TV

OVIEDO: *Hotel de la Reconquista.* ℗℗℗℗℗ AE DC MC V — 146
Calle Gil de Jaz 16, 33004 (Asturias). (*(98) 524 11 00.* FAX *(98) 524 11 66.*
A magnificent 18th-century building with a massive stone coat of
arms above the main entrance. The public rooms are arranged around
several arcaded and balconied courtyards. 🛏 ▤ TV

PECHÓN: *Don Pablo.* ℗℗ AE DC MC V — 30
Afueras, 39594 (Cantabria). (*(942) 71 95 00.* FAX *(942) 71 95 00.*
Three houses joined together look like an old ancestral mansion. The
hotel is close to the sea and is family-run, with cosy rooms and a warm
atmosphere. The two pretty attic bedrooms are popular. 🛏 TV

POTES: *El Jisu.* ℗℗ MC V — 9
Ctra Potes–Camaleño, 39587 (Cantabria). (*(942) 73 30 38.* FAX *(942) 73 03 15.*
A chalet hotel in the Liébana Valley, with views of the Picos de Europa.
The cosy sitting rooms are decorated with antiques. 🛏 TV

PRAVIA: *Casa del Busto.* ℗℗ AE DC MC V — 12
Plaza del Rey Don Silo 1, 33120 (Asturias). (*(98) 582 27 71.* FAX *(98) 582 27 72.*
In a beautiful town, and close to a beach, is this hotel in a 16th-century
house. It is tastefully furnished with period pieces. The bedrooms
overlook a central patio where meals can be served. 🛏 TV

QUIJAS: *Hostería de Quijas.* ℗℗ AE DC MC V — 33
Calle Barrio Vinueva, 39590 (Cantabria). (*(942) 82 08 33.* FAX *(942) 83 80 50.*
An 18th-century stone-built mansion on the Santander–Oviedo road,
near Torrelavega. It has broad eaves, bay windows, timbered ceilings
and a magnificent garden. The reception is in the former library. 🛏 TV

QUIJAS: *Posada de la Torre de Quijas.* ℗℗ AE DC MC V — 12
Calle Barrio Vinueva, 39590 (Cantabria). (*(942) 82 06 45.*
This hotel is in a restored, 19th-century stone house with wooden bay
windows. It is decorated with farming implements, which give it a
rustic atmosphere. The hotel is on a main road. 🛏

RIBADESELLA: *Gran Hotel del Sella.* ℗℗℗ AE DC MC V — 82
Calle Ricardo Cangas 17, 33560 (Asturias). (*(98) 586 01 50.* FAX *(98) 585 74 49.*
The former summer palace of the Marquis of Argüelles now has a
new wing and is a family-run hotel. It is outside town, on the beach,
and has a pool, tennis courts and vast gardens. 🛏 TV 🛗

SALAS: *Castillo de Valdés-Salas.* ℗℗ AE DC MC V — 12
Plaza de la Campa, 33860 (Asturias). (*(98) 583 22 22.* FAX *(98) 583 22 99.*
A 16th-century restored castle converted into a simple hotel retaining
much of the character of the original building. The local tourist
information desk is in the hotel reception. 🛏 TV

SANTANDER: *Las Brisas.* ℗℗℗ AE DC MC V — 13
Travesia de los Castros 14, 39005 (Cantabria). (*(942) 27 50 11.* FAX *(942) 28 11 73.*
A homely hotel in a 19th-century white villa close to the popular
Sardinero beach. Breakfast can be served on a seaside terrace. 🛏 TV

For key to symbols see back flap

Price categories for a standard double room per night, with tax, breakfast and service included:

Ⓟ   under 8,000 ptas
ⓅⓅ   8,000–12,000 ptas
ⓅⓅⓅ   12,000–16,000 ptas
ⓅⓅⓅⓅ   16,000–20,000 ptas
ⓅⓅⓅⓅⓅ   over 20,000 ptas

CREDIT CARDS
Indicates which credit cards are accepted: *AE* American Express; *DC* Diners Club; *MC* Master Card/Access; *V* Visa
PARKING
Parking provided by the hotel in a private car park or a private garage on the hotel site or very close by. Some hotels charge for use of private parking facilities.
SWIMMING POOL
Hotel pool outdoors unless otherwise stated.
GARDEN
Hotel with garden, courtyard or terrace, often providing tables for eating outdoors.

	CREDIT CARDS	NUMBER OF ROOMS	PRIVATE PARKING	SWIMMING POOL	GARDEN OR TERRACE
SANTANDER: *Hotel Real.* ⓅⓅⓅⓅ Paseo Pérez Galdós 28, 39005 (Cantabria). ☏ *(942) 27 25 50.* FAX *(942) 27 45 73.* An elegant, formal hotel, visible on the city's highest hill. It was built built late in the 19th century for nobility accompanying the royal family on holiday. The balconies give views over the bay. 🖥 📺 ♿	AE DC MC V	125	■		■
SANTILLANA DEL MAR: *Posada de Santa Juliana.* Ⓟ Calle Carrera 19, 39330 (Cantabria). ☏ *(942) 84 01 06.* FAX *(942) 84 01 70.* A small guest house located unpromisingly over a souvenir shop, but with charming attic rooms. Guests may eat in a bar across the street. 🖥 📺	AE DC MC V	6			
SANTILLANA DEL MAR: *Altamira.* ⓅⓅ Calle Cantón 1, 39330 (Cantabria). ☏ *(942) 81 80 25.* FAX *(942) 84 01 36.* A town-centre hotel in a restored 17th-century palace. The old wooden staircase leads to bedrooms with beams and polished floors. 🖥 📺	AE DC MC V	32			■
SANTILLANA DEL MAR: *Parador Gil Blas.* ⓅⓅⓅ Plaza Ramón Pelayo 11, 39330 (Cantabria). ☏ *(942) 81 80 00.* FAX *(942) 81 83 91.* This stone mansion, begun in the 15th century, has a pretty patio. Bare walls and tiled floors enhance the medieval atmosphere. 🖥 📺 ♿	AE DC MC V	56	■		■
SAN VICENTE DE TORANZO: *Posada del Pas.* ⓅⓅ Ctra N623 Burgos–Santander, 39699 (Cantabria). ☏ *(942) 59 44 11.* FAX *(942) 59 43 86.* An 18th-century stone mountain house in a green valley on the Santander–Burgos road accommodates this popular hotel. 🖥 📺	AE DC MC V	32	■	●	■
SOLARES: *Don Pablo.* ⓅⓅ Calle General Mola 6, 39710 (Cantabria). ☏ *(942) 52 21 20.* FAX *(942) 52 05 26.* A medieval monastery with an imposing façade and a chapel. The public rooms are spacious and the bedrooms comfortable. 🖥 📺	AE DC MC V	27	■		■
TARAMUNDI: *La Rectoral.* ⓅⓅⓅⓅ Taramundi, 33775 (Asturias). ☏ *(98) 564 67 67.* FAX *(98) 564 67 77.* A former priest's house deep in the Asturian countryside has been tastefully converted into a quiet and atmospheric hotel. The ample bedrooms all have views of the surrounding mountains. 🖥 🍴 📺	AE DC MC V	18	■		

BASQUE COUNTRY, NAVARRA AND LA RIOJA

	CREDIT CARDS	NUMBER OF ROOMS	PRIVATE PARKING	SWIMMING POOL	GARDEN OR TERRACE
ANGUIANO: *Abadía de Valvanera.* Ⓟ Monasterio de Valvanera, 26323 (La Rioja). ☏ *(941) 37 70 44.* FAX *(941) 37 70 44.* Queen Isabel I stayed in this Benedictine monastery in 1482. The surroundings are beautiful, the rooms simple, and the food good. 🖥	AE DC MC V	29	■		■
ARGOMÁNIZ: *Parador de Argomániz.* ⓅⓅ Carretera NI, 01192 (Álava). ☏ *(945) 29 23 00.* FAX *(945) 29 32 87.* Kings have lodged in this 17th-century stone palace. Its location on the slopes of Mount Zabalgaña is peaceful, with good views. 🖥 📺	AE DC MC V	53	■		
AXPE-ATXONDO: *Mendi Goikoa.* ⓅⓅⓅ Calle Barrio de San Juan 33, 48292 (Vizcaya). ☏ *(94) 682 08 33.* FAX *(94) 682 11 36.* Twin stone houses built in the 18th century have been converted into a pleasant hotel in the peaceful heart of the Valle de Atxondo. 🖥 🍴	DC MC V	12	■		
BAKIO: *Hostería del Señorío de Bizkaia.* ⓅⓅ Calle José María Cirarda 4, 48130 (Vizcaya). ☏ *(94) 619 47 25.* FAX *(94) 619 47 25.* A stone building with wooden balconies houses this hotel. In summer concerts are held in the garden. Bakio beach is nearby. 🖥 🍴 📺 ♿	AE DC MC V	16			■
BILBAO (BILBO): *Gran Hotel Ercilla.* ⓅⓅⓅⓅ Calle Ercilla 37–9, 48011 (Vizcaya). ☏ *(94) 410 20 00.* FAX *(94) 443 93 35.* Bilbao's largest hotel is centrally located, comfortable, welcoming and bustling with life. It has a very good restaurant. 🖥 🍴 📺	AE DC MC V	346	■		

DONAMARIA: *Donamaria'ko Benta.* ⓅⓅ · V · 5
Barrio Ventas 4, 31750 (Navarra). ☎ *(948) 45 07 08.* ℻ *(948) 45 09 25.*
This is a small, family-run hotel in a stone-built Pyrenean mountain house, with the five bedrooms in an annexe. The proprietors create a pleasant atmosphere and serve excellent food in the restaurant. 🔲🔲

ELIZONDO: *Casa Urrusca.* Ⓟ · 5
Barrio de Bearzun, 31700 (Navarra). ☎ *(948) 45 21 06.*
This isolated stone farmhouse at the head of a pretty valley is a family house offering beds and a breakfast of good fresh farm food.

EZCARAY: *Albergue de La Real Fábrica.* Ⓟ · AE V · 36
Carretera de Santo Domingo, 20280 (La Rioja). ☎ *(941) 35 44 74.*
This hotel, occupying a restored textile mill in a small town, is an economical place for a quiet night after hill walking. 🔲

FITERO: *Gustavo Adolfo Bécquer.* ⓅⓅ · V · 194
C/ Extramuros, Baños de Fitero, 31593 (Navarra). ☎ *(948) 77 61 00.* ℻ *(948) 77 62 25.*
One of two hotels on the site of the Roman baths – this hotel has a thermal spring in the basement. Bathing, massage and many treatments are available. The hotel also has extensive sports facilities. 🔲 🔲

HARO: *Los Agustinos.* ⓅⓅⓅ · AE DC MC V · 62
Calle San Agustín 2, 26200 (La Rioja). ☎ *(941) 31 13 08.* ℻ *(941) 30 31 48.*
A lounge in a vast, arched chamber hung with tapestries is one of the highlights of this hotel in a former Augustinian monastery. Another is the magnificent central patio in the old cloister. 🔲🔲🔲🔲

HONDARRIBIA (FUENTERRABÍA): *Pampinot.* ⓅⓅⓅ · AE DC MC V · 8
Calle Nagusia 5, 20280 (Guipúzcoa). ☎ *(943) 64 06 00.* ℻ *(943) 64 51 28.*
An atmosphere of warmth is achieved by the team of women who run this hotel in a 16th-century mansion in old Hondarribia. 🔲🔲🔲

HONDARRIBIA (FUENTERRABÍA): *Parador de Hondarribia.* ⓅⓅⓅⓅ · AE DC MC V · 36
Plaza de Armas 14, 20280 (Guipúzcoa). ☎ *(943) 64 55 00.* ℻ *(943) 64 21 53.*
This is an elegant parador in the town's restored fortress. Weapons and other memorabilia of its colourful history adorn the walls. 🔲🔲

LAGUARDIA: *Posada Mayor de Migueloa.* ⓅⓅⓅ · AE MC V · 7
Calle Mayor de Migueloa 20, 01300 (Álava). ☎ *(941) 12 11 75.* ℻ *(941) 12 10 22.*
A beautiful mansion in the pedestrianized old town. It was built in 1640 and has its original granite walls, beams and tiled floors. 🔲🔲🔲

LECUMBERRI: *Ayestarán.* Ⓟ · V · 91
Calle Aralar 22, 31870 (Navarra). ☎ *(948) 50 41 27.* ℻ *(948) 50 41 27.*
Part of this family-run hotel, on both sides of the Pamplona–San Sebastián road, was built in the 1920s. The service is extraordinarily friendly. 🔲🔲

LOGROÑO: *Herencia Rioja.* ⓅⓅⓅ · AE DC MC V · 83
Calle Marqués de Murrieta 14, 26005 (La Rioja). ☎ *(941) 21 02 22.* ℻ *(941) 21 02 06.*
A modern hotel near Logroño's historic quarter. It has comfortable cheerful bedrooms and a restaurant serving haute cuisine. 🔲🔲🔲🔲

MUNDAKA: *El Puerto.* ⓅⓅ · DC MC V · 11
Calle Portu Kalea 1, 48360 (Vizcaya). ☎ *(94) 687 67 25.* ℻ *(94) 617 70 64.*
A two-storey fisherman's house converted into a simple, cosy hotel. The windows give views over the sea. 🔲🔲

MUNDAKA: *Atalaya.* ⓅⓅⓅ · AE DC MC V · 15
Paseo de Txorrokopunta 2, 48360 (Vizcaya). ☎ *(94) 687 68 88.* ℻ *(94) 687 68 99.*
Next to the fishing port, at the mouth of a sea inlet, is this hotel built at the beginning of the 20th century. It has a clean and well-kept air, small but pleasant bedrooms, large window galleries and a garden. 🔲🔲

OLITE: *Casa Zanito.* ⓅⓅ · AE DC MC V · 15
Rua Mayor 16, 31390 (Navarra). ☎ *(948) 74 00 02.*
An unpretentious family-run restaurant-with-rooms in a narrow street in the lovely old centre of a historic town. 🔲🔲🔲

OLITE: *Parador de Olite.* ⓅⓅⓅⓅ · AE DC MC V · 43
Plaza de los Teobaldos 2, 31390 (Navarra). ☎ *(948) 74 00 00.* ℻ *(948) 74 02 01.*
Occupying part of the 15th-century castle and palace of Carlos III, king of Navarra, this parador has some modern bedrooms. There are some pricier but atmospheric rooms in the old part of the castle. 🔲🔲🔲🔲

For key to symbols see back flap

Price categories for a standard double room per night, with tax, breakfast and service included:

℗ under 8,000 ptas
℗℗ 8,000–12,000 ptas
℗℗℗ 12,000–16,000 ptas
℗℗℗℗ 16,000–20,000 ptas
℗℗℗℗℗ over 20,000 ptas

CREDIT CARDS
Indicates which credit cards are accepted: *AE* American Express; *DC* Diners Club; *MC* Master Card/Access; *V* Visa
PARKING
Parking provided by the hotel in a private car park or a private garage on the hotel site or very close by. Some hotels charge for use of private parking facilities.
SWIMMING POOL
Hotel pool outdoors unless otherwise stated.
GARDEN
Hotel with garden, courtyard or terrace, often providing tables for eating outdoors.

	CREDIT CARDS	NUMBER OF ROOMS	PRIVATE PARKING	SWIMMING POOL	GARDEN OR TERRACE
PAMPLONA (IRUÑA): *Tres Reyes.* ℗℗℗℗ Jardines de la Taconera, 31001 (Navarra). ((948) 22 66 00. FAX (948) 22 29 30. A large modern building between the old and new towns on the edge of the Taconera gardens. The bedrooms have balconies. The services range from a gym and a sauna to hairdressing and valeting. 🅿 ▤ 📺 ♿	AE DC MC V	168	■	●	
PUENTE LA REINA: *Mesón del Peregrino.* ℗℗ Ctra Pamplona–Logroño, 31100 (Navarra). ((948) 34 00 75. FAX (948) 34 11 90. A tasteful roadside restaurant-with-rooms in an old stone house near the junction of the two main pilgrim routes to Santiago. 🅿 ▤ 📺 ♿	MC V	16	■	●	
RONCESVALLES (ORREAGA): *La Posada.* ℗ Carretera de Francia, 31650 (Navarra). ((948) 76 02 25. In 1612 this historic inn opened to cater for pilgrims to Santiago de Compostela. Its austere bedrooms with tiled floors are still cheap. 🅿	V	18	■		
SAN SEBASTIÁN (DONOSTIA): *La Galeria.* ℗℗℗ Infanta Cristina 1–3, 20008 (Guipúzcoa). ((943) 21 60 77. FAX (943) 21 12 98. A new hotel on Ondarreta beach in a building that dates from the end of the 19th century. It has two charming attic rooms. 🅿 📺	MC V	23	■		
SAN SEBASTIÁN (DONOSTIA): *Niza.* ℗℗℗ Calle Zubieta 56, 20007 (Guipúzcoa). ((943) 42 66 63. FAX (943) 42 66 63. A seafront hotel in *belle époque* style on La Concha beach, with sunny bedrooms and a café terrace overlooking the beach. 🅿 📺	AE DC MC V	41	■		■
SAN SEBASTIÁN (DONOSTIA): *De Londres y de Inglaterra.* ℗℗℗℗ Calle Zubieta 2, 20007 (Guipúzcoa). ((943) 42 69 89. FAX (943) 42 00 31. A 19th-century palace in a privileged situation on La Concha beach, which was transformed into a hotel in 1902. Monarchs used to stay here for their summer holidays. 🅿 ▤ 📺 ♿	AE DC MC V	145			
SAN SEBASTIÁN (DONOSTIA): *Monte Igueldo.* ℗℗℗℗ Paseo del Faro 134, 20008 (Guipúzcoa). ((943) 21 02 11. FAX (943) 21 50 28. Superbly located on Monte Igueldo, this hotel has panoramic views across the city and the bay. It has a rooftop swimming pool. 🅿 ▤ 📺	AE DC MC V	125	■	●	
SAN SEBASTIÁN (DONOSTIA): *María Cristina.* ℗℗℗℗℗ Paseo República Argentina 4, 20004 (Guipúzcoa). ((943) 42 49 00. FAX (943) 42 67 70. A luxurious, well-sited hotel built in 1912 and decorated in *belle époque* style. It is the venue of the annual San Sebastián film festival. 🅿 ▤ 📺	AE DC MC V	136	■		■
SANTO DOMINGO DE LA CALZADA: *Parador de Santo Domingo.* ℗℗℗ Plaza del Santo 3, 26250 (La Rioja). ((941) 34 03 00. FAX (941) 34 03 25. A hospital founded in the 12th century for pilgrims to Santiago de Compostela has been converted into this parador. It has an imposing lounge divided by arches, and a beautiful carved ceiling. 🅿 ▤ 📺 ♿	AE DC MC V	61	■		
VITORIA (GASTEIZ): *General Álava.* ℗℗℗ Avenida Gasteiz 79, 01009 (Álava). ((945) 22 22 00. FAX (945) 24 83 95. A modern hotel with comfortable bedrooms in the new town near the Palacio de Congresos. The restaurant serves regional dishes. 🅿 ▤ ♿	AE DC MC V	114	■		
YESA: *Hospedería de Leyre.* ℗℗ Monasterio de Leyre, 31410 (Navarra). ((948) 88 41 00. FAX (948) 88 41 37. This hotel occupies part of an 11th-century monastery, spectacularly located beneath crags in a beautiful landscape. The rooms are plain and clean and the hotel has a good restaurant. 🅿 ▤	AE DC MC V	29	■		■
ZARAUTZ: *Karlos Arguiñano.* ℗℗℗℗℗ Calle Mendilauta 13, 20800 (Guipúzcoa). ((943) 13 00 00. FAX (943) 13 34 50. An elegant hotel in a stone tower-cum-mansion, with views of the sea. It is owned by a TV chef and has an excellent restaurant. 🅿 ▤ 📺	AE DC MC V	12	■		

BARCELONA

OLD TOWN: *Lloret*. **Map 5 A1.**
Rambla de Canaletes 125, 08002. **(** *(93) 317 33 66.* FAX *(93) 301 92 83.*
There are views of the city from the foyer of this popular hotel near
the Plaça de Catalunya – but streetside bedrooms can be noisy. The
old building retains many of its original decorative features.
Ⓟ · AE DC MC V · **52**

OLD TOWN: *Rembrandt*. **Map 5 A2.**
Carrer de Portaferrissa 23, 08002. **(** *(93) 318 10 11.* FAX *(93) 318 10 11.*
A clean, homely hotel in the Barri Gòtic, popular with students. A
tiled courtyard is a sitting area. Some bedrooms share bathrooms.
Ⓟ · **24** · ■

OLD TOWN: *Toledano*. **Map 5 A1.**
Ramblas 138, 08002. **(** *(93) 301 08 72.* FAX *(93) 412 31 42.*
A small hotel near the Plaça de Catalunya, with a lounge overlooking
the Ramblas. The rooms are basic and can be noisy.
Ⓟ · AE DC MC V · **17** · ■

OLD TOWN: *Atlantis*. **Map 2 F1.**
Carrer de Pelai 20, 08001. **(** *(93) 318 90 12.* FAX *(93) 412 09 14.*
This modern, inexpensive hotel is centrally located near the Plaça de
Catalunya. The bedrooms have a range of facilities.
ⓅⓅ · AE DC MC V · **42** · ■

OLD TOWN: *España*. **Map 2 F3.**
Carrer de Sant Pau 9–11, 08001. **(** *(93) 318 17 58.* FAX *(93) 317 11 34.*
Domènech i Montaner, the outstanding Modernista architect, designed
the lower floor of this hotel. The bedrooms are all modern.
ⓅⓅ · AE DC MC V · **84**

OLD TOWN: *Gaudí*. **Map 2 F3.**
Carrer Nou de la Rambla 12, 08001. **(** *(93) 317 90 32.* FAX *(93) 412 26 36.*
A pleasant hotel in a street adjoining the Rambla de Catalunya, near
Gaudí's Palau Güell, with comfortable, well-equipped rooms.
ⓅⓅ · AE DC MC V · **73** · ■

OLD TOWN: *Jardí*. **Map 2 F3.**
Plaça Sant Josep Oriol 1, 08002. **(** *(93) 301 59 00.* FAX *(93) 318 36 64.*
A popular hotel overlooking a leafy square. Some bedrooms have
been renovated and have good views; the others are cheaper.
ⓅⓅ · AE MC V · **38**

OLD TOWN: *Mesón Castilla*. **Map 2 F1.**
Carrer de Valdonzella 5, 08001. **(** *(93) 318 21 82.* FAX *(93) 412 40 20.*
A comfortable hotel, if a little old-fashioned, in a building with a
Modernista façade near the Casa de la Caritat arts centre.
ⓅⓅ · AE MC V · **60** · ■   ■

OLD TOWN: *San Agustín*. **Map 2 F3.**
Plaça de Sant Agustí 3, 08001. **(** *(93) 318 16 58.* FAX *(93) 317 29 28.*
An attractive hotel with a pleasant first-floor lounge and bar looking
across a square. Some bedrooms have Catalan furniture.
ⓅⓅ · AE DC MC V · **77**

OLD TOWN: *Oriente*. **Map 2 F3.**
Ramblas 45–7, 08002. **(** *(93) 302 25 58.* FAX *(93) 412 38 19.*
A former Franciscan friary makes a romantic setting for the Oriente.
The cloister has been converted into a ballroom. Some bedrooms have
balconies overlooking the Ramblas.
ⓅⓅⓅ · AE DC V · **142** · ■

OLD TOWN: *Suizo*. **Map 5 B2.**
Plaça del Ángel 12, 08002. **(** *(93) 310 61 08.* FAX *(93) 310 40 81.*
This hotel behind the cathedral has 19th-century Parisian style. The
attic bedrooms with skylights have great character.
ⓅⓅⓅ · AE DC MC V · **51** · ■

OLD TOWN: *Nouvel*. **Map 5 A1.**
Carrer de Santa Anna 18–20, 08002. **(** *(93) 301 82 74.* FAX *(93) 301 83 70.*
In a quiet street off the Ramblas, near the Plaça de Catalunya, this well-
kept, old-style hotel is tastefully decorated and furnished.
ⓅⓅⓅ · AE MC V · **54**

OLD TOWN: *Royal*. **Map 5 A1.**
Rambla dels Estudis 117, 08002. **(** *(93) 301 94 00.* FAX *(93) 317 31 79.*
This hotel, at the top of the Ramblas, has friendly staff and simple but
elegant rooms with spacious marble bathrooms.
ⓅⓅⓅⓅ · AE DC MC V · **108** · ■

OLD TOWN: *Arts*. **Map 6 E4.**
Carrer de la Marina 19–21, 08005. **(** *(93) 221 10 00.* FAX *(93) 221 10 70.*
A modern, super-luxurious beachside hotel in one of Spain's tallest
towers. It has a huge swimming pool and a fitness centre.
ⓅⓅⓅⓅⓅ · AE DC MC V · **455** · ■ ● ■

For key to symbols see back flap

Price categories for a standard double room per night, with tax, breakfast and service included:

  Ⓡ   under 8,000 ptas
  ⓇⓇ   8,000–12,000 ptas
  ⓇⓇⓇ   12,000–16,000 ptas
  ⓇⓇⓇⓇ   16,000–20,000 ptas
  ⓇⓇⓇⓇⓇ   over 20,000 ptas

CREDIT CARDS
Indicates which credit cards are accepted: *AE* American Express; *DC* Diners Club; *MC* Master Card/Access; *V* Visa
PARKING
Parking provided by the hotel in a private car park or a private garage on the hotel site or very close by. Some hotels charge for use of private parking facilities.
SWIMMING POOL
Hotel pool outdoors unless otherwise stated.
GARDEN
Hotel with garden, courtyard or terrace, often providing tables for eating outdoors.

	CREDIT CARDS	NUMBER OF ROOMS	PRIVATE PARKING	SWIMMING POOL	GARDEN OR TERRACE
OLD TOWN: *Colón.* Map 5 B2. ⓇⓇⓇⓇ Avinguda de la Catedral 7, 08002. 【 *(93) 301 14 04.* FAX *(93) 317 29 15.* From the Colón's front windows guests can watch the *sardana*, the traditional Catalan folk dance, performed in the Plaça de la Catedral, opposite, on Sunday mornings. 🖥 🍽 📺	AE DC MC V	147			
OLD TOWN: *Le Meridien.* Map 5 A1. ⓇⓇⓇⓇ Ramblas 111, 08002. 【 *(93) 318 62 00.* FAX *(93) 301 77 76.* An elegant hotel on the Ramblas, popular with rock and film stars; the Rolling Stones on tour once booked the whole hotel. It has an enormous presidential suite and a business centre. 🖥 🍽 📺 ⚙	AE DC MC V	208	■		
EIXAMPLE: *Felipe II.* Map 3 C4. Ⓡ Carrer de Mallorca 329, 08037. 【 *(93) 458 77 58.* A basic, clean hotel in an old apartment block in the Eixample, with a particularly fine antique lift. Some bedrooms share bathrooms. 🖥 📺		11			
EIXAMPLE: *Gran Vía.* Map 3 A5. ⓇⓇ Avda Gran Via de les Corts Catalanes 642, 08007. 【 *(93) 318 19 00.* FAX *(93) 318 99 97.* A hotel in a late 19th-century building with an ageing grandeur, north of the Plaça de Catalunya adjoining the Passeig de Gràcia. 🖥 🍽 📺 ⚙	AE DC MC V	53	■		
EIXAMPLE: *Catalunya Plaza.* Map 5 A1. ⓇⓇⓇ Plaça de Catalunya 7, 08002. 【 *(93) 317 71 71.* FAX *(93) 317 78 55.* A city-centre hotel popular with business people. The 19th-century building has large sitting rooms decorated with frescoes. 🖥 🍽 📺	AE DC MC V	46			
EIXAMPLE: *Duques de Bergara.* Map 5 A1. ⓇⓇⓇ Carrer de Bergara 11, 08002. 【 *(93) 301 51 51.* FAX *(93) 317 34 42.* A luxury hotel in an exquisite Modernista building, with its original halls and stairways, near the Plaça de la Catedral. It has spacious, well-furnished bedrooms and modern public rooms. 🖥 🍽 📺	AE DC MC V	56			■
EIXAMPLE: *Regente.* Map 3 A4. ⓇⓇⓇ Rambla de Catalunya 76, 08008. 【 *(93) 487 59 89.* FAX *(93) 487 32 27.* A hotel in a Modernista building, with magnificent stained-glass decoration and a small, rooftop pool overlooking Montjuïc. 🖥 🍽 📺	AE DC MC V	78	■	●	
EIXAMPLE: *Rivoli Ramblas.* Map 5 A1. ⓇⓇⓇ Rambla dels Estudis 128, 08002. 【 *(93) 302 66 43.* FAX *(93) 317 50 53.* An elegant hotel on the Ramblas decorated in contemporary style, with spacious bedrooms and city views from a roof terrace. 🖥 🍽 📺	AE DC MC V	89	■	●	
EIXAMPLE: *Clarís.* Map 3 B4. ⓇⓇⓇⓇ Carrer Pau Clarís 150, 08009. 【 *(93) 487 62 62.* FAX *(93) 215 79 70.* Antique kilims and elegant English and French furniture ornament this hotel off the Passeig de Gràcia. It occupies the converted Vedruna Palace and has a private museum of Egyptian art. 🖥 🍽 📺 ⚙	AE DC MC V	121	■	●	■
EIXAMPLE: *Condes de Barcelona.* Map 3 A4. ⓇⓇⓇⓇ Passeig de Gràcia 75, 08008. 【 *(93) 488 22 00.* FAX *(93) 488 06 14.* This Modernista hotel has an impressive pentagonal lobby with a marble floor, illuminated by a skylight. Book in advance. 🖥 🍽 📺	AE DC MC V	109	■	●	■
EIXAMPLE: *Gran Hotel Calderón.* Map 3 A5. ⓇⓇⓇⓇ Rambla de Catalunya 26, 08007. 【 *(93) 301 00 00.* FAX *(93) 317 31 57.* A modern hotel near the Plaça de Catalunya, with spacious, comfortable rooms, indoor and rooftop pools, and a good restaurant. 🖥 🍽 📺 ⚙	AE DC MC V	252	■	●	■
EIXAMPLE: *Majestic.* Map 3 A4. ⓇⓇⓇⓇ Passeig de Gràcia 70, 08008. 【 *(93) 488 17 17.* FAX *(93) 488 18 80.* A hotel in Neo-Classical style in a very chic street (adjoining the Carrer de Valencia). The bedrooms are well equipped and soundproofed. 🖥 🍽 📺	AE DC MC V	329	■	●	■

EIXAMPLE: *Palace.* **Map** 3 B5.   ₧₧₧₧₧   AE 161
Avda Gran Via de les Corts Catalanes 668, 08010. **(** *(93) 318 52 00.* **FAX** *(93) 318 01 48.*   DC
The most elegant of Barcelona's grand hotels, near the Plaça de Catalunya.   MC
The large, luxurious bedrooms are decorated in classic style. 🛏 ▤ TV   V

FURTHER AFIELD (NORTHWEST): *Gran Derby.*   ₧₧₧   AE 41
Loreto 28, 08029. **(** *(93) 322 32 15.* **FAX** *(93) 419 68 20.*   DC
Attractive suites are the only accommodation offered here. There is no   MC
restaurant; guests may dine in the Hotel Derby over the road. 🛏 ▤ TV   V

FURTHER AFIELD (WEST): *Princesa Sofía Intercontinental*   ₧₧₧₧₧   AE 506
Plaça de Pius XII 4, Avda Diagonal, 08028. **(** *(93) 330 71 11.* **FAX** *(93) 330 76 21.*   DC
A vast, luxury hotel decorated in marble, wood and bronze, with one   MC
of its several restaurants on the 19th floor, and a nightclub. 🛏 ▤ TV ♿   V

CATALONIA

ALBONS: *Albons Calm Hotel.*   ₧₧₧₧   AE 32
Ctra Figueres–La Bisbal, 17136 (Girona). **(** *(972) 78 82 99.* **FAX** *(972) 78 81 17.*   DC
An ultramodern, original hotel in the heart of the Empordà region.   MC
The bathrooms are spectacular and the cooking is excellent. Activities   V
include underwater swimming, gliding and horse riding. 🛏 ▤ TV

ANDORRA LA VELLA: *Andorra Park Hotel.*   ₧₧₧₧₧   AE 40
Les Canals 24 (Andorra). **(** *(07-376) 82 09 79.* **FAX** *(07-376) 82 09 83.*   DC
One of Andorra's most luxurious hotels, the Andorra Park is modern   MC
and built into a steep, wooded hillside. It has a library, a swimming   V
pool hewn out of rock, and is beside a department store. 🛏 TV ♿

ARTIES: *Parador Don Gaspar de Portolà.*   ₧₧₧   AE 52
Ctra a Baqueira-Beret, 25599 (Lleida). **(** *(973) 64 08 01.* **FAX** *(973) 64 10 01.*   DC
A modern, warm, comfortable parador, near the Vall d'Arán ski resorts,   MC
ideal for après-ski rest. Beside it is a medieval chapel. 🛏 TV ♿   V

AVINYONET DE PUIGVENTÓS: *Mas Pau.*   ₧₧₧   AE 7
Despoblado, 17500 (Girona). **(** *(972) 54 61 54.* **FAX** *(972) 54 63 26.*   DC
A beautiful hotel in a 17th-century house, surrounded by wooded   MC
farmland. The bedrooms and suites give on to a garden. 🛏 ▤ TV ♿   V

BAQUEIRA-BERET: *Royal Tanau.*   ₧₧₧₧   AE 30
Carretera de Beret, 25598 (Lleida). **(** *(973) 64 44 46.* **FAX** *(973) 64 43 44.*   MC
A luxurious hotel in the Tanau skiing area, with a ski lift to the pistes.   V
It has full après-ski facilities, from whirlpool baths to sun beds. 🛏 TV

BEGUR (BAGUR): *Aigua Blava.*   ₧₧₧₧   AE 85
Platja de Fornells, 17255 (Girona). **(** *(972) 62 20 58.* **FAX** *(972) 62 21 12.*   MC
A charming hotel on a small beach in an attractive spot on the   V
Costa Brava, from which there are marvellous sea views. 🛏 ▤ TV

BOLVIR DE CERDANYA: *Torre del Remei.*   ₧₧₧₧₧   AE 11
Camí Reial, 17463 (Girona). **(** *(972) 14 01 82.* **FAX** *(972) 14 04 49.*   DC
An Art Nouveau mansion with a large garden has become a refined   MC
hotel full of comforts, such as video players in bedrooms. 🛏 ▤ TV   V

CASTELLDEFELS: *Gran Hotel Rey Don Jaime.*   ₧₧₧₧₧   AE 240
Avenida del Hotel 22, 08860 (Barcelona). **(** *(93) 665 13 00.* **FAX** *(93) 665 18 01.*   DC
This hotel is in traditional Mediterranean style with arches and white-   MC
washed walls. It is on a hilltop giving views over the coast. 🛏 ▤ TV ♿   V

CASTELLÓ D'EMPÚRIES: *Allioli.*   ₧₧   AE 42
Urbanització Castell Nou, 17486 (Girona). **(** *(972) 25 03 20.* **FAX** *(972) 25 03 00.*   DC
A 17th-century Catalan farmhouse with considerable character, just off   MC
the main Rosas–Figueres road. The restaurant is a popular place for   V
Sunday lunch among the local people. 🛏 ▤ TV ♿

CUBELLES: *Llicorella.*   ₧₧₧₧   AE 15
Carrer Camí de Sant Antoni 101, 08880 (Barcelona). **(** *(93) 895 00 44.* **FAX** *(93) 895 24 17.*   DC
This elegant hotel has striking sculptures in its garden. Most of the   MC
bedrooms are luxurious and the restaurant is excellent. 🛏 ▤ TV   V

L'ESPLUGA DE FRANCOLÍ: *Hostal del Senglar.*   ₧   AE 40
Pl de Montserrat Canals 1, 43440 (Tarragona) **(** *(977) 87 01 21.* **FAX** *(977) 87 10 12.*   DC
A three-storey whitewashed hotel with a garden. A delicious menu of   MC
dishes traditional to the area is served in the restaurant. 🛏 TV ♿   V

Price categories for a standard double room per night, with tax, breakfast and service included:

℗ under 8,000 ptas
℗℗ 8,000–12,000 ptas
℗℗℗ 12,000–16,000 ptas
℗℗℗℗ 16,000–20,000 ptas
℗℗℗℗℗ over 20,000 ptas

CREDIT CARDS
Indicates which credit cards are accepted: *AE* American Express; *DC* Diners Club; *MC* Master Card/Access; *V* Visa

PARKING
Parking provided by the hotel in a private car park or a private garage on the hotel site or very close by. Some hotels charge for use of private parking facilities.

SWIMMING POOL
Hotel pool outdoors unless otherwise stated.

GARDEN
Hotel with garden, courtyard or terrace, often providing tables for eating outdoors.

	CREDIT CARDS	NUMBER OF ROOMS	PRIVATE PARKING	SWIMMING POOL	GARDEN OR TERRACE
L'ESPLUGA DE FRANCOLÍ: *Masía del Cadet.* ℗℗ Les Masies de Poblet, 43449 (Tarragona). ☎ *(977) 87 08 69.* FAX *(977) 87 03 26.* An inexpensive hotel near the monastery of Poblet in a tastefully renovated, 15th-century house. The bedrooms are austere and quiet. Traditional Catalan food is served in the restaurant. ⛁ ♿	AE DC MC V	12	■	●	■
LA GARRIGA: *Blancafort.* ℗℗℗ Carrer Banys 59, 08530 (Barcelona). ☎ *(93) 871 46 00.* FAX *(93) 871 57 50.* A 19th-century hotel in a relaxing spa town near Barcelona. There are simple bedrooms and games facilities in the lounges. ⛁ ▤ TV ♿	MC V	52	■	●	■
LA GARRIGA: *La Garriga.* ℗℗℗ Carrer Banys 23, 08530 (Barcelona). ☎ *(93) 871 70 86.* FAX *(93) 871 78 87.* Affluent people from Barcelona have been visiting this spa town for its waters since 1876. Children are not admitted to the hotel. ⛁ ▤ TV	AE MC V	22	■	●	■
GRANOLLERS: *Fonda Europa.* ℗℗℗ Carrer Anselm Clavé 1, 08400 (Barcelona). ☎ *(93) 870 03 12.* FAX *(93) 870 79 01.* This small hotel has been an inn for travellers since 1714. The rooms are on the second floor and are decorated in Art Deco style. ⛁ ▤ TV	AE DC MC V	7			
LLORET DE MAR: *Santa Marta.* ℗℗℗℗℗ Platja Santa Cristina, 17310 (Girona). ☎ *(972) 36 49 04.* FAX *(972) 36 92 80.* A modern hotel with tennis courts and other sporting facilities in its grounds. It is in a pine wood that extends to a quiet cove. ⛁ ▤ TV	AE DC MC V	78	■	●	■
MONTSENY: *San Bernat.* ℗℗℗ Finca El Cot, 08460 (Barcelona). ☎ *(93) 847 30 11.* FAX *(93) 847 31 02.* A big country house in the Sierra de Montseny, with a façade cloaked in greenery. There are beautiful grounds with lawns and a pond. ⛁ TV	AE DC MC V	20	■		■
PERAMOLA: *Can Boix.* ℗℗ Afueras, 25790 (Lleida). ☎ *(973) 47 02 66.* FAX *(973) 47 02 66.* Run by a family of distinguished restaurateurs, this simple, good-value hotel is convenient for walking in the Pyrenean foothills. ⛁ ▤ TV ♿	AE DC MC V	69	■	●	
S'AGARÓ: *Hostal de la Gavina.* ℗℗℗℗℗ Plaça de la Rosaleda, 17248 (Girona). ☎ *(972) 32 11 00.* FAX *(972) 32 15 73.* An elegant beach mansion in traditional Mediterranean style with an exclusive feel. It is set in its own estate, with beautiful gardens. ⛁ ▤ TV	AE DC MC V	73	■	●	■
SANTA CRISTINA D'ARO: *Mas Torrellas.* ℗℗ Carretera Platja d'Aro, 17246 (Girona). ☎ *(972) 83 75 26.* FAX *(972) 83 75 27.* An 18th-century country house hotel. Its most comfortable bedroom is in a distinctive yellow tower, built at a later date. ⛁ ▤ TV	AE DC MC V	17	■	●	■
SANT PERE DE RIBES: *Els Sumidors.* ℗℗ Carretera de Vilafranca, 08810 (Barcelona). ☎ *(93) 896 20 61.* On the southern slope of a hill, with views across the landscape of the fertile Penedès wine region, this rustic 18th-century house has atmosphere and a certain charm, but few comforts. ⛁ TV	MC V	9	■	●	■
LA SEU D'URGELL: *El Castell.* ℗℗℗ Carretera N260, 25700 (Lleida). ☎ *(973) 35 07 04.* FAX *(973) 35 15 74.* This sumptuous hotel is a low, modern building beneath the medieval castle of Seu d'Urgell. There are impressive views across the mountains of El Cadí and the ski slopes of Andorra are nearby. ⛁ ▤ TV	AE DC MC V	38	■	●	■
LA SEU D'URGELL: *Parador de La Seu d'Urgell.* ℗℗℗ Carrer Santdomenec 6, 2570 (Lleida). ☎ *(973) 35 20 00.* FAX *(973) 35 23 09.* Only the cloister, now the lounge, remains of a convent that occupied this site close to the 12th-century cathedral of La Seu. The dining room and indoor swimming pool have glass ceilings. ⛁ ▤ TV	AE DC MC V	78	■	●	

SITGES: *La Santa María.*   ₧₧ | AE DC MC V | 53
Passeig Ribera 52, 08870 (Barcelona). ((93) 894 09 99. FAX (93) 894 78 71.
A cheery modern hotel hidden behind an older, five-storey, moulded-plaster frontage. The restaurant has tables on the seafront. 🛏 🍽 TV ♿

SITGES: *Capri Veracruz.*   ₧₧₧ | AE DC MC V | 58
Avinguda de Sofía 13–15, 08870 (Barcelona). ((93) 811 02 67. FAX (93) 894 51 88.
Built in the 1950s near the beach, in one of the quieter parts of Sitges, this hotel has simple bedrooms and a family atmosphere. 🛏 TV

SITGES: *San Sebastián Playa.*   ₧₧₧₧ | AE DC MC V | 51
Carrer Port Alegre 53, 08870 (Barcelona). ((93) 894 86 76. FAX (93) 894 04 30.
This new hotel on the beach near the old part of the town has very attentive staff and comfortable bedrooms. 🛏 🍽 TV ♿

TAVÉRNOLES: *El Banús.*   ₧ | AE MC V | 6
El Banús, 08519 (Barcelona). ((93) 812 20 91. FAX (93) 888 70 12.
A small, partly 15th-century farmhouse, furnished with Banús family heirlooms, offering basic bedrooms, shared bathrooms, and breakfast.

TARRAGONA: *Lauria.*   ₧₧₧ | AE DC MC V | 72
Rambla Nova 20, 43004. ((977) 23 67 12. FAX (977) 23 67 00.
A modern, functional hotel in the town centre and close to the sea, with an elegant entrance under balustraded stone stairs. 🛏 🍽 TV

TORRENT: *Mas de Torrent.*   ₧₧₧₧₧ | AE DC MC V | 30
Afueras, 17123 (Girona). ((972) 30 32 92. FAX (972) 30 32 93.
A superbly converted, 18th-century country house in large, terraced gardens. It has magnificent views. 🛏 TV ♿

TORTOSA: *Parador Castillo de La Zuda.*   ₧₧₧₧ | AE DC MC V | 82
Castillo de la Zuda, 43500 (Tarragona). ((977) 44 44 50. FAX (977) 44 44 58.
A medieval castle built by the Moors makes a magnificent hilltop parador with views of the town and the Río Ebro valley. 🛏 🍽 TV

TREDÒS: *Hotel de Tredòs.*   ₧₧₧₧ | MC V | 37
Carretera a Baqueira-Beret, 25598 (Lleida). ((973) 64 40 14. FAX (973) 64 43 00.
Skiers and mountain walkers find this hotel in the Vall d'Arán good value. It is built of stone and slate in the local style. 🛏 TV ♿

VIELHA (VIELLA): *Parador Valle de Arán.*   ₧₧₧ | AE DC MC V | 135
Carretera del Túnel, 25530 (Lleida). ((973) 64 01 00. FAX (973) 64 11 00.
This modern parador has a semicircular lounge dominated by a large window from which there are magnificent mountain views. 🛏 TV

VILADRAU: *Hostal de la Glòria.*   ₧ | DC MC V | 23
Carrer Torreventosa 12, 17406 (Girona). ((93) 884 90 34. FAX (93) 884 94 65.
A hotel with a family atmosphere in a traditional Catalan house above the Sierra de Montseny. It is full of copper pots and brass lamps. 🛏 TV

VILANOVA I LA GELTRÚ: *César.*   ₧₧₧ | DC MC V | 32
Carrer Isaac Peral 8, 08800 (Barcelona). ((93) 815 11 25. FAX (93) 815 67 19.
This hotel, near the Ribes Roges beach, is owned by two sisters who pay great attention to detail, from the furniture and the fabrics in the bedrooms to the well-known restaurant. 🛏 TV

ARAGÓN

AINSA: *Casa Cambra.*   ₧ | | 17
Morillo de Tou, Ctra Barbastro–Ainsa, 22395 (Huesca). ((& FAX) (974) 50 07 93.
The hotel is one of three in a formerly abandoned Pyrenean village, rebuilt as a holiday complex with a large camp site, restaurants and bars. The village is a centre for almost every mountain sport. 🛏

ALBARRACÍN: *Arabia.*   ₧ | MC V | 21
Calle Bernardo Zapater 2, 44100 (Teruel). ((978) 71 02 12. FAX (978) 71 02 37.
A restored 17th-century school in a picturesque town. Some bedrooms have views of Albarracín's rooftops and its surrounding hills. 🛏 TV

ALBARRACÍN: *Casa de Santiago.*   ₧₧ | V | 9
Calle Subida a las Torres 11, 44100 (Teruel). ((978) 70 03 16.
Albarracín's most beautiful hotel, in a restored mansion near the Plaza Mayor. The cosy interior, decorated with lovely printed fabrics, has iron and wood furniture custom-made by local craftspeople. 🛏

For key to symbols see back flap

Price categories for a standard double room per night, with tax, breakfast and service included:

Ⓟ under 8,000 ptas
ⓅⓅ 8,000–12,000 ptas
ⓅⓅⓅ 12,000–16,000 ptas
ⓅⓅⓅⓅ 16,000–20,000 ptas
ⓅⓅⓅⓅⓅ over 20,000 ptas

CREDIT CARDS
Indicates which credit cards are accepted: *AE* American Express; *DC* Diners Club; *MC* Master Card/Access; *V* Visa
PARKING
Parking provided by the hotel in a private car park or a private garage on the hotel site or very close by. Some hotels charge for use of private parking facilities.
SWIMMING POOL
Hotel pool outdoors unless otherwise stated.
GARDEN
Hotel with garden, courtyard or terrace, often providing tables for eating outdoors.

	CREDIT CARDS	NUMBER OF ROOMS	PRIVATE PARKING	SWIMMING POOL	GARDEN OR TERRACE
ALBARRACÍN: *Albarracín.* ⓅⓅⓅ Calle Azagra, 44100 (Teruel). 🄲 (& FAX) (978) 71 00 11. A 16th-century Gothic mansion in a stepped street of medieval houses. The views from the windows are stunning. 🖪 TV	AE DC MC V	43		●	■
ALCAÑIZ: *Parador de Alcañiz.* ⓅⓅⓅ Castillo de Calatravos, 44600 (Teruel). 🄲 (978) 83 04 00. FAX (978) 83 03 66. This magnificent 12th-century monastery-castle once belonged to the Knights of Calatrava. It is on a hilltop, dominating the town. Its decor is a modern interpretation of medieval castle style. 🖪 ▤ TV 🄳	AE DC MC V	12	■		■
ALQUÉZAR: *Villa de Alquézar.* Ⓟ Pedro Arnal Cavero 12, 22145 (Huesca). 🄲 (974) 31 84 16. FAX (974) 31 84 16. An old house in a medieval village on the Río Vero, near the Sierra de Guara nature reserve. Some rooms have stunning mountain views. 🖪 TV	MC V	20	■		■
BENASQUE: *Ciria.* ⓅⓅ Avenida de los Tilos, 22440 (Huesca). 🄲 (974) 55 16 12. FAX (974) 55 16 86. An efficient, friendly family runs this Pyrenean hotel. It has cosy attic bedrooms and is good value. There are bicycles for hire. 🖪 TV	AE MC V	34	■		■
BIELSA: *Parador de Bielsa.* ⓅⓅⓅ Valle de Pineta de Bielsa, 22350 (Huesca). 🄲 (974) 50 10 11. FAX (974) 50 11 88. A mountain parador beautifully located in wooded country on the edge of Ordesa National Park, opposite Monte Perdido. Inside, it is warm and inviting, with a wood-panelled lounge with leather sofas. 🖪 TV	AE DC MC V	24			
CANFRANC-ESTACIÓN: *Santa Cristina de Somport.* ⓅⓅ Ctra de Francia N330, 22880 (Huesca). 🄲 (974) 37 33 00. FAX (974) 37 33 10. This hotel is near the Somport Pass, which is on one of the main pilgrim routes from France to Santiago de Compostela. In winter guests can hire skis; in summer the hotel arranges guided mountain walks. 🖪 TV 🄳	AE DC MC V	58	■		■
FUENTESPALDA: *Torre del Visco.* ⓅⓅⓅ Apto de Valderrobres, 44587 (Teruel). 🄲 (978) 76 90 15. FAX (978) 76 90 16. A 15th-century semi-fortified farmhouse in a remote river valley on the Teruel/Tarragona border is run as a hotel by an English couple. Room prices include breakfast and dinner based on produce from their farm. 🖪	V	8	■		■
HUESCA: *Pedro I de Aragón.* ⓅⓅⓅ Calle del Parque 34, 22003. 🄲 (974) 22 03 00. FAX (974) 22 00 94. A stylish modern hotel in the city centre, bristling with facilities. The bedrooms are soundproofed and ten have private terraces. 🖪 ▤ TV	AE DC MC V	130	■	●	■
JACA: *Conde Aznar.* ⓅⓅ Paseo de la Constitución 3, 22700 (Huesca). 🄲 (974) 36 10 50. FAX (974) 36 07 97. A simple, hospitable, good-value hotel in an old urban mansion on a classy avenue. It has a good restaurant serving local dishes. 🖪 TV	AE MC V	24			■
JACA: *Gran Hotel.* ⓅⓅⓅ Paseo de la Constitución 1, 22700 (Huesca). 🄲 (974) 36 09 00. FAX (974) 36 40 61. A modern hotel, centrally located next to a park, within reach of the ski slopes around Somport Pass. There is a charge for the car park. 🖪 TV	AE DC MC V	165	■	●	■
MORA DE RUBIELOS: *Jaime I.* ⓅⓅ Plaza de la Villa, 44400 (Teruel). 🄲 (978) 80 00 92. FAX (978) 80 00 92. A handsome stone building with wooden balconies and simple rooms in a town full of mansions on the edge of the Maestrazgo region. 🖪 TV	AE DC MC V	35			
NUÉVALOS: *Monasterio de Piedra.* ⓅⓅ Monasterio de Piedra, 50210 (Zaragoza). 🄲 (976) 84 90 11. FAX (976) 84 90 54. Beside a nature reserve is this former Cistercian monastery, now a hotel. Among its original details are alabaster window panes. 🖪 TV	AE DC MC V	61	■	●	■

SALLENT DE GÁLLEGO: *Almud.* ℗℗ AE DC V **8**
Espadilla 3, 22640 (Huesca). ☎ (& FAX) (974) 48 83 66.
A charming, homely hotel in the Pyrenees. All rooms are decorated
with antiques. The bar is in the former stables in the cellar. 🛏 TV

SALLENT DE GÁLLEGO: *Villa de Sallent.* ℗℗℗ AE DC MC V **40**
Urbanización El Formigal, 22640 (Huesca). ☎ (974) 49 02 23. FAX (974) 49 01 50.
At the foot of the pistes of Formigal ski resort, this family-run hotel is
welcoming at dusk. It has open fires and warm bedrooms. 🛏 TV 🚻

SOS DEL REY CATÓLICO: *Parador de Sos del Rey Católico.* ℗℗℗ AE DC MC V **65**
Paseo del Rey Católico, 50680 (Zaragoza). ☎ (948) 88 80 11. FAX (948) 88 81 00.
The parador, at one end of the medieval wall, blends with the town's
historic architecture and gives fine country views. 🛏 TV 🚻

TERUEL: *Parador de Teruel.* ℗℗℗ AE DC MC V **60**
Ctra a Zaragoza, 44080. ☎ (978) 60 18 00. FAX (978) 60 86 12.
This parador is in leafy surroundings a little outside the city, set back
from a main road. It has a pleasant, covered terrace-bar. 🛏 TV

TERUEL: *Reina Cristina.* ℗℗℗ AE DC MC V **81**
Paseo del Ovalo 1, 44001. ☎ (978) 60 68 60. FAX (978) 60 53 63.
The Reina Cristina is a modern, city-centre hotel, in easy reach of the
main monuments. Some of the bedrooms have terraces. 🛏 ▤ TV 🚻

VILLANÚA: *Faus Hütte.* ℗℗ AE DC MC V **10**
Ctra de Francia, 22870 (Huesca). ☎ (974) 37 81 36. FAX (974) 37 81 98.
This hotel deep in the Pyrenees is owned by a mountain guide. It is a
good base for skiing, hill-walking and other mountain activities. It is
also on the pilgrim's route to Santiago de Compostela. 🛏 TV

ZARAGOZA: *Conde de Aranda.* ℗℗℗ AE DC MC V **85**
Conde de Aranda 48, 50003. ☎ (976) 28 45 00. FAX (976) 28 27 17.
This hotel, not far from the city centre, is comfortable and popular with
business travellers. 🛏 ▤ TV 🚻

ZARAGOZA: *Gran Hotel.* ℗℗℗℗ AE DC MC V **140**
Calle Joaquín Costa 5, 50001. ☎ (976) 22 19 01. FAX (976) 23 67 13.
Zaragoza's city-centre grand hotel was opened in 1929 by Alfonso XIII.
It has colonnades and a magnificent domed salon. 🛏 ▤ TV

ZARAGOZA: *Tibur.* ℗℗℗ AE DC MC V **50**
Plaza de la Seo 2 & 3, 50001. ☎ (976) 20 20 00. FAX (976) 20 20 02.
The Tibur is conveniently located in the old heart of the city, with views
of the Basílica del Pilar. The bedrooms are well equipped. 🛏 ▤ TV 🚻

VALENCIA AND MURCIA

ÁGUILAS: *Carlos III.* ℗℗ AE DC MC V **32**
Calle Rey Carlos III 22, 30880 (Murcia). ☎ (968) 41 16 50. FAX (968) 41 16 58.
A modern town-centre hotel near the beach in a small Murcian resort.
The restaurant serves fish, seafood and other local dishes. 🛏 ▤ TV

ALICANTE (ALACANT): *Palas.* ℗℗ AE DC MC V **39**
Calle Cervantes 5, 03002. ☎ (96) 520 92 11. FAX (96) 514 01 21.
This hotel in an aristocratic mansion built late in the 19th century on
the Explanada, near the beach, the harbour and the city centre. 🛏 TV

ALICANTE (ALACANT): *Sidi San Juan.* ℗℗℗℗℗ AE DC MC V **176**
Playa de San Juan, 03540. ☎ (96) 516 13 00. FAX (96) 516 33 46.
A luxury hotel outside Alicante, with access to a beach through gardens.
The bedrooms have sea views and there is a health farm. 🛏 ▤ TV

ARCHENA: *Termas.* ℗℗℗ **71**
Ctra Balneario, 30600 (Murcia). ☎ (968) 67 01 00. FAX (968) 67 10 02.
Inside, this spa hotel is decorated in a glorious Mudéjar style, with
ornate plasterwork, domes and Moorish arches. Tunnels in the
basement are heated by water gushing from the ground. 🛏 ▤ TV 🚻

BOCAIRENT: *L'Estació de Bocairent.* ℗℗ AE DC MC V **14**
Parque de la Estación, 46880 (Valencia). ☎ (96) 290 52 11. FAX (96) 290 54 23.
A small, comfortable hotel set up by the regional tourist board in an
old railway station on the edge of a fascinating medieval town.
🛏 ▤ TV 🚻

For key to symbols see back flap

Price categories for a standard double room per night, with tax, breakfast and service included:

₧ under 8,000 ptas
₧₧ 8,000–12,000 ptas
₧₧₧ 12,000–16,000 ptas
₧₧₧₧ 16,000–20,000 ptas
₧₧₧₧₧ over 20,000 ptas

CREDIT CARDS
Indicates which credit cards are accepted: *AE* American Express; *DC* Diners Club; *MC* Master Card/Access; *V* Visa
PARKING
Parking provided by the hotel in a private car park or a private garage on the hotel site or very close by. Some hotels charge for use of private parking facilities.
SWIMMING POOL
Hotel pool outdoors unless otherwise stated.
GARDEN
Hotel with garden, courtyard or terrace, often providing tables for eating outdoors.

	Price	CREDIT CARDS	NUMBER OF ROOMS	PRIVATE PARKING	SWIMMING POOL	GARDEN OR TERRACE
CALP: *Venta la Chata.* Carretera de Valencia, 03710 (Alicante). **(** (96) 583 03 08. An old coaching inn on the main road between Alicante and Valencia. The bedrooms are simple, mixing old and new furniture, and some have terraces looking out on a pretty garden.	₧	DC MC V	17	■		■
CARTAGENA: *Los Habaneros.* Calle San Diego 60, 30202 (Murcia). **(** (968) 50 52 50. FAX (968) 50 52 54. Located on the edge of the old part of town, this hotel offers comfort at an affordable price. It also has a popular restaurant.	₧	AE DC MC V	63	■		■
CASTELL DE CASTELLS: *Pensión Castells.* Calle San Vicente 18, 03793 (Alicante). **(** (96) 551 82 54. An old house in an inland village not far from the Costa Blanca. All the rooms are given a loving touch. The British owners offer bed and breakfast, and they take guests walking in the surrounding hills.	₧		4			■
CHULILLA: *Balneario de Chulilla.* Afueras, 46167 (Valencia). **(** (96) 165 70 13. FAX (96) 165 70 31. This riverside spa hotel is an inexpensive place to stop while exploring the woods and hills of inland Valencia. It has all the facilities for a rest-cure, including a sauna, a gym, tennis courts and a Jacuzzi.	₧	V	60	■	●	■
DENIA: *Rosa.* Las Marinas, 03700 (Alicante). **(** (96) 578 15 73. FAX (96) 578 15 73. A modern white villa close to the beach. It was built and is run by a Parisian expatriate who works hard to please his guests. Comfortable rooms have sun-trapping, Florentine-style balconies.	₧₧	MC V	39	■	●	■
ELX: *Huerto del Cura.* Porta de la Morera 14, 03203 (Alicante). **(** (96) 545 80 40. FAX (96) 542 19 10. A secluded hotel in Europe's largest palm tree wood, surrounded by landscaped grounds. The bedrooms are all in Mediterranean-style bungalows. The restaurant is highly regarded.	₧₧₧	AE DC MC V	70	■	●	■
FORCALL: *Palau dels Ossets.* Plaza Mayor 16, 12310 (Castellón). **(** (964) 17 75 24. FAX (964) 17 75 56. A tastefully renovated 16th-century mansion on the main square of a quiet village at the heart of El Maestrat. It has wooden beams, tiled floors and well-equipped bedrooms.	₧₧	V	20	■		
FORTUNA: *Balneario.* Balneario de Fortuna, 30630 (Murcia). **(** (968) 68 50 11. FAX (968) 68 50 87. This hotel, used by visitors to a spa, has the atmosphere of a former grand hotel. It has Art Nouveau doors and a grand staircase. The swimming pool is naturally heated.	₧₧	AE MC V	58	■	●	
LA MANGA DEL MAR MENOR: *Príncipe Felipe.* Hyatt La Manga Club, 30385 (Murcia). **(** (968) 13 72 34. FAX (968) 13 72 72. A luxurious hotel, part of an exclusive resort complex built in the style of a Spanish village. It is surrounded by palm and olive groves, and has 3 golf courses, 18 tennis courts and 4 swimming pools.	₧₧₧₧₧	AE DC MC V	192	■	●	■
MORAIRA: *Swiss Hotel Moraira.* Urbanización Club Moraira, 03724 (Alicante). **(** (96) 574 71 04. FAX (96) 574 70 74. On an estate of holiday villas close to the coast is this exclusive hotel. The bedrooms are spacious with sunny terraces.	₧₧₧₧	AE DC MC V	25	■	●	■
MORATALLA: *Cenajo.* Embalse del Cenajo, 30440 (Murcia). **(** (968) 72 10 11. FAX (968) 72 06 45. At night, silence descends on this creamy-yellow hotel beside the Cenajo dam, in a part of rural Murcia where few foreign tourists stray. Horse riding is one of many activities available.	₧₧	MC V	76	■	●	■

MORELLA: *Cardenal Ram.*   ℗
Cuesta Suñer 1, 12300 (Castellón). ((964) 17 30 85. FAX (964) 17 32 18.
A renovated, 16th-century mansion with stone arches and beamed
ceilings, overlooking the main porticoed street of a historic town. 🚗 TV
MC V — 19

MURCIA: *Conde de Floridablanca.*   ℗℗℗
Princesa 18, 30002. ((968) 21 46 26. FAX (968) 21 32 15.
A comfortable, good-value hotel across the river from the city centre,
furnished with antiques and decorated with stained glass. 🚗 ▤ TV
AE DC MC V — 85

MURCIA: *Arco de San Juan.*   ℗℗℗
Plaza de Ceballos 10, 30003. ((968) 21 04 55. FAX (968) 22 08 09.
The restoration of this hotel near the cathedral has won awards. The
decor combines contemporary materials with antiques. 🚗 ▤ TV
AE DC MC V — 115

PENÁGUILA: *Mas de Pau.*   ℗℗
Ctra Alcoi–Penáguila, 03815 (Alicante). ((96) 551 31 11. FAX (96) 551 31 11.
A 19th-century house in a landscape of almond and olive trees near Alcoi.
It has small bedrooms, some overlooking the Sierra Aitana. 🚗 TV
AE MC V — 18

PEÑÍSCOLA: *Benedicto XIII.*   ℗℗
Urbanización Las Atalayas, 12598 (Castellón). ((964) 48 08 01. FAX (964) 48 95 23.
A white villa in a quiet private estate on a hillside above Peñíscola. Its
terraces and arched windows give views of the town. 🚗 TV &
AE DC MC V — 30

PEÑÍSCOLA: *Hostería del Mar.*   ℗℗℗
Avenida Papa Luna 18, 12598 (Castellón). ((964) 48 06 00. FAX (964) 48 13 63.
Many of the rooms in this modern beach hotel have sea views.
Animated medieval banquets are a.house speciality. 🚗 ▤ TV &
AE DC MC V — 86

PUZOL: *Monte Picayo.*   ℗℗℗℗
Autopista A7, exit 7, 46530 (Valencia). ((96) 142 01 00. FAX (96) 142 21 68.
A luxury hotel close to the Valencia bypass but surrounded by gardens,
with its own casino and bullring. Some of the bedrooms have a private
garden and swimming pool. 🚗 ▤ TV
AE DC MC V — 83

EL SALER: *Parador de El Saler.*   ℗℗℗
Avda de los Pinares 151, 46012 (Valencia). ((96) 161 11 86. FAX (96) 162 70 16.
A modern parador, peacefully situated beside the sea near L'Albufera
and surrounded by a renowned golf course. 🚗 ▤ TV &
AE DC MC V — 58

VALENCIA: *Ad Hoc.*   ℗℗℗
Calle Boix 4, 46003. ((96) 391 91 40. FAX (96) 391 36 67.
A chic hotel in a renovated, soundproofed, 19th-century building in the
historic quarter of the city, near the Río Turia gardens. 🚗 ▤ TV
AE DC MC V — 28

VALENCIA: *Inglés.*   ℗℗℗
Calle Marqués de Dos Aguas 6, 46002. ((96) 351 64 26. FAX (96) 394 02 51.
This convenient city-centre hotel is in the old palace of the Dukes
of Cardona, next to the National Ceramics Museum. All the bedrooms
look on to the street. The restaurant serves Valencian cuisine. 🚗 ▤ TV
AE DC MC V — 62

VALENCIA: *Reina Victoria.*   ℗℗℗℗
Calle Barcas 4, 46002. ((96) 352 04 87. FAX (96) 352 04 87.
In the city centre, near the Plaza del Ayuntamiento, this elegant hotel,
built in the late 19th century, has modern bedrooms. 🚗 ▤ TV
AE DC MC V — 97

LA VILA JOIOSA (VILLAJOYOSA): *El Montíboli.*   ℗℗℗℗
Partida El Montíboli, 03570 (Alicante). ((96) 589 02 50. FAX (96) 589 38 57.
This hotel is perched on a low cliff outside the town, and looks down
on a secluded beach. 🚗 ▤ TV &
AE DC MC V — 53

XÀBIA (JÁVEA): *Parador de Jávea.*   ℗℗℗
Calle Arenal 2, 03730 (Alicante). ((96) 579 02 00. FAX (96) 579 03 08.
A parador in the middle of Arenales beach. The dining room looks
across the terrace to splendid gardens, and the bedroom balconies
have sea views. There are water sports facilities nearby. 🚗 TV
AE DC MC V — 65

XÀBIA (JÁVEA): *Solymar.*   ℗℗
Montañar 1, Auda del Mediterraneo 83, 03730 (Alicante).
((96) 646 1919. FAX (96) 647 1907.
This small hotel lies between Jávea harbour and Arenal beach. It has
simple, but perfectly pleasant bedrooms, some of which have balconies
with sea views. 🚗 ▤ TV &
AE DC MC V — 38

For key to symbols see back flap

Price categories for a standard double room per night, with tax, breakfast and service included:

Ⓟ   under 8,000 ptas
ⓅⓅ   8,000–12,000 ptas
ⓅⓅⓅ   12,000–16,000 ptas
ⓅⓅⓅⓅ   16,000–20,000 ptas
ⓅⓅⓅⓅⓅ over 20,000 ptas

CREDIT CARDS
Indicates which credit cards are accepted: *AE* American Express; *DC* Diners Club; *MC* Master Card/Access; *V* Visa
PARKING
Parking provided by the hotel in a private car park or a private garage on the hotel site or very close by. Some hotels charge for use of private parking facilities.
SWIMMING POOL
Hotel pool outdoors unless otherwise stated.
GARDEN
Hotel with garden, courtyard or terrace, often providing tables for eating outdoors.

MADRID

	CREDIT CARDS	NUMBER OF ROOMS	PRIVATE PARKING	SWIMMING POOL	GARDEN OR TERRACE
OLD MADRID: *Hostal Buenos Aires.* **Map** 1 D1. Ⓟ Gran Vía 61, 28013. ☎ *(91) 542 01 02.* FAX *(91) 542 28 69.* A simple, economical hotel, conveniently located on the busy Gran Vía. The public rooms are pleasantly decorated. Each of the bedrooms has its own balcony or small terrace. 🛏 ▤ TV	AE DC MC V	25			
OLD MADRID: *Inglés.* **Map** 5 A1. ⓅⓅ Calle de Echegaray 8, 28014. ☎ *(91) 429 65 51.* FAX *(91) 420 24 23.* A good-value, family-run hotel with its own garage. The bedrooms facing the street are sunny but the back rooms are quieter. 🛏 TV	AE DC MC V	58	■		
OLD MADRID: *Regente.* **Map** 2 F2. ⓅⓅ Mesonero Romanos 9, 28013. ☎ *(91) 521 29 41.* FAX *(91) 532 30 14.* This convenient, centrally located hotel combines new facilities with old-style furniture. 🛏 ▤ TV	AE DC MC V	145	■		
OLD MADRID: *Carlos V.* **Map** 2 E3. ⓅⓅⓅ Calle Maestro Vitoria 5, 28013. ☎ *(91) 531 41 00.* FAX *(91) 531 37 61.* A city-centre hotel in a pedestrian street beside the Puerta del Sol, run by a family. There are interconnecting bedrooms, family rooms, rooms with balconies and top-floor rooms with sizeable sun terraces. 🛏 ▤ TV	AE DC MC V	67			
OLD MADRID: *Tryp Gran Vía.* **Map** 2 F2. ⓅⓅⓅ Gran Vía 25, 28013. ☎ *(91) 522 11 21.* FAX *(91) 521 24 24.* A chain hotel in one of the city's busiest streets. Some of the furniture is in the style of the 1960s and 1970s. 🛏 ▤ TV	AE DC MC V	174			
OLD MADRID: *Tryp Rex.* **Map** 2 E2. ⓅⓅⓅⓅ Gran Vía 43, 28013. ☎ *(91) 547 48 00.* FAX *(91) 547 12 38.* A chain hotel in an old building between the Plaza del Callao and the Plaza de España, close to a large public car park. It has spacious public rooms and well-equipped bedrooms, each with its own safe. 🛏 ▤ TV	AE DC MC V	144			
OLD MADRID: *Arosa.* **Map** 2 F2. ⓅⓅⓅⓅ Calle de la Salud 21, 28013. ☎ *(91) 532 16 00.* FAX *(91) 531 31 27.* This centrally located hotel off the Gran Vía and the Puerta del Sol is popular with international and business visitors to Madrid. All the bedrooms are comfortable and well soundproofed. 🛏 ▤ TV	AE DC MC V	139	■		
OLD MADRID: *Emperador.* **Map** 2 E2. ⓅⓅⓅⓅ Gran Vía 53, 28013. ☎ *(91) 547 28 00.* FAX *(91) 547 28 17.* A popular hotel, ideally placed for exploring the city centre. The spacious bedrooms are quiet, in spite of the traffic below. There is a rooftop swimming pool. 🛏 ▤ TV	AE DC MC V	232	■	●	
BOURBON MADRID: *Mora.* **Map** 5 C2. ⓅⓅ Paseo del Prado 32, 28014. ☎ *(91) 420 15 69.* FAX *(91) 420 05 64.* A 1930s hotel with an attractive entrance. Its rooms and facilities are functional, but its prices are low and it is centrally located, near the Jardín Botánico and the Prado. 🛏 ▤ TV	AE DC MC V	62			
BOURBON MADRID: *Palace.* **Map** 5 B1. ⓅⓅⓅⓅ Plaza de las Cortes 7, 28014. ☎ *(91) 360 80 00.* FAX *(91) 360 81 00.* This gracious *belle époque* hotel with a glass dome and a colonnade, has accommodated statesmen and the spy, Mata Hari. The bedrooms are elegant and the service welcoming and efficient. 🛏 ▤ TV ♿	AE DC MC V	455	■		■
BOURBON MADRID: *Pintor.* **Map** 3 D3. ⓅⓅⓅⓅ Calle Goya 79, 28001. ☎ *(91) 435 75 45.* FAX *(91) 576 81 57.* The lobby of this hotel, in a modern city block off the Plaza de Colón, a stroll from the Parque del Retiro, is in mock-Hawaiian style. 🛏 ▤ TV	AE MC V	176	■		

BOURBON MADRID: *Reina Victoria*. Map 5 A1. ⓅⓅⓅⓅ
Plaza Santa Ana 14, 28012. 【 *(91) 531 45 00.* FAX *(91) 522 03 07.*
Ernest Hemingway once lodged in this historic hotel, a graceful edifice
and a traditional haunt of bullfighting aficionados. 🖼 ▤ TV ♿
AE DC MC V — 201

BOURBON MADRID: *Ritz*. Map 5 C1. ⓅⓅⓅⓅ
Plaza de la Lealtad 5, 28014. 【 *(91) 521 28 57.* FAX *(91) 532 87 76.*
Inaugurated in 1910 as a hotel for aristocrats, the Ritz is still one of
Spain's most elegant hotels *(see p274).* It has an ornate, circular foyer
and a terrace garden, and offers musical teas and brunches. 🖼 ▤ TV
AE DC MC V — 158

BOURBON MADRID: *Suecia*. Map 3 B5. ⓅⓅⓅⓅ
Calle del Marqués de Casa Riera 4, 28014. 【 *(91) 531 69 00.* FAX *(91) 521 71 41.*
Centrally located near the Puerta del Sol, the Suecia has a small, seventh-
floor terrace for relaxing and sunbathing. 🖼 ▤ TV
AE DC MC — 128

BOURBON MADRID: *Suite Prado*. Map 5 A1. ⓅⓅⓅⓅ
Manuel Fernández y González 10, 28014. 【 *(91) 420 23 18.* FAX *(91) 420 05 59.*
A stylish apartment hotel of luxurious suites a short distance from the
Prado and the Museo Thyssen-Bornemisza. 🖼 ▤ TV
AE DC MC — 18

BOURBON MADRID: *Villa Real*. Map 5 B1. ⓅⓅⓅⓅ
Plaza de las Cortes 10, 28014. 【 *(91) 420 37 67.* FAX *(91) 420 25 47.*
Located close to the Prado, this stylish hotel is housed in an early 19th-
century building. The public areas are furnished with mahogany
reproduction furniture and embroideries of pastoral scenes. 🖼 ▤ TV
AE DC MC V — 115

BOURBON MADRID: *Wellington*. Map 4 F4. ⓅⓅⓅⓅ
Calle de Velázquez 8, 28001. 【 *(91) 575 44 00.* FAX *(91) 576 41 64.*
A stylish hotel built in the early 1950s close to the Parque del Retiro.
It is a meeting place for people interested in bullfighting. 🖼 ▤ TV
AE DC MC V — 288

FURTHER AFIELD (EAST): *Alcalá*. ⓅⓅⓅⓅ
Calle de Alcalá 66, 28009. 【 *(91) 435 10 60.* FAX *(91) 435 11 05.*
A hotel with a friendly atmosphere across the street from the Parque
del Retiro. The back bedrooms overlook a pretty garden. 🖼 ▤ TV
AE DC MC V — 153

FURTHER AFIELD (EAST): *Colón*. ⓅⓅⓅⓅ
Calle Doctor Esquerdo 119, 28007. 【 *(91) 573 59 00.* FAX *(91) 573 08 09.*
A comfortable hotel in a tower block between the Parque del Retiro
and the Parque de Roma. It has a gym and business facilities. 🖼 ▤ TV
AE DC MC V — 389

FURTHER AFIELD (NORTH): *Hostal Sil*. Map 3 A4. Ⓟ
Calle Fuencarral 95, 28004. 【 *(91) 448 89 72.* FAX *(91) 447 48 29.*
In a lively part of town, this is a comfortable, convenient hotel with
quality bedroom and bathroom furnishings, but low prices. 🖼 ▤ TV
AE DC MC V — 20

FURTHER AFIELD (NORTH): *Mónaco*. Map 3 B4. ⓅⓅ
Calle Barbieri 5, 28004. 【 *(91) 522 46 30.* FAX *(91) 521 16 01.*
The decor of this hotel, formerly Madrid's most famous high-class
brothel, is unashamedly kitsch. The bedrooms still have some of their
original decadent features. 🖼 ▤ TV
AE DC MC — 32

FURTHER AFIELD (NORTH): *Serrano*. Map 4 E1. ⓅⓅⓅⓅ
Calle de Marqués de Villamejor 8, 28006. 【 *(91) 435 52 00.* FAX *(91) 435 48 49.*
The grey façade belies the elegant interior, with some antiques among
the furniture. The bedrooms are large and comfortable. 🖼 ▤ TV
AE DC MC V — 34

FURTHER AFIELD (NORTH): *Castellana Intercontinental*. ⓅⓅⓅⓅ
Paseo de la Castellana 49, 28046. 【 *(91) 310 02 00.* FAX *(91) 319 58 53.*
This hotel in Madrid's commercial centre is a favourite with business
travellers. Guests can choose between two restaurants. 🖼 ▤ TV ♿
AE DC MC V — 313

FURTHER AFIELD (NORTH): *Miguel Ángel*. ⓅⓅⓅⓅ
Calle Miguel Ángel 31, 28010. 【 *(91) 442 81 99.* FAX *(91) 442 53 20.*
Beside the Paseo de la Castellana, the Miguel Ángel combines modern
comfort with classic style. One of its two fine restaurants holds dinner
dances until 3am. 🖼 ▤ TV ♿
AE DC MC V — 278

FURTHER AFIELD (NORTH): *Santo Mauro*. ⓅⓅⓅⓅ
Calle Zurbano 36, 28010. 【 *(91) 319 69 00.* FAX *(91) 308 54 77.*
This palace, built in 1894 in one of Madrid's most elegant streets, has
housed embassies. It has a swimming pool beneath a vaulted basement
ceiling, and a restaurant occupies the former library. 🖼 ▤ TV ♿
AE DC MC V — 36

Price categories for a standard double room per night, with tax, breakfast and service included:

Ⓟ under 8,000 ptas
ⓅⓅ 8,000–12,000 ptas
ⓅⓅⓅ 12,000–16,000 ptas
ⓅⓅⓅⓅ 16,000–20,000 ptas
ⓅⓅⓅⓅⓅ over 20,000 ptas

CREDIT CARDS
Indicates which credit cards are accepted: *AE* American Express; *DC* Diners Club; *MC* Master Card/Access; *V* Visa
PARKING
Parking provided by the hotel in a private car park or a private garage on the hotel site or very close by. Some hotels charge for use of private parking facilities.
SWIMMING POOL
Hotel pool outdoors unless otherwise stated.
GARDEN
Hotel with garden, courtyard or terrace, often providing tables for eating outdoors.

	CREDIT CARDS	NUMBER OF ROOMS	PRIVATE PARKING	SWIMMING POOL	GARDEN OR TERRACE
FURTHER AFIELD (NORTH): *Villamagna.* ⓅⓅⓅⓅ Paseo de la Castellana 22, 28046. 【 *(91) 587 12 34.* ℻ *(91) 575 95 04.* The Villamagna combines 18th-century decor with modern luxury, and is ringed by gardens. It is popular with business people. 🔌 ▤ TV ♿	AE DC MC V	182	▪		▪
FURTHER AFIELD (NORTHEAST): *Conde de Orgaz.* ⓅⓅⓅ Avenida Moscatelar 24, 28043. 【 *(91) 388 40 99.* ℻ *(91) 388 00 09.* A modern hotel, with big, comfortable bedrooms, near to the airport and the Campo de las Naciones Exhibition Centre. 🔌 ▤ TV ♿	AE DC MC V	90	▪		
FURTHER AFIELD (NORTHWEST): *Tirol.* ⓅⓅ Calle de Marqués de Urquijo 4, 28008. 【 *(91) 548 19 00.* ℻ *(91) 541 39 58.* A good-value hotel, conveniently located off the Plaza de España and near the student district. The bedrooms are spacious and clean. 🔌 ▤	MC V	97	▪		
FURTHER AFIELD (NORTHWEST): *Monte Real.* ⓅⓅⓅⓅ Calle Arroyo Fresno 17, 28035. 【 *(91) 316 21 40.* ℻ *(91) 316 39 34.* Situated in a residential area near the Puerta de Hierro golf course, this imposing modern hotel has a peaceful atmosphere. Its balconies overlook the swimming pool and gardens. 🔌 ▤ TV ♿	AE DC MC V	80	▪	●	▪
FURTHER AFIELD (SOUTHEAST): *Agumar.* Map 6 F4. ⓅⓅⓅ Paseo de Reina Cristina 7, 28014. 【 *(91) 552 69 00.* ℻ *(91) 433 60 95.* A stylish hotel near the big museums, with its own collection of good paintings and carpets from the Real Fábrica de Tapices. 🔌 ▤ TV	AE DC MC V	245	▪		
FURTHER AFIELD (SOUTHWEST): *Reyes Católicos.* Map 1 C5. ⓅⓅⓅ Calle del Ángel 18, 28005. 【 *(91) 365 86 00.* ℻ *(91) 365 98 67.* This modern, central hotel is popular and always very busy. Children are made welcome. The bedroom windows are double-glazed for soundproofing. There are views of the city from the roof terrace. 🔌 ▤ TV	AE DC V	38	▪		
MADRID PROVINCE					
ALAMEDA DEL VALLE: *La Posada de Alameda.* ⓅⓅⓅ Calle Grande 34, 28749. 【 *(91) 869 13 37.* ℻ *(91) 869 01 63.* A sensitively restored farmhouse in the tranquil Lozoya valley, about an hour's drive from Madrid. All the bedrooms are well equipped and some have views of the countryside. Two are in converted silos. 🔌 TV	AE MC V	22	▪		▪
CHINCHÓN: *Parador de Chinchón.* ⓅⓅⓅⓅ Avenida del Generalísimo 1, 28370. 【 *(91) 894 08 36.* ℻ *(91) 894 09 08.* This converted 17th-century monastery has immensely thick walls and is built round an airy green courtyard. Delightful details to look out for include *azulejos (see p420)*, frescoes and antiques. 🔌 ▤ TV	AE DC MC V	38	▪	●	▪
RASCAFRÍA: *Santa María de El Paular.* ⓅⓅⓅⓅ El Paular, 28741. 【 *(91) 869 10 11.* ℻ *(91) 869 10 06.* This hotel occupies part of a Benedictine monastery in a peaceful corner of the Guadarrama mountains. A *mesón* (bar-restaurant) offers an informal alternative to the dining room. 🔌 TV	AE DC MC V	58	▪	●	▪
SAN LORENZO DE EL ESCORIAL: *Victoria Palace.* ⓅⓅⓅⓅ Calle Juan de Toledo 4, 28200. 【 *(91) 890 15 11.* ℻ *(91) 890 12 48.* A short walk from the 16th-century palace of El Escorial, this stylish and elegant hotel offers magnificent views from the bedrooms. An open fire warms the lounge in winter. 🔌 TV	AE DC MC V	87	▪	●	
TORREJÓN DE ARDOZ: *La Casa Grande.* ⓅⓅⓅⓅ Calle Madrid 2, 28850. 【 *(91) 675 39 00.* ℻ *(91) 675 06 91.* This luxurious hotel in a 16th-century house is decorated with antiques which once belonged to the Russian royal family. Catherine the Great is said to have slept in the bed now in the main suite. 🔌 ▤ TV	AE DC MC V	9	▪		▪

CASTILLA Y LEÓN

	Price	Cards	Rooms			
AGUILAR DE CAMPOO: *Posada de Santa María la Real.* Avenida Cervera, 34800 (Palencia). ((979) 12 20 00. Part of the Institute of Romanesque Studies is in this monastery; the hotel entrance is at the back and not signposted. The bedrooms are small and plain, with garden views. The atmosphere is friendly. ☎ TV	₧	V	18	▪		▪
LA ALBERCA: *Las Batuecas.* Carretera de las Batuecas, 37624 (Salamanca). ((923) 41 51 88. FAX (923) 41 50 55. On the edge of a pretty village, deep in a green valley, this hotel is a base for touring the Sierra de la Peña de Francia. It is a stone and wood building with a first-floor covered terrace. ☎ ▤ TV	₧	V	24			▪
ASTORGA: *Gaudí.* Plaza Eduardo de Castro 6, 24700 (León). ((987) 61 56 54. FAX (987) 61 50 40. This stylish hotel is on the same square as Gaudí's Neo-Gothic Bishop's Palace. The bedrooms overlook the palace and the cathedral. ☎ TV &	₧₧	AE DC MC V	35	▪		
ÁVILA: *Hostería de Bracamonte.* Calle Bracamonte 6, 05001. ((920) 25 12 80. A charming, traditionally Castilian hotel with exposed beams and tiled floors. It is in a quiet location, close to the cathedral and the town walls. The bedrooms are attractively decorated. ☎ TV	₧₧	AE MC V	20	▪		
ÁVILA: *Parador de Ávila.* C/ Marqués de Canales de Chozas 2, 05001. ((920) 21 13 40. FAX (920) 22 61 66. A parador in a 15th-century mansion next to Ávila's walls. From some rooms guests can watch storks nest on a gateway in spring. ☎ ▤ TV	₧₧₧	AE DC MC V	61	▪		▪
ÁVILA: *Palacio Valderrábanos.* Plaza de la Catedral 9, 05001. ((920) 21 10 23. FAX (920) 25 16 91. A spacious, sedate hotel in a stately 15th-century mansion beside the cathedral. There is a suite in the watchtower. ☎ ▤ TV	₧₧₧₧	AE DC MC V	73	▪		
BENAVENTE: *Parador de Benavente.* Paseo de Ramón y Cajal, 49600 (Zamora). ((980) 63 03 00. FAX (980) 63 03 03. Only the Tower of the Snail remained of Benavente castle in the wake of Napoleon's troops. As part of the parador, it now accommodates an extraordinary lounge with a Mudéjar ceiling from a church. ☎ ▤ TV &	₧₧₧	AE DC MC V	30	▪		▪
EL BURGO DE OSMA: *Virrey II.* Calle Mayor 4, 42300 (Soria). ((975) 34 13 11. FAX (975) 34 08 55. A lavish hotel near the old town. It is very comfortable, spotlessly clean and has efficient, friendly staff and a good restaurant. It makes an excellent base for exploring the province of Soria. ☎ TV &	₧₧₧	AE DC MC V	52	▪		
BURGOS: *Mesón del Cid.* Plaza de Santa María 8, 09003. ((947) 20 87 15. FAX (947) 26 94 60. This stylish hotel, across a little square from the cathedral, is dedicated to the conquering medieval hero, El Cid. ☎ ▤ TV	₧₧₧	AE DC MC V	28	▪		
BURGOS: *Landa Palace.* Carretera Madrid–Irún, 09001. ((947) 20 63 43. FAX (947) 26 46 76. An extravagant hotel on the city outskirts. The authentic-looking stone vaults roofing the dining room and the pool are 1960s, not Gothic; but the medieval tower was transported from a nearby village. ☎ ▤ TV &	₧₧₧₧₧	MC V	42	▪	●	▪
CASTRILLO DE LOS POLVAZARES: *Cuca la Vaina.* El Jardín, 24718 (León). ((987) 69 10 78. FAX (987) 69 10 78. A quiet, charming hotel occupying a renovated, stylishly decorated stone house in a well-preserved village in the Maragato region. ☎	₧	V	7			
CIUDAD RODRIGO: *Parador de Ciudad Rodrigo.* Plaza del Castillo 1, 37500 (Salamanca). ((923) 46 01 50. FAX (923) 46 04 04. This, the first parador to be installed in a historic building, preserves some of the atmosphere of a 12th-century castle. The prize suite has a circular bedroom with a domed roof. ☎ ▤ TV	₧₧₧₧	AE DC MC V	27	▪		▪
COLLADO HERMOSO: *Molino de Río Viejo.* Carretera N110, 40170 (Segovia). ((921) 40 30 63. FAX (921) 40 30 51. A cosy hotel in an old mill among poplars beside the Río Viejo is a good base for exploring the countryside of Segovia province. There are horses available for riding enthusiasts. Booking is essential. ☎	₧₧	AE V	7	▪		▪

Price categories for a standard double room per night, with tax, breakfast and service included:

® under 8,000 ptas
®® 8,000–12,000 ptas
®®® 12,000–16,000 ptas
®®®® 16,000–20,000 ptas
®®®®® over 20,000 ptas

CREDIT CARDS
Indicates which credit cards are accepted: *AE* American Express; *DC* Diners Club; *MC* Master Card/Access; *V* Visa

PARKING
Parking provided by the hotel in a private car park or a private garage on the hotel site or very close by. Some hotels charge for use of private parking facilities.

SWIMMING POOL
Hotel pool outdoors unless otherwise stated.

GARDEN
Hotel with garden, courtyard or terrace, often providing tables for eating outdoors.

	Price	CREDIT CARDS	NUMBER OF ROOMS	PRIVATE PARKING	SWIMMING POOL	GARDEN OR TERRACE
COVARRUBIAS: *Arlanza.* Calle Mayor 11, 09346 (Burgos). 🕻 *(947) 40 64 41.* 📠 *(947) 40 63 59.* The Arlanza overlooks a cobbled pedestrian square in a medieval village. It offers simple accommodation in an old building with black beams and a handsome staircase. Mountain food is served, including wild boar. 🛏	®®	AE DC MC V	38			▦
HOYOS DEL ESPINO: *El Milano Real.* Toleo, 05634 (Ávila). 🕻 *(920) 34 91 08.* 📠 *(920) 34 91 56.* A personal touch, a relaxed atmosphere and silent nights make Milano Real a good holiday hotel. Excursions on horseback are organized along packhorse tracks in the picturesque Sierra de Gredos. 🛏 📺	®	DC V	14	▦		▦
LEÓN: *Alfonso V.* Avenida Padre Isla 1, 24002. 🕻 *(987) 22 09 00.* 📠 *(987) 22 12 44.* Inside, this comfortable hotel in the city centre is contemporary in style. An extravagant, curvaceous staircase giving some interesting perspectives is its most impressive feature. 🛏 ☰ 📺	®®®	AE DC MC V	62			
LEÓN: *Parador de León.* Plaza de San Marcos 7, 24001. 🕻 *(987) 23 73 00.* 📠 *(987) 23 34 58.* This parador is in the Hostal San Marcos, a former convent and one of Spain's loveliest Renaissance buildings. It has a magnificent hall with a coffered ceiling and luxurious old and modern bedrooms. 🛏 📺 ♿	®®®®®	AE DC MC V	229	▦		▦
NAVARREDONDA DE GREDOS: *Parador de Gredos.* Sierra de Gredos, 05132 (Ávila). 🕻 *(920) 34 80 48.* 📠 *(920) 34 82 05.* Inaugurated in 1928 by Alfonso XIII, this was the first parador in Spain. Its setting is a beautiful pine wood in the Sierra de Gredos. It is restful and a good base for exploring the surrounding mountains. 🛏 📺 ♿	®®®	AE DC MC V	77	▦		▦
PEDRAZA DE LA SIERRA: *El Hotel de la Villa.* Calle Calzada 5, 40172 (Segovia). 🕻 *(921) 50 86 51.* 📠 *(921) 50 86 53.* No two bedrooms in this charming hotel are alike. All are exquisitely decorated with floral wallpapers and furnished with antiques, four-poster beds and cosy armchairs. 🛏 ☰ 📺	®®®	AE DC MC V	24	▦		
PEDRAZA DE LA SIERRA: *La Posada de Don Mariano.* Calle Mayor 14, 40172 (Segovia). 🕻 *(921) 50 98 86.* 📠 *(921) 50 98 86.* It is hard to nominate the best hotel in this lovely village. Don Mariano and the Hotel de la Villa are the work of the same decorator. Every room looks like something out of a decor magazine. 🛏 📺	®®®	AE DC MC V	18			▦
PONFERRADA: *El Temple.* Avenida de Portugal 2, 24400 (León). 🕻 *(987) 41 00 58.* 📠 *(987) 42 35 25.* El Temple's façade is a replica of the town's Templar castle. The decor evokes the Middle Ages with antiques and stone walls. 🛏 ☰ 📺 ♿	®®®	AE DC MC V	114	▦		▦
SALAMANCA: *Las Torres.* Plaza Mayor 26, 37002. 🕻 *(923) 21 21 00.* 📠 *(923) 21 21 01.* The restaurant of this hotel overlooks Salamanca's magnificent Plaza Mayor. Guests can take advantage of many extras, from a rapid clothes valeting service to complementary toiletries. 🛏 ☰ 📺 ♿	®®®	AE DC MC V	44	▦		▦
SALAMANCA: *Rector.* Paseo del Rector Esperabé 10, 37008. 🕻 *(923) 21 84 82.* 📠 *(923) 21 40 08.* The façade looks old but the hotel was built in the 1940s by an architect who specialized in reproducing old styles. Inside, leather sofas and stained glass suggest restrained elegance. 🛏 ☰ 📺	®®®®	AE DC MC V	13	▦		
SALAMANCA: *Gran Hotel.* Plaza Poeta Iglesias 3, 37001. 🕻 *(923) 21 35 00.* 📠 *(923) 21 35 00.* A hotel with spacious, quiet bedrooms near the spectacular Plaza Mayor, popular with bullfighters and their entourages. 🛏 ☰ 📺 ♿	®®®®	AE DC MC V	137	▦		▦

Santa María de Huerta: *Santa María de Huerta.* ℗℗℗ MC V 40
Carretera NII, 42260 (Soria). ☏ *(975) 32 70 11.* FAX *(975) 32 70 11.*
Beside the Santa María de Huerta monastery is this former parador,
now a private hotel, with hand-painted bedroom furniture. Guests can
walk, fish and cycle in the locality. ▤ ▤ TV ⓑ

Santa María de Mave: *Hostería El Convento.* ℗ AE MC V 25
Santa María de Mave, 34422 (Palencia). ☏ *(979) 12 36 11.* FAX *(979) 12 54 92.*
Just off the N661 south of Aguilar is this family-run hotel in a former
convent in pretty countryside. Several public areas have decorative
stonework. Traditional Castilian food is served in the restaurant. ▤

Santo Domingo de Silos: *Tres Coronas de Silos.* ℗℗ AE MC V 16
Plaza Mayor 6, 09610 (Burgos). ☏ *(947) 39 00 47.* FAX *(947) 39 00 65.*
A modest inn in an 18th-century mansion dominating the village square,
with an arched doorway and a proud coat of arms. Bare stone walls
and seasoned wood lend atmosphere to the interior. ▤

Segovia: *Infanta Isabel.* ℗℗℗ AE DC MC V 29
Plaza Mayor, 40001. ☏ *(921) 44 31 05.* FAX *(921) 43 32 40.*
A modern hotel in *fin de siècle* style, complemented by traditional
Segovian decor. The bedrooms are cosy. ▤ ▤ TV

Segovia: *Los Linajes.* ℗℗℗ AE DC MC V 55
Calle Doctor Velasco 9, 40003. ☏ *(921) 46 04 75.* FAX *(921) 46 04 79.*
Hidden behind an ancient half-timbered, red-brick façade is a modern
hotel which steps down the hillside beside the city walls in eight levels.
The higher your room level, the better the view. ▤ TV ⓑ

Segovia: *Parador de Segovia.* ℗℗℗℗ AE DC MC V 113
Carretera de Valladolid, 40003. ☏ *(921) 44 37 37.* FAX *(921) 43 73 62.*
This luxury parador has been strategically sited just outside Segovia so
that guests can enjoy magnificent views of the city while sunbathing in
the gardens. Facilities include a gym and an indoor pool. ▤ ▤ TV ⓑ

Sigueruelo: *Posada de Sigueruelo.* ℗℗ V 6
Calle Badén 40, 40590 (Segovia). ☏ *(921) 50 81 35.*
Breakfast and dinner are included in the room price of this rural house.
The owners organize riding, cycling, walking and canoeing. ▤

Solosancho: *Sancho de Estrada.* ℗℗ AE DC MC V 12
Castillo de Villaviciosa, 05130 (Ávila). ☏ *(920) 29 10 82.* FAX *(920) 29 10 82.*
The medieval castle of Villaviciosa, built to defend the Roman roads
over the Sierra de Gredos, has been restored. There are coats of
arms and other medieval touches in the bedrooms. ▤ TV

Soria: *Parador de Soria.* ℗℗℗ AE DC MC V 34
Parque del Castillo, 42005. ☏ *(975) 24 08 00.* FAX *(975) 24 08 03.*
The image and examples of the work of the Spanish poet, Antonio
Machado, decorate the walls of this parador in a hilltop park. It over-
looks the wooded Duero valley. ▤ TV

Valladolid: *Lasa.* ℗℗ AE MC V 62
Calle Acera de Recoletos 21, 47004. ☏ *(983) 39 02 55.* FAX *(983) 30 25 61.*
A renovated, 19th-century apartment block in the city centre. The
bedrooms are double-glazed to reduce street noise. ▤ ▤ TV

Villafranca del Bierzo: *Parador de Villafranca.* ℗℗℗ AE DC MC V 40
Avenida de Calvo Sotelo, 24500 (León). ☏ *(987) 54 01 75.* FAX *(987) 54 00 10.*
This rural parador has well-kept gardens and an attractive dining room.
The town was founded by French pilgrims and is traditionally a stop
on the pilgrimage route to Santiago de Compostela. ▤ TV

Zamora: *Hostería Real de Zamora.* ℗℗℗ AE MC V 18
Cuesta de Pizarro 7, 49027. ☏ *(980) 53 45 45.* FAX *(980) 53 45 45.*
The Inquisition once occupied this 16th-century mansion beside the
city wall and near the Río Duero. Now it is a good-value hotel with a
pretty courtyard at its centre. Basque cooking is served. ▤ TV

Zamora: *Parador de Zamora.* ℗℗℗℗ AE DC MC V 52
Plaza de Viriato 5, 49001. ☏ *(980) 51 44 97.* FAX *(980) 53 00 63.*
A city-centre parador in a Renaissance mansion. From a magnificent
courtyard bordered by carved stone pillars, stone stairs lead to a
sunny gallery furnished with antiques and pot plants. ▤ ▤ TV ⓑ

Price categories for a standard double room per night, with tax, breakfast and service included:

Ⓟ under 8,000 ptas
ⓅⓅ 8,000–12,000 ptas
ⓅⓅⓅ 12,000–16,000 ptas
ⓅⓅⓅⓅ 16,000–20,000 ptas
ⓅⓅⓅⓅⓅ over 20,000 ptas

CREDIT CARDS
Indicates which credit cards are accepted: *AE* American Express; *DC* Diners Club; *MC* Master Card/Access; *V* Visa
PARKING
Parking provided by the hotel in a private car park or a private garage on the hotel site or very close by. Some hotels charge for use of private parking facilities.
SWIMMING POOL
Hotel pool outdoors unless otherwise stated.
GARDEN
Hotel with garden, courtyard or terrace, often providing tables for eating outdoors.

CASTILLA-LA MANCHA

	CREDIT CARDS	NUMBER OF ROOMS	PRIVATE PARKING	SWIMMING POOL	GARDEN OR TERRACE
ALARCÓN: *Parador de Alarcón.* ⓅⓅⓅ Avda Amigos de los Castillos 3, 16213 (Cuenca). ☎ (969) 33 03 15. FAX (969) 33 03 03. A medieval fortress stunningly located above the Júcar valley, on the edge of the plains of La Mancha. The lounge and dining room are vaulted chambers with thick walls. 🖫 ▤ TV	AE DC MC V	13	■		■
ALBACETE: *Los Llanos.* ⓅⓅⓅ Avenida de España 9, 02002. ☎ (967) 22 37 50. FAX (967) 23 46 07. A modern hotel overlooking a verdant park. It has a disco, bingo, a hair salon and a giant video screen in the TV room. 🖫 ▤ TV	AE DC MC V	102	■		
ALBACETE: *Parador de Albacete.* ⓅⓅ Carretera N301, 02000. ☎ (967) 24 53 21. FAX (967) 24 32 71. A purpose-built parador with shady terraces and a pool, decorated with ox yokes and other rural implements. 🖫 ▤ TV	AE DC MC V	70	■	●	■
ALMAGRO: *Almagro.* ⓅⓅⓅ Carretera de Bolaños, 13270 (Ciudad Real). ☎ (926) 86 00 11. FAX (926) 86 06 18. This chain hotel in the new town is a two-storey brick building with a balcony. It offers business services and bicycles for hire. 🖫 ▤ TV ♿	AE DC MC V	50	■	●	■
ALMAGRO: *Parador de Almagro.* ⓅⓅⓅⓅ Ronda de San Francisco 31, 13270 (Ciudad Real). ☎ (926) 86 01 00. FAX (926) 86 01 50. One of Spain's most charming paradors is in a 16th-century convent. Most bedrooms look on to one of 14 courtyards. A lace maker works in one courtyard, keeping the town's tradition alive. 🖫 ▤ TV	AE DC MC V	55	■	●	■
AYNA: *Felipe II.* Ⓟ Avenida Manuel Carrera 9, 02125 (Albacete). ☎ (967) 29 50 83. FAX (967) 29 51 12. The semicircular layout of this modern, family-run hotel in the mountains of Albacete allows every bedroom to have a balcony giving a panoramic view of the town and the valley. 🖫 TV		42	■	●	■
BALLESTEROS DE CALATRAVA: *Palacio de la Serna.* Ⓟ Calle Cervantes 18, 13432 (Ciudad Real). ☎ (926) 84 22 08. FAX (926) 84 22 24. An 18th-century farm on the plains of La Mancha, in a mix of Castilian and modern styles. It is quiet and comfortable. There are excursions on horseback and on mountain bikes into the nearby hills. 🖫 ▤ TV ♿	V	15	■	●	■
BETETA: *Los Tilos.* Ⓟ Extrarradio, 16870 (Cuenca). ☎ (969) 31 80 98. FAX (969) 31 82 99. This traditional whitewashed country house, near a mineral spring in the beautiful Serranía de Cuenca, offers basic, affordable rooms. It is popular with ramblers and nature lovers. Regional food is served. 🖫 TV	AE DC V	24	■		■
CUENCA: *Posada de San José.* ⓅⓅ Calle Julián Romero 4, 16001. ☎ (969) 21 13 00. FAX (969) 23 03 65. An original, charming hotel run by a Canadian-Spanish couple in a historic building in the old part of town. It is curiously labyrinthine, and lovingly decorated with antiques and frescoes. 🖫	AE DC MC V	30			■
CUENCA: *La Cueva del Fraile.* ⓅⓅⓅ Carretera Cuenca–Buenache, 16001. ☎ (969) 21 15 71. FAX (969) 25 60 47. In a green valley outside Cuenca, this hotel is built around a white patio. It has tennis courts and bicycles for hire. 🖫 TV	AE DC MC V	63	■	●	■
CUENCA: *Leonor de Aquitania.* ⓅⓅⓅ Calle San Pedro 58–60, 16001. ☎ (969) 23 10 00. FAX (969) 23 10 04. Hunting trophies are displayed in the lobby of this hotel in the old part of town. The bedrooms are welcoming and cosy, and some have views of the gorge of the Río Huécar. 🖫 ▤ TV	AE MC V	49			

CUENCA: *Parador de Cuenca.* ℗℗℗℗ | AE DC MC V | 62
Hoz del Huécar, 16001. 【 (969) 23 23 20. FAX (969) 23 25 34.
The 16th-century convent of San Pablo, on the opposite side of the
Río Huécar from the city, is an elegant parador. Cuenca's famous old
hanging houses *(see p367)* can be seen from the bedrooms. 🛏 ▤ TV

GUADALAJARA: *España.* ℗ | MC V | 40
Calle Teniente Figueroa 3, 19001. 【 (949) 21 13 03. FAX (949) 21 13 05.
A family-run hotel in a 19th-century mansion in the centre of the city.
The modernized interior is lightened by touches of originality, such as
a mural on the staircase. The staff can advise on sightseeing. 🛏 TV 🛇

MANZANARES: *Parador de Manzanares.* ℗℗℗ | AE DC MC V | 50
Ctra Madrid–Cádiz, 13200 (Ciudad Real). 【 (926) 61 04 00. FAX (926) 61 09 35.
In one of the main cities of La Mancha's principal wine region, this
parador is a base for exploring Don Quixote country. 🛏 ▤ TV

OROPESA: *Parador de Oropesa.* ℗℗℗℗ | AE DC MC V | 48
Plaza del Palacio 1, 45560 (Toledo). 【 (925) 43 00 00. FAX (925) 43 07 77.
The Sierra de Gredos forms a backdrop to this medieval fortress
rising above a plain of olive groves and vineyards. It has plenty of
modern comforts, including a Jacuzzi in one bedroom. 🛏 ▤ TV

OSSA DE MONTIEL: *Albamanjón.* ℗℗ | DC MC V | 8
Laguna de San Pedro 16, 02611 (Albacete). 【 (926) 69 90 48. FAX (926) 69 91 20.
This modern complex in a mix of local and Andalusian style is the best
hotel beside the Lagunas de Ruidera, La Mancha's string of attractive
turquoise lakes. It is decorated with tiles and climbing plants. 🛏 TV

PASTRANA: *Colegio San Buenaventura.* ℗℗ | MC V | 2
Calle Adolfo Martín-Gamero 20, 19100 (Guadalajara). 【 (949) 37 02 32.
A 16th-century school of sacred music in a town in the Alcarria has
become a tasteful guest house offering bed and breakfast. 🛏 🛇

PASTRANA: *Hospedería Real de Pastrana.* ℗℗ | AE MC V | 27
Convento del Carmen, 19100 (Guadalajara). 【 (& FAX) (949) 37 10 60.
A hotel in a wing of the Monasterio del Carmen, founded by St Teresa
of Ávila, with simple, quiet rooms. On one side is the valley of the Río
Tajo and on the other the picturesque town of Pastrana. 🛏 ▤ TV 🛇

PUERTO LÁPICE: *Aprisco de Puerto Lápice.* ℗ | DC MC V | 17
Carretera Madrid–Cádiz, 13650 (Ciudad Real). 【 (& FAX) (926) 57 61 50.
An economical overnight stop next to a popular, often crowded
restaurant on the Madrid–Andalusia road. The lounge has a rustic
decor and is crammed with ornaments, including a boar's head. 🛏

SIGÜENZA: *Parador de Sigüenza.* ℗℗℗℗ | AE DC MC V | 81
Plaza del Castillo, 19250 (Guadalajara). 【 (949) 39 01 00. FAX (949) 39 13 64.
Sigüenza's massive castle overlooks the town from a hilltop. Its former
VIP guests include the Catholic Monarchs *(see pp52–3)*. It is furnished
in regal style and the bedrooms surround a courtyard. 🛏 ▤ TV 🛇

TALAVERA DE LA REINA: *Beatriz.* ℗℗ | AE DC MC V | 161
Avenida de Madrid 1, 45600 (Toledo). 【 (925) 80 76 00. FAX (925) 81 58 08.
A modern hotel on the town's edge, on the road from Madrid. In the
cellar is an anti-nuclear refuge built by the owner. 🛏 ▤ TV 🛇

TOLEDO: *La Almazara.* ℗ | AE DC MC V | 21
Carretera Toledo-Argés, 45080. 【 (925) 22 38 66. FAX (925) 25 05 62.
This 16th-century country house hotel is high on a wooded hilltop
outside Toledo, and has a magnificent view. Obliging and informal
staff compensate for simple bedrooms and limited facilities. 🛏 🛇

TOLEDO: *Hostal del Cardenal.* ℗℗℗ | AE DC MC V | 27
Paseo de Recaredo 24, 45004. 【 (925) 22 49 00. FAX (925) 22 29 91.
Now a historic hotel by the city walls, this 18th-century mansion was
formerly the residence of the archbishop of Toledo. It has splendid,
sculpted ceilings and pretty brick courtyards. 🛏 ▤ TV

TOLEDO: *Pintor El Greco.* ℗℗℗ | AE DC MC V | 33
Calle Alamillos del Tránsito 13, 45002. 【 (925) 21 42 50. FAX (925) 21 58 19.
A 17th-century house in Toledo's former Jewish quarter has been
discreetly extended behind the original façade and patio. Wrought iron
and traditional ceramics add character to the hotel. 🛏 ▤ TV 🛇

For key to symbols see back flap

	CREDIT CARDS	NUMBER OF ROOMS	PRIVATE PARKING	SWIMMING POOL	GARDEN OR TERRACE
Price categories for a standard double room per night, with tax, breakfast and service included: ℗ under 8,000 ptas ℗℗ 8,000–12,000 ptas ℗℗℗ 12,000–16,000 ptas ℗℗℗℗ 16,000–20,000 ptas ℗℗℗℗℗ over 20,000 ptas	**CREDIT CARDS** Indicates which credit cards are accepted: *AE* American Express; *DC* Diners Club; *MC* Master Card/Access; *V* Visa **PARKING** Parking provided by the hotel in a private car park or a private garage on the hotel site or very close by. Some hotels charge for use of private parking facilities. **SWIMMING POOL** Hotel pool outdoors unless otherwise stated. **GARDEN** Hotel with garden, courtyard or terrace, often providing tables for eating outdoors.				
TOLEDO: *Parador de Toledo.* ℗℗℗℗ Cerro del Emperador, 45002. ▐ *(925) 22 18 50.* FAX *(925) 22 51 66.* There is a spectacular view of Toledo from the terrace of this parador on the brow of a hill overlooking the city. The hotel is popular with sightseers and photographers, so book in advance. 🛏 ▤ TV	AE DC MC V	76	■	●	■
TRAGACETE: *Hostal El Gamo.* ℗ Plaza de los Caídos 2, 16150 (Cuenca). ▐ *(969) 28 90 08.* FAX *(969) 28 92 28.* A good-value restaurant-with-rooms in a peaceful village among hills and woods in the Serranía de Cuenca, near the Río Cuervo's source. 🛏	MC V	35			■
VALDEPEÑAS: *Meliá El Hidalgo.* ℗℗℗ Ctra Madrid–Cádiz, 13300 (Ciudad Real). ▐ *(926) 31 30 88.* FAX *(926) 31 33 36.* A roadside motel built in the 1960s in a landscape of vineyards. The rooms are in large, bright bungalows, each with its own parking space and direct access to the swimming pool. 🛏 ▤ TV ♿	AE DC MC V	54	■	●	■

EXTREMADURA

	CREDIT CARDS	NUMBER OF ROOMS	PRIVATE PARKING	SWIMMING POOL	GARDEN OR TERRACE
BADAJOZ: *Río.* ℗℗℗ Avenida Adolfo Díaz Ambrona 13, 06006. ▐ *(924) 27 26 00.* FAX *(924) 27 38 74.* A comfortable, modern hotel in the city centre. As well as all the standard facilities it has a bingo hall and a solarium. 🛏 ▤ TV	AE DC MC V	85	■	●	■
CÁCERES: *Parador de Cáceres.* ℗℗℗℗ Calle Ancha 6, 10003. ▐ *(927) 21 17 59.* FAX *(927) 21 17 29.* A small parador in the converted 14th-century Palace of Torreorgaz. Inside it is a labyrinth of stairs, doors, patios and corridors. 🛏 ▤ TV	AE DC MC V	31	■		
CÁCERES: *Meliá Cáceres.* ℗℗℗℗℗ Plaza de San Juan 11, 10003. ▐ *(927) 21 58 00.* FAX *(927) 21 40 70.* This 16th-century mansion beside the city walls has been renovated by a hotel chain. Some of the bedrooms have vaulted ceilings. 🛏 ▤ TV	AE DC MC V	86			
GUADALUPE: *Hospedería del Real Monasterio.* ℗℗ Plaza de Juan Carlos I, 10140 (Cáceres). ▐ *(927) 36 70 00.* FAX *(927) 36 71 77.* The *hospedería* is part of the 16th-century Franciscan monastery which dominates Guadalupe. Many of the rooms which surround the stone courtyard were originally monks' cells. 🛏 ▤	MC V	47	■		
GUADALUPE: *Parador de Guadalupe.* ℗℗℗ C/ Marqués de la Romana 12, 10140 (Cáceres). ▐ *(927) 36 70 75.* FAX *(927) 36 70 76.* A pilgrim's hospice in the 16th century, this parador has a central courtyard planted with citrus trees. The rooms in the modern annexe are spacious, but those in the old building are more popular. 🛏 ▤ TV	AE DC MC V	40	■	●	■
JARANDILLA DE LA VERA: *Parador de Jarandilla.* ℗℗℗℗ Avenida de García Prieto 1, 10450 (Cáceres). ▐ *(927) 56 01 17.* FAX *(927) 56 00 88.* This imposing 15th-century castle, where the Emperor Carlos V stayed for a year, has been modernized without losing its medieval feel. It has rose gardens, a tennis court and a children's play area. 🛏 ▤ TV	AE DC MC V	53	■	●	■
JEREZ DE LOS CABALLEROS: *Tryp Los Templarios.* ℗℗ Carretera de Villanueva, 06380 (Badajoz). ▐ *(924) 73 16 36.* FAX *(924) 75 03 38.* A modern hotel named after the Knights Templar who played an important part in the history of the area. All the bedrooms have views over the valley. A wide terrace surrounds the pool. 🛏 ▤ TV	AE DC MC V	49	■	●	■
LOSAR DE LA VERA: *Antigua Casa del Heno.* ℗ Finca Valdepimienta, 10460 (Cáceres). ▐ *(927) 19 80 77.* A simple old stone farmhouse surrounded by oak trees and meadows. It offers bed and breakfast, and is most popular in the spring when the cherry trees come into blossom. 🛏	V	8	■		

LOSAR DE LA VERA: *Hostería Fontivieja.* ℝ
Calle Mártires 11, 10460 (Cáceres). ☎ (927) 57 01 08.
A small, family-run hotel in a peaceful olive grove outside the town.
Two bedrooms have terraces with views of the countryside. 🛏 ▤ TV

MC V — 12

MALPARTIDA DE PLASENCIA: *Cañada Real.* ℝℝℝ
Carretera Comarcal 511, 1060 (Cáceres). ☎ (927) 45 94 07. FAX (927) 45 94 34.
This modern hotel is in easy striking distance of Plasencia and the Montfrague
nature reserve. The bedrooms are comfortable and spacious. 🛏 ▤ TV ♿

AE MC V — 61

MÉRIDA: *Emperatriz.* ℝℝℝ
Plaza de España 19, 06800 (Badajoz). ☎ (924) 31 31 11. FAX (924) 31 33 05.
An austere-looking, 16th-century granite mansion on the main square,
with a cloistered courtyard and a bar in the cellar. Bedrooms with
balconies overlooking the square can be noisy in the day. 🛏 ▤ TV

AE MC V — 41

MÉRIDA: *Tryp Medea.* ℝℝℝ
Avenida de Portugal, 06800 (Badajoz). ☎ (924) 37 24 00. FAX (924) 37 30 20.
The semicircular shape of this modern hotel near the ancient Roman
bridge suggests an amphitheatre. The hotel has two swimming pools
(one indoors), a gym, a sauna and a squash court. 🛏 ▤ TV ♿

AE DC MC V — 126

MÉRIDA: *Parador de Mérida.* ℝℝℝℝ
Plaza de la Constitución 3, 06800 (Badajoz). ☎ (924) 31 38 00. FAX (924) 31 92 08.
A converted 17th-century Baroque convent on a shady square. Roman
columns, inscriptions in Arabic and Visigothic capitals have been
preserved. The lounge is in a former chapel. 🛏 ▤ TV ♿

AE DC MC V — 82

ORELLANA LA VIEJA: *Castillo de Orellana.* ℝ
Cerro de la Herrería, 06740 (Badajoz). ☎ (924) 86 70 02. FAX (924) 86 70 40.
A good-value holiday complex on the shores of the Orellana reservoir,
a bathing and picnicking spot in pretty countryside. 🛏 ▤ TV ♿

AE V — 70

PLASENCIA: *Alfonso VIII.* ℝℝ
Avenida Alfonso VIII 32, 10600 (Cáceres). ☎ (927) 41 02 50. FAX (927) 41 80 42.
A modern hotel, centrally located near the Parque de la Isla (where
there is a swimming pool), with very attentive staff. 🛏 ▤ TV

AE DC MC V — 57

TRUJILLO: *Mesón La Cadena.* ℝ
Plaza Mayor 8, 10200 (Cáceres). ☎ (927) 32 14 63.
This restaurant-with-rooms in an attractive granite house on the main
square offers a cheaper alternative to the parador. The bedrooms,
decorated with textiles made locally, are on the third floor. 🛏 ▤

AE MC V — 7

TRUJILLO: *Parador de Trujillo.* ℝℝℝℝ
Plaza Santa Beatriz de Silva, 10200 (Cáceres). ☎ (927) 32 13 50. FAX (927) 32 13 66.
This charming parador, built in the 1980s, incorporates parts of a 16th-
century convent, including the former cloister. The parador is within
walking distance of Trujillo's sights, but away from its noise. 🛏 ▤ TV

AE DC MC V — 46

ZAFRA: *Huerta Honda.* ℝℝℝ
Avenida López Asme 30, 06300 (Badajoz). ☎ (924) 55 41 00. FAX (924) 55 25 04.
Many regular guests feel this hotel offers accommodation as good as
the parador next door. The restaurant is also good value. 🛏 ▤ TV

AE MC DC V — 45

ZAFRA: *Parador de Zafra.* ℝℝℝ
Pl del Corazón de María 7, 06300 (Badajoz). ☎ (924) 55 45 40. FAX (924) 55 10 18.
This castle, with its round towers, was built in the 15th century on the
ruins of a Moorish fortress. A beautiful staircase leads from the courtyard, with an arcaded gallery, to the bedrooms. 🛏 ▤ TV

AE DC MC V — 45

SEVILLE

EL ARENAL: *La Rábida.* **Map 3 B1.** ℝℝ
Calle Castelar 24, 41001. ☎ (95) 422 09 60. FAX (95) 422 43 75.
This hotel in one of several old palaces in residential streets near the
cathedral has a few modern bedrooms. Its beautiful public rooms are
built round two courtyards, one with a stained-glass roof. 🛏 ▤ TV

AE DC MC V — 104

EL ARENAL: *Simón.* **Map 3 B2.** ℝℝ
Calle García de Vinuesa 19, 41001. ☎ (95) 422 66 60. FAX (95) 456 22 41.
A central hotel in an 18th-century mansion built round a pretty patio
planted with ferns. The bedrooms vary in size and quality. Some have
balconies overlooking the street. 🛏 ▤

AE DC MC V — 29

For key to symbols see back flap

Price categories for a standard double room per night, with tax, breakfast and service included:

Ⓟ under 8,000 ptas
ⓅⓅ 8,000–12,000 ptas
ⓅⓅⓅ 12,000–16,000 ptas
ⓅⓅⓅⓅ 16,000–20,000 ptas
ⓅⓅⓅⓅⓅ over 20,000 ptas

CREDIT CARDS
Indicates which credit cards are accepted: *AE* American Express; *DC* Diners Club; *MC* Master Card/Access; *V* Visa

PARKING
Parking provided by the hotel in a private car park or a private garage on the hotel site or very close by. Some hotels charge for use of private parking facilities.

SWIMMING POOL
Hotel pool outdoors unless otherwise stated.

GARDEN
Hotel with garden, courtyard or terrace, often providing tables for eating outdoors.

	Credit Cards	Number of Rooms	Private Parking	Swimming Pool	Garden or Terrace
EL ARENAL: *Álvarez Quintero.* Map 3 C1. ⓅⓅⓅ Calle Álvarez Quintero 9–13, 41004. ☎ (95) 422 12 98. FAX (95) 456 41 41. Although it is surrounded by the city's star sights, this hotel's regulars are business people. Behind a Sevillian mansion façade is a remodelled interior. Wines from the hotel's own bodegas are served. 🔒 ▤ TV	AE DC MC V	43	▪		▪
EL ARENAL: *Taberna del Alabardero.* Map 3 B1. ⓅⓅⓅⓅⓅ Calle Zaragoza 20, 41001. ☎ (95) 456 06 37. FAX (95) 456 36 66. An exquisite restaurant-with-rooms occupying a 19th-century mansion. The house is built round a central courtyard illuminated by a stained-glass roof. There are cosy bedrooms on the top floor. 🔒 ▤ TV ♿	AE DC MC V	7	▪		▪
SANTA CRUZ: *Las Casas de la Judería.* Map 3 D2. ⓅⓅⓅ Callejón de las Dos Hermanas 7, 41004. ☎ (95) 441 51 50. FAX (95) 442 21 70. Less a hotel, more a labyrinth of suites, some with a private terrace. This is a peaceful place to rest, away from the city rush. 🔒 ▤ TV ♿	AE DC MC V	56	▪		▪
SANTA CRUZ: *Hostería del Laurel.* Map 3 C2. ⓅⓅⓅ Plaza de los Venerables 5, 41004. ☎ (95) 422 02 95. FAX (95) 421 04 50. A hotel in a small square near the Hospital de los Venerables. The reception is in a covered courtyard, reached through an inn hung with hams and garlic. The rooms are simple but spacious. 🔒 ▤ TV	AE DC MC V	21			▪
SANTA CRUZ: *Murillo.* Map 6 E4. ⓅⓅⓅ Calle Lope de Rueda 7 & 9, 41004. ☎ (95) 421 60 95. FAX (95) 421 96 16. A pleasant, reasonably priced hotel in an old building off Plaza Alfaro, a short walk from the cathedral. Book well ahead for Holy Week and the April Fair. The management also let apartments nearby. 🔒 ▤	AE DC MC V	57			
SANTA CRUZ: *Doña María.* Map 3 C2. ⓅⓅⓅⓅ Calle Don Remondo 19, 41004. ☎ (95) 422 49 90. FAX (95) 421 95 46. This hotel is in a street running alongside the Palacio Arzobispal. Its terrace and swimming pool overlook the Giralda. Guests can choose from bedrooms decorated in a variety of styles. 🔒 ▤ TV ♿	AE DC MC V	68		●	▪
FURTHER AFIELD (LA MACARENA): *Baco.* Map 2 E5. ⓅⓅⓅ Plaza Ponce de León 15, 41003. ☎ (95) 456 50 50. FAX (95) 456 36 54. An old house has been transformed into a modern hotel in Sevillian style. A spiral staircase ascends from reception; the quieter back bedrooms overlook patios with tiles and potted plants. 🔒 ▤ TV	AE DC MC V	25			▪
FURTHER AFIELD (LA MACARENA): *Patio de la Cartuja.* Map 1 C4. ⓅⓅⓅ Calle Lumbreras 8 & 10, 41002. ☎ (95) 490 02 00. FAX (95) 490 20 56. A group of old houses has been converted into this hotel in La Macarena. It offers apartments of excellent quality at very competitive prices and a tranquil atmosphere in a busy city. 🔒 ▤ TV	AE DC MC V	34	▪		▪
FURTHER AFIELD (LA MACARENA): *San Gil.* Map 2 D4. ⓅⓅⓅⓅ Calle Parras 28, 41002. ☎ (95) 490 68 11. FAX (95) 490 69 39. A beautiful, early 20th-century mansion classed as one of Seville's 100 most important buildings. It has spacious, beautifully furnished rooms and a peaceful garden with palm trees and an old cypress. 🔒 ▤ TV ♿	AE DC MC V	39	▪	●	▪
FURTHER AFIELD (PARQUE MARÍA LUISA): *Alfonso XIII.* Map 3 C3. ⓅⓅⓅⓅⓅ Calle San Fernando 2, 41004. ☎ (95) 422 28 50. FAX (95) 421 60 33. Elegance and appropriately formal service are assured in Seville's grand hotel, built in Neo-Mudéjar style. Inside there are chandeliers and statuary; outdoors there are palm trees. 🔒 ▤ TV ♿	AE DC MC V	146	▪	●	▪
FURTHER AFIELD (SOUTH): *Ciudad de Sevilla.* Map 4 D5. ⓅⓅⓅⓅ Avenida Manuel Siurot 25, 41013. ☎ (95) 423 05 05. FAX (95) 423 85 39. Behind its old façade, this hotel, away from the centre, is modern. It has large, light rooms and a rooftop swimming pool. 🔒 ▤ TV ♿	AE DC MC V	94	▪	●	

ANDALUSIA

ALCALÁ DE GUADAIRA: *Hotel Oromana.* ⓅⓅⓅ
Avenida de Portugal, 41500 (Sevilla). 【 (& FAX) (95) 568 64 00.
On the edge of town, within easy reach of Seville, the Oromana is
shaded by pines. It is run by a team of women who are happy to
cater for families with children and for the disabled. 🚗 ▤ TV ⅋

| | AE MC V | 30 | | | |

ALMERÍA: *Torreluz IV.* ⓅⓅⓅ
Plaza Flores I, 04001. 【 (& FAX) (950) 23 47 99.
A smart, city-centre hotel with a spiral staircase and a rooftop pool.
The Torreluzs II and III, sister hotels nearby, are cheaper. 🚗 ▤ TV ⅋

| | AE DC MC V | 105 | | | |

ARACENA: *Sierra de Aracena.* ⓅⓅ
Gran Vía 21, 21200 (Huelva). 【 (959) 12 61 75. FAX (959) 12 62 18.
This quiet hotel is in the centre of the attractive town of Aracena.
The rooms at the back overlook the town's castle. 🚗 ▤ TV ⅋

| | AE DC MC V | 42 | | | |

ARACENA: *Finca Buen Vino.* ⓅⓅⓅⓅ
Los Marines, 21293 (Huelva). 【 (& FAX) (959) 12 40 34.
A stylish modern villa on a hilltop at the heart of a wooded nature
reserve. This is a private home open to guests and it has an informal
atmosphere. Cordon bleu cooking is served by candlelight. 🚗

| | AE DC MC V | 4 | | | |

ARCOS DE LA FRONTERA: *Cortijo Faín.* ⓅⓅⓅ
Carretera de Algar, 11630 (Cádiz). 【 (& FAX) (956) 23 13 96.
This 17th-century farmhouse stands majestically in an estate of olive
trees. The rooms are furnished with antiques and some have old brass
bedsteads. A swimming pool is hidden among the olive trees. 🚗 ▤ TV

| | AE MC V | 8 | | | |

ARCOS DE LA FRONTERA: *Parador de Arcos de la Frontera.* ⓅⓅⓅ
Plaza del Cabildo, 11630 (Cádiz). 【 (956) 70 05 00. FAX (956) 70 11 16.
A fine mansion, formerly a magistrate's house, on the main square. Its
terrace overhangs a precipice and has spectacular views. 🚗 ▤ TV ⅋

| | AE DC MC V | 24 | | | |

AYAMONTE: *Riu Canela.* ⓅⓅⓅ
Playa de Isla Canela, 21409 (Huelva). 【 (959) 47 71 24. FAX (959) 47 71 70.
With its three pools, one for children, the beachside Riu Palace is more
a summer holiday centre than a hotel. The hotel is on Isla Canela near
the Portuguese border, close to the Algarve. 🚗 ▤ TV ⅋

| | AE DC MC V | 350 | | | |

BAENA: *Hotel Zambudio.* Ⓟ
Carretera Baena–Zuheros, 14850 (Córdoba). 【 (& FAX) (957) 67 08 37.
A hotel-cum-restaurant near Baena with views of the hills around
Zuheros. It is quiet, comfortable and good value. 🚗 ▤ TV

| | AE MC V | 11 | | | |

BAEZA: *Hospedería Fuentenueva.* ⓅⓅ
Paseo Arca del Agua 11, 23440 (Jaén). 【 (953) 74 31 00. FAX (953) 74 32 00.
This Renaissance town has an unusual hotel in a converted women's
prison, run by a cooperative of five young hoteliers. The rooms are in
excellent taste; there is a quiet lounge with a domed ceiling. 🚗 ▤ TV

| | AE DC MC V | 12 | | | |

BENAOJÁN: *Molino del Santo.* ⓅⓅ
Calle Barriada Estación, 29370 (Málaga). 【 (95) 216 71 51. FAX (95) 216 73 27.
This converted water mill in the hills near Ronda is a relaxing sun trap
with an attractive swimming pool. The British owners are a mine of
tourist information. They keep mountain bikes for guests to rent. 🚗

| | AE DC MC V | 12 | | | |

BUBIÓN: *Villa Turística de Bubión.* ⓅⓅⓅ
Calle Barrio Alto, 18412 (Granada). 【 (958) 76 31 11. FAX (958) 76 31 36.
This mini-village is in the distinct building style of the Alpujarras, with
flat roofs and tall chimneys. You can cook in your kitchen or eat in the
informal restaurant. Horse riding and hikes are arranged. 🚗 ▤ ⅋

| | AE DC MC V | 43 | | | |

CARMONA: *Parador de Carmona.* ⓅⓅⓅ
Calle Alcázar, 41410 (Sevilla). 【 (95) 414 10 10. FAX (95) 414 17 12.
This clifftop parador was built as a fortress by the Moors and became
the palace of the Christian King, Pedro the Cruel. Historic Carmona is
a good base for exploring Seville province. 🚗 ▤ TV ⅋

| | AE DC MC V | 63 | | | |

CARMONA: *Casa de Carmona.* ⓅⓅⓅⓅ
Plaza de Lasso 1, 41410 (Sevilla). 【 (95) 414 33 00. FAX (95) 414 37 52.
This 16th-century converted palace, decorated in a blend of modern
and period styles, has featured in design magazines. 🚗 ▤ TV ⅋

| | AE DC MC V | 30 | | | |

For key to symbols see back flap

Price categories for a standard double room per night, with tax, breakfast and service included:

Ⓟ   under 8,000 ptas
ⓅⓅ   8,000–12,000 ptas
ⓅⓅⓅ   12,000–16,000 ptas
ⓅⓅⓅⓅ   16,000–20,000 ptas
ⓅⓅⓅⓅⓅ   over 20,000 ptas

CREDIT CARDS
Indicates which credit cards are accepted: *AE* American Express; *DC* Diners Club; *MC* Master Card/Access; *V* Visa
PARKING
Parking provided by the hotel in a private car park or a private garage on the hotel site or very close by. Some hotels charge for use of private parking facilities.
SWIMMING POOL
Hotel pool outdoors unless otherwise stated.
GARDEN
Hotel with garden, courtyard or terrace, often providing tables for eating outdoors.

	CREDIT CARDS	NUMBER OF ROOMS	PRIVATE PARKING	SWIMMING POOL	GARDEN OR TERRACE
CASTELLAR DE LA FRONTERA: *Casa Convento La Almoraima.* ⓅⓅⓅ Finca La Almoraima, 11350 (Cádiz). 📞 *(956) 69 30 02.* FAX *(956) 69 32 14.* One of Europe's largest country estates (now in public ownership) surrounds this hotel. The house was built by the dukes of Medinaceli in the 17th century and used by them as a hunting lodge. 🛏 🍽	AE DC MC V	17	■	●	■
CASTILLEJA DE LA CUESTA: *Hacienda de San Ygnacio.* ⓅⓅⓅⓅ Calle Real 194, 41950 (Sevilla). 📞 *(95) 416 04 30.* FAX *(95) 416 14 37.* A 17th-century Andalusian farmhouse built round a patio planted with palms. The dining room was once an olive oil mill. 🛏 🍽 📺	AE DC MC V	12	■	●	■
CAZALLA DE LA SIERRA: *Las Navazuelas.* Ⓟ Apartado 14, 41370 (Sevilla). 📞 *(95) 488 47 64.* FAX *(95) 488 47 64.* The rooms in this charming, family-run farmhouse are furnished with handworked fabrics. Staying here gives visitors a rare opportunity to experience living in an authentic Andalusian *cortijo* (farmstead). 🛏	MC V	8		●	■
CAZALLA DE LA SIERRA: *Hospedería La Cartuja.* ⓅⓅ Carretera Cazalla–Constantina, 41370 (Sevilla). 📞 *(95) 488 45 16.* FAX *(95) 488 35 15.* An old monastery has been eccentrically rehabilitated by its crusading owner as a refuge for artists. The walls are hung with their paintings. Organic produce from the farm is used in the cooking. 🛏	MC V	8		●	■
CAZORLA: *Molino de la Fárraga.* Ⓟ Apartado 1, 23470 (Jaén). 📞 *(953) 72 12 49.* A 200-year-old mill, recently renovated, near the Plaza Santa María, is a relaxing stop. An annexe can be rented as a self-catering apartment. 🛏		5		●	■
CAZORLA: *Parador de Cazorla.* ⓅⓅⓅⓅ Cazorla 23470 (Jaén). 📞 *(953) 72 70 75.* FAX *(953) 72 70 77.* The forests and mountains of the Sierra de Cazorla, a major Andalusian nature reserve, are the superb setting for this modern parador. 🛏 📺	AE DC MC V	33	■	●	■
CÓRDOBA: *Maestre.* Ⓟ Calle Romero Barros 4-6, 14003. 📞 *(957) 47 24 10.* FAX *(957) 47 53 95.* Near the Mezquita in the centre of Córdoba, this is a simple, very economically priced hotel with basic modern amenities. 🛏 🍽 ♿	AE DC MC V	26	■		
CÓRDOBA: *Occidental.* ⓅⓅⓅⓅ Calle Poeta Alonso Bonilla 7, 14012. 📞 *(957) 40 04 40.* FAX *(957) 40 04 39.* This is a modern hotel in a residential suburb in the north of the city, with coffered ceilings and smart brass lanterns. 🛏 🍽 📺 ♿	AE DC MC V	153	■	●	■
CÓRDOBA: *Alfaros.* ⓅⓅⓅⓅ Calle Alfaros 18, 14001. 📞 *(957) 49 19 20.* FAX *(957) 49 22 10.* In a busy street, but soundproofed against traffic noise, Alfaros has three attractive courtyards in Neo-Mudéjar style. 🛏 🍽 📺 ♿	AE DC MC V	133	■	●	■
DÚRCAL: *Cortijo la Solana.* Ⓟ La Solana Alta 3, 18650 (Granada). 📞 (& FAX) *(958) 78 05 75.* A country house with extensive grounds in a little-known valley in the mountains of Granada, offering bed and breakfast only.		4			
ÉCIJA: *Platería.* Ⓟ Calle Garcilópez 1–A, 41400 (Sevilla). 📞 *(95) 483 50 10.* FAX *(95) 483 50 10.* This hotel is in the former silversmiths' quarter and is named after it. Its large, cool rooms are relaxing in the searing summer heat. 🛏 🍽 📺 ♿	AE DC MC V	18	■		
GIBRALTAR: *The Rock.* ⓅⓅⓅⓅ 3 Europa Road. 📞 *(9567) 730 00.* FAX *(9567) 735 13.* Trading on old-fashioned colonial style and service, Gibraltar's first five-star hotel is elevated above the town and harbour and has views across the bay. Many celebrities have stayed here. 🛏 🍽 📺	AE DC MC V	127	■	●	■

GRANADA: *Reina Cristina.*   ₧₧ | AE | 42
Calle Tablas 4, 18002. ((958) 25 32 11. FAX (958) 25 57 28. | DC |
A glass-covered courtyard and a handsome balustrade are preserved in | MC |
this 19th-century mansion, once a hiding place of the poet García Lorca | V |
(see p31). The rooms are small but comfortable. ⬛ ▤ TV ♿

GRANADA: *América.*   ₧₧₧ | AE | 13
Calle Real de la Alhambra 53, 18009. ((958) 22 74 71. FAX (958) 22 74 70. | DC |
This cosy, affordable, family-run hotel beside the Alhambra is on the | MC |
same street as Granada's parador. In summer, home cooking is served | V |
in a plant-filled courtyard. Always book well in advance. ⬛ ▤

GRANADA: *Alhambra Palace.*   ₧₧₧₧ | AE | 140
Calle Peña Partida 2 & 4, 18009. ((958) 22 14 68. FAX (958) 22 64 04. | DC |
A gloriously kitsch mock-Moorish building on the same hill as the | MC |
Alhambra. A superb terrace has views of old Granada. ⬛ ▤ TV ♿ | V |

GRANADA: *Parador de Granada.*   ₧₧₧₧ | AE | 36
Calle Real de la Alhambra, 18009. ((958) 22 14 41. FAX (958) 22 22 64. | DC |
This elegant parador in the gardens of the Alhambra was a convent. | MC |
For a room in such a spot you must book months ahead. ⬛ ▤ TV ♿ | V |

GUALCHOS: *La Posada.*   ₧₧₧ | MC | 9
Plaza de la Constitución 3 & 4, 18614 (Granada). ((& FAX) (958) 65 60 34. | V |
This is primarily a restaurant, with a few cosy rooms scattered around
an interesting old building. It is on the square of an unspoilt village
in the hills above Granada's coast. ⬛

JAÉN: *Parador de Jaén.*   ₧₧₧ | AE | 45
Carretera del Castillo, 23001. ((953) 23 00 00. FAX (953) 23 09 30. | DC |
From this castle-parador above Jaén there are spectacular views of the | MC |
Sierra Morena. With its dimly lit corridors, small arched windows, huge | V |
doors and suits of armour, it retains a medieval atmosphere. ⬛ ▤ TV

LOJA: *La Bobadilla.*   ₧₧₧₧₧ | AE | 60
Finca La Bobadilla, 18300 (Granada). ((958) 32 18 61. FAX (958) 32 18 10. | DC |
Looking rather like a labyrinthine Andalusian village, surrounded by | MC |
its own estate, this is one of the most luxurious hotels in Europe. | V |
Guests can take part in a wide range of sports and activities. ⬛ ▤ TV

MÁLAGA: *Don Curro.*   ₧₧₧ | AE | 103
Calle Sancha de Lara 7, 29015. ((95) 222 72 00. FAX (95) 221 59 46. | DC |
The exterior may not be attractive, but inside, this hotel is charming | MC |
and comfortable, with a friendly, welcoming atmosphere. ⬛ ▤ TV | V |

MARBELLA: *El Fuerte.*   ₧₧₧₧ | AE | 263
Avenida El Fuerte, 29600 (Málaga). ((95) 286 15 00. FAX (95) 282 44 11. | DC |
El Fuerte was the first hotel built in Marbella and it is still one of the | MC |
best. Some rooms have mountain views and others look out to sea. | V |
The hotel has a heated, glassed-in pool and a health centre. ⬛ ▤ TV

MARBELLA: *Marbella Club Hotel.*   ₧₧₧₧₧ | AE | 129
Blvr Príncipe von Hohenlohe, 29600 (Málaga). ((95) 282 22 11. FAX (95) 282 98 84. | DC |
An exclusive, low-level, beachside complex between Marbella and | MC |
Puerto Banús. There are two pools, one indoors, and subtropical | V |
gardens with a choice of places to eat and relax. ⬛ ▤ TV

MAZAGÓN: *Parador de Mazagón.*   ₧₧₧₧ | AE | 43
Ctra Huelva–Matalascañas, 21130 (Huelva). ((959) 53 63 00. FAX (959) 53 62 28. | DC |
A modern parador on the Huelva coast, between a large, sandy beach | MC |
and a pine forest. It is in a good location for visiting the wildlife reserve | V |
of Doñana National Park nearby. ⬛ ▤ TV ♿

MIJAS: *Club Puerta del Sol.*   ₧₧₧ | AE | 130
Ctra Fuengirola–Mijas, 29650 (Málaga). ((95) 248 64 00. FAX (95) 248 54 62. | DC |
An elegant, low, U-shaped hotel on a foothill of the Sierra de Mijas. | MC |
From its gardens, pool and terraces there is an impressive view of | V |
Fuengirola and the coast. It has tennis courts and a gym. ⬛ ▤ TV ♿

MOJÁCAR: *Parador de Mojácar.*   ₧₧₧₧ | AE | 98
Playa de Mojácar, 04638 (Almería). ((950) 47 82 50. FAX (950) 47 81 83. | DC |
The architecture of this purpose-built parador on the dry, sunny coast | MC |
of Almería echoes that of the dazzling white cube houses in nearby | V |
Mojácar. There are facilities for water sports. ⬛ ▤ TV ♿

For key to symbols see back flap

Price categories for a standard double room per night, with tax, breakfast and service included:

- ℗ under 8,000 ptas
- ℗℗ 8,000–12,000 ptas
- ℗℗℗ 12,000–16,000 ptas
- ℗℗℗℗ 16,000–20,000 ptas
- ℗℗℗℗℗ over 20,000 ptas

CREDIT CARDS
Indicates which credit cards are accepted: *AE* American Express; *DC* Diners Club; *MC* Master Card/Access; *V* Visa

PARKING
Parking provided by the hotel in a private car park or a private garage on the hotel site or very close by. Some hotels charge for use of private parking facilities.

SWIMMING POOL
Hotel pool outdoors unless otherwise stated.

GARDEN
Hotel with garden, courtyard or terrace, often providing tables for eating outdoors.

	CREDIT CARDS	NUMBER OF ROOMS	PRIVATE PARKING	SWIMMING POOL	GARDEN OR TERRACE
NERJA: *Hostal Avalón.* Calle Punta Lara, 29780 (Málaga). ((95) 252 06 98. This small hotel above the coast road just outside Nerja has a friendly atmosphere, pleasant, clean bedrooms – all but one with views of the sea – and an informal lounge with comfortable sofas.	℗	8	■		
OJÉN: *Refugio de Juanar.* Sierra Blanca, 29610 (Málaga). ((95) 288 10 00. FAX (95) 288 10 01. A hunting lodge has been converted into this tranquil, cosy hotel. It is in the Sierras de Ojén, the wooded hills behind Marbella, a region of wildlife interest. The restaurant specializes in regional gastronomy.	℗℗	AE DC MC V	23	■	●	■
ORGIVA: *Taray.* Ctra Tablate–Albuñol, 18400 (Granada). ((958) 78 45 25. FAX (958) 78 45 31. A hotel in a garden of lawns and olive and orange trees. The bedrooms are large enough to be small apartments. The hotel is in good walking country and horse riding is organized.	℗℗	AE DC MC V	15	■	●	■
PALMA DEL RÍO: *Hospedería de San Francisco.* Avenida Pío XII 33, 14700 (Córdoba). ((957) 71 01 83. FAX (957) 71 07 32. Built in the 15th century as a Franciscan monastery, this hotel has some bedrooms in former monks' cells. They have hand-painted basins and bedcovers woven by nuns. Meals are served in the cloister.	℗℗	MC V	17	■		■
PECHINA: *Balneario de Sierra Alhamilla.* Pechina, 04259 (Almería). ((950) 31 74 13. FAX (950) 16 02 57. This spa hotel in peaceful hills has been restored to its 18th-century glory. There are Roman baths in the basement and, nearby, a naturally heated swimming pool.	℗℗	AE MC V	24	■	●	■
PINOS GENIL: *Labella María.* Carretera Sierra Nevada, 18191 (Granada). ((958) 48 87 46. FAX (958) 48 87 26. A modern, family-run hotel just outside Granada, well placed for visiting the city or the Sierra Nevada. The rooms are comfortable and airy. Some are large enough for a family of four.	℗	AE DC MC V	24	■		■
PRADO DEL REY: *Cortijo Huerta Dorotea.* Ctra Vilamartín–Ubrique, 11660 (Cádiz). ((956) 72 42 91. FAX (956) 72 42 89. On a hill surrounded by olive trees, near the white town of Prado del Rey, is this new hotel, run by a cooperative. Guests can choose rooms or log cabins. Riding is one leisure activity available.	℗	AE MC V	7	■	●	
EL PUERTO DE SANTA MARÍA: *Monasterio San Miguel.* Calle Larga 27, 11500 (Cádiz). ((956) 54 04 40. FAX (956) 54 26 04. An elegant, rather luxurious hotel, well placed for visits to Cádiz and Jerez de la Frontera. It has a faintly monastic atmosphere, recalling the former function of this Baroque building.	℗℗℗℗	AE DC MC V	150	■	●	■
EL ROCÍO: *Puente del Rey.* Avenida Canaliega, 21750 (Huelva). ((959) 44 25 75. FAX (959) 44 20 70. A country hotel on the edge of Doñana National Park. It is reasonably comfortable. Horse riding and excursions are organized.	℗℗	AE DC MC V	185	■	●	■
RONDA: *Reina Victoria.* Calle Jerez 25, 29400 (Málaga). ((95) 287 12 40. FAX (95) 287 10 75. The Reina Victoria, perched on a cliff edge, has spectacular views. It was Ronda's grand hotel until the parador was built.	℗℗℗	AE DC MC V	89	■	●	■
RONDA: *Parador de Ronda.* Plaza España, 29400 (Málaga). ((95) 287 75 00. FAX (95) 287 81 88. Edging up to Ronda's famous cliff, yet close to the town centre, this modern, purpose-built parador has stunning views over the gorge, especially from the top-floor suites.	℗℗℗℗	AE DC MC V	79	■	●	■

SAN JOSÉ: *San José.* ⓅⓅⓅ | MC V | 8

Calle Correo, 04118 (Almería). **(** (950) 38 01 16. **FAX** (950) 38 00 02.
A gaudy colour scheme, eccentric furnishings and a parrot lend charm to this hotel. It is near the beach in a small, developing resort, and close to the Cabo de Gata nature reserve. 🛏 📺

SANLÚCAR DE BARRAMEDA: *Los Helechos.* ⓅⓅ | AE DC MC V | 56

Plaza Madre de Dios 9, 11540 (Cádiz). **(** (956) 36 13 49. **FAX** (956) 36 96 50.
Decorated with tiles and pot plants, Los Helechos is a stylish, relaxing hideaway. Visits to Doñana National Park are arranged. 🛏 ▤ 📺

SANLÚCAR LA MAYOR: *Hacienda de Benazuza.* ⓅⓅⓅⓅ | AE DC MC V | 44

Virgen de las Nieves, 41800 (Sevilla). **(** (95) 570 33 44. **FAX** (95) 570 34 10.
Parts of this old hilltop house are said to be 1,000 years old. It is now a luxury hotel, furnished in traditional Andalusian style. It has several suites, three restaurants, a game reserve and a heliport. 🛏 ▤ 📺 ♿

SAN ROQUE: *La Solana.* ⓅⓅ | AE DC MC V | 18

Ctra Cádiz–Málaga N340, 11360 (Cádiz). **(** (956) 78 02 36. **FAX** (956) 78 02 36.
A useful stop en route to or from the Tangier ferry, this is a pleasant small hotel in a 200-year-old house set back from the motorway in its own small estate. The 12 rooms and 6 suites are all different. 🛏 📺

SIERRA NEVADA: *Santa Cruz.* ⓅⓅ | AE DC MC V | 66

Ctra Sierra Nevada, 18160 (Granada). **(** (958) 48 48 00. **FAX** (958) 48 48 06.
From the windows and balconies of this high-altitude hotel guests can contemplate the snowy peaks of the lovely Sierra Nevada. Open fires make the modern building cosy in winter. 🛏 📺 ♿

TARIFA: *Hurricane.* ⓅⓅⓅ | AE DC MC V | 33

Carretera N340, 11380 (Cádiz). **(** (956) 68 49 19. **FAX** (956) 68 03 29.
Tarifa is a mecca for windsurfers and the Hurricane is a temple to the sport and to physical fitness. It is an imaginative, open-plan building in subtropical gardens. There are views across the sea to Africa. 🛏

TORREMOLINOS: *Hotel Miami.* Ⓟ | | 26

Calle Aladino 14, 29620 (Málaga). **(** (95) 238 52 55.
The Miami, between Torremolinos and Málaga, gives welcome respite from the Costa del Sol's modern developments. It has whitewashed walls, tiles, iron grilles, balconies and plant pots. 🛏

TREVÉLEZ: *Mesón La Fragua.* Ⓟ | MC V | 14

Calle San Antonio 4, 18417 (Granada). **(** (958) 85 86 26. **FAX** (958) 85 86 14.
This *mesón* (inn) is in what claims to be the highest village in Spain. There are great views of the valley from the rooftop terrace. The rooms vary considerably in size and character. 🛏 📺

TURRE: *El Nacimiento.* Ⓟ | | 4

Cortijo El Nacimiento, 04639 (Almería). **(** (950) 52 80 90.
This remote and lovely old house is run by a friendly couple. They offer bed and breakfast, serving organic produce from their farm.

TURRE: *Finca Listonero.* ⓅⓅ | MC V | 5

Cortijo Grande, 04639 (Almería). **(** (950) 47 90 94. **FAX** (950) 47 90 94.
This hotel is in a restored farmhouse in the country near Mojácar. The breakfasts are generous; home-grown vegetables are served at meals.

ÚBEDA: *Palacio de La Rambla.* ⓅⓅⓅ | AE MC V | 8

Plaza del Marqués 1, 23400 (Jaén). **(** (953) 75 01 96. **FAX** (953) 75 02 67.
A 17th-century mansion run by its aristocratic owner as a small, central, exclusive hotel. The rooms, furnished with heirlooms, enclose a patio thought to be by the Renaissance architect, Vandelvira. 🛏 ▤ 📺 ♿

ÚBEDA: *Parador de Úbeda.* ⓅⓅⓅ | AE DC MC V | 31

Plaza Vázquez de Molina 1, 23400 (Jaén). **(** (953) 75 03 45. **FAX** (953) 75 12 59.
Presiding over Úbeda's monumental central square, this parador is in a former 16th-century aristocratic residence. Blue and white tiles adorn the façade and the house surrounds a pretty courtyard. 🛏 ▤ 📺

ZUHEROS: *Zuhayra.* Ⓟ | AE DC MC V | 18

Calle Mirador 10, 14870 (Córdoba). **(** (957) 69 46 93. **FAX** (957) 69 45 34.
The principal charm of this simple hotel is its location in a white town on the edge of a range of high hills. The building imitates the style of the noble mansion it replaced. Silence reigns at night. 🛏 ♿ .

For key to symbols see back flap

Price categories for a standard double room per night, with tax, breakfast and service included:

ℙ under 8,000 ptas
ℙℙ 8,000–12,000 ptas
ℙℙℙ 12,000–16,000 ptas
ℙℙℙℙ 16,000–20,000 ptas
ℙℙℙℙℙ over 20,000 ptas

CREDIT CARDS
Indicates which credit cards are accepted: *AE* American Express; *DC* Diners Club; *MC* Master Card/Access; *V* Visa
PARKING
Parking provided by the hotel in a private car park or a private garage on the hotel site or very close by. Some hotels charge for use of private parking facilities.
SWIMMING POOL
Hotel pool outdoors unless otherwise stated.
GARDEN
Hotel with garden, courtyard or terrace, often providing tables for eating outdoors.

THE BALEARIC ISLANDS

	Price	CREDIT CARDS	NUMBER OF ROOMS	PRIVATE PARKING	SWIMMING POOL	GARDEN OR TERRACE
FORMENTERA, ES PUJOLS: *Sa Volta.* Calle Miramar 94, 07871. ☎ *(971) 32 81 25.* FAX *(971) 32 82 28.* An inexpensive, family-run hotel in a modern three-storey block within walking distance of the beach in one of Formentera's main resorts. Each bedroom has its own terrace. 🛏 TV	ℙℙ	AE DC MC V	25			■
IBIZA (EIVISSA), IBIZA TOWN: *Hostal La Marina.* Calle Barcelona 7, 07800. ☎ *(971) 31 01 72.* FAX *(971) 31 39 11.* An old hotel, modernized inside but with much of its 1862 decoration. Airy front bedrooms overlook the harbour. Breakfast is not served. 🛏	ℙ	AE DC MC V	47			■
IBIZA (EIVISSA), IBIZA TOWN: *El Palacio.* Calle de la Conquista 2, 07800. ☎ *(971) 30 14 78.* FAX *(971) 39 15 81.* A theme hotel in the old town, with Marilyn Monroe penthouse suites, public rooms hung with movie memorabilia, and Hollywood Boulevard-style hand prints in the secluded garden. 🛏 ▤ TV	ℙℙℙℙℙ	AE DC MC V	7			■
IBIZA (EIVISSA), SANT ANTONI: *Pikes.* Camino Sa Vorera, 07820. ☎ *(971) 34 22 22.* FAX *(971) 34 23 12.* A chic hotel in a tastefully restored mansion on a hill planted with pines. Celebrities sometimes stay here. 🛏 ▤	ℙℙℙℙℙ	AE DC MC V	24	■	●	
IBIZA (EIVISSA), SANT MIQUEL: *Hacienda Na Xamena.* Apto 423, Urb Na Xamena, 07080. ☎ *(971) 33 45 00.* FAX *(971) 33 45 14.* There are stunning views from the bedrooms of this modern clifftop hotel built above a pretty, rocky cove, and from the elegant sun terrace round the swimming pool. 🛏 ▤ TV	ℙℙℙℙℙ	AE DC MC V	63	■	●	■
IBIZA (EIVISSA), SANTA EULÀRIA D'ES RIU: *Les Terrasses.* Apto 1235, Carretera de Santa Eulària, 07600 ☎ (& FAX) *(971) 33 26 43.* A country house decorated simply but beautifully in Ibizan style, painted white, blue and yellow. Each room is individually decorated. There are quiet corners inside and out to sit and read or relax. 🛏 ▤	ℙℙℙℙ	MC V	7	■	●	■
MALLORCA, ANDRATX: *Villa Italia.* Camino Sant Carles 13, Port d'Andratx, 07157. ☎ *(971) 67 40 11.* FAX *(971) 67 33 50.* A pink, Florentine-style villa built in the 1920s by an eccentric Italian millionaire for his lover. Inside there are stucco ceilings, marble floors and columns with Roman capitals. 🛏 ▤ TV	ℙℙℙℙℙ	AE DC MC V	16		●	■
MALLORCA, BANYALBUFAR: *Sa Baronía.* Calle Sa Baronia 16, 07191. ☎ *(971) 61 81 46.* FAX *(971) 61 81 46.* A family-run hotel built as a modern extension to a 17th-century baronial tower. It is in a small village on the island's unspoilt northwest coast. All the bedrooms have terraces with sea views. 🛏	ℙ	V MC	30	■	●	■
MALLORCA, BANYALBUFAR: *Mar i Vent.* Calle Mayor 49, 07191. ☎ *(971) 61 80 00.* FAX *(971) 61 82 01.* A hospitable hotel perched on a terrace above a rocky cove. The bedrooms in the annexe are large and quiet. 🛏	ℙℙ	MC V	23	■	●	■
MALLORCA, DEIÀ: *La Residencia.* Finca Son Canals, 07179. ☎ *(971) 63 90 11.* FAX *(971) 63 93 70.* Two magnificently restored, 16th-century manors on the outskirts of Deià have been made into an elegant hotel. Most bedrooms have four-poster beds and all have traditional Spanish furniture. 🛏 ▤	ℙℙℙℙℙ	AE DC MC V	64	■	●	■
MALLORCA, ESCORCA: *Santuari de Lluc.* Santuari de Lluc, 07315. ☎ *(971) 51 70 25.* FAX *(971) 51 70 96.* The Santuari de Lluc, high in the Tramuntana mountains, is accessible only by car. The simple bedrooms are in the monastery buildings. 🛏 ♿	ℙ	MC V	97	■	●	■

MALLORCA, PALMA DE MALLORCA: *Born.* ℗℗ | AE MC V | 29
Calle Sant Jaume 3, 07012. (*(971) 71 29 42.* FAX *(971) 71 86 18.*
The Marquis of Ferrandell's town mansion, built in the 16th century
and restored in the 18th, makes a splendid hotel. It has a typical
Mallorcan courtyard with palms and a grand staircase.

MALLORCA, POLLENÇA: *Illa d'Or.* ℗℗℗ | AE DC MC V | 119
Paseo de Colón 265, 07470. (*(971) 86 51 00.* FAX *(971) 86 42 13.*
Built in the 1930s for elite northern Europeans to summer on the
island, the hotel retains its original furniture and atmosphere.

MALLORCA, POLLENÇA: *Formentor.* ℗℗℗℗ | AE DC MC V | 127
Playa de Formentor, 07470. (*(971) 86 53 00.* FAX *(971) 86 51 55.*
The visitors' book of this luxury hotel in a beautiful spot on the
island's northwest tip is signed by writers, opera singers, film stars,
and the Dalai Lama. There is a health and beauty centre.

MALLORCA, RANDA: *Es Recó de Randa.* ℗℗℗ | AE MC V | 14
Font 13, 07629. (*(971) 66 09 97.* FAX *(971) 66 25 58.*
A restaurant-with-rooms in an old stone house in a quiet village at
the foot of the Puig de Randa mountain. There are views of the village
and the mountains from some of the bedroom windows.

MALLORCA, SES SALINES: *Es Turó.* ℗℗℗ | AE DC MC V | 10
Ses Salines, 07640. (*(971) 64 95 31.* FAX *(971) 64 95 48.*
Rural calm, tasteful comfort and timeless Mallorcan life are brought
together in this hotel in an old farmhouse. It contains a small museum
of local life and is surrounded by olive and almond orchards.

MALLORCA, SÓLLER: *Ca N'Aí.* ℗℗℗℗ | AE DC MC V | 11
Camí de Son Puça 48, 07100. (*(971) 63 24 94.* FAX *(971) 63 18 99.*
An old Mallorcan house built into the side of Sóller valley, which is
covered with orange and palm trees. Inside, the decor is refined. The
service has a personal touch and the cooking is excellent.

MALLORCA, VALLDEMOSSA: *Vistamar.* ℗℗℗℗ | AE DC MC V | 16
Ctra de Valldemossa–Andratx, 07170. (*(971) 61 23 00.* FAX *(971) 61 25 83.*
This is a peaceful clifftop hotel in a villa built early in the 20th century.
The bedrooms, furnished with antiques, overlook a courtyard. Chopin
and George Sand made the nearby monastery famous.

MENORCA, CIUTADELLA: *Hostal Residencia Ciutadella.* ℗ | AE DC MC V | 17
Calle San Eloy 10, 07760. (*(971) 38 34 62.* FAX *(971) 38 35 62.*
Just a few minutes' walk from the Plaça des Borne, this simple, modern
hotel offers good-value, no-frills accommodation. The rooms are
plainly furnished and spotless. Simple meals are served in the bar.

MENORCA, CIUTADELLA: *Patricia.* ℗℗℗ | AE DC MC V | 44
Paseo San Nicolás 90–92, 07760. (*(971) 38 55 11.* FAX *(971) 48 11 20.*
A modern, cream-coloured chain hotel with white bay windows
on one of the town's main avenues, near the harbour.

MENORCA, MAÓ: *Capri.* ℗℗ | AE DC MC V | 75
Calle San Esteban 8, 07703. (*(971) 36 14 00.* FAX *(971) 35 08 53.*
This is a central hotel in a modern, five-storey block close to shops,
the harbour and the beach. Most bedrooms have a terrace.

MENORCA, MAÓ: *Del Almirante.* ℗℗ | | 40
Carretera de Villacarlos, 07780. (*(971) 36 27 00.* FAX *(971) 36 27 04.*
Built in the 18th century in classic Georgian style, this house became
the home of Admiral Lord Collingwood, a friend of Admiral Nelson.
The hotel has a new wing built round the swimming pool.

MENORCA, MAÓ: *Mirador des Port.* ℗℗℗ | AE MC DC V | 70
Calle Dalt Villanova 1, 07700. (*(971) 36 00 16.* FAX *(971) 36 73 46.*
A modern, comfortable hotel at the western end of town with a view
across the harbour. Many bedrooms have shuttered terraces – ideal for
summer evenings. There is a chic designer bar downstairs.

MENORCA, MAÓ: *Port Mahón.* ℗℗℗℗ | AE DC MC V | 82
Fort de L'Eau 13, 07701. (*(971) 36 26 00.* FAX *(971) 35 10 50.*
Housed in an attractive red and white colonial-style building, this hotel
looks over Maó harbour. Its grounds include wide terraces and a
curving swimming pool surrounded by lawns.

For key to symbols see back flap

Price categories for a standard double room per night, with tax, breakfast and service included:

Ⓟ   under 8,000 ptas
ⓅⓅ   8,000–12,000 ptas
ⓅⓅⓅ   12,000–16,000 ptas
ⓅⓅⓅⓅ   16,000–20,000 ptas
ⓅⓅⓅⓅⓅ   over 20,000 ptas

CREDIT CARDS
Indicates which credit cards are accepted: *AE* American Express; *DC* Diners Club; *MC* Master Card/Access; *V* Visa
PARKING
Parking provided by the hotel in a private car park or a private garage on the hotel site or very close by. Some hotels charge for use of private parking facilities.
SWIMMING POOL
Hotel pool outdoors unless otherwise stated.
GARDEN
Hotel with garden, courtyard or terrace, often providing tables for eating outdoors.

THE CANARY ISLANDS

	CREDIT CARDS	NUMBER OF ROOMS	PRIVATE PARKING	SWIMMING POOL	GARDEN OR TERRACE
FUERTEVENTURA, ANTIGUA: *El Castillo.* ⓅⓅ Caleta de Fuste, 36610. 📞 *(928) 16 31 00.* FAX *(928) 16 30 46.* The attractive apartments in this village-style complex have direct access to a beach curving round a gentle bay, and to a central plaza of shops, cafés and restaurants. A popular location for water sports. 🚗 ♿	AE DC MC V	390	■	●	■
FUERTEVENTURA, CORRALEJO: *Tres Islas.* ⓅⓅⓅⓅ Grandes Playas, 35660. 📞 *(928) 53 57 00.* FAX *(928) 53 58 58.* All the bedrooms of this spacious hotel have balconies facing the sea. There are two huge pools set among gardens. 🚗 ■ 📺 ♿	AE DC MC V	365	■	●	■
FUERTEVENTURA, COSTA CALMA: *Fuerteventura Playa.* ⓅⓅⓅ Urb Cañada del Río, Polígono C1, 35627. 📞 *(928) 54 73 44.* FAX *(928) 54 70 97.* The two wings of this hotel curve round gardens and pools. It is in a secluded spot with direct access to the beach. All the bedrooms are large, with balconies overlooking the sea. 🚗 ■ 📺 ♿	AE MC V	300	■	●	■
LA GOMERA, PLAYA DE SANTIAGO: *Jardín Tecina.* ⓅⓅⓅⓅ Lomada de Tecina, 38811. 📞 *(922) 89 50 50.* FAX *(922) 89 51 88.* Its many facilities make this complex in the hills behind the Playa de Santiago virtually a self-contained resort. A cliffside lift takes guests down to the beach club. 🚗 ■ ♿	AE MC V	434	■	●	■
LA GOMERA, SAN SEBASTIÁN: *Parador de San Sebastián.* ⓅⓅⓅ San Sebastián de La Gomera, 38800. 📞 *(922) 87 11 00.* FAX *(922) 87 11 16.* On a clifftop above La Gomera's main town and port, this parador is in traditional style, with pitched ceilings. The bedrooms have dark wood fittings and tiled bathrooms, and there are tropical gardens. 🚗 📺	AE DC MC V	58	■	●	■
GRAN CANARIA, AGAETE: *Princesa Guayarmina.* Ⓟ Los Berrazales, 35480. 📞 *(928) 89 80 09.* FAX *(928) 89 85 25.* A small, plain hotel in the mountains. The simply furnished rooms overlook a tropical valley. It is excellent value and has friendly staff. 🚗	MC V	27	■	●	■
GRAN CANARIA, MASPALOMAS: *Maspalomas Oasis.* ⓅⓅⓅⓅⓅ Playa de Maspalomas 3, 35106. 📞 *(928) 14 14 48.* FAX *(928) 14 11 92.* In a prime, palm-shaded spot by the dunes is this quiet, secluded hotel. The guests are stylishly accommodated in split-level suites with spacious bedrooms. The staff are efficient and pleasant. 🚗 ■ 📺	AE DC MC V	334	■	●	■
GRAN CANARIA, LAS PALMAS: *Imperial Playa.* ⓅⓅⓅ Calle Ferreras 1, 35008. 📞 *(928) 46 88 54.* FAX *(928) 46 94 42.* A smart, comfortable business hotel in a modern block overlooking Las Canteras beach, close to the port and shops. 🚗 ■ 📺	AE DC MC V	142			
GRAN CANARIA, LAS PALMAS: *Santa Catalina.* ⓅⓅⓅⓅ Calle León y Castillo 227, 35005. 📞 *(928) 24 30 40.* FAX *(928) 24 27 64.* An long-established hotel in a large park. It is a traditional building of the Canary Islands, with carved wooden balconies and a colonial atmosphere. There is an opulent casino. 🚗 ■ 📺	AE DC MC V	200	■	●	■
GRAN CANARIA, PLAYA DEL INGLÉS: *Parque Tropical.* ⓅⓅⓅⓅ Avenida de Italia 1, 35100. 📞 *(928) 77 40 12.* FAX *(928) 76 81 37.* An attractive hotel in local style with comfortable rooms, direct access to the seafront and good sports facilities. Book ahead. 🚗	AE DC MC V	235	■	●	■
GRAN CANARIA, PUERTO DE MOGÁN: *Club de Mar.* ⓅⓅⓅ Puerto de Mogán, 35138. 📞 *(928) 56 50 66.* FAX *(928) 56 54 38.* Pretty buildings with rooms and apartments are ranged round a small bay with a sandy beach and a marina. There are pleasant grounds, a swimming pool and lively local bars. 🚗 ■ 📺	AE MC V	56	■	●	■

EL HIERRO, FRONTERA: *Punta Grande.*   ℙℙ   4
Las Puntas, 38911. 【 *(922) 55 90 81.* FAX *(922) 55 90 81.*
Guests are charmed to find themselves in the world's smallest hotel,
as listed in *The Guinness Book of Records*: four bedrooms and a sitting
room converted from what was once a customs store.

EL HIERRO, VALVERDE: *Parador El Hierro.*   ℙℙℙ   AE DC MC V   47
Valverde, 38910. 【 *(922) 55 80 36.* FAX *(922) 55 80 86.*
Black cliffs are the backdrop for this modern, pantiled hotel on an
isolated beach. It is attractively decorated and quiet, with an informal,
intimate atmosphere. A good base for a walking holiday.

LANZAROTE, ARRECIFE: *Lancelot.*   ℙ   AE DC MC V   113
Avenida Mancomunidad 9, 35500. 【 *(928) 80 50 99.* FAX *(928) 80 50 39.*
A stylish new hotel beside a beach of soft, pale sand. Coral reefs lie just
offshore. There are good restaurants in the hotel and the town.

LANZAROTE, COSTA TEGUISE: *Meliá Salinas.*   ℙℙℙℙ   AE DC MC V   310
Urbanización Costa Teguise, 35509. 【 *(928) 59 00 40.* FAX *(928) 59 03 90.*
A vast atrium with central water gardens and ornamental plants is the
focus of this contemporary hotel. It offers big, restful bedrooms,
boutiques, sports facilities and an attractive beach.

LANZAROTE, PUERTO DEL CARMEN: *Los Fariones.*   ℙℙℙ   AE DC MC V   249
Calle Roque del Oeste 1, 35510. 【 *(928) 51 01 75.* FAX *(928) 51 02 02.*
A secluded hotel on an attractive beach. It is relaxing and comfortable,
with spacious bedrooms and a good range of facilities.

LANZAROTE, YAIZA: *Lanzarote Princess.*   ℙℙℙ   AE DC MC V   407
Avenida Playa Blanca 35570. 【 *(928) 51 71 08.* FAX *(928) 51 70 11.*
A resort hotel, popular with families. It is cool and light, with split-level
areas ornamented with water gardens. There is a large pool.

LA PALMA, BARLOVENTO: *La Palma Romántica.*   ℙℙ   AE MC V   41
Calle Las Llanadas, 38726. 【 *(922) 18 62 21.* FAX *(922) 18 64 00.*
Nestling into a hillside high above the sea is this light, airy hotel with
spacious rooms. It has an indoor pool, a sauna and a solarium.

TENERIFE, LOS CRISTIANOS: *Estefanía.*   ℙℙℙ   AE DC MC V   32
Carretera de Arona, 38660. 【 *(922) 75 16 97.* FAX *(922) 75 15 93.*
A hotel in the hills behind the Playa de las Américas, with luxurious
bedrooms and a cool, stylish decor.

TENERIFE, LA OROTAVA: *Parador de Cañadas del Teide.*   ℙℙ   AE DC MC   23
Apto de Correos 15, Cañadas del Teide, 38300. 【 *(922) 38 64 15.* FAX *(922) 38 23 52.*
There are views of Mount Teide from this modern parador, which
looks like an Alpine chalet. It is inside the national park, and is a
useful centre from which to explore this volcanic region.

TENERIFE, PLAYA DE LAS AMÉRICAS: *Jardín Tropical.*   ℙℙℙℙ   AE DC MC V   315
Urbanización San Eugenio, 38660. 【 *(922) 75 01 00.* FAX *(922) 75 28 44.*
In the heart of the resort, with access to the seafront, this is an
imaginative modern hotel with turrets and tiled patios.

TENERIFE, PUERTO DE LA CRUZ: *Monopol.*   ℙℙ   AE DC MC V   100
Calle Quintana 15, 38400. 【 *(922) 38 46 11.* FAX *(922) 37 03 10.*
An old-style, family-run hotel with a plant-filled patio with wooden
balustrades. The bedrooms are modern and spacious, and there is a
basement restaurant. The staff are smart and efficient.

TENERIFE, PUERTO DE LA CRUZ: *Botánico.*   ℙℙℙ   AE DC MC V   282
Calle Richard J Yeoward, 38400. 【 *(922) 38 14 00.* FAX *(922) 38 15 04.*
The sea is some distance away from this restful hotel near the Botanic
Gardens, but it offers excellent leisure facilities.

TENERIFE, SANTA CRUZ DE TENERIFE: *Náutico.*   ℙℙℙ   AE DC MC V   40
Calle Profesor Peraza 13, 38001. 【 *(922) 24 70 66.* FAX *(922) 24 72 76.*
A small, modern block behind the port, close to a bus stop for Las
Teresitas beach. The small café serves a good Spanish breakfast.

TENERIFE, VILAFLOR: *Alta Montaña.*   ℙ   AE DC MC V   11
Calle Morro del Cano 1, 38613. 【 *(922) 70 90 49.* FAX *(922) 70 90 00.*
A small, homely hotel with spectacular views. It is run by a friendly
Belgian couple, who serve organic food in their restaurant.

For key to symbols see back flap

RESTAURANTS AND BARS

ONE OF THE JOYS of eating out in Spain is the sheer sociability of the Spanish. Family and friends, often with children in tow, can be seen eating out from early in the day until after midnight.

Spanish food has a regional bias. Traditional restaurants originated as taverns and tapas bars serving dishes based on local produce. Spain also has

Wall tile advertising a Barcelona restaurant

its fair share of top-quality gourmet restaurants, notably in the Basque Country.

The restaurants listed on pages 578–609 have been selected for their food and conviviality. Pages 574–7 illustrate some of the best tapas and drinks; and each of the book's five regional sections includes features on the area's unique food and wines.

Bodegas are bars that specialize in wines and do not serve food

RESTAURANTS AND BARS

THE CHEAPEST and quickest places to eat are the bars and cafés that serve tapas. Some bars, however, especially *pubs* (late-opening bars for socializing) serve no food.

Family-run *bar-restaurantes*, *ventas*, *posadas*, *mesones* and *fondas* – all old words for the different types of inn – serve inexpensive, sit-down meals. *Chiringuitos* are beachside bars. They open only during the summer season.

Spain's top restaurants tend to be clustered in the Basque Country, Galicia, Barcelona, Catalonia and Madrid.

Most restaurants close one day a week, some for lunch or dinner only, and most for an annual holiday. They also close on some public holidays. The main closing times of the restaurants on pages 578–609 are listed at the end of each entry. Always check these opening times, however, when phoning to book a table.

EATING HOURS IN SPAIN

THE SPANISH often have two breakfasts *(desayunos)*. The first is a light meal of biscuits or toast with olive oil or butter and jam and *café con leche* (milky coffee). A more substantial breakfast may follow between 10 and 11am, perhaps in a café. This may consist of a savoury snack, such as a *bocadillo* (sandwich) with sausage, ham or cheese, or a thick slice of *tortilla de patatas* (potato omelette). Fruit juice, coffee or beer are the usual accompaniments.

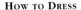

Decoration, Barcelona bar

From about 1pm people will stop in the bars for a beer or a *copa* (glass) of wine with tapas. By 2pm those who can will have arrived home from work for *la comida* (lunch), which is the main meal of the day. Others will choose to have lunch in a restaurant.

The cafés, *salones de té* (tea rooms) and *pastelerías* (pastry shops) fill up by about 5:30 or 6pm for *la merienda* (tea) of sandwiches, pastries or cakes, with coffee, tea or juice. Snacks like *churros* (fried batter sticks) can also be bought from stalls.

By 7pm, bars are crowded with people having tapas with sherry, wine or beer. In Spain *la cena* (dinner or supper), begins at about 9pm. Restaurants sometimes begin their evening service earlier for tourists. In summer, however, Spanish families and groups of friends often do not sit down to eat until as late as midnight. At weekend lunch times, especially in the summer, you may find that restaurants are filled by large and noisy family gatherings.

HOW TO DRESS

A JACKET AND TIE are rarely required, but the Spanish dress smartly, especially for city restaurants. Day dress is casual in beach resorts, but shorts are frowned on in the evenings.

The parador restaurant in Pedraza de la Sierra, Segovia (see p595)

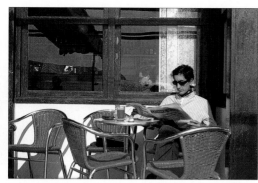

Pavement tables outside a cafetería, in Cadaqués on the Costa Brava

READING THE MENU

ASIDE FROM TAPAS, perhaps the cheapest eating options in Spanish restaurants are the fixed-price *platos combinados* (meat or fish with vegetables and, usually, chips) and the *menú del día*. A *plato combinado* is only offered by cheaper establishments. Most restaurants – but not all – offer an inexpensive, fixed-price *menú del día*, normally of three courses, but with little choice. Some gourmet restaurants offer a *menú de degustación* consisting of a choice of six or seven of the head chef's special dishes.

The Spanish word for menu is *la carta*. It starts with *sopas* (soups), *ensaladas* (salads), *entremeses* (hors d'oeuvres), *huevos y tortillas* (eggs and omelettes) and *verduras y legumbres* (vegetable dishes).

Main courses are *pescados y mariscos* (fish and shellfish) and *carnes y aves* (meat and poultry). Daily specials are chalked on a board or clipped to menus. Paella and other rice dishes may be served as the first course. A useful rule is to follow rice with meat, or start with *serrano* ham or salad and then follow with a paella.

Desserts are called *postres* in Spanish. All restaurants offer fresh fruit (the usual dessert in Spain) but otherwise the range of *postres* is generally poor. The better restaurants offer a limited choice, perhaps *natillas* (custard) and *flan* (crème caramel). Gourmet restaurants have more creative choices.

Vegetarians are rather poorly catered for in Spain. Some

vegetable, salad and egg dishes will be vegetarian, but may contain pieces of ham or fish, so ask before you order. All eating places welcome children and will serve small portions if requested.

Las Torres de Ávila *(see p185)*, a distinctive Barcelona bar

WINE CHOICES

DRY FINO WINES are perfect with shellfish, *serrano* ham, olives, soups and most first courses. Main courses are commonly accompanied by wines originating from Ribera del Duero, Rioja, Navarra or Penedès. A typical bar might serve wines from Valdepeñas or the local vineyards. Oloroso wines *(see p577)* are often ordered as a *digestif*.

SMOKING

IN FINE RESTAURANTS customers are offered *puros* (cigars) with their coffee and brandy. Many people in Spain smoke and very few restaurants have no-smoking areas or tables.

PRICES AND PAYING

IF YOU ORDER from *la carta* in a restaurant, your bill can soar way above the price of the *menú del día*, especially if you order pricey items, such as fresh seafood, fish or *ibérico* ham *(see p438)*. If there is an expensive fish such as sole or swordfish on the menu at a bargain price, it may be frozen. Sea bass and other popular fish and shellfish, such as large prawns, lobster and crab, are priced by weight as a rule.

La cuenta (the bill) includes service charges and perhaps a small cover charge. Prices on menus do not include seven per cent VAT *(IVA)*, which is usually added when the bill is totalled. The Spanish hardly ever tip restaurant waiters more than five per cent, often just rounding up the bill.

Cheques are rarely used in Spain. Travellers' cheques are usually accepted but you may be given a poor rate of exchange. The major credit cards and international direct debit cards are now accepted in most restaurants. However, do not expect to pay by credit card in smaller eating or drinking places like tapas bars, cafés, village *mesones*, road-side *ventas*, *pubs* or bodegas.

WHEELCHAIR ACCESS

SINCE RESTAURANTS are rarely designed for wheelchairs, phone in advance (or ask the hotel staff to call) to check on access to tables and toilets.

Early 20th-century decor in a Madrid bar

Choosing Tapas

TAPAS, SOMETIMES CALLED PINCHOS, are small snacks that originated in Andalusia in the 19th century to accompany sherry. Stemming from a bartender's practice of covering a glass with a saucer or *tapa* (cover) to keep out flies, the custom progressed to a chunk of cheese, or a few olives, being placed on a platter to accompany a drink. Once free of charge, tapas usually have to be paid for nowadays. Choose from a range of appetizing varieties, from cold meats or cheeses to elaborately prepared hot dishes of seafood, meat or vegetables.

Dry fino sherry

Fritura de pescado *is a mixture of fried fish and seafood served with lemon. It includes red mullet, squid and baby hake or other available fresh fish.*

Albondigas *(meatballs) are a hearty tapa and may be served with a zesty tomato sauce.*

Jamón serrano, *salt-cured ham dried in mountain* (serrano) *air, can be served unadorned in chunks* (tacos) *or in thin slices* (lonchas). *This basic tapas dish is often accompanied by bread.*

Gambas a la plancha *is a simple but flavourful dish of whole grilled unpeeled prawns.*

Tortilla a la española *is the ubiquitous thick Spanish omelette, a tasty dish of onion and potato, bound together with seasoned egg. It is served in wedges or small squares.*

Mejillones a la marinera *is a dish of mussels cooked in a tasty sauce of sautéed onion and garlic, white wine, olive oil, lemon juice and parsley.*

Almendras fritas *(fried salted almonds) are a common snack, since almond trees grow in many parts of Spain.* Pistachios (pistachios), *salted peanuts* (cacahuetes) *and sunflower seeds* (pipas) *can also be ordered to accompany a drink.*

Pollo al ajillo, *a widely available tapa, consists of small pieces of chicken (often wings or legs) browned in oil and then gently simmered in an appetizing garlic-flavoured sauce.*

Banderillas *a canapés skewered o toothpicks. Popular ingr dients include marinate fish and vegetables, har boiled egg, prawns, gherki and olives. The entire cana should be eaten at once, blend the flavours togeth*

Ensaladilla rusa *(Russian salad)* *is cold dish of tuna, prawns, potatoes, carrots and peas coated with mayonnaise. It may be topped with peppers or egg.*

Chorizo, *a popular sausage that is flavoured with garlic and paprika, is usually eaten cold; but some kinds are fried and served hot.*

Patatas bravas *is a piquant dish of potatoes fried in oil and coated in a spicy tomato sauce flavoured with onion, garlic, white wine, parsley and red chilli peppers. The bite-sized morsels are both delicious and filling.*

Olives *are common tapas, and come in several varieties. Gordals are fat Seville olives. Manzanillas may be pitted and stuffed with anchovies, almonds or pimientos. Some olives are marinated in herbs and oil or vinegar.*

Salpicón de mariscos *is a luxurious cold salad consisting of an assortment of fresh seafood, including lobster, crab and prawn, with chopped tomatoes. The salad is coated in a zesty vinaigrette flavoured with onion and red peppers.*

Calamares fritos *are squid rings which have been dusted with flour before being deep fried in olive or vegetable oil. They are served garnished with a slice of lemon.*

Ensalada de pimientos rojos *is a colourful cold salad of roasted red peppers and tomatoes. The juices from the roasting are combined with olive oil and vinegar to make a delicious sauce for the salad.*

Queso manchego, *sheep's cheese from La Mancha (see p321), is Spain's most popular cheese. It comes served with bread in either a mild, semisoft form (semicurado) or, when left to age, a tangy mature form (curado).*

TAPAS BARS

Even a small village will have at least one bar where the locals go to enjoy drinks, tapas and conversation with friends. On Sundays and holidays, the favourite places are packed with whole families enjoying the fare. In larger towns it is customary to move from bar to bar, sampling the specialities of each. A tapa is a single serving, whereas a *ración* serves two or three. *Bocadillos,* sandwiches filled with the same ingredients as tapas, can also be ordered. Tapas are generally eaten standing at the bar rather than sitting at a table, for which a surcharge is usually made.

Friends gathered for conversation and a selection of tapas in a local bar

What to Drink in Spain

SPAIN IS ONE OF THE WORLD'S largest wine-producing countries and many fine wines are made here, particularly reds in La Rioja and sherry in Andalusia. Many other beverages – both alcoholic and nonalcoholic – are served in bars and cafés, which provide an important focus for life in Spain. Spaniards are also great coffee drinkers. In the summer months a tempting range of cooling drinks is on offer, in addition to beer, which is always available. Brandy and a variety of liqueurs, such as *anís*, are drunk as apéritifs and *digestifs*, as is chilled pale gold fino sherry.

Customers enjoying a drink at a terrace café in Seville

Hot chocolate

A plate of *churros* (batter sticks)

Café con leche   Camomile   Lime flower

HOT DRINKS

CAFÉ CON LECHE is a large half-and-half measure of milk and coffee; *café cortado* is an espresso with a splash of milk; *café solo* is a black coffee. Hot chocolate is also popular and is often served with *churros* (batter sticks). Herbal teas include *manzanilla* (camomile) and *tila* (lime flower).

COLD DRINKS

IN MOST SPANISH TOWNS and cities it is safe to drink the tap water, but people generally prefer to buy bottled mineral water, either still *(sin gas)* or sparkling *(con gas)*. Besides soft drinks, a variety of other thirst-quenching summer beverages is available, including *horchata (see p243)*, a sweet, milky drink made from ground *chufas* (earth almonds). Another popular refreshing drink is *leche merengada* (iced milk with sweet meringue floating in it). *Gaseosa*, fizzy lemonade, can be drunk either on its own or as a mixer, usually with wine. *Zumo de naranja natural* (freshly squeezed orange juice) is an excellent thirst quencher.

Sparkling and still mineral water

Horchata, made from *chufas*

SPANISH WINE

Wine has been produced in Spain since pre-Roman times and there is a great variety on offer today, including famous types such as Rioja. The key standard for the industry is the *Denominación de Origen* (DO) classification, a guarantee of a wine's origin and quality. *Vino de la Tierra* is a classification of wines below that of DO in which over 60 per cent of the grapes come from a specified region. *Vino de Mesa*, the lowest category, covers basic unclassified wines. For more detailed information on Spain's principal wine producing regions, refer to the following pages: Northern Spain *(see pp74–5)*, Eastern Spain *(see pp192–3)*, Central Spain *(see pp322–3)*, and Southern Spain *(see pp402–3)*.

Penedès white wine   **Rioja red wine**   **Sparkling wine *(cava)***

SPIRITS AND LIQUEURS

Spanish BRANDY, which comes mainly from the sherry bodegas in Jerez, is known as *coñac*. Most bodegas produce at least three different labels and price ranges. Magno is a good middle-shelf brandy; top-shelf labels are Lepanto and Larios. *Anís*, which is flavoured with aniseed, is a popular liqueur. *Pacharán*, made from sloes, is sweet and also tastes of aniseed. Licor 43 is a vanilla liqueur. Ponche is brandy that has been aged and flavoured with herbs.

Anís   **Pacharán**   **Licor 43**   **Ponche**

BEER

Most SPANISH BEER *(cerveza)* is bottled lager, although you can sometimes find it on draught. Popular brands include San Miguel, Cruzcampo and Águila. To order a glass of beer in a bar ask for *una caña*. Alcohol-free lager *(cerveza sin alcohol)* is also available in most bars in Spain.

Bottled beers

SHERRY

Sherry IS PRODUCED in bodegas in Jerez de la Frontera (Andalusia) and in nearby towns Sanlúcar de Barrameda and El Puerto de Santa María *(see pp402–3)*. Although not officially called sherry, similar kinds of wine are produced in Montilla near Córdoba. Pale fino is dry and light and excellent as an apéritif. Amber amontillado (aged fino) has a strong, earthy taste while oloroso is full-bodied and ruddy.

Two brands of fino sherry

Red wine and lemonade

MIXED DRINKS

Sangria IS a refreshing mixture of red wine, *gaseosa* (lemonade) and other ingredients including chopped fruit and sugar. Wine diluted with lemonade is called *vino con gaseosa*. Another favourite drink is *Agua de Valencia*, a refreshing blend of *cava* (sparkling wine) and orange juice. Young people will often order the popular *cubalibres*, cola with rum or gin.

Cubalibre   **Vino con gaseosa**

Sangria

HOW TO READ A WINE LABEL

If you know what to look for, the label will provide a key to the wine's flavour and quality. It will bear the name of the wine and its producer or bodega *(see p619)*, its vintage if there is one, and show its *Denominación de Origen* (DO) if applicable. Wines labelled *cosecha* are recent vintages and the least expensive, while *crianza* and *reserva* wines are aged a minimum of two or three years – part of that time in oak casks – and therefore more expensive. Table wine *(Vino de Mesa)* may be *tinto* (red), *blanco* (white) or *rosado* (rosé). *Cava* is a sparkling wine made by the *méthode champenoise* in specified areas of origin.

Brand name

Company's crest

Capacity of the bottle

Estate-bottled rather than cooperative

The wine's *Denominación de Origen*

The vintage

Symbol for region

Choosing a Restaurant

THE RESTAURANTS in this guide have been selected across a wide range of price categories for their good value, exceptional food and interesting location. This chart lists the restaurants by region, starting with Galicia. Use the colour-coded thumb tabs, which indicate the regions covered on each page, to guide you to the relevant section of the chart.

	CREDIT CARDS	TAPAS BAR	FIXED-PRICE MENU	GOOD WINE LIST	OUTDOOR TABLES

GALICIA

BAIONA: *Moscón.* ₧₧
Calle Alférez Barreiro 2 (Pontevedra). ((986) 35 50 08.
Galician cuisine including a tasty fish *caldeirada* (casserole) spiced with paprika. The harbour view makes for a pleasant dining experience. 🍽 ♿

	AE DC MC V			●	

BETANZOS: *La Casilla.* ₧
Avenida de Madrid 90 (A Coruña). ((981) 77 01 61.
This old stone house by the roadside is famous throughout Spain for its omelettes. You can admire the garden from the terrace. ● Mon. ♿

	MC V		■	●	

BUEU: *A Centoleira.* ₧₧
Playa de Beluso 28 (Pontevedra). ((986) 32 08 96.
Choose your own lobster from the aquarium or try the hake with clams accompanied by a good Albariño wine. ● Mon & Oct. 🍽

	AE DC MC V	●	■	●	■

A CORUÑA: *La Penela.* ₧
Plaza de María Pita 12. ((981) 20 92 00.
Simple, unpretentious dining both indoors and out. The roast veal, Spanish omelette, and Galician-style monkfish are specialities. ● Sun. 🍽

	AE DC MC V			●	■

A CORUÑA: *Casa Pardo.* ₧₧
Calle Novoa Santos 15. ((981) 28 00 21.
This tavern by the fishing port is renowned for its monkfish, prepared in various ways. The blackberry crème caramel is also popular. ● Sun. 🍽

	AE DC MC V		■	●	

O GROVE: *Crisol.* ₧₧₧
Calle Hospital 10–12 (Pontevedra). ((986) 73 00 29.
A variety of seafood and shellfish dishes are served here, using first-class ingredients. The dining room overlooks the sea. 🍽

	AE MC V		■	●	

A GUARDA: *Anduriña.* ₧₧
Calle Calvo Sotelo 48 (Pontevedra). ((986) 61 11 08.
Watch the fishing boats bring in their catch as you enjoy fresh hake, turbot or a fish casserole in this port-side restaurant. 🍽 ♿

	AE DC MC V	●		●	■

LUGO: *Alberto.* ₧₧
Calle Cruz 4. ((982) 22 83 10.
Award-winning chef Alberto García's delicacies include beef entrecôte served in a green turnip sauce and sea bass with baby eels. ● Sun. 🍽

	AE DC MC V	●	■		

LUGO: *Verruga.* ₧₧₧
Calle Cruz 12. ((982) 22 98 55.
This restaurant offers a wide variety of seafood from its own hatchery. Try the red peppers stuffed with crab meat and the delicious home-made *filloas* (crêpes) prepared in different ways. ● Mon. 🍽 ♿

	AE DC MC V	●	■	●	

OURENSE: *Pingallo.* ₧
Rúa San Miguel 6. ((988) 22 00 57.
Wholesome home cooking, with Galicia's trademark dish of *lacón con grelos* (turnip greens with ham). Try the tasty cutlets of beef or kid. ♿

	AE MC V	●	■		■

OURENSE: *San Miguel.* ₧₧₧
Rúa San Miguel 12–14. ((988) 22 12 45.
Innovative Galician cuisine specializing in seafood dishes. Try the sea bass in crayfish sauce or the fresh oysters and cockles. ● Tue. 🍽

	AE DC MC V	●	■		

PADRÓN: *Casa Ramallo.* ₧₧
Calle Castro 5, Rois (A Coruña). ((981) 80 41 80.
Home-grown vegetables and hearty fish casseroles are served in this rustic house. The *xobiña guisada* is a tasty casserole of sardines with potatoes and tomatoes. The home-made desserts are delicious. ● Mon. 🍽

	AE DC MC V			●	■

Price categories for a three-course evening meal for one, including a half-bottle of house wine, tax and service:

ℙ under 3,000 ptas
ℙℙ 3,000–4,500 ptas
ℙℙℙ 4,500–6,000 ptas
ℙℙℙℙ over 6,000 ptas

TAPAS BAR
In addition to the main dining room, there is a bar serving tapas *(see p574–5)* and *raciones* (larger portions).

FIXED-PRICE MENU
A good-value, fixed-price menu is offered at lunch or dinner, or both, usually with three courses.

GOOD WINE LIST
Denotes a wide range of good wines, or a more specialized selection of local wines.

OUTDOOR TABLES
Facilities for eating outdoors, on a terrace, or in a garden or courtyard, often with a good view.

Restaurant	Price	Credit Cards	Tapas Bar	Fixed-Price Menu	Good Wine List	Outdoor Tables
PONTEVEDRA: *Doña Antonia.* Calle Soportales, Plaza de la Herrería 4. (*(986) 84 72 74.* Contemporary European cuisine in a refined setting overlooking the lovely Plaza de la Herrería. The lukewarm monkfish salad and the nougat ice cream with hazelnuts and pistachios are favourites. ● *Sun.* ▤	ℙℙℙ	MC V			●	
SAN SALVADOR DE POYO: *Casa Solla.* Avenida Sineiro 5 (Pontevedra). (*(986) 87 28 84.* Specialities of this elegant restaurant, housed in a lovely old *pazo* (manor house), include lobster salad with tomato vinaigrette and sea bass served on a bed of leeks. ▤ ♿	ℙℙℙ	AE DC MC V			●	▪
SANTIAGO DE COMPOSTELA: *Nixon.* Calle Santiago de Chile 15 (A Coruña). (*(981) 53 15 31.* Good home cooking, based on local recipes. The house specialities are river salmon, prepared in various ways, and sirloin steak. Try the *filloas* (crêpes) for dessert. Well-stocked wine cellar. ● *Sun.* ▤	ℙℙ	AE V		▪	●	
SANTIAGO DE COMPOSTELA: *Toñi Vicente.* Avenida Rosalía de Castro 24 (A Coruña). (*(981) 59 41 00.* Worshippers of Galician haute cuisine flock faithfully to Toñi's culinary temple. The marinated sea bass salad and the hake cooked in a shell of potato are just two of her creations. ● *Sun.* ▤ ♿	ℙℙℙℙ	AE DC MC V		▪	●	
SANXENXO: *La Taberna de Rotilio.* Avenida del Puerto (Pontevedra). (*(986) 72 02 00.* Located in the cellar of the hotel, this smart restaurant has gained fame for its innovative approach to Galician cuisine. The chef's creations include a monkfish *caldeirada*, an all-time favourite. ● *Mon & mid Dec–mid Jan.* ▤	ℙℙℙℙ	AE DC MC V		▪	●	
VEDRA: *Roberto.* Calle San Julián de Sales (A Coruña). (*(981) 51 17 69.* With an emphasis on fish and vegetables, Roberto Crespo uses home-grown produce to create interesting dishes such as sea bass with turnip greens. In the garden is a 300-year-old magnolia tree.	ℙℙℙ	AE MC V	●	▪	●	▪
VERÍN: *Gallego.* Carretera N525, Albarellos de Monterrei (Ourense). (*(988) 41 82 02.* Enjoy traditional Galician recipes, including a wide variety of seafood and shellfish, in this bright dining room with views of the countryside. ▤ ♿	ℙℙ	AE DC MC V	●	▪	●	▪
VIGO: *El Castillo.* Parque del Castro (Pontevedra). (*(986) 42 11 11.* There is a stunning view of Vigo and the ria from this elegant hilltop restaurant which specializes in grilled fish and meat. ● *Mon.* ▤	ℙℙℙ	AE DC MC V		▪		
VILAGARCÍA DE AROUSA: *El Lagar.* Pazo Sobrán, Villajuan de Arosa (Pontevedra). (*(986) 50 09 09.* Situated in a large 11th-century *pazo* (manor house), this building is reputedly older than the cathedral of Santiago de Compostela. Informal dining with good regional cooking. ♿	ℙℙ	AE MC V	●	▪		
VILAGARCÍA DE AROUSA: *Chocolate.* Avenida de Cambados 151 (Pontevedra). (*(986) 50 11 99.* Manolo Cores, a local personality and master of the grill, offers a balanced selection of seafood and meat. He is proud to tell you that his wife's savoury sweetcorn and cockle pies are unbeatable. ● *Sun.* ▤ ♿	ℙℙℙ	AE MC V			●	
VILLAFRAMIL: *La Villa.* Carretera Oviedo–A Coruña (Lugo). (*(982) 12 30 01.* This charming 300-year-old village house has been artfully restored and specializes in traditional regional food. The hake served with caviar and the tender Galician veal are recommended. ● *Tue.*	ℙ	AE DC MC V		▪	●	▪

Price categories for a three-course evening meal for one, including a half-bottle of house wine, tax and service:

® under 3,000 ptas
®® 3,000–4,500 ptas
®®® 4,500–6,000 ptas
®®®® over 6,000 ptas

TAPAS BAR
In addition to the main dining room, there is a bar serving tapas (see p574–5) and raciones (larger portions).
FIXED-PRICE MENU
A good-value, fixed-price menu is offered at lunch or dinner, or both, usually with three courses.
GOOD WINE LIST
Denotes a wide range of good wines, or a more specialized selection of local wines.
OUTDOOR TABLES
Facilities for eating outdoors, on a terrace, or in a garden or courtyard, often with a good view.

ASTURIAS AND CANTABRIA

		CREDIT CARDS	TAPAS BAR	FIXED-PRICE MENU	GOOD WINE LIST	OUTDOOR TABLES
AVILÉS: *Real Balneario de Salinas.* Calle Juan Sitges 3, Salinas (Asturias). (98) 551 86 13. This lovely restaurant in the seaside resort of Salinas is owned by a prestigious Avilés restaurateur. The emphasis of the seasonal menu is on seafood, and the baby eels are the house speciality. ▤ ♿	®®®	AE MC V		▦	●	▦
CANGAS DE ONÍS: *La Cabaña.* Calle Susierra 34 (Asturias). (98) 594 00 84. A popular grillroom with a wood fire where suckling pig and baby lamb are roasted to perfection. Finish with cheese or apple pie. ● *Thu.* ▤ ♿	®	AE DC MC V		▦		▦
CASTAÑEDA: *Hostería de Castañeda.* Calle Villabañez (Cantabria). (942) 59 81 13. After seeing the nearby caves at Puente Viesgo, relax in the converted stables of this 17th-century farmhouse. Tuck into the wild boar stew with fine herbs or the sirloin steak with mushrooms. ▤ ♿	®®	AE DC MC V	●	▦	●	▦
CASTRO URDIALES: *Mesón del Marinero.* Calle Correría 23 (Cantabria). (942) 86 00 05. This listed historic building houses a stylish seafood restaurant. The portions are generous and its proximity to the fishing port is evident in the freshness of the produce. Excellent wine list.	®®®	AE DC MC V	●	▦	●	
CASTROPOL: *El Risón.* Calle del Puerto (Asturias). (98) 563 50 65. Delightful rustic house with a terrace by the banks of the Eo ria where you can savour authentic Asturian cuisine. The shellfish crêpes (*frixuelos*) and sea bass in white Albariño wine are delicious. ● *Mon & Feb.*	®	AE DC MC V	●	▦	●	▦
COMILLAS: *El Capricho de Gaudí.* Barrio de Sobrellano (Cantabria). (942) 72 03 65. Antoni Gaudí's whimsical architectural wonder provides a unique setting for this sophisticated restaurant. The salmon in anchovy cream and the turbot with garlic sprouts are recommended. ● *Mon & mid Jan–mid Feb.* ▤	®®®	AE DC MC V		▦		▦
COSGAYA: *Mesón del Oso.* Carretera Potes–Fuente Dé (Cantabria). (942) 73 30 18. Delightful country hotel and restaurant by the Río Deva with splendid views of the Picos de Europa. The veal steaks and *cocido lebaniego* (a rich stew with chickpeas and pork) are local specialities. ● *Jan–mid Feb.*	®®	DC MC V		▦		▦
CUDILLERO: *Mariño.* Playa de la Concha de Arteido (Asturias). (98) 559 01 86. The fish casseroles, *calderadas*, are this restaurant's speciality. A typical dish is *curadillo* (a member of the shark family) served in sauce. ♿	®®	AE DC MC V	●	▦	●	▦
ESCALANTE: *San Román de Escalante.* Carretera Escalante–Castillo (Cantabria). (942) 67 77 28. This lovely old mountain house, set in gardens with a 12th-century chapel, is the elegant setting for French-style cuisine. ● *mid Dec–mid Jan.* ▤ ♿	®®®	AE DC MC V	●	▦	●	▦
LAREDO: *Risco.* Calle la Arenosa 2 (Cantabria). (942) 60 50 30. Book a table by one of the large panoramic windows with wonderful views of the bay and savour a hake stew with potatoes and clams in *salsa verde* (a garlic and parsley sauce), or cod prepared with fried red peppers.	®®®®	AE DC MC V	●		●	▦
LASTRES: *El Cafetín.* Calle Matemático Pedrayes (Asturias). (98) 585 00 85. Fresh sea produce is served together with regional specialities such as *pote asturiano* (a stew made with white beans and sausage meat). ● *Wed.*	®	DC MC V	●	▦		▦

LUARCA: *Villa Blanca.* ⓅⓅ
Avenida de Galicia 25–27 (Asturias). 🄲 *(98) 564 10 79.*
Try your hand at pouring cider in the rustic bar and then enjoy the *pitu de aldea* (chicken served with peas and small potatoes). 🍴 🛇

AE DC MC V

OVIEDO: *El Raitán.* ⓅⓅ
Plaza de Trascorrales 6 (Asturias). 🄲 *(98) 521 42 18.*
Discover the variety of Asturian cuisine with the nine-course lunch time *menú de degustación*, served by waiters in regional costume. ● *Sun.* 🍴

AE DC MC V

POTES: *Martín.* Ⓟ
Calle Roscabao, Urbanización Ivana (Cantabria). 🄲 *(942) 73 02 33.*
Authentic regional cooking including the hearty *cocido lebaniego* (a stew with chickpeas and pork) and peppers stuffed with local Treviso cheese. There are great views of the countryside from the dining room. ● *Jan.* 🛇

AE MC V

PRENDES: *Casa Gerardo.* ⓅⓅ
Carretera N632 (Asturias). 🄲 *(98) 588 77 97.*
This delightful restaurant reputedly serves the best *fabada* – a rich stew with white beans and black pudding – in all of Spain. ● *Mon.* 🍴 🛇

AE MC V

PUENTE ARCE: *El Molino.* ⓅⓅⓅ
Carretera Nacional (Cantabria). 🄲 *(942) 57 50 55.*
Aesthetically and gastronomically, this has to be the finest dining experience in the area. Housed in a converted mill, it offers sophisticated Cantabrian cuisine, with romantic views of the river. ● *Mon.* 🛇

AE DC MC V

RAMALES DE LA VICTORIA: *Río Asón.* ⓅⓅⓅ
Calle Barón de Adzaneta 17 (Cantabria). 🄲 *(942) 64 61 57.*
Off the beaten tourist track hides one of Cantabria's best restaurants. The salmon is caught in the nearby Río Asón, and the seasonal menu will delight even the most sophisticated of palates. ● *Mon & Jan.* 🍴 🛇

AE DC MC V

REINOSA: *Vejo.* ⓅⓅ
Avenida de Cantabria 83 (Cantabria). 🄲 *(942) 75 17 00.*
Tender veal is this modern restaurant's speciality. The sirloin with foie gras and truffles is delectable, and the Cantabrian cheese board will give you an idea why this region is renowned for its dairy products.

AE DC MC V

SANTANDER: *Bodega del Riojano.* ⓅⓅ
Calle Río de la Pila 5 (Cantabria). 🄲 *(942) 21 67 50.*
This colourful bodega is as famous for its decorative wine barrels, painted by Spanish artists, as it is for its delicious food. The stuffed red peppers are said to be "the best in the world." Good selection of tapas. 🍴

AE DC MC V

SANTANDER: *Zacarías.* ⓅⓅ
Calle Hernán Cortés 38 (Cantabria). 🄲 *(942) 21 23 33.*
Featuring authentic Cantabrian dishes, this popular restaurant and lively tapas bar will give you a complete taste of regional specialities. 🍴 🛇

AE DC MC V

TARAMUNDI: *El Mazo.* Ⓟ
Cuesta de la Rectoral (Asturias). 🄲 *(98) 564 67 60.*
This old rectory house offers simple, home cooking in an enchanting rural setting. Sirloin steak with local Cabrales blue cheese is one example. 🍴

AE DC MC V

BASQUE COUNTRY, NAVARRA AND LA RIOJA

AOIZ: *Beti Jai.* ⓅⓅ
Calle Santa Agueda 2 (Navarra). 🄲 *(948) 33 60 52.*
Old town house in the main square with views of the river, serving authentic Navarrese cuisine. The sheep's tripe *(menudicos)*, pig's trotters and the home-made sponge cake are local specialities. 🍴

MC V

AZPEITIA: *Kiruri Jatetxea.* ⓅⓅ
Barrio de Loiola 23 (Guipúzcoa). 🄲 *(943) 81 56 08.*
Enjoy the Guridi family's traditional Basque dishes such as *txangurro* (spider crab baked and served in the shell) or *lubina al txacoli* (sea bass cooked in the local white wine). 🍴 🛇

AE DC MC V

BILBAO (BILBO): *Zortziko.* ⓅⓅⓅⓅ
Calle Alameda Mazarredo 17 (Vizcaya). 🄲 *(94) 423 97 43.*
Contemporary haute cuisine served in a beautiful and elegant building, declared a historic monument. The menu is seasonal and the creative Basque elaborations are sublime. ● *Sun.* 🍴

AE DC MC V

For key to symbols see back flap

Price categories for a three-course evening meal for one, including a half-bottle of house wine, tax and service:

℗ under 3,000 ptas
℗℗ 3,000–4,500 ptas
℗℗℗ 4,500–6,000 ptas
℗℗℗℗ over 6,000 ptas

TAPAS BAR
In addition to the main dining room, there is a bar serving tapas (see p574–5) and raciones (larger portions).
FIXED-PRICE MENU
A good-value, fixed-price menu is offered at lunch or dinner, or both, usually with three courses.
GOOD WINE LIST
Denotes a wide range of good wines, or a more specialized selection of local wines.
OUTDOOR TABLES
Facilities for eating outdoors, on a terrace, in a garden or courtyard, often with a good view.

	CREDIT CARDS	TAPAS BAR	FIXED-PRICE MENU	GOOD WINE LIST	OUTDOOR TABLES
CINTRUÉNIGO: *Maher.* ℗℗℗ Calle Ribera 19 (Navarra). (*(948) 81 11 50.* Innovative cuisine is impeccably presented in this basement restaurant. Asparagus pudding, rice with hare, and suckling lamb ribs in a delicious mushroom sauce are all house specialities. ▤	AE DC MC V	●	■	●	
EGÜES: *Mesón Egües.* ℗℗℗ Carretera de Aoiz (Navarra). (*(948) 33 00 81.* Enjoy excellent meat and fish in this cosy restaurant with a rustic atmosphere. Specialities include turbot and chargrilled steaks, and delicious fresh foie gras. Good home-made desserts. ● Mon. ▤ &	AE DC MC V			●	
ELORRIO: *Nico.* ℗℗ Plaza Arbol de Guernika 4 (Vizcaya). (*(94) 682 04 69.* This old Vizcayan house with wooden beams and rustic decor is a popular eating spot serving simple yet tasty cooking. ● Mon & Aug.	MC V		■		
ESTELLA (LIZARRA): *Navarra.* ℗℗ Calle Gustavo de Maeztu 16, Los Llanos (Navarra). (*(948) 55 10 69.* Traditional regional cuisine is served in this grand house, with tiles depicting Navarra's former kings. The *blanca de navarra* (a lemon and honey ice cream, served with fresh cream and nuts) is superb. ● Mon. ▤	AE MC V	●	■	●	
EZCARAY: *Echaurren.* ℗℗ Calle Héroes del Alcázar 2 (La Rioja). (*(941) 35 40 47.* One of La Rioja's emblematic restaurants, run by the delightful Paniego family. The region's superlative vegetables are cooked to perfection and there is a great variety of Rioja and Albariño wines. ● Nov. ▤ &	AE DC MC V		■	●	
GALDÁCANO: *Aretxondo.* ℗℗℗ Calle Elexalde 20 (Vizcaya). (*(94) 456 76 71.* One of the region's best restaurants, this is a veritable showcase of sophisticated Basque cooking, and well worth the drive of 10 km (6 miles) from Bilbao. Reservations are advised. ● Mon. ▤ &	AE MC V		■	●	
GETARIA: *Elkano.* ℗℗℗℗ Calle Herrerita 2 (Guipúzcoa). (*(943) 14 06 14.* Pedro Arregui is famous for his grilled fish dishes. The squid served with its own ink and the turbot are both excellent. The best Basque brand of *txacoli* wine – Txomín Echaniz – is also available here. ▤ &	AE DC MC V			●	■
HARO: *Terete.* ℗℗ Calle Lucrecia Arana 17 (La Rioja). (*(941) 31 00 23.* This ancient wood-burning oven has been roasting lamb since 1877. Sit at the long wooden tables and savour the Riojan specialities, accompanied by a bottle of house wine. ● Mon. ▤ &	MC V		■	●	
HONDARRIBIA (FUENTERRABÍA): *Sebastián.* ℗℗ Calle Mayor 9–11 (Guipúzcoa). (*(943) 64 01 67.* A lovely 16th-century house in the historic part of town serving Basque-French cuisine. Game dishes are available in season. ● Mon & Nov. &	AE DC MC V		■		
KORTEZUBI: *Lezika.* ℗℗ Barrio Basondo 8, Santimamiñe (Vizcaya). (*(94) 625 29 75.* Close to the Santimamiñe caves is this delightful 18th-century country house serving traditional Basque cuisine, such as hake in *salsa verde*, and red beans with ham and sausage. Good selection of wines. ▤ &	AE DC MC V	●	■	●	■
LAGUARDIA: *Posada Mayor de Migueloa.* ℗℗℗ Calle Mayor de Migueloa 20 (Álava). (*(941) 12 11 75.* The elegant and beautifully restored 17th-century palace of Viana now houses one of La Rioja's best restaurants. The roast lamb and the Riojan potatoes *(a la riojana)* are just two of the specialities. ▤ &	AE DC MC V	●	■	●	■

LASARTE: *Martín Berasategui.* 🅟🅟🅟   AE DC MC V
Calle Loidi 4 (Guipúzcoa). (*(943) 36 64 71.*
One of the area's leading restaurants, in a converted farmhouse. The cold potato soup with smoked bacon is just one of Martín's creations. He will also design a menu to fit your budget. ● *Mon.* 🍽 🅱

LEKEITIO: *Mesón Arropain.* 🅟🅟🅟   AE DC MC V
Carretera de Marquina, Arropain, Ispaster (Vizcaya). (*(94) 684 03 13.*
A rustic farmhouse with an emphasis on seafood. Grilled turbot, baked crayfish and spider crab are all specialities. The home-made *cuajada* (a curd pudding) is typical of the region. ● *Wed & mid Dec–mid Jan.* 🅱

LOGROÑO: *El Cachetero.* 🅟🅟   DC MC V
Calle Laurel 3 (La Rioja). (*(941) 22 84 63.*
Home-style local cuisine is served in this cosy restaurant. The vegetable dishes are excellent, and it is also a good place to try roast kid. Desserts include *arroz con leche* (rice pudding). ● *Sun & mid Jul–mid Aug.* 🍽 🅱

OIARTZUN: *Zuberoa.* 🅟🅟🅟🅟   AE DC MC V
Calle Iturriotz Auzoa 8 (Guipúzcoa). (*(943) 49 12 28.*
Another of Spain's best restaurants, Zuberoa is set in a lovely 600-year-old farmhouse. The Arbelaitz brothers maintain a consistent level of culinary artistry, and their foie gras with chickpea sauce is a classic. ● *Mon.* 🍽 🅱

PAMPLONA (IRUÑA): *Sarasate.* 🅟🅟   MC V
Carretera de Irún, Olave (Navarra). (*(948) 33 08 20.*
This farmhouse just outside Pamplona serves great food at affordable prices. Grilled dishes are the speciality, and you can try their *guisado de toro* (bull stew) just after the Sanfermines bull-running fiesta. ● *Mon.* 🅱

PAMPLONA (IRUÑA): *Alhambra.* 🅟🅟🅟   AE DC MC V
Calle Bergamín 7 (Navarra). (*(948) 24 50 07.*
Typical Navarrese cooking is served in this welcoming restaurant. The artichokes, the truffle and vegetable purée and the mushroom risotto are all delicious appetizers. Good selection of local wines. ● *Sun.* 🍽

PASAI DONIBANE: *Casa Cámara.* 🅟🅟   MC V
Pasajes de San Juan 79 (Guipúzcoa). (*(943) 52 36 99.*
Choose your own live lobster from the aquarium or try the baked spider crab as you admire panoramic sea views. ● *Mon.* 🅱

PUENTE LA REINA: *Mesón el Peregrino.* 🅟🅟🅟   MC V
Carretera Pamplona–Logroño (Navarra). (*(948) 34 00 75.*
This charming country inn provides a peaceful setting to enjoy refined, regional cuisine. Savour veal cheeks in an onion sauce and finish off with a white chocolate mousse. ● *Mon.* 🍽

SAN SEBASTIÁN (DONOSTIA): *Akelaré.* 🅟🅟🅟🅟   AE DC MC V
Paseo Padre Orcolaga 56, Barrio de Igueldo (Guipúzcoa). (*(943) 21 20 52.*
A Spanish gastronomic temple with spectacular views of rolling hills which plunge into the sea. To savour the chef's star dishes, try the seven-course *menú de degustación*. Smart dress only. ● *Mon & Feb.* 🍽 🅱

SAN SEBASTIÁN (DONOSTIA): *Arzak.* 🅟🅟🅟🅟   AE DC MC V
Calle Alto del Miracruz 21 (Guipúzcoa). (*(943) 27 84 65.*
According to many gourmets, this is Spain's best restaurant. Master chef Juan Mari Arzak's international reputation for innovative Basque cuisine, rewarded with three Michelin stars, is well deserved. ● *Mon & Nov.* 🍽 🅱

TAFALLA: *Túbal.* 🅟🅟   AE DC MC V
Plaza de Navarra 6 (Navarra). (*(948) 70 08 52.*
This historic building has 18 balconies overlooking the square. Try the crêpes filled with borage, a traditional Navarrese vegetable. ● *Mon.* 🍽 🅱

VIANA: *Borgia.* 🅟🅟🅟   AE DC MC V
Calle Serapio Urra (Navarra). (*(948) 64 57 81.*
A small restaurant in the historic part of town with an interesting seasonal menu. The artichokes with foie gras served on a bed of watercress and the lamb marinated in herbs with a gin sauce are specialities. ● *Sun & Aug.*

VITORIA (GASTEIZ): *Dos Hermanas.* 🅟🅟🅟   AE DC MC V
Madre Vedruna 10 (Álava). (*(945) 13 29 34.*
Classic regional cooking with a seasonal menu. The tuna served on a bed of peppers and the oxtail stew are both delicious. ● *Sun.* 🍽 🅱

For key to symbols see back flap

Price categories for a three-course evening meal for one, including a half-bottle of house wine, tax and service:

Ⓟ under 3,000 ptas
ⓅⓅ 3,000–4,500 ptas
ⓅⓅⓅ 4,500–6,000 ptas
ⓅⓅⓅⓅ over 6,000 ptas

TAPAS BAR
In addition to the main dining room, there is a bar serving tapas (see p574–5) and raciones (larger portions).
FIXED-PRICE MENU
A good-value, fixed-price menu is offered at lunch or dinner, or both, usually with three courses.
GOOD WINE LIST
Denotes a wide range of good wines, or a more specialized selection of local wines.
OUTDOOR TABLES
Facilities for eating outdoors, on a terrace, or in a garden or courtyard, often with a good view.

		CREDIT CARDS	TAPAS BAR	FIXED-PRICE MENU	GOOD WINE LIST	OUTDOOR TABLES
VITORIA (GASTEIZ): *Ikea.* Portal de Castilla 27 (Álava). ⓒ (945) 14 47 47. José Ramón Berriozabal masterfully combines traditional Basque cuisine with a French influence. The hake fillet in *salsa verde* is a classic dish. The foie gras terrine and the Bresse pigeon are both exquisite. ● Mon. ▤	ⓅⓅⓅ	AE DC MC V		■	●	
BARCELONA						
OLD TOWN: *Agut.* **Map 5 A3.** Carrer Gignàs 16. ⓒ (93) 315 17 09. Painters used to exchange their artwork for a hearty, honest Catalan meal here. Nowadays the specialities include an aubergine terrine and succulent blood red steaks from Girona. ● Aug. ▤	Ⓟ	MC V		■	●	
OLD TOWN: *Cal Pep.* **Map 5 B3.** Plaça de les Olles 8. ⓒ (93) 310 79 61. According to some seafood fanatics, Pep's *pescado frito* (fried fish) is the best in the world! Other recommended dishes include clams with ham, fried baby squid, and crayfish with onion. ● Sun & Aug. ▤	Ⓟ	AE DC MC V	●			
OLD TOWN: *Egipte.* **Map 2 F2.** Carrer Jerusalem 3. ⓒ (93) 317 74 80. This lively place, once a monks' residence, serves Mediterranean specialities, and salt cod prepared in ten different ways. ▤	Ⓟ	AE DC MC V	●	■	●	
OLD TOWN: *Les Quinze Nits.* **Map 5 A3.** Plaça Reial 6. ⓒ (93) 317 30 75. Conveniently located, this attractive restaurant draws a young crowd and offers good Catalan dishes at reasonable prices. ▤ ♿	Ⓟ	AE DC MC V		■	●	■
OLD TOWN: *Romesco.* **Map 2 F3.** Carrer de Sant Pau 28. ⓒ (93) 318 93 81. A popular spot just off the Ramblas with home-style cooking, a lively atmosphere and unbeatable prices. The house speciality is *frijoles* (a Cuban dish of rice, black beans, fried banana and eggs). ● Sun & Jul.	Ⓟ		●	■		
OLD TOWN: *Amaya.* **Map 5 A1.** Ramblas 24. ⓒ (93) 302 10 37. This classic, popular Basque-Catalan restaurant offers a good selection of tapas at the bar and half portions of many dishes that appear on the encyclopedic menu. Fantastic wine list. ▤	ⓅⓅ	AE DC MC V	●	■	●	
OLD TOWN: *Can Culleretes.* **Map 5 A2.** Carrer Quintana 5. ⓒ (93) 317 64 85. The city's oldest restaurant, established in 1786, serves traditional Catalan dishes such as *pica pica de pescado* (a seafood medley). ● Mon & Jul. ▤ ♿	ⓅⓅ	AE DC MC V		■	●	
OLD TOWN: *Can Majó.* **Map 5 B5.** Carrer de l'Almirall Aixada 23. ⓒ (93) 221 54 55. This renowned seafood restaurant in Barceloneta serves great rice dishes such as a peeled shellfish paella and *suquet* (a delicious hot fish and potato stew). Extensive wine list. ● Mon. ▤ ♿	ⓅⓅ	AE DC MC V		■	●	
OLD TOWN: *Los Caracoles.* **Map 5 A3.** Carrer Escudellers 14. ⓒ (93) 302 31 85. Bustling restaurant in the Barri Xinès (Chinese Quarter) serving simple dishes such as paella, suckling lamb, and chicken roasted on a spit. ▤	ⓅⓅ	AE DC MC V	●		●	
OLD TOWN: *Fonda Senyor Parellada.* **Map 5 B3.** Carrer de la Argentería 37. ⓒ (93) 310 50 94. With wooden benches, old chandeliers, and candlesticks on the tables, this atmospheric restaurant is a great choice for authentic, reasonably priced Catalan cuisine. ● Sun. ▤ ♿	ⓅⓅ	AE DC MC V			●	

OLD TOWN: *Reial Club Marítim de Barcelona.* **Map 5 A4.** ⓅⓅ MC V
Moll d'Espanya. (*(93) 221 62 56.*
Classic nautical club restaurant with spectacular views of the port. The elaborate cuisine includes dishes such as aubergine terrine with goat's cheese, and gilthead with apples and a cider sauce. 🗒

OLD TOWN: *Casa Leopoldo.* **Map 2 F3.** ⓅⓅⓅ AE DC MC V
Carrer de Sant Rafael 24. (*(93) 441 30 14.*
This delightful restaurant, set in old stables and a carriage house, has been in the family since 1929 and the menu, featuring good quality regional dishes, has altered little since then. Good service. ● *Mon & Aug.* 🗒 &

OLD TOWN: *Llevataps.* **Map 5 B4.** ⓅⓅⓅ AE DC MC V
Plaça Pau Vila. (*(93) 221 24 33.*
Overlooking the marina, this modern restaurant is decorated with corkscrews and offers seven different fixed-price menus. 🗒 &

OLD TOWN: *Set Portes.* **Map 5 B3.** ⓅⓅⓅ AE DC MC V
Passeig de Isabel II 14. (*(93) 319 29 50.*
This lavishly decorated restaurant is reminiscent of an elegant Parisian café. Specialities include 11 different types of paella, and delicious home-made cannelloni. Efficient service and a good wine list. 🗒 &

OLD TOWN: *Talaia Mar.* **Map 6 E5.** ⓅⓅⓅⓅ AE DC MC V
Anexo Torre Mapfre, Carrer de la Marina 16. (*(93) 221 90 90.*
This stunning, sleek, circular shaped restaurant, with views of the marina, offers extremely good food. The menu varies with the season. You can order half portions *(pica pica)* of most dishes. 🗒 &

EIXAMPLE: *Roig Robí.* **Map 3 A2.** ⓅⓅⓅ AE DC MC V
Carrer de Séneca 20. (*(93) 218 92 22.*
Small, intimate restaurant offering authentic Catalan cuisine, with a lovely interior courtyard for summer. The terrines, fresh salads and any of the rice or seafood dishes are bound to please. ● *Sun.* 🗒 &

EIXAMPLE: *El Tragaluz.* **Map 3 A3.** ⓅⓅⓅ AE DC MC V
Passeig Concepció 5. (*(93) 487 06 21.*
Two different dining concepts are offered here: the second floor serves fast food and the third has contemporary Mediterranean cuisine. The restaurant's logo is by graphic designer Javier Mariscal. 🗒

EIXAMPLE: *La Venta.* ⓅⓅⓅ AE DC MC V
Plaça Doctor Andreu. (*(93) 212 64 55.*
At the foot of Tibidabo is this attractive restaurant. The glass covered terraces are open in summer and provide a bright, greenhouse setting in winter, with views of the city. Catalan-French cuisine. ● *Sun.* 🗒 &

FURTHER AFIELD (NORTHWEST): *Chicoa.* ⓅⓅ AE MC V
Carrer d'Aribau 73. (*(93) 453 11 23.*
A haven for lovers of salt cod, with more than ten different preparations of the celebrated *bacallà*. As well as many other seafood and meat dishes, there is a good Penedès rosé house wine. ● *Sun & Aug.* 🗒 &

FURTHER AFIELD (NORTHWEST): *Giardinetto Notte.* **Map 3 A2.** ⓅⓅ AE DC MC V
Carrer Granada del Penedès 22. (*(93) 218 75 36.*
Mediterranean and Italian dishes are served in this romantic setting. Try the home-made pasta with a bottle of Catalan wine. ● *Sun & Aug.* 🗒

FURTHER AFIELD (NORTHWEST): *Tiro Mimet.* ⓅⓅ AE MC V
Carrer de Sant Marius 22. (*(93) 211 77 66.*
The cuisine here can best be described as Catalan-French. Hot and cold duck livers are served as well as a wide variety of mushrooms, and game in season. Good selection of Catalan wines and *cavas*. ● *Sun & Aug.*

FURTHER AFIELD (NORTHWEST): *La Balsa.* ⓅⓅⓅ AE DC MC V
Carrer de Infanta Isabel 4. (*(93) 211 50 48.*
There are great views of Barcelona from the terrace of this restaurant. The Catalan cuisine includes an excellent goose liver as a starter. ● *Sun.*

FURTHER AFIELD (NORTHWEST): *Botafumeiro.* **Map 3 A2.** ⓅⓅⓅⓅ AE DC MC V
Carrer Gran de Gràcia 81. (*(93) 218 42 30.*
Fine quality seafood and Galician specialities are served in this stylish restaurant. The shellfish dishes are served in generous portions and the desserts are mouthwatering. Extensive wine list. ● *Aug.* 🗒 &

Price categories for a three-course evening meal for one, including a half-bottle of house wine, tax and service:

Ⓟ under 3,000 ptas
ⓅⓅ 3,000–4,500 ptas
ⓅⓅⓅ 4,500–6,000 ptas
ⓅⓅⓅⓅ over 6,000 ptas

TAPAS BAR
In addition to the main dining room, there is a bar serving tapas (see p574–5) and raciones (larger portions).
FIXED-PRICE MENU
A good-value, fixed-price menu is offered at lunch or dinner, or both, usually with three courses.
GOOD WINE LIST
Denotes a wide range of good wines, or a more specialized selection of local wines.
OUTDOOR TABLES
Facilities for eating outdoors, on a terrace, or in a garden or courtyard, often with a good view.

	CREDIT CARDS	TAPAS BAR	FIXED-PRICE MENU	GOOD WINE LIST	OUTDOOR TABLES
FURTHER AFIELD (NORTHWEST): *Jaume de Provença.* ⓅⓅⓅ Carrer de Provença 88. ☏ (93) 430 00 29. The chef's original and creative Catalan cuisine has established his restaurant as among the city's finest. Despite the business-like decor the food is excellent and the service attentive. ● Mon & Aug. ▤ ♿	AE DC MC V		■	●	
FURTHER AFIELD (WEST): *Peixerot.* **Map 1 B1.** ⓅⓅ Torre Catalunya, Carrera de Tarragona 177. ☏ (93) 424 69 69. First-class seafood predominates on the menu of this comfortable, modern restaurant. Great rice dishes and shellfish. ▤	AE DC MC V	●		●	
FURTHER AFIELD (WEST): *Neichel.* ⓅⓅⓅⓅ Beltrán i Rózpide 16. ☏ (93) 203 84 08. European haute cuisine with Catalan touches is served in one of the city's most prestigious establishments. It has an excellent selection of cheese and over 300 wine labels. ● Sun & Aug. ▤ ♿	AE DC MC V		■	●	
CATALONIA					
ALTAFULLA: *Faristol.* Ⓟ Carrer de Sant Martí 5 (Tarragona). ☏ (977) 65 00 77. Wine was once made in this delightful 18th-century house, now decorated with antiques. Try the the superb chocolate mousse. ● Oct–May: Mon–Thu.	DC MC V	●		●	■
ANDORRA LA VELLA: *Borda Estevet.* ⓅⓅ Carretera de la Comella 2 (Andorra). ☏ (07-376) 86 40 26. This old country house, decorated in rustic style, is still used for the traditional practice of drying tobacco from the nearby fields. Ask for the meat a la "llosa" (brought to you on a hot slate). ▤ ♿	AE MC V			●	
ARENYS DE MAR: *Hispania.* ⓅⓅⓅ Carrer Real 54, Carretera NII (Barcelona). ☏ (93) 791 04 57. Authentic Catalan cuisine which has won accolades from near and far. The classic clam suquet, similar to a fricassee, and the crema catalana (a rich caramel custard) are both delicious. ● Tue & Oct. ▤	AE DC MC V			●	
ARTIES: *Casa Irene.* ⓅⓅⓅ Hotel Valarties, Calle Mayor 3 (Lleida). ☏ (973) 64 43 64. Located in a picturesque village, this restaurant offers wonderful, French influenced food and three menús de degustación. ▤ ♿	AE DC MC V		■	●	
BERGA: *Sala.* ⓅⓅ Passeig de la Pau 27 (Barcelona). ☏ (93) 821 11 85. Classic Catalan dishes are offered here, many of which feature mushrooms. Game is available in season. ● Mon. ▤ ♿	AE DC MC V		■	●	
BLANES: *Can Patacano.* ⓅⓅ Passeig del Mar 12 (Girona). ☏ (972) 33 00 02. Delightful family-run establishment close to the sea, serving good, affordable fresh seafood and shellfish. Catalan specialities include the fish and potato suquet. ▤ ♿	DC MC V		■	●	
BOLVIR DE CERDANYA: *Torre del Remei.* ⓅⓅⓅⓅ Camí Reial (Girona). ☏ (972) 14 01 82. This stunning palace surrounded by gardens has been impeccably restored and now houses an elegant restaurant and hotel. The chef will delight you with his gourmet dishes and superb wine selection. ▤	AE DC MC V		■	●	■
CALAFELL: *Giorgio.* ⓅⓅ Carrer Ángel Guimerá 4 (Tarragona). ☏ (977) 69 11 59. Delicious Italian food with home-made pasta, bread and desserts, served on a terrace overlooking the sea. The lasagne is legendary but be sure to reserve since there are only ten tables. ♿			■	●	■

CAMBRILS: *Joan Gatell-Casa Gatell.* Ⓟ Ⓟ Ⓟ
Passeig Miramar 26, Cambrils Port (Tarragona). ((977) 36 00 57.
Seafood is the speciality of this establishment. The rice dishes, shellfish,
and lobster casserole are all first class. ● *Mon & mid Dec–mid Jan.* 🍴 &
AE DC MC V

CASTELL-PLATJA D'ARO: *Joan Piqué.* Ⓟ Ⓟ Ⓟ
Barri de Crota 3 (Girona). ((972) 81 79 25.
Lovely 14th-century *masía* (farmhouse), decorated in keeping with the
period, serving innovative cuisine of the Empordà region. The frogs' legs
served with celery in a pesto sauce is one example. ● *Tue & Nov.* 🍴 &
AE DC MC V

FIGUERES: *Ampurdán.* Ⓟ Ⓟ Ⓟ
Hotel Ampurdán, Carretera NII (Girona). ((972) 50 05 62.
Gourmets congregate here to enjoy Josep Mercader's legendary cuisine.
The fresh broad beans with mint and the salt cod with a garlic mousseline
are both exquisite. Delightful terrace for dining in the summer. 🍴 &
AE DC MC V

GIRONA: *El Celler de Can Roca.* Ⓟ Ⓟ Ⓟ
Carretera Taialá 40. ((972) 22 21 57.
The capital's best restaurant, where Juan Roca creates imaginative dishes
such as lamb stuffed with sweetbreads and cinnamon. ● *Sun.* 🍴 &
AE DC MC V

LLEIDA: *Forn del Nastasi.* Ⓟ Ⓟ
Carrer Salmerón 10. ((973) 23 45 10.
Excellent regional cuisine including chargrilled vegetables *(escalivada)*
and snails *a la llauna* (baked in the oven). ● *Mon.* 🍴 &
AE DC MC V

LLORET DE MAR: *El Trull.* Ⓟ Ⓟ Ⓟ
Ronda Europa, Cala Canyelles (Girona). ((972) 36 49 28.
Rustic dining room with marine motifs where you can choose your lobster
from the aquarium and then watch it sizzle on the open grill. The
arrosat (noodles prepared with seafood) is also a good choice. 🍴 &
AE DC MC V

MARTINET: *Boix.* Ⓟ Ⓟ Ⓟ
Carretera N260 (Lleida). ((973) 51 50 50.
A famous Catalan restaurant, located on the banks of the Río Segre,
serving roast leg of lamb so tender you can eat it with a spoon! ● *Tue.* 🍴
AE DC MC V

PERALADA: *Castell de Peralada.* Ⓟ Ⓟ Ⓟ
Casino Castell de Peralada (Girona). ((972) 53 81 25.
Dine in the incomparable medieval setting of this castle and try any of
the dishes of the Empordà region and the castle's own house wine. 🍴
AE MC V

REUS: *El Pa Torrat.* Ⓟ Ⓟ
Avinguda Reus 24, Castellvell del Camp (Tarragona). ((977) 85 52 12.
Good regional home cooking with dishes such as roast rabbit with *allioli*
(a garlic mayonnaise) and stuffed *calamares* (squid). ● *Tue.* 🍴 &
AE MC V

ROSES: *El Bulli.* Ⓟ Ⓟ Ⓟ Ⓟ
Cala Montjoi (Girona). ((972) 15 04 57.
Considered by many to be one of Spain's best restaurants and perhaps
one of Europe's most beautiful, El Bulli is a must on any gourmet's
itinerary. Expensive, but definitely worth the treat. ● *mid Oct–mid Mar.*
AE DC MC V

SANT CARLES DE LA RÀPITA: *Miami Can Pons.* Ⓟ Ⓟ
Avinguda Constitució 35 (Tarragona). ((977) 74 05 51.
Good quality Catalan cooking is served here by the Pons family. The
suquet and the *crema catalana* are just two of the specialities. ● *Feb.* 🍴
AE DC MC V

SANT CELONI: *El Racó de Can Fabes.* Ⓟ Ⓟ Ⓟ Ⓟ
Carrer de Sant Joan 6 (Barcelona). ((93) 867 28 51.
Santi Santamaría is considered one of Spain's best chefs and this delightful
country restaurant is a gastronomic paradise. The ever changing seasonal
menu combines many types of fresh regional produce. ● *Mon.* 🍴 &
AE DC MC V

SANT FELIÚ DE GUIXOLS: *Can Toni.* Ⓟ Ⓟ
Carrer Garrofers 54 (Girona). ((972) 32 10 26.
Enjoy traditional cooking of the Empordà region here. Many dishes
include mushrooms when in season (September–March). ● *Tue.* 🍴 &
AE DC MC V

SANT SADURNI D'ANOIA: *El Mirador de les Caves.* Ⓟ Ⓟ Ⓟ
Carretera Sant Sadurni–Ordal, Subirats (Barcelona). ((93) 899 31 78.
The duck with a foie gras and truffle sauce is one of the superb dishes
served here. Guests can enjoy views over the Penedès vineyards. 🍴 &
AE DC MC V

For key to symbols see back flap

Price categories for a three-course evening meal for one, including a half-bottle of house wine, tax and service:

(P) under 3,000 ptas
(P)(P) 3,000–4,500 ptas
(P)(P)(P) 4,500–6,000 ptas
(P)(P)(P)(P) over 6,000 ptas

TAPAS BAR
In addition to the main dining room, there is a bar serving tapas (see p574–5) and raciones (larger portions).
FIXED-PRICE MENU
A good-value, fixed-price menu is offered at lunch or dinner, or both, usually with three courses.
GOOD WINE LIST
Denotes a wide range of good wines, or a more specialized selection of local wines.
OUTDOOR TABLES
Facilities for eating outdoors, on a terrace, or in a garden or courtyard, often with a good view.

LA SEU D'URGELL: *El Castell.*   (P)(P)(P)
Carretera N260 (Lleida). ☎ (973) 35 07 04.
At the foot of Seu d'Urgell castle, surrounded by beautiful countryside, lies this idyllic hotel-restaurant serving modern Catalan cuisine. The wine list will delight even sophisticated wine lovers. ● mid Jan–mid Feb. ▤ &
Credit cards: AE DC MC V · FIXED-PRICE MENU · GOOD WINE LIST

SITGES: *EL Velero.*   (P)(P)
Passeig de la Ribera 38 (Barcelona). ☎ (93) 894 20 51.
A seaside restaurant whose creations include sole fillets on a bed of mushrooms and crab sauce, and lobster with a chickpea sauce. ▤ &
Credit cards: AE DC MC V · FIXED-PRICE MENU · GOOD WINE LIST

TARRAGONA: *El Merlot.*   (P)(P)
Carrer Callers 6. ☎ (977) 22 06 52.
Situated in the old part of town, this restaurant serves Mediterranean cuisine, based on first-class local produce. Specialities include game dishes (available in season) and home-made desserts. ● Mon & Feb. ▤
Credit cards: DC MC V · FIXED-PRICE MENU · GOOD WINE LIST · OUTDOOR TABLES

VALLS: *Masía Bou.*   (P)(P)
Carretera Lleida (Tarragona). ☎ (977) 60 04 27.
Many interesting dishes are on the menu. The speciality is *calçotadas* (onions charred over embers, served with *romesco* sauce). ● Tue. ▤ &
Credit cards: AE DC MC V · TAPAS BAR · FIXED-PRICE MENU · GOOD WINE LIST · OUTDOOR TABLES

VIC: *Floriac.*   (P)(P)
Carretera Manresa–Vic, Collsuspina (Barcelona). ☎ (93) 887 09 91.
A 16th-century *masía* (farmhouse) surrounded by woods, serving regional cuisine. The game dishes, available in winter, are excellent. ● Tue.
Credit cards: AE MC V · TAPAS BAR · FIXED-PRICE MENU · GOOD WINE LIST

VILAFRANCA DEL PENEDÈS: *Airolo.*   (P)(P)(P)
Rambla Nostra Senyora 10 (Barcelona). ☎ (93) 892 17 98.
Over 250 varieties of Penedès wine accompany the seasonal menu which includes duck served with *millefeuille* and aubergine. ● Mon & Aug. ▤ &
Credit cards: AE DC MC V · FIXED-PRICE MENU

ARAGÓN

AINSA: *Bodegas del Sobrarbe.*   (P)(P)
Plaza Mayor 2 (Huesca). ☎ (974) 50 02 37.
Get a taste of medieval history in the vaulted wine cellar of this 11th-century house. Typical Pyrenean dishes include game and *ternasco* (tender suckling lamb roasted on a wood fire). ● mid Dec–mid Mar.
Credit cards: AE DC MC V · FIXED-PRICE MENU · GOOD WINE LIST · OUTDOOR TABLES

ALCAÑIZ: *Meseguer.*   (P)(P)
Avenida del Maestrazgo 9 (Teruel). ☎ (978) 83 10 02.
Popular for its updated home-cooking at reasonable prices, Félix Meseguer's menu includes a delicious vegetable stew (*menestra*) and white beans with partridge. Good local wines. ● Sun. ▤ &
Credit cards: AE DC MC V · TAPAS BAR · FIXED-PRICE MENU · GOOD WINE LIST

BARBASTRO: *Flor.*   (P)(P)
Calle Goya 3 (Huesca). ☎ (974) 31 10 56.
Seasonal menu with fresh produce from the fertile Vero valley and an excellent wine cellar. The baked hake with garlic and the salad of tomato, fresh cheese and local black olives are recommended. ▤ &
Credit cards: AE DC MC V · FIXED-PRICE MENU · GOOD WINE LIST

BIESCAS: *Casa Ruba.*   (P)(P)
Calle Esperanza 18–20 (Huesca). ☎ (974) 48 50 01.
The Ruba family has been serving traditional Aragonese dishes here since 1884. This delightful mountain hotel offers game dishes in season and delicious mushroom and vegetable savoury pies. ● Oct. ▤ &
Credit cards: MC V · TAPAS BAR · FIXED-PRICE MENU

BORJA: *La Bóveda del Mercado.*   (P)
Plaza del Mercado 4 (Zaragoza). ☎ (976) 86 82 51.
Carefully restored 16th-century wine cellar where you can enjoy original dishes using Jewish and Arab recipes as a base. The *delicias de sartén* (fried pastry with aniseed and cinnamon) is one example. ● Mon & Feb.
Credit cards: MC V · GOOD WINE LIST

....

CANTAVIEJA: *Buj.*   ₧₧
Avenida del Maestrazgo 6 (Teruel). ((964) 18 50 33.
A simple, family-run restaurant by the roadside. The stuffed potatoes and
mushroom soup are always on the menu due to popular demand.
Game dishes are available in season. Open lunch times only. ● Feb. &

CARIÑENA: *La Rebotica.*   ₧   MC
Calle San José 3 (Zaragoza). ((976) 62 05 56.   V
Try any of the 58 varieties of local Cariñena wine available in this
converted village pharmacy. Most of the recipes are elaborated with
wine, such as the suckling pig sirloin in a white wine sauce. ● Mon.

ESQUEDAS: *Venta del Sotón.*   ₧₧   AE
Carretera Tarragona–San Sebastián (Huesca). ((974) 27 02 41.   DC
This wayside inn is one of Aragón's leading restaurants, with a creative   MC
cuisine including local specialities and excellent grilled dishes. ● Mon. ▤   V

HUESCA: *Las Torres.*   ₧₧₧   AE
Calle María Auxiliadora 3. ((974) 22 82 13.   DC
The Abadía brothers offer an interesting seasonal menu with innovative   MC
flourishes. The crispy grouper served on a bed of pig's trotters, with a   V
raisin and pine nut sauce, should give you an idea. ● Sun. ▤ &

LA IGLESUELA DEL CID: *Casa Amada.*   ₧   AE
Calle Fuente Nueva 10 (Teruel). ((964) 44 33 73.   MC
Straightforward regional cooking, a simple setting and affordable prices   V
ensure a steady crowd. Try the walnut crème caramel for dessert. ▤ &

JACA: *La Cocina Aragonesa.*   ₧₧   AE
Calle Cervantes 5 (Huesca). ((974) 36 10 50.   MC
One of the best restaurants in the area, serving elaborate regional cuisine.   V
In winter, the partridge stuffed with foie gras or the wild boar meatballs
can be enjoyed around the fireplace. ● Wed. ▤

NUÉVALOS: *Reyes de Aragón.*   ₧   AE
Hotel Monasterio de Piedra (Zaragoza). ((976) 84 90 11.   DC
Typical Aragonese cuisine is offered in this 12th-century monastery   MC
set in a beautiful nature reserve. The trout, fresh from the monastery's   V
own fish farm, served with a ham and almond sauce, is delicious. ▤ &

RUBIELOS DE MORA: *Portal del Carmén.*   ₧₧   AE
Calle Glorieta 2 (Teruel). ((978) 80 41 53.   DC
A former Carmelite monastery with a delightful cloister, specializing in   MC
regional food. The salmon and trout are from the nearby fish farms and   V
the *tocinillo de cielo* (a candied egg yolk dessert) is heavenly. ● Thu. &

SENEGÜÉ: *Casbas.*   ₧   AE
Carretera a Francia (Huesca). ((974) 48 01 49.   DC
A restaurant with a large wood fire where skiers and hikers congregate   MC
for a hearty meal. The typical mountain dessert of aged wine with sliced   V
peaches is a very popular choice. ● Sep. ▤ &

TERUEL: *La Menta.*   ₧₧   AE
Calle Bartolomé Esteban 10. ((978) 60 75 32.   DC
One of the best restaurants in the area, offering an original menu with   MC
Basque and Catalan influences. The delicious *pastel ruso* – a traditional   V
cake from Aragón – is made with egg yolks and almonds. ● Sun. ▤ &

UNCASTILLO: *Casa Sierra.*   ₧₧   DC
Calle Mediavilla 71 (Zaragoza). (& FAX (976) 67 94 81.   MC
Simple yet tasty regional dishes, such as dried white beans with olive   V
oil, and *migas a la pastora* (breadcrumbs with grapes).

ZARAGOZA: *La Rinconada de Lorenzo.*   ₧₧   AE
Calle la Salle 3. ((976) 55 51 08.   DC
Typical Aragonese cuisine is served here, such as *migas con jamón*   MC
(breadcrumbs with ham) and *ternasco al borno* (roast lamb). The   V
home-made desserts include *higos con nueces* (figs with nuts). ▤ &

ZARAGOZA: *Gayarre.*   ₧₧₧   AE
Carretera del Aeropuerto. ((976) 34 43 86.   DC
Lovely house with a pretty garden, just outside the city. The menu is   MC
seasonal with an emphasis on regional vegetables, such as borage, which   V
are used in a variety of salads. Good service and wine list. ● Mon. ▤ &

For key to symbols see back flap

Price categories for a three-course evening meal for one, including a half-bottle of house wine, tax and service:

ℙ under 3,000 ptas
ℙℙ 3,000–4,500 ptas
ℙℙℙ 4,500–6,000 ptas
ℙℙℙℙ over 6,000 ptas

TAPAS BAR
In addition to the main dining room, there is a bar serving tapas (see p574–5) and raciones (larger portions).
FIXED-PRICE MENU
A good-value, fixed-price menu is offered at lunch or dinner, or both, usually with three courses.
GOOD WINE LIST
Denotes a wide range of good wines, or a more specialized selection of local wines.
OUTDOOR TABLES
Facilities for eating outdoors, on a terrace, or in a garden or courtyard, often with a good view.

	CREDIT CARDS	TAPAS BAR	FIXED-PRICE MENU	GOOD WINE LIST	OUTDOOR TABLES
ZARAGOZA: *La Venta del Cachirulo.* ℙℙℙ Autovía de Logroño (Zaragoza). ((976) 33 16 74. A large, elegantly decorated Aragonese house. The beef cutlet is brought to you on a bed of glowing salt embers allowing you to grill it to perfection. There is a wide variety of vegetable dishes. 🍽 ♿	AE DC MC V			●	

VALENCIA AND MURCIA

	CREDIT CARDS	TAPAS BAR	FIXED-PRICE MENU	GOOD WINE LIST	OUTDOOR TABLES
ALICANTE (ALACANT): *Dársena.* ℙℙ Paseo del Puerto. ((96) 520 75 89. With 50 different rice dishes on the menu, you might be hard pressed to choose. The generous portions are served in individual paella pans. 🍽	AE DC MC V		■	●	■
ALICANTE (ALACANT): *Delfín.* ℙℙ Explanada de España 12. ((96) 521 49 11. Overlooking the harbour, the Delfín offers formal and informal dining areas, both serving imaginative Mediterranean cuisine. Try one of the rice dishes or the sea bass in a puff pastry crust with a lobster mousse. 🍽 ♿	AE DC MC V		■	●	■
ALTEA: *Raco de Toni.* ℙℙ Calle de la Mar 127 (Alicante). ((96) 584 17 63. Regional food including rice dishes and locally caught fish is served in this simple, cosy restaurant. The rice with salt cod and vegetables and the anchovies stuffed with peppers are two of the specialities. ● Nov. 🍽 ♿	AE DC MC V	●	■	●	
BENIDORM: *La Palmera-Casa Paco Nadal.* ℙ Avenida Penetración, Rincón de Loix (Alicante). ((96) 585 32 82. Agreeable place just outside Benidorm offering regional specialities. Of the 15 rice dishes, the rice with monkfish and clams is especially good. 🍽 ♿	AE DC MC V		■	●	■
BENIDORM: *El Molino.* ℙℙ Carretera Alicante–Valencia (Alicante). ((96) 585 71 81. Thousands of wine bottles decorate this restaurant, where chef Ivan serves traditional fare including *nayuscas* (grilled crêpes filled with ham and caviar). ● Mon. 🍽 ♿	AE DC MC V			●	■
BENIMANTELL: *L'Obrer.* ℙ Carretera de Alcoi 27 (Alicante). ((96) 588 50 88. A rustic-style restaurant, decorated with locally made ceramics. Enjoy roast lamb, followed by one of the home-made desserts. ● Fri & Jul. 🍽 ♿	AE MC V			●	
BENISSANO: *Levante.* ℙℙ Calle Virgen del Fundamento 15 (Valencia). ((96) 278 07 21. You can't leave Valencia without trying the excellent paellas here, cooked over a wood fire. One of the region's largest and best wine cellars is also at your disposal. Open lunch times only. ● Tue & mid Jul–mid Aug. 🍽 ♿	AE MC V			●	
BUÑOL: *Venta L'Home.* ℙℙ Carretera NIII Madrid–Valencia, Ventamina exit (Valencia). ((96) 250 35 15. A 17th-century coaching inn now housing a delightful restaurant decorated with rustic touches. Great Valencian cuisine such as rabbit with honey or lamb with olives. Good local wines. 🍽 ♿	AE DC MC V	●	■	●	■
CASTELL DE GUADALEST: *Venta la Montaña.* ℙ Carretera de Alcoi 9, Benimantell (Alicante). ((96) 588 51 41. A picturesque mountain inn decorated with antique farming implements where wholesome dishes, such as the typical *olleta de trigo* (a broth made with pork, vegetables and wheat), are served. ● Mon. 🍽 ♿	AE DC MC V	●	●	●	■
CASTELLÓ DE LA PLANA: *La Tasca del Puerto.* ℙℙℙ Avenida del Puerto 13, El Grao (Castellón). ((964) 28 44 81. Specialities include rice dishes, *fideuà* (noodles) and *calderetas* (fish casseroles). There are good views of the harbour and sea. ● Mon. 🍽 ♿	AE DC MC V		■	●	■

COCENTAINA: *L'Escaleta*. ℗℗ AE DC MC V
Avenida País Valenciano 119 (Alicante). ☎ *(96) 559 21 00*.
This basement restaurant, tastefully decorated with tiles and old brass items, serves imaginative dishes such as fillets of sole with *cava*. Excellent desserts – try the minted pears with honey ice cream. ● *Mon.* 🍽 ⚐

CULLERA: *Casa Salvador*. ℗℗ AE DC MC V
L'Estany de Cullera (Valencia). ☎ *(96) 172 01 36*.
Sited on a pretty inlet of a lake *(estany)*, this restaurant in two cottages serves 20 different rice dishes and fish specialities. Some of the fish are caught in the lake and the vegetables are home-grown. 🍽 ⚐

ELX: *Mesón El Granaíno*. ℗℗ AE DC MC V
Calle José María Buch 40 (Alicante). ☎ *(96) 546 01 47*.
The bar is very popular, offering more than 30 different tapas. The dining room, decorated in traditional Andalusian style, serves regional and southern dishes. The wine cellar contains over 5,000 bottles. ● *Sun.* 🍽

FORCALL: *Mesón de la Vila*. ℗ AE DC MC V
Plaza Mayor 8 (Castellón). ☎ *(964) 17 11 25*.
Enjoy affordable regional dishes in the vaulted basement of this 15th-century building, which was once the town hall. Try the rabbit, served with either truffles or white snails from the region. 🍽

GANDIA: *Gamba*. ℗℗℗ AE DC MC V
Carretera Nazaret–Oliva, Gandía-Playa (Valencia). ☎ *(96) 284 13 10*.
Although you can't see the sea from here, the fish and shellfish are fresh from the fishermen's nets. The set menu *(menú dirigido)* offers shellfish and a rice or noodle dish. Open lunch times only. ● *Mon & Nov.* 🍽 ⚐

MORAIRA: *Girasol*. ℗℗℗℗ AE DC MC V
Carretera Moraira–Calp (Alicante). ☎ *(96) 574 43 73*.
Joachim Koerper's innovative Mediterranean cuisine has won over gourmets throughout Europe and is perfectly complemented by the refined decoration of this seaside villa. ● *Mon & Feb.* 🍽 ⚐

MORELLA: *Casa Roque*. ℗℗ AE DC MC V
Calle Segura Barreda 8 (Castellón). ☎ *(964) 16 03 36*.
Diners come from near and far to savour Roque Gutiérrez's famous lamb stuffed with truffles. Or try the duck with red wine and bitter orange essence, and the mushrooms served with truffles. ● *Mon & Feb.*

MURCIA: *Las Cocinas del Cardenal*. ℗℗ AE MC V
Plaza del Cardenal Belluga 7. ☎ *(968) 21 13 10*.
In this restaurant you can opt for the fixed-price menu with a great variety of dishes, or enjoy excellent tapas at the bar. ● *Mon.* 🍽

MURCIA: *Hispano*. ℗℗℗ AE DC MC V
Calle Arquitecto Cerdán 7. ☎ *(968) 21 61 52*.
Regional cooking, including *caldero marinero del Mar Menor* (a typical seafood casserole). The vegetable paella and the gilthead cooked in salt are also delicious. Good selection of regional wines. 🍽 ⚐

ORIHUELA: *Casa Corro*. ℗ MC V
Palmeral de San Antón (Alicante). ☎ *(96) 530 29 63*.
A popular family-run establishment serving typical dishes such as *arroz con costra* (baked rice with a crust) and a hearty stew with meatballs. 🍽

POLOP DE LA MARINA: *Ca l'Angeles*. ℗℗ MC V
Calle Gabriel Miró 35 (Alicante). ☎ *(96) 587 02 26*.
Eat in one of three dining rooms, with wooden beams and rustic decor. Dishes include roast baby kid with almonds. ● *Tue & mid Jun–mid Jul.* 🍽 ⚐

SANTA POLA: *Batiste*. ℗℗ AE DC MC V
Avenida Pérez Ojeda 6, Playa de Poniente (Alicante). ☎ *(96) 541 14 85*.
Reasonably priced seafood and shellfish as well as delicious rices, such as *arroz a banda* (fish risotto), feature on the menu of this classic restaurant. The sea bass in puff pastry is also a speciality. 🍽 ⚐

TORREVIEJA: *Cabo Roig*. ℗℗℗ AE DC MC V
Urbanización Cabo Roig, Playas de Orihuela (Alicante). ☎ *(96) 676 02 90*.
Perched on top of the cliff with magnificent views of the Costa Blanca, Cabo Roig offers a great variety of seafood and rice dishes. The ancient watchtower houses a collection of over 20,000 bottles of wine.

Price categories for a three-course evening meal for one, including a half-bottle of house wine, tax and service:

℗ under 3,000 ptas
℗℗ 3,000–4,500 ptas
℗℗℗ 4,500–6,000 ptas
℗℗℗℗ over 6,000 ptas

TAPAS BAR
In addition to the main dining room, there is a bar serving tapas *(see p574–5)* and *raciones* (larger portions).
FIXED-PRICE MENU
A good-value, fixed-price menu is offered at lunch or dinner, or both, usually with three courses.
GOOD WINE LIST
Denotes a wide range of good wines, or a more specialized selection of local wines.
OUTDOOR TABLES
Facilities for eating outdoors, on a terrace, or in a garden or courtyard, often with a good view.

	Price	Credit Cards	Tapas Bar	Fixed-Price Menu	Good Wine List	Outdoor Tables
VALENCIA: *La Rosa.* Avenida del Neptuno 70. ☎ *(96) 371 20 76.* Typical beachside restaurant with around 30 different rice dishes and a good assortment of fresh fish and shellfish. Open lunch times only. 🍽 ⅏	℗℗	AE MC V			●	■
VALENCIA: *Albacar.* Calle Sorní 35. ☎ *(96) 395 10 05.* Enjoy innovative cuisine in attractive surroundings. Try the lukewarm salad of fish with tarragon vinaigrette, and finish with the excellent home-made apple *millefeuille* with ice cream. ● *Sun & mid Aug–mid Sep.*	℗℗℗	AE DC MC V			●	
VINARÒS: *El Langostino de Oro.* Calle San Francisco 31. ☎ *(964) 45 12 04.* Carefully selected seafood menu, including seafood *suquet*. The rice dishes and the *fideus rosetjats* (specially prepared noodles) are also very popular, and the home-made date tart excellent. ● *Mon.* 🍽 ⅏	℗℗℗	AE DC MC V		■	●	
MADRID						
OLD MADRID: *La Bola Taberna.* Map 2 D2. Calle de la Bola 1. ☎ *(91) 547 69 30.* A true bastion of the *cocido madrileño*, this restaurant dates back to 1870. Since then, little has changed in the preparation of the hearty stew, made with chickpeas and sausage, and served at lunch times only. ● *Sun.* 🍽 ⅏	℗			■	●	
OLD MADRID: *Casa Patas.* Map 5 A2. Calle Cañizares 10. ☎ *(91) 369 04 96.* Known for its flamenco shows in the evening, Casa Patas is also an original place to eat in the heart of Old Madrid. Well-stocked tapas bar and unbeatable fixed-price menu. ● *Sun & Aug.* 🍽 ⅏	℗	AE DC MC V	●	■	●	
OLD MADRID: *Casa Ciriaco.* Map 1 C4. Calle Mayor 84. ☎ *(91) 548 06 20.* A traditional tavern near the Royal Palace, renowned for its *gallina en pepitoria* (a chicken stew with egg and saffron). ● *Wed & Aug.* 🍽 ⅏	℗℗	DC MC V	●	■	●	
OLD MADRID: *Botín.* Map 2 E4. Calle de Cuchilleros 17. ☎ *(91) 366 42 17.* Reputedly the oldest restaurant in the world, dating back to 1725. The original wood-burning oven is still used to cook the traditional Castilian roast lamb and suckling pig. Reasonable fixed-price menu. 🍽	℗℗℗	AE DC MC V		■	●	
OLD MADRID: *Lhardy.* Map 2 F3. Carrera de San Jerónimo 8. ☎ *(91) 521 33 85.* Established in 1839 and conserving its true character with chandeliers, mirrors and dark wood-panelled walls, this restaurant serves what is arguably the most classic *cocido madrileño*. 🍽	℗℗℗℗	AE DC MC V	●	■	●	
BOURBON MADRID: *Champagnería Gala.* Map 5 B2. Calle Moratín 22. ☎ *(91) 429 25 62.* Admire the indoor patio and chandeliers and enjoy a generous set menu with Catalan specialities at an unbelievably reasonable price. 🍽	℗		●	■		■
BOURBON MADRID: *Hylogui.* Map 5 A1. Calle Ventura de la Vega 3. ☎ *(91) 429 73 57.* This traditional restaurant attracts families for Sunday lunch. The long menu includes typical dishes such as *callos a la madrileña* (tripe in a spicy tomato sauce). Service is efficient. ● *Aug.* 🍽 ⅏	℗	AE MC V	●	■	●	
BOURBON MADRID: *Teatriz.* Map 4 E3. Calle Hermosilla 15. ☎ *(91) 577 53 79.* A restaurant in the stalls of an old theatre, with a cocktail bar on the stage. Italian-inspired food, such as a salmon and sole *carpaccio*. ● *Aug.* 🍽 ⅏	℗℗	AE DC MC V	●	●	●	

BOURBON MADRID: *Al Mounia*. **Map 4** D4.   (R)(R)(R)
Calle de Recoletos 5. ((91) 435 08 28.
Madrid's finest Moroccan restaurant serving authentic couscous and *tajine* (lamb stew). If you have room, there is the rich house dessert, made with honey, almonds and orange blossom water. ● *Sun, Mon & Aug.* 🍴 ♿
Cards: AE, DC, MC, V

BOURBON MADRID: *Alkalde*. **Map 4** E3.   (R)(R)(R)
Calle Jorge Juan 10. ((91) 576 33 59.
Call in for Basque specialities in the dining room or at the lively tapas bar. The spider crab soup, the *chipirones* (small squid cooked in its ink) and the clams in a white wine, onion and garlic sauce are all good. ● *Aug.* 🍴
Cards: AE, DC, MC, V

BOURBON MADRID: *La Giralda*. **Map 4** E4.   (R)(R)(R)
Calle Claudio Coello 24. ((91) 576 40 69.
Andalusian cuisine is served in a restaurant decorated in Moorish style. Try the *pescado frito* (an assortment of fried fish) or any grilled fish. 🍴 ♿
Cards: AE, DC, MC, V

BOURBON MADRID: *Paradis*. **Map 5** B1.   (R)(R)(R)
Calle Marqués de Cubas 14. ((91) 429 73 03.
Part of a successful Catalan chain, offering high quality Mediterranean cuisine. The grilled vegetables and the rice dishes make delicious starters. They can be followed by any of the fresh fish. ● *Sun & Aug.* 🍴 ♿
Cards: AE, DC, MC, V

BOURBON MADRID: *El Amparo*. **Map 4** E4.   (R)(R)(R)(R)
Callejón de Puigcerdá 8. ((91) 431 64 56.
New Basque Cuisine in what many consider to be Madrid's nicest setting, with a skylight that lets you gaze up at the stars. The tuna mousse with lobster and parsley oil is just one creation. ● *Sun & Aug.* 🍴
Cards: AE, MC, V

BOURBON MADRID: *Viridiana*. **Map 6** D1.   (R)(R)(R)(R)
Calle Juan de Mena 14. ((91) 523 44 78.
Innovative Spanish cuisine complemented by an encyclopedic wine list is offered in this restaurant decorated with stills from Luis Buñuel's film *Viridiana*. The creative menu changes frequently. ● *Sun & Aug.* 🍴
Cards: AE, MC, V

FURTHER AFIELD (EAST): *La Taberna de la Daniela*.   (R)(R)
Calle General Pardiñas 21. ((91) 575 23 29.
A short but well-chosen menu is offered at this restaurant. The only thing served at lunch times is *cocido madrileño*, or you can choose from a wide range of tapas at the bar. Good home-made desserts. ● *Aug.* 🍴
Cards: V

FURTHER AFIELD (NORTH): *Casa Ricardo*.   (R)
Calle Fernando El Católico 31. ((91) 447 61 19.
This typical Spanish bar offers good, home-style dishes. The oxtail soup is delicious as are the baby squid prepared in their own ink. 🍴 ♿
Cards: MC, V

FURTHER AFIELD (NORTH): *La Barraca*. **Map 3** A5.   (R)(R)
Calle de la Reina 29. ((91) 532 71 54.
Over ten different Valencia-style rice dishes and paellas are on offer here, made with first class ingredients. Good home-made desserts. 🍴
Cards: AE, DC, MC, V

FURTHER AFIELD (NORTH): *El Puchero*. **Map 3** A2.   (R)(R)
Calle de Larra 13. ((91) 445 05 77.
Popular, unfussy restaurant offering hearty, home-style cooking. The baby broad beans with ham, the roast suckling pig and the game stews are legendary, along with the cantankerous waitresses. ● *Sun & Aug.* 🍴
Cards: AE, MC, V

FURTHER AFIELD (NORTH): *Goizeko Kabi*.   (R)(R)(R)(R)
Calle Comandante Zorita 37. ((91) 533 01 85.
Traditional Basque cuisine served in a refined setting. Excellent fresh produce and seafood are the basis of the chef's creations. Good wine list and delectable desserts. ● *Sun.* 🍴 ♿
Cards: AE, DC, MC, V

FURTHER AFIELD (NORTH): *Jockey*. **Map 4** D2.   (R)(R)(R)(R)
Calle Amador de los Ríos 6. ((91) 319 10 03.
Among Madrid's top five restaurants, frequented by gourmets and celebrities, Jockey offers a seasonal menu. Excellent poultry and game dishes and a superb wine list. Smart dress only. ● *Sun & Aug.* 🍴 ♿
Cards: AE, DC, MC, V

FURTHER AFIELD (NORTH): *Zalacaín*.   (R)(R)(R)(R)
Calle Álvarez de Baena 4. ((91) 561 48 40.
Considered to be Madrid's finest restaurant, Zalacaín lives up to its reputation with a luxurious setting, attentive service, and above all delicious Basque-oriented cuisine. Smart dress only. ● *Sun & Aug.* 🍴 ♿
Cards: AE, DC, MC, V

Price categories for a three-course evening meal for one, including a half-bottle of house wine, tax and service:

Ⓟ under 3,000 ptas
ⓟⓟ 3,000–4,500 ptas
ⓟⓟⓟ 4,500–6,000 ptas
ⓟⓟⓟⓟ over 6,000 ptas

TAPAS BAR
In addition to the main dining room, there is a bar serving tapas (see p574–5) and raciones (larger portions).

FIXED-PRICE MENU
A good-value, fixed-price menu is offered at lunch or dinner, or both, usually with three courses.

GOOD WINE LIST
Denotes a wide range of good wines, or a more specialized selection of local wines.

OUTDOOR TABLES
Facilities for eating outdoors, on a terrace, or in a garden or courtyard, often with a good view.

	CREDIT CARDS	TAPAS BAR	FIXED-PRICE MENU	GOOD WINE LIST	OUTDOOR TABLES
FURTHER AFIELD (NORTHEAST): *Sacha.* ⓟⓟⓟ Calle Juan Hurtado de Mendoza 11. 【 (91) 345 59 52. Decorated like a cosy bistro, this restaurant serves specialities such as partridge with rice and mushrooms. ● Sun & Aug. 目 ᕒ	AE DC MC V			●	■
FURTHER AFIELD (NORTHEAST): *Cabo Mayor.* ⓟⓟⓟⓟ Calle Juan Ramón Jiménez 37. 【 (91) 350 87 76. One of Madrid's finest seafood restaurants with Cantabrian-Navarrese cuisine. Try the delicious fresh pasta and prawn salad or the monkfish with mushrooms. Excellent wines and desserts. ● Sun. 目	AE DC MC V	●	■	●	■
FURTHER AFIELD (NORTHEAST): *El Olivo.* ⓟⓟⓟⓟ Calle General Gallegos 1. 【 (91) 359 15 35. Top of the line Mediterranean cuisine, with olive oil as the underlying culinary theme. The owner will advise you on which of the 40 different olive oils will best accompany your meal. ● Sun & Mon. 目	AE DC MC V		■	●	
FURTHER AFIELD (SOUTHWEST): *Malacatín.* Map 2 E5. Ⓟ Calle de la Ruda 5. 【 (91) 365 52 41. This old bar in the centre of the Rastro has only one item on the menu: *cocido madrileño*. It has to be ordered a day in advance, and is served in three separate stages. The price includes wine and dessert. ● Sun. 目		●	■		
FURTHER AFIELD (SOUTHWEST): *Casa Lucio.* Map 2 D5. ⓟⓟⓟ Calle Cava Baja 35. 【 (91) 365 32 52. This historic tavern serves Castilian specialities. The fried eggs with potatoes are exquisite and the rice pudding renowned. ● Aug. 目	AE DC MC V	●		●	
FURTHER AFIELD (SOUTHWEST): *Gure-Etxea.* Map 1 C4. ⓟⓟⓟ Plaza de la Paja 12. 【 (91) 365 61 49. Quality Basque cooking in a vaulted dining room. The *piperrada*, made with scrambled eggs, red peppers, green beans and ham, goes well with the sharp white Basque wine, *txacoli*. ● Sun & Aug. 目 ᕒ	AE DC MC V		■	●	
MADRID PROVINCE					
ARANJUEZ: *Casa Pablo.* ⓟⓟ Calle Almíbar 42. 【 (91) 891 14 51. A centrally located tavern offering solid home cooking. Try the pheasant with grapes or the fresh asparagus and strawberries. ● Aug. 目 ᕒ	AE MC V	●	■	●	
CHINCHÓN: *Mesón de la Virreina.* ⓟⓟ Plaza Mayor 28. 【 (91) 894 00 15. Traditional Castilian food, including *sopa castellana* (a garlic soup with chickpeas) and classic roast lamb, is prepared in this 16th-century building. The local *anís* makes an excellent *digestif*. 目 ᕒ	AE DC V MC	●	■	●	■
MORALZARZAL: *El Cenador de Salvador.* ⓟⓟⓟⓟ Avenida de España 30. 【 (91) 857 77 22. Many gourmets make the trek from Madrid to Moralzarzal just for the pleasure of dining in this lovely chalet. The exquisite seasonal cooking is bound to delight even the most refined taste buds. ● Mon. 目 ᕒ	AE DC MC V		■	●	■
PATONES DE ARRIBA: *El Poleo.* ⓟⓟⓟ Travesía del Arroyo 1–3. 【 (91) 843 21 01. This picturesque town with slate roofed houses boasts a wonderful restaurant offering Navarrese-style cuisine. Open Fri–Sun only. ● Aug. 目	AE DC MC V	●		●	■
SAN LORENZO DE EL ESCORIAL: *Taberna La Cueva.* ⓟⓟ Calle San Antón 4. 【 (91) 890 15 16. Juan de Villanueva, architect of the Prado, designed this 18th-century inn whose specialities include the *huevos a la cueva* (fried eggs and ham served in a nest of straw potatoes). ● Mon.		●	■	●	

CASTILLA Y LEÓN

ARANDA DE DUERO: *Mesón La Villa.*
Plaza Mayor 3 (Burgos). ((947) 50 10 25. ⓅⓅⓅ
High-quality regional cooking with a great variety of Castilian dishes, such as pickled partridge, sweetbreads with mushrooms, and *menestra de verduras* (vegetable stew). Impressive selection of local wines. ● *Mon.* 🍽

AE DC MC V

ARÉVALO: *Asador La Cubas.*
Calle Figones 9 (Ávila). ((920) 30 01 25. Ⓟ
This converted wine cellar with clay casks embedded in the walls offers delicious suckling lamb and pig roasted in the wood-burning oven, and tasty regional desserts such as sweet custard fritters *(leche frita)*. 🍽

AE DC MC V

ASTORGA: *La Peseta.*
Plaza de San Bartolomé 3 (León). ((987) 61 72 75. Ⓟ
A family-run restaurant with a tradition for hearty, healthy cooking. Try the rabbit and potato stew accompanied by a local Bierzo wine. ♿

AE MC V

ÁVILA: *Mesón del Rastro.*
Plaza del Rastro 1. ((920) 21 12 18. ⓅⓅ
Authentic regional dishes are offered in this truly Castilian restaurant nestled in the city wall. The *Judías de El Barco de Ávila* (dried white beans served in a thick sauce with chorizo) is an all-time favourite. 🍽 ♿

AE DC MC V

BURGOS: *Casa Ojeda.*
Calle Vitoria 5. ((947) 20 90 52. ⓅⓅⓅ
The city's most traditional restaurant serving classic dishes such as roast suckling lamb, and *morcilla* (a black blood sausage) with red peppers. There is an extensive choice of Ribera del Duero and La Rioja wines. 🍽

AE DC MC V

COVARRUBIAS: *El Galín.*
Plaza de Doña Urraca 4 (Burgos). ((947) 40 30 15. Ⓟ
The Galín is a simple, busy restaurant in the main square, preparing succulent baby lamb and other hearty regional dishes such as *olla podrida* (a thick, bean based broth). Good tapas bar. ● *Tue & Sep.*

AE DC MC V

FRÓMISTA: *Hostería de Los Palmeros.*
Plaza San Telmo 4 (Palencia). ((979) 81 00 67. ⓅⓅ
This ancient inn on the Road to Santiago has been agreeably restored. The menu offers good Castilian dishes including baby pigeon casserole and *tocinillo de cielo* (sweet candied egg yolks) for dessert. 🍽

AE DC MC V

LA GRANJA DE SAN ILDEFONSO: *Hilaria.*
Carretera Valladolid–Madrid, Valsaín (Segovia). ((921) 47 02 92. ⓅⓅ
The owners of this family-run restaurant still use an original recipe for their white bean stew. Good roast suckling lamb and pig. ● *Mon.* 🍽 ♿

AE MC V

LEÓN: *Mesón Leonés del Racimo de Oro.*
Calle Caño Vadillo 2. ((987) 25 75 75. ⓅⓅ
Enjoy traditional cooking in the stables of a 16th-century inn. In winter there are game dishes and stews, such as the *cocido leonés* (a hearty broth of chickpeas, potatoes and bacon, blood sausage and cabbage). ● *Tue.* ♿

AE MC V

MEDINACELI: *Las Llaves.*
Plaza Mayor 13 (Soria). ((975) 32 63 51. ⓅⓅ
A small, cosy restaurant decorated with antiques, in the centre of windy Medinaceli. The lentil stew with curry and the oven-cooked veal stew are just two of the specialities. ● *Mon & mid Jan–mid Feb.* ♿

AE MC V

PALENCIA: *Casa Damián.*
Calle Ignacio Martínez de Azcoitia 9. ((979) 74 46 28. ⓅⓅ
A reliable restaurant with provincial specialities including a fresh *menestra de verduras* and delicious *buñuelos* (sweet fritters). ● *Mon & Aug.* 🍽 ♿

AE DC MC V

PEDRAZA DE LA SIERRA: *Hostería Pintor Zuloaga.*
Calle Matadero 1 (Segovia). ((921) 50 98 35. ⓅⓅ
Located in a former Inquisition house, this restaurant serves traditional Castilian fare such as roast pork and lamb, and hearty stews. ● *Tue.* 🍽

AE DC MC V

PONFERRADA: *Azul-Montearenas.*
Carretera NVI Madrid–A Coruña (León). ((987) 41 70 12. Ⓟ
Simple, home-style cooking is prepared in this restaurant with mountain views. Try the chard filled with shrimp and monkfish. 🍽 ♿

AE DC MC V

Price categories for a three-course evening meal for one, including a half-bottle of house wine, tax and service:

ℙ under 3,000 ptas
ℙℙ 3,000–4,500 ptas
ℙℙℙ 4,500–6,000 ptas
ℙℙℙℙ over 6,000 ptas

TAPAS BAR
In addition to the main dining room, there is a bar serving tapas (see p574–5) and raciones (larger portions).

FIXED-PRICE MENU
A good-value, fixed-price menu is offered at lunch or dinner, or both, usually with three courses.

GOOD WINE LIST
Denotes a wide range of good wines, or a more specialized selection of local wines.

OUTDOOR TABLES
Facilities for eating outdoors, on a terrace, or in a garden or courtyard, often with a good view.

	Price	Credit Cards	Tapas Bar	Fixed-Price Menu	Good Wine List	Outdoor Tables
QUINTANA DE RANEROS: *Bodega El Cercao.* Calle de la Bodega 4, Finca El Cercao (León). ℂ (987) 28 01 28. This huge 17th-century wine cellar is one long maze of underground passages and rustic dining rooms. Enjoy any of the traditional dishes, such as *morcilla* (blood sausage) with locally grown red Bierzo peppers.	®®	AE DC MC V	●	■	●	
SALAMANCA: *Río de la Plata.* Plaza del Peso 1. ℂ (923) 21 90 05. A tiny, popular restaurant next to the Plaza Mayor, serving a great variety of fresh fish and Castilian dishes, all of superb quality. ● Mon & Jul. 🍽	®®®	AE MC V	●	■		
SANTA MARÍA DE MAVE: *Hostería El Convento.* Santa María de Mave (Palencia). ℂ (979) 12 36 11. This ancient Benedictine monastery on the banks of the Río Pisuerga now houses an inn serving traditional Castilian fare, including lamb roasted in a wood-burning oven and *sopa castellana* (a rich garlic soup). ♿	®®	AE MC V	●	■		■
SANTO DOMINGO DE SILOS: *Casa Emeterio.* Hotel Tres Coronas de Silos, Plaza Mayor 6 (Burgos). ℂ (947) 39 00 47. After admiring the monastery you can relax in the rustic dining room of this large, 18th-century house and enjoy good, regional cooking. ♿	®®	AE MC V	●	■		
SEGOVIA: *Mesón de Cándido.* Plaza del Azoguejo 5. ℂ (921) 42 81 03. Don't leave town without visiting Mesón de Cándido, *the* place to eat in Segovia. The restaurant has good views of the Roman aqueduct and serves local specialities such as roast lamb and suckling pig. 🍽 ♿	®®	AE DC MC V	●		●	■
SEPÚLVEDA: *Cristóbal.* Calle Conde de Sepúlveda 9 (Segovia). ℂ (921) 54 01 00. Enjoy impressive views of the Duratón gorges as you dine on traditional hearty stews and, reputedly, the best roast lamb in the region. ● Tue. 🍽	®®	AE DC MC V	●	■	●	
TORDESILLAS: *El Torreón.* Calle Dimas Rodríguez 11 (Valladolid). ℂ (983) 77 01 23. Specializing in first class grilled meats, El Torreón has a reproduction of the Convento de Santa Clara's beautiful ceiling. Reservations advised. 🍽	®®®	AE DC MC V			●	
TORO: *Casa Lorenzo.* Puerta del Mercado 21 (Zamora). ℂ (980) 69 11 53. Typical Zamoran dishes, including peppers stuffed with cod, and baked asparagus with smoked salmon. Try the potent local wine. ● Sep. 🍽 ♿	®®	AE DC MC V	●	■		
TORRECABALLEROS: *El Rancho de la Aldegüela.* Carretera N110 (Segovia). ℂ (921) 40 10 46. A country house with rustic decor serving regional specialities such as *revuelto de morcilla* (scrambled eggs with blood sausage). ● Mon.	®®	AE DC V	●	■		■
VALLADOLID: *La Fragua.* Paseo de Zorrilla 10. ℂ (983) 33 87 85. The rich garlic soup, lamb casserole in white wine and spring vegetables, and the veal stew are all proof that this is a truly Castilian restaurant. Fish is a speciality too. Great tapas bar. ● Mon & Aug. 🍽 ♿	®®®	AE DC MC V	●		●	■
VILLAFRANCA DEL BIERZO: *La Charola.* Carretera NVI Madrid–A Coruña (León). ℂ (987) 54 00 95. A family-run restaurant by the side of the road, serving generous portions of regional dishes. Simple, reliable and inexpensive. 🍽 ♿	®	AE DC MC V	●	■	●	
ZAMORA: *Pizarro.* Cuesta de Pizarro 7. ℂ (980) 53 45 45. Once used as an Inquisition palace, this 16th-century building serves regional and Basque specialities such as sole with anchovy sauce. ♿	®®	AE MC V		■	●	

CASTILLA-LA MANCHA

ALBACETE: *Nuestro Bar.* ℗℗ AE DC MC V
Calle Alcalde Conangla 102. 【 (967) 24 33 73.
The dining room serves regional dishes and a *menú de degustación* which includes specialities of La Mancha such as *gazpacho manchego* (a rich game stew thickened with biscuits). Great tapas bar. ● *Jul.* 目

ALMAGRO: *El Corregidor.* ℗℗ AE DC MC V
Calle Jerónimo Ceballos 2 (Ciudad Real). 【 (926) 86 06 48.
This delightful old house, with many dining rooms and a central patio, is one of Castilla-La Mancha's prettiest restaurants. Creative, regional cuisine including the town's speciality, pickled aubergines. ● *Mon.* 目

ALMANSA: *Mesón de Picelín.* ℗℗ AE DC MC V
Calle Norias 10 (Albacete). 【 (967) 34 00 07.
Considered by many to be one of the region's best restaurants. You can try authentic regional dishes including their famous *gazpacho manchego* made with chicken, rabbit and partridge. ● *Mon & Aug.* 目 ㋫

BETETA: *Hotel Los Tilos.* ℗ AE MC V
Extrarradio (Cuenca). 【 (969) 31 80 98.
A simple, unfussy hotel restaurant serving typical mountain dishes, such as onion soup, venison stew and *morteruelo* (a mixed game pâté). ㋫

BRIHUEGA: *Asador El Tolmo.* ℗℗ MC V
Avenida de la Constitución 26 (Guadalajara). 【 (949) 28 04 76.
The traditional Castilian decor is in keeping with the cuisine, which includes roast kid, beans with partridge and home-made desserts. 目 ㋫

CIUDAD REAL: *Gran Mesón.* ℗℗ AE MC V
Ronda de Ciruela 34. 【 (926) 22 72 39.
Ample set menu with regional specialities such as *gachas* (gruel), *pisto* (a vegetable mix), suckling pig and local cheese and wines. 目 ㋫

CUENCA: *Marlo.* ℗℗ AE MC V
Calle Colón 59. 【 (969) 21 11 73.
Fish and shellfish feature predominantly on the modern menu here, and there are also good meat dishes. Try the stuffed partridge, the fillet steak in a cheese sauce, or the aubergine and cheese pie. 目

CUENCA: *Mesón Casas Colgadas.* ℗℗℗ AE DC MC V
Calle Canónigos. 【 (969) 22 35 09.
Dine above the gorge in one of Cuenca's famous hanging houses. Unbeatable views combined with great regional cuisine, including game dishes, make this an experience you won't want to miss. 目

GUADALAJARA: *Minaya.* ℗℗ AE MC V
Calle Mayor 23. 【 (949) 21 22 53.
A wonderful 16th-century palace with period furniture. The short seasonal menu has an emphasis on grilled meats and roast kid. ● *Sun.* 目

GUADALAJARA: *Amparito Roca.* ℗℗℗ MC V
Calle Toledo 19. 【 (949) 21 46 39.
This pleasantly decorated house offers traditional Spanish cuisine with innovative touches. The venison sirloin served in a mushroom sauce and the scrambled eggs with potato and salmon are examples. ● *Sun.* 目 ㋫

JADRAQUE: *El Castillo.* ℗℗ AE DC MC V
Carretera de Soria (Guadalajara). 【 (949) 89 02 54.
After visiting the castle, stop here for delicious roast kid or any of the other classic Castilian dishes prepared in this typical *mesón* (inn).

MANZANARES: *Mesón Sancho.* ℗ AE MC V
Calle Jesús del Perdón 26 (Ciudad Real). 【 (926) 61 10 16.
This simple, down-to-earth restaurant serves typical, robust dishes such as garlic soup, *duelos y quebrantos* (scrambled eggs with pork) and rabbit *a la manchega* (in a sauce), washed down with local wine. 目 ㋫

LAS PEDROÑERAS: *Las Rejas.* ℗℗℗ AE DC MC V
Avenida de Brasil (Cuenca). 【 (967) 16 10 89.
Spain's garlic capital also has a first class restaurant with an appetizing seasonal menu and an unforgettable garlic soup. Many dishes feature regional produce. Try the fresh *manchego* cheese salad. ● *Mon.* 目 ㋫

For key to symbols see back flap

Price categories for a three-course evening meal for one, including a half-bottle of house wine, tax and service:

® under 3,000 ptas
®® 3,000–4,500 ptas
®®® 4,500–6,000 ptas
®®®® over 6,000 ptas

TAPAS BAR
In addition to the main dining room, there is a bar serving tapas *(see p574–5)* and *raciones* (larger portions).
FIXED-PRICE MENU
A good-value, fixed-price menu is offered at lunch or dinner, or both, usually with three courses.
GOOD WINE LIST
Denotes a wide range of good wines, or a more specialized selection of local wines.
OUTDOOR TABLES
Facilities for eating outdoors, on a terrace, or in a garden or courtyard, often with a good view.

	Price	Credit Cards	Tapas Bar	Fixed-Price Menu	Good Wine List	Outdoor Tables
PUERTO LÁPICE: *Venta del Quijote.* Autovía de Andalucía (Ciudad Real). ☎ (926) 57 61 10. Set in the heart of Don Quixote territory, this legendary inn evokes Cervantes' masterpiece. Sit around the pebbled courtyard and enjoy any of the Manchegan specialities or have tapas at the bar. ♿	®®	AE DC MC V	●	■	●	■
SIGÜENZA: *El Motor.* Avenida Juan Carlos (Guadalajara). ☎ (949) 39 08 27. As well as the typical roast suckling pig and lamb you can also try the fried breadcrumbs *(migas)* or the garlic soup *(sopa castellana)*. ▤ ♿	®	AE MC V	●	■	●	
TALAVERA DE LA REINA: *Antonio.* Avenida de Portugal 8 (Toledo). ☎ (925) 80 40 17. A bar serving good quality tapas at reasonable prices, and a dining room offering great regional food, make this place very popular. ▤ ♿	®	AE DC MC V	●	■	●	
TOLEDO: *Hostal del Cardenal.* Paseo de Recaredo 24. ☎ (925) 22 08 62. Once the summer residence of Cardinal Lorenzana, this 18th-century palace retains its beautiful garden, enclosed by the city walls. It serves garlic soup, suckling pig and the famous Toledo *mazapán* (marzipan). ▤	®®	AE DC MC V		■	●	■
TOLEDO: *La Lumbre.* Calle Real de Arrabal 3. ☎ (925) 22 03 73. A lovely old house with wooden beams, next to the Puerta de Bisagra. The meat dishes, such as roast suckling pig and lamb, are especially good, and there is delicious *manchego* cheesecake for dessert. ● *Sun.* ▤	®®	AE MC V		■	●	
TOLEDO: *Adolfo.* Calle de Granada 6. ☎ (925) 22 73 21. Set in the heart of Toledo's Jewish quarter, the Adolfo, with its tiles, columns, antiques and a wonderful 15th-century Mudéjar coffered ceiling, serves game in winter and fresh trout from the Río Tajo. ▤ ♿	®®®	AE DC MC V	●	■	●	
TRAGACETE: *El Gamo.* Plaza de los Caídos 2 (Cuenca). ☎ (969) 28 90 08. This mountain inn has a simple, family-run restaurant where you can try home-style cooking, such as venison stew and *morteruelo.* ♿	®	MC V		■		■
VALDEPEÑAS: *Baviera.* Calle 6 de Junio 30 (Ciudad Real). ☎ (926) 32 40 84. A centrally located restaurant serving authentic cuisine of La Mancha. The *galianos* (a typical dish made with game) and the mountain rabbit with garlic are two specialities. Good selection of Valdepeñas wines. ● *Tue.* ▤	®	AE DC MC V	●	■	●	
VILLALBA DE LA SIERRA: *Nelia.* Ruta de la Ciudad Encantada (Cuenca). ☎ (969) 28 10 21. A wood and stone restaurant on the banks of the Río Júcar. The wild boar meatballs, the marinated venison and the vegetables in puff pastry are all superb. Good Valdepeñas wines. ● *Wed & mid Jan–mid Feb.* ▤ ♿	®®	AE MC V	●	■	●	●

EXTREMADURA

	Price	Credit Cards	Tapas Bar	Fixed-Price Menu	Good Wine List	Outdoor Tables
ALMENDRALEJO: *Nando.* Calle Ricardo Romero 12 (Badajoz). ☎ (924) 66 12 71. The dining room serves generous portions of rice with rabbit, *judiones* (locally grown beans prepared with pig's knuckle or partridge) and fresh fish. Good tapas bar for trying local specialities. ● *Sun.* ▤	®	AE MC V	●	■		
BADAJOZ: *Los Gabrieles.* Calle Vicente Barrantes 21. ☎ (924) 22 00 01. Regional cooking including roast lamb and *revuelto mixto*, composed of scrambled eggs, mushrooms, shrimp and white truffles. ▤ ♿	®	AE DC MC V	●	■		

BADAJOZ: *Aldebarán.* ⓅⓅⓅ
Avenida de Elvas, Urbanización Guadiana. ꧁ (924) 27 42 61.
One of Badajoz province's finer restaurants, with elaborate cuisine in an
elegant setting. Creations include the pickled Iberian pork salad, ravioli
filled with mushrooms and liver, and pigeon in wine sauce. ● Sun. ▤ ♿
AE DC MC V

CÁCERES: *El Figón de Eustaquio.* ⓅⓅ
Plaza de San Juan 14. ꧁ (927) 24 81 94.
Simple restaurant in the historic part of town where you can sample
genuine Extremaduran cooking such as trout *a la extremeña* (stuffed with
ham) and the house soup of tomato with poached egg. ▤ ♿
AE DC MC V

CÁCERES: *Atrio.* ⓅⓅⓅ
Avenida de España 30. ꧁ (927) 24 29 28.
Innovative, contemporary cuisine offset by elegant decor in Cáceres' most
sophisticated restaurant. The tender venison fillets served with muscat
grapes and pears is just one of the chef's creative combinations. ♿
DC MC V

GUADALUPE: *Hospedería del Real Monasterio.* Ⓟ
Plaza de Juan Carlos I (Cáceres). ꧁ (927) 36 70 00.
Owned by the Franciscan order, this restaurant offers simple regional
cooking. The tomato soup, the roast kid and the *migas extremeñas*
(breadcrumbs with pork) are all recommended. ● mid Jan–mid Feb. ▤
MC V

GUADALUPE: *Mesón El Cordero.* Ⓟ
Calle Alfonso Onceno 27 (Cáceres). ꧁ (927) 36 71 31.
Regional specialities are served in the cosy wood-panelled dining room.
Enjoy the fresh vegetable *menestra* (stew) or the partridge casserole as
you admire the view of the mountains. ● Mon & mid Sep–mid Oct. ▤ ♿
AE MC V

JARANDILLA DE LA VERA: *Cueva de Puta Parió.* Ⓟ
Calle Francisco Pizarro 8 (Cáceres). ꧁ (927) 56 03 92.
A lively and popular tavern with good regional dishes including tomato
soup and lamb casserole, and locally produced house wine. ● Mon. ▤
AE DC MC V

JEREZ DE LOS CABALLEROS: *La Ermita.* Ⓟ
Calle Doctor Benítez 9 (Badajoz). ꧁ (924) 73 14 76.
This 17th-century chapel converted into a wine cellar now houses a
restaurant serving local dishes. Sample the partridge stew or the typical
revuelto de espárragos, made with scrambled eggs and asparagus tips. ♿
V

LOSAR DE LA VERA: *Carlos V.* Ⓟ
Avenida de Extremadura 45 (Cáceres). ꧁ (927) 57 06 36.
Home cooking and lovely views of the mountains and the Tiétar valley.
The *revuelto con criadillas de tierra* (scrambled eggs with white truffles),
the roast kid and the steaks are all house specialities. ▤ ♿
AE MC V

MÉRIDA: *Nicolás.* ⓅⓅ
Calle Félix Valverde Lillo 13 (Badajoz). ꧁ (924) 31 96 10.
You might want to visit the small brick wine cellar for an apéritif before
tucking into the regional specialities such as the delicious lamb with
plums or the pork sirloin with peppers. Pretty garden and terrace. ▤
AE DC MC V

MÉRIDA: *Parador de Mérida.* ⓅⓅⓅ
Plaza de la Constitución 3 (Badajoz). ꧁ (924) 31 38 00.
This lovely old convent now houses a parador and a restaurant well
worth a visit. Savour regional specialities such as Extremaduran cheeses,
cold meats, and the *caldereta de cordero* (lamb casserole). ▤ ♿
AE DC MC V

PLASENCIA: *Alfonso VIII.* ⓅⓅⓅ
Avenida Alfonso VIII 32 (Cáceres). ꧁ (927) 41 02 50.
Creative cuisine, relying heavily on local produce and updated
traditional recipes. Try the kid stew or the Iberian ham. ▤ ♿
AE DC MC V

PLASENCIA: *El Rincón Extremeño.* ⓅⓅⓅ
Calle Vidrieras 8 (Cáceres). ꧁ (927) 41 11 50.
Traditional Plasencian dishes including frogs in *salsa verde*, lizard
(in season) and more "usual" fare such as suckling pig. Be sure
to try the raspberry, cheese and honey dessert called *Tío Pichu*. ▤ ♿
AE DC MC V

PUEBLA LA REINA: *Mesón La Jara-Casa Andrés.* Ⓟ
Calle Luis Chamizo 14 (Badajoz). ꧁ (924) 36 00 05.
This charming *mesón* has become a sanctuary of authentic regional food.
Those with stamina can try the 14-course meal. ● Mon. ▤
DC MC V

For key to symbols see back flap

Price categories for a three-course evening meal for one, including a half-bottle of house wine, tax and service:

ℙ under 3,000 ptas
ℙℙ 3,000–4,500 ptas
ℙℙℙ 4,500–6,000 ptas
ℙℙℙℙ over 6,000 ptas

TAPAS BAR
In addition to the main dining room, there is a bar serving tapas (see p574–5) and raciones (larger portions).
FIXED-PRICE MENU
A good-value, fixed-price menu is offered at lunch or dinner, or both, usually with three courses.
GOOD WINE LIST
Denotes a wide range of good wines, or a more specialized selection of local wines.
OUTDOOR TABLES
Facilities for eating outdoors, on a terrace, or in a garden or courtyard, often with a good view.

		CREDIT CARDS	TAPAS BAR	FIXED-PRICE MENU	GOOD WINE LIST	OUTDOOR TABLES
TRUJILLO: *Mesón La Troya.* Plaza Mayor 10 (Cáceres). ☎ *(927) 32 13 64.* A typical *mesón* dating back to the 16th century, serving regional food in hearty portions. The *migas* (breadcrumbs) with pork, the dried white beans in sauce, and the lamb in its own juice are all recommended. ▤	ℙ	MC V	●	■	●	■
TRUJILLO: *Pizarro.* Plaza Mayor 13 (Cáceres). ☎ *(927) 32 02 55.* The decor in this restaurant has changed little since it opened before the Civil War. Enjoy traditional dishes such as tomato soup with figs and grapes, and chicken stuffed with truffles. ● *Tue.* ▤	ℙℙ	MC V		■	●	
ZAFRA: *Barbacana.* Hotel Huerta Honda, Avenida López Asme 30 (Badajoz). ☎ *(924) 55 41 00.* This 16th-century house, finely decorated with antiques, provides a lovely backdrop for good regional and Basque cuisine, including roast suckling lamb with rosemary and fillet of hake with clams. ● *Mon.* ▤	ℙℙ	MC V		■	●	

SEVILLE

		CREDIT CARDS	TAPAS BAR	FIXED-PRICE MENU	GOOD WINE LIST	OUTDOOR TABLES
EL ARENAL: *Bodegón Torre del Oro.* **Map 3 B2.** Calle Santander 15. ☎ *(95) 422 08 80.* This combined bar and dining room specializes in *raciones*. Try the *garbanzos con espinacas* (chickpeas with spinach), *puntillitas* (tiny grilled cuttlefish) or the *punta de solomillo* (fillet tip). ⑁	ℙℙ	AE DC MC V	●	■		■
EL ARENAL: *Enrique Becerra.* **Map 3 B1.** Calle Gamazo 2. ☎ *(95) 421 30 49.* This plush restaurant-bar attracts well-heeled customers for apéritifs and meals. Besides a fine selection of fish and meat dishes, the daily specials feature Andalusian home-style cooking. ● *Sun.* ▤	ℙℙ	AE DC MC V	●	■	●	
EL ARENAL: *El Burladero.* **Map 3 B1.** Hotel Colón, Calle Canalejas 1. ☎ *(95) 422 29 00.* Decorated with bullfighting memorabilia, this restaurant offers caviar and filet mignon as well as local dishes such as *puchero* (meat-in-a-pot). ▤ ⑁	ℙℙℙ	AE DC MC V	●	■	●	
EL ARENAL: *La Isla.* **Map 3 B2.** Calle Arfe 25. ☎ *(95) 421 26 31.* An attractive, centrally located restaurant featuring superb seafood: turbot, bream and delicacies such as *percebes* (sea barnacles). ● *Mon & Aug.* ▤	ℙℙℙ	AE DC MC V	●	■	●	
SANTA CRUZ: *Las Meninas.* **Map 3 D1.** Calle Santo Tomás 3. ☎ *(95) 422 62 26.* Hearty food and good prices make this a popular place. A variety of excellent local dishes, such as braised bull's tail, *potaje* of chickpeas and cod, and gazpacho may be on the menu. ▤	ℙ	AE DC MC V	●	■		
SANTA CRUZ: *Casa Robles.* **Map 3 C1.** Calle Álvarez Quintero 58. ☎ *(95) 456 32 72.* Right in the heart of Seville, this lively place has three small dining rooms. Fish is a speciality – fried, baked or with rice – and there is an excellent choice of fresh shellfish. Good meat dishes and tapas. ▤	ℙℙ	AE DC MC V	●	■	●	
SANTA CRUZ: *Corral del Agua.* **Map 3 C2.** Callejón del Agua 6. ☎ *(95) 422 48 41.* Dine on the cool patio in a lee of the Reales Alcázares gardens. The menu emphasizes seasonal specialities, carefully prepared and served. ● *Sun.*	ℙℙ	AE DC MC V		■		■
SANTA CRUZ: *Hostería del Laurel.* **Map 3 C2.** Plaza de los Venerables 5. ☎ *(95) 422 02 95.* Rustic decoration, with wooden barrels and colourful wall tiles. Try local specialities: *serrano* ham and *tortilla de patatas* (potato omelette). ▤ ⑁	ℙℙ	AE DC MC V	●	■	●	■

SANTA CRUZ: *Mesón Don Raimundo.* Map 3 C1. ⓟⓟ
Calle Argote de Molina 26. ((95) 422 33 55.
This restaurant is set in a 17th-century convent and decorated with ceramics and tapestries. Traditional Andalusian cuisine, based on game from the marshes of the Guadalquivir, as well as seafood dishes. 🗐 ⑤
AE DC MC V

SANTA CRUZ: *La Albahaca.* Map 3 D2. ⓟⓟⓟ
Plaza de Santa Cruz 12. ((95) 422 07 14.
This 1920s mansion furnished with 17th-century antiques makes a fine setting to enjoy good Basque-influenced food. ● Sun. 🗐 ⑤
AE DC MC V

SANTA CRUZ: *Egaña Oriza.* Map 3 C3. ⓟⓟⓟⓟ
Calle San Fernando 41. ((95) 422 72 11.
Tucked against the walls of the Alcázar gardens is this stylish place. Fish is a speciality, and both the meat dishes and desserts are superb. ● Sun. 🗐
AE DC MC V

FURTHER AFIELD (WEST): *Río Grande.* Map 3 B3. ⓟⓟ
Calle Betis. ((95) 427 83 71.
Terrific location, where you can enjoy the gazpacho or the *rabo de toro* (braised bull's tail) on a terrace overlooking the Guadalquivir. 🗐 ⑤
AE DC MC V

FURTHER AFIELD (WEST): *Ox's.* Map 3 C3. ⓟⓟⓟ
Calle Betis 61. ((95) 427 62 75.
A small and intimate *asador* (grill room) specializing in grilled meats. Clams with artichokes and *angulas* (tiny baby eels) are specialities. 🗐 ⑤
AE DC MC V

ANDALUSIA

ALJARAQUE: *Las Candelas.* ⓟⓟ
Carretera Huelva–Punta Umbria (Huelva). ((959) 31 84 33.
An attractive restaurant with a rustic dining room serving fine local seafood and excellent meat dishes. ● Sun. 🗐
AE DC MC V

ALMERÍA: *Rincón de Juan Pedro.* ⓟ
Calle Federico Castro 2. ((950) 23 58 19.
Andalusian meat and seafood specialities, and local dishes such as *trigo a la cortijera* (a stew with wheat berries, meat and sausage). ● Mon. 🗐 ⑤
AE DC MC V

ALMERÍA: *Bellavista.* ⓟⓟ
Urbanizacion Llanos del Alquián. ((950) 29 71 56.
This restaurant outside the city offers top quality fish and shellfish prepared in various ways. It is also a good place to try baby kid. 🗐
AE DC MC V

ALMERÍA: *Club de Mar.* ⓟⓟ
Calle Muelle 1. ((950) 23 50 48.
Enjoy fresh fish and shellfish right on the seafront. The *bullabesa* (Spanish bouillabaisse) and *fritura* (mixed fried fish) are specialities. 🗐
AE DC MC V

ALMUÑÉCAR: *Playa Cotobro.* ⓟⓟ
Calle Rio Playa (Granada). ((958) 63 18 02.
The food here has a French touch, with specialities such as pastry with prawns and leeks, and angler fish gratin with spinach. ● Mon.
MC V

ANTEQUERA: *La Espuela.* ⓟ
Plaza de Toros (Málaga). ((95) 270 26 76.
Uniquely situated in a bullring, this restaurant prepares Andalusian dishes including the town speciality, *porra* (a thick gazpacho). ⑤
AE DC MC V

BAEZA: *Juanito.* ⓟⓟ
Avenida Arca del Agua (Jaén). ((953) 74 00 40.
Right in the heart of the olive belt, Juanito offers a selection of olive oils to accompany your meal. Specialities include spinach casserole. 🗐
V

BAEZA: *Andrés de Vandelvira.* ⓟⓟⓟ
Calle San Francisco 14 (Jaén). ((953) 74 81 30.
Located in a 16th-century monastery built by Andrés de Vandelvira, Jaén's Renaissance architect, this restaurant serves typical regional food: *cardos* (cardoons, a type of artichoke) in a cream sauce, and partridge salad. 🗐
AE DC MC V

BAILÉN: *Zodíaco.* ⓟⓟ
Carretera Madrid–Cádiz (Jaén). ((953) 67 10 58.
Cold soups feature on the menu in summer, such as *ajo blanco* (white garlic) with almonds. Other specialities include the *revuelto* (scrambled eggs with ham, asparagus, prawns and elvers) and partridge. 🗐 ⑤
AE DC MC V

	CREDIT CARDS	TAPAS BAR	FIXED-PRICE MENU	GOOD WINE LIST	OUTDOOR TABLES

Price categories for a three-course evening meal for one, including a half-bottle of house wine, tax and service:

Ⓟ under 3,000 ptas
ⓅⓅ 3,000–4,500 ptas
ⓅⓅⓅ 4,500–6,000 ptas
ⓅⓅⓅⓅ over 6,000 ptas

TAPAS BAR
In addition to the main dining room, there is a bar serving tapas (see p574–5) and raciones (larger portions).
FIXED-PRICE MENU
A good-value, fixed-price menu is offered at lunch or dinner, or both, usually with three courses.
GOOD WINE LIST
Denotes a wide range of good wines, or a more specialized selection of local wines.
OUTDOOR TABLES
Facilities for eating outdoors, on a terrace, or in a garden or courtyard, often with a good view.

LOS BARRIOS: *Mesón El Copo.* ⓅⓅⓅ Calle Almadraba 2, Palmones (Cádiz). 【 *(956) 67 77 10.* Dine on superb seafood, from fried anchovies to lobster and sea bass. Order a few shellfish dishes *para picar* (to share as a starter) and follow with the *dorada al horno* (bream casserole with potatoes). ● *Sun.* ▤	AE DC MC V	●	▨	●	
BUBIÓN: *Villa Turística de Bubión.* Ⓟ Calle Barrio Alto (Granada). 【 *(958) 76 31 11.* This restaurant in the Alpujarras serves typical mountain food such as *plato alpujarreño* (potatoes with egg, sausage, ham and pork loin). ▤ ♿	AE DC MC V		▨		▨
CÁDIZ: *La Costera.* ⓅⓅ Calle Doctor Fleming 8. 【 *(956) 27 34 88.* Fish dominates the menu at this restaurant, but the meat dishes are also good. You can order tapas at the bar or on the lovely terrace. ▤ ♿	AE DC MC V	●		●	▨
CÁDIZ: *Ventorillo del Chato.* ⓅⓅ Carretera Cádiz–San Fernando. 【 *(956) 25 00 25.* This old rustic inn offers seafood, venison and a stew of the day such as *berza* (vegetable and sausage) or *menudo* (tripe). ● *Sun.* ▤ ♿	AE DC MC V		▨	●	
CÁDIZ: *El Faro.* ⓅⓅⓅ Calle San Félix 15. 【 *(956) 21 10 68.* Classic restaurant with a warm atmosphere. The menu, a superb blend of modern and traditional dishes, changes daily but always features local seafood, as in the *tortillitas de camarones* (fritters of tiny shrimps). ▤ ♿	AE DC MC V	●	▨	●	
CÓRDOBA: *Federación de Peñas.* Ⓟ Calle Conde y Luque 8. 【 *(957) 47 54 27.* Inexpensive local food. Try the *rabo de toro* (braised bull's tail), a house speciality, or the *cardos* (cardoons) with clams. ● *mid Jan–mid Feb.* ♿	MC V	●	●		▨
CÓRDOBA: *Almudaina.* ⓅⓅ Jardines de los Santos Mártires 1. 【 *(957) 47 43 42.* Once the palace of Bishop Leopold of Austria, this mansion serves typical dishes from the Sierra Morena, including venison and boar. ▤	AE DC MC V		▨	●	
CÓRDOBA: *El Churrasco.* ⓅⓅ Calle Romero 16. 【 *(957) 29 08 19.* The speciality here is charcoal-grilled meat, but vegetable dishes such as *salmorejo* (a thick tomato soup served with crisp wafers of aubergine) are also good. Sip an apéritif in the wine cellars a few doors away. ● *Aug.* ▤	AE DC MC V		▨	●	
CÓRDOBA: *Taberna Pepe de la Judería.* ⓅⓅ Calle Romero 1. 【 *(957) 20 07 44.* Sit in the dining rooms festooned with photos of notable customers and try the gazpacho or the *flamenquín* (fried rolls of veal and ham). ▤ ♿	AE DC MC V	●	▨		▨
CÓRDOBA: *El Blasón.* ⓅⓅⓅ Calle José Zorilla 11 (Córdoba). 【 *(957) 48 06 25.* The ground-floor café in this charming old house, situated near Córdoba's main shopping area, is an ideal place for light meals. ▤	AE DC MC V	●	▨	●	▨
CÓRDOBA: *Caballo Rojo.* ⓅⓅⓅ Calle Cardenal Herrero 28 (Córdoba). 【 *(957) 47 53 75.* A lovely restaurant offering traditional dishes, including many adapted from Moorish and Sephardic recipes. Enjoy lamb with honey or *Sefardi* salad of wild mushrooms, asparagus, roasted peppers and salt cod. ▤ ♿	AE DC MC V		▨	●	
ESTEPONA: *La Alborada.* ⓅⓅ Puerto Deportivo de Estepona (Málaga). 【 *(95) 280 20 47.* This quayside eatery serves excellent paella and other rice dishes, such as *arroz a la banda* (fish risotto), plus fish and steaks. ● *Wed & Nov.* ♿	AE DC MC V				▨

FUENGIROLA: *Portofino.* ⓅⓅ
Edificio Perla 1, Paseo Marítimo (Málaga). ((95) 247 06 43.
This seafront restaurant is popular for its friendly service and good
Italian food, such as the fish and shellfish brochette. ● *Mon.* 🍽 ⎸
AE DC MC V

GRANADA: *Las Brasas.* Ⓟ
Calle Generalife 54, Cenes de la Vega. ((958) 48 60 35.
Besides steaks, try the *plato alpujarreño*, with its red and black sausages,
or the *patatas arrugadas* (fried potatoes with garlic). ● *Wed & Aug.* ⎸

GRANADA: *Casa Bienvenido.* Ⓟ
Calle Cádiz–San José 1, Monachil. ((958) 50 05 03.
Home-style cooking, using vegetables and meat grown on the farm.
The daily specials include lentils with rice and sausages. ● *Mon.* 🍽 ⎸
DC MC V

GRANADA: *Don Giovanni.* Ⓟ
Avenida de Cádiz 65. ((958) 81 87 51.
It is hard to beat Don Giovanni's prices for oven baked pizzas and the
wide variety of pastas, meat dishes and salads. ● *Mon.* ⎸

GRANADA: *Chikito.* ⓅⓅ
Plaza Campillo 9. ((958) 22 33 64.
Built on the site of a café where Lorca and his contemporaries used to
meet, Chikito serves broad beans with ham and Sacromonte omelette
as specialities. Try the *piononos* (anise-scented cake). ● *Wed.* 🍽 ⎸
AE DC MC V

GRANADA: *Mirador de Morayma.* ⓅⓅ
Calle Pianista García Carrillo 2. ((958) 22 82 90.
Situated in the Albaicín with views of the Alhambra, this restaurant
specializes in typical dishes of Granada, such as *remojón* (a salad of
oranges and codfish) and *choto albaicinero* (kid fried with garlic). 🍽
AE MC V

GRANADA: *Velázquez.* ⓅⓅ
Calle Emilio Orozco 1. ((958) 28 01 09.
The ambience here is warm and the food imaginative, with modern
interpretations of such Moorish dishes as *bstella* (a meat pastry with pine
nuts and almonds), and savoury almond cream soup. ● *Sun & Aug.* 🍽 ⎸
AE DC MC V

GRANADA: *Ruta del Veleta.* ⓅⓅⓅ
Carretera Sierra Nevada 50, Cenes de la Vega. ((958) 48 61 34.
The decoration, with typical Alpujarran textiles and ceramic jugs, goes
well with the traditional cuisine – roast baby kid and good seafood. 🍽
AE DC MC V

HUELVA: *El Estero.* ⓅⓅ
Avenida Martín Alonso Pinzón 13. ((959) 25 65 72.
A good, centrally located restaurant, serving local fare. Enjoy *chocos con
habas* (cuttlefish and beans) or sole stuffed with oysters. ● *Sun.* 🍽 ⎸
AE DC MC V

ISLA CRISTINA: *Casa Rufino.* Ⓟ
Avenida de la Playa (Huelva). ((959) 33 08 10.
A popular beachside place whose *el tonteo* menu (for four) comprises
eight different fish in sauces, including angler fish in raisin sauce. ⎸
AE DC MC V

JABUGO: *Mesón Sánchez Romero Carvajal.* Ⓟ
Carretera San Juan del Puerto (Huelva). ((959) 12 15 15.
Fine Jabugo hams are made here and the adjoining bar-restaurant is a
good place to sample them. Besides dishes featuring ham and sausage,
try the fresh *ibérico* pork dishes, such as *presa de paletilla al mesón.* 🍽 ⎸
MC V

JAÉN: *Casa Vicente.* ⓅⓅ
Calle Francisco Martín Mora 1. ((953) 23 28 16.
Vicente serves typical dishes from Jaén – lamb stew, spinach casserole,
artichokes in sauce – in a classic setting with a central patio. 🍽 ⎸
MC V

JEREZ DE LA FRONTERA: *Gaitán.* ⓅⓅ
Calle Gaitán 3 (Cádiz). ((956) 34 58 59.
Gaitán's innovative chef combines Basque and Andalusian influences
to create dishes such as hake confit with roasted vegetables and laurel,
and breast of chicken with foie gras and pine nuts. 🍽
AE DC MC V

JEREZ DE LA FRONTERA: *La Mesa Redonda.* ⓅⓅ
Calle Manuel de la Quintana 3 (Cádiz). ((956) 34 00 69.
A charming small restaurant, where the dedication to fine cooking is very
much in evidence. Try the *mojama* (cured tuna) as a starter. ● *Sun.* 🍽 ⎸
AE DC MC V

For key to symbols see back flap

<table>
<tr><td colspan="2">

Price categories for a three-course evening meal for one, including a half-bottle of house wine, tax and service:

Ⓟ under 3,000 ptas
ⓅⓅ 3,000–4,500 ptas
ⓅⓅⓅ 4,500–6,000 ptas
ⓅⓅⓅⓅ over 6,000 ptas

</td><td colspan="5">

TAPAS BAR
In addition to the main dining room, there is a bar serving tapas *(see p574–5)* and *raciones* (larger portions).
FIXED-PRICE MENU
A good-value, fixed-price menu is offered at lunch or dinner, or both, usually with three courses.
GOOD WINE LIST
Denotes a wide range of good wines, or a more specialized selection of local wines.
OUTDOOR TABLES
Facilities for eating outdoors, on a terrace, or in a garden or courtyard, often with a good view.

</td></tr>
</table>

	CREDIT CARDS	TAPAS BAR	FIXED-PRICE MENU	GOOD WINE LIST	OUTDOOR TABLES
LOJA: *La Finca.* ⓅⓅⓅⓅ Hotel La Bobadilla, Autovía Granada–Sevilla (Granada). 【 *(958) 32 18 61.* Worth a detour off the *autovía*, this exceptional restaurant is a place for fine dining. The chef makes creative use of fresh vegetables, capon and pork grown on the farm, game (in season) and seafood. 📱	AE DC MC V		■	●	■
MÁLAGA: *Marisquería Santa Paula.* ⓅⓅ Avenida de los Guindos, Barriada Santa Paula. 【 *(95) 223 65 57.* One of Málaga's traditional seafood bars, Santa Paula serves a great *fritura* (mixed fish fry) and *mariscada* (selection of shellfish). 📱 ♿	AE DC MC V	●	■		
MÁLAGA: *Mesón Astorga.* ⓅⓅ Calle Gerona 11. 【 *(95) 234 68 32.* Creative flair using Málaga's superb local produce makes this restaurant popular. Try the fried aubergine drizzled with molasses, or the salad of fresh tuna with sherry vinegar dressing. Lively tapas bar. ● *Sun.* 📱 ♿	AE DC MC V	●		●	■
MANILVA: *Macues.* ⓅⓅ Puerto de la Duquesa (Málaga). 【 *(95) 289 03 95.* At this restaurant, with its covered terrace overlooking the yacht harbour, your fish will be brought round for inspection before it is cooked. Fish baked in salt is a speciality, and the meat is good too. ● *Mon & Feb.* 📱 ♿	AE DC MC V			●	■
MARBELLA: *Triana.* ⓅⓅ Calle Gloria 11 (Málaga). 【 *(95) 277 99 62.* An intimate restaurant, right in the centre of Marbella's old town, specializing in Valencia-style rice dishes. Apart from paella, there is *caldoso con langosta* (soupy rice with lobster). ● *Mon & mid Jan–Mar.* 📱	AE DC MC V				
MARBELLA: *Santiago.* ⓅⓅⓅ Paseo Marítimo 5 (Málaga). 【 *(95) 277 43 39.* This is probably the best place for seafood on the Costa del Sol. On any day, there will be 40 to 50 fish and shellfish dishes, including paella, and good meat dishes such as pig and suckling lamb. ● *Nov.* 📱 ♿	AE DC MC V	■		●	■
MARBELLA: *Toni Dalli.* ⓅⓅⓅ El Oasis, Carretera de Cádiz (Málaga). 【 *(95) 277 00 35.* This lovely white palace flanked by palms, right on the beach, makes for a great night out. The Italian-influenced food includes home-made pastas, meat and fish. Live music is sometimes provided by Toni himself. ♿	AE DC MC V			●	
MARBELLA: *La Hacienda.* ⓅⓅⓅⓅ Urbanización Hacienda Las Chapas, Ctra Cádiz (Málaga). 【 *(95) 283 12 67.* Set in a gracious villa, the restaurant has gardens with sea views. The food – Andalusian with French touches – includes specialities such as guinea fowl with raisin sauce, and game in season. ● *mid Nov–mid Dec.* ♿	AE DC MC V		■	●	■
MARBELLA: *La Meridiana.* ⓅⓅⓅⓅ Camino de la Cruz (Málaga). 【 *(95) 277 61 90.* Situated in Marbella's rarefied heights, La Meridiana has a canopied garden room and adjoining patio bar. The menu features dishes such as swordfish *carpaccio*, artichokes with foie gras, and game in season. ● *Jan.* 📱 ♿	AE DC MC V		■	●	■
MIJAS: *El Mirador.* ⓅⓅ La Alcazaba, Plaza de la Constitución (Málaga). 【 *(95) 259 00 97.* In this picturesque hill town there are regrettably few good restaurants. However, this one has great sea views and offers excellent meat dishes and Valencia-style paella. ● *Tue.* 📱 ♿	AE DC MC V				■
MOTRIL: *Tropical.* ⓅⓅ Avenida Rodríguez Acosta 23 (Granada). 【 *(958) 60 04 50.* Both seafood, such as bass with *ajo verde* (green garlic), and meat, such as *choto a la brasa* (roast baby kid), are specialities here. ● *Sun & Jun.* 📱	AE DC MC V		■		

PALMA DEL RÍO: *Hospedería de San Francisco.*   ₽₽   MC V
Avenida Pío XII 33 (Córdoba). ((957) 71 01 83.
Dine in the cloisters of this out-of-the-way former monastery. The ever-
changing menu features superb Basque specialities. ● *Sun.*

EL PUERTO DE SANTA MARÍA: *Las Bóvedas.*   ₽₽   AE DC MC V
Monasterio de San Miguel, Calle Larga 27 (Cádiz). ((956) 54 04 40.
Dine in style under the vaulted brick ceilings of a former monastery.
Fish and shellfish are specialities, as is the dessert *tocino de cielo*
("heavenly bacon"), made from egg yolks by nuns.

EL PUERTO DE SANTA MARÍA: *El Faro del Puerto.*   ₽₽₽   AE DC MC V
Carretera de Rota (Cádiz). ((956) 87 09 52.
The menu here offers refined interpretations of modern dishes. Not to be
missed are the desserts, especially the oloroso sherry ice cream.

LA RÁBIDA: *Hostería de la Rábida.*   ₽₽   MC V
Paraje de la Rábida (Huelva). ((959) 35 03 12.
This restaurant, beside the 14th-century monastery where Christopher
Columbus once stayed, has good meat and seafood specialities.

RONDA: *Pedro Romero.*   ₽   AE DC MC V
Calle Virgen de la Paz 18 (Málaga). ((95) 287 11 10.
Facing Ronda's graceful bullring, this restaurant serves well-prepared
country food. Try the rabbit with thyme or the braised bull's tail.

SAN FERNANDO: *Venta Vargas.*   ₽₽   AE MC V
Avenida Puente Zuazo (Cádiz). ((956) 88 16 22.
This popular small town eatery has lots of flamenco atmosphere. Order
raciones of classics such as *aliñadas* (potato salad). ● *Mon.*

SAN ROQUE: *Los Remos en Villa Victoria.*   ₽₽₽   AE DC MC V
Ctra San Roque–La Línea, Gibraltar Campamento (Cádiz). ((956) 69 84 12.
Housed in a restored mansion with Mediterranean decor, this restaurant
serves exquisite dishes, with a focus on first-rate seafood. A sampling
menu includes shrimp fritters and sea nettles. ● *Sun.*

SANLÚCAR DE BARRAMEDA: *Casa Bigote.*   ₽₽   AE DC MC V
Bajo de Guía (Cádiz). ((956) 36 26 96.
At the mouth of the Río Guadalquivir, this typical sailors' *taberna* is the
place to sample *langostinos de Sanlúcar* (large, sweet, striped prawns)
and fresh fish from the day's catch, such as baby eels. ● *Sun.*

SANLÚCAR LA MAYOR: *La Alquería.*   ₽₽₽   AE DC MC V
Hacienda de Benazuza, Virgen de las Nieves (Sevilla). ((95) 570 33 44.
The chef at this beautiful country hacienda offers a choice of innovative
and simple dishes, all based on quality produce. ● *mid Jul–Sep.*

TORREMOLINOS: *Bar Restaurante Casa Juan.*   ₽   AE DC MC V
Calle Mar 14, La Carihuela (Málaga). ((95) 238 41 06.
A popular beachfront restaurant offering favourites such as fish baked
in salt and *fritura malagueña* (mixed fish fry). ● *Jan.*

TORREMOLINOS: *Frutos.*   ₽₽   AE DC MC V
Urbanización Los Álamos, Carretera a Cádiz (Málaga). ((95) 238 14 50.
The *grande dame* of Costa del Sol restaurants, serving superb meat and
fish. Enjoy suckling pig and follow with *arroz con leche* (rice pudding).

VERA: *Terraza Carmona.*   ₽₽   AE DC MC V
Calle Manuel Giménez 1 (Almería). ((950) 39 07 60.
The specialities here are excellent seafood, and unusual regional dishes
such as *gurullos con conejo* (pasta with rabbit). ● *Mon.*

THE BALEARIC ISLANDS

FORMENTERA, ES PUJOLS: *Sa Palmera.*   ₽   AE MC V
Playa Es Pujols. ((971) 32 83 56.
Freshly caught seafood is served at this seafront restaurant. Try the mixed
fish paella or the shellfish casserole *(zarzuela de mariscos).* ● *Nov–Jan.*

IBIZA (EIVISSA), IBIZA TOWN: *Ca'n Alfredo.*   ₽   AE DC MC V
Paseo Vara de Rey 16. ((971) 31 12 74.
Regional cuisine is served in this popular establishment. Choose from
numerous rice dishes or the *borrida de ratjada* (ray stew).

Price categories for a three-course evening meal for one, including a half-bottle of house wine, tax and service:

® under 3,000 ptas
®® 3,000–4,500 ptas
®®® 4,500–6,000 ptas
®®®® over 6,000 ptas

TAPAS BAR
In addition to the main dining room, there is a bar serving tapas (see p574–5) and raciones (larger portions).

FIXED-PRICE MENU
A good-value, fixed-price menu is offered at lunch or dinner, or both, usually with three courses.

GOOD WINE LIST
Denotes a wide range of good wines, or a more specialized selection of local wines.

OUTDOOR TABLES
Facilities for eating outdoors, on a terrace, or in a garden or courtyard, often with a good view.

	CREDIT CARDS	TAPAS BAR	FIXED-PRICE MENU	GOOD WINE LIST	OUTDOOR TABLES
IBIZA (EIVISSA), IBIZA TOWN: *El Cigarral.* ®® Calle Fray Vicente Nicolás 9. ((971) 31 12 46. A family-run restaurant where the menu changes according to what is fresh in the market. Delicious grilled steaks and fish, complemented by one of the largest selections of wines in Ibiza. ● mid Aug–mid Sep. ▤ ⛨	AE DC MC V			●	
IBIZA (EIVISSA), SANT ANTONI: *Sa Capella.* ®®® Carretera Can Germà. ((971) 34 00 57. Housed in a former chapel, this restaurant offers an international menu, including good fish and steaks. Open for dinner only. ● Nov–Apr. ⛨	DC MC V	●		●	
IBIZA (EIVISSA), SANT JOSEP: *Cana Joana.* ®®® Carretera Ibiza–Sant Josep. ((971) 80 01 58. One of the island's most interesting gastronomic offers. The seasonal menu, with Catalan and Mediterranean influences, includes dishes such as *pan palles* (toasted bread with tomato and olive oil). ● Nov–Jan. ⛨	AE MC V			●	▪
IBIZA (EIVISSA), SANTA EULÀRIA D'ES RIU: *Doña Margarita.* ®® Paseo Marítimo. ((971) 33 06 55. A port-side restaurant offering fresh fish, perfectly prepared, and a delicious yogurt mousse with raspberry sauce as dessert. ● Nov. ▤ ⛨	AE DC MC V			●	▪
IBIZA (EIVISSA), SANTA GERTRUDIS: *Ca'n Pau.* ®® Carretera de Sant Miquel. ((971) 19 70 07. Rustic Ibizan *masía* (farmhouse) serving good Catalan cuisine. Tender roast kid, quail with cabbage, and rabbit are a few of the house specialities, and there is a good selection of Catalan wines. ● Mon. ⛨	AE MC V			●	▪
MALLORCA, ALCÚDIA: *Mesón Los Patos.* ®® Carretera Sa Pobla–Alcúdia. ((971) 89 02 65. An agreeably decorated family restaurant with a garden and a children's playground. Simple and traditional Mallorcan dishes, including *arroz brut* (a soupy rice served with meat). ● Tue & mid Jan–Feb. ▤ ⛨	AE DC MC V	●	▪	●	▪
MALLORCA, CALA D'OR: *Port Petit.* ®® Avenida Cala Llonga. ((971) 64 30 39. Enjoy creative Mediterranean cuisine overlooking the marina. The salmon and monkfish *carpaccio* and the turbot in a mustard sauce are classics, along with the rich chocolate fondue. Open for dinner only. ● Nov–Apr.	AE DC MC V			●	
MALLORCA, CALA RATJADA: *Ses Rotges.* ®®® Calle Rafael Blanes 21. ((971) 56 31 08. This lovely old stone mansion, surrounded by palm trees and azaleas, is an ideal setting for sophisticated dining on French cuisine prepared using local produce. Good local wines. ● Dec–Feb. ⛨	AE DC MC V		▪	●	▪
MALLORCA, DEIÀ: *Bens d'Avall.* ®® Urbanización Costa Deià. ((971) 63 23 81. Perched on top of a cliff, this restaurant offers wonderful views of the coastline. Traditional, regional recipes are given modern touches, creating dishes such as shrimp *carpaccio* with pesto and Parmesan. ● Nov–Mar. ⛨	AE DC MC V		▪	●	▪
MALLORCA, DEIÀ: *El Olivo.* ®®®® Hotel la Residencia, Finca Son Canals. ((971) 63 90 11. One of the island's best restaurants, with delightful decoration and views of the mountains. Delicious *nouvelle cuisine* incorporating Mediterranean influences, with dishes such as lamb baked with olives. ▤ ⛨	AE DC MC V		▪	●	▪
MALLORCA, INCA: *Celler Ca'n Amer.* ®® Calle Pau 39. ((971) 50 12 61. This wonderful old wine cellar is now home to one of the island's most authentic regional dishes, *sopa mallorquina*, made with bread and braised vegetables. Good rice dishes and roast suckling pig. ● Sun. ▤	AE MC V			●	

MALLORCA, PAGUERA: *La Gran Tortuga.*　　　　　　　　　　Ⓟ Ⓟ
Aldea Cala Fornells 1. ☎ *(971) 68 60 23.*
There is a great sea view from the terrace, where you can try home-made
foie gras or monkfish stuffed with smoked salmon in a spinach sauce.
The atmosphere is agreeable and the service efficient. ● *Mon & Dec–Jan.*

MALLORCA, PALMA DE MALLORCA: *Ca'n Carlos.*　　　　　　Ⓟ
Calle del Agua 5. ☎ *(971) 71 38 69.*
Old Balearic recipes have been revived, providing diners with an
authentic version of the islands' food. The oven-roasted suckling lamb
and the grouper with cabbage are just two examples. ● *Sun.* 🗏

MALLORCA, PALMA DE MALLORCA: *Porto Pí.*　　　　　　　Ⓟ Ⓟ
Calle Garita 25. ☎ *(971) 40 00 87.*
This elegant old house, surrounded by gardens, is an ideal spot to savour
creative Mediterranean cuisine using first-class ingredients. ● *Sun.* 🗏

MALLORCA, POLLENÇA: *Celler Ca Vostra.*　　　　　　　　Ⓟ Ⓟ
Carretera Alcúdia–Port de Pollença. ☎ *(971) 86 55 46.*
This former wine bar is still decorated with wine barrels. Typical local
food, with fresh fish and *escudella* (a vegetable stew). ● *Wed.* 🗏 ♿

MALLORCA, PORT D'ANDRATX: *Layn.*　　　　　　　　　　Ⓟ Ⓟ
Calle Almirante Riera Alemany 19. ☎ *(971) 67 18 55.*
This restaurant has its own fishing boat to ensure the freshest of sea fare.
There are also meat specialities including roast suckling pig and beef
with cabbage. Views of the sea from the terrace. ● *Mon & mid Dec–Jan.*

MALLORCA, PORT D'ANDRATX: *Miramar.*　　　　　　　　Ⓟ Ⓟ
Avenida Mateo Bosch 22. ☎ *(971) 67 16 17.*
A family-run restaurant with views of the marina, offering good seafood
and impeccable service. Specialities include *arroz negro* (black rice, made
with squid's ink) and shrimps in rock salt. ● *Mon & mid Dec–mid Jan.*

MALLORCA, SÓLLER: *El Guía.*　　　　　　　　　　　　Ⓟ Ⓟ
Calle Castañer 2. ☎ *(971) 63 02 27.*
People come from near and far for El Guía's artichokes stuffed with
spinach. Good, tasty, home cooking at excellent prices. 🗏 ♿

MALLORCA, SON SERVERA: *S'Era de Pula.*　　　　　　　Ⓟ Ⓟ
Carretera Son Servera–Capdepera. ☎ *(971) 56 79 40.*
A rustic Mallorcan country house in a peaceful spot with mountain
views. The interesting mix of continental and local cuisine features
dishes such as cod with crystallized garlic. ● *Mon & mid Jan–mid Mar.* 🗏 ♿

MENORCA, CIUTADELLA: *Ca's Quintu.*　　　　　　　　Ⓟ Ⓟ
Plaza de Alfonso III 4. ☎ *(971) 38 10 02.*
This centrally located restaurant serves traditional Menorcan food, with an
emphasis on fresh fish. Try the house speciality, *caldera de langosta*
(lobster casserole) or *caldera de mariscos* (the shellfish version). 🗏 ♿

MENORCA, CIUTADELLA: *Casa Manolo.*　　　　　　　Ⓟ Ⓟ Ⓟ
Calle Marina 117. ☎ *(971) 38 00 03.*
A lively restaurant in the harbour with a delightful terrace overlooking
the marina. Regional seafood dishes including a selection of grilled
Menorcan fish, rice with seafood, and lobster casserole. 🗏 ♿

MENORCA, FORNELLS: *Es Cranc.*　　　　　　　　　Ⓟ Ⓟ Ⓟ
Calle Escoles 31. ☎ *(971) 37 64 42.*
This establishment deserves the reputation it has throughout the island
for the freshness and preparation of its seafood. The lobster *caldereta* and
the succulent grilled shrimp are two examples. ● *Wed & Dec–Feb.* 🗏 ♿

MENORCA, MAÓ: *Jágaro.*　　　　　　　　　　　　　Ⓟ Ⓟ
Moll de Levant 334. ☎ *(971) 36 23 90.*
Enjoy an excellent view of the harbour from this restaurant where seafood
dishes predominate in the summer and hearty stews in the winter. The
potato pie and almond pie are popular choices for desserts. ♿

MENORCA, ES MERCADAL: *Ca'n Aguedet.*　　　　　　Ⓟ Ⓟ
Calle Lepanto 23–30. ☎ *(971) 37 53 91.*
Authentic Menorcan dishes such as rabbit with figs, cuttlefish with shrimp
and pine nuts, and *arroz de tierra* (a rice and meat dish dating back to
Moorish times). Try a wine from the proprietor's own vineyard. 🗏

For key to symbols see back flap

Price categories for a three-course evening meal for one, including a half-bottle of house wine, tax and service:

Ⓟ under 3,000 ptas
ⓅⓅ 3,000–4,500 ptas
ⓅⓅⓅ 4,500–6,000 ptas
ⓅⓅⓅⓅ over 6,000 ptas

TAPAS BAR
In addition to the main dining room, there is a bar serving tapas (*see p574–5*) and raciones (larger portions).
FIXED-PRICE MENU
A good-value, fixed-price menu is offered at lunch or dinner, or both, usually with three courses.
GOOD WINE LIST
Denotes a wide range of good wines, or a more specialized selection of local wines.
OUTDOOR TABLES
Facilities for eating outdoors, on a terrace, or in a garden or courtyard, often with a good view.

THE CANARY ISLANDS

	CREDIT CARDS	TAPAS BAR	FIXED-PRICE MENU	GOOD WINE LIST	OUTDOOR TABLES
FUERTEVENTURA, PUERTO DEL ROSARIO: *Benjamín.* Calle León y Castillo 139. 【 *(928) 85 17 48.* Innovative Canary Islands cooking relying exclusively on local produce. The potatoes with *mojo* (a spicy sauce), the goat's cheese, and sorbet made from prickly pear fruit are all recommended. ● *Sun.* Ⓟ			■	●	
FUERTEVENTURA, PUERTO DEL ROSARIO: *La Casa del Jamón.* La Asomada. 【 *(928) 53 00 64.* Decorated like a traditional Spanish *mesón*, this family-run restaurant offers a mix of Basque and regional dishes including roast kid and a tasty variety of cheeses and Iberian cold meats. ● *Sep.* 🔥 Ⓟ	AE DC MC V			●	
LA GOMERA, SAN SEBASTIÁN DE LA GOMERA: *Casa del Mar.* Avenida Fred Olsen 2. 【 *(922) 87 12 19.* Simple seafood dishes are served in this family-style restaurant close to the harbour. You can have fish in a stew, in a paella or grilled. ● *Sun.* Ⓟ	AE DC MC V	●			
GRAN CANARIA, CRUZ DE TEJEDA: *Hostería Cruz de Tejeda.* Cruz de Tejeda. 【 *(928) 66 60 50.* Gran Canaria's famed parador restaurant dominates the lovely central mountains. Try the traditional roast kid or rabbit terrine, and the delicious *bienmesabe* (almond cake) with ice cream for dessert. 🔥 ⓅⓅ	AE DC MC V	●	■	●	●
GRAN CANARIA, MASPALOMAS: *Orangerie.* Hotel Palm Beach, Avenida Oasis. 【 *(928) 14 08 06.* A lush, tropical setting where you can dine on creative, up-market cuisine either indoors or out. Open for dinner only. ● *Thu & Sun.* ▤ ⓅⓅⓅⓅ	AE DC MC V		■	●	■
GRAN CANARIA, LAS PALMAS: *Casa Carmelo.* Paseo de las Canteras 2. 【 *(928) 46 90 56.* The sleek first-floor dining room gives a grandstand view of Las Palmas' superb seafront, which is particularly beautiful at night. The emphasis here is on chargrilled meat and fresh local fish. ▤ ⓅⓅ	AE DC MC V		■	●	
GRAN CANARIA, LAS PALMAS: *Mesón La Cuadra.* Calle General Mas de Gaminde 32. 【 *(928) 24 33 80.* Choose from either the tempting variety of tapas at the bar, or the truly "home-grown" menu. The proprietor's own farm produces the tender suckling lamb, the goat's cheese and the milk curd dessert. ● *Mon.* ▤ 🔥 ⓅⓅ	AE DC MC V	●	■	●	
GRAN CANARIA, PLAYA DEL INGLÉS: *Tenderete II.* Avenida Tirajana 5. 【 *(928) 76 14 60.* Typical Canary Islands cooking with an emphasis on fresh seafood. The fish prepared in rock salt and the *potaje de berros* (watercress broth) are house specialities. Try the locally grown *manga*, similar to mango. ▤ 🔥 ⓅⓅ	AE DC MC V		●	●	■
GRAN CANARIA, SANTA BRÍGIDA: *Las Grutas de Artiles.* Las Meleguinas. 【 *(928) 64 05 75.* A restaurant set in caves, offering authentic Canary Islands specialities and grilled meat. The gardens and swimming pool are ideal for children. ⓅⓅ	AE DC MC V	●	■	●	■
GRAN CANARIA, VEGA DE SAN MATEO: *Museo Cho-Zacarías.* Avenida de Tinamar. 【 *(928) 66 06 27.* Old farmers' cottages provide a unique setting for this restaurant. The traditional Canary Islands menu features *cherne* (a local fish) served in a coriander sauce, and watercress broth. Open lunch times only. ● *Mon.* Ⓟ	AE MC V			●	■
EL HIERRO, LA RESTINGA: *Casa Juan.* Calle Juan Gutiérrez Monteverde 23. 【 *(922) 55 71 02.* Local families flock to this inexpensive, no frills restaurant. Delicious fresh fish such as *vieja* and *cherne*, accompanied by a *mojo* sauce. Ⓟ		●			

LANZAROTE, ARRECIFE: *Castillo de San José.*
Castillo de San José. (*(928) 81 23 21.*
A converted 16th-century fortress, now housing a contemporary art
gallery and restaurant. Enjoy international and regional specialities
as you admire the art on the walls and the views of the harbour.
(₱₱ — AE MC V)

LANZAROTE, COSTA TEGUISE: *Mesón La Jordana.*
Centro Comercial de Lanzarote, Lanzarote Bay. (*(928) 59 03 28.*
A popular and attractive spot where you can sample local fare given a
French touch. Try the fresh *cherne* or the roast kid. ● *Sun & Sep.* 目
(₱₱ — AE MC V)

LANZAROTE, PUERTO DEL CARMEN: *Colón.*
Centro Comercial Mata Gorda. (*(928) 51 25 54.*
Decorated in traditional style, this restaurant serves international and
regional cuisine. The menu includes fresh duck foie gras and fish
dishes of the highest quality. Excellent wine list. 占
(₱₱ — AE DC MC V)

LANZAROTE, YAIZA: *Casa Salvador.*
Avenida Playa Blanca. (*(928) 51 70 25.*
Located right on the beach, this establishment serves freshly caught fish
and shellfish, as well as good grilled steaks and paellas.
(₱ — AE DC MC V)

LANZAROTE, YAIZA: *La Era.*
Calle El Barranco 3. (*(928) 83 00 16.*
La Era is set in one of the few old country houses to survive the island's
volcanic eruptions of 1730 to 1736. Enjoy regional specialities such as
lamb, kid or lentil stew in one of the pretty, rustic dining rooms.
(₱₱ — AE DC MC V)

LA PALMA, SANTA CRUZ DE LA PALMA: *Chipi Chipi.*
Calle Juan Mayor 42. (*(922) 41 10 24.*
Just 6 km (3.5 miles) out of town, this restaurant, with dining rooms
around a pretty patio, specializes in grilled meats and local dishes such
as chickpea soup. Good selection of island wines. ● *Wed, Sun & Oct–Nov.* 占
(₱ — AE MC V)

TENERIFE, ADEJE: *El Patio.*
Hotel Jardín Tropical, Urbanización San Eugenio. (*(922) 75 01 00.*
An enchanting setting for a special evening out. The lovely, flower-filled
patio is ideal for balmy summer nights. Imaginative, modern dishes are
created using local produce. Open for dinner only. 目
(₱₱₱₱ — AE DC MC V)

TENERIFE, LA OROTAVA: *Los Corales.*
Carretera General del Norte 130, Santa Úrsula. (*(922) 30 19 18.*
Genuine Canary Islands food with creative flourishes and wonderful
views of the valley. The meat or fish *carpaccio* and the traditional
conejo en salmorejo (rabbit terrine) are recommended. ● *Mon.* 占
(₱₱ — AE DC MC V)

TENERIFE, PUERTO DE LA CRUZ: *Mi Vaca y Yo.*
Calle Cruz Verde 3. (*(922) 38 52 47.*
A typical Canary Islands house, in the old part of town, agreeably
decorated with plants. There is a lively atmosphere in which to enjoy
a seafood paella or the house speciality, lobster casserole. ● *Jun.* 占
(₱ — AE DC MC V)

TENERIFE, PUERTO DE LA CRUZ: *Magnolia "Felipe el Payés".*
Avenida Marqués de Villanueva del Prado. (*(922) 38 56 14.*
Assured Catalan cooking, including the traditional *pan con tomate* (bread
with tomato) and *suquet* (fish stew), served in a flamboyant modern
dining room or in the gardens. 目 占
(₱₱₱ — AE DC MC V)

TENERIFE, SANTA CRUZ DE TENERIFE: *Café del Príncipe.*
Plaza del Príncipe de Asturias. (*(922) 27 88 10.*
Sample any of the good local dishes in this pretty restaurant which
overlooks the square in the centre of town. ● *Mon & Jun.* 占
(₱ — MC V)

TENERIFE, SANTA CRUZ DE TENERIFE: *El Coto de Antonio.*
Calle General Goded 13. (*(922) 27 21 05.*
Excellent regional specialities are served in this simple restaurant near the
bullring. The black potato salad, with salt cod, peppers and olive oil, and
the *vieja* in a coriander sauce are favourites among the clientèle. 目 占
(₱₱₱ — AE DC MC V)

TENERIFE, TEGUESTE: *El Drago.*
Urbanización San Gonzálo 1. (*(922) 54 30 01.*
This delightful 18th-century farmhouse provides a rustic setting for
excellent Canary Islands cooking including traditional watercress broth,
puchero (vegetable and meat broth) and fish casserole. ● *Mon & Aug.* 占
(₱₱ — AE DC MC V)

For key to symbols see back flap

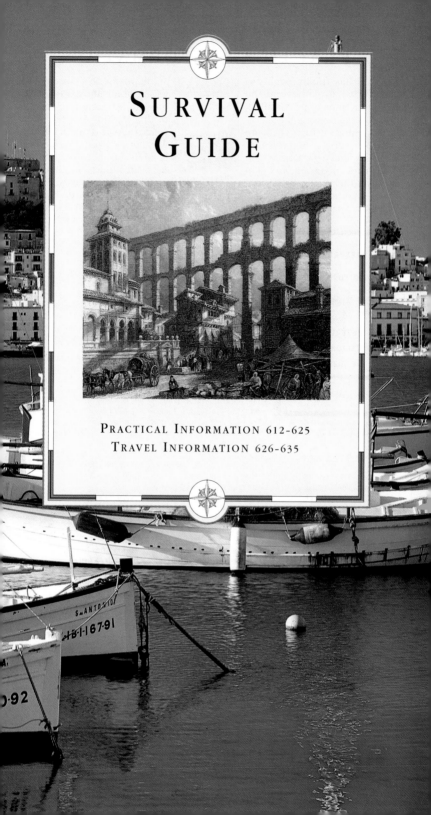

SURVIVAL
GUIDE

PRACTICAL INFORMATION

Spain has finally begun to market itself beyond the attractions of its coastline, and now has a solid tourist information infrastructure. There are national tourist offices in every large city, and regional offices in the smaller towns. All offer help with finding accommodation, restaurants and activities in their area. August is Spain's main holiday month.

Old street signs

Many businesses close for the whole month and roads are very busy at the beginning and end of this period. At any time of year, try to find out in advance whether your visit coincides with local fiestas, because although these are attractions, they often entail widespread closures. It is a good idea to plan leisurely lunches, as most of Spain stops from 2pm to 5pm.

A bilingual Basque/Castilian reserved parking sign

LANGUAGE

THE MAIN LANGUAGE of Spain, *Castellano* (Castilian), is spoken by almost everyone. There are three main regional languages: Catalan, spoken in Catalonia, *Gallego* (Galician) in Galicia and *Euskera* (Basque) in the Basque Country. Variants of Catalan are spoken in the Valencia region and also in the Balearic Islands.

People who speak English are often employed in places that deal with tourists.

MANNERS

THE SPANISH greet and say goodbye to strangers at bus stops and in lifts, shops and other public places. They often talk to people they do not know. People shake hands when introduced and whenever they meet. Women usually kiss on both cheeks when they meet, and friends and family members may kiss or embrace briefly.

VISAS AND PASSPORTS

VISAS ARE NOT required for citizens of EU countries, Iceland or Norway.

A list of entry requirements, which is available from Spanish embassies, specifies 35 other countries, including New Zealand, Canada and the USA, whose nationals do not need to apply for a visa if visiting Spain for less than 90 days. Thereafter they may apply to the *Gobierno Civil* (a local government office) for an extension. You usually need proof of employment or of sufficient funds to support yourself during a long stay.

Visitors from other countries, including Australia, must obtain a valid visa before travelling.

If you intend to stay for a long time in Spain, you should contact your nearest Spanish embassy several months in advance about your needs.

British visitors should note that a Visitor's Passport is no longer available. A full passport must be obtained.

TAX-FREE GOODS AND CUSTOMS INFORMATION

NON-EU RESIDENTS can reclaim *IVA* (VAT) on single items worth over 15,000 pesetas bought in shops displaying a "Tax-free for Tourists" sign. (Food, drink, tobacco, cars, motorbikes and medicines are exempt.) You pay the full price and ask the sales assistant for a *formulario* (tax exemption form). On leaving Spain, you ask customs to stamp your *formulario* (this must be within six months of the purchase). You receive the refund by mail or on your credit card account.

Banco Exterior branches at Barcelona, Madrid, Málaga, Mallorca, Oviedo, Santander and Seville airports will give refunds on *formularios* stamped by customs.

TOURIST INFORMATION

ALL MAJOR CITIES and towns have *oficinas de turismo*. They will provide town plans, lists of hotels and restaurants, information about the locality and details of activities and events for tourists.

There is a **Spanish National Tourist Office** in several large cities abroad.

OPENING HOURS

MOST MONUMENTS and museums close on Mondays. On other days they generally open from 10am to 2pm, close from 2pm to 5pm, and, in some cases, reopen from 5pm to 8pm. Churches may follow these opening hours or only be opened for services. Admission is charged for most museums and monuments.

In smaller towns it is common for churches, castles and other sights to be kept permanently locked. The key, available to visitors on request, will be lodged with a caretaker in a neighbouring house, in the town hall, or perhaps with the owners of the local bar.

 OFICINA DE TURISMO

Spanish tourist office sign with distinctive "i" logo

◁ **The old town of Ibiza enclosed by its 16th-century walls, seen from the harbour**

Students enjoy reduced admission fees to many museums and galleries

FACILITIES FOR THE DISABLED

SPAIN'S NATIONAL association for the disabled, the Confederación Coordinadora Estatal de Minusválidos Físicos de España (COCEMFE), has a tour company, Servi-COCEMFE *(see p533)*, which publishes guides to facilities in Spain and will help plan a holiday to individual requirements. Tourist offices and the social services departments of town halls can provide information on local conditions and facilities. A travel agency, **Viajes 2000**, specializes in holidays for disabled people. RADAR and Holiday Care Service in the UK *(see p533)* offer limited information on facilities for the disabled in Spanish resorts.

COCEMFE sign for disabled access

SPANISH TIME

IN WINTER, Spain is one hour ahead of Greenwich Mean Time (GMT) and in summer an hour ahead of British Summer Time (BST). The Canary Islands are on GMT in winter and an hour ahead in summer. Spain uses the 24-hour clock, so 1pm = 13:00.

La madrugada is the small hours. *Mañana* (morning) lasts until the late Spanish lunch time at about 2pm and *mediodía* (midday) from about 1–4pm. *La tarde* is the afternoon and evening.

STUDENT INFORMATION

HOLDERS OF THE International Student Identity Card (ISIC) are entitled to benefits, such as discounts on travel and reduced entrance charges to museums and galleries. Information is available from all national student organizations and, in Spain, from the local government-run **Centros de Información Juvenil (CIJ)** in large towns. **Turismo y Viajes Educativos (TIVE)** specializes in student travel.

ELECTRICAL ADAPTORS

SPAIN'S ELECTRICITY supply is 220 volts, but the 125-volt system still operates in some old buildings. Plugs for both have two round pins. A three-tier standard travel converter enables you to use appliances from abroad on both supplies. Heating appliances should be used only on 220 volts.

CONVERSION CHART

Imperial to metric
1 inch = 2.54 centimetres
1 foot = 30 centimetres
1 mile = 1.6 kilometres
1 ounce = 28 grams
1 pound = 454 grams
1 pint = 0.6 litre
1 gallon = 4.6 litres

Metric to imperial
1 millimetre = 0.04 inch
1 centimetre = 0.4 inch
1 metre = 3 feet 3 inches
1 kilometre = 0.6 mile
1 gram = 0.04 ounce
1 kilogram = 2.2 pounds
1 litre = 1.8 pints

DIRECTORY

EMBASSIES

Australia
Paseo de la Castellana 143,
28046 Madrid.
(91) 579 04 28.

United Kingdom
Calle de Fernando El Santo 16,
28010 Madrid.
(91) 319 02 00.

SPANISH TOURIST OFFICES

Madrid
Calle de la Princesa 1,
28008 Madrid.
(91) 541 23 25.

Barcelona
Gran Via de les Corts
Catalanes 658,
08010 Barcelona.
(93) 301 74 43.

Seville
Avenida de la Constitución 21b,
41004 Seville.
(95) 422 14 04.

Australia
International House,
Suite 44,
203 Castlereagh St,
Level 2,
PO Box A-685,
Sydney, NSW 2000.
(612) 264 7966.

United Kingdom
56 St James's Street,
London
SW1A 1LD.
(0171) 499 0901.

DISABLED

Viajes 2000
Paseo de la Castellana 228,
28046 Madrid.
(91) 323 10 29.

YOUTH/STUDENT

CIJ
Calle de Alcalá 31,
28013 Madrid.
(91) 580 42 42.

TIVE
Calle Fernando el Católico 88,
28015 Madrid.
(91) 543 74 12.

Personal Security and Health

IN SPAIN, AS IN MOST EUROPEAN countries, rural areas are generally safe, but certain parts of cities are subject to petty crime. Carry cards and money in a belt and never leave anything visible in your car when you park it.

If you are unwell, Spanish pharmacists are qualified to advise and sometimes to prescribe. Emergency phone numbers vary from region to region. The most important ones are given on the opposite page. If you lose your documents, contact your consulate or the local police.

Spanish pharmacy sign

IN AN EMERGENCY

ONLY THE *Policía Nacional* operate a nationwide emergency phone number. Call it even if you need some other service and they will assist you in getting help. Telephone directories list local emergency numbers under *Servicios de Urgencia*, and they appear on tourist maps and leaflets.

For emergency medical treatment call the Cruz Roja (Red Cross), look under *Ambulancias* in the phone book, or go to a hospital casualty department *(Urgencias)*.

MEDICAL TREATMENT

ALL EU NATIONALS are entitled to Spanish social security cover. To claim, you must obtain Form E111 from the UK Department of Health or from a post office before you travel. You give this form to anyone who treats you, so you may need several photocopies. It comes with a booklet, *Health Advice for Travellers*, which

explains exactly what health care you are entitled to and where and how to claim. You may have to pay and reclaim the money later.

Not all treatments are covered by Form E111 and some are costly, so arrange for medical cover before travelling.

If you want private medical care in Spain, ask at a tourist

Sign identifying a Cruz Roja (Red Cross) emergency treatment centre

office, or at your embassy or hotel for the name and number of a doctor. If necessary, ask for one who speaks English.

PHARMACIES

SPANISH PHARMACISTS have wide responsibilities. They can advise and, in some cases, prescribe without consulting a doctor. In a non-emergency a *farmacéutico* is a good

person to see first. It is easy to find one who speaks English.

The *farmacia* sign is a green or red illuminated cross. Those open at night in a town are listed in the windows of all the local pharmacies. Do not confuse them with *perfumerías*, which sell toiletries only.

PERSONAL SECURITY

VIOLENT CRIME is rare in Spain but visitors should avoid walking alone in poorly lit areas. Wear a bag or camera across your body, not on your shoulder. Men occasionally make complimentary remarks *(piropos)* to women in public, particularly in the street. This is an old custom and not intended to be intimidating.

SPANISH POLICE

THERE ARE ESSENTIALLY three types of police in Spain. The *Guardia Civil* (National Guard) mainly police rural areas. Their uniform is olive green but there are local and regional variations. They impose fines for traffic offences.

The *Policía Nacional*, who wear a blue uniform, operate in towns with a population of more than 30,000. The *Policía Nacional* have been replaced with a regional force, the *Ertzaintza*, in the Basque country, and with the *Mossos d'Esquadra* in Catalonia. These can be distinguished by their respective red and blue berets.

The *Policía Local*, also called *Policía Municipal* or *Guardia Urbana*, dress in blue. They operate independently in each town and also have a separate branch for city traffic control.

All three services will direct you to the relevant authority in the event of an incident requiring police help.

Guardia Civil   **Policía Nacional**   **Policía Local**

DIRECTORY

EMERGENCY NUMBERS

Policía Nacional
[091 *(nationwide)*.

Fire Brigade (Bomberos)
[080 *(Madrid, Barcelona and Seville)*.

Ambulance: (Red Cross, Cruz Roja)
[*(91) 522 22 22 (Madrid)*.
[*(93) 300 20 20 (Barcelona)*.
[*(95) 435 01 35 (Seville)*.

For emergency services outside these cities, consult the local telephone directory.

Patrol car of the Policía Nacional, Spain's main urban police force

Policía Local patrol car, mainly seen in small towns

Cruz Roja (Red Cross) ambulance

The emergency number on the side of fire engines varies regionally

LEGAL ASSISTANCE

SOME INSURANCE POLICIES cover legal costs, for instance after an accident. If you are not covered, telephone your nearest consulate.

You can also contact the *Colegio de Abogados* (lawyers' association) of the nearest town or city, which can advise you where to obtain legal advice or representation locally.

If you need an interpreter, consult the *Páginas Amarillas (Yellow Pages)* telephone directory for the region under *Traductores* or *Intérpretes.* Both *Traductores Oficiales* and *Traductores Jurados* are qualified to translate legal or official documents.

PERSONAL PROPERTY

HOLIDAY INSURANCE is there to protect you financially from the loss or theft of your property, but it is always best to take obvious precautions against loss and theft.

If you have to carry large sums of money with you, take traveller's cheques and, if you have two credit cards, do not carry them together. Never leave a bag or handbag unattended anywhere and do not put down a purse or handbag on the tabletop in a café.

The moment you discover a loss or theft, report it to the local police station. To claim insurance you must do this immediately, as many companies give you 24 hours only. Ask the police for a *denuncia*

(written statement), which you need to make a claim. If your passport was one of the items stolen, or if you lose it, report it to your consulate.

PUBLIC CONVENIENCES

PUBLIC PAY-TOILETS are rare in Spain. Department stores are often good places to try, as are bars and restaurants where you are a customer. On motorways, there are toilets at service stations. You may have to ask for a key *(la llave)*, not only at the service stations but also in some bars in country areas. It is best to bring your own tissues, too. The term generally used for toilets in Spain is *los servicios.*

OUTDOOR HAZARDS

SPAIN is prey every summer to forest fires fanned by winds and fuelled by bone-dry vegetation. Be sensitive to fire hazards and use car ashtrays. Broken glass can start a fire so be careful to take your empty bottles away with you.

The sign *coto de caza* in woodland areas identifies a hunting reserve where you must follow the country codes. *Toro bravo* means "fighting bull" – do not approach. A *camino particular* sign indicates a private driveway.

If you are climbing or hill-walking go properly equipped and let someone know when you expect to return.

Banking and Local Currency

YOU MAY ENTER SPAIN with any amount of money, but if you intend to export more than one million pesetas, you should declare it. Eurocheques are widely accepted in Spain. Traveller's cheques may be exchanged at banks, *cajas de cambio* (bureaux de change), some hotels and some shops. Banks generally offer the best exchange rates. The cheapest exchange may be offered on your credit or direct debit card, which may be used in cash dispensers displaying the appropriate sign.

24-hour cash dispenser

BANKING HOURS

SPANISH BANKS are beginning to extend their opening hours, but expect extended hours only at large central branches in the big cities.

As a rule of thumb, banks are open from 8am to 2pm on weekdays. Some open until 1pm on Saturdays. Most close on Saturdays in August; in the south they also close on Saturdays from May to September.

Bureau de change

CHANGING MONEY

MOST BANKS have a foreign exchange desk with the sign *Cambio* or *Extranjero*. Always take your passport as ID to effect any transaction.

You can draw up to 50,000 pesetas on major credit cards at a bank. If you bank with **Barclays** or **NatWest**, it is possible to cash a cheque in the usual way at one of their branches in Spain.

Bureaux de change, with the sign *Caja de Cambio* or "Change", invariably charge higher rates of commission than banks, but they are often open after hours. They are commonly found in the tourist areas of Spanish towns and cities.

Cajas de Ahorro (savings banks) also exchange money. They open from 8:30am to 2pm on weekdays and also on Thursday afternoons from 4:30pm to 7:45pm.

CHEQUES AND CARDS

TRAVELLER'S CHEQUES can be purchased at American Express, Thomas Cook or your bank. All are accepted in Spain. If you exchange AmEx cheques at an AmEx office, commission is not charged. You can purchase cheques in pesetas from any bank.

You can write a cheque in pesetas using Eurocheques, which may also be used to change money at a bank. You must show your Eurocard or Mastercard and your passport.

The most widely accepted card in Spain is the **Visa** card. **Mastercard** (Access)/Euro-card and **American Express** are also useful currency. The major banks will allow cash withdrawals on credit cards.

When you pay for goods or services with a card, cashiers will usually pass your card through a reading machine. Sometimes, however, you will be asked to punch your PIN into a small keypad attached to the machine.

Credit card reader with PIN keypad

CASH DISPENSERS

IF YOUR CARD is linked to your home bank account, you can use it with your PIN to withdraw money from cash dispensers. These are widespread and nearly all take Visa or Mastercard (Access) cards.

When you enter your PIN, instructions are displayed in English, French, German and Spanish. These days, many dispensers are inside buildings and to gain access you will have to run your card through a door-entry system.

Cards with Cirrus and Maestro logos can also be widely used to withdraw money from cash machines.

DIRECTORY

FOREIGN BANKS

Barclays Bank
Plaza de Colón 1, 28046 Madrid.
((91) 336 10 00.

Banco NatWest March
Calle Príncipe de Vergara 125,
28002 Madrid.
((91) 321 71 00.

LOST CARDS AND TRAVELLER'S CHEQUES

American Express
((07 44) 1273 696933 (toll free reversed charge international call).

Diners Club
((07 44) 1252 513500 (toll free reversed charge international call).

Mastercard (Access)
((07 44) 1268 298178.

Visa
((900) 99 12 16 (toll free).

CURRENCY

THE CURRENCY of Spain is the peseta, usually abbreviated to "pta", or "ptas". It is common to speak of *duros* in popular speech (1 *duro* is 5 pesetas). *Cinco* (5) *duros* equal 25 pesetas and *mil* (1,000) *duros* is 5,000 pesetas. Shop assistants giving change often round the figure up or down to the nearest 5 pesetas.

Spanish coins are often a source of confusion. For only nine denominations, 58 different coins are in circulation. However, many of these are now being phased out and from January 1997 only coins minted after 1986 will be in use. (The almost worthless 1-peseta and 2-peseta coins will be removed from circulation.)

The seven denominations of coin that will be in circulation after 1997 will be easy to distinguish by shape and colour, but the designs will change each year. A 200-peseta coin minted in 1992 shows King Juan Carlos and his son Prince Felipe on one side, and the statue of a bear in Madrid's Puerta del Sol on the other; paintings by Velázquez and Goya appear on the 1994 coin.

A 2,000-peseta coin, minted in silver to commemorate Spain's presidency of the EU Council of Ministers in 1996 is available as a collectors' item. One side shows the Royal Palace in Madrid and the other has the King's head.

1,000 pesetas

2,000 pesetas

Bank Notes
Spanish bank notes are in four denominations. The 1,000-peseta note (two designs, both in green), is the smallest, followed by the 2,000-peseta note (pink), the 5,000-peseta note (ochre with brown and purple) and the 10,000-peseta note (blue).

5,000 pesetas

10,000 pesetas

Coins
Spanish coins, shown here at actual size, are in denominations of 5 ptas, 10 ptas, 25 ptas, 50 ptas, 100 ptas, 200 ptas and 500 ptas. The 500-pta, 100-pta, 25-pta and 5-pta coins are all a dull gold. The 200-pta, 50-pta and 10-pta coins are all silvered.

5 pesetas   **10 pesetas**   **25 pesetas**

50 pesetas   **100 pesetas**   **200 pesetas**   **500 pesetas**

Shopping

Shopping in Spain is a pleasurable activity, particularly if you approach it in a leisurely way, punctuating it with frequent breaks for coffee. In small, family-run shops especially, people will go out of their way to fulfil your smallest request. Markets sell the freshest of produce and quality wines can be found at almost any grocer. Leatherwork is still highly regarded among Spain's many traditional crafts. Spanish design has come to the forefront in both fashion and decor. Below is a size conversion chart for clothes and shoes, and suggestions to help you make the most of shopping in Spain.

A drinking vessel or glass *porrón*

Fresh produce in a market in Pollença (Mallorca)

OPENING HOURS

Shops usually open at 10am, close at 2pm and reopen from 5pm to 8pm. Bakeries and bars generally open earlier, at around 8am. Hypermarkets and department stores stay open over lunchtime.

Markets are held in the morning only. In some regions Sunday trading is just limited to the bakeries, *pastelerías* and newspaper kiosks, but in many holiday resorts shops open on Sunday.

Fans are still in daily use as well as being costume accessories

PAYING

Cash and credit cards are the usual methods of payment in Spain. Cheques are rarely accepted. Visitors can reclaim the *IVA* (VAT) charged on all purchases except food, drink, motor vehicles and medicines *(see p612)*. Money-changing and currency are explained on pages 616–17.

LARGER SHOPS

The hipermercados are sited outside towns and can usually be found by following signs to the *centro comercial.* The best known are Alcampo, Continente and PRYCA.

Spain's leading department store is El Corte Inglés. It has branches in all cities and most of the larger regional towns.

Major seasonal sales are advertised by the word *Rebajas* displayed in shop windows.

SPECIALIST SHOPS

Specialist shops often represent generations of family business. *Panaderías* (also called *bornos*) are bakeries selling bread, *bollos* (sweet buns) and rolls. Cakes and pastries are sold in *pastelerías;* many sell chocolates, as well. You buy fresh meat from a *carnicería,* but for the best cold meats go to a *charcutería,* which also sells cheese. *Charcuterías* are often found in or near markets. *Pescaderías* sell fish and shellfish, although the best fish is often sold on market stalls.

For fruit and vegetables, a *frutería* or *verdulería* will have better produce, because they stock only what is in season.

Hardware stores are called *ferreterías. Librerías* are in fact bookshops, not libraries, and *papelerías* are stationers.

Anything you buy as a *regalo* (gift) will be gift-wrapped on request. When you buy flowers from a *floresteria,* the assistant will expect to arrange them.

MARKETS

Every large town has a daily market *(mercado),* open from 9am to 2pm. Small towns have one or more market days a week. This guide lists market days for all towns featured.

Markets usually have the best fresh produce, but they sell all types of food, including *frutos secos* (dried fruits) and seasonal produce, such as mushrooms, soft fruit and game. There are also usually other types of goods on sale, such as flowers, hardware and clothes.

Antiques and flea markets *(rastros)* are held everywhere in Spain, but the largest is in Madrid *(see p292).*

Display of hand-painted ceramics in Toledo

REGIONAL PRODUCTS

SPANISH REGIONAL specialities are often better value when bought where they are made. Each region produces its own type of sausage. In Burgos, for example, *morcilla* (blood sausage) is made and a fiery red chorizo comes from Guijelo, Extremadura. Andalusia is renowned for olives and olive oil and Galicia for its cheeses.

Seasonal delicacies include *rovellons* (huge golden mushrooms) in Catalonia and tiny fiery peppers, *pimientos de Padrón*, in Galicia.

Some crafts originated with the Moors, such as Toledo's filigree metalwork and the *azulejos* (ceramic tiles) of Andalusia. Paterna and Manises near Valencia, and Talavera de la Reina in Castilla-La Mancha are towns well known for their ceramics.

Lace from the villages of the Sierra de Gata in Extremadura and Galicia's Costa do Morte is prized. Carved fiddles and clogs are Cantabrian crafts. Spanish crafts, such as guitars, fans and flamenco shoes, are sold in major cities.

Basketware is sold in all parts of Spain

WINE AND OTHER BEVERAGES

WINE IS SOLD in grocers and supermarkets, but only specialist dealers do justice to Spain's many vine-growing areas. Local wines can be bought by the litre at a town or village shop (bodega); they can also be bought directly from the vineyard (also called bodegas), but you have to make an appointment to visit.

Spain's most famous vine-growing regions are La Rioja and Navarra *(see pp74–5)*; Penedés, where *cava* (sparkling wine) is produced *(see pp192–3)*; Valdepeñas *(see pp322–3)*; Ribera del Duero *(see pp322–3)*; and Jerez, the sherry region *(see pp402–3)*.

Among the many Spanish liqueurs are *Pacharán (see p577)*, made from sloes, and *licor de bellota*, from acorns.

A range of olives, some flavoured with herbs, on a market stall

HOUSEHOLD AND KITCHEN GOODS

DEPARTMENT STORES have a good selection of household goods, but the *ferreterías* (small hardware shops) often have the more authentic selection. Traditional pottery, such as red clay *cazuelas* (dishes) that can be used in the oven and on the hob are cheap. Paella pans have always been made of iron or enamel, but now come in stainless steel or with non-stick finishes. Table linen is often good value on market stalls. Spanish lighting design is widely admired and sold in *lampisterías*. Traditional wrought-iron goods, such as candlesticks and door furniture, are always popular.

CLOTHING AND SHOES

THE LARGER CITIES naturally offer the widest selection of clothes shops, but Spanish designer labels can be found even in the smaller towns.

If you wish to purchase an item which needs altering, it is still usual for shops to offer the services of a seamstress for a very modest fee. Most can be persuaded to return your item within two days.

Leather shoes and accessories can be inexpensive and there is a wide range in terms of quality and price. It is the practice in mid-range shops for customers to choose from the selection in the window and give the sales assistant the code number indicated and your *talla* (size). If you want an all-leather shoe, look for *cuero*, the hide label mark. Leather clothes are also good quality and well designed.

SIZE CHART

Women's dresses, coats and skirts

Spanish	40	42	44	46	48	50	52 (size)
British/Australian	8	10	12	14	16	18	20 (size)
British	32	34	36	38	40	42	44 (inches)
Australian	86	91	95	100	105	110	120 (cm)

Women's shoes

Spanish	36	37	38	39	40	41
British	3	4	5	6	7	8
Australian	5	6	7	8	9	10

Men's suits

Spanish	44	46	48	50	52	54	56	58 (size)
British	34	36	38	40	42	44	46	48 (inches)
Australian	87	92	97	102	107	112	117	122 (cm)

Men's shirts (collar size)

Spanish	36	38	39	41	42	43	44	45 (cm)
British	14	15	15$\frac{1}{2}$	16	16$\frac{1}{2}$	17	17$\frac{1}{2}$	18 (inches)
Australian	36	38	39	41	42	43	44	45 (cm)

Men's shoes

Spanish	39	40	41	42	43	44	45	46
British	6	7	7$\frac{1}{2}$	8	9	10	11	12
Australian	6	7	7$\frac{1}{2}$	8	9	10	11	12

Communications

TELEFONICA, THE SPANISH telecommunications company, has improved its service since it was digitized in 1995, and the state monopoly is to be removed in 1998. Public telephones are easy to find and most operate with a card or coins, but international calls have a high charge.

The postal service, Correos, is identified by a crown insignia in red or white on a yellow background. Registered post and telegrams can be sent from all Correos offices *(see pp622–3)*. They sell stamps as well, but most people buy them from state-run *estancos* (tobacconists). There are no public phones in Correos offices.

Logo of the Spanish telecom system

USING A COIN AND CARD TELEPHONE

1 Lift the receiver, and wait for the dialling tone and for the display to show *Inserte monedas o tarjeta.*

2 Insert either coins *(monedas)* or a card *(tarjeta).*

3 Key in the number firmly, but not too fast – Spanish phones prefer you to pause between digits.

4 As you press the digits, the number you are dialling will appear on the display. You will also be able to see how much money or how many units are left and when to insert more coins.

5 When your call is finished, replace the receiver. The phonecard will then re-emerge automatically or any excess coins will be returned.

A 1000-peseta phonecard

Denominations of pesetas accepted in coin-operated telephones

TELEPHONING IN SPAIN

AS WELL AS PUBLIC telephone boxes *(cabinas)*, there are nearly always payphones in bars. Both types take coins of 5, 25 and 100 pesetas. There will be a high minimum connection charge, especially for international calls, so make sure that you have plenty of change at the ready.

Phonecards are far more convenient and can be bought at newsstands and *estancos*. Some phones are equipped with multilingual electronic instruction displays.

There are public telephone offices called *locutorios* where you can make a call and pay for it afterwards. They are usually quieter than phone booths and you do not need coins. Telefónica run the official ones, which are the cheapest type; private ones, often located in shops, are pricier.

There are four charge bands for international calls: EU countries; non-EU European countries and Northwest Africa; North and South America; and the rest of the world. With the exception of local calls, using

USEFUL SPANISH DIALLING CODES

- To make a call within a province, dial the number directly.
- To call another province, first dial the area code (beginning with 9; e.g. Madrid 91). Area codes are listed in the A-K phone book or obtained from directory enquiries.
- To make an international call, dial 07, wait for the tone, then dial the country code, the area code and the number.
- Country codes are: UK 44; Eire 353; France 33; USA and Canada 1; Australia 61; New Zealand 64. It may be necessary to omit the initial digit of the destination's area code.

- For operator/directory service, dial 003.
- For international directories, dial 025.
- To make a reversed-charge (collect) call within the EU, dial 900 99 00 followed by the country code; to the USA or Canada, dial 900 99 00 followed by 11 or 15 respectively. Numbers for other countries can be found in the front of the A-K telephone directory under *Modalidades del Servicio Internacional.*
- To report technical faults, dial 002.
- For the speaking clock dial 093, for the weather 094, for a wake-up call 096.

the telephone system can be expensive, especially from a hotel, which may add a surcharge. A call from a *cabina* or a *locutorio* costs 35 per cent more than one made from a private phone in someone's home. Reversed-charge calls made to EU countries may be dialled directly, but most other reversed-charge calls must be made through the operator.

The Spanish dialling code system works on a provincial basis, with each area code prefixed by the number 9. For example, Barcelona is 93. When dialling from outside Spain, you omit the 9. The international code for Spain is always 34 so, to get through to Barcelona, you dial 34 3.

Phone numbers in Spanish cities generally have seven digits, but in smaller towns and in country areas they have six.

Public payphone booth, easily visible in a city street

TELEVISION AND RADIO

TELEVISION ESPAÑOLA, Spain's state television company, broadcasts two channels which are called TVE1 and TVE2.

Several of the *comunidades* (*see pp622–3*) have their own publicly owned television channels which broadcast in the language of the region.

There are three national independent television stations: Antena 3, Tele-5 (Telecinco) and Canal+ (Canal Plus). Some Canal+ programmes are only

Spanish daily papers

available on payment of a subscription for a station decoder.

Most foreign films shown on Spanish television (and in cinemas) are dubbed and subtitled films are listed as *V.O. (versión original).*

Several satellite channels, such as CNN, Eurosport and Cinemanía, can be received throughout Spain.

The state radio station is Radio Nacional de España. Radio Clásico and Radio 2 broadcast music.

Some stations in tourist areas rebroadcast BBC World Service programmes in English. They are: Radio Mijas; Coastline Radio in Torrox; Onda Cero Radio in Marbella and Tenerife; Radio Maspalomas in Gran Canaria; and Sunshine Capital Radio in Palma de Mallorca.

NEWSPAPERS AND MAGAZINES

NEWSAGENTS and kiosks in town centres often stock periodicals in English. The newspapers available on publication day are the *International Herald Tribune*, the *Financial Times* and the *Guardian International*. Other English-language and European titles are on sale, but usually not until a day after they have been published.

The European newspaper and popular weekly news magazines such as *Time, Newsweek* and *The Economist* are readily available throughout the country. The most

Logo of Radio Nacional de España

widely read of the Spanish newspapers, in descending number of sales, are *El País, El Mundo, ABC* and *La Vanguardia* (in Catalonia). *El Mundo* is oriented more towards features and aimed at a younger market than the other three, which cover international news more thoroughly. Weekly listings magazines for arts and events are published in Barcelona *(see p184)*, Madrid *(see p306)* and Seville. They are the *Guía del Ocio* in Barcelona and Madrid, and *El Giraldillo* in Seville. Several other cities also have listings magazines.

Local newspapers in Spanish, such as *Levante* in Valencia and *La Gaceta de Canarias* in the Canary Islands, are a useful source of information on local and regional events.

Foreign-language periodicals are published by expatriates in Madrid and in the country's main tourist areas. Examples in English include *Sur* on the Costa del Sol, the *Costa Blanca News* and the *Mallorca Daily Bulletin*. One of the longest-running magazines is *Lookout*. Published in Fuengirola, it features in-depth reports covering all aspects of life in Spain.

A *prensa* (press) sign identifies a newsstand

POSTAL SERVICE

CORREOS, the postal service in Spain, is rather slow. Mail sent to an address in the city where it is posted can take three to four days to arrive and

Shops with this sign sell stamps

a national or international delivery may take more than a week. Send any urgent or important post by *urgente* (express) or *certificado* (registered) mail. To be sure of fast delivery it is wise to use a private courier.

Post can be registered and telegrams sent from all Correos offices. However, it is much more convenient to buy stamps for letters and postcards from an *estanco* (tobacconist). Postal rates fall into four price bands: the EU; the rest of Europe; the USA; and the rest of the world. Parcels have to be weighed and stamped by Correos and must be securely tied with string or a charge may be made at the counter to have them sealed by a clerk.

The main Correos offices open 8am–9pm from Monday to Friday and 9am–7pm on Saturday. Branches in the suburbs of cities and in villages open 9am–2pm from Monday to Friday and 9am–1pm on Saturday.

Standard issue postage stamps

ADDRESSES

IN SPANISH ADDRESSES the house number follows the name of the street. The floor of a block of flats comes after a hyphen. Therefore 4-2' means a flat on the second floor of number four. All postcodes have five digits, the first two being the province number.

SPAIN'S LOTTERIES

Lottery fever is greater in Spain than in any other European country. The Lotería Nacional runs prize draws most Saturdays, plus a few special ones, the *extraordinarios*, of which the biggest is El Gordo ("the Fat One") at Christmas *(see p39)*. It is common to buy a *décimo* (one-tenth of a number), rather than a full ticket. Punters can also try their luck with the ONCE lottery, which has draws daily, the Thursday Lotería Primitiva, and the Bono-loto, with four draws a week.

ONCE lottery booth

LETTERS AND FAXES

LETTERS POSTED at a central post office usually arrive more quickly than if posted in a postbox (*buzón*). Post-boxes in cities are yellow pillar boxes; in towns and villages they are usually small, wall-mounted postboxes. Poste restante letters should be addressed care of the *Lista de Correos* and the town. You can collect them from main post offices. To send and receive money by post ask for a *giro postal*.

When dealing with businesses in Spain, it is best to phone or fax. The post tends to be used only as a last resort. There are fax facilities in some *locutorios (see p620)* and in hotels and many private shops. Look for a *telefax* sign.

Spanish postbox

LOCAL GOVERNMENT

SPAIN is one of Europe's most decentralized states. Many powers have been devolved to the 17 regions, *comunidades autónomas*, which have their own elected parliaments. These regions have varying degrees of independence from Madrid, with the Basques and Catalans enjoying the most autonomy. The *comunidades* provide some services – such as the promotion of tourism – which were once carried out by central government.

The country is subdivided into 50 provinces, each with its *diputación* (council). The affairs of each of the Balearic and Canary islands are run by an island council.

Every town, or group of villages, is administered by an *ayuntamiento* (town council – the word also means town hall) which is supervised by an elected *alcalde* (mayor) and a team of councillors.

Murcia's town hall (*ayuntamiento* or *Casa Consistorial*)

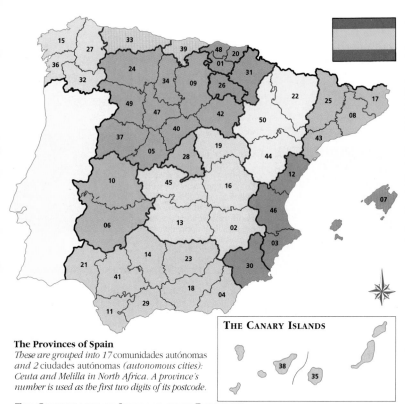

The Provinces of Spain

These are grouped into 17 comunidades autónomas and 2 ciudades autónomas (autonomous cities): Ceuta and Melilla in North Africa. A province's number is used as the first two digits of its postcode.

THE CANARY ISLANDS

THE COMUNIDADES OF SPAIN AND THEIR PROVINCES

NORTHERN SPAIN

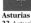

Galicia
15 A Coruña
27 Lugo
32 Ourense
36 Pontevedra

Asturias   Cantabria
33 Asturias
39 Cantabria

Basque   Navarra   La Rioja
Country
Basque Country (Euskadi)
01 Álava
20 Guipúzcoa
48 Vizcaya
Comunidad Foral de Navarra
31 Navarra
La Rioja
26 La Rioja

EASTERN SPAIN

Catalonia
08 Barcelona
25 Lleida
17 Girona
43 Tarragona

Aragón
22 Huesca
44 Teruel
50 Zaragoza

Valencia   Murcia
Comunidad Valenciana
03 Alicante
46 Valencia
12 Castellón
Murcia
30 Murcia

CENTRAL SPAIN

Madrid
28 Comunidad de Madrid

Castilla-La Mancha
02 Albacete
13 Ciudad Real
16 Cuenca
19 Guadalajara
45 Toledo

Extremadura
06 Badajoz
10 Cáceres

Castilla y León
05 Ávila
09 Burgos
24 León
34 Palencia
37 Salamanca
40 Segovia
42 Soria
47 Valladolid
49 Zamora

SOUTHERN SPAIN

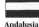

Andalusia
04 Almería
11 Cádiz
14 Córdoba
18 Granada
21 Huelva
23 Jaén
29 Málaga
41 Sevilla

SPAIN'S ISLANDS

The Balearic Islands (Islas Baleares)
07 Baleares

The Canary Islands (Islas Canarias)
35 Las Palmas
38 Santa Cruz de Tenerife

Sports and Outdoor Activities

SPAIN IS ONE OF EUROPE'S most geographically diverse countries. Its mountain ranges, woodlands and deltas are all fertile ground for scenic tours and sports holidays as alternatives to a break on the beach. It also has a full calendar of seasonal and annual events and activities *(see pp36–9)*. Tourist offices will provide lists of leisure and sporting activities in their region. These pages give an idea of the range of activities there is to choose from.

A game of golf on a course on Ibiza in the Balearic Islands

SPECIALIST HOLIDAYS

ALL SPANISH tourist offices provide details of special interest holidays. Cookery, wine and painting holidays, and tours led by professional historians and archaeologists, are increasingly popular. There is a wide choice for nature lovers and photographers, particularly in Spain's many national parks.

Information about courses in Spanish language and culture is provided by **Canning House** in London and by the **Instituto Cervantes**.

GOLF AND TENNIS

SPAIN NOW HAS an abundance of golf courses, some with activities for non-golfers. The **Real Federación Española de Golf** will give locations and more detailed information.

In most tourist areas there are tennis courts for hire by the hour and some hotels have tennis courts for their guests *(see pp536–71)*. Travel agents arrange tennis holidays for enthusiasts. For more information contact the **Real Federación Española de Tenis**.

WALKING, CYCLING AND HORSE RIDING

MANY tour operators now specialize in outdoor holidays. The **Federación Hípica Española** and Spanish tourist offices have information on horse riding and pony trekking in most regions.

The road to Santiago de Compostela *(see pp78–9)* is Spain's most famous walk and some national parks *(see pp26–7)* have spectacular routes for mountain-walking. Picturesque minor roads in many regions of Spain are excellent for cycle-touring.

Walking along the Río Cares in the Picos de Europa in Asturias

MOUNTAIN SPORTS

SPAIN'S MOST POPULAR resorts for downhill skiing are in the Vall d'Aran in Catalonia *(see pp200–201)*, and in the Sierra Nevada, near Granada *(see p461)*. Downhill skiing is often possible in the Sierra de Guadarrama north of Madrid, and there is cross-country skiing in other mountain areas.

Every region of this mountainous country has a climbing association. The **Federación Española de Montañismo** will supply details. This national organization has information about climbing and many other mountain sports.

AIR SPORTS

A PRIVATE pilot's licence is valid in Spain for up to six months. The **Federación Nacional de Deportes Aéreos** will send information about Spanish airfields and clubs where visitors can practise flying *(vuelo)*, gliding *(vuelo sin motor)* and parachuting *(salto en paracaídas)*.

The organization also gives information on places where tourists can go ballooning *(volar en globo)*, hang-gliding *(ala delta)* and paragliding *(parapente)*. Parts of Castilla y León and Castilla-La Mancha are recognized internationally as excellent venues for hang-gliding, and the Valle de Abdalajis, north of Málaga, is well known for paragliding.

Paragliding above the Vall d'Aran in the eastern Pyrenees

White water rafting in the Spanish Pyrenees

WATER SPORTS

THERE IS WHITE WATER RAFTING and canoeing on rivers in Catalonia, Aragón and many other regions of Spain. Sort, a village in the Catalonian Pyrenees, is one of Europe's prime river sports resorts.

Boating, sailing and windsurfing are very popular. The tourist offices at the coastal resorts of the mainland and in the islands give information about local hire of boats and sailboards. Experienced windsurfers head for Tarifa *(see p444)*, whose windswept location has made it one of Europe's windsurfing capitals.

Information on sailing is available from the **Federación Española de Vela**.

Beaches, marinas and ports that meet strict European standards of cleanliness and safety are permitted to fly a *bandera azul* (blue flag).

Windsurfing off Fuerteventura in the Canary Islands

NATURISM

CONTACT THE **Federación Española de Naturismo**, or coastal tourist offices for the location of nudist beaches.

Fly-fishing in the rivers of Castilla y León, famous for their trout

FIELD SPORTS

IF YOU WANT TO HUNT or shoot in Spain you must first apply for a licence and be properly insured. To obtain a licence you apply to the *comunidad* (regional government) of the area where you want to hunt. The fees tend to be high.

Permits for river or sea fishing for any length of period from one day to one year, and for fishing competitions, are issued by the *comunidades*. The **Federación Española de Caza** (for hunting) and the **Federación Española de Pesca** (for fishing) give information on where each different field sport is permitted, the dates of open seasons, and advise on licences. Travel agents and hotels specializing in hunting and fishing trips will obtain licences for clients.

DIRECTORY

Canning House
2 Belgrave Square,
London SW1X 8PJ.
((0171) 235 2303.

Federación Española de Caza
Calle Francos Rodriguez 70-2°,
28039 Madrid.
((91) 311 14 11.

Federación Española de Montañismo
Calle Alberto Aguilera 3,
28015 Madrid.
((91) 445 13 82.

Federación Española de Naturismo
Apartado 301, Almería.
((950) 25 40 44.

Federación Española de Pesca
Calle Navas de Tolosa 3-1°,
28013 Madrid.
((91) 532 83 52.

Federación Española de Vela
Calle Luis Salazar 12,
28002 Madrid.
((91) 519 50 08.

Federación Hípica Española
Plaza del Marqués de Salamanca 2,
28006 Madrid.
((91) 577 78 92.

Federación Nacional de Deportes Aéreos
Calle Ferraz 16,
28008 Madrid.
((91) 547 59 22.

Instituto Cervantes
Calle Libreros 23, 28801
Alcalá de Henares (Madrid).
((91) 885 61 00.

22–3 Manchester Square,
London W1M 5AP.
((0171) 935 1518.

Real Federación Española de Golf
Calle Capitán Haya 9,
28020 Madrid.
((91) 555 26 82.

Real Federación Española de Tenis
Avinguda Diagonal 618-3°D,
08021 Barcelona.
((93) 200 53 55.

TRAVEL INFORMATION

SPAIN HAS AN INCREASINGLY EFFICIENT transport system. All the major cities have airports and flights from all over the globe arrive at those of Madrid and Barcelona. Both the road and rail networks were greatly improved during the 1980s and in the run-up to Expo and the Olympics in 1992 *(see p65)*. Intercity rail services are efficient, but coaches are a faster and more frequent option between smaller towns. In much of rural Spain, however, public transport is limited and a car is the most practical solution for getting about. Ferries connect mainland Spain with the UK, North Africa and the Balearic and Canary islands.

Sign for an airport

Duty-free shopping at Barcelona's El Prat airport

ARRIVING BY AIR

SPAIN IS SERVED by most international airlines. **Iberia**, the national airline, has scheduled flights daily into Madrid and Barcelona from all west European capitals (but just four times a week from Dublin), and once or twice weekly from most east European capitals. **British Airways** is currently the only UK airline offering scheduled flights to Spain. It serves Madrid and Barcelona daily from London Heathrow and London Gatwick; also Madrid from Manchester, and Barcelona from Birmingham.

Of the several US airlines serving Spain, **Delta Airlines** and **TWA** fly to both Madrid and Barcelona. Iberia has a more comprehensive service from the USA, as well as direct flights to many destinations in Spain from the cities of Toronto and Montreal. There are no airlines operating direct flights between Spain and Australasia.

BARAJAS AIRPORT, MADRID

Madrid's airport is 13 km (8 miles) from the city centre. The international terminal (which is connected to the domestic terminal) is illustrated here. Arrivals are on the ground floor; departures, check-in and boarding on the first floor. A shuttle bus runs every 12 minutes to the centre of Madrid, stopping at six stops, the most central of which are Calle de Velázquez and Plaza de Colón. Alternatively, you can take a taxi (allow half an hour to the centre) or, at much greater expense, a chauffeur-driven car.

SECOND FLOOR

Departure gates 1–16

Bank

FIRST FLOOR

To domestic terminal

KEY

- Departures/transit area
- Arrivals
- Public access
- Check-in
- Customs
- Passport control
- Passengers only
- Restricted access
- Airline companies

Bank

GROUND FLOOR

Meeting point

Car hire

Bank

INTERNATIONAL AIRPORTS

THE MOST REGULAR international services operate from Madrid and Barcelona. The busiest international airports for scheduled and charter flights in Spain are marked on the map on pages 10–11.

Palma de Mallorca, Tenerife Sur, Las Palmas de Gran Canaria, Málaga, Lanzarote, Ibiza, Alicante, Fuerteventura and Menorca handle large amounts of holiday traffic. The first four are especially busy – Palma topped 12 million passengers in 1993. Most is seasonal traffic, mainly from north European countries, and at peak summer holiday time these airports can get crowded. Details of public transport to and from Spain's most important airports are given on page 628.

All the Balearic and Canary islands have international airports, except Hierro, which has a domestic one, and La

Iberia plane on the tarmac of Seville airport

Gomera, which has no airport. Melilla and Ceuta are served by domestic flights only.

AIR FARES

AIR FARES for flights to Spain vary through the year, depending on demand. They are generally highest during the summer months. Special deals, particularly for weekend city breaks, are often offered in the winter and may include a number of nights at a hotel. Look out for Iberia's "Bravo"

air fares, and also promotions by **Viva Air**, an Iberia franchise. Christmas and Easter flights are almost always booked up well in advance.

Charter flights from the UK serve airports such as Alicante, Málaga and Girona near beach resorts. These can be very cheap, but less reliable, and often fly at unsociable hours. Make sure your agent is ABTA bonded before booking. Local car hire companies may offer good deals at resort airports, but read rental terms carefully.

EL PRAT AIRPORT, BARCELONA

Barcelona's airport is 12 km (7 miles) from the city centre. Terminal A handles international arrivals and foreign airlines' departures. Terminals B and C are for departures on Spanish airlines and arrivals from European Union countries. Trains to the Plaça de Catalunya in the city centre leave every 30 minutes. For intercity rail services get off at Sants mainline station. There is also a shuttle bus, the Aerobús, running every 15 minutes, which will also leave you in Plaça de Catalunya.

FIRST FLOOR — Terminal C

Terminal B

GROUND FLOOR

Terminal A

Bank

Car hire

KEY

| Departures
| Arrivals
| Public access
| Check-in
| Customs
| Passport control
| Passengers only
| Restricted access

Car hire

Meeting point

Bank

Car hire

Bank

Insignia of Spain's national airline

DOMESTIC FLIGHTS

M OST OF Spain's domestic flights have traditionally been operated by **Iberia** and **Aviaco**, its affiliated airline. In recent years, however, this monopoly has been broken to encourage competition. The two main alternative carriers are **Air Europa** and **Spanair**.

The most frequent shuttle service is the Puente Aéreo, run between Barcelona and Madrid by Iberia. It flies every 15 minutes at peak business times, hourly at other times. A self-ticketing machine allows passengers to buy tickets up to 15 minutes before a flight departs. When a flight is full, waiting passengers are always offered a seat on the next available shuttle. The flight usually takes 50 minutes.

Aviaco, Air Europa and Span-air services between Madrid and the regional capitals are not as frequent as the Puente Aéreo, but their prices are usually slightly lower. They operate in a similar way to

Apex tickets: the earlier the booking is made, the greater the discount. The cheapest ticket, which must be booked a week in advance, can save up to one-third of the full price. Flights to the provincial cities usually operate in the morning and evening. They can be expensive, costing as much as 20,000 pesetas for a one-way trip. Pressure from the intercity rail services may eventually result in lower air fares.

Self-ticketing machine

Flights to the Balearic and Canary islands, and island-hopping flights between them, are operated by two Iberia-affiliated companies: **Binter**, and an air charter company, **Viva**. Travel agencies often offer a variety of special deals on internal flights, which may include one night or more in a hotel. These deals are advertised in the Spanish press.

Some flights from domestic airports are billed as international flights but they do not go directly to foreign destinations. Instead, they stop en route at Madrid or Barcelona.

The departures concourse in Seville Airport

AIRPORT	[C] INFORMATION	DISTANCE TO CITY CENTRE	PUBLIC TRANSPORT TIME TO CITY CENTRE
Alicante	(96) 691 90 00	15 km (9 miles)	Bus: 20 mins
Barcelona	(93) 298 38 38	15 km (9 miles)	Rail: 20 mins Bus: 25 mins
Bilbao	(94) 486 93 00	10 km (6 miles)	Bus: 30 mins
Madrid	(91) 305 83 43	15 km (9 miles)	Bus: 30 mins
Málaga	(95) 204 88 38	10 km (6 miles)	Rail: 15 mins Bus: 20 mins
Palma de Mallorca	(971) 78 90 00	9 km (5.5 miles)	Bus: 30 mins
Las Palmas de Gran Canaria	(928) 57 90 00	20 km (12 miles)	Bus: 30 mins
Santiago de Compostela	(981) 54 75 00	10 km (6 miles)	Bus: 30 mins
Seville	(95) 444 90 23	8 km (5 miles)	Rail: 15 mins Bus: 30 mins
Tenerife Sur – Reina Sofía	(922) 75 92 00	69 km (43 miles) to Santa Cruz	Bus: 60 mins
Valencia	(96) 370 95 00	8 km (5 miles)	Rail: 20 mins Bus: 30 mins

ARRIVING BY SEA

FERRIES connect the Spanish mainland to the Balearic and Canary islands, to North Africa and to the UK. All the important routes are served by car ferries. It is always wise to make an advance booking, especially in summer.

Two routes link Spain with the UK. **Brittany Ferries** sails between Plymouth in the UK and Santander in Cantabria; and **P&O European Ferries** sails from Portsmouth into Santurce harbour, near Bilbao in the Basque Country. The crossings take over 24 hours. Each ship has cabins, chairs to sleep on, a restaurant, cafés and a cinema. Discos are sometimes held on board.

FERRIES TO THE ISLANDS

FREQUENT CROSSINGS run from Barcelona and Valencia on the mainland to the three main Balearic islands. The crossings, on **Trasmediterránea** ferries, take about eight hours. The same company also operates frequent inter-island services; and small operators take day-trippers (passengers only) from Ibiza to Formentera. Storms are rare in this part of the Mediterranean and crossings are, therefore, usually calm and comfortable.

Trasmediterránea operates a weekly service from Cádiz in Andalusia to the main ports of the Canary Islands – Las Palmas de Gran Canaria and Santa Cruz de Tenerife. Crossings normally take 39 hours.

Ferry in port at Los Cristianos (Tenerife) in the Canary Islands

Car ferries link the islands with each other. Trasmediterránea also runs passengers-only services between the islands of Gran Canaria, Tenerife and Fuerteventura, and between Tenerife and La Gomera.

The ferries to Spain's islands have cabins, cafés, restaurants, bars, shops, cinemas, pools and sunbathing decks for the summer. They are also fitted with lifts and other facilities for people with special needs, and they even have kennels. A variety of entertainment, such as films and discos, is provided on the long crossing from the mainland to the Canary Islands.

Trasmediterránea Ferries logo

FERRIES TO AFRICA

TRASMEDITERRANEA operates ferries daily to the Spanish territories in North Africa: from Málaga and Almería to Melilla, and from Algeciras to Ceuta. Ferries also cross to Tangier in Morocco from Algeciras.

DIRECTORY

IBERIA, AVIACO, BINTER AND VIVA AIRLINES

International flights
((901) 33 32 22 in Spain.

Domestic flights
((901) 33 31 11 in Spain.

UK
((0171) 830 0011.

USA
((800) 772-4642.

OTHER AIRLINES

Air Europa
((91) 542 73 38 in Spain.

Spanair
((902) 13 14 15 in Spain.

British Airways
((91) 436 59 00 in Spain.
((0181) 759 2525 in UK.

GB Airways
((350) 79300 in Gibraltar.
((0345) 222111 in UK.

TWA
((91) 310 30 94 in Spain.
((800) 892-4141 in USA.

Delta Air Lines
((91) 577 07 53 in Spain.
((800) 221-1212 in USA.

TRASMEDITERRÁNEA

Barcelona
((93) 443 25 32.

Valencia
((96) 367 65 12.

Cádiz
((956) 22 74 21.

Algeciras
((956) 66 52 00.

Almería
((950) 23 61 55.

Palma de Mallorca
((971) 40 50 14.

Santa Cruz de Tenerife
((922) 28 78 50.

UK
((0171) 491 4968.

OTHER FERRIES

Brittany Ferries
((0990) 360 360 in UK.
((942) 22 00 00 in Spain.

P&O European Ferries
((0990) 980 980 in UK.
((94) 423 44 77 in Spain.

Trasmediterránea car ferry to the Balearic Islands in Barcelona harbour

Travelling by Train

THE SPANISH STATE RAILWAY, **RENFE** (*Red Nacional de Ferrocarriles Españoles*), operates a service that is continually improving, particularly between cities. The fastest intercity services are called the TALGO and the AVE – their names are acronyms for the high-speed, luxury trains that run on these routes. *Largo recorrido* (long-distance) and *regionales y cercanías* (regional and local) trains are notoriously slow, many stopping at every station. They are much cheaper than the high-speed trains but can take hours longer.

Logo of the Spanish national railways

ARRIVING BY TRAIN

THERE ARE SEVERAL routes to Spain from France. The main western route runs from Paris through Hendaye in the Pyrenees to San Sebastián. The eastern route from Paris runs via Cerbère and Port Bou to Barcelona. The trains from London, Brussels, Amsterdam, Geneva, Zurich and Milan all reach Barcelona via Cerbère. At Cerbère there are connections with the TALGO and the *largo recorrido* (long-distance) services to Valencia, Málaga, Seville, and other major destinations. If you book a sleeper on the TALGO from Paris, you travel to your destination without having to change trains.

EXPLORING BY TRAIN

SPAIN OFFERS many options for train travellers. In the last ten years, the TALGO high-speed services have belied Spain's reputation for inefficiency and it is now possible to travel the long distances between the main cities extremely quickly. Ticket prices compare very favourably with the cost of high-speed train fares in many other countries. AVE is the efficient high-speed rail service between Madrid and Seville via Córdoba. The full journey normally takes just under three hours.

The *largo recorrido* (long-distance) trains are so much slower you usually need to travel overnight. You can

Logo for a high-speed rail service

AVE high-speed trains at Estación de Santa Justa in Seville

choose between a *cochecama* (compartment with two *camas* or beds) or a *litera*, one of six seats in a compartment which converts into a bunk bed. You reserve these when booking and pay a supplement. You should book at least a month in advance, but bear in mind that it is difficult to change a ticket you have paid for.

Regionales y cercanías (the regional and local services) are frequent and very cheap. You buy the tickets from machines on the station.

Some cities have more than one station. In Madrid the major stations for regional and long-distance trains are Atocha, Chamartín and Norte. The AVE runs from Atocha, the TALGO from all three. Sants and Francia are Barcelona's two principal stations. In Seville Santa Justa is the only station for regional and international services.

DIRECTORY

RENFE INFORMATION AND RESERVATIONS

Madrid
((91) 328 90 20.

Barcelona
((93) 490 02 02.

Seville
((95) 454 02 02.

Credit Card Bookings
((91) 374 38 24.

REGIONAL RAILWAYS

ET
((943) 45 01 31.

FEVE
((98) 534 24 15.

FF CC
((93) 205 15 15.

FGV
((96) 347 37 50.

Iberrail
((93) 310 15 12.

FARES

SPANISH RAILWAYS offer a ten per cent discount on specified days to encourage people to travel. They are called *días azules* (blue days) and are indicated in the timetables in blue.

Fares for rail travel in Spain are structured according to the speed and quality of the service. Tickets for the TALGO and AVE are most expensive.

Interrail tickets for people under 26, and Eurodomino tickets for people over 26, are available from major travel agencies in Europe and from RENFE ticket offices in Spain. Always take proof of your identity when booking.

Iberrail holidays offer rail-plus-hotel deals for travelling between Spanish cities at very economical prices.

REGIONAL RAILWAYS

THREE OF THE *comunidades autónomas* have regional rail companies. Catalonia and Valencia each has its own *Ferrocarrils de la Generalitat:*

SPAIN'S PRINCIPAL RENFE NETWORK

KEY

- ● Main station
- ○ Other station
- — Principal rail route
- ▬ AVE route

Spain's national rail network operates a wide variety of services. Check a RENFE brochure or a train timetable before you buy your ticket.

respectively the **FF CC** and the **FGV**; and the Basque Country has the **ET** (*Eusko Trenbideak*).

Iberrail markets tickets for two special trains similar to the Orient Express. One is the Al Andalus Expres, which tours Andalusia, stopping at Seville, Córdoba, Granada, Jerez and Ronda. The other is the Transcantábrico, run by **FEVE** (*Ferrocarriles de Vía Estrecha*), which leaves San Sebastián to travel the length of Spain's north coast, ending its journey in Santiago de Compostela. Passengers travel in style in 14 period carriages built between 1900–30 and since restored.

The regional tourist offices publicize unusual rail services, such as the narrow-gauge lines to Inca and Sóller in Mallorca.

BOOKING TICKETS

Talgo, AVE and any other tickets for *largo recorrido* travel by train may be booked and bought at any of the major railway stations from the *taquilla* (ticket office). They are also sold by all travel agents in Spain, who will charge a commission. RENFE tickets are sometimes sold by travel agents in other countries. Telephone reservations may be made directly to all RENFE

Ticket machine for local and regional lines

ticket offices using a credit card number. A booking may be made or a special pass purchased as long as 59 days ahead of travel. Tickets for local and regional services are purchased from the station *taquilla*. In larger stations they can be bought from ticket machines but these only accept coins. Tickets for *cercanías* (local services) cannot be reserved. For a one-way journey ask for *ida* and for a return ask for *ida y vuelta*.

TIMETABLES

Renfe timetables change in May and October each year. They are not very easy to obtain outside Spain, but your travel agent will be able to provide the correct times of trains for your journey. In Spain timetables are available from RENFE offices. Most come in the form of leaflets and are broken down into the various types of journey: intercity, *largo recorrido* and *regionales*. *Cercanías* timetables are posted on boards at local railway stations.

Atocha, one of Madrid's largest mainline railway stations

Travelling by Road

S PAIN'S FASTEST ROADS are its *autopistas*. They are normally dual carriageways and are subsidized by *peajes* (tolls). *Autovías* are similar but have no tolls. The *carretera nacional* is the countrywide network of main roads or highways with the prefix N. Smaller minor roads are generally less well kept but are often a more leisurely and enjoyable way to see rural areas of Spain. These pages tell you how to use the roads, tolls and parking meters, how to buy petrol, and explain important driving regulations.

Sign for national highway N110

Cambio de sentido (slip road)
300 m (330 yd) ahead

ARRIVING BY CAR

M ANY PEOPLE drive to Spain via the French motorways. The most direct routes across the Pyrenees, using the motorways, pass through Hendaye on the western flank and Port Bou in the east. Other, rather more tortuous routes may be used, from Toulouse through the Vall d'Aran, for instance. From the UK there are car ferries from Plymouth to Santander and from Portsmouth to Bilbao in northern Spain (*see p629*).

WHAT TO TAKE

A GREEN CARD and a bail bond from a motor insurance company are needed in order to extend your comprehensive cover to Spain. The RAC, the AA and Europ Assistance have sound rescue and recovery policies with European cover.

Spanish law requires you to carry with you at all times your vehicle's registration document, a valid insurance certificate and your driving licence. You must always be able to show a passport or a national identity card as ID. You must also display a sticker with the car's country of registration on the rear of the vehicle.

The headlights of right-hand drive vehicles will have to be adjusted or deflected. This is done with stickers that can be bought at ferry ports and on ferries. You risk on-the-spot fines if you do not carry a red warning triangle, spare light bulbs and a first-aid kit.

In winter you should carry chains if you intend to drive in mountain areas. In summer, it is a good idea to take drinking water with you if you are travelling in a remote area.

BUYING PETROL

I N SPAIN *gasolina* (petrol) and *gasóleo* (diesel) are priced by the litre. *Gasolina sin plomo* (unleaded petrol) is available everywhere. All cost more at the *autopista* service stations. Self-service stations, where you fill up yourself, are common. You must wait for service if there are attendants. They will ask *¿cuánto?* (how much?); you should reply *lleno* (fill the tank) or specify an amount in pesetas: *dos mil pesetas por favor*. Small stations do not all accept credit cards. If you use your credit card to pay at a motorway service station you will be asked to show your passport or ID. Modern pumps sometimes operate by credit card. You run your card through the machine, press the buttons to indicate the amount of petrol you want in pesetas, and then serve yourself.

Speed limit 60 km/h (37 mph)

Pedestrian crossing sign

RULES OF THE ROAD

M OST TRAFFIC regulations and warnings to motorists are represented on signs by easily recognized symbols. But Spain has a few road rules and signs that may be unfamiliar to some drivers from other countries.

To turn left at a busy junction or across oncoming traffic you may have to turn right first and cross a main road, often by way of traffic lights, a bridge or an underpass. If you are going the wrong way on a motorway or a main road with a solid white line, you are allowed to turn round where you see a sign for a *cambio de sentido*.

At any crossing you must give way to the right unless a sign indicates otherwise. It is compulsory always to wear seat belts if they are fitted in front and rear seats. Oncoming drivers may flash their headlights at you to mean "you go"; "danger"; "your lights are on unnecessarily"; or (most often) "speed trap ahead".

A filling station run by a leading chain with branches throughout Spain

SPEED LIMITS AND FINES

SPEED LIMITS on the roads in Spain for cars without trailers are as follows:
• 120 km/h (75 mph) on *autopistas* (toll motorways).
• 100 km/h (62 mph) on *autovías* (non-toll motorways).
• 90 km/h (56 mph) on *carreteras nacionales* (main roads) and *carreteras comarcales* (secondary roads).
• 60 km/h (37 mph) in built-up areas.

Speeding fines are imposed on the spot at the rate of 1,000 pesetas for every kilometre per hour over the limit. Fines for other traffic offences (such as turning the wrong way into a one-way street) depend on the severity of the offence and the whim of a police officer.

Tests for drink-driving and fines for drivers over the blood alcohol legal limit, which is 80 mg per millilitre, are now imposed frequently throughout the country.

Blue *autopista* (motorway) sign for motorists approaching the A6

MOTORWAYS

SPAIN HAS more than 2,000 km (1,240 miles) of *autopistas*, and many more are planned. They are toll roads and they are rather expensive to use. The long-distance tolls are calculated per kilometre and the rate varies from region to region. Among the busiest and most expensive are the A7 along the south coast to Alicante and the A68 Bilbao-Zaragoza *autopista*.

There are service stations every 40 km (25 miles) or so along the *autopistas*, marked by a blue and white parking sign (P) or a sign indicating the services available. About 1 km (550 yd) from a service station, a sign indicates the distance to the next one and lists its services. Most have fuel, toilets, a shop for maps,

Driving through the Sierra Nevada along one of Europe's highest roads

coffee and snacks, and a café which serves full meals.

Emergency telephones occur every 2 km (1.25 miles) along the *autopistas*.

USING AUTOPISTA TOLLS

IF YOU ARE TRAVELLING a long distance on the *autopista* you pick up a ticket from a toll booth *(peaje)* as you drive on to it and give it up at a booth as you exit. Your toll will be calculated according to the distance you have covered. Over some short stretches of motorways near to cities a fixed price is charged. Tolls can be paid either in cash or by credit card.

You must join one of three channels at the *peaje* leading to different booths. Do not drive into *telepago*, a credit system for which you need a chip on your windscreen. *Automático* has machines for you to pay by credit card or with exactly the right coins. In *manual* an attendant in the booth takes your ticket and your money.

PEAJE TOLL

***Autopista* toll booths ahead**

The *peaje manual* channel, with attendant

OTHER ROADS

CARRETERAS NACIONALES, Spain's main roads, have black and white signs and are designated N *(Nacional)* plus a number. Those with Roman numerals (NIII) start at the Puerta del Sol, Madrid. The distance from the Kilometre Zero mark in the Puerta del Sol *(see p262)* appears on kilometre markers. Those with ordinary numbers (N6) have kilometre markers giving the distance from the provincial capital. Some *carreteras nacionales* are dual carriageways, but most are single-lane roads and can be slow. They tend to be least busy at lunch time, from 2–5pm, when many lorry drivers stop for lunch.

Autovías are new roads built in recent years to motorway standard to replace N roads. They have blue signs similar to *autopistas*. Because they have no tolls they are busier than *autopistas*.

Carreteras comarcales, secondary roads, have a number preceded by a letter C. Other minor roads have numbers preceded by letters representing the name of the province such as the LE 1313 in Lleida. On any road in winter, watch out for signs indicating whether a mountain pass ahead is open *(abierto)* or closed *(cerrado)*.

CAR HIRE

As well as the international car hire companies, a few Spanish companies, such as **Atesa**, operate nationwide. You can probably negotiate the best deal with an international company from home. There are also fly-drive and other package deals, including car hire. Fly-drive, an option for two or more travellers, can be arranged by travel agents.

There are car hire desks at airports and offices in the large towns. Alternatively, if you wish to hire a car locally for, say, a week or less, you can arrange it with a local travel agent. A car for hire is called a *coche de alquiler*.

For chauffeur-driven cars in Spain, **Avis** offer deals from major cities. Car-hire prices and conditions vary according to the region and locality.

Some of the leading car-hire companies operating in Spain

MAPS

Fold-out road maps can be obtained at airports, on the ferries and from tourist offices. The Spanish Ministry of Transport publishes a comprehensive road map in book form, the *Mapa Oficial de Carreteras*. Campsa, the oil company, publishes the *Guía Campsa*, a road map and restaurant guide in one book. Michelin publishes a useful series of maps (440–448, with orange covers) at a scale of 1:400,000 (1 cm:4 km), which covers Spain in eight sections, including the islands. They are sold at bookshops and petrol stations all over Spain.

A series of more detailed maps at 1:200,000 for cycling, walking and other specialist uses is published by Plaza y Janés. Military maps at scales of 1:50,000 and 1:100,000 are available from **Stanfords Travel Bookshop** in London and from specialist bookshops

and some local bookshops in Spain. Tourist offices in towns and cities usually have a giveaway street map of the town showing the principal sights.

There are detailed street maps of central Barcelona on pages 176–81, of Madrid on pages 298–303 and of Seville on pages 430–33 of this guide.

PARKING

The hours for which drivers have to pay for parking in Spain are 8am until 2pm and 4pm until 8pm on Mondays to Saturdays.

As a rule, you may not park where the pavement edge is painted yellow or where a no parking sign is displayed. Occasionally there is a no parking sign on both sides of a city street, one saying "1–15" and the other "16–30". This means that you can park on one side of the street only for the fortnight indicated on the sign.

In the cities, non-metered, on-street parking is generally hard to find, but there are blue pay and display parking spaces. To use them you buy a ticket from the machine and display it on the inside of your windscreen. The cost varies, but averages about 200 pesetas per hour. You can usually park at the same spot for up to two hours. The penalties for infringements vary from town to town.

Major cities have many large underground car parks. You collect a ticket when you enter, retain it, and pay the attendant as you drive out.

City taxis with their logo and official numbers

A parking ticket machine

No parking at any time of day

TAXIS

There is no central system for taxis in Spain. Every city and/or region has its own design and tariffs for its taxis. All will display a green light if they are free. Most taxis are metered and at the start of the journey a minimum fee will be shown on the meter. In smaller villages the taxi service may well be run by a resident driving an unmetered private car. Ask at the hotel reception or in a nearby shop for the name and number of a local driver. It is best to negotiate a price for the trip before you set off.

In the cities there are taxi ranks at the airports, the railway and bus stations and usually in the main shopping areas. Tips of 50–100 pesetas will be acceptable.

ROAD CONDITIONS AND WEATHER FORECASTS

To hear recorded road and traffic information call the national toll-free number for **Información de Tráfico de Carreteras**. This service is in Spanish only. Ask your hotel receptionist to call for you if you need a translation. The RAC offers route-planning services tailored to individual requirements, which may include current road conditions. The weather information service, **Teletiempo Nacional**, gives forecasts for the regions and provinces, as well as the national weather. It also provides information on maritime and mountain conditions.

ARRIVING BY COACH

OFTEN THE CHEAPEST WAY TO reach and travel around Spain is by coach. **Eurolines** operates routes throughout Europe and runs daily services to Madrid and Barcelona.

Coaches from the UK depart from London Victoria Coach Station. Tickets may be bought from National Express offices or travel agents, or a credit card booking may be made by phone. The journey to both cities takes about 24 hours.

TRAVELLING AROUND SPAIN BY COACH

THERE IS NO Spanish national coach company, but private regional companies operate routes around the country. The largest coach tour company, **Autocares Juliá**, which acts as an

Alsina Graells, a regional coach service

agent for Eurolines in Spain, offers itineraries, coach holidays and sightseeing trips nationwide. Other coach companies operate in particular regions – Alsina Graells, for instance, covers most of the south and east of Spain. Tickets and information for long-distance travel are available at all main coach stations and

CYCLING

Cycling is popular in Spain and there are bicycles for hire in most tourist spots but there are few cycle lanes, even in towns. Bicycles may be carried on *cercanías* trains after 2pm on Fridays until the last train on Sunday night, on any *regional* train

Cycle touring, a popular holiday activity

with a goods compartment, and on all long-distance over-night trains. If you need to take your bicycle long-distance at other times, you should check it in an hour before the train departs. You may have to send it as luggage and pay a baggage charge based on its weight. It might not travel with you so you will have to collect it when it arrives.

from travel agents but they cannot always be booked in advance. In Madrid there are several coach stations. The biggest of them are **Estación Sur**, which serves the whole of Spain; **Terminal Auto Res**, serving Valencia, Extremadura and Andalusia; and **Terminal Continental Auto**, for destinations in the north.

LOCAL BUSES

LOCAL BUS routes and time-tables are posted at bus terminuses and stops. You pay on the bus or buy strips of ten tickets called *billetes bonabús* from *estancos* (tobacconists).

Indicators for Seville's circular bus routes

DIRECTORY			

CAR HIRE

Atesa
((93) 302 45 78 in Barcelona.
((94) 442 32 90 in Bilbao.
((91) 305 86 60 in Madrid.
((95) 441 97 12 in Seville.

Avis
((0181) 848 8733 in UK.
((900) 13 57 90 toll-free in Spain.

Europcar
((0345) 222 525 in UK.
((91) 721 12 22 in Spain.

Hertz
((0345) 555 888 in UK.
((900) 10 01 11 toll-free in Spain.

COACH OPERATORS

Autocares Juliá
((93) 402 69 00 in Barcelona.

Eurolines
((0171) 730 8235 in UK.
((93) 490 40 00 in Barcelona.
((91) 528 11 05 in Madrid.

COACH STATIONS

Madrid
Estación Sur
Calle Canarias 17.
((91) 468 42 00.

Terminal Auto Res
Calle Fernández Shaw 1.
((91) 551 72 00.

Terminal Continental Auto
Calle Alenza 20.
((91) 533 04 00.

Barcelona
Estació del Nord
Calle Ali Bei 80.
((93) 265 65 08.

Estació de Sants
Calle Viriato.
((93) 490 40 00.

Seville
Estación Plaza de Armas
Calle Arjona.
((95) 490 80 40.

MAPS

Altair S.A.
Calle Balmes 69,
08006 Barcelona.
((93) 454 29 66.

Instituto de Información Geográfica de España
C/ General Ibáñez Ibero 3,
28003 Madrid.
((91) 554 14 50.

Stanfords
12–14 Long Acre,
London WC2E 9LP.
((0171) 836 1321.

WEATHER FORECASTS

Teletiempo Nacional
((906) 36 53 65 toll-free.

Teletiempo Provincial
((906) 36 53 + first two digits of provincial post-code. Toll-free.

TRAFFIC AND ROAD CONDITIONS

Información de Tráfico de Carreteras
((900) 12 35 05 toll-free.

General Index

Acknowledgments

DORLING KINDERSLEY would like to thank the following people whose contributions and assistance have made the preparation of this book possible.

MAIN CONTRIBUTORS
JOHN ARDAGH is a journalist and writer, and the author of several books on modern Europe.

DAVID BAIRD, resident in Andalusia from 1971 to 1995, is the author of *Inside Andalusia*.

VICKY HAYWARD, a writer, journalist and editor, lives in Madrid, and has travelled extensively in Spain.

ADAM HOPKINS is an indefatigable travel writer and author of *Spanish Journeys: A Portrait of Spain*.

LINDSAY HUNT has travelled widely and has contributed to several Eyewitness Travel Guides.

NICK INMAN writes regularly on Spain for books and magazines.

PAUL RICHARDSON is the author of *Not Part of the Package*, a book on Ibiza, where he lives.

MARTIN SYMINGTON is a regular contributor to the *Daily Telegraph*. He also worked on the *Eyewitness Travel Guide to Great Britain*.

NIGEL TISDALL, contributor to the *Eyewitness Travel Guide to France*, is the author of the *Insight Pocket Guide to Seville*.

ROGER WILLIAMS has contributed to Insight Guides on Barcelona and Catalonia, and was the main contributor to the *Eyewitness Travel Guide to Provence*.

ADDITIONAL CONTRIBUTORS
Mary Jane Aladren, Pepita Aris, Emma Dent Coad, Rebecca Doulton, Harry Eyres, Josefina Fernández, Anne Hersh, Nick Rider, Mercedes Ruiz Ochoa, David Stone, Clara Villanueva, Christopher Woodward, Patricia Wright.

ADDITIONAL ILLUSTRATIONS
Arcana Studio, Richard Bonson, Louise Boulton, Martine Collings, Brian Craker, Jared Gilbey (Kevin Jones Associates), Paul Guest, Steven Gyapay, Claire Littlejohn.

ADDITIONAL PHOTOGRAPHY
Tina Chambers, Geoff Dann, Phillip Dowell, Mike Dunning, Neil Fletcher, Steve Gorton, Frank Greenaway, Derek Hall, Colin Keates, Alan Keohane, Dave King, D Murray, Cyril Laubsouer, Stephen Oliver, J Selves, Mathew Ward.

CARTOGRAPHY
Lovell Johns Ltd (Oxford), ERA-Maptec Ltd.

DESIGN AND EDITORIAL ASSISTANCE
Rosemary Bailey, Vicky Barber, Teresa Barea, Gretta Britton, Peter Casterton, Elspeth Collier, Carey Combe, Jonathan Cox, Martin Cropper, Linda Doyle, Des Hemsley, Tim Hollis, Michael Lake, Erika Lang, Rebecca Lister, Sarah Martin, Jane Oliver, Simon Oon, Mike Osborn, Malcolm Parchment, Anna Streiffert, Helen Townsend, Andy Wilkinson.

PROOFREADER
Stewart J Wild.

INDEXER
Hilary Bird.

SPECIAL ASSISTANCE
DORLING KINDERSLEY would like to thank all the regional and local tourist offices, *ayuntamientos*, shops, hotels, restaurants and other organizations throughout Spain for their invaluable help. Particular thanks are also due to Dr Giray Ablay (University of Bristol); María Eugenia Alonso and María Dolores Delgado Peña (Museo Thyssen-Bornemisza); Ramón Álvarez (Consejería de Educación y Cultura, Castilla y León); Señor Ballesteros (Santiago de Compostela Tourist Office); Carmen Brieva, Javier Campos and Luis Esteruelas (Spanish Embassy, London); Javier Caballero Arranz; Fernando Cañada López; The Club Taurino of London; Consejería de Turismo, Castilla-La Mancha; Consejería de Turismo and Consejería de Cultura, Junta de Extremadura; Mònica Colomer and Montse Planas (Barcelona Tourist Office); María José Docal and Carmen Cardona (Patronato de Turismo, Lanzarote); Edilesa; Klaus Ehrlich; Juan Fernández, Lola Moreno and others at El País-Aguilar; Belén Galán (Centro de Arte Reina Sofía); Amparo Garrido; Adolfo Díaz Gómez (Albacete Tourist Office); Professor Nigel Glendinning (Queen Mary and Westfield College, University of London); Pedro Hernández; Insituto de Cervantes, London; Victor Jolín (SOTUR); Joaquim Juan Cabanilles (Servicio de Investigación Prehistórica, Valencia); Richard Kelly; Mark Little (Lookout Magazine); Carmen López de Tejada and Inma Felipe (Spanish National Tourist Office, London); Caterine López and Ana Roig Mundi (ITVA); Julia López de la Torre (Patrimonio Nacional, Madrid); Lovell Johns Ltd (Oxford); Josefina Maestre (Ministerio de Agricultura, Pesca y Alimentación); Juan Malavia García and Antonio Abarca (Cuenca Tourist Office); Mario (Promoción Turismo, Tenerife); Janet Mendel; Javier Morata (Acanto Arquitectura y Urbanismo. Madrid); Juan Carlos Murillo; Sonia Ortega and Bettina Krücken (Spain Gourmetour); Royal Society for the Protection of Birds (UK); Alícia Ribas Sos; Katusa Salazar-Sandoval (Fomento de Turismo, Ibiza); María Ángeles Sánchez and Marcos; Ana Sarrieri (Departamento de Comercio, Consumo y Turismo, Gobierno Vasco); Klaas Schenk; María José Sevilla (Foods From Spain); The Sherry Institute of Spain (London); Anna Skidmore (Fomento de Turismo, Mallorca); Philip Sweeney; Rupert Thomas; Mercedes Trujillo and Antonio Cruz Caballero (Patronato de Turismo, Gran Canaria); Gerardo Uarte (Gobierno de Navarra); Fermín Unzue (Dirección General de Turismo, Cantabria); Puri Villanueva.

ARTWORK REFERENCE
Sr. Joan Bassegoda, Catedral Gaudí (Barcelona); José Luis Mosquera Muller (Mérida); Jorge Palazón, Paisajes Españoles (Madrid).

PHOTOGRAPHY PERMISSIONS
THE PUBLISHER would like to thank the following for their kind assistance and permission to photograph at their establishments:
© Patrimonio Nacional, Madrid; Palacio de la Almudaina, Palma de Mallorca; El Escorial, Madrid; La Granja de San Ildefonso; Convento de Santa Clara, Tordesillas; Las Huelgas Reales, Burgos; Palacio Real, Madrid; Monasterio de las Descalzas; Bananera "El Guanche S.L."; Museo Arqueológico de Tenerife-OACIMC del Excmo. Cavildo Insular de Tenerife; Asociación de Encajeras de Acebo-Cáceres; Museo de Arte Abstracto Español, Cuenca; Fundación Juan March; Pepita Alia Lagartera; Museo Naval de Madrid; © Catedral de Zamora; Museo de Burgos; Claustro San Juan de Duero, Museo Numantino, Soria; San Telmo Museoa Donostia-San Sebastián; Hotel de la Reconquista, Oviedo; Catedral de Jaca; Museo de Cera, Barcelona; Museu D'Història de la Ciutat, Barcelona; © Capitol Catedral de Lleida; Jardí Botànic Marimurtra, Estació Internacional de Biologia Mediterrània, Girona; Museo Arqueológico Sagunto (Teatro Romano-Castillo); Museo Municipal y Ermita de San Antonio de la Florida, Madrid. Also all the other churches, museums, hotels, restaurants, shops, galleries and sights too numerous to thank individually.

PICTURE CREDITS
Key: t=top; tl=top left; tlc=top left centre; tc=top centre; trc=top right centre; tr=top right; cla=centre left above; ca=centre above; cra=centre right above; cl=centre left; c=centre; cr=centre right; clb=centre left below; crb=centre right below; cb=centre below; bl=bottom left; br=bottom right; b=bottom; bc=bottom centre; bcl=bottom centre left; bcr=bottom centre right; (d)=detail.

Every effort has been made to trace the copyright holders. Dorling Kindersley apologizes for any unintentional omissions and would be pleased, in such cases, to add an acknowledgement in future editions.

Works of art have been published with the permission of the following copyright holders: *Dona i Ocell* Joan Miró © ADAGP, Paris & DACS, London 172tl; *Guernica* Pablo Ruiz Picasso 1937 © DACS 1996 289cb; *Morning* George Kolbe © DACS 1996; *Peine de los Vientos* Eduardo Chillida 118b; Various works by Joaquín Sorolla © DACS 1996 295t; *Rainy Taxi* Salvador Dalí © DEMART PRO ARTE BV/DACS 1996 205tr; *Tapestry of the Foundation* Joan Miró 1975 © ADAGP, Paris & DACS, London; *Three Gypsy Boys* © Joan Rebull 1976 140bl.

The publisher would like to thank the following individuals, companies and picture libraries for their kind permission to reproduce their photographs: ACE PHOTO AGENCY: Bob Masters 22b; Mauritius 19t; Bill Wassman 306b; AISA ARCHIVO ICONOGRAFICO, BARCELONA: 18t, 32bl, 42l, 44ca, 44cb, 45bl, 45br, 46cra, 46cb, 47tl, 48cla, 48bl(d), 50bl, 50br, 50 cla, 50–51, 51cl, 51cra, 51bl, 52bl, 57br, 61tr, 63tl, 63b, 264t, 293b, 337bl, 405bl, 405br, 406cl, 465 br; Biblioteca Nacional, Madrid *Felipe V* Luis Meléndez 67bl; Catedral de Sevilla *Ignacio de Loyola* Alonso Vázquez 120bl(d); *Camilo José Cela* Álvaro Delgado 1916 © DACS 1996 31br (d); *La Tertulia del Pombo* José Gutiérrez Solana 1920 © DACS 1996 289t; Museo de América, Madrid *Vista de Sevilla* Alonso Sánchez Coello 54cb; Museo de Bellas Artes, Seville *Sancho Panza y El Rucio* Moreno Carbonero 56ca; Museo de Bellas Artes, Valencia *Ecce Homo* Juan de Juanes 242br; Museo Frankfurt *La Armada* 55tl; Museo de Historia de México *Hernán Cortés* S.E. Colane 54bl(d); Museo Histórico Militar, San Sebastián *Guerra Carlista* 59br(d); Museo Lázaro Galdiano, Madrid *Lope de Vega* Caxes 280tr; Museo Nacional del Teatro *Poster for "Yerma"* (FG Lorca) Juan Antonio Morales y José Caballero © DACS 1996 31tr; Museo del Prado, Madrid *La Rendición de Breda* Diego Velázquez 57cb, *El Tres de Mayo de 1808 en Madrid* Francisco de Goya y Lucientes 58-59(d), La Reina María Luisa María Francisco de Goya 58cla, *Carlos IV* Francisco de Goya 67bc, *Los Borrachos* Diego de Velázquez 282t, *Saturno devorando a un hijo* Francisco de Goya 284tr, *El Descendimiento* Van der Weyden 285b; Real Academia de Bellas Artes de San Fernando, Madrid *El Sueño del Caballero* Antonio de Pereda 56–57(d); AKG, London: 63cr; ALLSPORT: Stephen Munday 38cr; AQUILA: Adrian Hoskins 200cla, 200clb; Mike Lane 325clb; James Pearce 195bl; ARXIU MAS: 32br, 33bl, 47crb, 52tl, 53cl, 53br(d); Museo del Prado, Madrid *Felipe II* Sánchez Coello 66br(d); Patrimonio Nacional 55cl,55b(d).

BIOFOTOS: Heather Angel 76cla, 76bl; BRIDGEMAN ART LIBRARY: *St Dominic enthroned as Abbot* Bartolomé Bermejo 284tl; Index/Museo del Prado, Madrid *Auto-da-fé in the Plaza Mayor* Francisco Rizi 264c; Musée des Beaux Artes, Berne *Colossus of Rhodes* Salvador Dalí 1954 DEMART PRO ARTE BV/DACS 1996 29tr; Museo del Prado, Madrid *Charles IV and his Family* Francisco de Goya y Lucientes 29cb, *The Adoration of the Shepherds* El Greco 282tc, *The Annunciation* Fra Angelico 282cb, *The Clothed Maja* Francisco de Goya y Lucientes 283t, *The Naked Maja* Francisco de Goya y Lucientes 283ca, *The Three Graces* Peter Paul Rubens 283cb, *The Martydom of St Philip* José de Ribera 283b; Museo Picasso, Barcelona *Las Meninas, Infanta Margarita* Pablo Ruiz Picasso 1957 © DACS 1996 28tl; *Children On the Beach* Joaquin y Bastida Sorolla © DACS 1996 285t; Phoenix Galleries, London *Rooftops, Fortna Luxt, Majorca* Frederick Gore 8-9; MICHAEL BUSSELLE: 197r, 199b, 200t.

CENTRO DE ARTE REINA SOFIA: *Bertsolaris* Zubiaurre © DACS 1996 121cb, *Paisaje de Cadaqués*

Salvador Dalí 1923 © DEMART PRO ARTE
BV/DACS 1996 288cb, *Accidente* Ponce de León
288b; CEPHAS: Mick Rock 25bl, 38t, 74t, 192tr,
192cl, 193tr, 322tr, 402tr, 403br, 403cr; Roy Stedall
403tr; COCOMFE: 613b; BRUCE COLEMAN: Eric
Crichton 194tr; José Luis González Grande 195tr;
Werner Layer 325tl; Andy Purcell 27ca; Hans
Reinhard 76crb; Norbert Schwirtz 195tl; Colin
Varndell 195crb; DEE CONWAY: 407cl, 407cr; SYLVIA
CORDAIY PHOTO LIBRARY: Chris North 34tl; JOE
CORNISH: 24ca, 328, 346b, 354tr; GIANCARLO COSTA:
33bc; COVER: Genin Andrada 36b, 39b; Angel
Bocalandro 624tl; Austin Catalan 64bl; Juan
Echeverria 27cra, 37br, 521bl; Pepe Franco 182c;
Quim Llenas 121ca, 305tl; Matías Nieto 39c; José R
Platón 624tr; F J Rodríguez 121bl.

J D DALLET: 65tr,440tl, 575br.

EDEX: 47bl, 387b; EDILESA: 334b; EL DESEO: Pedro
Almodóvar 295b; PACO ELVIRA: 26crb; EMI:
Hispavox 358b; EQUIPO 28: 407t; ET ARCHIVE: 48br;
EUROPA PRESS: 19c, 64tl, 65ca; MARY EVANS PICTURE
LIBRARY: 9t, 52cla, 59bl, 69t, 133r, 187t, 255r,
264bl, 317, 397r, 447b, 479, 529t, 611r; Explorer
406t; EYE UBIQUITOUS: James Davis Travel
Photography 17t, 208br.

FIRO FOTO: 153c; 509t; FOTOTECA: IFEMA: Philipe
Imbault 304br; FUNDACION CÉSAR MANRIQUE: 524br;
FUNDACION COLECCION THYSSEN-BORNEMISZA:
Madonna of Humility Fra Angelico 173t, *La
Virgen del Árbol* Petrus Christus 278tr, *Harlequin
with a mirror* Pablo Ruiz Picasso 1923 © DACS
1996 278c, *Hotel Room* © Edward Hopper 1931
278bl, *Portrait of Baron HH Thyssen-Bornemisza*
© Lucian Freud 1981–82 278br, *Venus y Cupido*
Peter Paul Rubens (after 1629) 279tl, *Saint Jerome
in the Wilderness* Tiziano c.1575 279tr, *Santa
Casilda* Francisco de Zurbarán 1640–1645 279c,
Autumn Landscape in Oldenburg Karl Schmidt-
Rottluff 1907 © DACS 1996 279b; FUNDACIO JOAN
MIRO, BARCELONA: *Flama en L'espai i dona nua*
Joan Miró 1932 © ADAGP, Paris and DACS,
London 1996 168t.

GODO FOTO: 210b, 211t, 215t, 239b, 245t, 315bl;
RONALD GRANT ARCHIVE: *For a Few Dollars More*
© United Artists 476b.

ROBERT HARDING PICTURE LIBRARY: 15t, 137tr, 156ca,
168b, 169b, 239t, 293t, 487br; Julia Bayne
186–187; Nigel Blythe 15b, 145c; Bob Cousins
22clb; Robert Frerck 439tr; James Strachan 270tl;
MARIA VICTORIA HERNANDEZ: 509b; HULTON DEUTSCH
COLLECTION: 62b, 373br.

IBERDIAPO: Triangle 500–501; THE IMAGE BANK,
London: Andra Pistolesi 170; Mark Romanelli
136bl; Mathew Weinreb 157b; IMAGES COLOUR
LIBRARY: 629b; A.G.E Fotostock 24tr, 25tr, 26cra,
26ca, 26br, 32tr, 33ca, 36c, 38cl, 118b, 164, 183t,
183c, 201br, 223ca, 223br, 304t, 307c, 325cla, 331
tr, 403cl, 406br, 442b, 473t, 507t, 533tr, 625c,
625b; Horizon International 32-33, 136cb; INCAFO:
J A Fernández & C De Noriega 71bl, 121br; Juan

Carlos Muñoz 378b, 473b; A Ortega 26bl; INDEX:
30tl, 44c, 44b, 45c, 45cb, 46tl, 49b, 50cra, 52br
(d), 55tr, *Los Moriscos suplicando al rey Felipe III*
57c, 60–61, 61b, 63 cl, *Carlos I* 66tc, 66 bl, 67br,
467ca; Bridgeman, London 54cra; CCJ 19b;X
Correa 44tl; *Garrote Vil* José Gutiérrez Solana
1931 © DACS 1996 61clb(d); Galería del Ateneo,
Madrid *Lucio Anneo Seneca* Villodas 46cla (d);
Galeria Illustres Catalonia, Barcelona *Joan Prim I
Prats* J Cusachs 59ca(d); Image *José Zorilla* 31bl;
Instituto Valencia de Don Juan, Madrid *Carlos V*
Simón Bening 55crb; Iranzo 52cra; Mithra 48clb,
54br (d), 60tl; Museo de América, Madrid *Indio
Yumbo y Frutas Tropicales* 55cra; Museo Lázaro
Galdiano, Madrid *Lope de Vega* Anonymous 30c,
Félix Lope de Vega Francisco Pacheco 56br(d);
Museo Municipal, Madrid *Fiesta en la Plaza
Mayor de Madrid* Juan de la Corte 57tl; Museo
del Prado, Madrid *Ascensión de un globo
Montgolfier en Madrid* Antonio Carnicero
58cra(d), *José Moreño Conde de Floridablanca*
Francisco de Goya 58br(d), *Flota del Rey Carlos
III de España* A Joli 59t(d); National Maritime
Museum, Greenwich *Batalla de Trafalgar*
Chalmers 58cb; A Noé 52cb; Palacio del Senado,
Madrid *Alfonso X "El Sabio"* Matías Moreno
30b(d), *Rendición de Granada* Francisco Pradilla
52–53(d); Patrimonio Nacional 52t(d); Private
Collection, Madrid *Pedro Calderón de la Barca*
Antonio de Pereda 57bl(d); Real Academia de
Bellas Artes de San Fernando, Madrid *San Diego
de Alcalá dando de comer a los pobres* Bartolomé
Esteban Murillo 57ca(d), *Fernando VII* Francisco
de Goya 67tl(d), *Isabel* II 67tc, *Self Portrait*
Francisco de Goya 229b; A Tovy 65cb; NICK
INMAN: 194bc, 612t, 615cb, 622tr, 631b; INSTITUT
TURISTIC VALENCIÀ: 235br.

CÉSAR JUSTEL: 335b.

ANTHONY KING: 281t.

L'ESTARTIT TOURIST BOARD: 207c; LIFE FILE
PHOTOGRAPHIC: 207c; Tony Abbott 324cla; Xavier
Catalan 137cb; Emma Lee 137cra, 402tl, 635tr;
NEIL LUKAS: 440cb, 440b.

MAGNUM: S Franklin 64cb; Jean Gaumy 64br, 65tl;
JOHN MILLER: 196l, 478–479, 481cb, 505r, 514b,
519b, 524t, 525b; MUSEO ARQUEOLOGICO DE
VILLENA: 44–45; MUSEU NACIONAL D'ART DE
CATALUNYA: Museu d'Art Modern *El Tombant del
Loing* Alfred Sisley 151t; MUSEO NACIONAL DEL
PRADO: *El Jardín de las Delicias* 282b; MUSEU
ARQUEOLOGIC DE BARCELONA: 167c; MUSEU PICASSO
BARCELONA: *Auto Retrato* Pablo Ruiz Picasso
1899–1900 © DACS 1996 148b; *Las Meninas*
Pablo Ruiz Picasso 1957 © DAC S 1996 149b.

NATURPRESS: Oriol Alamany 27bl; J L Calvo & J R
Montero 325crb; José Luis Grande 441b; Walter
Kwaternik 26clb, 27bc, 324cra, 325cra; Francisco
Márquez 441cb, 398bl; Aurelio Martín 27br,
Sebastián Martín 325bc; José A Martínez 76tr,
324clb, 324crb; © NATIONAL MARITIME MUSEUM:
54–55; Network: Bilderberg/W Kunz 403tl; NHPA:

Laurie Campbell 76cra; Stephen Dalton 77cl; Vicente García Canseco 27cla; Manfred Daneggar 76br, 77br; NATURAL SCIENCE PHOTOS: Nigel Charles 104tl; C Dani & I Jeske 100b, 325br; J Plant 222cb; Richard Revels 324br; Brian Sutton 324bl; W Tarboton 324tl; P & S Ward 222br.

OMEGA FOTO: 106tl, Manuel Pinilla 38b, 119b; ORONOZ: 4, 29br, 32 cl, 33br, 43b, 45t, 46b, 49t, 49clb, 49crb, 50tl, 50cb, 51t, 51br, 54tl, 54cla, 56cb, 61tl, 64ca, 65c, 78tl, 108t, 295cr, 337br, 345br, 352b, 416bl, 423bl, 443tl, 455t, 456l, 465bl; Biblioteca Nacional, Madrid *Isabel la Católica* Luis Madrazo 66tl(d); *El Espíritu de los Pájaros o Pájaros Volando* Eduardo Chillida 1953 © DACS 1996 289b; Iglesia Santo Tomé, Toledo *El Entierro del Conde de Orgaz* El Greco 28ca; *Portrait II* Joan Miró 1938 © ADAGP, Paris and DACS, London 1996 288t; Monasterio Santa Maria, Barcelona *Virgen con Niño* Ferrer Bassa 28clb(d); Museo de Bellas Artes, Cádiz *San Bruno en Éxtasis* Zurbarán 443tr; Museo Casa Gredo, Toledo *Carlos II* Miranda Correño 66tr(d); Museo del Ejército, Madrid *Isabel II* Madrazo 58tl; Museo Municipal de Bellas Artes, Tenerife *Retrato de Boabdil o Abu Abdala* 53tr(d); Museo Nacional de Escultura, Valladolid *Natividad* Berruguete 349tr; Museo Naval, Madrid *Desembarco de Colón* José Garnelo 53tl; Museo Naval Laminas, Madrid *Carabelas de Colón* Monleón 53bl(d); Museo del Prado, Madrid *El Salvador* José de Ribera 28crb, *Las Meninas o Familia de Felipe V* Diego Velázquez 28–29, *Felipe III* Pedro A Vidal 56bl, *Felipe V* 58bl, *Guernica* Pablo Ruiz Picasso 1937 © DACS 1996, 62–63, *Felipe IV* Diego Velázquez 66bc(d), *Bodegón* Zurbarán 284b, *David Vencedor de Goliat* Caravaggio 285c; Palacio Moncloa *Interior de la Catedral de Santiago* Villaamil Pérez 78–79; *Mujer en Azul* Pablo Ruiz Picasso 1901 © DACS 1996 288ca; Private Colection, Palma *Oleo Sobre Lienzo* Joan Miró 1932 © ADAGP, Paris and DACS, London 29ca; Real Academia de Bellas Artes de San Fernando *Fray Pedro Machado* Zurbarán 271tr.

PANOS PICTURES: Adrian Evans 64–65; JOSÉ M PÉREZ DE AYALA: 26cr, 440tr, 440ca, 441t, 441ca; THE PHOTOGRAPHERS LIBRARY: 499tr; PICTURES COLOUR LIBRARY: 18b, 26tr, 158-159, 248b, 398cl; PRISMA 60ca , 61crb, 62ca, 62cb, 63tr, 93t, 136br, 229c, 240t, 307t, 435, 492br, 508cl, 515clb, 515cb, 515crb, 515bl, 519t, 527bl, 527br; Franco Aguiar 67tr; *El ingenioso hidalgo Don Quixote de la Mancha* 1605 Ricardo Balaca 377br; Diputación de Madrid *Francisco Bahamonde Franco* Enrique Segura 62tl; Domenech & Azpiliqueta 114t; Albert Heras 182b; Marcel Jaquet 507b, 517b; Hans Lohr 459b; *Los Niños de la Concha* Bartolomé Esteban Murillo 29bl(d); Museo de Arte Moderno, Barcelona *Pío Baroja* Ramón Casas 60cb(d); Museo de Bellas Artes, Bilbao *Condesa Mathieu de Noailles* Ignacio Zuloaga y Zubaleta © DACS 1996 114b; Museo de Bellas Artes, Zaragoza *Príncipe de Viana* José Moreno Carbonero 126b (d); Mateu 185c; Palacio del Senado, Madrid *Alfonso XIII* Aquino © DACS 1996 67cr; Patrimonio Nacional Palacio de Riofrío, Segovia: 60br; *Auto Retrato* Pablo Ruiz Picasso 1907 © Succession Picasso DACS 1996 61ca; Marta Povo 626t; Real Academia de Bellas Artes de San Fernando, Madrid *Las Bodas de Camacho* José Moreno Carbonero 31tl(d), *Procession of the Flagellants* Francisco de Goya 264br(d); *Emilio Castelar* Joaquin Sorolla © DACS 1996 60bl. REX FEATURES: Sipa Press 205cb; © ROYAL MUSEUM OF SCOTLAND: Michel Zabé 43t.

MARIA ÁNGELES SANCHEZ: 34tr, 35b, 39t, 75t, 94cl, 14l, 280tl, 294b, 369c, 387tr, 508t, 508cr, 508b, 512c, 523t; SCIENCE PHOTO LIBRARY: Geospace 10l; 6 TOROS 6: 33cb; SPANISH TOURIST BOARD: 245c; SPECTRUM COLOUR LIBRARY: 132–133, 136tr, 528–529; STOCKPHOTOS, Madrid: Marcelo Brodsky 36t; Campillo 625t; Heinz Hebeisen 37bl; Mikael Helsing 624b, 314tl; David Hornback 17b; Javier Sánchez 314tl; Werner Otto Reisefotografie 629t; JAMES STRACHAN: 281b, 292t, 292c, 294t; TONY STONE WORLDWIDE: Doug Armand 16b; Jon Bradley 304bl; Robert Everts 422ca.

VISIONS OF ANDALUCIA: Michelle Chaplow 406–407; JD Dallet 379tr; VU: Christina García Rodero 2–3, 16c, 34b, 35c, 35t, 128cl, 246–247, 350l, 413cr.

CHARLIE WAITE: 116–117, 470–471; WERNER FORMAN ARCHIVE: Museo de Arte Hispanomusulmán 48t; Museum of Catalan Art, Barcelona 326tl; National Maritime Museum, Greenwich 48cr; ALAN WILLIAMS: 74b; PETER WILSON: 254–255, 272, 444b, 445c, 451t, 457t; WORLD PICTURES: 305c, 488t;

ZEFA: 1.

Front endpaper: All special photography except JOE CORNISH cbl; JOHN MILLER tr; SPECTRUM COLOUR LIBRARY ca; PETER WILSON cbr.

Jacket: All special photography except INDEX: spine cb; ORONOZ front cbl; ZEFA: front t.

Phrase Book

IN AN EMERGENCY

Help!	¡Socorro!	soh-**koh**-roh
Stop!	¡Pare!	**pah**-reh
Call a doctor!	¡Llame a un médico!	**yah**-meh ah **oon meh**-dee-koh
Call an ambulance!	¡Llame a una ambulancia!	**yah**-meh ah **oonah** ahm-boo-**lahn**-thee-ah
Call the police!	¡Llame a la policía!	**yah**-meh ah lah poh-lee-**thee**-ah
Call the fire brigade!	¡Llame a los bomberos!	**yah**-meh ah lohs bohm-**beh**-rohs
Where is the nearest telephone?	¿Dónde está el teléfono más próximo?	**dohn**-deh ehs-**tah** ehl teh-**leh**-foh-noh mahs prohx-ee-moh
Where is the nearest hospital?	¿Dónde está el hospital más próximo?	**dohn**-deh ehs-**tah** ehl ohs-pee-**tahl** mahs prohx-ee-moh

COMMUNICATION ESSENTIALS

Yes	Sí	see
No	No	noh
Please	Por favor	pohr fah-**vohr**
Thank you	Gracias	**grah**-thee-ahs
Excuse me	Perdone	pehr-**doh**-neh
Hello	Hola	**oh**-lah
Goodbye	Adiós	ah-dee-**ohs**
Good night	Buenas noches	**bweh**-nahs **noh**-chehs
Morning	La mañana	lah mah-**nyah**-nah
Afternoon	La tarde	lah **tahr**-deh
Evening	La tarde	lah **tahr**-deh
Yesterday	Ayer	ah-**yehr**
Today	Hoy	oy
Tomorrow	Mañana	mah-**nya**-nah
Here	Aquí	ah-**kee**
There	Allí	ah-**yee**
What?	¿Qué?	keh
When?	¿Cuándo?	**kwahn**-doh
Why?	¿Por qué?	pohr-**keh**
Where?	¿Dónde?	**dohn**-deh

USEFUL PHRASES

How are you?	¿Cómo está usted?	**koh**-moh ehs-**tah** oos-**tehd**
Very well, thank you.	Muy bien, gracias.	mwee bee-**ehn grah**-thee-ahs
Pleased to meet you.	Encantado de conocerle.	ehn-kahn-**tah**-doh deh koh-noh-**thehr**-leh
See you soon.	Hasta pronto.	ahs-tah **prohn**-toh
That's fine.	Está bien.	ehs-tah bee-**ehn**
Where is/are . . .?	¿Dónde está/están . . .?	**dohn**-deh ehs-**tah**/ehs-**tahn**
How far is it to . . .?	¿Cuántos metros/ kilómetros hay de aquí a . . .?	**kwahn**-tohs meh-trohs/kee-**loh**-meh-trohs **eye** deh ah-**kee** ah
Which way to . . .?	¿Por dónde se va a . . .?	pohr **dohn**-deh seh bah ah
Do you speak English?	¿Habla inglés?	**ah**-blah een-**glehs**
I don't understand	No comprendo	noh kohm-**prehn**-doh
Could you speak more slowly please?	¿Puede hablar más despacio por favor?	pweh-deh ah-**blahr** mahs dehs-pah-thee-oh pohr fah-**vohr**
I'm sorry.	Lo siento.	loh see-**ehn**-toh

USEFUL WORDS

big	grande	**grahn**-deh
small	pequeño	peh-**keh**-nyoh
hot	caliente	kah-lee-**ehn**-teh
cold	frío	**free**-oh
good	bueno	**bweh**-noh
bad	malo	**mah**-loh
enough	bastante	bahs-**tahn**-teh
well	bien	bee-**ehn**
open	abierto	ah-bee-**ehr**-toh
closed	cerrado	thehr-**rah**-doh
left	izquierda	eeth-key-**ehr**-dah
right	derecha	deh-**reh**-chah
straight on	todo recto	toh-doh **rehk**-toh
near	cerca	**thehr**-kah
far	lejos	**leh**-hohs
up	arriba	ah-**ree**-bah
down	abajo	ah-**bah**-hoh

early	temprano	tehm-**prah**-noh
late	tarde	**tahr**-deh
entrance	entrada	ehn-**trah**-dah
exit	salida	sah-**lee**-dah
toilet	lavabos, servicios	lah-**vah**-bohs, sehr-**bee**-thee-ohs
more	más	mahs
less	menos	**meh**-nohs

SHOPPING

How much does this cost?	¿Cuánto cuesta esto?	**kwahn**-toh kwehs-tah **ehs**-toh
I would like . . .	Me gustaría . . .	meh goos-ta-**ree**-ah
Do you have?	¿Tienen?	tee-**yeh**-nehn
I'm just looking.	Sólo estoy mirando, gracias.	soh-loh ehs-**toy** mee-**rahn**-doh **grah**-thee-ahs
Do you take credit cards?	¿Aceptan tarjetas de crédito?	ah-**thehp**-tahn tahr-**heh**-tahs deh **kreh**-dee-toh
What time do you open?	¿A qué hora abren?	ah keh oh-rah **ah**-brehn
What time do you close?	¿A qué hora cierran?	ah keh oh-rah thee-**ehr**-rahn
This one.	Éste.	**ehs**-teh
That one.	Ése.	**eh**-seh
expensive	caro	**kahr**-oh
cheap	barato	bah-**rah**-toh
size, clothes	talla	**tah**-yah
size, shoes	número	**noo**-mehr-oh
white	blanco	**blahn**-koh
black	negro	**neh**-groh
red	rojo	**roh**-hoh
yellow	amarillo	ah-mah-**ree**-yoh
green	verde	**behr**-deh
blue	azul	ah-**thool**
antiques shop	la tienda de antigüedades	lah tee-**ehn**-dah deh ahn-tee-gweh-**dah**-dehs
bakery	la panadería	lah pah-nah-deh-**ree**-ah
bank	el banco	ehl **bahn**-koh
book shop	la librería	lah lee-breh-**ree**-ah
butcher's	la carnicería	lah kahr-nee-theh-**ree**-ah
cake shop	la pastelería	lah pahs-teh-leh-**ree**-ah
chemist's	la farmacia	lah fahr-**mah**-thee-ah
fishmonger's	la pescadería	lah pehs-kah-deh-**ree**-ah
greengrocer's grocer's	la frutería la tienda de comestibles	lah froo-teh-**ree**-ah lah tee-**yehn**-dah deh koh-mehs-**tee**-blehs
hairdresser's	la peluquería	lah peh-loo-keh-**ree**-ah
market	el mercado	ehl mehr-**kah**-doh
newsagent's	el kiosko de prensa	ehl kee-**ohs**-koh deh **prehn**-sah
post office	la oficina de correos	lah oh-fee-**thee**-nah deh kohr-**reh**-ohs
shoe shop	la zapatería	lah thah-pah-teh-**ree**-ah
supermarket	el supermercado	ehl soo-pehr-mehr-**kah**-doh
tobacconist	el estanco	ehl ehs-**tahn**-koh
travel agency	la agencia de viajes	lah ah-**hehn**-thee-ah deh bee-**ah**-hehs

SIGHTSEEING

art gallery	el museo de arte	ehl moo-**seh**-oh deh **ahr**-teh
cathedral	la catedral	lah kah-teh-**drahl**
church	la iglesia la basílica	lah ee-**gleh**-see-ah lah bah-**see**-lee-kah
garden	el jardín	ehl hahr-**deen**
library	la biblioteca	lah bee-blee-oh-**teh**-kah
museum	el museo	ehl moo-**seh**-oh
tourist information office	la oficina de turismo	lah oh-fee-**thee**-nah deh too-**rees**-moh
town hall	el ayuntamiento	ehl ah-yoon-tah-mee-**ehn**-toh
closed for holiday	cerrado por vacaciones	thehr-**rah**-doh pohr bah-kah-thee-**oh**-nehs
bus station	la estación de autobuses	lah ehs-tah-thee-**ohn** deh owtoh-**boo**-sehs
railway station	la estación de trenes	lah ehs-tah-thee-**ohn** deh **treh**-nehs

STAYING IN A HOTEL

Do you have a vacant room?	¿Tienen una habitación libre?	tee-**eh**-nehn oo-nah ah-bee-tah-thee-**ohn** lee-breh
double room	habitación doble	ah-bee-tah-thee-**ohn doh**-bleh
with double bed	con cama de matrimonio	kohn **kah**-mah deh mah-tree-**moh**-nee-oh
twin room	habitación con dos camas	ah-bee-tah-thee-**ohn** kohn dohs **kah**-mahs
single room	habitación individual	ah-bee-tah-thee-**ohn** een-dee-vee-doo-**ahl**
room with a bath	habitación con baño	ah-bee-tah-thee-**ohn** kohn **bah**-nyoh
shower	ducha	**doo**-chah
porter	el botones	ehl boh-**toh**-nehs
key	la llave	lah **yah**-veh
I have a reservation.	Tengo una habitación reservada.	tehn-goh **oo**-na ah-bee-tah-thee-**ohn** reh-sehr-**bah**-dah

EATING OUT

Have you got a table for . . .?	¿Tienen mesa para . . .?	tee-**eh**-nehn meh-sah pah-**rah**
I want to reserve a table.	Quiero reservar una mesa.	kee-eh-roh reh-sehr-**bahr** oo-nah **meh**-sah
The bill please.	La cuenta por favor.	lah **kwehn**-tah pohr fah-**vohr**
I am a vegetarian	Soy vegetariano/a	soy beh-heh-tah-ree-**ah**-no/na
waitress/ waiter	camarera/ camarero	kah-mah-**reh**-rah kah-mah-**reh**-roh
menu	la carta	lah **kahr**-tah
fixed-price menu	menú del día	meh-**noo** dehl **dee**-ah
wine list	la carta de vinos	lah **kahr**-tah deh **bee**-nohs
glass	un vaso	oon **bah**-soh
bottle	una botella	oo-nah boh-**teh**-yah
knife	un cuchillo	oon koo-**chee**-yoh
fork	un tenedor	oon teh-neh-**dohr**
spoon	una cuchara	oo-nah koo-**chah**-rah
breakfast	el desayuno	ehl deh-sah-**yoo**-noh
lunch	la comida/ el almuerzo	lah koh-**mee**-dah/ ehl ahl-**mwehr**-thoh
dinner	la cena	lah **theh**-nah
main course	el primer plato	ehl pree-**mehr plah**-toh
starters	los entremeses	lohs ehn-treh-**meh**-sehs
dish of the day	el plato del día	ehl **plah**-toh dehl **dee**-ah
coffee	el café	ehl kah-**feh**
rare	poco hecho	**poh**-koh **eh**-choh
medium	medio hecho	**meh**-dee-oh **eh**-choh
well done	muy hecho	mwee **eh**-choh

MENU DECODER

al horno	ahl **ohr**-noh	baked
asado	ah-**sah**-doh	roast
el aceite	ah-**thee-eh**-teh	oil
las aceitunas	ah-theh-**toon**-ahs	olives
el agua mineral	**ah**-gwa mee-neh-**rahl**	mineral water
sin gas/con gas	seen gas/kohn gas	still/sparkling
el ajo	**ah**-hoh	garlic
el arroz	ahr-**rohth**	rice
el azúcar	ah-**thoo**-kahr	sugar
la carne	**kahr**-neh	meat
la cebolla	theh-**boh**-yah	onion
la cerveza	thehr-**beh**-thah	beer
el cerdo	**therh**-doh	pork
el chocolate	choh-koh-**lah**-teh	chocolate
el chorizo	choh-**ree**-thoh	red sausage
el cordero	kohr-**deh**-roh	lamb
el fiambre	fee-**ahm**-breh	cold meat
frito	**free**-toh	fried
la fruta	**froo**-tah	fruit
los frutos secos	**froo**-tohs seh-kohs	nuts
las gambas	**gahm**-bahs	prawns
el helado	eh-**lah**-doh	ice cream
el huevo	oo-**eh**-voh	egg
el jamón serrano	hah-**mohn** sehr-**rah**-noh	cured ham

el jerez	heh-**rehz**	sherry
la langosta	lahn-**gohs**-tah	lobster
la leche	**leh**-cheh	milk
el limón	lee-**mohn**	lemon
la limonada	lee-moh-**nah**-dah	lemonade
la mantequilla	mahn-teh-**kee**-yah	butter
la manzana	mahn-**thah**-nah	apple
los mariscos	mah-**rees**-kohs	seafood
la menestra	meh-**nehs**-trah	vegetable stew
la naranja	nah-**rahn**-hah	orange
el pan	**pahn**	bread
el pastel	pahs-**tehl**	cake
las patatas	pah-**tah**-tahs	potatoes
el pescado	pehs-**kah**-doh	fish
la pimienta	pee-mee-**yehn**-tah	pepper
el plátano	**plah**-tah-noh	banana
el pollo	**poh**-yoh	chicken
el postre	**pohs**-treh	dessert
el queso	**keh**-soh	cheese
la sal	sahl	salt
las salchichas	sahl-**chee**-chahs	sausages
la salsa	**sahl**-sah	sauce
seco	**seh**-koh	dry
el solomillo	soh-loh-**mee**-yoh	sirloin
la sopa	**soh**-pah	soup
la tarta	**tahr**-tah	pie/cake
el té	teh	tea
la ternera	tehr-**neh**-rah	beef
las tostadas	tohs-**tah**-dahs	toast
el vinagre	bee-**nah**-greh	vinegar
el vino blanco	**bee**-noh **blahn**-koh	white wine
el vino rosado	**bee**-noh roh-**sah**-doh	rosé wine
el vino tinto	**bee**-noh **teen**-toh	red wine

NUMBERS

0	cero	**theh**-roh
1	uno	**oo**-noh
2	dos	dohs
3	tres	trehs
4	cuatro	**kwa**-troh
5	cinco	**theen**-koh
6	seis	says
7	siete	**see**-eh-teh
8	ocho	**oh**-choh
9	nueve	**nweh**-veh
10	diez	dee-**ehth**
11	once	**ohn**-theh
12	doce	**doh**-theh
13	trece	**treh**-theh
14	catorce	kah-**tohr**-theh
15	quince	**keen**-theh
16	dieciséis	dee-eh-thee-**seh-ees**
17	diecisiete	dee-eh-thee-see-**eh**-teh
18	dieciocho	dee-eh-thee-**oh**-choh
19	diecinueve	dee-eh-thee-**nweh**-veh
20	veinte	**beh**-een-teh
21	veintiuno	beh-een-tee-**oo**-noh
22	veintidós	beh-een-tee-**dohs**
30	treinta	**treh**-een-tah
31	treinta y uno	treh-een-tah ee **oo**-noh
40	cuarenta	kwah-**rehn**-tah
50	cincuenta	theen-**kwehn**-tah
60	sesenta	seh-**sehn**-tah
70	setenta	seh-**tehn**-tah
80	ochenta	oh-**chehn**-tah
90	noventa	noh-**vehn**-tah
100	cien	thee-**ehn**
101	ciento uno	thee-**ehn**-toh oo-noh
102	ciento dos	thee-**ehn**-toh dohs
200	doscientos	dohs-thee-**ehn**-tohs
500	quinientos	khee-nee-**ehn**-tohs
700	setecientos	seh-teh-thee-**ehn**-tohs
900	novecientos	noh-veh-thee-**ehn**-tohs
1,000	mil	meel
1,001	mil uno	meel **oo**-noh

TIME

one minute	un minuto	oon mee-**noo**-toh
one hour	una hora	oo-na **oh**-rah
half an hour	media hora	**meh**-dee-a **oh**-rah
Monday	lunes	**loo**-nehs
Tuesday	martes	**mahr**-tehs
Wednesday	miércoles	mee-**ehr**-koh-lehs
Thursday	jueves	hoo-**weh**-vehs
Friday	viernes	bee-**ehr**-nehs
Saturday	sábado	**sah**-bah-doh
Sunday	domingo	doh-**meen**-goh

BARCELONA TRANSPORT MAP

The metro is the quickest way of getting around Barcelona. It runs from 5:30am–11pm on weekdays; 6:30am–11:30pm on Sundays and public holidays. In the stations the lines are identified by number and colour; platform signs display the name of the last station on the line. You can buy a one-journey ticket (*bitllet*) or a discounted, ten-trip *tarjeta*: the T-1, which is valid for the metro only; or the T-2, which is valid for the metro and the buses. Tickets for the interconnecting FF CC suburban rail network, which runs from the city centre out to the airport and to Barcelona's environs, and for the funiculars, must be purchased separately.

KEY

▬▬▬	Metro line 1
▬▬▬	Metro line 2
▬▬▬	Metro line 3
▬▬▬	Metro line 4
▬▬▬	Metro line 5
▬▬▬	FF CC train line (Ferrocarrils de la Generalitat de Catalunya)
▬▬▬	RENFE airport train line
✛✛✛	Funicular railway
═══	Tramvia Blau (Blue Tram)
○	Interchange station
⚡	RENFE main line rail station